Laurel Wagner

5 25

W9-BNG-817

pg. 135-140

MUSIC IN HISTORY

H. D. McKinney

ORPHEUS, THE GOD OF MUSIC

Statue by Carl Milles in Stockholm

MUSIC IN HISTORY

THE EVOLUTION OF AN ART

HOWARD D. McKINNEY and W. R. ANDERSON

Authors of *Discovering Music*

There is no truer truth obtainable
By man, than comes of music.

ROBERT BROWNING

AMERICAN BOOK COMPANY · New York · Cincinnati
Chicago · Boston · Atlanta · Dallas · San Francisco

MUSIC IN HISTORY

E.P. 6

MADE IN U.S.A.

Prelude

NO MERE introduction to such an art as music can satisfy an eager student. After becoming aware of his capacity for participating in the great heritage of the world's musical experience, it is natural that to his enthusiasm he should wish to add knowledge; and that he should desire to increase his modest ability by every available means. This work has been written to help him fulfill such purposes.

Prepared along the lines of a general historical survey of the whole subject, it is meant for the average listener of today who has secured a start on his journey of discovery into the extensive land of music and would go further. It is not a work for the specialist who desires to become versed in the intricate details of the historical development of his subject. The writing of this book was motivated by the same pedagogic principle that governed the shaping of the material in *Discovering Music*, namely, *the study of an art can " educate " only if it can be made to give a sense of pleasure*. The authors feel that the most potent reason for a music listener's wanting to learn more of the rich heritage of his art is the greatly increased sense of pleasure and satisfaction that he will derive from the music he hears; and they have kept this viewpoint in mind throughout.

Most works that treat of the story of the development of music employ a different procedure. They are content to convey information by a chronological arrangement of facts, with little attempt to relate these to general cultural backgrounds and none whatever to make them live by means of actual listening experience. The authors have avoided this stereotyped method of arrangement and have adopted several cardinal principles for their work which differentiate it in aim and scope from the older types of musical histories:

First. Reading or hearing about music without being able to listen to it is largely a profitless experience; the *music* is always the important thing. Therefore the authors have arranged their treatment so as to embrace, for the most part, only those works from the various composers which are available in standard phonograph recordings, so that the student can actually know what he is reading about, without merely taking the authors' word for it. The developments of the art are traced by discussions of general periods, such as Medieval, Gothic, Renaissance, and Romantic, as well as by study of the works of its greatest composers — Palestrina, Bach, Haydn, Mozart, Beethoven, Schubert, Liszt, Brahms, Wagner, Strauss, Stravinsky — together with those of such significant though less eminent men as Monteverdi, Scarlatti, Telemann, and so forth. Thus the reader gradually becomes familiar with a large and varied listening repertoire.

Second. None of the arts — and this is especially true of music — has developed in a void, unassociated with its time and period. Even the specialists, once content largely to dig up facts and pigeonhole them so that they might be used to verify or refute other facts, have become conscious of the need for relating these neat parcels of data to the larger influences which have shaped all the periods of history. To understand music as we have it today, it is necessary to know something of the forces which have shaped and conditioned the various epochs of its growth. Music reflects the temper of the time that gives it birth and has a definite relationship to the political, economic, and cultural conditions that surround its composers and practitioners. Therefore this treatment has been planned to show the outstanding social and aesthetic characteristics of the great epochs in art history — Greek, Early Christian, Romanesque, Gothic, and the rest. All the music has been discussed against the general backgrounds of its time and co-ordinated with some of the other arts — painting, literature, sculpture, and architecture. In a word, the authors have tried to show that music is an integral element of the general spirit which informs the whole exterior or interior world of a period. In carrying out this scheme they have used a large number of pictures in order to give the reader a wider conception of the part which the other arts have played in the life of man.

Third. Owing to its very nature, music, in so far as the average individual is concerned, is more a matter of emotional significance than of intellectual understanding. Real interest in music begins, therefore, for everyone except the specialists, with the works of the eighteenth century. While recognizing this fact, the authors have paid the music written before that time more attention than is usually accorded it in a work of this kind. They have also given an adequate description of the backgrounds out of which our modern music has come, with as complete reference as possible to the works involved.

Fourth. An important factor in forming any good historical perspective in art is the judgment of contemporary opinion. A wise essayist has said that the best history of music that could be written would be one composed entirely of contemporary judgments — extracts from letters and autobiographies of musicians and persons having musical experience. As many of these as is practicable have been included in this work, covering the most important periods and movements.

Fifth. An attractive style not only helps understanding but increases enthusiasm. The authors have therefore tried to make their writing alive and interesting as well as informing; they have avoided textbook phraseology and have not hesitated to use many quotations. This book thus provides a humanistic background for the study of music, the comprehension of which will increase the understanding and heighten the enjoyment of every piece of music the average listener may hear, whether it be by Guillaume de Machaut, Johannes Brahms, or Paul Hindemith; whether it stem from the believing twelfth, the brilliant sixteenth, the gallant eighteenth, or the cynical twentieth century.

Acknowledgments

The authors herewith offer thanks to the following, who have kindly given permission to reproduce copyrighted material. Specific credits for illustrations are given with the pictures themselves.

American Book Company for selections from *Fluctuation of Forms of Art,* Volume I of " Social and Cultural Dynamics " by Pitirim A. Sorokin and *The National Mind* by Michael Demiashkevich.

Breitkopf & Härtel, Berlin, for the selection from *Geschichte der Motette* by Hugo Leichtentritt. By kind permission of Breitkopf & Härtel, owners of the copyright.

The Clarendon Press, Oxford, for extracts from *The Works of Lucian of Samosata,* translated by H. W. and F. S. Fowler and *The Mediaeval Stage* by E. K. Chambers. By permission of The Clarendon Press, Oxford.

The Cordon Company, Inc. for the extract from *An Intellectual and Cultural History of the Western World* by Harry Elmer Barnes.

Covici Friede, Inc. for the excerpt from *Fool of Venus; The Story of Peire Vidal,* translated by George Cronyn.

F. S. Crofts & Company for the paragraph from *Hellenic Civilization* by Maurice Croiset, translated by Paul B. Thomas.

Dodd, Mead & Company, Inc. for selections from *International Cyclopedia of Music and Musicians; Debussy, Man and Artist* by Oscar Thompson; and *Palestrina, His Life and Times* by Zoe K. Pyne. All are reprinted by permission of the publishers, Dodd, Mead & Company, Inc.

Gerald Duckworth & Co., Ltd. for the extract from *Southern Baroque Art* by Sacheverell Sitwell.

E. P. Dutton & Co., Inc., New York, for selections from *The Caedmon Poems,* translated by Charles W. Kennedy; *Monteverdi, His Life and Work* by Henry Prunières; *Gluck* by Alfred Einstein; *Letters of Mozart,* edited by Hans Mersman and translated by M. M. Bozman; and *Raggle-Taggle* by Walter Starkie.

Newman Flower for the extract from *George Frideric Handel.*

Harcourt, Brace and Company, Inc. for an excerpt from the Introduction to *The American Songbag* by Carl Sandburg.

William Heinemann, Ltd. for a selection from *Giuseppe Verdi* by Francis Toye.

Henry Holt and Company, Inc. for a selection from *The Social Forces in German Literature* by Kuno Francke.

Houghton Mifflin Company for the poem from *A Tropical Morning at Sea* by Edward Rowland Sill and an extract from Virgil's *The Aeneid,* translated by T. C. Williams.

Kegan Paul, Trench, Trubner & Co., Ltd., London, for the excerpt from *Gustav Mahler* by Bruno Walter.

Alfred A. Knopf, Inc. for selections from *Franz Schubert and His Times* by Karl Kobald, translated by Beatrice Marshall; *Memoirs, 1808–1865, of Hector Louis Berlioz,* translated by Rachel and Eleanor Holmes and revised by Ernest Newman; and *Jean Sibelius* by Karl Ekman.

H. Laurens Publishing Company, Paris, for the selection from *Le Ballet de Cour avant Lully* by Henry Prunières.

J. B. Lippincott Company for an excerpt from *The Civilization of Babylonia and Assyria* by Morris Jastrow.

Liveright Publishing Corporation for the lines from *Collected Poems of H. D.* (Hilda Aldington), published by Liveright Publishing Corporation.

London *Observer* for selections by Basil de Sélincourt, April, 1933, and William Glock, July 26, 1936.

Longmans, Green & Co. for a passage from *The Theatre* by Sheldon Cheney.

The Macmillan Company for selections from *Art and Society* by Herbert Read; Gluck's Preface to *Alceste* in *Music & Nationalism* by Cecil Forsyth; *Beyond Good and Evil* by Friedrich Wilhelm Nietzsche, translated by Helen Zimmern; *Music Study in Germany* by Amy Fay; and the map adapted from *A Political and Cultural History of Modern Europe, Volume I,* by C. J. H. Hayes. These selections are used by permission of The Macmillan Company, publishers.

Music & Letters, London, for the selection by Eva Mary Grew, January, 1938.

Musical Courier for "My Dream" by Franz Schubert, translated by César Saerchinger.

New York Herald Tribune for the item by Lawrence Gilman; the Schönberg item translated by J. D. Bohm; and the item signed "J. S., May 25, 1939."

The New York Sun for the article by W. J. Henderson.

The New York Times for the excerpt from Olin Downes's interview with Ernest Bloch, January 22, 1939.

Novello & Company, Ltd., London, for the extract from *The Organ Works of Bach* by Harvey Grace.

Oxford University Press, London, for selections from *The Music of Bach* by C. Sanford Terry and *The Oxford History of Music, Volume I,* edited by H. W. Wooldridge.

Oxford University Press, New York, for the quotation from Shaw's translation of *The Odyssey* and the poem by Ford Madox Ford from his *Collected Poems.*

Duncan Phillips, author, for part of his article on Giorgione from *The Enchantment of Art.*

G. P. Putnam's Sons for selections from *The Dance; A Short History of Classic Theatrical Dancing* by Lincoln Kirstein.

Random House, Inc. for a paragraph from *Beloved Friend* by C. S. Bowen and B. von Meck.

G. Schirmer, Inc. for selections from the following articles in *The Musical Quarterly:* "The Social Condition of Violinists in France before the Eighteenth Century" by Marc Pincherle, "Music and the Centenary of Romanticism" by Julien Tiersot (in which he quotes from Victor Basch), "Gluck and the Encyclopaedists" by Julien Tiersot, "Haydn and the Viennese Classical School" by Guido Adler, "Early Spanish Music for Lute and Keyboard Instruments" by Willi Apel, and "Polyphonic Music of the Gothic Period" by Rudolf Ficker.

Charles Scribner's Sons for selections from *The Dawn of Conscience* by James H. Breasted and *The Opera, Past and Present* by William F. Apthorp.

Bernard Shaw and Constable & Company, Ltd., London, for quotations from *Music in London*.

Sheed and Ward, Inc. for the selection from *In Search of Mozart* by Henri Ghéon.

Miss Dorothy Thompson for the excerpt from her article on "The Grouse on the English," *New York Herald Tribune*, May 12, 1937.

Ives Washburn, Inc. for the selection from *Dufay to Sweelinck* by Edna R. Sollitt.

A Table of Contents

THE HISTORICAL PAST

THE PROBLEMATIC PRESENT

THE ARTS IN HISTORY

The Arts in History

Art must be recognized as the most certain mode of expression which mankind has achieved. As such it has been propagated from the very dawn of civilization. In every age man has made things for his use and followed thousands of occupations made necessary by his struggle for existence. He has fought endlessly for power and leisure and for material happiness. He has created languages and symbols and built up an impressive fund of learning; his resource and invention have never been exhausted.

And yet all the time, in every phase of civilization, he has felt that what we call the scientific attitude is inadequate. The mind he has developed from his deliberate cunning can only cope with objective facts; beyond these objective facts is a whole aspect of the world which is only accessible to instinct and intuition. The development of these obscurer modes of apprehension has been the purpose of art; and we are nowhere near an understanding of mankind until we admit the significance and indeed the superiority of the knowledge embodied in art.

We may venture to claim superiority for such knowledge because whilst nothing has proved so impermanent and provisional as that which we are pleased to call scientific fact and the philosophy built on it, art, on the contrary, is everywhere, in its highest manifestations, universal and eternal.

— Herbert Read: *Art and Society*

THE VALUE OF HISTORY

WE must have a knowledge of what has been going on and how and why it came to be if we are to be as wise and as happy as possible — in a word, if we are to possess the world in which we live. The sum of such knowledge, order made out of a vast number of facts, the significant separated from the inconsequential, is what we call *history* — social, economic, political, and cultural.

Our generation is making an earnest attempt, as is shown by the new titles appearing constantly in our bookstores, to see, as a whole, the course of those forces which have brought about its present social and economic crises. It is also turning from material insecurity and a loss of confidence in the established social order to an attempt at realizing something of the supersubstantial heritage of the human race. Such projects as federal support of artists, municipal museums and orchestras, and art and music high schools are some of the varied manifestations of this effort we are making to appropriate art as a spiritual resource.

Goethe once said that if we are ever to possess that which we inherit from our forefathers, we must earn it for ourselves. The possession of art in this sense means that we must look on its history not merely as definite and literal information on what has been accomplished in the past but as a description of the social, political, and artistic milieu out of which grew the music, painting, architecture, and sculpture of the various periods and which explains how they came to be what they are.

DIVERSE PHILOSOPHIES OF HISTORY

The idea of the division of man's achievements into certain definite periods has been used in historiography since early times. The philosophers of Greece — Plato, Aristotle, and the rest — thought of human developments as occurring in a series of historical cycles, which always returned to the original starting point. The Middle Ages looked to the ancients as the source of all wisdom, and so the historical outlook was a static one. It was the rationalistic seventeenth century, led by René Descartes and his followers, which developed a philosophy of history based on the idea of a cultural evolution, the various elements of which were closely integrated.

Prior to the nineteenth century the most enthusiastic exponent of the doctrine of history as progress was the Marquis Marie Jean de Condorcet, who tried to show " through reasoning and through facts that nature has assigned no limits to the perfecting of the human faculties, that the perfectibility of man is truly indefinite, and that the progress of this perfectibility, henceforth independent of any power that might wish to arrest it, has no other limit than the duration of the globe on which nature has placed us."

The philosophers of nineteenth-century Romanticism added their individual conceptions to this idea of history as a series of periods, each representing definite progress. The need for a science based on the facts of human relationships rather than on the abstract reasonings of philosophers was first expressed by Count Claude Henri de Saint-Simon and developed as a system by his pupil and associate, Auguste Comte. In the latter's *Positive Philosophy*, published in 1851–1854, history is divided into epochs, each of which shows socialized progress. It was Herbert Spencer in England who merged the idea of such sociological progress with the new theory of cosmic evolution. From this resulted the materialism and confidence in progress so largely current up to the time of the World War. The doubts arising from the collapse of this optimism have led to a number of other theories of sociological fluctuations.

With or without the concept of "perfectionism," most anthropologists, sociologists, and historians have used some scheme of periodizing — of dividing historical changes into certain phases in each of which there is definite social and cultural integration. Let us put it in another way: the observer, as he watches the long scroll of history unroll before his eyes, is impressed by the fact that there are certain periods when man's achievements in science, philosophy, religion, and the arts indicate that there were characteristic patterns in thinking and acting, patterns which are repeated and which show that the various phases of activity were part of one living unity and the manifestation of one spirit. This was recognized by the eighteenth-century philosopher Turgot, when he said: "The same senses, the same organs, the spectacle of the same universe have everywhere given to men the same ideas, just as the same needs and the same propensities have everywhere taught them the same arts." A recent and impressively documented sociological study by Dr. Sorokin of Harvard University has gone so far as to maintain that the theories of social and cultural development generally held are not valid, and to suggest a new classification of the fluctuation of the forms of art, systems of truth, ethics, and law, as well as those of social relationships, war, and revolution. But even this newest of sociological theories depends for its validity on the fact that the various phases of the cultures studied are logically and closely integrated. Sorokin states that not only the arts but all the main components of a culture — its science and philosophy, its ethics and law, its forms of social, political, and economic organization — are interrelated and have changed their form at the same time and in the same direction.

Most historians of art have followed some such periodizing as a matter of course and have evolved in the process a great many "catalogue histories" of painting, architecture, music, and so forth. These are of importance if one wishes to know who painted a certain picture and when he did so, how many operas Boieldieu wrote, how many symphonies Stamitz produced, or where the great buildings of the world are located; but they give little understanding of these things as works of art. Art, even considered in the most abstract way, is the result of the desire of the artist to create something that will satisfy himself through the manipulation of certain arrangements of shape, size, mass, time, and so forth — what the aestheticians call *beauty*. And all the arts, especially music, have tended to express the sense of beauty in certain periods according to definite ideals. Which means that the conception of beauty has been a constantly changing idea during the ages, one which has altered itself to suit the ideals of the historical period during which it was produced. It means also that in order to appreciate the manifestations of a work of art, we should know the general life and thought of the period which brought it into being and how the sonata, the sonnet, the cathedral, the painting, reflecting this life and thought, are related to the other intellectual products of the time.

THE SEVENTEENTH CENTURY, A PRACTICAL EXAMPLE

A concrete example may help to make this clear. No period in the history of Europe was more active in liberating man's powers and shaping our modern life than was the seventeenth century. It was then, we must remember, that some of the greatest discoveries in science were made: when Francis Bacon set the current of man's thought turning toward material things, after it had dwelt so long on spiritual ones; when

Galileo, the creator of experimental science, swept the heavens with his telescope, discovering the Milky Way to be a track of countless separate stars and the moon a dead satellite owing its light merely to a reflection of the sun's rays; when Isaac Newton, through the observation of an apple's fall, worked out the laws of universal gravitation; when Harvey published his discovery of the circulation of the blood and Pascal his treatise on vacuum. This was the time when Shakespeare, Milton, Corneille, and Molière lived and wrote; when Rubens, Rembrandt, Velásquez, and Van Dyck carried out to the full the traditions which had been handed down by the masters of the Renaissance. If we realize all this and can sense something of the great intellectual curiosity of the period, something of its tremendous zest for living, then we can understand the developments that took place at this time in music. It was during this era that the Italians invented and developed their colorful and spectacular *new music*, the opera. In Venice church music of gorgeous quality and luxuriant richness was being produced for both choirs and orchestras. In St. Peter's in Rome, Frescobaldi, the greatest organist of the time, was playing to crowds of thousands of people; so great was his popularity that his audiences followed him from city to city. In England a musical culture so varied and rich that it has never again been equaled in that country was in full flower; everywhere instruments were freeing themselves from the shackles of being merely " consorts for the voice " and were developing a new and outstanding kind of expression for themselves; it was at this time that the violin came into its own and the keyboard instruments first attained their popularity. All this was part and parcel of the daring, experimental attitude of mind that was common to the age, an attitude which completely changed during the next hundred years but which explains the operas of Monteverdi, the church music of the Gabrielis and Schütz, the instrumental works of Corelli and Purcell.

" BIGGER AND BETTER "

It is through describing the characteristic thought and feeling of the various periods in history and the sense of form and ideals of beauty manifested in the art works of these periods that a history of art can best help one to share the delight of those who produced them. In the writing of such a history the traditional precedent of periodizing may be followed, provided it is realized that overlapping is unavoidable and that pigeonholing everything exactly and definitely is impossible. The concept of rationalists and early sociologists that history is a series of episodes inevitable in their progress must also be avoided. It is not a matter of a sort of grand triumphal procession from something simple and elemental to the superior and complex result that we know today. Such a conception has been rudely upset by recent events in all phases of life; and recent discoveries show that it has always been absolutely untenable in so far as art is concerned.

Until 1895 the outstanding intellects of western Europe had dedicated themselves definitely to the conviction that the culture of their time represented the highest to which man had attained — that everything which had been produced before the beginning of history could only be primitive and insignificant in comparison with the developments that had taken place since, which culminated in the glories of the nineteenth century. Then, from a French scholar, there came accounts of a newly discovered series of rock paintings in Spain and France, paintings which showed that the men living in the ice age, thousands of years before our era, had possessed a significant culture and produced an art so advanced as to be not far removed from that of modern times — an art to which later sculptors and painters were to turn for inspiration.

Many historians of art have planned their works according to this concept of inherent growth, a growth in which "individual events and men sink into insignificance in comparison with the drama of which they are only acts and actors" (Daniel Gregory Mason). Without making any attempt to settle the question of creative evolution, we can undoubtedly say that this is not true. If it were, it would be necessary to consider the Gregorian chant (a type of music which we have come to appreciate as one of our most precious tonal treasures), or the secular and sacred polyphonic music of the Renaissance, or even the works of the great Sebastian Bach, as merely steps in an orderly progress from the primitive music of the savages to the contemporary "perfection" of Stravinsky and Schönberg. And we should have to think of the lovely lute songs of the seventeenth century as being but the early products of an evolutionary process which was to lead to the later glories of Schubert and Wolf, whereas these early songs are fully developed entities, beautifully expressive of their time and period.

The best thought on the subject, while recognizing the reality of the spiritual development of the human race, regards history as a process of flowering rather than one of continual progress, one of practical and cultural change rather than of constant improvement. Such changes are due to a number of causes; but they do not necessarily make any one period greater or more developed than another. Faure has said that the Egyptian civilization was the equal of any that has yet appeared on the earth; and from many aspects this is true, though it reached its zenith, you will remember, in the fifteenth century B.C. There is no good reason why we should try to think of the music of Palestrina either as superior to or inferior to that of Beethoven. Our enjoyment of either is enhanced if we know why the music of each is typical of the religious, social, and general intellectual trends of the time in which it was written and how it differs from the other things of the same period. Then we realize why it affects us as it does.

Malvina Hoffman, the American sculptress, has said in her autobiography, *Heads and Tales*, that the beauty of the Greek civilization as revealed to her in the architecture and sculpture in Athens made her "stagger, as if under a series of blows," a statement which all lovers of visual beauty will understand. But she does not infer that this beauty was greater than that which was made manifest during the Renaissance or than that which is being produced today. It was simply different, suggestive of the ideals of the culture which gave it birth. And so it has been through all history.

DANGERS TO BE REALIZED

There are, of course, certain dangers in any attempt to integrate the arts; the process is not so simple as it seems. In the course of development, each art has naturally followed certain technical procedures peculiar to itself, which may or may not have their counterparts in the

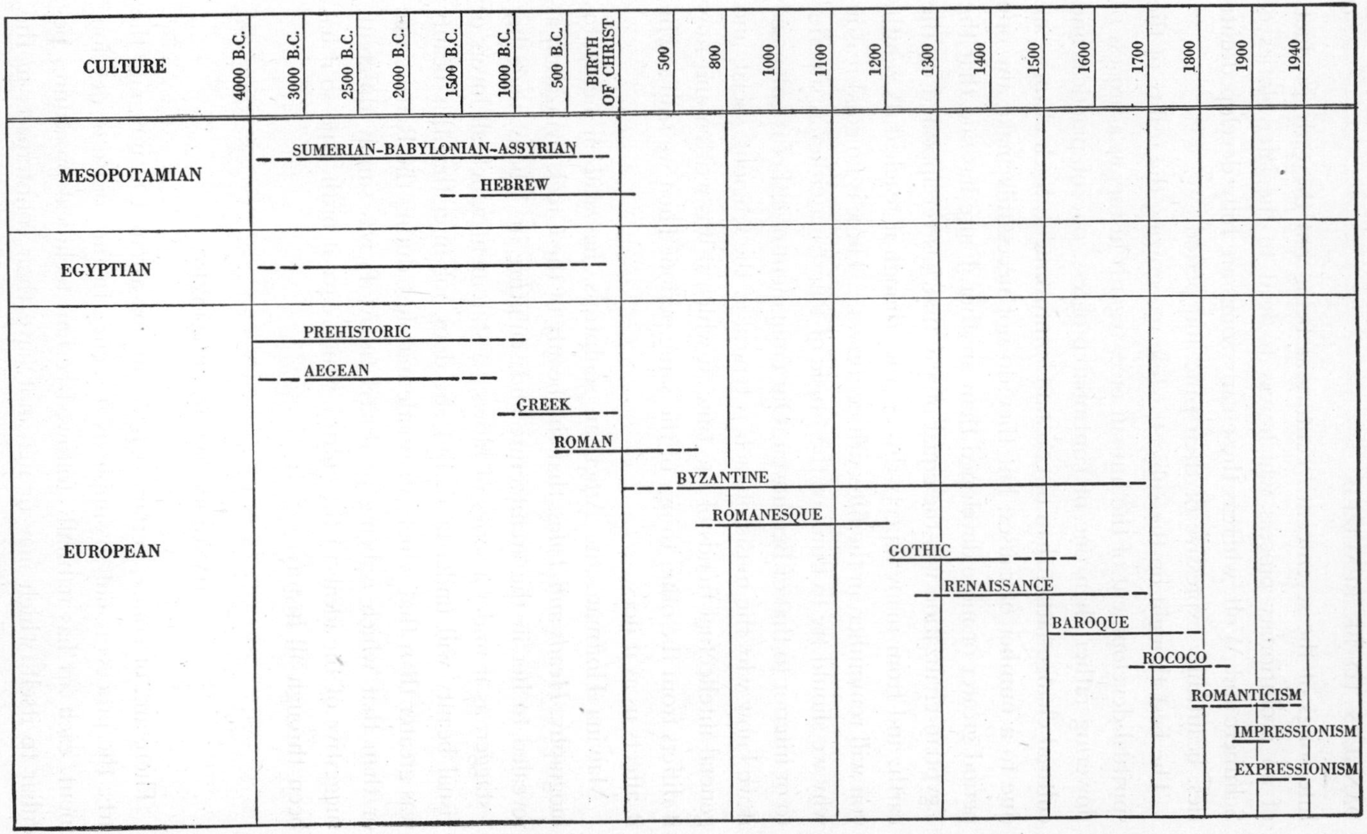
CULTURE
4000 B.C.
3000 B.C.
2500 B.C.
2000 B.C.
1500 B.C.
1000 B.C.
500 B.C.
BIRTH OF CHRIST
500
800
1000
1100
1200
1300
1400
1500
1600
1700
1800
1900
1940
MESOPOTAMIAN
SUMERIAN-BABYLONIAN-ASSYRIAN
HEBREW
EGYPTIAN
EUROPEAN
PREHISTORIC
AEGEAN
GREEK
ROMAN
BYZANTINE
ROMANESQUE
GOTHIC
RENAISSANCE
BAROQUE
ROCOCO
ROMANTICISM
IMPRESSIONISM
EXPRESSIONISM

other arts; and an attempt to interpret these according to the same principles is bound to result in confusion and misunderstanding.

And there are other difficulties. For one thing, history refuses to be divided arbitrarily: at the time when the Gothic period was gradually losing its force and vigor, the Renaissance was nearly at its height and the Baroque was in the process of being born. Likewise certain styles appeared earlier and developed more rapidly in some countries than in others: the Gothic ideal arose in the north and was never fully understood in the south of Europe; the Baroque was essentially an Italian style and never really reached England at all; and we are apt to think of the Rococo as a purely French influence. Nevertheless the clearer understanding that results from an integrated treatment of the arts against the general background of history justifies the employment of such a historical method, no matter what the difficulties.

In making the differences between the various periods as clear as possible, we have followed the usual procedure and chosen the epochs shown on the chart on page 10 as most representative and of scope wide enough to include all the materials pertinent to the treatment of our subject. The dates given are, of course, only approximate.

Various classifications of the arts have been made during these different culture periods. Without maintaining that it can be absolutely justified, we have followed the conventional distinction, usually taken for granted today, between what have come to be known as the "major" and the "minor" arts, and have confined our discussions to the former as being more highly expressive and self-sufficient than the latter. The difference between these two groups may be realized by comparing the finest products of the silversmith or the cabinetmaker with the best architectural, musical, or literary productions. When we refer in general to *art*, we mean the arts of music, the dance, architecture, sculpture, painting, and literature.

THE CONJECTURAL BEGINNINGS

The Origins of Art

They are content to be naked, but ambitious to be fine.
— Captain Cook, in writing of the savages of Tierra del Fuego

ART — WHAT IS IT?

PHILOSOPHIES differing widely in point of time and conception of ideas have been in general agreement as to the importance in the life of man of that which we have come to call *art*. From the time of man's earliest existence on earth, even perhaps before he had developed a written language, he has been possessed of an impulse to surround himself with beauty. Sometimes he seems to have been largely concerned with merely making designs for the pure pleasure of creation; at other times he has tried to provide himself with beautiful examples of the things he had to use every day. As he has developed in experience, he has attempted, through the expression of his emotions, to establish some sort of contact between himself and the outer world — "to bring into order the whole world of the gods."

We can find these various aspects of art in the earliest phases of human development and can trace them through all conditions of society. As man emerges from the dark chaos of the prehistoric centuries and starts to form tribes, cities, nations, through all the simple as well as the complex processes which have transformed and shaped his life and made and destroyed his civilizations — the power and magnificence of the Egyptians, the glory that was Greece and the grandeur that was Rome, the turbulence and strife of the Middle Ages, the splendor of the Renaissance, the exuberance of the Baroque, the grace of the Rococo, the warmth and sentiment of the Romantic years, into the machine age of today — there has persisted this simple yet essential impulse of man to produce art. Man seems to have been endowed from the first with a certain intuition which has impelled him to create things according to the laws of proportion and rhythm and has enabled him to invest his symbols and sounds with eternal beauty and mystery.

Yet, because words are necessarily such poor instruments for conveying thought, the same expressions being sometimes employed for diametrically opposed ideas, and because in this case the ideas themselves are so intangible, any exact definition of art seems impossible, although many have been attempted. The Alexandrian philosopher Plotinus, writing in the third century after Christ, said that art deals with things that are beyond human definition; nevertheless, his successors through the ages have spent a great deal of time and energy trying to explain just what they considered art to be and how it affects the human consciousness. It remains today, however, like electricity, one of those great forces which have tremendous influence on our lives and yet which elude all attempts at satisfactory definition.

If, however, we are to base such a work as this on the premise that art is one of the supreme achievements of human endeavor and a representative activity of the various epochs of human history, we must make some sort of attempt at describing its characteristics. The best way of doing this is through an inquiry into the possible origins of this activity in man. For art has remained essentially the same in spirit throughout the centuries of its existence, and if we can learn something of the interplay of forces to which it owes its beginnings, we can be brought to realize its essential characteristics and can better explain some of its later, complex developments.

ANTHROPOLOGY'S CONCLUSIONS

There are two main sources for the materials of such a study: first, the speculations of the anthropologists [1] and the archaeologists [2] regarding those remains of prehistoric art that have come down to us — such

[1] In its fullest sense *anthropology* means the study of man in general, his relation to his physical character, environment, and culture; in practice it is usually limited to the study of man in the earliest stages of his advance to full development.

[2] *Archaeology* treats of man's past life and activities as shown by the relics and monuments he has left behind him.

Courtesy of The American Museum of Natural History, New York

THE ART OF PREHISTORIC MAN

This shows the entrance to one of his caves as a modern artist conceives it. The wall paintings have been found deep in the recesses of such caves. (From a model of Castillo Cave, Northern Spain)

things as the pictures drawn and painted on the walls of caves and on rocks in the various parts of Europe and Africa inhabited by the Stone Age men and their descendants, as well as the many sculptured objects which they left behind; and second, the observation of such primitive societies as still exist, living an elementary hunting life in the wilds of Africa and the other places of the globe not yet pre-empted by civilization.

An enormous amount of research has been made along these lines by various societies and individuals, notably by Professor Frobenius and his Institute for the Morphology of Civilization, founded at Frankfort on the Main, Germany. These researches seem to prove that the art which once existed in Europe lives on today among the descendants of its originators in Africa. So that our knowledge of primitive man, now richer than ever, gives us definite information from which to draw reasonable conclusions regarding the life and art of his prehistoric prototypes.

Using all the information at their disposal, anthropologists have decided that man appeared in Europe sometime during the first of three

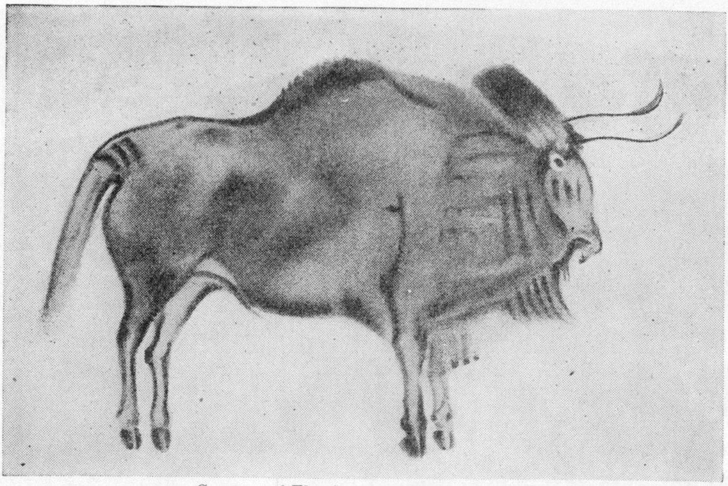

Courtesy of The American Museum of Natural History, New York

POLYCHROME PAINTING OF A BISON (Altamira Cave, Spain)

interglacial or warm periods, which are thought to have occurred between the four great glaciated epochs when ice covered most of our globe.[3] The first beginnings of art that have survived — the rock paintings and sculpture just mentioned — are assumed to have occurred during the last of these periods, in what is designated as the later Paleolithic period, extending from about 20,000 to 10,000 B.C. These paintings, although they were executed by men who were still primitive savages living in caves in the earth, their food provided entirely through the hunt, and who had no conception of the great benefits that were to come later through the development of agriculture, writing, and so forth, are nevertheless masterpieces far removed from whatever may have been the primi-

[3] In a recently published book, Earnest A. Hooton, Professor of Anthropology at Harvard University, has made an interesting graphic " time clock " of the three billion years which are supposed to represent the age of our earth. By reducing these to the twelve hours which it takes for the hands to go around the face of a clock, he shows that man has lived on the earth — he is thought to have appeared some four millions of years ago — for only the last 21 seconds of the whole twelve-hour period. If again we stretch this 21 seconds over a clockface, Mr. Hooton shows that it was nine o'clock before man began to make his rough stone axes; that at 11.54 he began to draw and paint pictures, and that fewer than 37 seconds before midnight he discovered the use of iron. What we speak of as modern times are, in such a scheme, merely a fraction of the final second!

tive sources of art. At what stage, then, in man's long ascent from a purely animal dependence on nature can we say that conscious art made its appearance, and what was the nature of its origin? These are questions that can hardly be given anything like scientific answers; but it is possible to speculate somewhat on these origins in a larger sense and to trace psychologically some of the probable forces to which the art impulse owes its origin.

THE ORIGINS OF ART

If we strip art of the intellectual connotations which civilized man has given it and try to see it, as far as we can, from the viewpoint of mentalities many epochs removed from ours, we realize that it is an activity of the senses — "elemental as the primary emotions of love, hate, and fear." We can reasonably conclude that such an activity arose in different localities as the result of a number of varied influences. Among these were probably:

(1) The innate desire of prehistoric man for ornamenting and decorating himself
(2) The serving of some definitely utilitarian purpose
(3) The impulse to imitate nature and the pleasure to be derived from it
(4) The expression of some kind of sex-consciousness
(5) The usefulness of art as an adjunct to a religion of idolatry
(6) The expression of some emotional necessity which had no direct connection with ordinary life

ART AS ORNAMENT

There are many who agree with the contentions of Ernst Grosse, who, in his book *The Beginnings of Art,* maintains that the first manifestations of an art impulse in prehistoric man came through his desire to make himself as beautiful and as attractive as possible by painting or tattooing his body and decorating it with such ornaments as necklaces, hairdresses, loincloths, and so forth. Such pleasure in adornment is to be found among all modern primitive peoples: we find them smearing their bodies with striped bands of paint until they resemble American barber poles; they blacken their teeth, pull out their ear lobes and pull down their lips; they pile up their hair into all sorts of odd shapes. All this activity seems to lead naturally to an elemental development of various kinds of patterns and compositions.

That this impulse to decorate was transferred to the utensils and implements used by early man may readily be seen by examining the lance heads, throwing sticks, magic wands, and daggers he left behind. Among the abundant examples of lance heads of worked flint that have been found in the caves of prehistoric man, there is a set in the British Museum which shows that these heads were often made with a view to appearance as well as usefulness as weapons, for they have a beautiful form and show a delicate manipulation of surface structure. One of the best-known single examples of early mobiliary art is a piece of reindeer horn which clearly shows the anatomy of a crouching deer, treated in such a way as to make an admirable dagger handle, the beautifully formed animal figure lending itself perfectly to the grip of the human hand! A similar love of design and ornamentation is to be found on early pottery and woven stuffs; whether or not it was accidental in origin is of little moment.[4] Whatever its first occasion, there is no doubt that the decorative impulse was a strongly determining force in the art of all primitive peoples.

ART ARISING FROM USE

Those who believe that the beginnings of art, as well as all its later developments, served some definitely practical or utilitarian purpose, argue that the painting of pictures, the making of sculptured objects, the practice of dancing, even self-adornment, were not isolated phenomena, unrelated to the life of primitive man, but a part of the very

[4] It has been suggested by some that the geometrical designs on early pottery and baskets go back to thumbprints or the imprint of instruments necessary to the process of baking the clay, or to the necessity for using various types of grasses or threads in the process of weaving.

texture of his existence, connected in various ways with such elemental activities as the obtaining of food, the making of war, and the propagation of the species. Man decorated his weapons and wove his baskets as he did in order to increase their usefulness. He tattooed his body in order to increase its sexual attractiveness and to enable him to stand out as superior to his fellows.

ART AS AN IMITATION OF NATURE

Two of the oldest theories as to the origin of art maintain that it arose from this source. First, Aristotle [5] observed that from his earliest childhood man is an imitative animal, naturally drawing likenesses of himself and his surroundings (we can all remember our own childish activities in this line) and delighting in being able to recognize the original in the copy. Second, Lucretius [6] traced the origins of music back to an imitation of natural sounds, such as the songs of birds and the roar of the wind.

The earliest art we know is full of imitative drawings and paintings which show that our cave-man ancestors possessed alert powers of observation as well as considerable technical ability as painters. Modern savages display the same tendencies, tracing or drawing the likenesses of animals and fish with evident pleasure. The mimetic dances described later in this chapter, with their imitative poses and suggestive gestures, are excellent examples of the importance of imitation as a genetic factor in art; but we must guard against considering it as the only, or even the most important, factor. While recognizing the importance of truth to nature in the representative arts, modern theorists are apt to look on imitation as a means for achieving beautiful and significant form rather than as a purely genetic force.

[5] The Greek philosopher (384–322 B.C.) who discoursed in his *Poetics* on the arts of poetry, music and the dance, sculpture, and painting, but significantly says nothing about architecture. It would be difficult indeed to attribute a mimetic origin to this, the most practical of the arts.

[6] A Latin poet (96–55 B.C.) whose great poem *De rerum natura* strove to free his countrymen from the trammels of superstition and to raise them above their natural weaknesses.

ART AS AN EXPRESSION OF THE SEX IMPULSE

There are various ways in which this universal human impulse has affected the production of art, ranging from the sophisticated "compensatory satisfactions" derived by civilized man from such things as his manner of dress, his practice of religion, his creation of art, to the simplest and most obvious means of all, that of excelling in the matter of sex rivalries. Primitive man, as we have already observed, used ornamentation and decoration and dress as means for sex attraction. He tried to please by showing his prowess in singing a love song or in doing an athletic dance or in fighting his rivals. And it is natural to suppose that the primitive woman of the Paleolithic era used much the same means to attract her man as her modern sister does today.

All sorts of erotic and suggestive dances are common in primitive societies, as are symbolic painting and sculpture. When we examine the art work of primitive peoples we find sex characteristics greatly overemphasized. And many of the large communal religious ceremonies of primitive, as well as of civilized, peoples have been frankly sexual both in imagery and in design — the ceremonies of the aboriginal natives as well as the phallic worship of the cultivated Greeks.

Because the popular doctrines of certain sects hold that all art is a sort of disguised manifestation of inarticulate sex feelings, rebellious because thwarted, the theory that art is closely related to sex has been recently overemphasized. There is no doubt that there is a close connection of a subtle as well as a direct type. The sexual impulse can be made to account for some of the loveliest things in art; but we must remember that a great deal of art has not been touched by it at all.

THE ARTIST AS PRIEST

Another theory of the beginnings of art, one which until recently has had a wide vogue and which serves to explain many of the details of that art with which we are primarily concerned — music — treats all art as an adjunct to and outgrowth of magic and religion. The sculptured figures which primitive man left behind him are thought to have been some sort of idols or fetishes intended as offerings to the gods; the paintings on the cave walls were designed to insure, through the practice of a kind of magic power, the capture of animals necessary for existence; and music was thought to have grown out of a type of dancing that was originally ritualistic in its import.

ART AS AN INDIVIDUALISTIC EXPRESSION OF THE FEELINGS AND EMOTIONS

But there are many for whom none of these explanations, singly or all together, are satisfactory: they feel that art has arisen from something more than mere utility, sex, or the impulse to adorn or to imitate. In the previously mentioned book, *The Beginnings of Art,* Grosse expresses this idea by saying that an artistic activity is not necessarily entered upon as a means toward any end, but it is an " indefeasible faculty of man " and exists as an end in itself, without any connection with practical activities. Dr. Hirn of Helsingfors thus sums up the opinions of most writers on aesthetics on this subject:

" Most metaphysicians as well as psychologists, Hegelians as well as Darwinians, all agree in declaring that a work or performance which serves any utilitarian, nonaesthetic object cannot be considered as a genuine work of art. True art has its one end in itself, and rejects every extraneous purpose: that is the doctrine which, with more or less exactness, has been stated by Kant, Schiller, Spenser, and others, and popular opinion agrees in this respect with the conclusions of science."

This may be interpreted to mean that art is an individualistic rendering in a communicable form of the spiritual reactions established between man and the outer world, an objectified representation of some experience through which he has lived or by which he has been stimulated. While these expressions have nothing to do with practical realities, they are communicated in such a vivid way as to arouse in the reader, hearer, or observer reactions which in varying measure correspond to those which moved the artist. It is this power of art to stir feeling, to arouse emotions, to influence attitudes, and to affect thought which has made it one of the most important factors in human history.

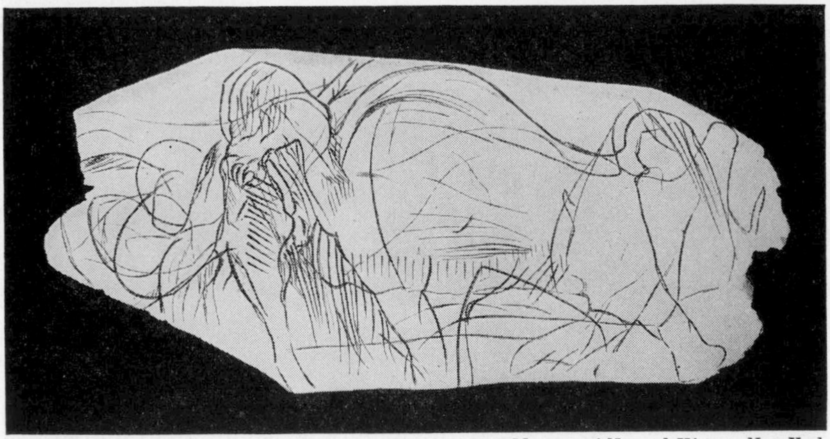

Courtesy of The American Museum of Natural History, New York

A prehistoric artist has made his conception of a mammoth conform to the size and shape of the elephant tusk on which he has drawn it, thus producing a real work of art. (From Dordogne, France; now in the Museum of Archaeology, Paris)

THE PURPOSE OF ART

Fortunately any rational study of the early manifestations of the art spirit in primitive peoples makes us realize that we do not need to hold exclusively to any of these beliefs. If we trace the manifold causes and influences which account for the significant importance of artistic creation in the world today, we can but conclude that it is impossible to select one of these exclusively to the neglect of the others. We need not believe either that art is strictly utilitarian, something woven into the very stuff of human existence and always associated with other values, such as religion, morality, and idealism, nor that it is entirely ideological, existing only for its own sake. The evidences made available through comparatively recent discoveries of prehistoric art objects in Europe and in Africa point to the fact that, at least from the Stone Age on, art has served both purposes and has been influenced by many factors.

The naturalistic paintings and carvings of the cave dwellers of two hundred centuries ago may have been created for the sheer delight which their achievement gave to those who placed them on the dark walls of their caves; but they also probably had a practical, utilitarian purpose — that of a magical propitiation of the gods or of acquisition of a command over animals desired for food. Primitive man probably thought of these painted animals as some sort of magic symbols and put them where he did in order to assure the capture of the real ones.

The magnificent temples and monumental sculpture of Egypt were but means for assuring the souls of the kings a life after death. "Sculpture and painting to the Greeks were not merely a medium for aesthetic pleasure; they were means for expressing and interpreting national life. As such they were subordinated to religion: the primary end of sculpture was to make statues of gods and heroes; the primary end of painting was to represent mythological scenes; and in either case the purely aesthetic pleasure was also a means to the religious experience" (Croiset: *Hellenic Civilization*). It is not necessary to do more than remind ourselves of the fact that architecture, music, sculpture, and painting of the Christian era up to the time of the Renaissance were conditioned almost entirely by the aims and beliefs of the Church; yet we can hardly say that the artists who executed these art works were not sincerely concerned with them from the aesthetic point of view, as expressions of pure beauty.

Richard Wagner was certainly moved by the erotic instinct to write some of his greatest music, and there is no doubt that sex played an important role in producing the salty exuberance of Rabelais; but to say that neither artist was seriously concerned with the production of work of highest aesthetic value is gravely to misunderstand these men.

THE BEGINNINGS OF MUSIC: RHYTHM

A close study of the origins of our own art will show the same duality of purpose. Among the earliest peoples the arts which we have come to distinguish as music, poetry, and the dance were united in one common whole the regulating force of which was rhythm, a factor which determined alike words, music, and dance figures. This united art played as important a role in the ideological and religious life of these early people as it did in their everyday existence.

In his book *Arbeit und Rhythmus* Karl Bücher has established the fact that the dance was a constant and persevering feature of the life of

DANCE OF WOMEN

Rock painting from South Africa (Copied by George W. Stowe, 1867)

The following remarks by a present-day Bushman help in interpreting this early painting: " They seem to be dancing, for they are stamping with their legs. This man who stands in front seems to be showing the people how to dance, that is why he holds a stick. He feels that he is a great man, so he holds the dancing stick, because he is one who dances before the people, that they may dance after him. The people know that he is one who dances first, because he is a great sorcerer."

primitive man. " All people dance," he says,[7] " dance till they are in a frenzy and their physical powers exhausted, often until the dancers sink fainting to the earth." Such a dance might have developed out of some sort of unco-ordinated, spontaneous movement of the body, perhaps arising from a surplus of animal vigor, resulting in the kind of capering and flinging about of the body, with accompanying shouts and cries, that we see when a boy and his dog take their morning walk together. Or the early dancers may have imitated the appearance and movements of animals as they had observed them while hunting, a procedure that can be observed in the play of young children and which illustrates Aristotle's theory as to artistic creation being an imitation of nature.

[7] Another writer on early music, Wallaschek, has said that there has never been dance without music of some sort.

But whatever the beginnings, nothing in the way of art was achieved until some sort of control was applied to such movements. By applying the principle of the rhythmic beat (the repetition of a measured sequence of strokes or sounds), our progenitors systematized and co-ordinated the movements of their dances so as to make them pleasurable and effective. That there is a psychological effect in the repetition of rhythms for the production of emotional states was probably discovered early. The hypnotic effect of monotonous repetition and the exciting effect of acceleration of speed and vehemence can still be observed in the ritualistic dances of primitive peoples — both orgiastic dances and war dances. The realization of these effects may well have been the source of dance rhythm. At any rate, rhythm probably antedated melody, since it seemed capable of satisfying both emotional and intellectual instincts of primitive man such as were shown in his simple ordering of the objects he strung together in a necklace or the making of patterns in his drawings.

AN ADDED FACTOR: MELODY

Many theories have been advanced as to how man first began to make melody. Herbert Spencer thought that singing was the result of some intense emotion influencing the organs of speech and respiration so strongly as to produce sounds, a fact that is shown by our natural grunting while working or screaming when in pain. Darwin thought that it originated in some sort of love call from man to his mate. Grosse believed that song, as we have suggested of the dance, was some form of play. Others have thought that it may have resulted from some biological necessity or the attempts of the members of a group to co-ordinate their work so as to make it most effective. A more recent theory, one which does little honor to the memory of the great names in German philosophy, is that which bears the striking imprint of the Nazi *Kultusministerium* to the effect that the art which this people has so signally enriched had its beginnings in the strident war calls of the early Teutonic nations, echoing and re-echoing from hilltop to hilltop. It is hardly necessary to add that such a theory would receive scant credence outside the intensely nationalistic circles of the totalitarian states.

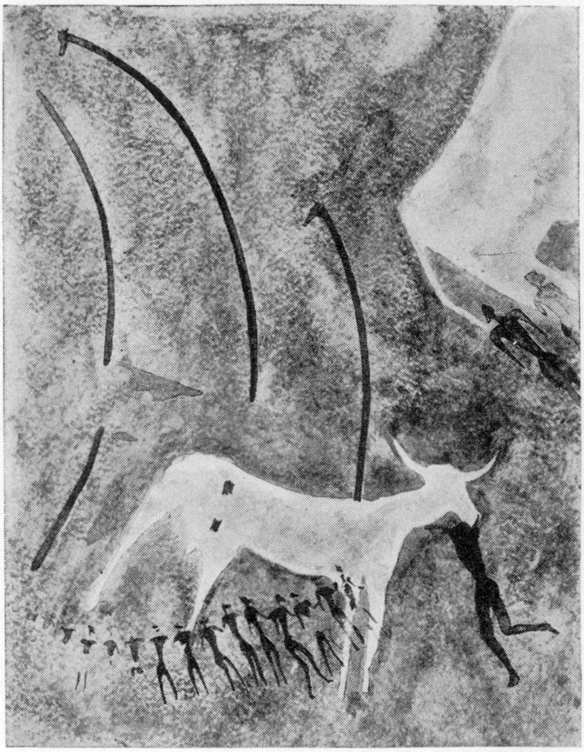

Courtesy of The Museum of Modern Art

This picture of the dancing men behind a cow, with the fragments of three large giraffes in the background, was found in one of the greatest of African deserts, the Libyan. Dynamic and colorful, it is an example of the Levant tradition.

MUSIC AND MAGIC

There is probably some truth in all these ideas. Sorokin has well said that it is likely that primitive people sang when they became excited or when they had an overabundance of energy or merely because they enjoyed it, because singing and dancing are pleasant and biologically useful. But undoubtedly one of the principal uses which primitive man found for music and dancing was in the performing of acts of magic. Religion was of great significance in the life of prehistoric society, just as it is today in primitive communities. In its practice, as we have pointed out, one of the chief activities was that of the performance of certain occult formulas and prescribed rituals in order to obtain the favor of the gods. These rites seemed to have been carried out according to certain contracts which it was believed the gods had revealed and to which man had agreed. Some of the tribes came in time to believe that the objects of their desire could be obtained through the potency of the magic rites themselves, without participation of the gods. It was in this manner that music came to be thought of as having a special meaning.

Combarieu maintains that, if we are to believe the evidence of modern primitives, there were in these prehistoric societies magic dance incantations for all purposes — for communicating with the spirits, for subduing animals, for obtaining rain or good weather, for inspiring love, for aid in childbearing, for assuring the birth of a boy, for obtaining vengeance, for bringing back the spirits of the dead, for appeasement of evil spirits, and so on. We have no idea, of course, as to the musical nature of these incantations, aside from assuming that they were much like those used among modern primitive peoples. But there is little doubt that prehistoric man attached definite significance not only to the sounds themselves but to the religious-magical values they represented.

So, too, with the dance movements associated with these rites. Savages have a large number of magic dances, many of which are accompanied by both vocal and instrumental music — dances of the chase, where the figures imitate animals such as kangaroos, bears, wolves, and otters; war dances, in which the actual movements of battle are imitated in order to inculcate courage and insure victory; dances for celebrating the conclusions of treaties between tribes, and so on. One of the most important writers on the origins of civilization, Lubbock, says that among savages and uncultured people the dance was never thought of as an amusement without significance but always as a serious occupation and a necessary factor in all the activities of communal life.

Travelers in uncivilized parts of the globe have brought back plenty of accounts of such dances. Brown has cited some of them, notably one taken from a book published in 1878, *The Aborigines of Victoria,* according to which the assembly dances of the natives of Central Australia were held around a large fire, in front of which stood the conductor or leader, a native of distinction, who indicated the rhythm by means of

Attilio Gatti-Pix

A PRESENT-DAY MAMBUTI PYGMY

He enacts in dance pantomime the fight which he had with a leopard whose hide is seen in the foreground.

the two staves of office which he struck together. On one side were the women, squatting on the ground with opossum skins stretched between their knees, upon which they beat with their fists. We do not have to follow the description of the dance in its details to realize that all its movements, engaged in simultaneously by a large number of individuals, were performed in perfect time. At one moment there was a uniform shout from all the performers, and the description suggests that it sounded as if it had been uttered by a single throat.

Another dance described was of a mimetic kind and represented with the utmost accuracy the browsing of a herd of cattle in a glade, the movements of the creatures being reproduced with careful attention to detail; then came a raid by a party of whites, perfectly camouflaged, and a combat between them and the natives. Very likely such mimetic dances were used in paleolithic days, for there are a number of figures in the

Attilio Gatti-Pix

VICTORY BALL

Music for the dance celebrating a successful hunt is supplied by tom-toms on which the Mambuti drummers beat a rhythm with the palms of their hands.

art of the period which suggest such practices. How highly organized they were and whether they were carried out in strict time we have no way of knowing; but that they were, in contrast to the modern gymnastic conception of the art, of magical nature, we are certain. When or how they developed into such a form as that shown by the Greeks we do not know, but it is likely that the change came rather early.

THE USE OF INSTRUMENTS

From the very beginnings of his music making man was furnished by nature with two very serviceable instruments, his voice and his hands. The wind instruments which he developed, flutes and reeds, are but " prolongations " of the voice, means to increase its natural force and quality. So the various percussive instruments which he made, drums, castanets, and so forth, were developments of the idea of clapping together his hands or beating in gorilla-fashion on his breast, for the purpose of indicating rhythm. The origin of the stringed instruments was possibly the hunter's bow with which he shot his arrows. Even today the savages of Central Africa speak of the bow as the source of all music.

Modern archaeological research has unearthed in Mesopotamia what is supposed to be the oldest instrument known to man — a double pipe made of bone. This was probably human, since it was the custom of primitive man to use parts of the human skeleton for such a purpose. The experts have figured that this instrument was made during the Chalcolithic Age, a period between the Bronze Age and the Stone Age, some three thousand years before Christ. It seems that all three of the instruments which appear first in history — the pipe, the drum, and the harp — originated in Asia and were quickly distributed over the world then known.

IN CONCLUSION

Even such a cursory survey of the probable beginnings of art as this should show the student that although it is impossible to say just when and in response to what forces it first appeared, it has always been one of the most important factors in the life of man. Nor is it necessary to dogmatize regarding such a long-continuing, universal, and diverse force. From the very beginning man's creative tendencies in art seem to have taken two definite directions, the ideological leading to abstractions and the utilitarian leading to achievement of material, realistic form. The proportion of each of these has varied in the different arts in different countries at different times: at one period there has been a dominance of one ideal; at another, the opposite has prevailed. But if we can realize that from the very first these aims have existed concurrently and that both have been important factors in the production of art, we shall avoid many of the misunderstandings that inevitably seem to result from works on the appreciation of art.

Music in the Life of the Near East

Thy dawning is beautiful in the horizon of heaven,
O living Aton, Beginning of life!
When thou risest in the eastern horizon of heaven
Thou fillest every land with thy beauty.

— From a hymn by Amenhotep (Ikhnaton)

THE CRADLE OF CIVILIZATION

THERE is a wide and so far unexplained gap between the arts we have described as having been produced by primitive man and those created by the earliest "civilized" peoples. What happened in between has long been the subject of continued research on the part of eager archaeologists anxious to solve the riddle of how the cave man developed into the Egyptian architect or the Sumerian poet. As Durant has remarked, there are not many finer things in man's rather sorry existence than this noble curiosity, this restless passion for understanding his past.

These researchers have come to the conclusion that the beginning of civilization took place in the restricted area lying at the eastern end of the Mediterranean somewhere around 5000 B.C.[1] As to just which civilization was the earliest to develop or what people first evolved the idea of conscious art, opinion seems divided. Both the Mesopotamian valley and the Egyptian valley have their supporters among the scholars; but the majority of opinions at present seem to favor the first and to suggest that at the time our Stone Age forefathers in Europe were still without written language or organized communities, there had developed in the Mesopotamian peninsula a technique of life which was later transferred to posterity intact in all its essentials.

to 2300 BC

China + Far East

[1] Professor Woolley of the University of Pennsylvania, in his researches at Ur, estimated that the Sumerians appeared to have reached civilization by 4500 B.C.

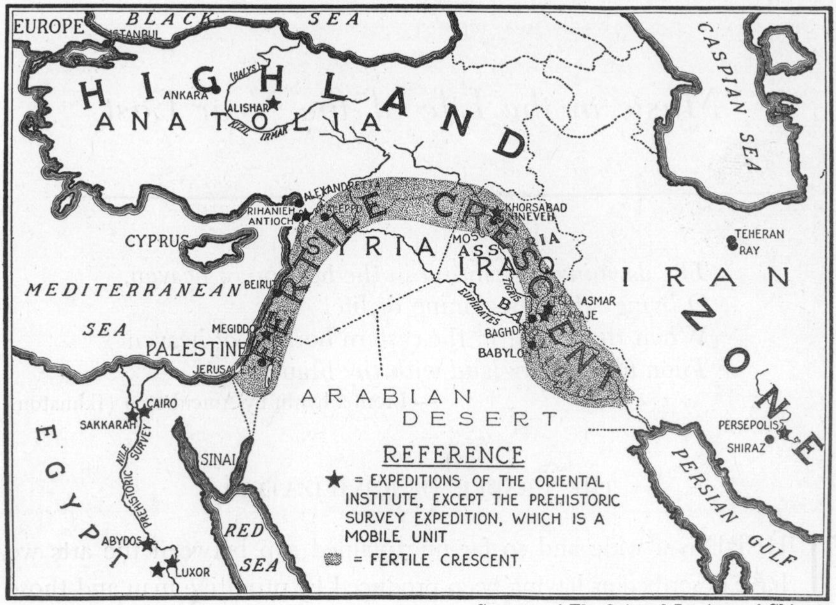

Courtesy of The Oriental Institute of Chicago

Directly east of the Mediterranean Sea lies the so-called Fertile Crescent, the region where the early civilizations worked out the techniques of life which they transmitted to the modern world through Greece and Rome.

THE SUMERIANS

One of the great romances of archaeology, a science in which there is much more of romance than the layman generally realizes, has been the recent unearthing of this civilization which represents the first evidences we have of anything like a complete culture and which was, until these investigations were undertaken during the latter part of the last century, entirely unknown. The manner in which this discovery was made seems almost fantastic.

During their study of the cuneiform writing of the Babylonians, archaeologists gradually became convinced that much of this writing, because of its non-Semitic character, must have been borrowed from an earlier race; and, without knowing that such a people had actually existed, the scholars posited them and gave them the name of Sumerians.

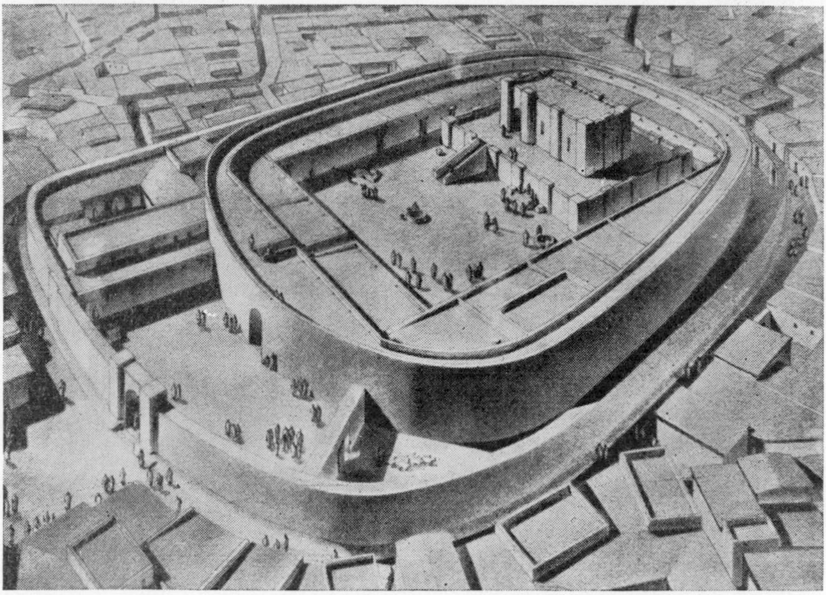

Courtesy of The Oriental Institute of Chicago

Aerial photography has been an invaluable aid to the modern archaeologist, since it reveals the lines of old cities which are invisible from the ground. This picture is an air view of a reconstruction of Khafaje, the great oval enclosing a Sumerian temple of 3000 B.C.

A few years later, two English archaeologists, working in the Tigris-Euphrates Valley, uncovered the sites of a number of cities in which some pre-Babylonian race had lived — Ur, which was already rich and powerful in the year 3000 B.C., Eridu, and Urak. Later investigations have revealed other important cities of these people, among them Kish, the seat of the oldest culture so far found in these regions, and Agade, capital of the ancient kingdom of Akkad.

Owing to the fortunate fact that by the time the Sumerians had made their brief appearance on the rapidly changing stage of history the art of writing had become fully developed, we have been able to reconstruct this earliest of civilizations in detail. In spite of the fact that Sumerian research is still in its infancy, we know much of its historical background, its economic and social life, its religious beliefs and practices, and its government, arts, and letters.

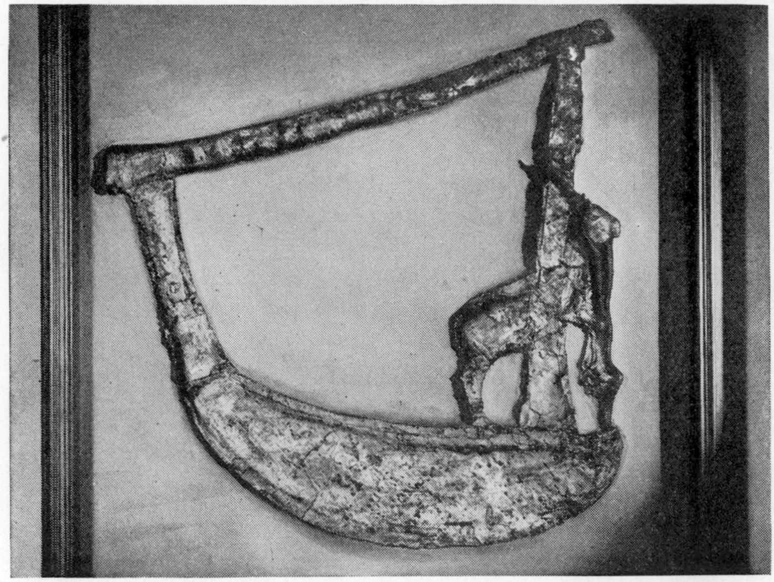

Courtesy of The University Museum, Philadelphia

SILVER BOAT-SHAPED LYRE
(From the Royal Tombs at Ur, about 3000 B.C.)

The Sumerian epoch, stretching roughly from 4000 B.C. to 2300 B.C., has been called a synthesis of beginnings. In some respects primitive enough, it nevertheless represents many " firsts " among man's activities — his first-known codes of law, his first use of irrigation, his first states and seigniories, his first use of gold and silver as tokens of value, his first business practices, including the use of a credit system, his first literature, and his first architectural vault and dome. The most striking feature of this epoch was, as we have intimated, the use of writing, evidently considered in the beginning merely as a tool for such business transactions as the production of bills, receipts, and shipments. Then it was taken up by the priests, who used it for the preservation of their magic formulas, ritualistic rubrics, hymns, and prayers; and so it became literature. The known origins of this art may be sought in such Sumerian hymns and prayers as that of the great Gudea, noblest of the Sumerian kings, addressed to the patron goddess of Lagash, his city, and written about 2600 B.C.:

"O my Queen, the Mother who established Lagash,
The people on whom thou lookest is rich in power;
The worshiper on whom thou lookest, his life is prolonged.
I have no mother — thou art my mother;
I have no father — thou art my father . . .
My goddess Bau, thou knowest what is good;
Thou hast given me the breath of life.
Under the protection of thee, my Mother,
In thy shadow I will reverently dwell."

— Translated by Jastrow in *The Civilization of Babylonia and Assyria*

If we can trust the accounts on the thousands of clay tablets on which the Sumerian priests recorded the history of their civilization, it is likely that such prayers and hymns were chanted to music. There are a number of descriptions of worship in which these were used, accompanied by pipe, lyre, and drum.

THE SIGNIFICANCE OF MUSIC AMONG THE SUMERIANS

As has been true all through its history, one of music's principal uses in this early civilization was in connection with religion. We have already spoken of the fact that primitive man was certainly cognizant of the peculiar capacity of music for stirring the emotions. A Sumerian clay tablet of the twenty-sixth century B.C. attributes the same power to it:

"To fill with joye the Temple court
And chase the Citie's gloome awaie,
The harte to still, the passions calme,
Of weeping eyes the teares to staie."

— Translated by Francis W. Galpin [2]

[2] In his book *The Music of the Sumerians and Their Immediate Successors, the Babylonians & Assyrians*. This is by far the most exhaustive study yet made of the music of these early peoples. In it Galpin appraises the effect of Sumerian music and song and states definitely that the Sumerians or their compatriots, the Akkads, had discovered a means of writing down their music centuries before the Greeks, to whom we have hitherto looked for the earliest efforts in this direction, evolved their systems of notation.

The book contains an example of a Sumerian hymn of creation transcribed into our modern notation by Galpin, who thinks that it was based on a seven-tone diatonic scale with the fourth step augmented — C,D,E,F♯,G,A,B,C — and that its rhythm

Courtesy of The University Museum, Philadelphia

A LARGE TEMPLE LYRE FROM UR (about 2700 B.C.)

The bull's head is of gold, with lapis-lazuli beard and shell inlays.

There was only the loosest sort of political unity in the Sumerian government, each group maintaining its own *patesi* or priest king and acknowledging the power of a principal emperor only when one arose with personality enough to make them his subjects. So in the Sumerian religion there was no universal god, but rather a diverse number of deities belonging to the different city-states and associated with the various phases of human activity.

---

and stress were entirely dependent on the words, which must have been delivered, in part at least, in a sort of free recitative.

It should be added that scholars do not agree on this matter. Dr. Curt Sachs in the *Archiv für Musikwissenschaft*, April, 1925, maintains that this notation, found on a tablet at Assur, shows the Sumerian scale to have had a nonchromatic pentatonic basis.

Most of these gods lived in temples, where they were liberally provided by their priests with money, food, and even wives. In addition to the gods there were spirits, beneficent as well as evil, seeking to possess the Sumerian soul. Music was used in the worship of these temples, where the priests were wont to deliver the revealed word of the god to the people to the solemn accompaniment of the harp, a fact which caused this instrument to be thought of as that of the "decision of fate." There were likewise music forces of liturgists and psalmists, both men and women, in the temples, trained to sing and play in praise of the god. A late account describes these forces as consisting of an orchestra, led by a harp, with a seven-stringed lyre, a two-stringed lute, pipes, and so forth, and a large group of singers.

That there was Sumerian secular music as well as sacred music is shown clearly by a catalogue which has been found of a music library of the time, listing, in addition to liturgical and psalmodic music, folk songs for craftsmen and shepherds, poems of victory and heroism, and love songs for both sexes. All these, according to Galpin's ideas, were without the modal characteristics which are to be found in later music and would sound more congenial to modern ears than would, for instance, the music of the Greeks.

Their musical scale is not the only thing in the Sumerian culture which would seem congenial to modern man; for many Sumerian ideals were absorbed by later peoples and so have become the common heritage of the ages. The exorcising power of music, later exemplified by the playing of the Hebrew shepherd David before King Saul; the attribution of some of man's powers to animals, an idea which persisted in the Orpheus legend and which is to be found as late as Gothic times, when the sculptors and wood carvers loved to depict animals playing instruments; the "blowing up of the trumpet in the new moon," a later religious practice of the Jews; the story of the Flood, adopted by the writers of the Old Testament — all these were part of Sumerian consciousness and so were absorbed into history.

The significant fact for musicians, however, is that the Sumerian art when it first appears in known history occupies a position that was not very different from that of later times. In other words, when music made its advent, it was as a fully established art, one which played an important role in the life of its time and established its standing for centuries to come. It was used in connection with religious services; it was thought to possess definite powers of magic; officially it was recognized by the state and religious authorities, although there are evidences that it was likewise pursued for pleasure's sake, in a " wine, woman, and song " sense; it was both vocal and instrumental, employing the services of many instruments, among them harps, lyres (both these types favorite instruments for accompanying the voice), flutes, drums, reed pipes, double as well as single, and, in a later, more decadent phase, trumpets, timbrels, and rattles (sistra); it passed through various developments, reaching a " golden " period, after which it became more and more sensual. In all these characteristics it differed little from its use in the other civilizations which appeared in the Near East — Egyptian, Babylonian, Assyrian, and Hebrew.

THE EGYPTIANS

A modern archaeologist has said that we know more about the details of the daily life in the Egypt of the fourteenth century B.C. than we do about those of England in the fourteenth century A.D. But such knowledge unfortunately does not extend to the field of music. There are two reasons for this: first, the fact that the Egyptians interested themselves a great deal more in the arts of sculpture and architecture than they did in music; and second, the fact that the musical practices were largely in the hands of the priests, who regarded them as magical and sacred influences in the lives of the people and hence as something to be carefully and secretly protected. No change or development was to be thought of. They would not even take the chance of revealing their secret by writing it down. As in other early cultures, the whole musical system of Egypt was subjected to such " rigid religious and hierarchal laws that it remained at its primitive form . . . and represents an immovable block which resists the assault of the centuries " (H. Wollett).[3]

[3] He is writing of Chinese music, but his statement applies with equal truth to Egyptian.

Archives Photographiques

FRAGMENT OF A SUMERIAN BAS-RELIEF

This shows what is evidently a religious procession. Several of the figures bear in their hands utensils that were dedicated to the rites of that time. Underneath, two figures provide accompanying music: one seems to be singing, and the other playing a large lyre similar to that recently discovered at Ur.

We have already said that scholars are not agreed as to the priority of Sumerian to Egyptian civilization and that some of them, notably the great American Egyptologist Breasted, consider that it was the other way about — that whatever ideas of agriculture and civilization the Sumerians may have possessed came to them from Egypt. However that may be, with the exception of music the Egyptians developed that which they may have borrowed from their neighbors to the northeast into a civilization which was not only one of the most robust and powerful but also one of the most polished in history. In spite of the advanced conditions in agriculture and industry which were to be found in ancient Egypt, its remarkable developments in science and letters, its well-organized system of government, with a longer record of duration than any other people has since attained, its advancement of science and education, the greatest achievements of Egyptian civilization, everything considered, were its architecture, sculpture, painting, and applied art. It is quite possible, as Faure has said, that "Egypt, through the solidarity, the unity, and the disciplined variety of its artistic products, through the enormous duration and the sustained power of its effort, offers the spectacle of the greatest civilization that has yet appeared on the earth." And Herr Ranke in his introduction to that book which gives the best of all possible records of this civilization, *The Art of Ancient Egypt*, agrees that this art, in the course of the transformation which it underwent during the three kingdoms,[4] represents one of the greatest achievements of human creation.

THE ARTS OF EGYPT

During the whole period of Egyptian history, from its earliest fixed date of 4241 B.C., art seems to have served the material and spiritual needs of the people: each tomb or statue or carving had a definite purpose to serve. The chief use of art was in religion, where it was em-

[4] The term *kingdom* is not used here in its usual sense; it refers rather to long periods of time, each of them comprising several dynasties. The usual division is as follows: Old Kingdom, 2980–2475 B.C.; Middle Kingdom, 2160–1788 B.C.; New Kingdom, 1580–1150 B.C.

King Khephren with Royal Headdress and Sacred Falcon

King Amenemhet as Sphinx (about 1820 B.C.)

Hall of Granite Pillars in the Lower Part of King Khephren's Funerary Temple (about 2850 B.C.)

Courtesy of The Metropolitan Museum of Art

Colonnade of the Temple of Queen Hatshepsut (about 1500 B.C.)

THE ART OF THE OLD AND MIDDLE KINGDOMS

ployed to manifest the belief of man's continued life after his existence here upon earth. The tombs of the prehistoric chieftains were filled with objects which were thought to be of use in their life after death. The huge Old Kingdom Pyramids of Cheops and Khephren were attempts to memorialize the names of their creators in an impressive fashion that man could never forget, as well as to provide an eternal resting place for the bodies of these god kings. The rock tombs of the Middle Kingdom, the mural paintings and funerary statues, the figures and articles of jewelry and utensils placed in the tombs, which now give us a detailed picture of the life of the time, all fulfilled the same purpose of serving the dead. It is in the New Kingdom that the greatest glory is to be found: royal funerary temples hidden in out-of-the-way valleys; temples at Luxor and Karnak built for the luxury-loving monarchs in honor of the foremost of all gods, Amon; beautiful fresco paintings adorning the tomb walls with scenes from real life; and curiously modern sculptural portrait heads and figures.

One of the outstanding developments of this New Kingdom was the attempt of the "heretic king," Ikhnaton, to abandon the traditional religion and social organizations which he had received from his fathers in favor of a monotheism which transcended national bounds. This spiritual and social rebellion brought about an aesthetic revolution which, instead of following the impersonal conventions of the traditional sculpture and painting, inspired a series of portrait sculptures which are among the most amazing and enjoyable things in the whole range of the art. But Ikhnaton, a poet and a visionary rather than a practical ruler, was far ahead of his time, and after him Egypt returned to the old order of imperialism and artistic convention. The priests deliberately destroyed all the manifestations of Ikhnaton's reforming spirit and saw to it that the old order of privilege and prosperity was restored. Slow decay ensued, a decay which paralleled the gradual lessening of the energy of the nation, a decay which, however, was stayed long enough for the artists and sculptors and poets of the Saite period (663–525 B.C.) to gather together the traditions of their great predecessors, and so prepare them for transference to the Greek, Persian, and Roman conquerors who were to come.

Courtesy of The Metropolitan Museum of Art

COLONNADE IN THE TEMPLE OF KARNAK (about 1250 B.C.)

Notice the luxuriant style of the New Kingdom in comparison with the architecture of the Old and Middle Kingdoms.

Ägyptisches Museum, Berlin

KING AMENHOTEP (Ikhnaton)
About 1370 B.C.

Thus rooted in the religious conceptions and practical needs of the people, Egyptian architectural and sculptural art flourished. We see it early freeing itself from archaic rigidity and rising to heights which have hardly been surpassed by the artistic achievements of any other country.

THE PLACE OF MUSIC

We can hardly say the same about Egyptian music. There is abundant evidence in the tomb paintings, bas-reliefs, and so forth, that it played much the same role in the lives of the Egyptians as it had in those of the Sumerians. During the first and second kingdoms the priests looked upon it as invaluable in approaching the gods and in invoking their aid for assuring immortality. As in Sumeria, these priests lived in the luxurious temples of the gods; they ate and drank the sacrifices and libations offered to the gods; their considerable revenue was derived from the rental of temple lands and the fees which they demanded for their services; they were exempt from most taxation and from all enforced labor. Such prestige, together with their learning, gave them a position of great influence. In time they came into concurrence with the civil power. The king was looked upon as the chief priest of the faith, and thus both church and state, as in so many later civilizations, secured continuance.

The chief duties of the priests were the performance of rites and the invocation of spells designed to secure the help of the gods. Among the rites with which we are familiar was one which Plato thought must have been invented by a god, for its "ingenuity was entirely divine" — the Dance of the Stars. This was a special sort of ritual, evidently designed to show the whole cosmic order rather than to supplicate any special divinity, and was danced entirely within the temple precincts, without audience. Kirstein (in his book *The Dance, a Short History of Classic Theatrical Dancing*) describes its choregraphy as probably devised by astronomer priests and centering about a fixed altar which represented the sun, the dancers, clad in brilliant robes, making signs of the zodiac with their hands and turning rhythmically from east to west, following the course of the planets. After the completion of each circle, the dancers remained immobile in representation of the constancy of the earth. Thus, by combining miming and plastic movements, the priests represented the harmonies of the celestial system and the laws of the universe in a manner that must have been much like that of the modern abstract ballet. Bands of female singing dancers were kept in all the temples for the honoring of the god, and the royal and princely houses maintained similar groups, which were often used for secular purposes as well. Thus music existed in the life of the Egyptians, as in that of the other early civilizations, as an accessory but not as an independent art.

Flutes and harps (the latter an Egyptian invention, first found in the monuments of the fourth dynasty, the time of the building of the Pyramids) were the chief instruments used. At first hand clapping accompanied the dances. To this was later added the more subtle means of accentuating the rhythm afforded by the sistrum (a sort of rattle that was made of wood, porcelain, or enamel) and the drum, both of which instruments first appeared about 2500 B.C. If we are to judge by appearances, these religious rites demanded slow music and graceful dances.

But music during the first two kingdoms was no prerogative of the priests. A picture dating from 4000 B.C. shows a secular use of the flute — a child in a fox's skin trying to attract the attention of other animals by playing a flute (the Orpheus concept again!). And Ptah-hotep, prime minister of the fifth dynasty and, incidentally, author of the oldest work on philosophy known to us, gives a description of how he enjoyed his music while being barbered, manicured, and pedicured. There is an atmosphere of almost Hollywoodian luxuriance about the scene — pet animals, including monkeys, wander about as he sits in his palace; there are flowers and fruits in front of him, servants wait on him, and musicians play for him.

NEW-KINGDOM LUXURIANCE

The New Kingdom marked the zenith of Egyptian glory: Thutmosis III in a series of fifteen campaigns made his country the master of the world then known, conquering and annexing the Syrians and drawing their enormous wealth into Egypt for the creation of art and for the preparation of new conquests. It was during this period that Asiatic luxuries were introduced — such instruments as the cithara with its five to eighteen strings, played either with a plectrum or the fingers; the oboe; the guitar, with two or three strings and a long neck (thought to be so effeminate by the priests that they tried to prohibit its use); the harp, which in its earlier form had been only about five feet high and possessed six or eight strings, now taking a larger form, having ten, fifteen, or even twenty strings and a highly decorated frame ornamented with inlays of gold, silver, or lapis lazuli; and the drum, which was enlarged and, together with the trumpet (of small scale and sounding, according to Plutarch, like the "bray of an ass") was used for military purposes. Music lost its former simplicity and the dances evidently became much livelier. Significant is the fact that, beginning with the New Kingdom, the bas-reliefs show only women as flute players. Instrumental music at least seemed to have become the sole privilege of feminine musicians, perhaps on the theory that it was considered beneath the dignity of men.

We see, in the mural tomb decorations of this period, fashionable people sitting at banquets and being amused by flute players and dancing girls. We hear the song of a blind harper, accompanied by flutes and strings, a song filled with the inscrutable mystery of death:

"The generations pass away,
While other remain,
Since the time of the ancestors,
The gods who were aforetime,
Who rest in their pyramids,
Nobles and the glorious departed likewise,
Entombed in their pyramids . . .
Their place is no more. . . .

"Behold the places thereof;
Their walls are dismantled,
Their places are no more,
As if they had never been.

"None cometh from thence
That he may tell us how they fare;
That he may tell us of their fortunes,
That he may content our heart,
Until we too depart
To the place whither they have gone."

—Translated by Breasted in *The Dawn of Conscience*

But there is no reason to believe that the collective mind of Egypt dwelt only thus imaginatively on the long sleep of death; for Weigall has shown conclusively that the Egyptians were at heart a gay people, given to the pleasures of this life. If their speculations led them to ponder the inevitability of death, they came to the conclusion that while man is here on earth he might as well enjoy himself. And so, this Egyptologist insists, there was in Egypt sunshine, laughter, and feasting as well as mystic contemplation. Music was a means for increasing enjoyment: there are hieroglyphs signifying "songs of the harem" and "songs by domestic singers" as well as "songs by the singers of god." We know even the names of some of these pleasure-providing singers; and the boasts of Snefru and Remery-Ptah that they have "fulfilled every wish of the king by their beautiful singing" sound strangely like those of later times!

Rijksmuseum, Leyden, Holland

THE BLIND HARPER

Accompanied by strings and flutes, the blind harper plays and sings his song of the mystery of death, while a priest offers sacrifices. The words of the song are inserted above. This is the finest record now extant of music's place in the life of ancient Egypt. (XVIII Dynasty, about 1350 B.C.; from a limestone relief)

THE BABYLONIANS AND THE ASSYRIANS

There remains little to be added regarding the music of the powerful Babylonian and Assyrian civilizations which developed out of the earlier Sumerian beginnings in Mesopotamia, the fertile land between the rivers. The relationship of these three cultures is a difficult one to establish, for there was a great deal of warfare, conquest, and interpenetration. Durant has said that in general Sumeria stood in the same relation to Babylon and Babylon to Assyria as Crete to Greece and Greece to Rome: the first created a civilization; the second developed it to its height; the third inherited and protected it and passed it on as a " dying gift " to the world which was to come. The center of this civilization moved from Ur to Babylon and from Babylon to Nineveh.

At the very beginning of Babylonian history stands the great lawgiving king Hammurabi (2123–2081 B.C.), a contemporary of the Middle Egyptian Kingdom, whose historic code of laws, like that of Moses later, was supposed to have descended from heaven. It laid the foundations of order and serenity upon which the rich empire of Babylon reared itself. Shortly after the death of Hammurabi, Babylon was captured by a hardy non-Semitic tribe from the east, the Kassites, who continued as rulers for over six centuries. They in turn were supplanted by the Assyrians, who destroyed almost completely the glories of Babylon. But these were revived again under Nebuchadrezzar (605–562 B.C.), who in his reign of forty-three years made Babylon the largest and most luxurious city of the ancient world, surrounded, according to Herodotus, with a wall 56 miles in length. This was the city of the hanging gardens, one of the wonders of the world; its very name became synonymous with a sort of vicious luxuriance.

Essentially traders, businessmen, and warriors, the Babylonians achieved more success in science than in art: their commerce made necessary the development of mathematics, and out of their religious beliefs came the foundations of the modern sciences of astronomy and medicine. It was their laws that became the pattern for all ancient society. Their legends, through adoption by the Hebrews, became known to the whole world. Yet in the visual arts and music they accomplished little that was new. Because of the necessity for using bricks as building material, there being no stone available in the flat country of Babylon, the Babylonian architecture was heavy and uninspired. Painting never acquired any importance as an independent art; and sculpture, with the exception of some fine bas-reliefs, remained undeveloped, stereotyped, and crude; the best artistic results of the Babylonians seem to have been achieved in ceramics, glazed tile, and pottery. Their music is but an elaboration of Sumerian practices. They used, perhaps, more and bigger instruments — harps, citharas, lutes, single and double flutes, reeds, trumpets, drums, cymbals, and tambourines. As in Egypt, the singers sang and the orchestras played both in the temples and in the palaces of the rich; but again, no real examples of Babylonian music have come down to us, and so we know nothing of its character.

Shortly after Nebuchadrezzar's death in 562 B.C. the Babylonian empire fell apart and thus became a ready prey for Cyrus and his conquering Persians, who captured it in 538 B.C. and made it an essential part of their ambitious imperial scheme. Then two hundred years later came Alexander; and through him the cultural elements of the civilization of the Land between the Rivers were dispersed to become a part of the great heritage of mankind.

The great man of Assyria, the imperial power to the north, was Ashurbanipal (?–626 B.C.), whose empire at the height of its power embraced Assyria, Babylonia, Armenia, Palestine, Syria, Phoenicia, Sumeria, and Egypt. This empire was founded, as all such domains must be founded, on military power. It recognized frankly that government is the "nationalization of force," and its chief contributions — if they can be called contributions — to the progress of man were in the art of war. So we can hardly expect any important developments in Assyrian art. Except in their magnificent bas-reliefs filled with scenes from their wars and hunts, the Assyrians did not distinguish themselves as artists. They copied or imported everything from Babylon.

The one outstanding illustration of the use of music in the Assyrian civilization is the great decorative relief (now in the British Museum) from the time of Ashurbanipal, showing the royal musicians celebrating the triumphant return of the king from one of his wars. In this proces-

© British Museum

SCENE FROM AN ASSYRIAN WALL RELIEF

The relief is one from the time of the empire's greatest glory under Ashurbanipal, 668–626 B.C.

sion are players on double flutes and harps, a player on a percussive instrument, and singers, one of them, according to Combarieu, holding his hand to his throat in such a way as to produce the nasal tone so characteristic of oriental music, the others marking the rhythm by clapping their hands.

THE JEWS

The history of the Semitic people, the Hebrews, has become familiar not so much because of their importance as a people as through the influence which they exerted on the later history of the world. As someone has said, they did not make history; history made them. They were settled on a narrow strip of land bordering the Mediterranean, between Egypt and Assyria, and their country was the natural high road between these powers. Their significance is due to the fact that, influenced by the great civilizations to the south and east, they produced a written literature, a history of the world which records their developing concept of God, a collection of laws, songs, and religious rites, all of which were incorporated into the Christian Bible and thus became known to the whole Western world.

The music of the Hebrews was probably similar to that of their neighbors and largely bound up with the ritual of their worship. It was King David who assigned to one of the Jewish tribes the sole duty of providing music in the temple, although there had long been a special caste of "singers with instruments of music, psalteries, harps, and cymbals." It was the Levites who sang and played and danced before the Lord; and many of the texts which they probably used are to be found in the Psalms.[5] These are of interest to us today not only because of the superb lyricism of their poetry but also because they represent the sort of liturgical texts that were probably used by the Egyptians and the Babylonians. Commentators believe, for instance, that the rolling lines of the Twenty-fourth Psalm were a liturgical chant performed when the ark of the covenant arrived in front of the Temple, the priest singing half of each verse, and the choir the remainder:

> "The earth is the Lord's and the fullness thereof,
> the world and they that dwell therein.
> For he hath founded it upon the seas;
> and established it upon the floods."

It is the opinion of scholars that the last four verses of this magnificent psalm are the oldest:

> "Lift up your heads, O ye gates, and be ye lifted up, ye everlasting doors;
> And the King of Glory shall come in.
> Who is this King of Glory?
> The Lord strong and mighty, the Lord mighty in battle."

[5] Modern research seems to show that Solomon's Temple (which he built on Mount Moriah, a broad plateau east of Jerusalem, in order to provide a fitting setting for the sacrifices of his people to Jehovah and a permanent shelter for the ark of the covenant) consisted of a group of buildings surrounded by a strong fortress wall and surmounted by a high, golden-roofed tower. This tower, about two hundred feet high, contained the holy inner chamber where rested the tablets of the Ten Commandments; before it was an inner court which contained the great altar where the priests offered the sacrifices of animals and crops, required three times a year of every Jew. It was probably before this inner court that the musical ceremonies of the temple took place. The Levites, which were the singers (under King David 4000 men out of a tribe of 38,000 were musicians), "being arrayed in fine linen, having cymbals and psalteries and harps, stood at the east end of the altar, and with them an hundred and twenty priests sounding with trumpets."

And again, in ecstasy:

" Lift up your heads, O ye gates, even lift them up, ye everlasting doors;
And the King of Glory shall come in.
Who is the King of Glory?
The Lord of Hosts, he is the King of Glory. Selah."

These magniloquent lines call for mighty music. How impressive they must have sounded accompanied by the sweep of harps, the sound of trumpets, and the clash of cymbals! Then it must have been that the " trumpeters and singers were as one, to make one sound to be heard in praising and thanking the Lord; and when they lifted up their voice with the trumpets and cymbals and instruments of music . . . the house was filled with a cloud, even the house of the Lord. The glory of the Lord had filled the house of God."

The Jews believed that all music possessed this magic power. The prophet Samuel, when he anointed Saul to be king, said to him: " It shall come to pass . . . that thou shalt meet a company of prophets coming down from the high place with a psaltery and a tabret and a pipe and a harp before them; and they shall prophesy. And the spirit of the Lord will come upon thee, and thou shalt prophesy with them and shalt be turned into another man." And it was when the " evil spirit from God was upon Saul that David took a harp, and played with his hand; so Saul was refreshed, and was well, and the evil spirit departed from him."

The Bible gives many evidences that secular music and dances were likewise commonly employed by the Jews; war and work songs, laments and rejoicings are mentioned. Wandering minstrels, of whom Jubal, the " father of all such as handle the harp," was first, sang to the people. After such national triumphs as the passing of the Red Sea or the conquering of Goliath by David, there was rejoicing in song, with dancing and tambourine beating by the women.

It is interesting to speculate as to the nature of this music. The more recent research which has been done along this line has been able to establish definitely the character of the liturgy used in the ancient Jewish synagogues or meetinghouses established by the Jews at the time of their

Babylonian captivity (586–538 B.C.).[6] There were portions of scripture taken from the Pentateuch and the Prophets, sung in free rhythm to traditional tunes of a highly decorated character (the process was called *cantillation*) in a manner strongly resembling the later practices of the Christians. There was also the great *Shema* or Credo; and there were special prayers and psalms for various occasions. Certain Jewish scholars, particularly A. Z. Idelsohn and Lazare Saminsky, have proved, to their own satisfaction at least, that the synagogical modes and melodies used by the modern Transcaucasian Jews are much the same as those in use during the great days of Jewish worship. These Babylonian and Persian communities of Jews were established long before the beginning of the Christian era and have kept themselves isolated from European influences. Their religious songs and cantillations reveal an astounding similarity of melodies and scales, entirely different from those used by the Jews whose religious music has been subject to Arabic and European influences. And so their religious music probably established a real contact with the traditional practices of pre-Christian times.

Canon Douglas (in his fine book *Church Music in History and Practice*) has summarized the essential features of this Jewish Bible music, features which were taken over by the early Christians into their musical practices:

(1) The basic principle of monotonic recitation, or what we call *chanting*
(2) Congregational refrains to the singing of the Psalms
(3) Elaborate musical exfoliations (melismata) on certain vowels
(4) The establishment of the principle that the rhythm of the music depends on the rhythm of the prose
(5) A musical style of noble dignity, sharply distinguished from secular melodies

H. G. Wells is fond of saying that the Hebrew's place in history has been magnified out of all proportion to its real significance; and he likes

[6] These stood in somewhat the same relation to the Temple as the modern parish churches to the Cathedral. At the time of the destruction of the Temple in 70 A.D. there were over 400 of these meetinghouses in Jerusalem alone. They were the scenes of the preaching and worship of Jesus and of St. Paul.

to remind us that even Solomon's Temple in all its glory was not much larger, if the measurements given in the Bible are correct, than a good-sized modern barn. Undoubtedly the accounts of Jewish magnificence and importance as given in the Books of Kings and Chronicles have been exaggerated by patriotic writers in an attempt to show that a small, provincial people was able to keep up with the magnificence of its rich and powerful neighbors. But even if this is true, the Jewish ritual and music, representing, as they well may, something of the characteristics of the music of the other civilizations of the Near East, deserve our special consideration. For they are the nearest elements that we possess to a living link with that great past.

The Music of the Hellenic Age

The nodding promontories, and blue isles,
And cloudlike mountains, and dividuous waves
Of Greece, basked glorious in the open smiles
Of favoring heaven: from their enchanted caves
Prophetic echoes flung dim melody.

— Shelley: "Ode to Liberty"

I cannot rest from travel: I will drink
Life to the lees . . .
For always roaming with a hungry heart
Much have I seen and known: cities of men,
And manners, climates, councils, governments,
Myself not least, but honored of them all . . .
I am a part of all that I have met;
Yet all experience is an arch wherethro'
Gleams that untravel'd world, whose margin fades
Forever and forever when I move.

— Tennyson: "Ulysses"

THE SOURCES OF HELLENIC THOUGHT AND CULTURE

WITH the entrance of Greece into the arena of history, a new force made itself felt in the world: a force which, by casting off the dead weight of the superstitions of the past and by developing an insatiable curiosity for penetrating the unknown future, achieved in a few short centuries a cultural supremacy which, spreading over western Europe, has remained down to this day one of man's greatest heritages. While largely devoted to intellectual speculation, this spirit of free inquiry of the Greeks enabled them to make important contributions to the sciences as well as to the arts. It was Pythagoras who about 550 B.C., after experimenting with strings, first founded the science of mathematical acoustics and discovered the octave; and other Greeks made many fundamental contributions to the sciences of astronomy, medicine, and biology, contributions which, generally speaking, were not transcended until the seventeenth century. It is interesting to speculate as to what might have happened if this intellectually curious people had been possessed of a greater inclination for real scientific experimentation.

Modern historians like to remind us that these unique contributions which Greece passed on to later civilizations were by no means original with her but were based on the rich inheritances which she in her turn had received from earlier peoples. It was Egypt and Mesopotamia which, as Barnes has said, cleared the road and set up the cultural and intellectual signposts for the civilizations that were to follow; and through her whole history Greece maintained constant contact with her eastern neighbors, a fact which explains many of the characteristics of her art.

There were three sources which influenced the development of Greek culture as we know it: first, that which developed on the island of Crete in the Mediterranean and which later spread to the mainland of Asia Minor, where its center was Troy, and into Greece, with its center at Mycenae; second, the wandering tribes of fair-haired Aryans who lived in central and southeastern Europe and who came down from there into the Aegean cities; and third, the Phoenicians, those sea-Semitic traders, wanderers, and colonizers who roamed the whole Mediterranean from their bases at Tyre and Sidon. All three of these stand in the background as a sort of preludial introduction to the great symphony whose opening movement begins with the development of Greece.

THE MINOANS

According to the reckoning of the archaeologists, the Cretan or Minoan civilization goes back as far as the Bronze Age (around 2500 B.C.), and its early development coincides with that of the Old Kingdom in Egypt. A high degree of culture grew up early, and these pre-Grecian people achieved some astonishingly beautiful results in painting, sculpture, and such minor arts as bronze working and pottery making. The chief feature of their rich and civilized settlement at Knossos in Crete was the huge palace of King Minos, built about 1500 B.C., a structure which evidently housed not only the monarch but the people as well. Recent excavations of its ruins have given us a great deal of important information regarding this almost forgotten civilization. We know that it delighted in great festivals and shows, including a kind of bullfighting much like that developed also in Spain. That there were dances and gymnastic displays we are certain, Crete being looked upon by the writers of antiquity as the cradle of their dances. One of the earliest ritualistic dances known was found in the so-called Hymn of the Kouretes (young men just come to maturity), discovered at Palaikastro in Crete. There have been found terra-cotta figures dancing in circles, which the archaeologists date from the sixteenth century before Christ. Frescoes of dancing ladies decorated the palace of Minos. Indeed the excavations made show that this whole structure was filled with an existence generously enlivened by the arts.

Perhaps music played as important a role in the happy, civilized life of Minos at Knossos as it did in that of his contemporaries in Babylon;

Courtesy of The University Museum, Philadelphia

MINOAN ART — A restored fresco from the palace at Knossos

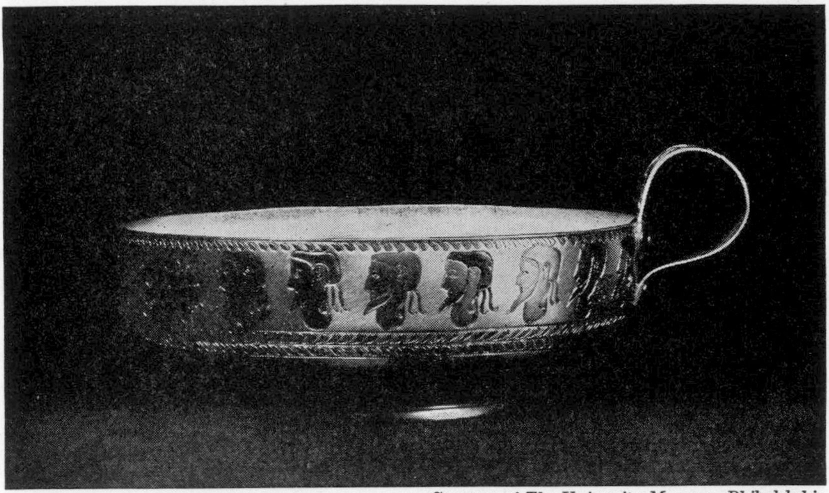

Courtesy of The University Museum, Philadelphia

MINOAN ART — Silver boat from the grave of the tower citadel, Mycenae

but aside from such discoveries as have been mentioned, little is known about it. The last stages of this culture, contemporary with the Homeric age, developed on the mainland. Fortified palaces became a necessity during this time because of the inroads of the Phoenicians and the Greeks; it is significant that these structures clearly anticipate the shape and general style of the later Greek temples. So, too, the Greek musical theories may have come from this Minoan people, whose civilization seems to have come to a sudden and awful end around 1400. The great palace at Knossos was destroyed, probably as the result of a Greek invasion, and was never rebuilt; and after it was gone, the center of civilization shifted to the south.

THE ARYANS

The Greek tribes who may have thus ended the Cretan civilization were descendants of the wandering Aryans who about 2000 B.C. lived in the forests and cleared lands of a large part of central Europe and western Asia and whose existence was hardly known to their civilized Babylonian and Egyptian contemporaries. Wells has given a good picture of this Nordic people, which was destined to play such an important part in the later history of the world. With their cattle pulling the rough wagons on which they heaped their simple belongings, they wandered over all northern Europe, settling down temporarily, raising crops of wheat, plowing and cultivating the land in a primitive way, building huts of wattles and mud. Their community life was social rather than religious; their leaders were chieftains rather than priests.

Music was a real part of the life of the Aryans. They have been well called a "vocal people," for by way of enlivening their wanderings they would foregather for communal feasts, on which occasions, in addition to a great deal of eating and drinking, there would be entertainment by their national poets, the bards. Their minds crowded with the memories of the great events of tribal history, these poets went about among their fellows reciting and singing the words they had composed, accompanying their lines by their own harp playing. Thus originated that great series of epics and sagas which has contributed so much to the world's enjoyment and which includes such masterpieces as *The Iliad, The Odyssey, The Nibelungenlied,* and *The Kalevala.*

The Dorians, a branch of this Aryan stem, came down into Greece from the north sometime before 1000 B.C. and, after capturing and destroying the cities and civilization established there by the Minoan peoples, settled themselves on the Aegean Islands and the narrow fringes of the Mediterranean coast line. The direct ancestors of the classic Greeks, these early tribes bore little resemblance to their famous descendants. They were a barbarian people, living in open villages which they built on the ruins of the civilized towns they had destroyed; and although they adopted some of the ideas and habits of the peoples they had conquered, they were without real culture. The first three centuries of the life of these tribes in Greece (from about 1000 to 700 B.C.) were largely given over to their establishment as an agricultural and commercial people. They earned their living from the fringes of coastal plain and river valleys bordering the mountainous chain which comprises so much of the Aegean archipelago and took to the sea in order to trade and barter with their neighbors. During this time there were slowly laid the foundations of the religious and social life out of which came the glories of the Athenian age.

THE PHOENICIANS

Ethnologists seem to be completely baffled as to the origin of the Phoenicians, the people who in pre-Hellenic times lived on the narrow strip of land along the east coast of the Mediterranean, whose ships sailed every known sea, and whose bartering merchants were to be found in every port. They were probably a western branch of the Semitic tribes of Arabia who had conquered Sumeria and helped set up the Babylonian empire. Forced by the geographical position of their country to make their living from the sea, they became the means of spreading the culture of Asia Minor among the countries of Europe.

As early as 2800 B.C. we find their ships in the Mediterranean, and they soon became the busiest merchants in the world. They manufactured various sorts of artistic objects, glass, metalware, jewelry, and so forth; and they became well known for extracting from the sea animals along their coasts the famous purple dye which was much in demand. In addition, they transported the products of India and the Near East to all the cities along the Mediterranean, carrying in return metals, ivory, and wood, as well as slaves for the service of those who could afford them. Their two great cities, Tyre and Sidon, rose to a place among the richest and most powerful in the world; according to the account of the prophet Ezekiel, they were "perfect in beauty and in them was sealed the sum of all wisdom." Their culture and art, drawn from Egypt, Crete, and the Near East, was carried abroad, along with their goods and merchandise; and we owe a great debt to this commercial people for introducing, among many other things, the Egyptian alphabet to the nations of antiquity.

Music seems to have occupied much the same place in their civilization as it did among their neighbors: we hear of its use at princely feasts, played on the same instruments as in Egypt and Assyria. The Phoenicians used the aulos, a kind of double reed pipe made of wood with mouthpiece of ivory or metal, which was later very popular in Greece. It is thought that those elements of theory and practice which entered the Greek music system from the East, elements which survived in the

The Louvre

GREEK POET HOLDING HIS LYRE

names of two of the Greek scales, the Phrygian and the Lydian,[1] were transmitted through the Phoenicians.

[1] Phrygia and Lydia were two of the nations which became powerful in Asia Minor, in the district to the east of Assyria, sometime after the ninth century B.C. They linked the civilization of the ancient Hittites, who came from India, with that of Greece. Whatever the Phrygian or Lydian musicians had inherited or found out as to the structure of instruments or schemes of tonality had its echo or application in Greece.

THE ARTS IN GREECE

Not only Hellenic art but also European literature begins on a note of epic grandeur, the Homeric poems. It is quite appropriate that the origin of such grandeur should be shrouded in mystery: whether or not there was a blind poet by the name of Homer, who, according to popular legend, composed the two great epics of *The Odyssey* and *The Iliad*, no one knows. Probably these epics were the result of the long accumulation of many generations of Aryan ballads, which may have been set down by one man sometime during the eighth or seventh century B.C. These great works deal with the adventures of the early Greeks in their warfare with the Minoans and tell of the last years of the siege of Troy, as well as of the adventures of Odysseus upon his return from these wars. Written in flexible hexameters (lines of six feet) these two epics have given rise to a great deal of discussion as to just how they were presented in Homeric times. We know that they were accompanied by the lyre, an instrument originally made by stretching strips of an animal's skin over a tortoise shell and adding branches from the side, joined by a crosspiece. Probably the words were delivered in a free sort of recitative, accompanied by the lyre. When in later centuries the renditions of the Homeric epics had become events of national importance, the *rhapsodes*, those who made the renditions, wore distinguishing costumes — long flowing cloaks of crimson when they recited *The Iliad*, blue when they declaimed *The Odyssey*. The accompaniment consisted of a prelude played on the lyre, a modest unisonal background for the voice,[2] and interludes between verses, with a postlude at the end of the performance.

THE FUNCTION OF MUSIC

The word *music* is of Greek origin (mousikē) and meant originally *of the Muses;* it was applied to a combination of poetry, music, and dancing, of which poetry was considered the ruler, music an accompaniment,

[2] The term *harmony* employed by many of the Greek writers on music always meant accompaniment at the unison. Chords, harmony, and counterpoint in our modern sense did not exist in ancient times. Plato speaks of the introductions to these accompanied poems (nomos) as having been composed with " remarkable art."

Furtwangler-Reichold: Griechische Vasenmalerei

GREEK SCHOOL

(From a vase now in Berlin)

This vase, dating from the youth of Sophocles, shows boys being taught to read, write, recite poetry, sing to the aulos, and play the lyre.

and dancing an integral part and not a mere spectacle.[3] Although such an association limited its own development as an art, it made music of tremendous significance in the life of the people. We have seen how the epics of Homer were always declaimed to musical accompaniment; other uses of music in this heroic age of Greek history, an age which extended down to 600 B.C., were in connection with religious and civic festivals, a fact that is commemorated by the survival of the names of the various musical forms used.

The mixed races which had settled on the islands and the lands bordering the Aegean Sea had, by the seventh century, founded a number of cities, the most important of which were Athens, Sparta, Corinth, Thebes, Samos, and Miletus. The last named, situated in Asia Minor, was the most important of them all. These cities grew rapidly in size and significance, but they never formed any strong political coalescence. Among the chief influences which gave them a certain amount of common interest and which held them together in a political sense was their religion. Basically borrowed from the cults of preceding civilizations, the Greek religion early developed its own rich mythology and striking theogony. In many of their dealings with the spirits who became their gods, the Greeks made music a necessary feature, regarding it as a sort of charm between man and the Invisible, and as possessing special effectiveness for their communications with the naturalistic inhabitants with which they had peopled Olympus, the home of their deities.

A number of accompanied chants, which went by the general name of *nomos*, were used in honor of the various members of this pantheon. Special forms of these were used on occasion: the *dithyramb*, at festivals of Dionysos, the wine god, wild and boisterous; the *paean*, a chant to Apollo, the god of music; *prosodies*, marchlike chants used to accompany religious processions; *threnodies*, perhaps the most primitive of all the chant forms, employed in lamenting the death of an individual (*The Iliad* closes with three magnificent examples sung on the death of Hector);

[3] Among the Greeks the term *musician* had a special significance, one somewhat similar to that of the eighteenth-century *honnête homme*: a well-rounded individual rather than a specialist. The study of music with the Greeks meant a training in singing and playing, dancing and verse. It was considered to be the backbone of education and to be closely associated with ethical and moral principles.

songs of joy and thanksgiving, used after recovery from illness or for invoking the protection of the gods in matters of health or in the midst of battle or as part of a religious ceremony at a banquet.[4]

THE FIRST OF THREE GREAT PERIODS: THE ARCHAIC

In the Homeric days the worship of these pantheistic people centered about smoking, open-air altars and included the enjoyment of song and dance, with sound of pipe and lyre. As they progressed toward a more unified culture, the Greeks designated certain spots, such as Delphi, as sacred places; and people came from far and near to sacrifice to the gods, to consult the oracle who was supposed to reside there, and to enjoy themselves generally while attending to their religious duties. Gradually permanent buildings arose in these sacred places, shrines, " treasuries," and monumental temples designed to give an appearance of dignity and impressiveness. The spontaneous games and play, the dancing and the singing of earlier days were developed into huge festivals in honor of Dionysos, Apollo, Aphrodite, or some other deity, festivals which came to be considered among the most important functions in the country. At first these festivals were concerned with elaborate pantomimic dancing celebrating events in the life of the gods or of the human heroes who

[4] Nothing gives the real character of these early religious rites better than does Homer's description of such a banquet:

" Then they orderly employ'd
The sacred offering, washed their hands, took salt cakes; and the priest
With hands held up to heaven, thus pray'd:
O thou that all things seest . . .
Hear thy priest, and as thy hand, in free grace to my prayers,
Shot fervent plague-shafts through the Greeks, now hearten their affairs
With health renewed and quite remove th' infection from their blood.
He pray'd; and to his prayers again the God propitious stood.
All, after prayer, cast on salt cakes, drew back, kill'd, flay'd the beeves,
Cut out and dubb'd with fat their thighs, fair dress'd with doubled leaves,
And on them all the sweetbreads prick'd. The priest, with small, sere wood,
Did sacrifice, pour'd on red wine; by whom the young men stood,
And turn'd, in five ranks, spits . . . which, roasted well, they drew.
The labor done, they served the feast in, that fed all to satisfaction.
Desire of meat and wine thus quench'd, the youths crown'd cups of wine
Drunk off, and fill'd again to all. That day was held divine,
And spent in paeans to the Sun."

The Louvre

LADY OF AUXERRE

This is one of the oldest Greek statues known.

were raised almost to the rank of deities. There are long lists of these dramatic dances performed for celebrating such events as the birth of Zeus, the marriage of Zeus and Hera, or the battle of Apollo and the python.[5] They were always performed to music. The aulos, the flute, and the cithara were the instruments employed, and there seems to have been

[5] One of the old authorities, Meursius, names over two hundred dances known to him. He refers in many cases to steps rather than to whole dances; but in any event the number is large. There were athletic, military, religious, and social dances.

THE DORIC TEMPLE AT PAESTUM
(Middle of the fifth century B.C.)

a background of singing. Gestures were used as means for heightening the effect of the words that were being sung. It was out of beginnings such as these that the popular Attic drama, both tragic and comic, developed.

The character of this early music was, of course, entirely religious. There was not a hint of the subjects with which the later Greek *mousikē* was so concerned — romantic love, or man's gigantic and helpless struggle against the Invisible. The choristers, always men, sang their parts in unison (the Greeks had no idea of part music as we know it), with the instruments playing the melody either in unison with the voices or an octave above them, sometimes using a simple variation. The combination of instruments beloved of the ancient civilizations, such as string, wind, and percussion, were not used by the Greeks. They especially stressed simplicity. Considering the large audiences which heard their musical performances, the means they employed seem meager enough — from sixteen to twenty-four choristers and dancers and one or two auloi.

The other arts were as much concerned during this archaic period with religious and mythological subjects as was music. In both painting and sculpture the technique employed was simple in the extreme and made no attempt to create a visual illusion of the objects rendered. The subjects used were the gods and incidents in Olympian life, straightforwardly and almost geometrically conceived. Architecture was largely concerned with the erection of temples serving the gods and the dead, simply and yet beautifully proportioned, of modest style, and using with great effectiveness the Doric column, an architectural feature which, because of its structural and organic unity, has never been surpassed for beauty. So, up to the sixth century B.C. we may say that the great concern of all the arts was that of the conveying of religious and ideational concepts.

THE SECOND PERIOD: THE LYRIC AGE

Then there came a change. With the gradual expansion of the city-states, the leadership of which was strongly maintained by the Ionians on the western coast of Asia Minor and on the adjacent islands, trade became more general, wealth increased, and intellectual interests became general. Man was no longer concerned only with his gods but began to take more interest in himself. Consequently, art became more personal, expressive, emotional, and visual. This was the great age of lyric poetry (the very derivation of the term *lyric* shows that this poetry was written to be sung). The poets Archilochus, Simonides of Ceos, Sappho the Lady of Lesbos, Anacreon, Pindar, and the great Athenian lawgiver Solon sang with such ecstasy and beauty as to insure for their lays a permanent place in the affections of lovers of poetry. No less a critic than Swinburne has said that he " agreed with all Grecian tradition in thinking Sappho to be beyond all question and comparison the very greatest poet that ever lived." And such simple beauty, a beauty which comes through even in an English translation, as is found in her fragment written about a girl who has remained unmarried, gives reason for such a sweeping judgment:

" Like the sweet apple which reddens upon the topmost bough,
Atop on the topmost twig, which the pluckers forgot, somehow,
Forgot it not, nay, but got it not, for none could get it till now.

" Like the wild hyacinth flower which on the hills is found,
Which the passing feet of the shepherds forever tear and wound,
Until the purple blossom is trodden in the ground."

— Translated by Rossetti

All this poetry was sung, much of it by solo voices accompanied by the lyre. Such things as the odes which Pindar wrote commemorating the victories of athletes in the games which by his time had become such an essential part of the religious festivals were chanted by a dancing chorus, the movements of which were carefully prescribed. Like Sappho, Pindar made his poetry a vehicle for individual expression rather than a matter of group sentiment, as his predecessors had done. Anacreon's chief business seems to have been the writing of banquet songs on the subjects of love and wine.[6] His " Address to a Dove," given below in Samuel Johnson's translation, is characteristic of his graceful style:

" Lovely courier of the sky
Where and whither dost thou fly?
Scattering, as thy pinions play,
Liquid fragrance all the way.
Is it business? Is it love?
Tell me, tell me, gentle Dove.

" Soft Anacreon's vows I bear,
Vows to Myrtale the fair;
Traced with all that charms the heart,
Blessing nature, sounding art . . ."

[6] J. C. Stobart, in *The Glory That Was Greece*, reflects at some length on the melancholy fact that these Anacreontics " were composed — according to the poet's own prescription — on ten parts of water to five of wine."

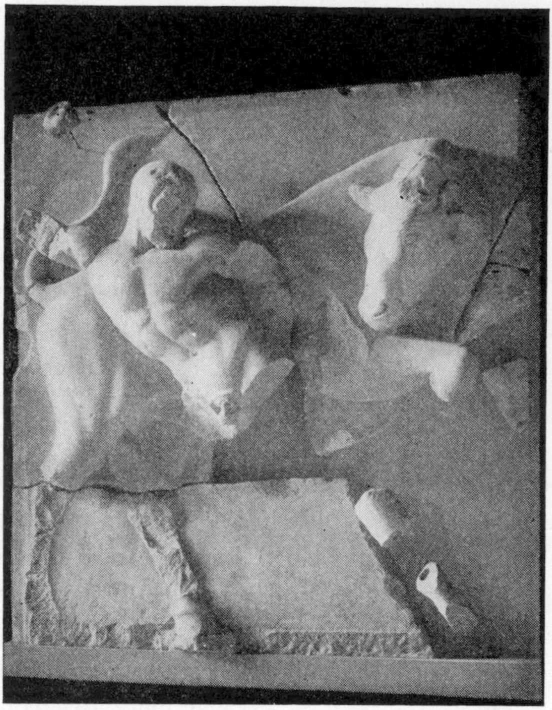

The Louvre

A GROUP FROM THE TEMPLE OF ZEUS, OLYMPIA

CULMINATION IN THE GOLDEN AGE

The golden age of Greek life and art came during the sixth and fifth centuries B.C., when Athens, after turning back the invaders from Persia who were intent on conquering Greece, assumed the leadership of all the Greek cities and established herself as the head of the Delian League and the center of Greek life and culture, attracting money and scholars and artists from the entire known world. During this fabulous period there occurred such a development in the drama, sculpture, and architecture as the world has never experienced since. Originating in the mimetic dances and chanted choruses of the religious festivals, especially those connected with Dionysos, Greek drama, from its earliest stages musically accompanied, may be said to have started with the works of

De Cou from Ewing Galloway, New York

THE PARTHENON AT ATHENS

Aeschylus (525–456 B.C.), who was the first playwright to introduce individual characters into his plays and thus make them capable of expressing personal ideas. Before his time, one character delivered formal speeches against a background of the chorus, which commented upon the action for the benefit of the spectators. Aeschylus kept the chorus but reduced its importance, for he could carry on the action by means of his few characters.

From the time of these early Aeschylian plays, the Greek dramas were always chosen in open competition and produced at the time of the great religious festivals, which included, in addition, processions, games, religious rites, and contests in singing and playing. Participation in these festivals was looked on as a religious rather than a social exercise, and during the spring days on which they were held the Greeks put aside their other affairs for the time being. They loved competitions of all sorts, dramatic and musical as well as athletic, and no greater honor could come to one of them than the prize, a vase or a wreath, given to the winner of one of these play competitions. Kirstein reminds us that a great deal of the extraordinary fertility of the Greek poets — of whose work only a small part has survived — was due to the interest taken in these competitions. He describes in detail the most important of these festivals, that of the feast of Dionysos Eleutherios:

"The poet who won here could gain no greater prize. It was celebrated on five days at the end of March, close to the spring equinox, when the seas were again navigable after the winter winds, and the streets of Athens would be full of visitors from the provincial leagues. Foreign emissaries came especially for the tragic games, which were regulated by the state under a delegated officer charged with each particular festival. On him lay the responsibility of selecting competing dramatists; at first three, and later five. On him lay the choice of actors, the distribution of roles, and the preparation of the plays, but generally he would appoint or have chosen a special *choregos* or chorus leader for detailed tasks.

"On the first day there was a grand Dionysiac parade, which, exhibiting the god's image, left it standing in his theater. The tragic, comic, and satiric contests were followed by lyric competitions in the dithyramb. These choirs were selected from the ten main tribes, and a victory for a chorus meant a triumph for its tribe. Our first date for a competition, virtually the very first record of a theatrical performance in history, is the year 535 B.C.

"The populace had an intense interest in the theater. There were no books then, nor films for a wide audience. No one was satiated by going to see plays at dawn, watching tetralogies of independent or related subjects till sundown. Besides, it only happened once a year. The audience met in the theater around the break of day, well provided with food which was consumed during the tedious parts and the intermissions. Herald trumpeters announced the commencement of the performance."

These plays [7] were given in outdoor amphitheaters that were built in natural beauty spots about a circular stage, structures wonderfully suited to their purpose. Originally merely a circle of benches about a level

[7] Exclusive of fragments, forty-seven of these Greek plays have survived — seven of Aeschylus, seven of Sophocles, nineteen of Euripides, eleven of Aristophanes, and three of Menander.

THE THEATER AND TEMPLE OF APOLLO AT DELPHI

These are beautifully situated on the slopes of Mt. Parnassus.

State Museum, Berlin

A GREEK DANCER FROM A FIFTH-CENTURY RELIEF

earthen stage tamped smooth for dancing, by the fifth century these structures had developed into gently sloping tiers of seats arranged about the *orchestra* and set into the slope of a hill in such a way as to provide a beautiful and extensive view beyond the limits of the stage. On the far side of the semicircular orchestra there was built the *skene*, a simple, two-storied building which served as a background for the actors and the chorus. The scenery was rudimentary, and there were few properties. The actors were originally amateurs, the poet always acting in his plays and writing the music for them as well as the lines. By the time of Aeschylus, acting had developed as a separate art, and the poet called in other specialists to help in producing his play. The actors wore masks and used a chanted recitative, making necessary a slow timed and artificial style.

The chorus, with its members chosen from among the free citizens, played an important role throughout the development of Greek drama. Up until the time of Euripides its interludes of music, poetry, and dance were an essential part of the dramatic design, and a definite plan was always followed as to its use. After a spoken *prologue* came the *parados*, or chorus entrance, an impressive procession led by *coryphees* or leaders and accompanied by aulos players. Two by two its members came into the orchestra, their pace slow and majestic, their faces proudly serious, their flowing robes forming a sort of visual bas-relief against which the action would be played out. The rhythm of this entrance was that of a march, and the words sung were always anapaestic. Defiling around the circular orchestra, the members finally came to rest in front of the skene, to remain there until the end of the drama, commenting from time to time on its development in solemn chant, lively song, or graceful dance. Through it, often, the dramatist expressed his ideas on religion.

The action of the play was developed by means of a series of *episodes* between the characters, interspersed with these *stasima* or musical chants. As there was no division into intervals, the play going on from its beginning to its inevitable and frequently awful conclusion, some such relief from the stormier heights of the action was absolutely necessary. In the earlier works, these dance-song episodes constituted the main design of the drama; and even in the time of Euripides they were beautifully decorative additions to its structure. Such a chorus as this from *Iphigenia in Aulis* may not be necessary to the development of the plot; but what a lovely accessory it must have made when chanted and danced!

> "May no child of mine
> Nor any child of my child
> Ever fashion such a tale
> As the Phrygians shall murmur,
> As they stoop at their distaffs,
> Whispering with Lydians,
> Splendid with weight of gold —
> Helen has brought this,
> They will tarnish our bright hair.
> They will take us captives
> For Helen . . . if men speak truth.

> "But still we lament our state,
> The descent of our wide courts.
> Even if there be no truth
> In the legends cut on ivory,
> Nor in the poets
> Nor the songs."
>
> — Translated by Hilda Aldington

The choregraphy of the chorus interpreted the sense of the words it sang. The dancing was not dancing in the sense we know it; for it possessed none of the characteristics of the modern ballet or social dance — no *pirouettes* or *pointes* or *demi-pointes*. There was no coupling of figures among the dancers, for there were no women interpreters; the movements were measured and graceful, well-proportioned and carefully balanced, and made use of the hands in a plastic manner that was suggestive of sculpture. It must have been a superb art, this dancing of the Greek chorus; and we find ourselves brooding with Euripides, who asks,

> "Will they ever come to me again, ever again
> The long, long dances,
> On through the dark till the dim stars wane?
> Shall I feel the dew on my throat, and the stream
> Of wind in my hair? Shall our white feet gleam
> In the dim expanses?"
>
> — *The Bacchae*, translated by Gilbert Murray

Sophocles (496?–406 B.C.) introduced more characters into his dramas — he wrote over a hundred and won productions for eighteen of them and so was able to achieve more of a dramatic plot in the modern sense, through the development of climax and suspense and the expression of conflict between his protagonists. Although the characters gave vent to emotions that were personal and individual, they did so in a manner that had universal significance. The story of Oedipus the King, doomed by the gods to marry his own mother, as it proceeds from disaster to disaster, is characteristic of Sophocles's treatment and is as simple, inevitable, and dignified as the sculptured figures of his contemporary, Phidias. With Euripides (480–406 B.C.) the individual, personal element became even more pronounced: the dramatic conflict was drawn between men and not gods: feminine characters were humanized, and the element of love was for the first time adequately treated. Euripides was in fact a romantic artist, emphasizing the personal and expressive, in rebellion against the classic restraints of his predecessors. He was the last of the great tragedists. After him came Aristophanes and the writers of comedy, who, in dealing with the ordinary social problems of living, held them up to the ridicule of the multitudes.

The character of the music changed with that of the drama. No longer concerned with purely sacerdotal aims, it became more human and elaborate, and there crept into it an evident desire to please as well as to edify. The classic balance, so carefully maintained between the chorus and the actors in the works of Aeschylus and Sophocles, was gradually destroyed by the introduction of more individual performers and the use of music expressive of the passions and the emotions. In Euripides, whenever an emotion was expressed by one of his heroines, the regular dramatic rhythm gave place to one more adaptable for lyric singing. Such a love song as the following, for instance, must have called for a musical utterance far different from that used in the classic dramas:

> "One with eyes the fairest
>   Cometh from his dwelling,
> Someone loves thee, rarest,
>   Bright beyond my telling.
> In thy grace thou shinest
> Like some nymph divinest,
> In her caverns dewy: —
> All delights pursue thee,
> Soon pied flowers, sweet-breathing,
> Shall thy head be wreathing."

— Translated by Shelley

MUSIC IN PRIVATE LIFE

It should not be thought that because the Greek citizen was so interested in the music and dancing used in religious and public festivals he neglected them in private life. On the contrary, we find that from the earliest days the Greeks loved to participate in and watch these dances.

We remember the famous description of the "chain dance" in *The Iliad*, one of the first accounts of dancing that we have:

"And with great skill he made a dancing floor, like that which Daedalus had done in broad Knossos for blonde Ariadne. These youths and maidens worth many oxen were dancing, holding each other's hands by the wrist. Of these some wore delicate linen dresses and others golden swords hanging from silver belts. At one time they moved rapidly in a circle with cunning feet, right easily, just as when a potter, seated, tries the wheel fitted to the hand, to see whether it runs; at another time they moved rapidly in file.

"And a great crowd stood round the charming dance, enjoying the spectacle; and amongst them a divine bard sang to the cithara; and two tumblers, when he began his song, whirled about in the middle."

And again, this time in *The Odyssey*, Homer tells of the love of his people for dancing:

"They leveled the dancing ground, making its ring neat and wide. The herald arrived with the minstrel's singing lyre. Demodocus advanced into the cleared space. About him grouped boys in their first blush of life and skillful at dancing, who footed it rhythmically on the prepared floor. . . . Then Alcinoüs ordered Halias and Laodomas to dance, by themselves, for never did anyone dare join himself with them. They took in their hands the fine ball, purple-eyed, which knowing Polybus had made them, and played. The first, bending his body back, would hurl the ball towards the shadowy crowds: while the other in his turn would spring high into the air and catch it gracefully before his feet touched ground. Then, after they had made full trial of tossing the ball high, they began passing it back and forth between them, all the while they danced upon the fruitful earth. The other young men stood by the dancing and beat time. Loudly their din went up."

— Translated by T. E. Shaw

In later times there came a sharper distinction between the professional dancers, who appeared at such functions as dinner parties and banquets, purveying entertainment and amusement to the guests, and the amateurs who danced for pleasure, either in social or religious groups. Speaking generally, the Greeks were by nature participants, in contrast to the later Romans, who were always spectators; and so they naturally looked on the professional musicians and dancers as little better than courtesans.

THE OLYMPIEION (second century A.D.)

THE THIRD PERIOD: DECLINE

After the Golden Age all the arts — music, the drama, sculpture, and architecture — underwent changes that paralleled those which took place in the religious beliefs and the civil practices of the various city-states. After the earlier devotion of the arts to purely religious purposes, there came during the great Athenian period a happy balance between religion and pure art, an equilibrium which was lost during the so-called Hellenistic times, after Athens had lost her supremacy and the center of Hellenic culture had moved to Alexandria and the cities of Asia Minor. The political and economic stability which had been the background of the period of Athenian greatness passed, and there came transformations in all phases of Greek life. Athens, and, with her, all Greece, came on troublous times. The philosophers, Plato, Socrates, Aristotle, and the rest, tried to explain the reasons for these adverse circumstances. Instead of the Olympian objectivity of the sculpture of Phidias and his contemporaries, we find an increasing desire for the achievement of grace and beauty, a desire which

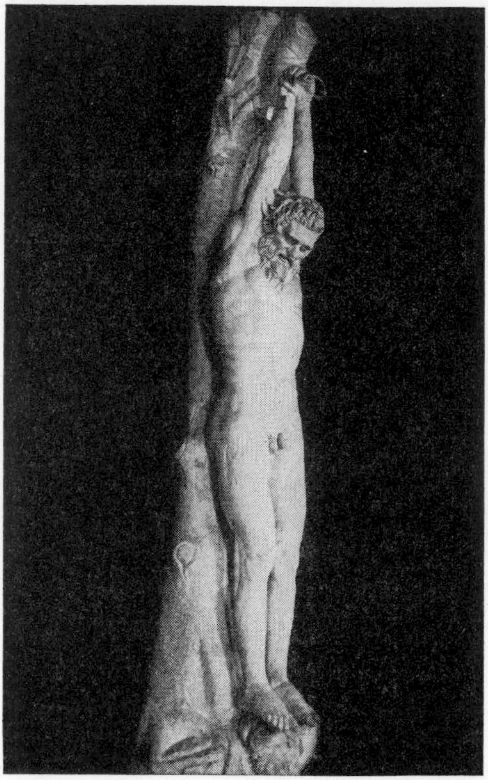

The Louvre

A SATYR SUSPENDED ON A PINE-TREE TRUNK (second century)

finally brought about a sentimentality that was about as antipodal to the severe virility and graceful serenity of the fifth century as can be imagined. The older tragedies gave way to comedies which, with their spirited and witty satirization of contemporary foibles and their absorption in the controversial issues of the day, made existence seem more bearable, if less sublime. Architecture became more and more colossal and grandiose, the Corinthian order being preferred above others because it seemed so exuberant and afforded chance for theatrical effectiveness. Music became more secular, sensual, and individual: the main aim of the musician of the fourth century seemed to be, as Aristoxenus said, "to get the applause of the multitude." No longer concerned with religious ceremony or dramatic expression, the musician was principally interested in developing, with an ever-increasing complexity of technique, the theme of the common man and his everyday affairs. Professionalism among both the composers and the performers increased. The dramas had to be commercially sponsored, and traveling companies were formed for playing them throughout Greece. The auloi were capable of " rivaling the trumpet's tone "; large citharas with as many as fifteen strings were used; all sorts of liberties were taken with the scales and rhythms; instrumental music became disassociated from choral music, and large concerts, with hundreds and even thousands of players, were given. Program music came into vogue, and at all the festival games competitions between virtuoso artists were instituted, musicians coming to compete from all parts of the world then known. It has been estimated that at some of the games organized by Alexander the Great as many as three thousand artists came together. Music, in a word, became a popular, sensual means for pleasure, indulged in for its own sake and cultivated more as a social fad than as an inherent necessity of life. Aestheticians and philosophers wrote long treatises on music, some of them dealing with speculations as to its nature, others with its psychological powers.

It is impossible to speak of Greek music as if it were an art possessing uniform characteristics. Within the space of some seven hundred years it passed through a cycle which, beginning with the stark simplicity of the Homeric epics, developed into the dithyrambic lyrics and religious chants of the classic age. Later came the marvelously co-ordinated unity of the fifth-century music-drama-dance form, the humanization of the Hellenistic period, which led eventually to the completely commercial and social debasements of the Alexandrian times. Modern European music has passed through much the same sort of changes, but it has taken nearly two thousand years for the process. When we speak of Greek music, we think of that of the Golden Age, without realizing, perhaps, that the later periods of its history brought changes as demoralizing and debasing as any that have occurred in later times.

Perhaps this is as well. For, as Alfred Einstein has pointed out, the knowledge which we have of the place which music occupied in Greek life, together with our wonder at the highly developed style which it

Photo Roseman

THE VICTORY OF SAMOTHRACE (about 300 B.C.)

eventually reached, has suggested to us that it must have possessed a unique and exalted character. It was this valuation which so strongly influenced later centuries, from the Middle Ages down to the time of Wagner, by "blazing up at important crises and stirring men's minds"; and its effect has been all the more potent in that no concrete examples of the music have survived. For all practical purposes, the music of the Greeks remains the "dim melody" of which Shelley sings.[8]

A SUMMARY

There is no calculating the debt which Western civilization owes to Hellenic culture. Taking the material advances which had been made before their time as a basis, these people of Ionia, Aeolis, Doris, and Athens[9] developed a set of intellectual and emotional concepts which, in their freedom from superstition and intolerance, their bold hypotheses regarding the universe, their balanced rationalism, and their challenge to the future, have never been surpassed. It was their ability to combine a definite feeling of humanity with a high degree of imagination that enabled the Greeks to produce such expressive and lasting art. The Attic citizen, altogether a very human individual,[10] while he may have possessed few of the qualities of the superman that have been attributed to him, nevertheless exemplified in his everyday life such real devotion

[8] A few melodic fragments have survived, eleven in all. But these are of little value for conveying any real idea of what Greek music of the Golden Age sounded like; for they are mostly from later periods, some of them dating from the Christian epoch. And there is no agreement as to how they should or could be interpreted by modern musicians. We are still very much in the dark as to how Greek music actually sounded. It is significant that even in such a highly specialized work as Dr. Margarete Bieber's *The History of the Greek and Roman Theater* (Princeton University Press, 1939), no elucidation or even discussion of the nature of the music so intimately associated with the production of Greek plays is attempted.

[9] It was the poets, philosophers, and intellectual inhabitants of these and a few other Greek states who made the great contributions to the progress of civilization attributed in general to the Greeks. The majority of their city-states, as Barnes reminds us, were no more cultivated than the regions of the Hottentots.

[10] It was Plato who told of some Athenian gentlemen who debated during the course of a banquet as to whether they should spend the night in revelry or in philosophic discussion. They decided on the latter, but the end of the discussions found at least two of the guests under the table!

to the principles of truth and beauty and such freedom of mind as to make his conduct a desirable prototype for all time.

The education of Greek citizens was such as to make them aware that what we call "culture" was an essential part of living and not something that was to be extraneously sought after once the material demands of life had been taken care of. It has been said that every free man in Athens could play the aulos; and he was also trained to take his part as a member of the chorus in the drama. The plastic and architectural beauties of the Athenian Acropolis were matters of ordinary experience to these men. No wonder that creative art flourished as it did, and reached heights of excellence that have seldom been equaled or surpassed!

In summarizing the debt of Western civilization to Hellenic thought and culture, Barnes has said that the greatest weakness of the Greeks was their failure to develop a technology and an economic system that was equal to these intellectual and artistic attainments. The material foundations of Greek life being inadequate, the whole structure collapsed. Today, after we have devoted most of our attention to the securing of such material foundations, we are, compared with the Greeks, culturally speaking, poverty-stricken. Is there no hope of achieving a balance?

OUR MUSICAL HERITAGE FROM THE GREEKS

Inasmuch as it was the Greek conception of intervals, scales, and modes that affected all later music, the reader of music history should know something regarding it. Pythagoras, a Greek mathematician, has the distinction of being the first man in history to explain the laws of proportion in music — how changing the length of a vibrating body affects the pitch of the musical tone it gives. Experimenting with sounding strings, he found that dividing them in half raised their pitch an octave; and this he established as the most important relationship in music. Dividing his string at a point two thirds of its length he found would raise the pitch by a perfect fifth; and this he considered the second important relationship of intervals. Dividing the string at three quarters of its length, he raised the pitch a perfect fourth; and this he established as another fundamental relationship.

These intervals of an octave, a fifth, and a fourth remain today, twenty-four hundred years after the experiments of Pythagoras, the fundamental intervals of music. The other ratios established may be stated as follows:

Octave — 1:2; fifth — 2:3; fourth — 3:4; major third — 4:5; minor third — 5:6

The unit of the system devised by Pythagoras was the tetrachord, a group of four sounds, its name being derived from the early four-stringed form of the cithara or the lyre. There were three kinds of these tetrachords: the *diatonic,* composed of tones and half tones as in our modern system; the *chromatic,* made up of an interval greater than a tone (minor third) and two half tones; and the *enharmonic,* derived from the East, in which a major third and two quarter tones were used. The diatonic genus was that most often used, especially in vocal music; but after the Golden Age, when music became progressively more and more complex, the chromatic and even the enharmonic genera crept into vocal use, after it had long been very popular with the instrumentalists.

Tone Tone Semi-tone
Diatonic

Minor third Semi-tone Semi-tone
Chromatic

Major third Quar-ter tone Quar-ter tone
Enharmonic

Today we ordinarily use but two scales in our music; but the Greeks employed a wealth of scales, the diatonic ones being formed by a conjoining and overlapping of tetrachords, always thought of in a descending series, contrary to modern practice. The most important of these scales, named after the different Greek tribes, were the Dorian, Phrygian, and Lydian. Others, among them the Mixolydian, Hypodorian, Hypophrygian, and Hypolydian, were derived from these principal scales.

Tetrachords
Dorian
Each tetrachord is composed of the same interval sequence.

Lydian

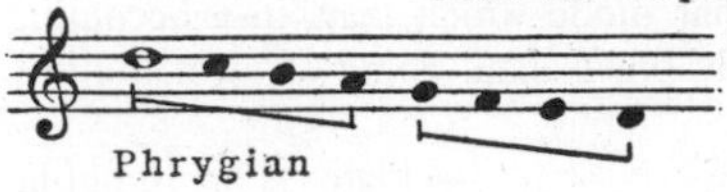
Phrygian

There is not enough evidence to show which of these scales the Greeks considered the ideal for melodic expression. We moderns must always remember that they did not use these scales, as we do ours, as foundations for harmony, but only as a sort of framework into which the melodies were fitted. The difference in general pitch and in the intervals used, as well as the fact that the melodies clustered about different centers in the different modes, gave the Greeks their doctrine of *ethos*, which regarded each mode as capable of a distinct general impression. The Dorian, for example, was considered suitable for virile, energetic music; the Lydian was thought to be effeminate and likely to induce poor morals. The modes which came from the East were used for amusement purposes, for banquet and dance music.

Much of the treatment of the subject of music on the part of the Greek philosophers consisted in elaborations of this idea that these various scales were capable of calling forth definite emotions within the listener. This aesthetic doctrine of the ethos, established by the Pythagoreans, was later given great attention by Plato and Aristotle,[11] who considered music as a valuable and important factor in educating the people; and later the Peripatetics developed it still further. In the second century of the Christian era, Ptolemaeus compiled a summary of the whole philosophic and aesthetic theories of the Greeks, which served as the basis of later treatises by the Romans. So the Greek theoretical conceptions regarding music have affected our present system in ways of which we are hardly conscious. Even the doctrine of the ethos survives in the investigations which have been made into the possibilities of music as a

[11] "By some of them [the modes], as for example the Mixolydian, we are disposed to grief and depression; by others, as for example the low-pitched ones, we are disposed to tenderness of sentiment."

— Aristotle

"'Which of the Harmoniai [modes] then are soft and convivial?'

'The Ionian,' he replied, 'and Lydian, and such as are called relaxing.'

'Can you make any use of these, my friend, for military men?'

'By no means,' replied he.

'Then, it seems, you have only yet remaining the Doric and the Phrygian. I do not know,' said I, 'the modes; but leave me that mode which may, in a becoming manner, imitate the voice and accents of a truly brave man, going on in a military action, and every rough adventure.'"

— Plato: *The Republic*

therapeutic agent, possibilities about which modern scientists by no means agree.[12]

Some scholars maintain that the most important discovery in Greek music was the invention of musical notation — a way of designating by written symbols the notes which were being played or sung. Some of the Eastern peoples may have antedated them in this, but the Greek system is the first clearly defined musical notation in history. Each sound could be registered in two ways, one for instruments and one for voices. The characters used were mostly derived from the Greek alphabet, there being 16 instrumental signs, capable of showing quarter tones, and 24 vocal ones. Some of these had slight rhythmic significance, although in the vocal music the rhythm depended entirely on that of the words. In general, we may conclude that rhythms meant much more to the Greeks, so far as the general effect was concerned, than did melody. Aristides Quintilian said that rhythm is masculine, melody feminine, and implied that the latter must always be subordinate to the former.

In this, as in other matters concerning Greek music, we can only theorize; all possibility of recovering the expressive value it once possessed has been forever lost.

[12] The Greeks had no doubts, however. It is reported that Thaletas of Crete destroyed the power of an epidemic through the sweetness of his lyre playing. Contemporary with the very important discoveries which the Greeks made in science and medicine, as well as in music, we find such curious theories as those of Aesculapius, who treated disorders of the ear with music; Theophrastus, who testified to the value of soft aulos music (it had to be in the Phrygian mode) for the relief of pain; and Caelius Aurelianus, who claimed that the agonies of sciatica could be mitigated through music.

State Museum, Berlin

A GREEK GATEWAY

Roman and Early Christian Music

Let others melt and mold the breathing bronze
To forms more fair, aye, out of marble bring
Features that live; let others plead causes well;
Or trace with pointed wand the cycled heaven,
And hail the constellations as they rise;
But thou, O Roman, learn with sovereign sway
To rule the nations.

— Virgil: *The Aeneid*, translated by Theodore C. Williams

THE ROMAN SPIRIT

WRITERS on the history of music are wont to dismiss the subject of the Romans with a brief epitome to the effect that since this mighty people took its artistic ideals from the Greeks and contributed nothing in the way of characteristic development, it is not worthy of any extended consideration in a history of art. This, like most generalizations, is only half true. The contributions of the Romans to world culture may not have been so striking as those of the Greeks; but they were nevertheless important and individual.

Perhaps nothing illustrates the general opinion of Roman art better than the well-known and oft-repeated tale of the general who, while engaged in removing to Rome some of the art relics which he had captured in one of the Greek cities, warned his soldiers and slaves that if they broke any of the statues they would be kept at work until they produced others as good. Even if this incident never actually happened, it would have been necessary to invent it, for it tells us so much about the Romans: that they were a proud, mercenary, conquering people, who thought that culture could be produced by "subjugation, borrowing, or compulsion"; that they never acquired that attitude towards life from which inspired artistic creation naturally and freely springs; and

Courtesy of German Tourist Information Office

A ROMAN GATEWAY

It would be difficult to find a better illustration of the essential difference between the spirit of Greek and Roman art than two gateways now in the Pergamon Museum, Berlin. The first (see page 92), built in the second century B.C. in a Greek colony in Asia Minor, reflects the calm spirit and austere restraint of the best Greek art. The second, from the Roman colony of Milet, built about 150 A.D., is obviously copied from the Greek style; but in comparison it is grandiose and overlavish.

that their art, like so much of that of recent times, came largely out of practical necessities or expressed a desire for luxurious display rather than any inner spiritual convictions.

The incidents which constitute the Roman episode in history are well known to everyone and hardly need retelling here. They represent, broadly speaking, the attempt of a nation made up largely of landowners and farmers to capture and control the entire European world. It started with a small city-state on the banks of the Tiber around 400 B.C., the first territorial additions to this tiny beginning being made because of the necessity of keeping off the enemy from its borders. Once started by the suppression of its neighbors to the north, the Etruscans, a race which had come from the East and settled in central Italy, this accretive process never ceased until at the time of its greatest extent the Roman Empire embraced such widely separated territories as Britain to the north, Spain to the west, Egypt to the south, and Mesopotamia to the east. In addition to the Etruscans, the Greeks and the Carthaginians and the Gauls were overcome and amalgamated into this enormous world state. Such a process of conquest and subjection was made possible, of course, by using a tremendous force of arms; and in order to form the innumerable legions necessary for their conquests, the patricians, or the older landowning class, granted more and more power and political privileges to the plebeians, or the free citizens of the middle class. The continuing wars and increasing possessions multiplied the wealth of all, including that of a third class which quickly arose, the business and official class, made up of merchants, politicians, bankers, moneylenders.

A background such as this, of military conquest, narrow-minded and hidebound aristocracy, petty officialdom, political intrigue, and social corruption on a large scale, does not offer a promising field for cultural development. The Roman intellect was at bottom, Barnes says, a farmer's intellect. And he attributes to its lack of imagination and flexibility not only the fact that Rome never produced any distinctive creative art — excepting a grandiose type of structural engineering — but also the fact that she was never able to cultivate sufficient commercial enthusiasm and financial wisdom to carry the tremendous load of world empire which she assumed. And so her doom was inevitable.

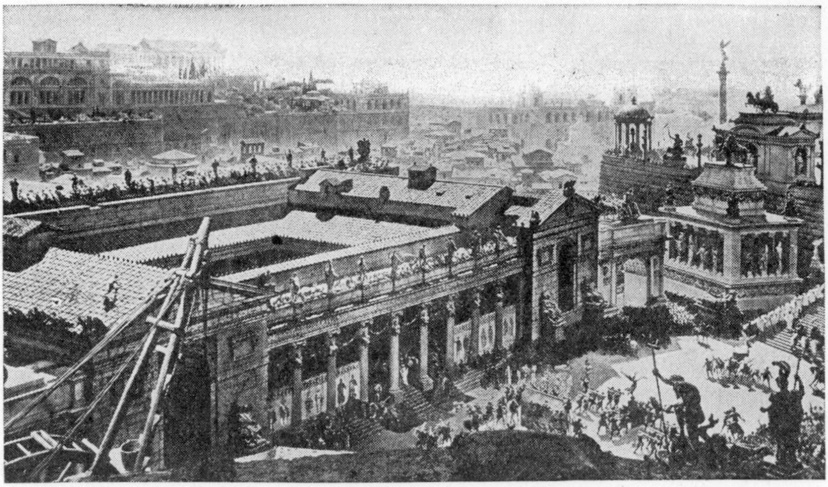

RECONSTRUCTION OF THE CIRCUS MAXIMUS, ROME

Nevertheless, the riches and the power acquired by the Romans, together with the fact that the presence of one sovereign political power enabled widely spread peoples to exchange and merge their cultural contributions, produced what one historian has called the most successful and extensive assimilation of culture achieved up to that time. Rome's great contributions to civilization were, of course, in the fields of law and politics. But the art fields were all enriched by Roman contributions of such a character as to affect strongly the generations that followed.

The austere beauty and the fine restraint characteristic of the best Greek art made little appeal to Roman taste, it is true; and when the Romans copied Hellenic models, they usually chose those of a decadent period, for they loved grandiose magnificence more than artistic restraint. Building was largely devoted to providing large public meetinghouses and law courts (basilicas), baths, theaters, sports arenas, monumental bridges, commemorative arches, and superb aqueducts. A desire for Gargantuan grandeur seemed to be an overwhelming passion: the great Circus Maximus, a sort of "multiple political club, lounge, social rendezvous," had accommodations for hundreds of thousands of spectators.

Sculpture was devoted largely to a literal copying of personal attributes — the making of a huge number of portrait busts of senators, gen-

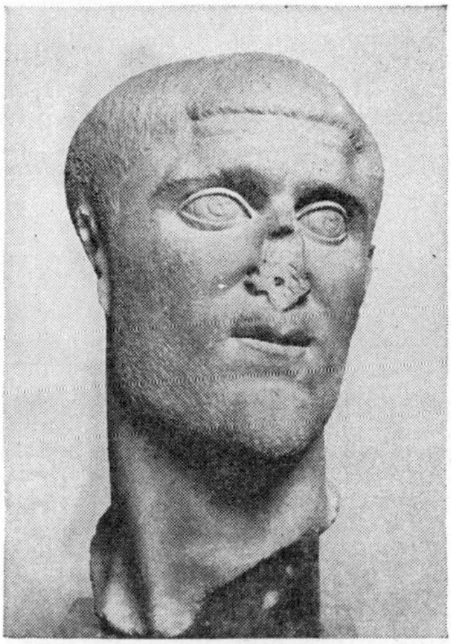

State Museum, Berlin

THE EMPEROR MAXIMINUS

A fine example of the Roman portrait bust

erals, and merchants — or to some sort of elaborate architectural ornamentation. The best examples combined some of the Greek ideals with an inherent desire for naturalism, but as a whole they were not very impressive. It was this architecture and sculpture which so strongly affected nineteenth-century European and American art. Any visitor to Paris, London, or New York cannot help realizing how architects and sculptors have based some of their most monumental creations on these Roman models. In painting, the Roman artist tried to attain the same naturalistic effects, simulating the appearance of depth by the devices of perspective, and achieving some important atmospheric results.

The Greek dramas were not imitated. Instead, we hear of farces given by the *mimi*, and of pantomimic dance dramas divorced entirely from words, and of the gorgeous spectacles of circus and arena which, controlled and exploited by the politicians, constituted one of the most powerful influences in Roman life. Artists were looked on as minor personages, many of them being slaves who had been captured from subject countries celebrated for excellence in learning or creative ability.

BORROWED IDEALS

So not much is to be expected in the way of musical development on the part of the Romans. They borrowed their ideas and ideals from the Greeks, but instead of developing them, they degraded them. Their poetry was not recited to musical accompaniment as it had been, at least in classic times, in Greece. In their productions of drama there was no orchestra or choir, the monodies of the actors being accompanied only by the aulos; these actors did not always sing their own part but kept the declamation and dialogue as speaking roles and hired a singer for the choral parts. One of the chief uses of instruments was in warfare, the cornu and the tuba being especially developed for this purpose. In the dance pantomimes into which the old tragedies had deteriorated, and which became more and more popular as they became more and more licentious and obscene, instruments were used for accompaniment. The band consisted of players on the tibia (a sort of double flute), the Pan-pipe (syrinx), the lyre, and cymbals; and each player had two metal plates fastened under his foot, so that he could mark out the time and thus keep the band together.

Lucian of Samosata, who lived in the second century A.D., wrote an essay on Roman dancing in which he makes one of his characters ask how anyone can

" sit still and listen to the sound of a flute and watch the antics of an effeminate creature got up in soft raiment to sing lascivious songs and mimic the passions of prehistoric strumpets to the accompaniment of twanging string and shrilling pipe and clattering heel? "

And another answers:

" The pantomime is above all things an actor: that is his first aim, in the pursuit of which he resembles an orator, and especially the composer of ' declamations,' whose success, as the pantomime knows, depends like his own upon verisimilitude, upon the adaptation of language to character: prince or tyrannicide, pauper or farmer, each must be shown with the peculiarities that belong to him. I must give you the comment of another foreigner on this subject. Seeing five masks laid ready — that being the number of parts in the piece — and only one pantomime, he asked who were going to play the parts. He was informed that the whole piece would be performed by a single actor. 'Your humble servant, sir,' cried our foreigner to the artist, 'I observe that you have but one body: it had escaped me, that you possessed several souls.' . . .

"Other entertainments of eye or ear are but manifestations of a single art: 'tis flute or lyre or song; 'tis moving tragedy or laughable comedy. The pantomime is all-embracing in the variety of his equipment: flute and pipe, beating foot and clashing cymbal, melodious recitative, choral harmony. Other arts call out only one half of a man's powers — the bodily or the mental: as a physical exercise, there is meaning in his movements; every gesture has its significance; and therein lies his chief excellence. The enlightened Lesbonax of Mytilene called pantomimes 'manual philosophers,' and used to frequent the theater, in the conviction that he came out of it a better man than he went in. . . .

"All professions hold out some object, either of utility or of pleasure: Pantomime is the only one that secures both these objects; now the utility that is combined with pleasure is doubled in value. [A typical Roman viewpoint!] Who would choose to look on at a couple of young fellows spilling their blood in a boxing match, or wrestling in the dust, when he may see the same subject represented by a pantomime, with the additional advantages of safety and elegance, and with far greater pleasure to the spectator? The vigorous movements of the pantomime — turn and

A GLADIATORIAL COMBAT TO THE ACCOMPANIMENT OF MUSIC OF TUBA, HORN, AND ORGAN

(From the mosaics of the Amphitheater in Zliten. About 70 A.D.)

twist, bend and spring — afford at once a gratifying spectacle to the beholder and a wholesome training to the performer; I maintain that no gymnastic exercise is its equal for beauty and for the uniform development of the physical powers — of agility, suppleness, and elasticity, as of solid strength."

— Translated by H. W. and F. S. Fowler

Enough has been written about the splendors and terrors of the Roman public games with which the consuls, and afterwards, the emperors, won the favor of the people — at their own expense. These imperial side shows might include anything that was exciting enough or barbarous enough to form an absorbing spectacle: chariot races and gladiatorial combats, fights between slave-manned galleys in the flooded arena, hundreds of trumpeters playing in a chorus, wild African lions let loose to be shot by specially imported archers, and so forth. Sad to relate, music played an ignominious role of accompaniment to all this Roman splendor, dismayingly like that which it occupies in similar Hollywoodian revels. All the noisy instruments they could find were used by the Romans in providing music for these spectacles, including tubas, horns, and organs, the latter being known in Alexandria as early as 100 B.C.

LATER TRENDS

In the Augustan times and afterwards art began to be cultivated by "the" people — both nobles and *bourgeoisie*. Artists and singers and players were sought after by Roman society and often received the favors of princes. A knowledge of music was looked upon as essential to social climbers who wished to get into society, and by the time of the first century A.D. all the former prejudices against professional artists had disappeared. Music was even cultivated by the emperors. We remember Nero's aspirations along this line; he devoted much time and patience to the cultivation of his "feeble, veiled voice," as one of his contemporaries described it, by going through long periods of fasting or of eating only pears and by exhibiting other foibles peculiar to singers. He had other claims to fame, especially the spectacular punishments which he devised for the Christians, a "sort of people who held a new and impious superstition," dressing them, according to Tacitus, in the skins of wild beasts and exposing them to be torn to pieces by dogs in the public games. Christians were sometimes crucified, sometimes condemned to be burned, according to the dictates of Nero's fancy; and at nightfall they sometimes served in place of lamps to lighten the darkness.

Loving to appear in public as a singer, Nero inflicted himself upon audiences all over Italy; and in order to be sure of his reception, "he chose young men of the equestrian order, and about five thousand robust young fellows from the common people, on purpose to learn various kinds of applause, called *bombi, imbrices,* and *testae,*[1] which they were to practice in his favor, whenever he performed. They were divided into several parties and were remarkable for their fine heads of hair, were extremely well dressed, with rings upon their left hands. The leaders of these bands had salaries of forty thousand sesterces allowed them" (Kirstein: *The Dance*).

Nothing better illustrates the depths of degradation to which Roman art finally descended; for here, as Kirstein has remarked, we have the spectacle of a spontaneous actor directing artistic applause, rather than spontaneous applause given to an artistic actor! Legend has given a final, aesthetically consistent denouement to this demoniacal career in the story of Nero's setting Rome aflame for the sheer enjoyment of tragic beauty, and fiddling while he watched it. Such a legend may have little historic basis, but it shows into what disrepute music had fallen at that time.

THE EARLY CHURCH

The history of the world has seen nothing more dramatic than the sudden reversal of the fortunes of that devoted group of religionists which took the name of Christians during the first centuries of the present era. Jesus of Nazareth, who was considered a god by many of his followers, but who was looked upon by the Roman officials of the time as simply another of the fanatical Jews who had given them so much

[1] The term *bombi* was derived from the humming of bees, and meant a confused din made by the hands or mouth; *imbrices* meant the sound of rain or hail on the roofs; *testae,* the smashing of terra-cotta jars. Here are old ideas which have been neglected by the modern purveyors of applause, the *claques!*

trouble, was crucified in Jerusalem in the year 30 A.D. About thirty years later another Jew who had taken part in the spread of the religion of Jesus, Saul of Tarsus, was put to death in Rome. In another ten years Jerusalem itself was razed to the ground and its inhabitants scattered over the face of the earth. Hundreds of its people were paraded through the streets of Rome as prisoners in celebration of what the Romans must have considered the end of the Judean fanatic and his religion.

But they were wrong: Christianity increased rapidly in popularity and in numbers during the first three centuries of its existence. The reasons why it was able to achieve such significant triumph over its powerful rival religions are many and complex. It happened to fit the needs of its time better than did any of the others; it possessed an assured and positive dogma; and it owed a great deal to the splendid organizing and disciplining power of the missionary Paul, as he was called after his conversion from Judaism. It was he who took the rather metaphysical teachings of Jesus, addressed as they had been to a small circle, and adapted them as the basis for a well-organized religion of universal appeal.

It would be apart from our purpose to attempt any complete account of the details of Christianity's triumph over Roman paganism. It is sufficient to note the fact that from a simple communal society formed from the followers who were left after the Crucifixion of Christ — a society that had no need of extensive organization, for it expected Jesus to return soon to earth — it developed rapidly, especially among the urban middle classes, during these first years, and in the process aroused the strong suspicions of the Romans. Any comparative study of religions will show that many of the fundamental doctrines which Christianity adopted during these years of its early existence are common to most of them and were inherited directly from the beliefs of the Jews who, in turn, borrowed them from earlier prototypal religions. The Jews also contributed to Christianity the fundamental idea of a Jehovah God and the hope of a Messiah to save humanity from its sins — an idea which Breasted has traced to Egyptian philosophy. The scholastic Greeks of the early Christian centuries introduced the element of abstract reasoning into the very personal, intimate teachings of Jesus. In their hands, as has

PAINTINGS FROM AN EARLY CHRISTIAN CATACOMB IN ROME
The subjects are figures from Christian mythology painted in Roman terms.

been said, Christian theology took on the color of Greek metaphysics, centering about Jesus and his place in the world rather than about Plato and his conception of truth. The religious practices of the Greeks contributed also to the shaping of parts of the Christian ritual, notably the rites of the Eucharist and baptism. The Persians are thought to have been the first to believe in man's immortality, a belief that was absorbed into Christianity through its becoming a constituent part of the Jewish faith. Rome itself made a mighty contribution to the new religion, that of its policy of organization and administration: as the Christian Church spread over the eastern and central parts of Europe, it effectually adopted for its own purposes the system of administration that had been found to work well within the empire. Drawn from all parts of the world, borrowing its ideas from all known cults, Christianity was able to impose such a strong element of emotional symbolism and didactic persuasiveness into its teachings as to make them quickly popular.

During its earliest days the Church had little interest in art of any kind; for not only were many of the converts of the new faith drawn from the middle classes, who were unused to artistic expression, but also in the minds of these early members of the Church, art stood for everything to which the new faith was opposed. It was the symbol of a godless, corrupt, pagan, and doomed world — a world to which the early return of Christ would bring a merciful close. Music especially was associated with the Antichrist, and painting was used merely to represent visually some of the events connected with Old Testament history. The close connection which these early Christian paintings had with texts used in the services of the dead shows that they were meant to be sort of visual prayers, the worshiper asking the Lord to receive the soul of the departed one for whose tomb the painting had been made, just as the Lord had accomplished the miracles depicted in the picture. The fact that the motifs used often had a double significance — a figure, for example, being capable of representing Orpheus to a casual pagan visitor who might see the painting and Christ to the believing worshiper — did not change the essential nature of the art. It was purely a case of "safety first." The same walls on which were painted in Roman terms the imploring figures of Christian mythology may have reverberated to a simple kind of chant adapted to the purposes of the Church from Hebraic and Greek sources.

THE "HYMN OF JESUS"

There are only the vaguest indications of the actual use of music in the Church during these first centuries. Not content with merely taking over some of the usages of the Jewish synagogues which had sprung up in all the important towns in Asia Minor, Syria, and even in Rome itself after the destruction of the temple in Jerusalem by the Roman Titus, the new religion early began to develop its own chants. Besides the Jewish psalms, these early Christians sang hymns similar in character to those connected with the Greek mysteries and used for the same purpose, that of invoking the god and coming into exalted, mystic contact with him. There is a definite record of such a hymn in the Apocryphal

"Acts of John" known, according to the Catholic Dictionary, to St. Augustine; it is supposed to date from about 160 A.D. and from its content we are justified in imagining that the music used must have been of a Hellenic nature and that not only music but dancing formed a part of the liturgical practices of the new sect:

"Before Jesus was taken by the Jews and unbelievers who hold to Satan's law, he gathered us together and said: Before I am delivered over to them, let us sing a hymn to the Father. We will then go to them, together. Then he asked us to form a circle: we took each by the hand, he being in the middle and said: Amen, Follow me; and he commenced the hymn.

Jesus: Glory be to the Father (and we who were circling him responded): Amen. [Thus let it be.]

Jesus: Glory be to thee — the word. Glory be to thee — the grace.
Disciples: Amen.
Jesus: Glory to thee — the Holy Ghost — praise be to thy glory.
Disciples: Amen.
Jesus: We praise thee, Father — we render thanks to thee, light where no shadows dwell.
Disciples: Amen.
Jesus: Of that unto which we render thee thanks I speak — to be saved is my desire and I desire to save.
Disciples: Amen.
Jesus: To be delivered is my desire, and I desire to deliver.
Disciples: Amen.
Jesus: To be blessed is my desire, and I wish to bless.
Disciples: Amen.
Jesus: To be born is my desire, and I wish to engender.
Disciples: Amen.
Jesus: To be nourished is my desire, and I wish to nourish.
Disciples: Amen.
Jesus: To hear is my desire, and I wish to be heard.
Disciples: Amen.
Jesus: To understand is my desire, with all my intelligence.
Disciples: Amen.
Jesus: To be cleansed is my desire, and I wish to cleanse.
Disciples: Amen.
Jesus: Forgiveness is our *choragus* [dance leader] — to sing is my desire, let us dance together.

Disciples: Amen.
Jesus: I wish to be grieved for, weep you all.
Disciples: Amen.
Jesus: I am thy light, ye who see me. I am the gate, ye who enter.
The twelve disciples now dance.
Jesus: Those who do not dance will not comprehend what shall befall.
Disciples: Amen.
Jesus: Then all of you join my dance. You who dance, see what I have accomplished."

We know that the spontaneous, ecstatic sort of songs that are characteristic of rather primitive religious rites (and which survive in the Negro camp-meeting extemporizations and Salvation Army gatherings of today) had a part in the early worship of the Church; they were accepted as a valuable adjunct to the services by Paul himself, who, however, insisted that they be intelligible to the rest of the congregation. None of the melodies of this period have survived; but they were probably of small compass and employed a simple form of melismatic decoration.

The third century was a period marked by a slow strengthening and a gradual development of the Church's resources. As the social and economic conditions of the Roman Empire became progressively worse, in spite of the reorganizing reforms and efficient administration of a few emperors, the collapse of that once powerful institution was seen to be inevitable; but there was little change in its official attitude toward the Christians. The members of the new sect were regarded at all times during these early centuries of the Church's existence with suspicion and dislike in the empire and were subjected to intermittent persecutions in the hope of breaking their morale. But in vain: the Christians continued to flourish, especially in Alexandria and the eastern part of the empire; important communities were founded, and many of the rich and learned professed the new faith.[2] By the year 300 the problem of the Christian Church was not so much that of defying the imperial power of Rome as it was of securing a unity of organization for itself. This was the great period of heretical discussion. There arose so many diverse

[2] "Let cruelty, envious or malignant," cries Cyprian, "hold you here in bonds and chains as long as it will; from this earth and from these sufferings you shall speedily come to the Kingdom of Heaven." (C. H. Dawson: *The Making of Europe*)

opinions as to what should constitute the essential doctrines of the Church that its very life was threatened. For it was obvious enough that if the new organization was not to split up at the very beginning of its existence into a number of irreconcilable sects, each differing from the others in some essential way, some method of repressing these individualistic spirits must be found. And so it was necessary to deal summarily and harshly with such heresies as Arianism, a dispute revolving around a difference of interpretation brought about by the change of a single letter in one Greek word; Gnosticism, an attempt to make the Christian faith conform to Greek metaphysics; Montanism, which preached the immediate second coming of Christ; and many others of a similar nature. One of the historians of this period has made the statement that these quarrels within the Church " made five or six times as many martyrs in fifty years as the pagan emperors had in two hundred and fifty years! "

DEMONIAC SONGS

Some of these heretical sects used propaganda songs, which they introduced on occasion into the worship of the Church, perhaps something in the manner in which the Salvation Army makes such effective use of modern melodies and rhythms. One of the problems of the early Church Fathers was how best to deal with such matters; indeed, they were sorely troubled as to what the general attitude of the Church should be toward this disturbing matter of music, so popular with the people and so pagan in its associations. They realized well enough its power to arouse feelings and stir passions;[3] they heard on every side its secular use, in work songs, sailor chanteys, lullabies, and so forth, and were worried about the effect which this sort of music might have on the hearts and minds of the faithful. They knew that the pagan shows and pantomimes were still popular with church members, both young and old, and they ranted about the " demoniac and satanic songs " to be heard on such occasions. St. John Chrysostom observes bitterly that if a youth of the time was asked to sing a psalm, he wouldn't know it; but if he was asked to hum one

[3] " Nothing so lifts the soul, gives it wings, frees it from earthly things, as a holy song, in which rhythm and melody form a true symphony." (St. John Chrysostom)

of the popular revue songs from the current pantomime, he would be sure to have it by heart! The councils of the Church tried to counteract these evil influences by decreeing that no person connected in any way with a circus or pantomime could be baptized and that any church member attending the theater on holy days would be excommunicated — rules which, if they had been strictly enforced, would have thrown half Christendom, including a good part of the clergy, out of the Church's communion:

> "From east to west, in Constantinople, in Antioch, in Alexandria, in Rome, the mimic drama flourished, uniting together old pagans and new Christians in the one common enjoyment of pure secularism."
>
> — Allardyce Nicoll: *Masks, Mimes and Miracles*

THE PROBLEM OF INSTRUMENTS

Another problem which taxed the ingenuity of the Fathers was that concerned with the use of instruments in the services; if some of their rulings seem strange to us today, we must always remember the infelicitous association which music had for them. In the beginning, all the Christian musical practices were vocal, if for no other reason than the very practical one that it was necessary to use great caution while conducting the services; and so no loud instruments could be tolerated. Later on, the lyre and the cithara were allowed, at least in private meetings; but even Clement of Alexandria, one of the most broad-minded of the early churchmen and one well versed in all the amenities of instrumental music, went on record to the effect that the Christians did not need to use instruments in their services, their word "being peace and not the psaltery, trumpet, aulos, and cymbals of those who prepared for war." The early bishops did not hesitate to compare the aulos to the evil serpent which tempted Mother Eve, and we read of their inveighing against such pagan uses of music as those in a church in Asia Minor, where they beat the hands, sounded little bells, and employed choregraphic movements of the body in accompanying the holy chants.

The Old Testament contains, of course, numerous references to the use of instruments in the worship of God's house; and the tortuous and symbolical means of explaining these away on the part of the good Fathers of the early Church make amusing reading. The injunction of Holy Writ to "praise God with the timbrel and the dance and all instruments of music" meant, according to their ingenious explanations, that the "members of the body are like strings in accord in praising the Lord, and its thoughts like cymbal's chime." St. Basil saw in the ten strings of the psaltery a likeness to the ten commandments, and therefore that instrument was permitted, especially since it was severe looking and in no sense resembled the instruments used in theatrical performances. Moreover, its upper strings were the ones which resounded the best and not the lower, as in the lyre and the cithara; therefore it represented a higher, purer form of music, and its use might be condoned.

Since music was the only one of the arts even mildly approved by the early Church, it seems probable that its emotion-releasing effect was much more powerful than if it had been one amongst various arts serving as the handmaid of religion. We can thus better understand the anxiety of the early Church Fathers to rationalize (as we would now say) the effects of music and to explain them away in symbolic terms.

THE CHURCH'S POSITION

Out of all these backgrounds there crystallized very gradually the general psychological attitude which the Church assumed towards music — an attitude which was to influence the history of the art for the next thousand years and shape its general development for an even longer period. With the Greeks, music was thought of as a moral and political force, capable of exerting a tremendous influence on the lives of the people; but it was also used as a means for giving pleasure. The Church Fathers, who were strongly influenced by Greek thought in so many things, adopted only part of this attitude. To them, as to the Hebrews, all art was justifiable only in the sense that it could be made to serve God; they never thought of it under any circumstances as existing for its own sake. Therefore it must be brought under the control of the Church. Even pleasure in its use for the glory of God was to be frowned upon: an early manuscript now in the Library at Vienna tells of an

Egyptian abbot named Paulo who at the beginning of the fourth century retired to the desert with some of his followers and of how one of them, on being sent to Alexandria on business, returned with accounts of the scandalous goings on in the churches there — the praises of God were actually being *sung*. Thereupon the old monk holds forth on the iniquity of seeking divers melodies and diverse rhythms for the worship of God. "When we stand in the presence of God we should assume an attitude of contrition and not employ the voice of praise. Can there be any spirit of penitence in a monk who, in church or cell, makes his voice resound like that of a bull?" So even the honest pleasures of the anchorite enjoying the fine resonance of his cell as he sang the praises of his Creator were to be denied him.

All these early chants of the Church, most of them confined to the settings of the Psalms, were probably simple in character, their melodies confined to the limits of the tetrachord and with no definite feeling of tonality. Athanasius (296?–373), who formulated the doctrine of the Trinity that was finally adopted by the Church, ordered that the Psalms were to be sung with so little variety that they sounded, according to St. Augustine, more like speaking than singing. There was an evident effort on the part of the early authorities to keep the use of music simple and avoid all extravagances.[4] Not only was music to be confined to the worship of God, but its use in this connection must be so carefully controlled that no suggestion of its paganistic implications might appear.

It was not until after the triumphant emergence of Christianity from the catacombs and its adoption as the Roman state religion that a more liberal attitude prevailed and ritualistic music assumed something of the importance it deserved in the worship of the Church. But that is another story and belongs to another chapter.

[4] The fourth-century abbot, Silvain, in rebuking a monk who had confessed to having fallen asleep during vigils, said that undoubtedly his sin was the result of too much fancy psalm chanting. Song, he maintained, had sent many a man (and some priests as well) to hell, so impure were the passions it aroused.

THE HISTORICAL PAST

Monodic Music of a Thousand Years

MUSIC IN THE CHURCH

Take nonspecialists in music and non-Catholic clergymen; take contemporaries, whether farmers, laborers, college students, college professors, journalists, scientists, etc. Play the records of the Gregorian chant on a phonograph without telling what it is, and then ask the listeners whether they like it or not. I venture to say that at least 95, if not 100, per cent would answer negatively. And in a sense they could not be blamed. Because, from the standpoint of a sensually audible criterion, the chant is no music at all; it is something queer, unenjoyable, primitive, dry; in brief, it has none of the earmarks of what we are accustomed to style music — neither measure, nor harmony, nor polyphony.

— Pitirim A. Sorokin: *Fluctuation of Forms of Art*

ART IN THE EARLY CHURCH

IT was the fourth century which brought about the dramatic change in the fortunes of the Christian religion which was to make it one of the greatest forces in European civilization. In the beginning years of this century, members of the strange new sect were being thrown to the lions in the arenas because of their refusal to bow down to the gods of the Romans; before the century was out, the same gods were thrown down and dragged in the dust during the festivities attendant upon the crowning of a Christian emperor. The citizens of Rome of the year three hundred were accustomed enough to the sight of the persecution of the Christians. Not many years later, the descendants of these citizens were crowding the Christian altars, praying to their new God for the forgiveness of their pagan fathers. The change came suddenly, almost in the manner of a theatrical climax — one decade, furtive secrecy and clandestine worship; the next, triumph, victory, and honor.

By the year 300 A.D. the Christians had become so numerous that the Roman emperors realized that further persecution would be useless. In 311 the emperor Galerius revoked the edict of persecution and introduced an era of tolerance. In 313 Constantine signed the famous Edict of Milan, an act which legalized Christian worship throughout the Roman Empire. He moved his capital from Rome to Byzantium, which was later called Constantinople, and from there he directed the practical realization of his dream of a Holy Roman Empire and pushed it onto the world stage. In 337, just before his death, this first Christian emperor received the rites of baptism at the hands of a bishop of the Church. Twenty-five years later, his nephew Julian died, after making a vain attempt to re-establish the pagan religion in Rome, murmuring, so the story goes, *Vicisti, Galilaee* (Thou hast conquered, O Galilean).

For nearly two hundred years, during which time the Church was able to consolidate her gains and lay the firm foundations for her future developments, she rejoiced in her triumph; then in 476 came the banishment of the last of the western emperors (whose name was, ironically enough, Romulus Augustus the Little) and the final collapse of the Roman civilization under the impact of the invading barbarian hosts. For a number of centuries the future of church as well as state seemed dark enough; "western European culture retrogressed to the level of the Cretan and Mycenaean civilizations" (Barnes) which had preceded both Greece and Rome. But the years between the conversion of Constantine and the coming of the Lombards form one of the great epochs in the Church's history and one of tremendous importance to art. It was during this first brilliant flush of its power and wealth that the foundations of Christian liturgy, legendry, and art were laid, the site of these early developments being Byzantium.

At the time the emperors of the West were still officially engaged in persecuting the followers of Christ, the Church in the East had already come to a state of maturity as a result of cultural traditions that reach back to the beginnings of history. We are sometimes likely to forget that the very beginnings of Christianity are Asiatic — Christ and the Jews lived in Palestine, not in Europe. So, too, the backgrounds of Christian culture are Eastern and not Western. It was in Egypt, with its capital of

AN EARLY CHRISTIAN–BYZANTINE CHURCH

At the top is shown the rear view of the ruins of the Basilica at Turmanin in North Syria, built during the sixth century; at the bottom, a front view of its reconstruction.

Alexandria, the center of the learning of the time, in Syria, with its mixed Hebraic, Greek, and Mesopotamian inhabitants, and in Persia that its first important development took place. Long before the Western Church dared to worship openly above ground rather than in the dark catacombs and secret places where it had furtively gathered, the Church in the East had started on a brilliant period of growth, a development which made necessary new buildings and suitable textiles, murals, and sculptures for their decoration, as well as elaborate liturgies and appropriate music which could be used in the services.

Out of the attempt to meet these artistic needs of the Church there came a glorious amalgam: the influence of the art of the Orient (an influence which, of course, was strongly felt in this part of the world), with its love of color, its stylized patterns, its rigid conventions, its sensuous feeling for mystical expression, was blended with the demands and ideals of the new religious sect and the remains of the Greco-Roman tradition. The result was the style which has come to be known as Byzantine, a style with so many cross-purposes and varying racial characteristics as to make any attempt at exact classification impossible. Cheney has characterized it well by saying that it was Christian in purpose and Oriental in expression. The churches which these Asiatic Christians built had Eastern domes and Eastern barrel vaults; they were decorated with painted murals and tapestries whose flattened composition, peculiar iconography, rich color, and closely intertwined motives all suggest an Eastern origin; their walls were covered with mosaics — designs worked out by setting small squares of colored glass or stone into a cement foundation. Everything about this art, its depths of infinite color, its sumptuous richness suggestive of the gold and jewels and spices of the Orient, aroused the spirit of mystic exaltation and emotional fervor which the Church wished to cultivate. So, in spite of later attempts on the part of Europeans to purge the Church of this gorgeous Eastern art, it exerted a strong influence on religious developments from the second century clear down to the twentieth century.

Not the least important of these influences has been that on music. Most modern investigators are agreed that it was here in these Eastern communities that the type of Church music which has come to be known as the Gregorian chant had its origin; and that it was later introduced into the Roman Church, there to become one of the great foundation stones on which the structure of European music was erected. Anyone familiar with this chant as it is still used in the Roman Catholic Church [1] today is often startlingly reminded of these Eastern influences by the frequent use which is made of the rich, florid vocal figures of the type known as *melisma* — a term which has come to be used for any decorative passage in which the original melody is spun out into embellishments. The people of the East have always had a strong predilection for this sort of vocalization, and it can still be heard in the music of India and the Orient. It was the practice in all the Eastern religions for the cantor (the trained leader of the choirs) to embellish the melodies he sang. The musicians of the early Church adopted the same idea, and melismatic singing in which oftentimes a veritable torrent of florid vocalization occurs has been a constituent part of Christian music from earliest times.

SOURCES OF EARLY CHRISTIAN MUSIC

We have but to listen to some of the traditional chants of the Jewish liturgy — such, for example, as that of the Passover *Kaddish* or the Day of Atonement *Abodah* — to realize how close is the bond between early Christian and Jewish music. In our discussions in an earlier chapter we have stated the features which were taken over into the music of the Christian Church from the practices of the synagogue. Prominent among these was the singing of the Psalms and Canticles, a feature of the oldest portion of the Church's liturgy, used in the so-called "Offices of the Hours" performed at fixed times during the day and night. The Church kept the responsorial character of the Jewish psalmodic singing, a phrase sung by the solo cantor or precentor being answered by the choir or congregation; and this practice has been maintained to the present day.[2]

[1] It has also made notable progress in the present-day Anglican communion in Great Britain and the Episcopal Church in the United States.

[2] It may be that we have here the beginnings of "prima donnaism," for it is clear historically that the cantor in both synagogue and church employed a certain element of melismatic coloratura.

A comparison of the music system of the early Christian Church with that of the Greeks will also reveal many likenesses. It can easily be shown that some of the Christian chants resemble the Greek melodies that have been preserved; and there is little doubt that the general musical traditions of those lands at the eastern end of the Mediterranean, traditions which the new sect derived from the Greek practices, had a great deal to do with the forming of the earliest music used in its worship.

In fact, it has come to be generally agreed that the music which came into use in the Church is an elevation of materials received from three sources: the Jewish synagogical liturgy, the usages of Greco-Roman antiquity, and the spontaneous developments that occurred among the early Eastern and Western Christian congregations. It was the result, in the words of Artur Schnabel, the well-known pianist, of the crossbreeding of paganism, Hellenism, and Christianity.

THE MYSTICAL POWER OF GREGORIAN CHANT

But, we must always remember, there was something more: the raising of music from a secondary to a sovereign role in the life of the early Christian peoples came about because of a recognized spiritual necessity. If we listen carefully to such a chant as that which has become traditional for use on Holy Thursday,[3] a setting of the words " Christ became obedient for us unto death, even to the death of the cross; for which cause God hath exalted him and hath given him a name which is above every name," we shall note that the general effect is that of a quiet, simple statement in which the melodic and textual divisions accord exactly. From time to time there are melismatic embellishments of the melody which give it added intensity, as if the simple melodic line could not sufficiently express the emotional fervor of the words. It is evident enough that the Church was able to create out of the material it borrowed from earlier sources an art which is distinctly its own, a perfect medium for the conveyance of its ideals and doctrines. The first part of this chant suggests, as clearly as does anything in pictorial art, the humiliation and

[3] *Christus Factus Est.*

sufferings of the cross; the second, the triumphal exaltation of which this suffering was the necessary preliminary. Thus the unknown composers of this melody would sum up the doctrine of the Church as to the efficacy of the redemption of mankind through Christ's death upon the cross.

In listening to this music we find ourselves far removed from the secular surroundings and hurrying bustle of the world. It is a fitting counterpart to the beauty of the architecture, the majestic, varicolored pageant of the ritual, the visual impressions of the incense mounting to heaven like the prayers of the righteous, with which the Church surrounded her worshipers from early times, seeking thereby to supplement and stimulate their natural emotions and lift them out of themselves into a region completely detached from everyday existence.

THE DEVELOPMENT OF PLAINSONG [4]

It must not be thought that all the chants of the early Church were as fully developed or as expressive as this. The history of early Christian music is inextricably bound up with that of the development of the liturgy, that is, the public rites and services used in the Church's worship. The earliest of these liturgies, together with the music used in it, came out of the East, and for the first few centuries of the Church's existence innumerable local and territorial liturgies were used, all of them different — Syrian, Egyptian, Persian, Byzantine, Gallic, Hispano-Gallic. Even the Roman liturgy, which later supplanted the others and remains today (with a few exceptions [5]) the standard in the Roman Catholic Church throughout the world, was at first Greek in form and language. By the seventh century this had become homogenized, had adopted Latin as its official language, and had gathered to itself a vast body of effective music of scope wide enough to cover the needs of all those who

[4] This term is usually applied to the whole traditional ritual melody of the Western Church; it is derived from *cantus planus*, implying a plain melody without counterpoint, and is used interchangeably with the term "Gregorian," which comes from the name of one of the greatest exponents of the chant, Gregory the Great, elected Pope in 590.

[5] Notably the Ambrosian liturgy, still in use at Milan, and the Mozarabic rites in Spain: each of these has its own peculiar type of music, differing from Gregorian plainsong.

participated in the services. By this time, bishop, cleric, choir, and congregation each had an important and individual part in the common worship, with a definite type of music adapted to the particular requirements.

There was, first of all, the essentially dramatic dialogue, set to simple chants, which took place between the Celebrant of the Mass (the official name of the Eucharistic Sacrifice and of its liturgy of prayers and ceremonies) and the entire congregation. Then there were the more elaborated chants sung by the choir, set to psalm texts, with refrains varied for the seasons and feasts of the liturgical year — such things as the Gradual and Alleluia responds, the Introit, the Offertory, and so forth. Finally there were those parts of the Mass (three in number at this time, the *Kyrie eleison*, the *Gloria in Excelsis Deo*, and the *Sanctus* [6]) designed for singing by the congregation alone and therefore set to very simple chants which strongly contrasted in character with those sung by the trained choir.

These developments were not accidental; they came about over a long period of time and through the agencies of a number of individuals. Leaders in the movement were (1) St. Ambrose, Bishop of Milan, the man generally credited with introducing the musical usages of the Eastern Church into the West (he it was who brought order out of the great confusion arising from the use of so many liturgies and who codified, from the usages of the time, four scales to be used in singing); and (2) Pope Gregory, who at the end of the sixth century again had the entire matter reviewed, added four more scales, and collected and recast, in his *Antiphonale Missarum*, the whole repertoire of chants then available.

An important factor in this standardization of the plainchant during these centuries was the great Roman *Schola Cantorum*, a school of singing founded, according to tradition, during the fourth century, immediately after the Edict of Milan, which officially freed the Christians from Roman persecutions. For nearly eight hundred years this institution

[6] The first of these was taken bodily from the Greek liturgy; the second and third were adaptations from Greek and Hebrew sources. The final details of the Mass as we know it today were not complete until the eleventh century, by which time two other portions were added, the *Credo* and the *Agnus Dei*. These portions are referred to as the Ordinary of the Mass, and to them are added the choral parts with variable texts, called the Proper — introits, graduals, alleluias, and so forth.

AN EARLY CHRISTIAN CHURCH: ST. CLEMENTE, ROME

In the center of the nave is the space reserved for the singers.

maintained its identity and helped spread the traditional manner of singing the music of the Church throughout all her domains, even as far afield as England. As Douglas puts it, in all that welter of migration, war, political turmoil, and social transformation which we call the Dark Ages, the " Song Schools of many a monastery and cathedral, faithful children of a great mother, preserved the ideals and advanced the practice of purely religious music. We are in their debt today for a very large part of what is best in our choral worship."

TECHNICAL CHARACTERISTICS OF PLAINSONG

These chants contained in the Gregorian *Antiphonale Missarum* still stand as a model and standard for the worship of the Church. But their melodies are bound to sound somewhat foreign to modern ears, and their general lack of rhythm, in the sense in which we understand it today, accentuates this strangeness. As we listen to these melodies, we are conscious of the fact that they seem to have been designed to emphasize the modulations of the natural speaking voice, like the changes in pitch of the voice of any speaker who has to make his words carry through large spaces — for instance, a train announcer in a huge modern terminal. No more practical means could have been found for the conveying of thought throughout the reaches of the large churches of the time. The chants use musical scales that are entirely diatonic (that is, made up of only tones and half tones), thereby giving the senses a feeling of peaceful assurance that is far removed from the restlessness and strivings of secular music with its colorful variety of chromatic intervals. There are no wide skips or nervous leaps in melody; everything proceeds by steps which suggest the quiet inflections of the voice in normal speaking. None of the effects of modern rhythm, with its regularly recurring stresses of accent, are present here; our impression is rather that of a wavelike flow of melody, uniting the various textual elements into a series of intelligible phrases. There are delicate dramatic effects, but nothing that is strained or overpowering. The whole feeling of this music is one of secure peacefulness, yet of strange mystery. All its elements — melodies, rhythm, and dynamics — flow from a single idea, simply because they sprang from the mood which best expresses this idea. They do for the text what faith does for the reason — carry it beyond its own limitations. According to the ideals of the Church this chant music has been made the true language of the worshiping soul.

Whereas modern music makes most frequent use of but two scales — the major and the minor, each of which has its own characteristics — the Church chant used eight scales, each with its individual flavor. The different feasts of the Church year vary naturally in mood — some joyful in character (Christmas and Easter), some hopeful (Advent), some sorrowful (Lent), some triumphant (Ascension). So the music that was composed for these various occasions was joyful, hopeful, sorrowful, triumphant in turn, and those who composed the chant melodies employed different scales to express this. They considered the first and second scales ("modes," they called them) as producing music of a "discreet, restrained, grave, contemplative character." The third and fourth they regarded as the modes of ecstasy, giving as much an impression of humanity as this impersonal music ever gave. The fifth and sixth modes, strongly resembling our modern major scale, they thought of as imparting a bright and spirited character to the music, filling it with hopeful buoyancy. The seventh, according to an authority, was the mode of solemn affirmation. The eighth mode was the " musical expression of that serenity of mind which is the characteristic feature of the wise." It is certain that our modern ears will never hear all that these old writers felt in their ancient scales; but it is interesting to know how they believed in these various possibilities and chose their modes carefully to suit the type of expression they wished to convey.

It is obvious enough that theoretical conceptions such as these were transplanted from the ideals of the Greeks. The two men who seem to have been largely responsible for transmitting these classical conceptions of musical theory into the Middle Ages were the Late Roman philosophers, Boethius and Cassiodorus,[7] both of the sixth century. Somewhere in this process the names of the Greek modes, *Dorian, Phrygian, Lydian,* and *Mixolydian,* were misapplied to the medieval scales, so that which in Greek music had been called *Dorian* was called *Phrygian* in medieval music, and that which had been known as *Lydian* was called *Ionian.* This false nomenclature was generally adopted and remained as the basis of musical theory for many centuries, the error being retained in order to avoid still further confusion. Boethius and Cassiodorus were thoroughly convinced of the validity of the Greek ideal of ethos in music, and their writings contain complete enumerations of the moral powers of music, its exhilarating and calming effects — ideals which were adopted to their needs by the Fathers of the Church.

The medieval theorists developed also a system of notation, at first merely using *neumes,* small signs placed above the words, giving a visual representation of the rise and fall of the melodies. Out of this came our

[7] Boethius, a minister at the court of Theodoric the Great, wrote five books on music, *De musica,* which remained the standard textbooks on music during the Middle Ages in Europe. Cassiodorus, who also had a public career at Theodoric's court in Ravenna, retired into a monastery where he had collected all that he could find of the fast disappearing ancient culture, in order that he might preserve as much of it as possible for posterity.

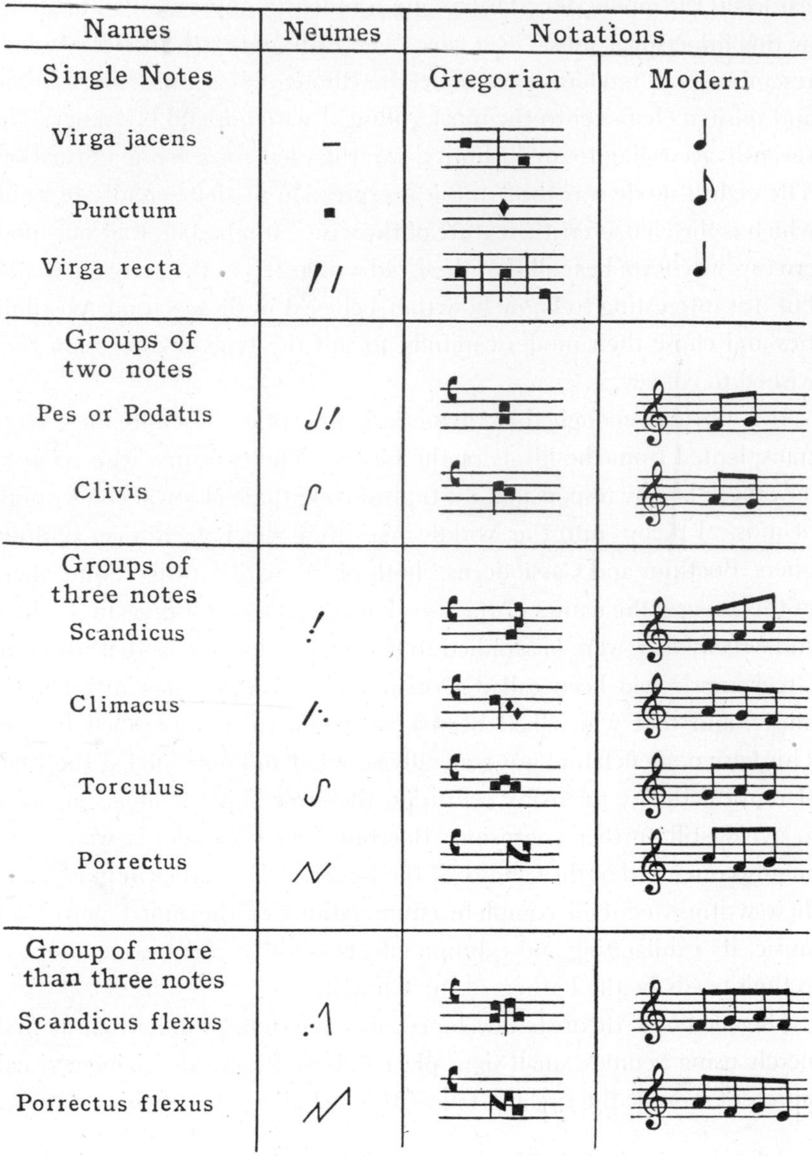
Names
Neumes
Notations
Gregorian
Modern
Single Notes
Virga jacens
Punctum
Virga recta
Groups of two notes
Pes or Podatus
Clivis
Groups of three notes
Scandicus
Climacus
Torculus
Porrectus
Group of more than three notes
Scandicus flexus
Porrectus flexus

A TABLE SHOWING HOW THE NEUMES WERE NAMED, AND THEIR EQUIVALENTS IN NOTATIONS modern notation, the greatest step forward being taken in the time of Guido d'Arezzo, a noted Benedictine theoretician of the eleventh century, when there was adopted the simple device of placing the neumes on lines representing fixed pitches.

As used by the medieval theorists, the Church scales made use of the same notes that we employ in our major scale — C, D, E, F, G, A, B, C — each mode commencing on successive notes of the scale and extending over the compass of one octave. Thus:

Four Principal Modes

First (Dorian): D, E, F, G, A, B, C, D
Third (Phrygian): E, F, G, A, B, C, D, E
Fifth (Lydian): F, G, A, B, C, D, E, F
Seventh (Mixolydian): G, A, B, C, D, E, F, G

Four Secondary Modes

Second (Hypodorian): A, B, C, D, E, F, G, A
Fourth (Hypophrygian): B, C, D, E, F, G, A, B
Sixth (Hypolydian): C, D, E, F, G, A, B, C
Eighth (Hypomixolydian): D, E, F, G, A, B, C, D

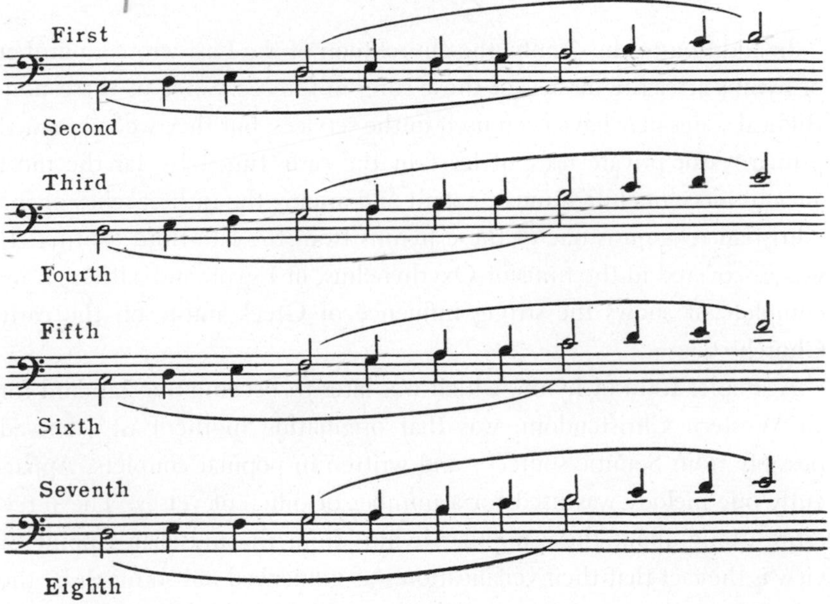

Later Glareanus, a sixteenth-century theorist, added four more modes — the Aeolian, starting on A (with its derived Hypoaeolian), and the Ionian, starting on C (with its derived Hypoionian).

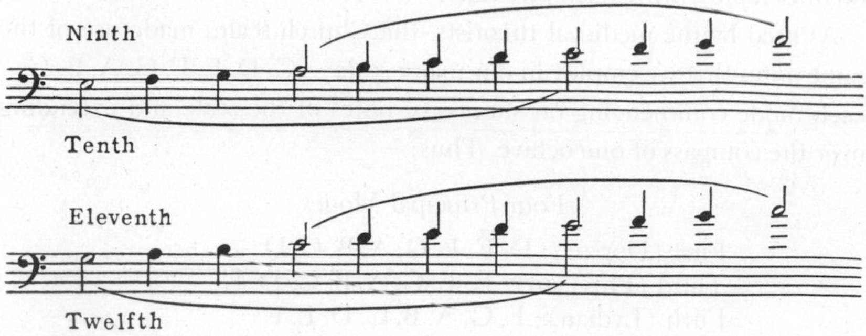

NOTE. It may be added that, since the secondary modes (*plagal*, Gregory called them) were borrowed from the principal modes, there was bound to be some overlapping. For example, although the Dorian and the Hypomixolydian modes use the same notes (see page 125), the latter is in reality the Mixolydian mode extended in a different compass. Therefore the melodies written in it have a different nature from those in the Dorian mode.

EARLY HYMNS

In addition to the chants, the churchmen of the East wrote a number of hymns after the models of those sung in Greece. Some of these non-Biblical songs may have been used in the services; but they were designed primarily for private uses, at least in the early times. By far the most ancient piece of church music extant and among the earliest relics of the Christian religion is one of these hymns from the late third century. It was discovered in the ruins of Oxyrhynchus, in Egypt, and, although incomplete, it shows the strong influence of Greek music on the early Church style.

A simpler form of hymn, which was later to become the standard for all Western Christendom, was that originating in the East (derived possibly from Semitic sources) and written in popular couplets. Apparently one melody was used for a number of different verses. The interesting thing about these popular hymns from the musician's point of view is the fact that their versification was influenced not so much by the quantity or length of the vowel sounds as by their being patterned according to regular rhythmic formulas made up of an alternation of accented and unaccented syllables. Such a hymn as this of St. Ambrose, Bishop of Milan, calls for a simple musical structure that is very much like that of the later folk songs and is entirely different from that of the freer chant melodies:

Ae - ter - ne re - rum con - di - tor, Noc -
tem di - em - que qui re - gis Et
tem - po - rum Das tem - po - ra, Ut al - le -
ves fas - ti - di - um.

From Hymnary of Pairis (Bibl. Colmar 442)

These hymns became extremely popular with the people when introduced into the services, for they represented something in which the whole congregation could heartily join. Many of them were written in the East. Their authors included men that are well known in ecclesiastical history, and their vogue extended into the sixth century.

A modern writer, Dom Cabrol, has imaginatively described the use of these hymns in the services of the Church of St. Sophia in Constantinople — that magnificent structure, an everlasting monument to the glory of Byzantine art, which was built by the emperor Justinian in the sixth century in an attempt to create a single building that should stand as the largest and finest in Christendom:

"These poems, conceived in the quiet of the cloister, were sung amidst surroundings and by congregations of great splendor: into the Church of St. Sophia came the people of Constantinople, together with the emperor and his brilliant cortege of officers, priests, dignitaries, and ladies

THE INTERIOR OF SANTA SOPHIA, CONSTANTINOPLE

of his palace. Here in the midst of a most astonishing profusion of precious marbles, mosaics, gold and silver decorations, the liturgical office commences. The priests defile in long processions, their ranks reaching even to the throne of the patriarch, that second ruler of the land.

"The moment arrives for the singing of the poet friar's hymn: the master of the choristers gathers his forces and prepares to direct their singing; the reader mounts the tribune, holding in his hand a roll of parchment on which the poem is written in clear, brilliant colors. The people come to attention, for they love this part of the service. The liturgical spectacle has renewed their ancient faith and made them ready for the inspiration that comes from music. Their eagerness is real; the song commences, line succeeds line, verse follows verse, the words outlined and made more significant by the appealing melody. The opening lines suggest with vividness the liturgical significance of the day; the succeeding stanzas are more general in their meaning. The singers reply to the reader, the scene being enlivened by the appearance in the dialogue of varied characters: the angels, the prophets, the saints of both the Old and New Testament, Adam, Noah, the good Joseph, even the devils themselves, speak one to another. It is in reality a *mystery*, the form which the later Latin Church was to develop centuries after."

— Translated from Dom Cabrol: *Le cardinal Pitra*, Paris, 1893

It was Ambrose,[8] Bishop of Milan and defender of the faith against the Arian heretics, who introduced these hymns into the Western usage. He wrote a number of them which breathe a spirit of clarity and optimistic confidence. Many of the great Occidental Church Fathers followed his example and made contributions to the liturgy of the Church in the way of Latin hymns full of austere beauty, yet pulsating with warm religious fervor. Gregory the Great (540?–604), Venantius Fortunatus (in the second part of the sixth century), Magnentius Arabanus Maurus (776–856), and St. Thomas Aquinas (1225?–1274?), "perhaps the most perfect master of lyric thought which the Occident ever possessed"

[8] The most comprehensive source of information regarding this early music of the church is St. Augustine of Hippo, who, around 388, wrote a long treatise, *De musica*, which shows how great was the difference between the ancient and the modern conceptions of music. The early musicians concentrated their attention largely on the rhythm and meter of the Latin verses they set. Augustine states in detail the differences between twenty-eight varieties of metrical feet; nevertheless he admits that the melody has certain purely musical laws of its own which it should obey. It is upon his authority (in his *Confessions*) that St. Ambrose is credited with organizing the music of the western European church.

KING DAVID AND POPE GREGORY

A Byzantine ivory miniature

(Max Fischer: *Mediaeval Hymns*), all wrote ardent, fervid poems which were popular in their day, but only a few of which, unfortunately, have found their way into Christian usage.

GROWING MAGNIFICENCE IN ART AND RITUAL

Music was not the only art to be strongly influenced by the opulent splendor of the East. During the great golden age of Byzantium the Roman Church split officially with the Eastern Church, but there came out of the great producing centers, Constantinople, Salonika, Nicaea, Ephesus, and the rest, such a flood of ivories, illuminations, textiles, goldsmith's work, and colored enamels as to transform completely the whole European conception of art. Prominent among these Byzantine influences was that which affected the building of churches: through all Christendom there arose magnificent buildings which combined the

THE BYZANTINE CHURCH OF S. VITALE IN RAVENNA (526 A.D.)
This shows the altar, choir, and presbytery. Notice the mosaic of Justinian's Procession.

plan of the basilicalike structures of the West with the love of glowing colors and rhythmic patternings of the East. The result was what one historian of art has described as the most "glorious manifestation of colorfulness in the whole of world architecture" (Cheney: *A World History of Art*). We get some idea of the glories of this period from such churches as those which have survived in Ravenna, on the east coast of Italy, or in Palermo, Sicily — cities which borrowed their artists from Byzantium — with their enormous spaces, their glowing mosaics spread over all the available walls, and their characteristic stiff formalism.

LATER PHASES OF GREGORIAN HISTORY

With the completion of these buildings, there arose the necessity of providing a more colorful and elaborate liturgy for the services held in them. We have already described in some detail the full collection of music suitable for this purpose available at the beginning of the seventh century. The crude and widely varied chants and songs of the earlier days gave way at the time of Gregory to a homogeneous and coherent body of music, which fitted the Latin text like a glove and was of extraordinary beauty. We know the names of some of the composers of the chants of this great period, which lasted until the tenth century. It was during this time that many of the chants in use today were written, characteristic ones that have come down to us being those comprising the two mass settings, *Orbis factor* and *Lux et origo,* to be found in *The Kyriale,* the authorized Vatican collection of chants.

The eleventh century saw a veritable throng of new composers; but none of them achieved the simplicity, the grandeur, and the originality of the earlier epoch. Technique was developed at the expense of clarity and direct appeal, the composers delighting in " difficult intonations and eccentric melodies which mounted high and descended low." During the twelfth century, St. Bernard of Clairvaux, the Church's great mystic, issued an *Antiphonaire* and a *Gradual,* collections and anthologies of chants which contained some new materials and certain modifications of the older usages. The names of most of these composers have been lost; we do know, however, the writer of the melody for such a hymn as the Easter *Victimae Paschali* — Wipo, chaplain of Conrad III.

It was during this period that there developed under the aegis of the Western Church two forms which were frequently interpolated into the Mass: the *sequence,* a text fitted to elaborate melismatic melodies suitable for a solo voice, the words emphasizing some particular phase of the liturgy or celebrating some special occasion; and the *trope,* additional words supplied to the liturgical text, making a devotional comment on it, set in such a way as to provide a syllable for each note of the chant used. These forms are no longer largely used, since they are felt to be out of character with the traditional style of the Mass.[9] But they are of great

[9] It was the Council of Trent (1545–1563) which ruled against the abuse of these liturgical additions: the use of tropes was forbidden, but four sequences were allowed to remain — the *Dies Irae,* the *Veni Sancte Spiritus,* the *Victimae Paschali,* and the *Lauda Sion.* Later another, the *Stabat Mater dolorosa,* was added.

Not being allowed in the Gregorian service books, the tropes were collected in great books called *Tropers.* These show the advances made for centuries.

Archives Photographiques

HIGH MASS IN THE CHAPEL OF SAINTE CHAPELLE, PARIS

Fifteenth-century miniature from the *Heures* of the Duc de Berry historical interest, for out of them grew the liturgical drama, the beginnings of the modern theater. Certain of the Easter and Christmas sequences and tropes were treated in the form of dramatic dialogues, with questions put by one priest and answered by others or by the choir. These in turn became the medieval Miracle and Mystery plays with which the Church sought to dramatize her essential doctrines.

The decadence of the chant began in the fourteenth century and was due largely to the influence of the new measured, contrapuntal style which had by this time become popular. By the seventeenth century this decadence was complete, each diocese adopting its own practices of chanting, thus insuring complete confusion throughout the Church. The Council of Trent tried vainly to remedy matters, but things went from bad to worse. The seventeenth and eighteenth centuries, fruitful enough in so far as the production of measured music is concerned, saw the nadir of plainchant. Its rhythm became heavy and measured; influenced, of course, by the other music, sharps and flats were introduced so as to make the traditional melodies conform to the major and minor modes and free them entirely from the bonds of the ecclesiastical tones. It was not until the comparatively recent careful study of such experts as Dom Jumilhac, Dom Mocquereau, Dom Pothier, that anything like the honorable traditions of the earlier centuries has been restored. Even after all the study which these modern Benedictine monks have made of the ancient sources, there remains a great deal of difference of opinion as to how Gregorian chants are best interpreted.

GREGORIANS, A UNIVERSAL LANGUAGE OF THE SOUL

For those who have the spiritual interests of the Church at heart, this music stands as a means for an exalted type of religious expression, an expression which, by providing liturgical beauty, helps the congregations to love truth and practice goodness. For the historian, the vital simplicity and melodic severity of this music is of interest because it instituted strong foundations on which many of the later developments were erected. Yet we need not go to the Gregorian chants for either religious or historical reasons alone; for they possess beauty as pure music, even though it is a beauty, as Prunières has rather plaintively remarked, that demands a certain initiation on the part of the hearer. The very process of listening without sharing the ecstasy of these chants or taking an intimate part in their essence is derogatory to appreciating their full beauty. This art of the Christian Church in music, as is true of so many other kinds of art, demands a certain quality of exhilaration that must be recaptured, if we are to understand it fully and really like it. And this is particularly difficult in the case of an art so far removed from reality and modern thought as this music of the first ten centuries of the Christian era.

The Gregorian plainsong fulfills two great roles and represents two well-defined moments in music. In its own right and in its many varied forms, it stands as music of special beauty and great sincerity of expression, the sung prayer of the Church in her intercourse with God. One of the greatest modern exponents of the chant, Dom Mocquereau, whose research as to the way in which it should be interpreted has gone far toward restoring its pristine beauty, has said of this music: "It appeals to what is highest in the soul; its beauty and nobility come from the fact that it borrows nothing, or as little as possible, from the world of the senses." The Gregorian chant represents also the basis for all the great changes that were wrought in the music of the period from the eleventh to the sixteenth century. To know it in each of these capacities is greatly to enrich our musical experience and heighten our sense of musical perspective.

MONODIC MUSIC OUTSIDE THE CHURCH

THE UNIVERSALITY OF FOLK MUSIC

FRENCH writers on music assume that the history of secular music begins with the troubadours and trouvères. If we are to believe such modern German historians as Moser and Mayer, the Nordic races were largely responsible for the familiar principles underlying all popular music. According to a present-day Italian, influenced no doubt by the ideology of the time, his people have always been first in every phase of musical development; therefore, without question, they must have produced the first composers of what we have come to call *folk music*. And the English, with their customary reticence, simply point to the account of a medieval traveler, one Giraldus Cambrensis, who, while journeying through Britain in the twelfth century, heard the people singing their own part songs: so there must have been popular music in Britain long before that!

As a matter of fact, no such chauvinistic claims need be made for the origin of folk music; for human beings have always been fundamentally the same everywhere and have had a common spontaneous desire to express themselves in song and dance. They have composed tunes as they worked and have danced while they played, the men roistering together in taverns and inns and the women crooning their little ones to sleep with lullabies in much the same fashion the world over. The characteristics which separate the music of the various countries became gradually fixed, not because of any great differences in the nature of the peoples but because of the social circumstances in which they lived. The songs of the people of France are different from those of Germany and England, not because the *genus homo* is fundamentally different in France from what it is in Germany or Great Britain, but because the people we call French, through their inherited prejudices, traditions, beliefs, and the history that is back of them, are so different from those we call Germans or Italians.

No one knows, of course, when secular music actually began. There are direct references in some of the Greek plays which show that certain songs were then known and sung by everybody; but there must have been popular songs long before this. We can reasonably assume that they existed in the earliest days of music and were sung by the people of civilizations which appeared at the very dawn of history. It is not unreasonable to suppose that the laborers in the Egyptian and Babylonian civilizations had their work and play songs; and we know for certain that there was folk music among the Hebrews and Greeks — work songs, rhythmic chanteys for the oarsmen, and so forth. But it is not until early medieval times that we have evidences of the important role which music played in the lives of the common people.

THE CHURCH'S OPPOSITION

The activities of the Christian Church of the fourth, fifth, and sixth centuries were largely concerned with the conversion of the various peoples with whom it came into contact — first the Romans themselves, then the huge hordes of Celts, Teutons, and other pagan tribes of northern Europe. Hundreds of thousands of those who accepted Christianity as a religion understood it hardly at all but accepted it merely as a means for convenient or temporal advantage in their relationships with Rome. These people, although adhering outwardly to the doctrines of the Church, still kept many of their old beliefs — beliefs in supernatural spirits, household deities, the powers of magic, and so forth. It is in the vigorous discourses which the Church dignitaries found it necessary to make on the subject of these pagan survivals among the Gallo-Roman Christians that we frequently come upon mention of the music and dancing which went on outside the Church; aside from these pronouncements, secular music was not recognized by the ecclesiastical authorities.

Evidently horrid and pagan practices were mingled with the observation of certain Christian feast days, especially those which the Church found it wise to synchronize with former religious festivals, such as Midsummer's Day, May Day, St. John's Day, and so on. From the time of the fourth century down to the fifteenth, we hear a great deal about the diabolical practices of dancing and singing at such times. What is more, these *cantica diabolica, amatoria, et turpia* were sung and danced in the churchyards — the only common gathering places the people had — and sometimes even in the churches themselves. In these dances the people joined hands and moved around in a ring, with one of the women acting as leader. " As a cow which precedes the rest carries a bell on its neck," writes a medieval observer, " so the woman who sings and leads the dance has the Devil's bell bound to her neck. For the dance is round, the Devil is its center, and all turn to the left, because all are going to eternal death. When the Devil hears the sound, he is reassured, and says, ' I have not lost my cow yet.' " (The Church considered the Devil as the inventor and ruler of dancing, and for this reason struggled so valiantly to keep out of her music all suggestiveness of popular rhythms.)

The Church Fathers tried their best to stop such profane songs and carols, as the ring dances were called, by making announcement that disaster was sure to follow in the wake of those who participated in them. Their warnings were sprinkled with accounts of people being struck dead, consumed by fire, stricken with disease, and so on, but their efforts were all in vain. The evil practices still went on. There are stories of priests who, exasperated by the heathen conduct of their parishioners, were brought to the extremity of cursing them, so that they were to dance for a whole year. This the dancers had to do, sinking exhausted on the ground and dying after their release from the curse. Giraldus Cambrensis tells of an English priest who became so obsessed with the rhythmic refrain of one of the dance songs which he had heard the people singing all night long, that at morning mass he involuntarily substituted for the words *Pax vobiscum* the opening line of the song, *Swete lemman dhin are* — " Sweet love, thy lover needs thine aid." The consternation of his superiors and the delight of his congregation can be imagined.

All the later medieval folk songs and dances were the survivals of these pagan ritualistic performances. The earliest music we have of this kind, dating from the thirteenth century, shows a strongly rhythmic character. No wonder that it was beloved of the people and obnoxious to the Fathers of the Church!

SACRED FOLK MUSIC

But not all this folk music was of such a diabolic tinge. The Venerable Bede (673–735) tells in his famous *Ecclesiastical History of the English People* of a lay brother in one of the English monasteries, Caedmon by name, who received in the year 680 the " free gift of song, for which reason he never would compose any trivial or vain poem. [The same Caedmon is looked upon by scholars as the father of English poetry.] For having lived in the secular habit until he was well advanced in years, he had never learned anything of versifying; and for this reason sometimes at a banquet, when it was agreed to make merry by singing in turn, if he saw the harp come towards him, he would rise up from the table and go out and return home. Once having done so and gone out of the house where the banquet was, to the stable where he had to take care of the cattle for the night, he there composed himself to rest at the proper time. Thereupon one stood by him in his sleep and saluting him and calling him by name, said, 'Caedmon, sing me something.' But he answered, 'I cannot sing, and for this cause I left the banquet and retired hither, because I could not sing.' Then he who talked to him replied, 'Nevertheless thou must needs sing to me.' 'What must I sing?' he asked. 'Sing the beginning of creation,' said the other. Having received this answer he straightway began to sing verses to the praise of God the Creator."

This song, out of the dream of Caedmon, may be said to be the first known English poem; as translated by Kennedy, it runs:

"Praise we the Lord
Of the heavenly kingdom,
God's power and wisdom
The works of his hand;
As the Father of glory,
Eternal Lord,
Wrought the beginning
Of all his wonders!
Holy Creator!
Warden of men!
First, for a roof,
O'er the children of earth,
He stablished the heavens,
And founded the world,
And spread the dry land
For the living to dwell in.
Lord Everlasting!
Almighty God!"

These songs of a religious nature were popular in all the countries in medieval times and were widely sung by the people. The gentle St. Francis of Assisi was an important leader in developing the taste of the ordinary people for such songs. He founded singing societies, the *laudisti*, each of them under the direction of a *capitain*; and the mighty sweep of the lines in his own song calling upon all things to praise the Lord — Sun, Moon, Earth, and even Death — shows how effective these *laudi* (songs of praise) could be. They were generally very simple in structure, with a refrain at the beginning and at the end, and were sung in unison.

It was natural enough for the people themselves to imitate, in some of the songs they made up, the style and language of the Church. We find that many of the earliest folk songs we know, for example *Christ ist erstanden* and *Gelobet seist du, Jesu Christ,* end with the Greek expression *Kyrie eleison* — " Lord have mercy on us." From earliest times this phrase was one that the Church encouraged its congregations to sing; and so the people took it for their own, often setting new words to the Kyrie melodies they knew and always ending them with this plea for mercy. Later they translated Latin hymns in the vernacular (*O filii et filiae* is an example), sometimes mixing Latin and vernacular phrases in a most incongruous and quite amusing fashion.

But beyond this they did not go for some time. In the twelfth century, even if the common people had been able to imagine a different world of their own, one entirely outside the influence of the clergy and the nobility, who would have thought of recording these imaginings? The thoughts and feelings of gentlemen were, of course, another matter, one worthy of record. And so we have handed down to us the songs of the troubadours and trouvères, the minnesingers and minstrels, songs that still have a fascination after the lapse of many centuries. These will be discussed in another chapter.

The Music of the Middle Ages

ROMANESQUE MUSIC

THE ART CALLED ROMANESQUE

THE era between the sixth and the twelfth century is usually designated by art historians as the period of the Romanesque,[1] in spite of the fact that the characteristics of the life of the period had little relation to Rome. The Christian art that was produced during this epoch was of mixed ancestry and was drawn more largely from the barbarian north and the Asiatic East than from ancient Greece and imperial Rome. Its history was inextricably intertwined with the important historical changes of the time: the decline and fall of the Roman Empire, the consequent overrunning of Europe by the barbarians from the north, and the shifting of political and social prestige from Rome to Constantinople, which became, after the fifth century, the center of the civilized culture of Europe.

For almost ten centuries, while most of Europe was struggling toward a rebirth of power and wealth, during the time which has come to be known as the Dark Ages, Constantinople was a bright spot in a general picture of economic misery and political bankruptcy. It was for this reason that there came into the Western Church from the flourishing and prosperous East a number of ideals which were to shape and mold all the art which it produced. The round arches, sculptural moldings, and heavy walls that characterize the Romanesque churches of Europe were derived from the pre-Byzantine structures of Persia and Syria as well as from the engineering constructions of the Romans. The formalized

[1] Historians generally interpret the term *Romanesque* as indicating a derivation from the term *Roman* in the same sense that the development of the so-called Romance languages, all of them based on Latin, arose from the various divisions of the Roman Empire.

Courtesy of Bibliothèque Nationale

CHRIST IN MAJESTY

This is a fine manuscript from the eighth-century evangelistary of Charlemagne.

designs of the Church's richly illuminated manuscripts, the beautifully decorated and jeweled book covers, the enameled reliquaries glowing with color — all show the abstract, patterning instinct of Eastern art.

Combined with this Byzantine influence was still another infusion, that of the primitive and virile traditions of the northern barbarians. There is little doubt that the Lombards and the Franks brought with them out of the depths of their northern forests certain art aptitudes, marked by a love of design and vigorous adornment, which had a strong effect on the tastes of the time. They may well have had a type of music that was more rhythmic and melodic than that allowed in the Christian Church, and so more appealing to the people at large. It has been too generally assumed that our present-day music had a purely Greco-Roman-Christian ancestry. Somewhere in its past there was likewise added a strain of barbarian blood, which contributed considerably to its strength and vigor.

THE CAROLINGIAN PEAK AND AFTER

It was under Charlemagne (742–814), King of the Franks, that these various Roman, Eastern, and Teutonic influences were blended into a kind of formal "style." A mighty warrior and a clever statesman, Charlemagne was also a patron of the arts, learning, and music. He built a great many churches and palaces after the Byzantine manner, decorating them with mosaics and frescoes and filling them with music. Through conquest of Italy he came into direct touch with the culture of that land, a contact which further intensified the blend of northern, southern, and eastern characteristics in the art of the time. He saw to it that music schools were established in the various Church centers of his empire, so that the music of the Church might be sung according to the best traditions of Rome; and he gathered together a collection of the popular songs and hymns of the Franks, so that posterity might have a record of the music of his time. Unfortunately this collection was ordered destroyed by his son and successor, Louis the Pious, who thought it too "pagan."

The feeble flickerings of light at the time of the Carolingian Empire proved to be a false dawn: Charlemagne's sons were incapable of holding together his enormous empire, and soon all was again confusion and turmoil. It was not until the eleventh century — " one of the greatest periods in the unfolding of the human spirit " — that the real Romanesque day came. Through the gradual re-establishment of something like law and order in a Europe that had seen so much of the art and civilization of the Roman world disappear in a barbarous welter, the repulsion of further barbarian invasions, the discovery of silver in Germany, the growth of trade and commerce following the building of roads into the wilderness, the re-education of men in mind, manners, and morals by the Church, and the reclaiming of the land and the establishment of an agricultural society through the devoted and tremendous labors of the monks, a foundation for a new civilization was laid, a civilization that again gave opportunities for the development of art.

History has shown again and again that the activity which gives birth to the arts is possible only in a well-organized and fairly wealthy society. In the eleventh century this society was largely centered in the monastic establishments of the Church. And so the architecture, sculpture, illuminations, painted glass, literature, and music of the time were the products of the cloister. Not only were the monasteries the conservers of the remnants of antique culture and the recipients of whatever the riches of Byzantium offered; they were also the ateliers where the blend of this confusion of styles was achieved. Within their walls so many new churches were planned that an eleventh-century observer was moved to remark that it seemed as if God had snowed churches upon the land, so many and so fair were they; " for without exaggeration the countryside may be said to have clothed itself with a white garment of churches."

THE SPIRIT OF THE ROMANESQUE

In order to provide fireproof buildings that were suitable for the safekeeping of the various precious relics which the Church had by this time accumulated, as well as to accommodate the huge congregations, often made up largely of pilgrims, the Romanesque architects and builders, all of them monks and friars, adopted a stone arch of great solidity and strength, capable of bearing tremendous weights. The heavy-

Courtesy of The Pennsylvania Museum of Art, Philadelphia

THE CLOISTER OF THE ABBEY OF SAINT GENIS DES FONTAINES

The abbey was built in the Romanesque style of the twelfth century.

vaulted and thick-walled Romanesque church, with its small windows and dark interior, its walls covered with stylized paintings in the Byzantine tradition, indicates the severe asceticism of its builders. Its impressive distances and gloomy spaces suggest a spirit of quiet renunciation of the world and an unquestioning faith in the life of the future. It is a place devoted to the worship of God. There is none of the cheerful brightness of the later Gothic style in these Romanesque interiors; in the dim twilight of their aisles one feels the very presence of the Most High and the shadow of the Almighty.

The same spirit pervades the other arts of the period: that of the monkish illuminators who sang God's praises through the copying of Byzantine manuscripts; of the sculptors and glass painters who pictured Biblical and religious scenes in the stone and glass of the churches; and of the musicians, who, no longer satisfied with the principle of monodic melody with which to worship God, began to experiment with new means.

ROMANESQUE MUSIC

The twelfth century saw the music of the Church dividing into two branches: the one, leading to polyphony, tentative and hesitating at first, but giving promise of a great future; the other, the universal Gregorian chant, strong and steadfast, the mature result of over five-hundred years of steady growth, an art whose monumental development at this time represents one of man's most significant achievements. Except for the magnificent Romanesque churches there was nothing in contemporary art that could stand comparison with this music. It represents a spirit of solemn and intense religiosity, its measured cadences and harmonious proportions reminding us strongly of the spatial rhythms and solid dimensions of the buildings in which it was sung.

Most of us will agree with Professor Leichtentritt that structures such as the Abbey Church at Beaulieu, France, one of the finest examples of twelfth-century architecture left to us, represent Gregorian chant translated into terms of architectural construction. In both cases a highly developed and refined art is reduced to the simplest possible terms, which are carefully calculated to give full expression of its spiritual justification for existence. As both these types of art are a blend of Eastern and Western traditions, there is nothing of the extraordinary or fantastic about them: while their elements glow warmly and are deeply felt, everything is held in balance and proportion, no one feature being allowed to preponderate over another.

SPECULATIONS ON POLYPHONIC BEGINNINGS

Yet if we search carefully, we may find in these characteristics of Romanesque art the inherent ideals from which came the great developments of polyphonic music. The best modern research seems to indicate that the experiments which led toward this new type of music were begun somewhere around the eighth century, just at the time when the developing Byzantine art was being most strongly influenced by the Oriental love of patterned design. The Eastern illuminated manuscripts of this period show a blend of classic Greek and Eastern Byzantine styles, but

Archives Photographiques

THE ABBEY CHURCH AT BEAULIEU, FRANCE

One of the finest examples of twelfth-century Romanesque architecture

Archives Photographiques

A MINIATURE OF THE EIGHTH CENTURY

The illumination, from a Greek lectionary in Leningrad, shows the blend of classic Greek and Eastern Byzantine styles.

the Oriental interest in pattern and rhythmical design is always predominant. Is it too much to assume that the monkish musicians who first began experimenting with part music looked to their brother artists for inspiration? We are certain at least that the earliest music of this kind that we know, music to which the names *organum* and *diaphony* seem to have been applied indiscriminately, was purely decorative harmony, the musical counterpart of the Romanesque mosaics and illuminations of the time.

This early polyphonic music consisted in a majestic paralleling of the monodic liturgical chant by other melodies at certain fixed intervals above and below it. The singing of the Gregorian chant had not been, in a strict sense of the word, homophonic; for it was sung in octaves whenever men and women or men and boys joined in singing the same melody, and such singing had to be limited in range so that the lower voices could sing the higher notes and vice versa. The first part singing in other than this octave practice came when the second group of voices paralleled the first at a distance of a fifth, that is, when some of the singers sang the same tune beginning on the dominant [2] rather than on the tonic. The result was similar to the patterned organization of decorative lines in the mosaics that flash from the walls of the Byzantine and Romanesque churches or in the stylized manuscript illuminations of the period.

The integrating principle of such a duplication of a melody at different pitches is exactly the same as that to be found in so much of the visual art of the period; both consist of a succession of parallel features and both result in a solemn, impersonal effect that is well suited to the

[2] Dom Anselm Hughes, a leading spirit of the English Plainsong and Medieval Music Society, has an interesting explanation of the way this came about. Gregorian music of the year 1000 was regarded as something sacred, to be handed down in an authentic and received text from one generation to another, and was preserved with scrupulous accuracy in identical form from Vienna to Scotland and from Italy to Sweden. Since it was not lawful to tamper with the chants, the creative genius of man was driven to seek new means of expression.

There is reason to suppose, Hughes argues, that part singing first evolved at a point in the Mass where it was traditional for singers to expand the existing resources, the Alleluia respond between the Epistle and the Gospel. Musicians began to add wordless tunes here, consisting of a repetition of musical phrases by each side of the choir (in the antiphonal manner adopted from the Hebraic services), with a final phrase sung in chorus by both sides. This new type of melody, to which the name *sequela* (sequence) was given, was a repetition of the theme of the Alleluia in various ways, one of which consisted in raising the pitch of the melody by the interval of a fifth. So one side of the choir would sing the *sequela* tune, followed by the other a fifth higher, and then finally both would sing it simultaneously at their different pitches.

At least this is exactly the process that is described by the theorists of the time as recorded in the *Musica Enchiriadis*, a theoretical work that was probably written sometime before the tenth century. If we gather up the manuscripts of the earliest specimens of this new part style, we shall find, according to Hughes, that they are in the majority of cases settings of the sequences or their close relatives, the tropes. His article is in the April, 1938, *Musical Quarterly*.

portrayal of the transcendent ideals of the Christian faith. Here are two examples of this early organum taken from the *Musica Enchiriadis*. With enough voices and instruments, their effect in the resonant Romanesque interiors must have been impressive indeed.

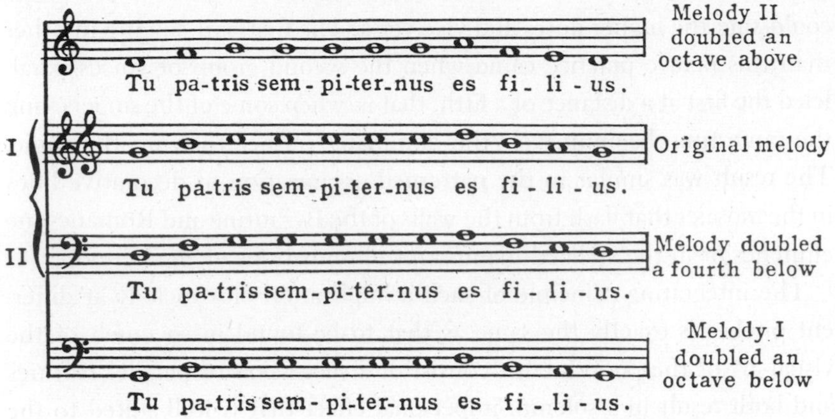

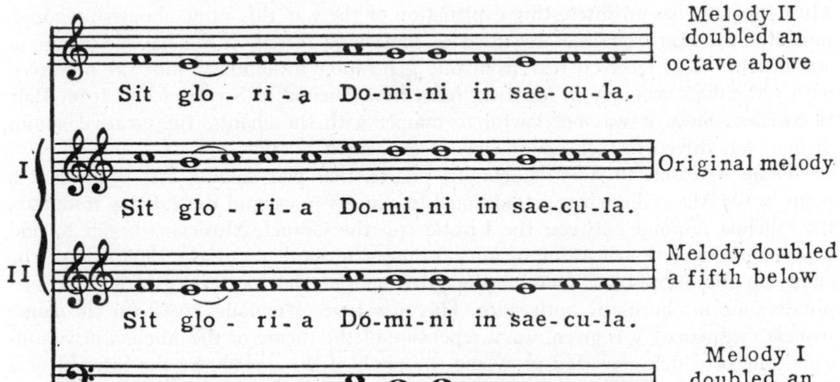

The *Musica Enchiriadis* records a method of avoiding the interval of an augmented fourth when it resulted from such a parallel duplication of voices. This interval (from F natural to B natural) was regarded with particular aversion by the medieval musicians: they did not seem to object to its occurring in close proximity in a melody, but when sounded simultaneously in the organum, it was thought to be a *diabolus in musica* — the very devil in music! This famous early musical treatise suggests that a good way of avoiding this *diabolus* is to keep one part stationary while moving the other. Thus was the first step taken toward making the various parts independent. Canon Douglas compares the importance of this step in the annals of history with the momentous occasion when the American, Wilbur Wright, made his first flight in a self-propelled airplane. Both these experiments permanently transformed the usages of man and opened up vistas that before had been undreamed of.

LIVING EXAMPLES

The late Sir Richard Terry of London made an interesting experiment in imitating this early method of writing part music: taking a Gregorian chant for Whitsuntide, *Veni Sancte Spiritus,* he supplied additional parts to it in the manner described by the *Musica Enchiriadis.* In listening to a rendition of such an arrangement, we should do so with the ears of the eleventh-century faithful rather than with those of the twentieth-century sophisticate. Then the effect will not seem " hollow " or " horribly cacophonous," as suggested by some writers, but strong, massive, valiant, crying out, like the architecture and mosaics of the time, that God is nigh. The difficulty for our ears lies, of course, in the fact that the intervals used, fifths and fourths, are necessarily bare. If we were to sing the simplest and most euphonious parallel accompaniment to a tune, we should do so in thirds, in places varied with sixths; the addition of a fifth or a fourth occasionally would give strength, but a succession of nothing except these intervals can only seem unusual. It is not difficult to realize, however, how well this befitted the severity of the great Romanesque churches.

This type of organum or diaphony, then, was the first attempt of which we have record of sounding two voices together. Giraldus Cambrensis,[3] writing at the end of the twelfth century, describes a similar

[3] Giraldus Cambrensis (Gerald of Wales) wrote his famous description in 1188; the quotations are from an early nineteenth-century translation of this work.

custom of singing popular music in parts of Wales and North England, a custom which seems to have been long established, introduced perhaps originally from Scandinavia. Speaking of the Northumberland method of singing two-part songs, Cambrensis says that it consisted of not more than " two varieties of pitch in the voices, one murmuring the lower, the other the upper part, in a manner both soothing and delightful." This seems a fair enough description of the music which has come down to us in the theoretical treatises of the time. The Welsh, however, did not utter the tunes uniformly as was done elsewhere, but " manifoldly, and in many manners and notes; so that in a multitude of singers, such as it was the custom of this people to gather together, so many songs are to be heard as there are singers to be seen, and a great diversity of parts, which finally come together in one consonance." This latter would seem to indicate, even if we make the necessary allowance for reportorial exaggeration, a much freer practice than the methods of uniform progression described in the theoretical writings of the churchmen.

These worthies seem to have been strangely silent in respect to the developments of symphonious singing which took place toward the end of the Romanesque period. Guido [4] wrote, as has often been recorded, a detailed description of the methods of organum employed in his time (the beginning of the eleventh century), which suggests that the two voices had acquired some individual freedom, not always keeping at exactly the same intervalic distance from each other, with now and then a suggestion of contrary movement. But from the time of his death (1050) until the beginning of the twelfth century, no description of contemporary methods has been found; however, several specimens of the work of that period have been discovered by the musicologists. These indicate that great progress toward a real art of composition was made during this time and that the foundations for future developments were firmly laid.

Coussemaker, one of the leading authorities on the music of this period, has published in his *Histoire de l'harmonie au moyen âge* a rendering

[4] Guido, a Benedictine monk of the monastery of Pomposa near Ravenna, Italy, is credited with a number of important " discoveries " in music, among them being the system of teaching sight singing by means of *hexachords*, groups of notes with the tones and semitones arranged exactly alike. He is also supposed to have developed the two-line staff into our present one of five lines.

into modern notation of one of these few surviving examples of eleventh-century polyphony. If we examine this setting of the words *Mira lege, miro modo* in any detail, we shall find that the two voices no longer move in parallel motion, the added voice sounding at intervals of not only the octave and fifth from the original melody but also of thirds, sixths, and seconds. Thus there is a deliberate mixing of discord with concord. The principle of contrary motion between the voices, one of the fundamentals of later part music, is completely developed here; but although the notes of the added voice do not always correspond exactly in metrical value with those of the *vox principalis,* there is no feeling of measure in this *discant,* as this form of polyphony is called. That is, essentially different rhythmic patterns are not employed in the two voices at the same time. And so, in spite of the new principles of freedom in contrary motion and intentional discord which this music possessed, it was necessary to free the parts from the bonds of rhythmic similarity before anything further could develop in the way of polyphonic independence. This was the next step.

THE EARLY GOTHIC MUSIC

Twelfth and Thirteenth Centuries

How high the sea of human happiness rose during the Middle Ages we know now only from the barriers built to restrain it.

— Gilbert K. Chesterton

THE GOTHIC AWAKENING

THE Gothic era, in many respects one of the greatest ages in the history of the world, grew naturally out of the Romanesque. Once referred to by the enlightened intellects of the Renaissance as *barbare,* the twelfth and thirteenth centuries stand for us today as a period of intellectual and spiritual awakening comparable to the time of Pericles in Greece. Within a few generations they brought forth the Crusades, the Gothic cathedral, and Thomas Aquinas. The great names of the Gothic

Archives Photographiques

CARCASSONNE

The medieval town in southern France dates back to the twelfth century.

period are legion: Abélard, John of Salisbury, Bernard of Clairvaux, Roger Bacon, Duns Scotus, St. Francis of Assisi, St. Dominic, Dante. These were the centuries which produced the *Chanson de Roland,* the Arthurian romances, and the *Divine Comedy*. Never before or since have architects and builders been fired with such zeal or produced such results: it has been carefully estimated that between the years 1170 and 1270 eighty great cathedrals and nearly five hundred churches of cathedral dignity were built in France alone, among them some of the greatest structures ever reared by man. Here is the paradox of a religion that was concerned with otherworldliness being able to manifest itself in so much beauty that was of this world: architecture, sculpture, music, joined in a magnificent symphony of which the leading theme was *Deus vult*.

Those most familiar with this period, however, assure us that Gothic art was not only mystic and otherworldly; it was also concerned with expressing satisfaction and joy in the abundant life here below. Out of a very limited population youths by the tens of thousands flocked to the great teachers of that era; and out of the ensuing intellectual ferment there came the universities, centers of learning in the various countries:

Paris in France, Bologna in Italy, Salamanca in Spain, Oxford and Cambridge in England. No one who has read the history of the Crusades, those exciting adventures in religion, art, love, and conquest, can maintain that they were concerned only with holy aims! Even the cathedrals were not entirely dissociated from worldly relations: they may have been built to the glory of God, but they were also monuments of local pride and gathering places for the processions, pilgrimages, and even secular festivities of the people of the time.

It was a complex and paradoxical period; its leitmotiv was unquestionably religious in character, in spite of the fact that the nobility were developing a conception of life and art independent of, and even contradictory to, that of the Church. This new freedom of thought, characterized by the struggle between State and Church which runs through the whole period, is but another manifestation of the Gothic spirit and had a powerful and, indeed, irresistible influence on the striking development of the individual which took place in the fourteenth and fifteenth centuries. There had arisen by this time a great body of secular songs and ballads, the influence of which on later music is only beginning to be realized and the importance of which is hardly suggested by the few examples that have come down to us. The songs of the troubadours and trouvères have long been appreciated for the quality of their poetry; their music is likewise worthy of our attention, combining as it does both the religious and the popular characteristics of the time and so reflecting the life and the spirit of medieval Europe.

No one who has ever heard or sung the old English round, *Sumer is icumen in*, supposed to have been written by a monk of the early thirteenth century, can doubt that it represents a new spirit in music, one which was trying wings for much finer flights than had so far been attempted. This marvel of the Middle Ages remains, alas, alone as something extraordinary, beyond the range of time. It is a song about the freshening season of the year that sounds quite modern in scale. Although three parts had long been the limit, this is written in six parts, four of which are in canon, each taking up the tune a little after the others; it stands as an intricate and formal piece of construction that finds no parallel until more than two centuries later. The two lowest parts repeat over and over a "ground bass," a short passage that does not vary and that goes with the canoning of the four upper parts to make a gay, open-air piece that is as delightful in spirit as it is clever in craftsmanship.

Although this piece seems to stand alone, the manuscript which contains it (now in the British Museum) has also a list of other music that links it definitely with the work of composers writing at that time in Paris. We can say truly enough that the freshened spirit and clever workmanship of this rondel is representative of the new Gothic feeling that entered the world with the twelfth century. The Crusades of the preceding years had brought stimulating contact with the East, and with the gradual revival of general prosperity, commerce developed, merchants became more important, and towns arose whose inhabitants, although they were always united by their religion, nevertheless developed a new sense of independence that had no direct relation with the Church.

The visible world became a more pleasant place to live in, for life was felt to be more enjoyable for its own sake. Religion warmed to the influence of St. Francis of Assisi and his followers, who were more popular for their humanism and love of man and nature than they were for their asceticism. Learning was increasingly cherished, and it, too, realized the grandeur and significance of nature and of man in all his activities. The Romanesque world had been largely in the hands of the monks; that of Gothic times centered in the communes, the large towns which sprang up everywhere in France and England, their inhabitants friendly to both bishop and king and yet not dependent on either.

THE CATHEDRAL, THE GREATEST EXPRESSION OF THE GOTHIC ERA

We have already remarked on the strong sentiment for religion which pervaded all classes of society at this time: its greatest expression was the Gothic cathedral of the twelfth and thirteenth centuries. One of the first complete expressions of this type of architecture may be seen at the very gates of Paris, in the royal abbey church of St. Denis, where many of the kings of France sleep their long, last sleep. Instead of the massive walls and heavy pillars which the Romanesque builders found necessary for

ABBEY CHURCH OF ST. DENIS

One of the earliest Gothic churches, this still stands outside Paris.

their huge structures, the Gothic architects, by developing the Romanesque system of construction, were able to turn their fanes into armatures of stone, with slender piers soaring aloft and merging into pointed arches that seem to reach up into boundless space. In place of the small windows in the thick-walled Romanesque structures, these builders of

ANALYSIS OF GOTHIC CONSTRUCTION
Rheims Cathedral (from Gailhabaud)

the north filled every interstice of their buildings with glowing glass, whose gorgeous colors were expressive of their warm faith. There remained nothing of the heavy gloom of the monastic churches, everything about these communally built structures being light and animated.

From the Ile de France, Gothic architecture spread over most of Europe. Such buildings as Notre Dame in Paris, the cathedrals of Chartres and Amiens, and York Minster in England express this new, freer spirit of the times in their design and in the decorative glass, carving, and tapestry. The people could not read, but they had spread before them a marvelous fabric, which expressed their love of God and their joy in humanity; the Gospel story was narrated for them in thousands of sculptured images. No such symbolization of faith has ever been achieved as in these Gothic buildings; a contemporary writer expressed it thus:

"My beloved son, thou hast approached God's house in all faith, and adorned it with such abundant comeliness; and having illuminated the vaults of the walls with divers works and colors, thou hast in a manner shown forth to the beholders a vision of God's paradise, bright as springtide, with flowers of every hue, and fresh with green grass and leaves, refreshing the souls of the saints with crowns proportioned to their divers merits, whereby thou makest them to preach his wonders in his works. For man's eyes knoweth not whereon first to gaze: if he looks up at the vaults, they are as mantles embroidered with spring flowers; if he regard the walls, there is a manner of paradise; if he consider the light streaming through the windows, he marvelleth at the priceless beauty of the glass and the variety of this most precious work. Work, therefore, now good man — kindle thyself to a still ampler art, and set thyself with all the might of thy soul to complete that which is yet lacking in the gear of the Lord's house, without which the divine mysteries and the ministries of God's service may not stand."

— Quoted in *Burlington Magazine*, September, 1912

THE GOTHIC SPIRIT IN ART

It is this spirit of achievement in creation, of trying to acquire a unity of expression through using an infinite variety of means, that is most characteristic of these Gothic times: it pervaded every form of artistic activity. To the thirteenth-century artist the thousands of details in a Gothic cathedral were simply means for expressing the essential unity of his faith. So with the illuminators who spent their lives in decorating the manuscripts of the period; they loved to work into their designs all sorts of seemingly eccentric and unrelated details, representations of beasts

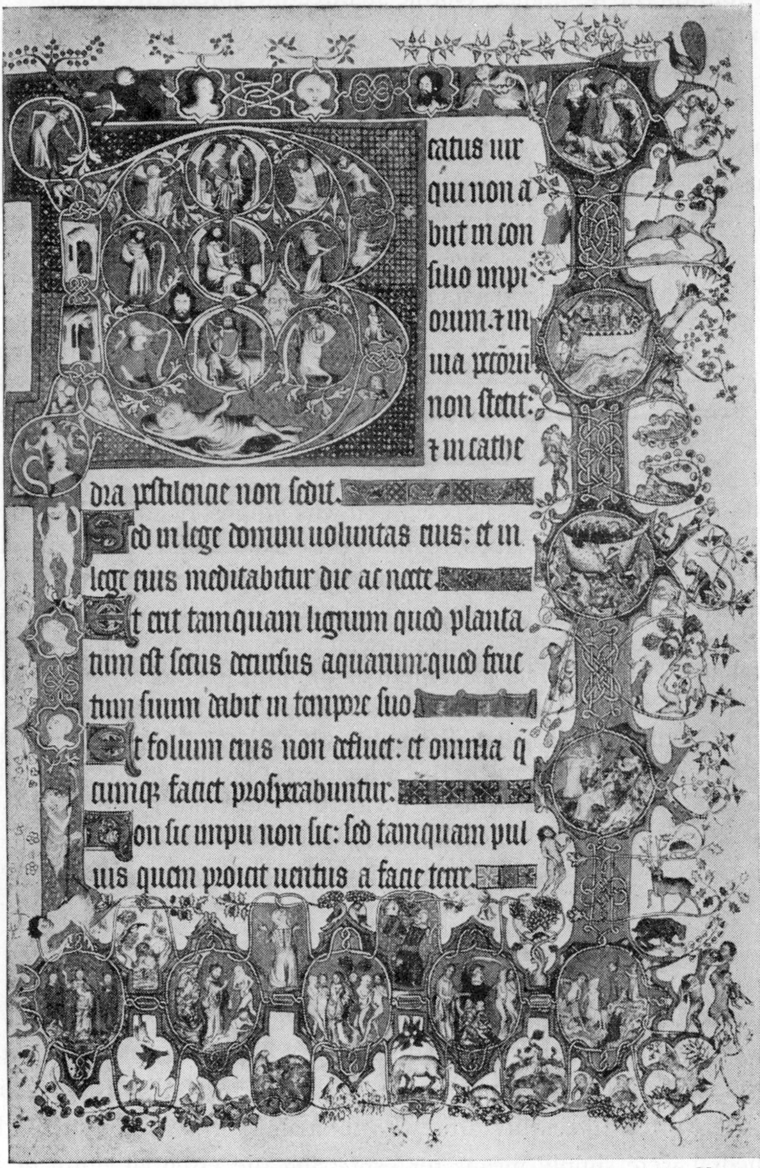

Courtesy of the British Museum

GOTHIC ART

The Beatus Page from the Psalter of the St. Omer Family is a fine example of Gothic illuminated manuscript showing a multitude of seemingly unrelated details.

and birds and flowers that had no connection with the text they were illustrating. Yet to these artists nothing was unimportant; they saw significance and beauty in all things and were able to "sense the infinite in

A THIRTEENTH-CENTURY ROSE WINDOW

the particular." The sculptor loved to crowd every possible space with his figures, feeling them all to be component parts in a unified design. The glassmaker wrought out of gorgeous bits of color intricate patterns that were expressive of the universality of his beliefs.

EARLY GOTHIC MUSIC

The makers of music followed exactly the same ideals. If we examine some of the music of the thirteenth century — a large amount of which has been preserved in a manuscript, the *Antiphonarium Mediceum,* now in the Laurentian Library, Florence — we shall find the same attempt at elaborate construction and infinite detail that appears in the visual arts of the time. The unknown composers of this music were really craftsmen working at their melodic ornamentation in precisely the same way as the illuminator did on his manuscript or the goldsmith on his monstrance. For the first time we find in this music a strong contrast in rhythm between the parts: above a rigid, unmeasured *tenor* (the original melody) there has been constructed a decorative melismatic series of notes — we can hardly call it a melody — which completely throws the original into the background.

This *organum purum,* one of the most important forms of music at this time, with its unmeasured tenor notes (probably often given to instruments) and its completely free upper voice, was largely cultivated at the abbey of St. Martial in Limoges, at Chartres, as well as in Paris, which later became the principal center for polyphonic music during the Gothic era, as it had long been of architecture.

Here we first learn of definite composers: the two earliest mentioned are Léonin and Pérotin, both of whom lived and worked in Paris about 1200, a little before its intellectual center, the famous Sorbonne, was founded. Léonin was the choirmaster at Notre Dame and wrote a whole cycle of *organa pura* for the various occasions of the church year, calling it *Magnus liber organi de Gradali et Antiphonario.* This was somewhat remodeled by his follower, Pérotin, who likewise wrote some three-part and four-part organa. The most famous of these are the four-part *Viderunt* and *Sederunt* organa: of colossal dimensions, they are full of tremendous rhythmic energy. Their powerful massed tones and chords, sung by both men's and boys' voices and played on various sorts of instruments, must have had a tremendous effect in the wide, resonant spaces of the Gothic cathedrals. As Dr. Ficker has described it: "Above a syllabic chant of mystic profundity there flows a far-flung stream of

By Burton Holmes from Ewing Galloway

THE GOTHIC INTERIOR

Chartres has "armatures of stone, with slender piers soaring aloft and merging into pointed arches that seem to reach up into boundless space."

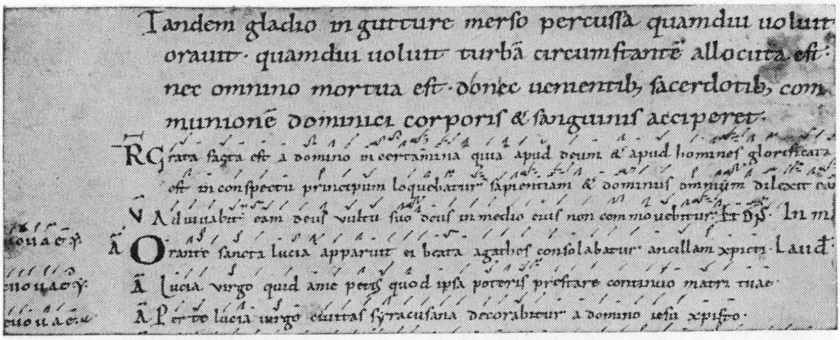

Neumes without staff (tenth century)

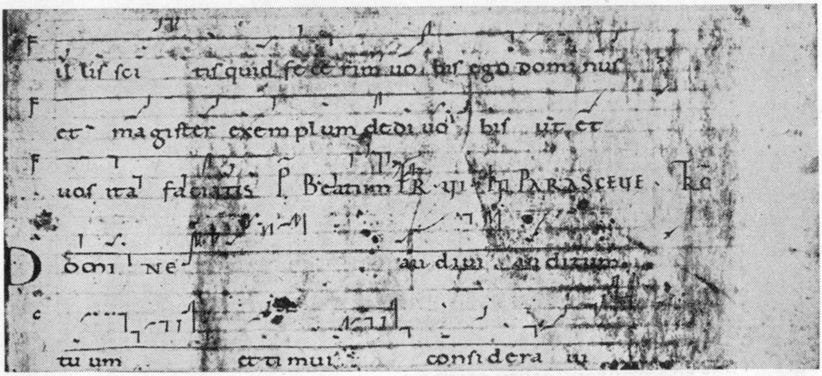

Gothic choral notation on a three-line to four-line staff (eleventh century)

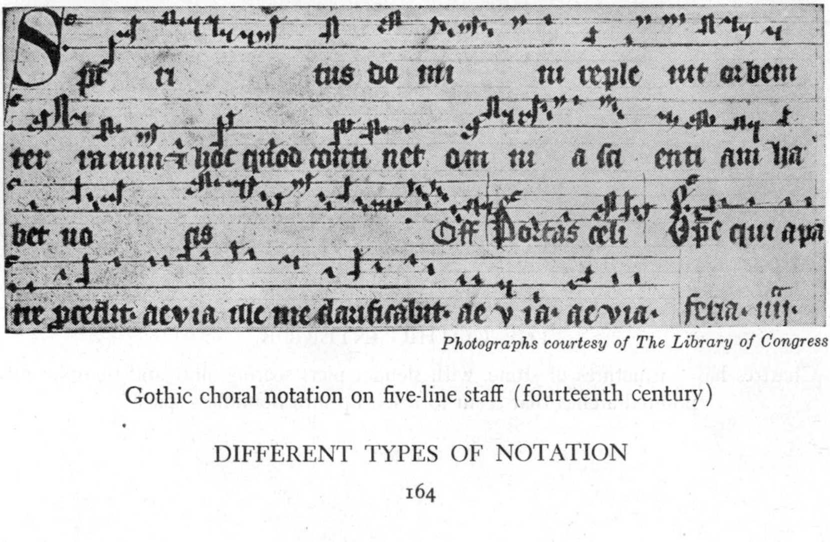

Photographs courtesy of The Library of Congress

Gothic choral notation on five-line staff (fourteenth century)

DIFFERENT TYPES OF NOTATION

interwoven tones, now like shadowy, fugitive apparitions, now swelling to an orgiastic rout." Again the Gothic love of elaborated construction and infinite detail is felt expressing the might of a religious idea; and we can well credit an ancient report concerning the effect of this music on the common people, who "listened in awe-stricken and trembling admiration to the strident creaking of the organ bellows and the shrill clangor of the cymbals, the harmony of the flutes."

There arose the necessity for finding some means of more exactly writing down what the composer wanted to be sung and played; for up to this time the manuscripts were able to serve only as a sort of sketch and were not by any manner of means a precise indication for the performers as to numbers and kinds of singers and instrumentalists, tempi, dynamics, tonalities, accidentals, and so on. The performers really improvised on the bare outline left by the composer, and the effect they achieved depended largely on their own artistic abilities. Léonin is credited with being one of the first composers who actually marked down the different time value of notes, thus establishing "mensural music," sound lengths accurately measured. This was worked out in more detail by the theorists and taken up gladly by the composers, who then could demand from the performers a more exact rendering of what they had conceived than had been possible under the improvisatory method.

One of the outstanding features of all this music was the use of a liturgical melody for a *cantus firmus*, that is, the melody around which the composer wove his other parts. There was a good psychological reason for this, for these liturgical melodies possessed for the devout congregations an ideal significance, one far removed from things of the world; hence any music built on them was lifted beyond the realm of mundane expression into an atmosphere of spiritual significance. But in the early part of the thirteenth century composers began to use original melodies for their *cantus firmus*, so that the whole piece was pure composition. This resulted in what was called the *conductus*. Pérotin has left us many of these compositions, in which the cantus is freely invented and no longer consists of long-held notes but possesses plenty of rhythmic variety, with the added voices keeping the same fundamental rhythm that underlies the cantus.

THE MOTET

Pérotin was evidently a man of many parts; for not only did he write voluminously and effectively in the Gothic forms already mentioned, but he is credited with being the initiator of the chief form by which Gothic music of this period became famous, the *motet*, a term not to be confused with its use by later composers. The difficulty of providing structural unity between the various parts of the organa led to the adoption of this motet form as described by a writer of the thirteenth century (Johannes de Grocheo, quoted in Leichtentritt's *Geschichte der Motette*):

"The motet is made up of several interwoven voices which have either their own texts or kind of syllable division, and which sound together in consonances. There may be three or four of these interweaving voices, each of them having its syllables, with the exception of the *tenor*, which in some motets has a text, in many others does not.

"The various parts have different names: *tenor, motetus, triplum, quadruplum*. . . . The part upon which the others are built, as a house is built upon its foundation, is the *tenor*; it determines the character and the size of the motet, just as foundation does the building.

"The voice immediately above the tenor is called the *motetus*; it usually begins on the fifth above the tenor and keeps about that relationship to it, although it may go to the octave.

"The voice which begins at the octave above the tenor and keeps about that same relationship to it is named the *triplum:* whenever necessary, however, the triplum may go either above or below this range.

"The *quadruplum* is a voice sometimes added to make the harmony perfect, although there are some motets having only three voices in which the harmony may be said to be perfect."

Thus we have a real architectural structure made up of a number of seemingly incongruous members, unified according to Gothic ideals, in somewhat the following manner: (To us it may seem anything but unified to have the tenor an instrumental part based on a Gregorian motif, *Veritatem* . . . , the motetus singing a melody to the words *Verbum caro factum est;* and the triplum one to *Salve virgo nobilis*. But to the Gothic artist it was evidently the height of reasonableness.)

The true characteristic of these Gothic motets was this placing together of the most incongruous elements, each voice often having a different text, sometimes in a different language. Just as the illuminator called into being a peculiar set of fantastic creatures, half real and half unreal, which had no direct connection with the text of the manuscript he was illustrating, and the architect his fantastic race of gargoyle demons, so the musician did not hesitate to intermingle the most startlingly varied elements in his motets. Dr. Ficker describes one which has a *tenor* part based on a fragment of a Gregorian chant, set to the word *regnat* (he reigns), thus providing a sort of constant underlying reminder of God's sovereignty. The *motetus* sings a text suggestive of a moral lecture addressed to a roistering drunkard, exhorting him to change his ways, the implication being that otherwise he cannot expect to escape the chastening hand of him who reigneth over all; and the *triplum* has a melody similar to the *motetus* without any text at all; it may have used the same words.

Even this fragmentary connection is often lacking. Secular words and melodies were added to the most solemn tones of a Gregorian-chant tenor; there was thought to be nothing incongruous in the combination of a Latin hymn in praise of the Virgin with a drinking song in a second part and an erotic love song in a third, and in the placing of all this above a *tenor* based on a slow-moving Gregorian melody. There is a famous thirteenth-century motet with its tenor a Kyrie from a Gregorian Mass, its *motetus* having reference to the birds that sing in the spring, tra-la, and its *triplum* descriptive of the perils of bigamy! Later motets written in the so-called Burgundian style often had the melody in the upper voice, this being the only one with words, the other parts being accompanimental, often played on instruments — in reality, a monody accompanied by two subordinate voice parts.

To try to comprehend all this we must again recall the peculiar mental attitude of this age and all the incongruities of the other arts. Typical also were the scenes of ribaldry and frivolity that were often enacted in the churches on great feast days, which it is difficult to reconcile with the spirit that created the beautiful interiors. The congregation did not hesitate to burlesque the sacred mysteries to such an extent that, during the twelfth century when celebrating the " Feast of the Ass," they would in procession bring an animal into the church. Then, with much drinking and reveling, they would proceed to represent the flight into Egypt. After a rollicking hymn, set to one of the Church's melodies, in praise of the ass, a Mass would be celebrated, with imitations of the animal's braying interpolated at suitable places. In the same spirit of naïve realism, the sculptors and wood carvers working in the cathedrals did not hesitate to use all sorts of peculiar and amusing animal and human monstrosities in their designs. So we should not wonder too much at the Church's attempt to draw within her circle all phases of human activity, trying thus to make them subserve her own purposes and unifying them in so far as the attitude of the time was concerned.

USE OF INSTRUMENTS

Those who live in one age can never fully understand the music of another: for example, we who are accustomed to instrumental music that has reached an advanced stage of development find it almost impossible to realize how primitive its earliest stages must have been. These beginnings are to be found in the period under discussion; it must be remembered that, although the scores did not always lay forth the parts for instruments as well as voices, instrumental accompaniments were freely used during this period. (This subject is treated in more detail in another place.) But there is plenty of evidence in the sculptures and pictures of the period that instruments often played along with the voices in these polyphonic compositions, and we have examples of some of them that have both prelude and postlude for instruments alone. Organs were certainly used in the churches, together with such bowed instruments as *fiedels* and viols, and, in addition, lutes, harps, reed instruments, and trumpets. All these added their not overdelicate tones to the harmony, sometimes to the critical disapproval of the more sensitive-eared listeners. If a voice part had not its singer or a sufficient number of singers, instruments were used to fill in; there seemed to be no hesitancy in spoiling the effect of the vocal lines. But we can hardly say that the instrumental parts as yet assumed any real independence.

It is extremely difficult for us, with our present-day conceptions of tone color and harmonic relationships, to realize what this music must have sounded like to the Gothic ear. If, as Ficker has suggested, we can, in looking at some of these scores, let our minds conceive how the " metallic boy voices were mingled with all the gentle tintinnabulation of the glockenspiel, cymbals, triangle, etc. then in use, together with the dulcet tones of the viols, while the long-sustained notes of the lower parts were sung by smooth tenor voices supported by manifold wind instruments," we can perhaps get an idea of the dazzling effect of these Gothic motets and organa. " Fancy yourself," he bids us, " attending one of the great assemblies of the estates honored by the regent's presence and accompanied by the most lavish display, for which the courts of France and Burgundy were then conspicuous. All the bewildering splendor radiated by the cerebral action finds an echo in the scintillant rhythms and interlinked tones of this music." [5]

[5] For those who would pursue further the spirit of this fascinating time, we recommend two books: *Mont-Saint-Michel and Chartres* by Henry Adams and *Cathedral; A Gothic Pilgrimage* by Helen H. Parkhurst.

THE MUSIC OF CHIVALRY

The Troubadours and Their Fellows

I can play the lute, the violin, the pipe, the bagpipe, the syrinx, the harp, the gigue, the gittern, the symphony, the psaltery, the organistrum, the regals, the tabor, and the rote. I can sing a song well and make tales to please young ladies and can play the gallant for them if necessary. I can throw knives into the air and catch them without cutting my fingers. I can do dodges with string, most extraordinary and amusing. I can balance chairs and make tables dance. I can throw a somersault and walk on my head.

— *Les deux Menèstriers*, Bodleian Library, Oxford

A ROMANTIC MOVEMENT IN MEDIEVAL TIMES

THE songs of the troubadours were the direct result of a wave of emotionalism which swept over Europe during the twelfth century, an emotionalism that was engendered by the new contacts that the Europeans made with the East and its highly developed civilization. The Moorish conquest of Spain and the seven crusading journeys [6] that were made in order to rescue the Holy Land from the profane hands of the infidel occasioned a new interest on the part of the aristocratic European world in the more delicate and refined things of life: poetry and music began to be cultivated for themselves, and a new code of chivalry, with ideals of fealty to God, King, and Lady, was adopted:

" A Dieu mon âme,	My soul to God,
Mon cœur aux dames,	My heart to the ladies,
Ma vie au roi,	My life to the king,
L'honneur pour moi."	Honor for myself.

[6] Even a casual reading of history shows how confused were these centuries of the Crusades. " The most distant islands and savage countries," writes a historian of the time, " were inspired with the same ardent passion. The Welshman left his hunting, the Scotchman his fellowship with vermin, the Dane his drinking party, the Norwegian his raw fish " in order to help rescue the Holy Places of the East. Perhaps the most monstrous folly of all the seven crusades was that of the Children, in 1212, when scores of thousands of youths were persuaded to embark on this " holy mission," only to find themselves in the end sold into slavery, their goal still unrealized.

Wide World Photos, Inc.

A GRIM REMINDER OF THE POPULARITY OF THE CRUSADES

Crac-des-Chevaliers, a vast fortress that was built in the twelfth century on a thousand-foot eminence near Homs in Syria, was for over a hundred years one of the outposts of the Knights of St. John of Jerusalem, who built it with the help of artisan pilgrims from France.

The center of this Romantic influence was France; but it had no peculiarly nationalistic background and spread rapidly through all Europe, producing some great literature and poetry in France, England, and Germany. Its chief spokesmen were the troubadours (as they were called in the language of the south), the trouvères (the term used in the north — both *troubadour* and *trouvère* have the same significance, that of inventing or making poetry), and the minnesingers (as they were called in Germany). These were men sometimes born in high estate, sometimes in low, who gave their lives to the production of poetry and music in celebration of the beauty and loveliness of women, for the purpose of reciting deeds of chivalry and relating epic tales, both of men and of gods. The medieval biographer of William, Count of Poitiers, the earliest troubadour mentioned in history, said of him that he was "one of the most courteous men in the world and one of the greatest deceivers of ladies — a valiant knight in warfare and bounteous in love and gallantry.

TWO JONGLEURS, FROM A TWELFTH-CENTURY MANUSCRIPT

At the left is a shawm player and at the right a juggler. According to tradition each jongleur had to be able to play at least nine instruments.

And he knew well to sing and make poetry, and long time went through the world beguiling ladies" — a description which could be made to serve for most of his successors! The names of some four hundred troubadours and two hundred trouvères have come down to us, as well as a great deal of their poetry, consisting of ordered sequences of couplets and refrains, together with a number of the melodies they used.

The fact that these musician poets treated subjects that were quite outside the Church and upon which the clergy frowned, and which therefore found no place in the process of education that was entirely monopolized by the Church, was a tremendously important influence in the secularization of music. The nobles, increasingly reacting against the dominance of the Church, began to look elsewhere for artistic materials and found them in the common songs and dances of the people.

While the troubadours were essentially poets, they usually composed the melodies of their songs; but it was obviously important to the dignity of a nobleman that he should have an attendant trained to perform his master's works. These accompanists and musical scribes (the more skillful of whom acted as "ghosts" for their masters) were called *ménestrels* or *jongleurs*; being of the common people, they would naturally be influenced by popular melodies. Someone has called them the beloved vagabonds of the thirteenth century, for they passed constantly from one world to another, from noble castle to rustic inn.[7]

[7] The minstrels "wandered at will from castle to castle, and in time from borough to borough, sure of their ready welcome alike in the village tavern, the guildhall and the baron's keep. They sang and jested in the market places, stopping cunningly at a critical moment in the performance to gather their harvest of small coins from the bystanders. In the great castles, while lords and ladies supped or sat around the fire, it was theirs to while away many a long bookless evening with courtly *gests* or witty sally. At wedding or betrothal, baptism or knight dubbing, treaty or tournament, their presence was indispensable. The greater festivities saw them literally in the hundreds, and rich was their reward in jewels, in costly garments, and in broad acres.

"They were licensed vagabonds, with free right of entry into the presence chambers of the land. You might know them from afar by their coats of many colors, gaudier than any knight might respectably wear, by the instruments on their backs and those of their servants, and by the shaven faces, close-clipped hair, and flat shoes of their profession. This hen-speckle appearance, together with the privilege of easy access, made the minstrel's dress a favorite disguise in ages when disguise was imperative."

— E. K. Chambers: *The Mediaeval Stage*

Such songs as these, taken from the manuscript of an unknown jongleur of the thirteenth century, and now in the National Library, Paris, show this folk influence clearly enough. They were probably dance songs of the time, popular with commoner and noble alike.

I

II

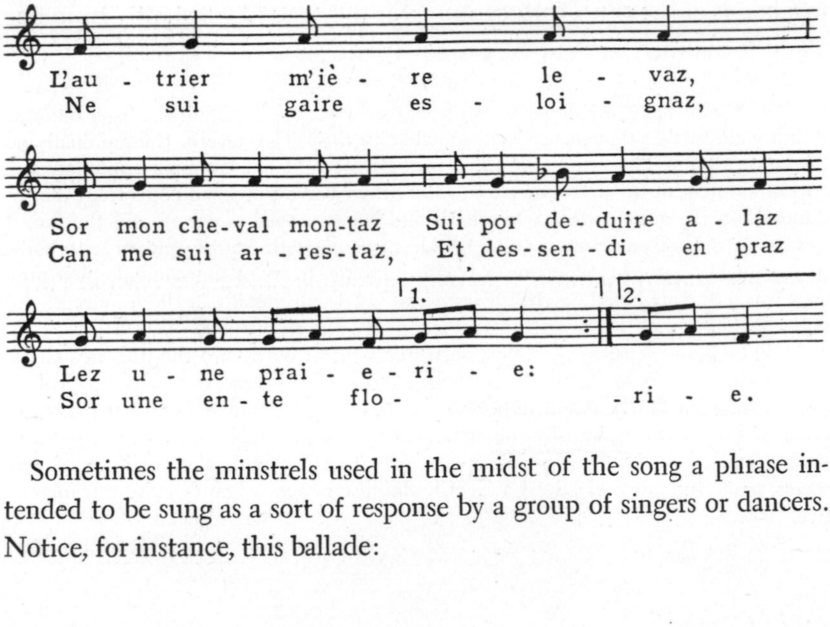

Sometimes the minstrels used in the midst of the song a phrase intended to be sung as a sort of response by a group of singers or dancers. Notice, for instance, this ballade:

A l'en-tra - da del tens clar, E - y - a,
Per joi - a re - co - men-çar, E - y - a,
E per je - los ir - ri-tar, E - y - a,
Vol la re - gi - na mos-trat Qu'el 'es si a - mo -
ro - sa A la vi', A la vi -
a, Je - los, Lais - saz nos, Lais - saz nos,
Bal - lar en - tre nos, En - tre nos.

TYPES OF TROUBADOUR ART

The gallant music of the troubadours, written for use in court and castle, was something quite different. Springing out of the current chivalric Romanticism, the same spirit that produced the Arthurian romances, these troubadour songs fall naturally into two groups: *chansons à personnages*, general in manner and written according to strict conventions; and *poésie courtoise*, addressed by the troubadour directly to his lady. Included in the *chansons à personnages* were various conventional types: *chansons de toile*, work songs; *chansons de malmariee*, a most fruitful subject; *pastourelles; chansons de danse*, like those already mentioned;

reverdies, or spring songs; and *chansons d'aube*, morning songs. The more personal utterances of the poet were marked by passionate, often extravagant, devotion to the service of love; the troubadour, anxious to establish himself in favor with the lady of his choice, spent a great deal of his time imploring her favor in carefully designed stanzaic schemes:

"Lady, if Mercy help me not, I ween
That I to be thy slave am all too mean,
    For thy great worth small hope to me has given
Aught to accomplish meet for dame so rare —
Yet this I would, and nowise will despair;
    For I have heard, the brave, when backward driven,
Strive ever till the conquering blow they deal,
So strive I for thy love by service leal.

"Though to such excellence I come not near,
Nor eke of one so noble am the peer,
    I sing my best, bear meekly Love's hard burden,
Serve thee and love thee more than all beside,
Shun ill, seek after good whate'er betide;
    Wherefore, methinks, fair dame should liefer guerdon
With her dear self a valiant knight and true,
Than the first lord that haughtily may woo . . ."

— Raymond of Miraval

And more to the same purport. If the fair lady decided to "guerdon with her dear self" the valiant knight, a ceremony was arranged, modeled on that of a vassal pledging himself to his lord. "The lover, kneeling down with clasped hands before his lady, vowed fidelity to her; she then lifted him up, gave him a ring, and kissed him, as a token that she 'retained' him." Such a union, strange as it may seem in the light of today's monogamous ideals in marriage — for the troubadour's lady was almost sure to be the wife of someone else — was considered so solemn a matter as to call for blessing by a priest.

Indeed the whole period is difficult of modern comprehension; if we are to realize the beauty of some of these troubadour songs, we must detach ourselves from present-day connotations and immerse ourselves in the atmosphere evoked by the accounts of the lives of these gallants.

REINMAR, THE FIDDLER

He plays for dancing (from the Manesse Manuscript, Heidelberg University Library).

(It was the custom of medieval times to head the collection of a troubadour's poems with the story of his life; and so we have plenty of contemporary evidence available.) Take, for example, such a biography as that of Raimbaut de Vagueiras (*d.* 1207), one of the most distinguished of the Provençal poets, whose likely *Estampie* is quoted later on:

"Raimbaut de Vagueiras was the son of a poor knight of Provence, of the Castle of Vagueiras, one named Peirors, who passed for mad. And Raimbaut became a jongleur, and abode full long with the Prince of Orange, William of Baux. Well did he know how to sing and to make coblas and sirventes; and the Prince of Orange did him great good, and great honor, and advanced him, and made him to be known and prized of all good folk. And afterwards, Raimbaut departed from him, and gat him to Montferrat — to the court of my Lord the Marquis Boniface, and therein dwelt full long, growing in wisdom, in knowledge, and in prowess. And he became enamored of the sister of the Marquis, the which hight my Lady Beatrice, wife of Lord Henry of Carret, and he made many fair songs, calling her therein, 'Fair Knight,' and men weened she loved him well. Now well have ye heard who was Raimbaut de Vagueiras, and how he came to honor, and by whom; but now I will tell you how that when the Marquis had dubbed him knight, Raimbaut became enamored of my Lady Beatrice, sister of the Marquis and my Lady Azalais of Salutz.

"Greatly did he love her and desire her, having care that none should know of it, and much did he spread abroad her fame, and many a friend did he win for her. And she was wont to bear herself full graciously towards him, yet the while he was dying for desire and fearfulness, for he durst neither beseech her for her love nor show that he strove therefor, until as one sore pressed, he told her that he loved a lady of great excellence, yet durst not make known the goodwill and love he bore her, nor seek for hers in exchange, in such fear was he of her great excellence; and he besought her for God's sake to tell him whether she held it meet that he should speak his mind, or he should die loving the lady privly. Then that noble lady — my Lady Beatrice — when she heard this, and knew the goodwill he bore her, having also ere now full well perceived that he was, from great yearning for her, nigh unto death, was moved by love and pity, and spake, and said:

"'Raimbaut, full meet it is that the true love of a gentle lady should fear to show his love, but or ever he die, I read him to tell it to her, and pray her to take him for servant and lover; and I will warrant, that if she be wise and courteous she will in nowise hold it for an ill and shameful thing of him; rather will she prize him the more, and hold him the better man for it. Likewise I read you to speak your mind and will to her you love, and to bid her take you for her knight, since you are such as no lady in the world should scorn for knight and servant; for my Lady Azalais, Countess of Saluza, suffered Peire Vidal, and the Countess of Burlatz, Arnaut de Marvoil, and my Lady Maria, Gaucelm Faidit, and the Lady of Marseilles, Folquet; wherefore I give you counsel and license that you, by my word and surety, may beseech her for her love.'

"Then Raimbaut, hearing the counsel and assurance she gave, and the license, that she promised him, told her *she* was verily the lady that he so much loved, even she of whom he had sought counsel; whereat my Lady

Beatrice told him that he was come in a happy hour, and that if he strove after worth, and after the doing and speaking of good things, she would indeed choose him for knight and servant. So Raimbaut strove to the uttermost to increase her fame, and it was then that he made the canzona which says:

'Now demand of me her bearing and demeanor.'

"And after this it befell that the Marquis, with his host, passed over into Romania, and with great help from the Church conquered the kingdom of Salonica, and then it was that Raimbaut, for his valorous deeds, was made knight; and there the Marquis gave him rich lands and revenues, and there also did he die."

Unlike Raimbaut, most of these poet musicians were of knightly origin; but whether of humble or noble birth, they all conformed strictly to the aristocratic style of their period; in addition to those already mentioned the most famous of them were Bertran de Born, who lived around 1180; Peire Vidal (1175–1215), perhaps the most celebrated of the whole lot, known everywhere as the "terror of husbands"; Bernard de Ventadour (1201–1253), and Gaucelm Faidit (*d.* 1220). The trouvères were able to include kings in their number, notably Richard Cœur de Lion[8] (1157–1199) and Thibaut, King of Navarre (1201–1253); but the most

[8] Richard's interest in minstrelsy is one of the pleasantly accepted legends of history. Just how many songs he did write is open to question; but there seems no reason to doubt the authenticity of the one which still survives in the Laurentian Library, in a manuscript volume of Provençal poetry. This was probably composed in 1193 when the king was a captive in an Austrian castle on the Danube, and seems to have been written with some definite tune in mind:

"Never can captive make a song so fair
As he can make that has no cause for care,
Yet may he strive by song his grief to cheer.
I lack not friends, but sadly lack their gold!
Shamed are they, if unransomed I lie here,
A second Yule in hold.

"My men and barons all, full well they know,
Poitevins, English, Normans, Gascons, too,
That I have not one friend, however poor,
Whom I would leave in chains to save my gold,
I tell them this, but blame them not therefor;
Though I lie yet in hold . . .

"Sister and Countess, God give you good cheer!
And keep my Lady, whom I love dear;
For whom I lie in hold."

RICHARD THE LIONHEARTED AND HEINRICH VI

While Richard was the prisoner of the Emperor (1193–1194) he wrote his *Reis Rizard.*

famous of all the northern singers was the hunchbacked minstrel, Adam de la Halle (1238?–1288), whose little pastoral play *Le Jeu de Robin et Marion* is one of the landmarks of French dramatic history. The centers of this musical culture of the Middle Ages were the courts of Provence, Toulouse, and Poitou, and of the dukes of Flanders and Brabant, as well as of the kings of England, France, and Spain.

How much of the art of the troubadours was of their own invention and how much came from their paid assistants, the jongleurs, we cannot tell.[9] Probably the latter, who wrote down the music, made a far greater

[9] A contemporary account describes a troubadour's voice as being "so supple that the nightingale was amazed to hear it." But there is plenty of evidence that such vocal gifts were by no means usual, the troubadours leaving to their jongleurs the singing of the songs they had composed. Wolfram von Eschenbach confessed that he could neither read nor write — perhaps a statement somewhat exaggerated for effect — but we do know that the troubadour Ulrich von Liechtenstein dictated his songs to a scribe. There are conflicting reports concerning the ability of the jongleurs. An early

contribution to the history of music than did their masters; but it was the masters who were the glamorous figures, the men who received all the honor and glory, and so it is their names that have become attached to the whole movement. The jongleurs accompanied these songs by some instrument, usually the vielle (a bowed instrument, the direct ancestor of the violin) or the harp. In writing down these songs after they had perfected them, these scribes used a notation of the plainsong type; but this was defective, for while the rise and fall of the notes was shown, their length was a matter of rough rule, regulated by the syllables to which they were set. And so there has resulted a great deal of confusion in the modern transcription of these early songs and dances, most authorities letting the melody change occasionally to two and four pulses to the measure, instead of keeping it always in three, as suggested by the regular alternation of long and short syllables in the texts used.

Set to words according to modern principles of accent, and using melodies that are strongly suggestive of our present-day major and minor scales,[10] these troubadour songs make a more definite appeal to most

---

ecclesiastic said that many of his own brethren that were charged with uttering the noble words of God took less care and were far less keen about their work than were these players of the cithara and the flute. Petrarch, writing to Boccaccio in 1366, says: "they [that is, the jongleurs] are men of spirit, far from mediocre, gifted with good memory — very lavorious sort of persons with plenty of cheek," a description which might well be used of some of their modern descendants! Guiraut de Cabreiar was probably more concerned with rhetorical effect than with stating the truth, when he said to his jongleur: "You play the viol vilely; you sing even worse; you can't make a beautiful final cadence to save your life; even less can you contrive embellishments." But these complaints are rather common, especially against bad singers, so the technical efficiency of the musicians was probably none too good.

[10] Julián Ribera, a Spanish scholar with a vast knowledge of Arabic literature as well as of Spanish history, has an interesting explanation for this. He states, in his book *La música de las cantigas*, that music followed the general course of the other arts which, as we are just beginning to realize, after their origin in Egypt and the Sumerian civilizations and their development in Greece and Rome, went back to western Asia and reached a new high point of development in Persia during the eighth and ninth centuries A.D. The fundamental characteristics of this music, according to Ribera, based on the classic Greek models, were the use of the diatonic scale, of simple harmonies in the modern sense of the term, the possession of definite rhythmic patterns suited to the metrics of the verses to which they were set, and emphasis on "expression" — all of them characteristics likewise of the music of the troubadours.

Jean Beck and other workers in the field of troubadour music and poetry have never been able to explain satisfactorily the sources of the instruction and technique of these of us than do the mystic chants of the Church. Contrast this *Estampie* of Raimbaut de Vagueiras, based on a courtly dance rhythm, with the music of the Church which we have already heard:

Kalenda maya
Ni fuelhs de faya
Ni chanz d'auzelh ni flors de glaya
Non es quem playa,
Pros domna guaya,
Tro qu'un ysnelh messatgier aya
Del vostre bel cors, quem retraya,
Plazer novelh qu'Amors m'atraya,
E jaya
Emtraya
Vas vos, domna veraya;
E chaya
De playa
L'gelos, ans quem n'estraya.

It is the age-old, yet ever-new complaint:

"The joys of May, the new leaves on the trees, the songs of the birds, the blossoming of the flowers — all these can mean nothing to me, my noble and lovely one, until I see your messenger come with some token of your love for me, till I see my jealous foe struck by the lightning of your wrath."

---

poet composers. The words *troubadour* and *trouvère* mean literally "finder" or "inventor," but it is hardly safe to assume that such a description is to be taken literally. This new style of music came from somewhere; Ribera says the matter is simple enough, and explains it in this fashion:

The classic music of the Arabic countries was brought to Spain during the Moorish occupation (which lasted roughly from the eighth to fifteenth centuries), became established there, and was brought to a high state of perfection through the work of a number of important Spanish composers; so that by the twelfth century it was known throughout Europe. The Iberian Peninsula was, as everyone who has studied the troubadours knows, a sort of chosen country for them from the earliest beginnings of the Provençal school. This predilection, Ribera says, explains the sources of the troubadour melodies and verses. They went to Spain because of this new "popular" art they found there and because they wanted to perfect themselves in it. Thus Spain became one of the great highways for the diffusion of a world culture and played an important role in the introduction of the popular features of music into Europe.

Señor Ribera's work is thoroughly scholarly and carefully documented; it has been recently published in an English translation by Eleanor Hague and Marion Leffingwell (Stanford University Press).

A suggestion of modern tonality and rhythm is present in the two well-known little lyrics from Adam de la Halle's *Robin et Marion, J'ai encore un tel pâte* and *Robin m'aime*. These were undoubtedly popular melodies of the day, preserved for posterity by the charm of the art of this trouvère. That these fragrant reminders of this gallant period can still please is evidenced by the fact that they often are placed on modern programs. Perrin d'Angicourt's charming *Quand voi an la fin d'estey* and Blondel de Nesle's *A l'entrant d'esté* (both available in the *Anthologie Sonore*) are perhaps more of their period; they show clearly enough the influence of Eastern ideals and have a decidedly courtly atmosphere.

The texts of many of these lovely songs of the Provençal poets and musicians have luckily been preserved. Some of them have great simplicity, such as this, fresh as the breath of spring itself:

Quand le rossignol chante — qui nous charme par son chant —
Pour ma belle, douce amie — Je vois mon cœur rossignolant —
Jointes mains je la supplie — Car jamais je n'aimai tant; —
Je sais bien, que, si elle m'oublie — C'en est fini de mon bonheur.

— Translated into modern French by J. Beck

Others are stormy and turbulent like Peire Vidal's

Atressi co.l perilans
Que sus nn' laiga balansa . . .

As a mariner, sea-tossed,
Capsized in desperate plight,
Gives himself up for lost,
Yielding to craven fright,
Then sees a sudden light
And feels a rescuing hand
Drawing him safe to land;
So I, distraught, downcast
By heavy doubt, and long
Love-hungry, find at last
A splendid theme for song.

Beneath her beauty's mask
If I could know her mind
I'd have no need to ask,
Is she no more than kind,
And am I somewhat blind,
To steer my passion's bark
Through the uncharted dark,
Trusting to her regard
Without assurance? Dear
Lady, be not so hard,
But make the sailing clear!

— Translated by George Cronyn

Unfortunately many of the tunes to which these songs were sung have been lost. In the case of the trouvères we are more fortunate, for oftentimes several of their melodies are found set to the same words.

THE GERMAN COUNTERPART

We have spoken of the minnesinger as the German counterpart of the troubadour and trouvère. In reality the minnesinger, literally a love singer, was a somewhat later development in point of time, and his art lasted almost a whole century longer than that of his French brothers in song. The whole of this German art was tinctured with a religious element, for the delicacy of the love sentiment allowed it to be, in part, sublimated into a worship of the Virgin Mary; and this element is accentuated in the songs of the minnesingers by their melodic derivation from Church sources. Thus we have another link between secular and sacred song, the modes of the Church exercising their restraining influence on the music, which in the troubadour minstrelsy had shown a well-developed tendency to step into the path of what we know as the major keys.

The most famous minnesinger was without doubt Walter von der Vogelweide (c. 1170–1230). Many of his poems are known today, none of them more personal or characteristic than the one beginning:

Unter den Linden, An der Heide, Wo ich mit meiner Trauten sass, Da mögt ihr finden, Wie wir beide Die Blumen brachen und das Gras. Vor dem Wald mit süssem Schall Tandaradei! Sang im Tal die Nachtigall.	Under the lindens on the heather, There was our double resting place, Side by side and close together Garnered blossoms, crushed, and grass Nigh a shaw in such a vale: Tandaradei! Sweetly sang the nightingale.

— Translated by Ford Madox Ford

One of the few authentic melodies of Walter's is that of a *Crusader's Song*, written during his journey to the Holy Land in 1228, only two years before his death. The music is suggestive of Gregorian influence, and the words express the lyric joy of the poet on at last reaching the goal of his desire — the Holy Land.[11]

[11] Wagner brings the medieval spirit of chivalry and the culture of this period strikingly before us in his operas *Tannhäuser* (in which is staged a contest of song and poetry for the hand of a lady) and *Lohengrin*.

THE MINNESINGER HEINRICH FRAUENLOB (*d.* 1318)
(From the Manesse Manuscript, Heidelberg University Library)

A SINGING TRIAL OF THE MASTERSINGERS

In this scene from a seventeenth-century miniature we see the markers sitting at the left on the podium; in the pulpit at the right, the candidate is singing, and the mastersingers are sitting in the foreground.

The Meistersinger (mastersingers) carried on the art of the minnesingers, though with less brilliance, from about the middle of the fifteenth century to the early part of the seventeenth. They were local musicians of the bourgeois class, organized into guilds according to strict rules and regulations, and they allowed the artificiality and stiffness of these academic bonds to hamper their music. There were definite gradations of rank in this order — apprentice, pupil, singer, poet, and master — each of them subject to careful examination as to the ability of the candidate. Although Hans Sachs of Nuremberg, the best known of the mastersingers, wrote some beautiful melodies that are strangely suggestive of the later chorales, most of the work of these bourgeois musicians was uncouth and prosaic, the satisfaction of rules being more important to them than the expression of poetic or musical thought. Wagner's glorious opera, *Die Meistersinger*, draws a genial portrait of their weaknesses.

HANS SACHS (1494–1576)

He was the most famous of the mastersingers — " *Schumacher und Poet dazu.*"

DANCE SONGS OF THE TIME

The period of the troubadours produced also a definite art of instrumental music in the aristocratic and courtly dances that were so popular. As Dr. Sachs has asked, what more significant expression of this peculiar world of love and intrigue could be found than these *fêtes galantes,* when during the dances the barriers between knights and the ladies they loved were temporarily dropped? Modern research has made available some of this music and has shown how strong was its pull toward a regular rhythmic pulse.

Among the most interesting of these medieval dances described by Johannes de Grocheo, in his contemporary treatise on popular music,[12] is the *ductia* — a light, rapid tune that falls and rises gracefully and thus is

[12] Johannes de Grocheo was a music scholar and writer of the thirteenth century living in Paris. His *Theoria* is a rich source of the forms of medieval music.

A RENAISSANCE COURT DANCE: "THE DANCE WITH FLAMBEAUX"

(From a wood engraving by Dürer)

well suited for both singing and dancing. A good example of this has been preserved in a manuscript now in the Bodleian Library at Oxford. It is of the thirteenth century and consists of a number of short *vers* (verses) with the melody ending in a half close; the same tune is then repeated, ending in a full close on the tonic. During each repetition the dancers evidently returned in their steps to where they had begun each *vers*.

Another dance described by this author, who seems to have been a professor in the Sorbonne, is the *stantipes,*[13] which he says was so difficult of execution that it "served to restrain the youths from wicked

[13] The Latin term for a medieval dance piece played before courtly listeners; it was called *estampida* in the Provençal dialect, and Boccaccio calls it *stampita*. It was played *stehenden Fusses* in contrast to the *ductia*, where the players led in a round dance.

thoughts." An amusing example of this, with a primitive contrapuntal second part, is preserved in the British Museum. The *saltarello* and *Lamento di Tristano* came from Italy. The latter had a changing rhythm and was the sort of compound dance that is still found in country districts. The *vers* was in triple time, according to Sachs, and probably marked a step in which the whole company participated. The *rotta,* which followed, was in lively double time, and suggests an interlude for individual steps and interpolated pantomime.

There are a few other medieval dance tunes known today, but these we have mentioned are representative. It does not require a great deal of imagination when listening to their music to re-create the colorful background of courtly chivalry and graceful intrigue; and in their peculiar instrumentation we hear again the voice of a fascinating age long forgotten.

A TRANSITIONAL PERIOD

The Fourteenth and Fifteenth Centuries

The period which carried Europe from scholasticism to humanism, once regarded as arid and sterile, is now looked upon as one of the great turning points in intellectual history. It marked the actual transition from medievalism to the modern age. . . . The older conception of a sudden classical 'renaissance' in the fifteenth century, and of an almost precipitate development of natural science between 1550 and 1700 has been supplanted by a more truly historical perspective which stresses the continuity of cultural development between the late twelfth and the fifteenth centuries.

— Barnes: *An Intellectual and Cultural History of the Western World*

A PERIOD OF TRANSITION

ONE of the consistent phenomena of history is the appearance between eras of exceptional physical, mental, and spiritual activity (such as the one we have just been considering) of what may be called *fluctuational periods* — zones of a comparatively undetermined quality, sharing the characteristics of both the preceding and the following epochs, without having any decided ones of their own. Feeling the stirrings of the new times ahead, and yet unable to throw off the trappings of the old ones behind, these fluctuational periods are likely to be marked by attention to *law* rather than to *spirit*. In an attempt to hide the lack of real motivating forces, they are concerned with the development of technical perfection, of learning for its own sake, of oversophistication. Some historians consider the fourteenth and fifteenth centuries, lying between the apex of the Middle Ages and the High Renaissance, as such a period.

The medieval concept of the world was that of its being a God-inspired mystery that was capable of being expressed in terms of great beauty; that of the Renaissance was that it was rather a man-made rationality, worthy of cultivation for its own sake. In between there came these two centuries. Because both the old and the new were present in them, the old slowly perishing, the new slowly struggling for life, they were troubled enough. Symbolic is the fact that they produced both Dante's *Divine Comedy*, designed, as someone has said, largely for preparing the reader for the life to come, and Boccaccio's *Decameron*, which had as its purpose the preparation for life on this earth.

Gone was the sustaining faith of the eleventh and twelfth centuries; in its place arose a type of intellectuality which has made the term *scholasticism* one of contempt. The soaring Gothic beauty of the medieval churches degenerated into an overdeveloped, flamboyant style, which suggested a technical art of decoration rather than a spiritual means of expression. There developed a fashion for strict, artificial lyric forms in poetry, which, although possessing a certain charm, were not very significant in content. The Church seemed to have lost its hold on heaven as well as its grip on earth. The clergy were often corrupt beyond belief, some of them actively practicing piracy when not engaged in reading their services; ecclesiastical preferment was openly obtained by a process of barter and trade; the papacy had lost its moral and political power, not to speak of its spiritual significance, and at one time three popes were engaged in the edifying spectacle of trying to excommunicate one another.

Moreover, in these centuries occurred the Black Death and the Hundred Years' War between France and England. It is difficult to say which was cause and which effect; but to these two major catastrophes in man's

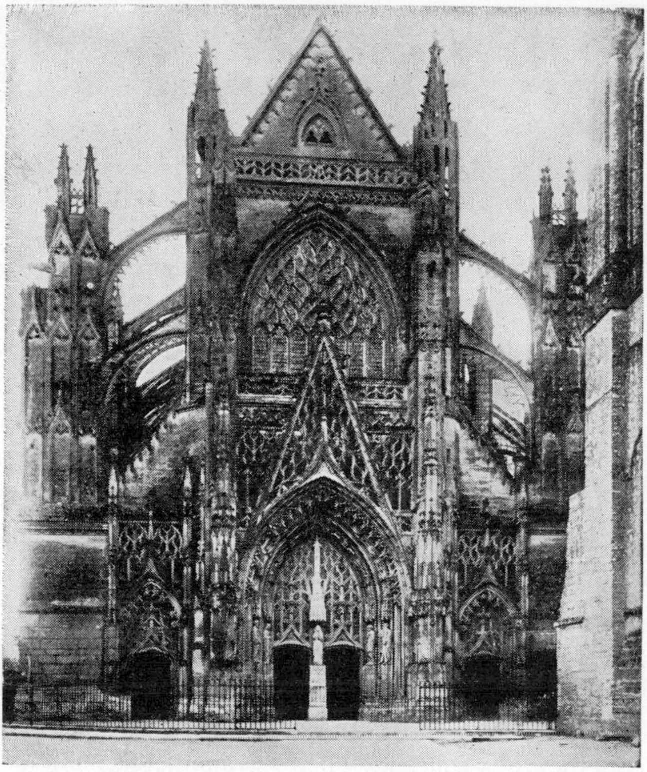

Archives Photographiques

FLAMBOYANT GOTHIC ARCHITECTURE — La Trinité, Vendome, France

What an overinsistence on technique did to the Gothic style: this twisted, crackling façade is far removed from the quiet, exalted beauty of Chartres.

history can be laid a great deal of the sad gloom, the sin, and the suffering of this period. Between them these two cataclysms cost Europe uncounted thousands of its inhabitants, drained it of a great deal of its wealth, and deprived it of manners and morals, faith and reason. No wonder that a favorite theme of the time was the brevity of life and the consequent need for immediate pleasure. The *Danse macabre* became a sort of universal symbol: in verse and wall paintings and actual dance ceremonial, every type of society was portrayed — pope, emperor, cardinal, prince, archbishop, baron, lady, squire, abbot, prior, lawyer, scholar,

DANSE MACABRE IN THE CHURCH OF LA CHAISE DIEU,

deacon, merchant, monk, thief, physician, minstrel, and common workingman — marching forward in a sort of inevitable parade, each in his place according to his rank, with Death dancing grotesquely among all, questioning them and demonstrating the certainty of his final triumph.

But we must not overemphasize the dark side of the picture; if the old was dying, the new was being born. For out of the confusion and disillusionment of these years there came new ideals. New political units, the states, emerged, shaped by the common national sentiment of the various peoples and governed by central rulers. The medieval unifying forces which had held sway for so long — the Holy Roman Empire, the Catholic Church, the feudal system — gradually lost power and influence in the face of these new concepts. There was another factor in the decline of medieval ideals during this time, the development of commerce and the consequent growth of a prosperous bourgeois class with its particular ideology. The commercial relationships of these trading merchants led "straight to the discovery of America and the origins of the modern age."

Nowhere is the dual nature of the period better shown than in the art it produced. On the one hand, there was the interest in virtuosity and a tendency to be content with a sort of sensuous enjoyment mixed with a touch of humorous and ironical philosophy, a let-us-eat-drink-and-be-merry-for-tomorrow-we-die attitude. We have mentioned some of the characteristic results of this — the flamboyance of the northern architecture, the technical perfection and artificiality of fourteenth-century poetry. A symptomatic portrait is that given by the gilded youths of Boccaccio's *Decameron,* who while away their time in the pleasant countryside near plague-stricken Florence telling stories and singing ballads.

Archives Photographiques

Haute-Loire, France (by an unknown artist of the fifteenth century)

On the other hand, these centuries mark the rise of a new interest — or, better, a renewed interest — in man as an individual and a curiosity regarding the world in which he lives. The religious concepts of the Middle Ages are no longer completely satisfying; artists begin to portray man as a natural, human being and not merely as an abstract religious symbol. This is the period of the great sculptors Ghiberti, Verrocchio, and Donatello, the latter one of the great realists of Italian art; of the painters Giotto, Masaccio, Uccello, and Fra Filippo Lippi, a distinguished line which brought the art out of its medieval limitations and, by concentrating on such matters as draughtsmanship, color, and perspective, laid the foundations for its modern development. In Italy Brunelleschi and his follower, Michelozzo, designed buildings which show a definite attempt to return to older, more humanistic ideals. In literature, Chaucer and Boccaccio introduced a new secular spirit derived from a wide knowledge of the world and its inhabitants. The poets Petrarch and Villon infused new feeling into old forms and represent the humanistic tendencies of the time, as does Dante its more medievalistic aspects. In music we find a strong consciousness of the traditions of the past, as well as a great enthusiasm for the new expressive powers which suddenly opened up. Philippe de Vitry's treatise, *Ars nova*, was much more than a mere proclamation of a new art; it provided a fresh outlook by emphasizing new rhythmic schemes and secured thereby a significant advance in emotional expressiveness and humanistic interest.[14] His ideals were carried on by the

[14] It is in De Vitry and other theorists of the *Ars nova* that we first find the rule which so strongly affected all music written after their time — that of forbidding consecutive fifths or octaves in two parallel contrapuntal parts. This was in direct contrast to the general practice of the time.

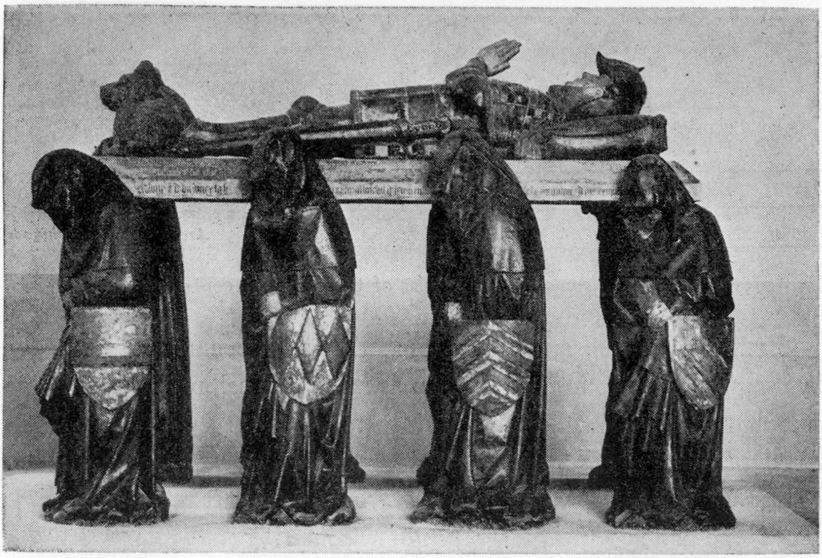

Archives Photographiques

TOMB OF THE "GRAND SÉNÉCHAL" PHILIPPE POT

The new spirit in the Gothic is shown in this fifteenth-century work.

Florentine organist, Francesco Landino, and the intricate developments of the Netherlandish polyphonic composers.

There were a number of reasons for the exhaustion of the burning, driving intensity of the Gothic spirit of creative enthusiasm which came toward the end of the thirteenth century. First of all was the feeling of doubt and often complete agnosticism engendered in the minds of many churchmen by the teachings of the Greek scholastic philosophy which preceded the Renaissance. Then the frightful ignorance and open corruptness of the clergy made the Christian religion an object of scorn and derision over the whole of Europe. The long years of struggle between France and England caused most of the wealth which these countries had formerly lavished on the building and decoration of churches to be levied for the purposes of war. And, as a tragic climax, came the paralyzing horrors of the Black Death, the terrible pestilence which originated in China, spread over India, Asia Minor, and Egypt, and reached Europe in 1347.

These physical events in the history of Europe had a marked effect on man's spiritual development; for with the weakening of the authority and

CHOIR GALLERY IN THE CATHEDRAL, FLORENCE, 1433–1438
(By Donatello)

power of the Church, upon which man had learned to lean for so long, there came a corresponding unfolding of man's personality. No longer entirely dependent on either Church or State, man began to realize how he could make his own spiritual approach to God and find his own place in the world about him. It was a time of stirring interest and teeming ideas, this close of the medieval period; there came, after a long time of subordination to the wishes and desires of the Church, a release of new power, a zest for the realities of life, and a love for the things of the world. This spirit was everywhere manifest, but especially in Italy; and it had its reflection in art, as might be expected. No longer satisfied with the composite expression of the Cathedral, the individual began to seek out ways to express his definite and personal viewpoint. The emphasis was thus shifted from a collective, symbolic, and, therefore, impersonal spirit of artistic expression to a more subjective, realistic, and personal one. From this time the individual begins to stand out more and more in art, and the period of the so-called "easel picture," made by a single artist for a single person, begins.

THE RISE OF ARTISTIC PERSONALITIES

It was not until the fourteenth and fifteenth centuries, then, that definite personalities began to emerge in Christian art — among others, the painters Giotto, the Van Eyck brothers, with their curiously wrought Gothic multiplicity of detail, the gentle Memling, the sculptors Donatello and Ghiberti, and the musicians Guillaume de Machaut in the north and Francesco Landino in the south. But before tracing the achievements of these earliest individual composers, it will be interesting to note briefly an attempt made by the Church to reassert something of its old authority and to reinstate something of its old austere beauty into its ritual. From Avignon, the French city to which the papacy had been temporarily withdrawn, Pope John XXII issued in 1324 his famous decree on the misuse of music in the churches. In this he attempted to take the art back to where it had been four hundred years before; for the only intervals he would allow in the church were the octave, the fifth, and the fourth. The language of this document, which in purpose was much like that of the later *Motu proprio* issued by Pius X, is clear:

"Certain disciples of the new school, much occupying themselves with the measured dividing of the *tempora*, display their probation in notes which are new to us, preferring to devise methods of their own rather than to continue singing in the old way; the music therefore of the divine offices is now performed with semibreves and minims, and with these notes of small value every composition is pestered. Moreover, they truncate the melodies with hockets,[15] they deprave them with discants, sometimes even they stuff them with upper parts made out of secular songs. So that often they must be losing sight of the fundamental sources of our melodies in the Antiphonal and Gradual, and may thus forget what that is upon which their superstructure is raised. They may become entirely ignorant concerning the ecclesiastical tones, which they already no longer distinguish, and the limits of which they even con-

[15] It may be added in passing that the *hocket* was a musical embellishment popular at the time, consisting of a quick alternating of the same melody between two parts. It was thus satirically described by a contemporary writer: "Sometimes thou mayest see a man with an open mouth, not to sing, but as it were breathe out his last gasp, by shutting in his breath, and by a certain ridiculous interception of his voice to threaten silence, and now again to imitate the agonies of a dying man, or the ecstasies of such as suffer."

found, since, in the multitude of their notes, the moderate risings and temporate descents of the plainsong, by which the scales themselves are to be known one from another, must be entirely obscured. Their voices are incessantly running to and fro, intoxicating the ear, not soothing it, while the men themselves endeavor to convey by their gestures the sentiment of the music which they utter. As a consequence of all this, devotion, the true end of worship, is little thought of, and wantonness, which ought to be eschewed, increases.

" This state of things, hitherto the common one, we and our brethren have regarded as standing in need of correction; and we now hasten therefore to banish those methods, nay, rather to cast them entirely away, and to put them to flight more effectual than heretofore, far from the house of God. Wherefore, having taken counsel with our brethren, we straitly command that no one henceforward shall think himself at liberty to attempt those methods, or methods like them, in the aforesaid Offices, and especially in the canonical Hours, or in the solemn celebration of the Mass.

" And if any be disobedient, let him, on the authority of this canon, be punished by a suspension from office of eight days; either by the Ordinary of the diocese in which the forbidden things are done or by his deputies in places not exempt from episcopal authority, or, in places which are exempt, by such of their offices as are usually considered responsible for the correction of irregularities and excesses, and such like matters.

" Yet, for all this, it is not our intention to forbid, occasionally — and especially upon feast days or in the solemn celebrations of the Mass and in the aforesaid divine offices — the use of some consonances, for example the eighth, fifth, and fourth, which heighten the beauty of the melody; such intervals therefore may be sung above the plain *cantus ecclesiasticus*, yet so that the integrity of the *cantus* itself may remain intact, and that nothing in the authoritative music be changed. Used in such sort the consonances would much more than by any other method both soothe the hearer and arouse his devotion, and also would not destroy religious feeling in the minds of the singers."

— *The Oxford History of Music, Volume I*

THE CASUISTRY OF THE FALSE BASS

Professor Wooldridge, one of the authors of *The Oxford History of Music*, thinks that this attempt of the Church to simplify its music at this time was the origin of what was known as *faulx bourdon* (false bass).[16] In an attempt to circumvent this decree of Pope John's, the Church musicians developed a method of organizing which consisted in inserting a third voice between a simple two-part organum at the fifth. This was written at an equal distance from the outer voices and thus resulted in the interval of a third with each:

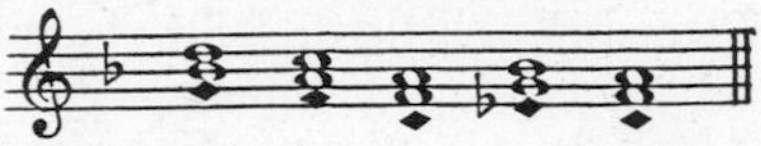

But — and this is where the ingenuity of frustrated man shows itself — in singing such an arrangement, the lowest part was given to a high voice, which would transpose it up an octave, and it would sound thus:

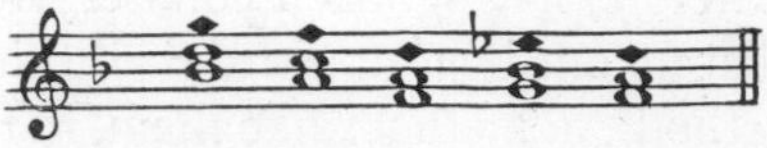

This resulted in an agreeable series of consecutive thirds and sixths, which were not in accord with John's decree, as well as a fourth, which was; but officialdom evidently closed its ears and was satisfied with what its eyes suggested was obedience to the letter of the law, since the highest part was always written as a false bass below the others. This use of parallel thirds and sixths spread over the whole of Europe by the end of the fourteenth century and was especially cultivated in England.

The development of *faulx bourdon* was not the only sign that music was beginning to strain at the leashes that had so long been imposed upon it by the Church. In 1325 Philippe de Vitry, bishop, poet, and composer, issued a work to which he gave the proud title *Ars nova* (The New Art); and this gave the name to the whole century, which was a period of steady development and humanizing of the art. During this time there took place a remarkable change in rhythmic procedure, for the theoreticians awakened to the possibilities of duple time, and the composers began to use it as well as triple, which had up to this time reigned supreme. The contrast between long and short notes became more clearly established; there was a further development of music forms and a tendency to use more and more instrumental music. This whole movement was, in fact, really a continuation of the ideals of the troubadours and trouvères.

16 Often spelled *faux bourdon* or *faburden*. Other authorities give different versions of its origin.

Courtesy of The National Library, Paris

THE INSPIRATION OF GUILLAUME DE MACHAUT

Attributed to an unknown painter of the court of Charles V, this scene from a contemporary miniature represents Love bringing Sweet-thoughts, Pleasure, and Hope to Machaut.

MACHAUT, A TYPICAL GOTHIC COMPOSER

The life of Machaut, who lived from 1305(?) to 1377, was an extremely brilliant one. Born in Champagne, he became a courtier in the service of the warrior king, John of Luxembourg and Bohemia, and later entered the service of the French court. An important figure in the development of the technique of the writing of French verse, Machaut, in addition to his musical activities, became a canon of the Church and when he died was considered the most influential spiritual leader of his time. In music he expressed himself most freely in the form of the *ballade*, the important secular form of the period, consisting of a vocal song or duet set to several verses of rather elaborate and stilted type and supported by one or two purely ornamental parts. One of his best essays in this form, *Ma chère dame*, shows clearly enough, even to our modern sophisticated ears, that he attempted to practice what he preached, namely, that " he who writes and composes without feeling spoils both his words and his music," the first desire for a humanized ideal that we come across in music. His great work was the writing of a musical setting of the Mass, probably the first one ever to include the entire Ordinary.[17] For years this has been an almost legendary work, unknown even to the musicologists. Now it has been gathered together from various fragments and different sources, and part of it has been recorded in Dr. Sachs's collection *Anthologie Sonore*. In form it is a gigantic motet in the medieval sense, its four voices weaving a constructional unity out of a confusing number of tangled architectural elements in true Gothic fashion. Because of its length and the fact that the various parts are connected by means of a melodic nucleus, it represents better than any other single work the Gothic conception of collective expression and so should be heard by everyone who would know what this music was like. But in it are present, too, an impassioned melodic movement and a rhythmic liberty characteristic of the *ars nova*.

A CONTEMPORARY COLLECTION

The so-called *Roman de Fauvel*, one of the outstanding works both in early French literature and in music, contains a number of motets, ballads, and other examples of contemporary Gothic musical forms written

[17] The Mass deserves special attention as an " art form," for it was the first of the larger forms to develop and has been of great importance in the history of music. Up to the time of Machaut the Ordinary of the Mass — that portion which is invariable whatever the seasons of the Church's year — had been sung to plainsong melodies but not combined in any fixed work. (The fact that modern editions group these Gregorian chants in fixed Masses should not confuse the issue; they do so purely for convenience. Such groupings are arbitrary and vary in different editions.)

Machaut's was the first entirely composed Mass; its settings of the *Kyrie, Gloria, Credo, Sanctus*, and *Agnus Dei* constitute a new fivefold art form comparable in importance, as Douglas says, to the great parallel form which evolved from instrumental dance music — the symphony. A large number of composers followed Machaut's example, among them some of the greatest in music. Bach's noble *B Minor Mass*, one of the world's masterpieces of choral art, is a direct descendant of this Gothic work of the fourteenth century.

in a style that is suggestive of Machaut's. This work, which dates from the beginning of the fourteenth century, is perhaps the most important manuscript of the time which has come down to us and contains an unusual combination of literature, music, and painting.

THE ARS NOVA IN THE SOUTH

We have already suggested the special importance of Italy and Italian artists in this new humanizing movement of the fourteenth and fifteenth centuries. We must always remember that this was the time when Dante, Petrarch, and Boccaccio did so much there to free mankind from the stultifying and often hypocritical interpretations of the medieval theologians and to awaken in him a new delight in the things of this earth. It was natural that the *ars nova* should thrive in this southern clime: a new style of writing developed in which fifths, unisons, and octaves were evidently forbidden and which was strongly influenced by the popular music of the day. A large number of forms were used, the composers contriving settings to fit such contemporary poetic forms as the *madrigal* (derived from troubadour poetry and representing the art song of the period) and the *ballata* (a composition for combined singing, playing, and dancing). The Italian love of elaborate *fioriture* (embellishments) in melody is everywhere evident in these works, and frequent use was often made of instrumental preludes, interludes, and postludes. One of the most popular forms was the *caccia*, a canon for two voices over an instrumental bass, its text descriptive of some animated scene, such as a hunt or the cries of a street.

The records of the time show an amazing prolificness on the part of at least thirty composers in northern Italy, there being still extant hundreds of specimens of the work of this period. Among the names that have survived are those of Vincenzo da Rimini, Giovanni da Cascia, Jacopo da Bologna; but at the head of all is Francesco Landino, the organist of San Lorenzo in Florence (c. 1325–1397), "blind of body but enlightened in spirit, one who understood both the theory and practice of his art, the best singer of his time, a player of every instrument and especially the organ, by means of which he was wont to delight his many

ADORATION OF THE MAGI by Stephan Lochner

listeners," to use the words of a contemporary writer. Over a hundred and fifty of his works have come down to us, written in all the forms used at the time and showing the characteristics which made them so popular during the composer's life. A contemporary writer already quoted, Giovanni da Prato, has, like Boccaccio, left behind him a clear picture of Florentine life in his romanza, *Il paradiso degli Alberti;* included in this are stories of Francesco and a description of an occasion when the blind musician played his love verses so sweetly that the listeners' hearts "almost burst from their bosoms." But Francesco's chief glory — like that of many another composer who followed after him — came from his skill as a virtuoso organist and his powers of improvisation. A number of the works of this composer, as well as others of the Italian *ars nova,* have been preserved in the so-called "Squarcialupi Manuscript" now in the Laurentian Library at Florence.

The fifteenth century saw a further intensification of this late Gothic spirit of humanism. The love of grace and susceptibility to form, which is natural to the Italians, produced new loveliness in the art and music of the south, and these ideals were retransferred to the artists of the north. If we look at the fifteenth-century pictures of such Italian painters as Fra Angelico and Fra Filippo Lippi we shall see in them the same love of harmonious color, attention to exquisite detail, refined grace, sweep of rhythmic line, and spirit of lyric happiness that are found in the works of the Flemish Van der Goes and Memling and the German Stephan Lochner. This is natural enough, for during the century in which they worked, communication between the flourishing trade centers of Italy and Flanders was frequent, and the artists of one country mingled freely with those of another. This explains the cosmopolitan influences so strongly present in the music of Guillaume Dufay, a composer born in the Low Countries, who traveled and studied as a youth in Italy and who spent most of his life as composer to the rich and art-loving dukes of Burgundy.

A BURGUNDIAN MASTER

The duchy of Burgundy, a territorial organization which comprised parts of modern France, the Netherlands, and Belgium, was a country dominated by French influence and civilization. Its court at Dijon was French in nature; its intellectual language and predilections were French; its duke was the first peer of the realm and exerted a great deal of influence on the internal policies of France. The great artistic centers of the country, however, were its rich and populous cities in the Low Counties—Brabant, Flanders, and Hainault; and it was here that the celebrated Burgundian School (often called the School of the Netherlands) originated. For many years the music in these wealthy cities of Philip the Good and Charles the Bold, the two outstanding members of the Burgundian ducal family, was considered by contemporary critics to be the best in the world, quite the equal of the famous painting and sculpture fostered by these art-loving dukes. The centers for this music were the churches and chapels maintained by the princes. The chapel service of Philip the Good, modeled on that of the Papal Chapel, was for nearly a century the most important influence in the cultivation of the music of the time. These rich ducal patrons made it possible for Dufay to settle in the city of Cambrai from 1450 to the end of his life, devoting his time to composition and travel. His existence there has been described as that of a great personage, honored and respected by all intellectual and artistic Europe. He must have been particularly happy; for Cambrai had a special reputation as a music center, one of Dufay's contemporaries describing its cathedral as having the best singing in Europe.

It was for such surroundings that Dufay composed. He is supposed to have been influenced by the Englishman, John Dunstable, whose music reflected the English love of thirds and sixths in parallel movement. Such motets of Dufay's as *Conditor alme siderum* show plainly enough his ability to make the rather awkward parallelism of the *faulx bourdon* suit his own needs; for this music, although it still retains the general effect of parallel motion, has real emotional feeling. Like all musicians of his generation, Dufay composed a number of settings for various parts of the Mass; and like all the others he did not hesitate to use as as a *cantus firmus* for these settings such popular ballads of the time as *Se la face ay pâle* or *L'homme armé*. But to his Gothic imagination there was nothing incongruous in this, and he was able to conceal these melodies in such a musical framework of decorative workmanship that we are hardly aware of their presence. In such a lovely motet as his *Alma redemptoris mater* he shows his preference for the upper voice, giving it the most important melodic burden in the Italian manner and treating the other parts as purely accompanying voices, to be either sung or played. In his effective setting of the Mass fragment *Gloria ad modum tubae*, he is both daring and vivid. While two vocal parts pursue their singing of the words *Gloria in excelsis*, one strictly copying the other a little way behind it, there is an accompaniment of two trumpets under the whole, quickening towards the end as if to urge on the voices in their melodic flight. This effective bit is an excellent example of the manner in which instruments were used with vocal music at the time.

Although he was connected with a religious establishment, Dufay by no means confined himself to the writing of sacred music. Indeed, his use of the secular forms of the period, particularly the *chanson française*, the

ycy sont ceulx z celles . qui ont
fait le psaultier .

Bibliothèque Arsenal

MINIATURE FROM A FIFTEENTH-CENTURY PSALTER

A concert of contemporary instrumental music at one of the courts is suggested by this miniature.

most favored form of aristocratic music, shows some of his most characteristic attributes. These *chansons* were the northern counterparts of the Italian secular forms and, like them, were governed in their structure by literary formulas. Dufay cultivated all the styles of these, writing *ballades, rondeaux,* and *virelais* with equal success. Characteristic are the melancholy *Le jour s'endort,* in which the top part cleverly reproduces in shortened note values the melody of the cantus, and his *Pourrai-je.*

The achievements of Dufay were all characteristic of music's general trends; in one of them he took the art a long way forward on the road leading to the modern devices of the sonata and the symphony. He was the first to use the unifying scheme of basing the different sections of his Mass settings on one melody, a *cantus firmus* that was sometimes secular, sometimes sacred in origin; by building all his sections around this one theme, he gave his work as a whole a musical unity that was comparable to the liturgical unity provided by the words.

The more one hears of the music of this Burgundian master, strange as it may seem at first to modern ears, the more one realizes that it was but part and parcel of the vivid life of its time. In writing of Dufay, a modern Dutch critic has said that it is necessary, if we are to appreciate his music to the full, to picture ourselves in the setting of the luxurious court of Philip the Good in Dijon, with its Gothic rooms covered with multicolored tapestries and filled with elaborate and infinitely varied costumes, the hats and headdresses original almost to the point of extravagance. Only then can we realize that Dufay's music, with its delicate melodic parts and slightly dissonant counterpoint, was just the type to please an aristocracy which prided itself on being fully abreast of the times, aesthetically eager to take up the newest and finest creations.

JOSQUIN DES PRÉS, CREATOR OF A UNIVERSAL EXPRESSION

One of Dufay's enthusiastic contemporaries speaks of him as having written the "first music worthy of being heard." Most modern listeners would probably reserve this honor, in so far as it implies emotional expressiveness in music, for Josquin des Prés, who lived from 1450 to 1521.

Midway between these masters stands Johannes Ockeghem, Dufay's principal pupil, who until recently has been regarded chiefly as a composer largely given over to the working out of ingenious technical problems — to the " cultivation of crabbed canons," as one writer has put it. Recent research and the publication of a great deal of his music, however, tend to absolve Ockeghem from such a stigma. He and his contemporaries did write some music that reminds us of tonal puzzles to be solved by the application of intricate rules; but they also wrote much that is beautiful and worthy to be classed with the best music of their time.

Ockeghem has been overshadowed by the figure of his great pupil, Josquin des Prés, who was, like Dufay, a man of international importance, having been born in the north but active for much of his life in Italy and France. He employed all the constructive skill and craftsmanship developed by his predecessors; but he was able to impart much more expressiveness to his music.

Like Beethoven, Josquin lived and wrote in two epochs: in him was united the Gothic ideal of art, the ability of creating a universal expression out of a multiplicity of individual elements, with that of the Renaissance, the idea of creating art for its own sake. He may be said to have been the first composer to express in music the ideals of the Renaissance. His imagination was able to seize on the spirit of a text, whether solemn or majestic, passionate or serious, secular or sacred, and to express it with something like definite exactness. Luther's remark on Josquin, who was his favorite composer, sums it up well: " He is the master of his notes: they have to do as he bids them; other composers have to do as the notes will."

Several of Josquin's best-known shorter works illustrate this. The familiar *Ave verum* is full of an expressive beauty wonderfully suited to the mystic quality of its text. A setting which he made of the fifteenth century hymn, *Ave coelorum Domina* — " Hail, thou Queen of Heaven, who fillest all earth and space with joy and givest us salvation " — is, on the other hand, light and lilting in character, with a charm that is quite captivating and exactly fits the words. And certainly there is nothing more moving in all music than the *Incarnatus* from the Credo of the Mass *Ave regina coelorum*. Filled with a deep brooding and a sense of mystery,

Courtesy of Communal Museum, Bruges

ADORATION OF THE MAGI by Hans Memling, Des Prés contemporary

it perfectly interprets the spirit of the words: "He was conceived . . . of the Virgin Mary and made man." This little gem has been well called the most moving thing in early music; like all the best works of Des Prés, it is suggestive of the peculiar beauty to be found in the paintings of his contemporary countryman, Memling. In the work of both these artists there is a simple charm of style and a decided intensity of expression that makes them stand out far above the general level of the period. Both happened to serve the Church, for the influence of that powerful factor in the development of art was still very potent; yet we can but feel that both men were essentially interested in making their art beautiful as art, developing its technical resource not merely for the joy of craftsmanship, but so that with it they could better increase its human expressiveness. Thus were they true forerunners of the Renaissance.

Altogether Des Prés wrote more than thirty Masses, besides many motets and secular chansons. In his own day his work was regarded as unique, and every composer of the period was affected by it.[18] There were a number of other men in both the Netherlands and German schools of this time who showed that they were likewise able to combine constructive skill and craftsmanship with profound expression. Among them were Pierre de la Rue, Fevin, Mouton, and Compère in France and the Netherlands; Finck, Isaak, and Senfl in Germany.

A great deal of the influence which these late Gothic composers exerted on one another came about through the invention of musical printing about this time: the work and style of one man was thus made immediately available to the others. Ottaviano dei Petrucci perfected a process of printing music from movable types in Venice in 1498, about fifty years after Gutenberg's first work; and three years later this printer issued a comprehensive collection of motets by Josquin and his contemporaries. Although Venice long remained the center for the printing of music, the invention rapidly spread over all Europe and had an incalculable effect on the development of the art.

THE GOTHIC PERIOD IN GENERAL

Thus the Gothic period, which began within the cloistered walls of the church, ended in a burst of rich and joyfully exuberant humanistic invention that was a fitting precursor of the Renaissance. Through it all is manifest the same spirit, a conscious joy in the seeking of elaboration and complexity, a richness and vitality, a love of brilliance that was manifested in the use of colors in the illuminating of manuscripts, in the glitter of gold and jewelry, in the richness of architectural ornament, in the sweep of melismatic melodies. For most of these medieval artists art was that which could be applied to those practices which contributed toward

[18] "Through all the restraint of Church ritual and the art methods of that early time, there speaks in the music of Josquin a warm sensitiveness, a capacity for urgent emotion, a mystic awe of worship. His Masses are noble with the nobility of the heart's depth. In his other works, the abstract, elevated style of earlier composers is broken up by his prism into a glowing play of many colors. Here is sadness, pain, and bitter revolt; and here is intimate love, tender, sympathetic, and playful jest. It is an unprecedented stride forward which occurs in Josquin's music; in him there is lived through an art development such as is found in no artist previously and very few since."

— Ambros; translated and quoted in Sollitt: *Dufay to Sweelinck* and produced the necessities of life, to use the expression of St. Thomas Aquinas; and for most of the period, the greatest necessity in life was man's religion. The usefulness of architecture was therefore that of providing a beautiful setting for the worship of God; the object of the figurative arts was to illustrate suitable religious teachings and history; and music, as it gradually took on sensuous charm and rich complexity as well as a touch of humanistic feeling, did so the better to exemplify the truth and beauty of religious experience.[19]

[19] A contemporary glimpse of the artistic outlook of this whole period may be had through the eyes of one of its greatest musical theorists, the Fleming Johannes de Verwere (Latinized, Tinctoris), who lived from 1446 to 1511 and was active at the Court of Ferdinand I in Naples. He says: "Before I began to write, I strove to equip myself with the necessary knowledge of the various things pertaining to music, partly through listening to others and partly through my own incessant work. However, I do not write to bring honor to myself, but for the benefit of others who wish to study music, and further in order not to bury the talent which God has bestowed upon me. And therefore I have now undertaken to write briefly about counterpoint — which is made up of well-sounding consonances — in God's honor and for the use of those who are striving for skill in this excellent art. Before I proceed now with the work, I will not hide the fact that I have studied what the ancient philosophers, such as Plato and Pythagoras, as well as their successors, Cicero, Macrobius, Boethius, and Isidore, believe concerning the harmony of the spheres. Since, however, I have found that they differ very much from each other in their teachings, I have turned from them to Aristotle and the more modern philosophers, and no one shall make me believe that musical consonances arise through movements of the heavenly bodies, for they can only be produced by means of terrestrial instruments. The ancient musicians, Plato, Pythagoras, Nicomachus, Aristoxenus, Archytas, Ptolemaeus, and many others, indeed including Boethius himself, dealt exclusively with the consonances, and yet we do not know at all how they arranged and classified them. And if I must now refer to that which I have seen and learned, I must confess that some old compositions of unknown composers have come into my hands, pieces that sound quite simple and tasteless, so that they rather disturb than please the ear. However, what surprises me especially is that only in the last forty years are there compositions which, in the judgment of the specialist, are worth listening to. Today, however, we have blossoming forth, quite apart from the large number of famous singers — whether it be on account of heavenly influences or particularly zealous studies — an almost unlimited number of composers, for example Johannes Ockeghem, Johannes Regis, Antonius Busnois, Firminus Caron, Guilelmus Faugues, and all can boast of having had as teachers the musicians who died recently, Johannes Dunstable, Egidius Binchois, and Guilelmus Dufay. Nearly all the works of these masters excel in pleasant sound; I never hear or look at their compositions without rejoicing in them or being instructed by them, and therefore I, too, in my own compositions, adhere entirely to the approved style."

— Translated by Coussemaker

THE INSTRUMENTS OF THE MIDDLE AGES AND THEIR MUSIC

TO the modern mind, the term *music* means sounds produced on instruments. How often we hear the distinction made, in describing the forces employed in some concert, between *musicians* and *singers!* Our present-day musical practices are so predominantly instrumental that popular opinion is inclined to designate musicians as those who are able to play some instrument or other, while vocalists are assigned to a sort of intermediate twilight zone of benevolent toleration, as being occasional necessary accessories to a well-established fact. Yet we have seen that the early developments in Western European music were almost entirely vocal in character; the modern predominance of instrumental style is a comparatively recent thing, dating from about the beginning of the eighteenth century.

Up to the sixteenth century instruments were used only as accompaniments for vocal music or interchangeably with it. Such an idea as letting instruments express their individuality or voice their independence was never even thought of. We shall see how the lute music of Spain and France was the first purely instrumental music ever written, in the sense that it showed the real possibilities of instruments as means for expressing musical ideas. A little later the organists succeeded in working out a style well suited to their instruments, and they in turn were followed by the writers for the clavichord and the harpsichord. During the seventeenth century a genuine type of orchestral music developed out of the court and popular dances of the time, and then followed the deluge of music for instruments, both solo and ensemble, that has continued up to the present.

OBSCURE ORIGINS

But what happened before this era of instrumental precedence set in? It is obvious enough that instruments have existed from the earliest periods of history, and there is plenty of evidence that man has always enjoyed himself playing them. Why was instrumental music, then, so slow in developing in comparison with that used by singers?

We have already speculated a bit as to the ways in which the various types of instruments may have been introduced to man; beyond this it is hardly necessary to go, aside from mentioning the fact that the historical records of all the early civilizations are full of references as to the ways by which man learned to use these instruments of music. The Greek account of the invention of their national instrument, the lyre, is characteristic: Mercury found one day a tortoise of which he took the shell, made holes in the opposite sides of it and passed cords through them. His instrument was thus complete, with one cord for each of the Muses.

We have also referred to the fact that when music first appeared in known history, among the Sumerians, it was produced by a wide variety of instruments: the harp, the lyre, the flute, the reed pipe, the drum, and even the trumpet. As we have seen, instrumental music played an important part in the great civilizations that grew up along the banks of the Nile and on the Assyrian plains of western Asia. We know a great deal about the instruments used by both the Greeks and the Romans; but there is little definite information as to just how and when the ancestors of the various instruments we use today were introduced. It is quite certain that at the beginning of the Christian era musical instruments of every kind were excluded from the services of the Church; yet one of the miniatures in the manuscript of an illustrated ninth-century Psalter, now in the library of the University of Utrecht, provides a lively picture of singers and players against a decorative background suggestive of a church mural, these figures being evidently engaged in providing music for Christian worship. Sometime between the third and the ninth century stringed, wind, and percussion instruments came into general use in the Church. The organ, which the early Christians had associated with their Roman persecutors, must early have been introduced into the Christian service, for it was in special favor with the Church during the ninth century if we are to judge by the important place given to it in this famous medieval miniature. It forms the central feature of the illustration from the Utrecht Psalter, with its two players greatly concerned over the wind supply that is being furnished by four hard-working blowers.

Bibliothèque Arsenal

MINIATURE FROM THE UTRECHT PSALTER (860 A.D.)

This miniature illustrates the One Hundred Fiftieth Psalm.

INSTRUMENTS IN MEDIEVAL PAINTING

Our most reliable source of information regarding the use of instruments during the Middle Ages is that left behind by many of the artists of this period. They show stringed instruments, such as lutes, guitars, mandolins, psalteries, harps, and *fiedels,* in amazing and confusing profusion; wind instruments, such as flutes, schalmeis, trumpets, and horns; percussive triangles, xylophones, and drums; and, in addition, organs and organistrums. These were played, if we are to trust the artists' power of observation, in any sort of combination, being used sometimes with and sometimes without singers.

When we find in a twelfth-century manuscript in the British Museum a depiction of Christ surrounded by twenty-four elders playing various instruments — organs, psalteries, oliphants (carved horns), *fiedels,* harps, and so on — it may mean nothing more than that these particular instruments happened to please the artist's fancy; but we are certain of the fact that they must have been used at the time.

Hans Memling, a Flemish painter who was the contemporary of Josquin des Prés, just at the beginning of the great choral era, has left us two pictures that he painted for the decoration of an organ case in a Spanish church. These contain depictions of the instruments that we may safely conclude to have been in common use at that time (1480).

DECORATION FOR AN ORGAN CASE BY MEMLING (1430–1495)
1 2 3 4 5

(1) *Psaltery* (Zither). Introduced into European music somewhere around the eleventh or twelfth century and much used as an accompanying instrument. When a keyboard was added, the psaltery became the harpsichord of Renaissance music.

(2) *Tromba marina* (Nun's fiddle). A peculiar, one-stringed instrument, whose thick, heavy string was played in its "harmonics" only, by touching its nodes rather than by stopping it in the ordinary way. Rather mercifully, now obsolete, for its tone was loud and brassy. Used up until the time of Mozart.

(3) *Lute*. Probably of Oriental origin, introduced into Europe around 300 A.D. With pear-shaped body and from 6 to 13 strings, this became one of the favorite Renaissance instruments and was made in many sizes, the four-stringed *chitarra* being the smallest and the *chitarrone* (often with 24 strings), the largest.

(4) *Trumpet*. A relic of the Roman military instruments, its clear piercing tone being of great effectiveness for outdoor use. Gradually it increased in length and folded on itself.

(5) *Bomhart*. The ancestor of our modern reed instruments, descended in turn from the Asiatic *schalmei*. This double-reed instrument was used

The fifteenth-century painter depicted contemporary instruments.

6 7 8 9 10

by both Greeks and Romans and came into new significance at the beginning of the second century A.D., when it developed into a complete family called *shawms* or *pommers*. This was the nucleus of the ensemble groups before the strings assumed their modern pre-eminence.

(6) *Busine*. The ancestor of our trombone and an instrument of great length. A " slide " was added about the end of the fourteenth century, and the altered instrument was called a *sackbut*.

(7) *Trumpet*.

(8) *Portative organ*. We first hear of the organ in the third century before Christ. It is the only instrument that shows a continuous development from very early times. These small organs, with one or two sets of reed pipes and capable of being carried about, were very popular for home use.

(9) *Harp*. One of the most widely diffused types of instruments, in use (as we have seen) from the earliest days of man's history.

(10) *Fiedel*. A representative of the generic bowed string family from which have descended our modern violin, viola, cello, and bass. Called by various names, this type of instrument was in wide use during medieval and Renaissance times.

SECULAR USES

There is likewise much iconographical evidence that the instrumental style was popular in the secular music of the Middle Ages, both for furnishing the accompaniments for such songs as the troubadours used and for the dances of the people. The great *Heidelberg Songscript*, for instance, by far the most valuable of the minnesinger manuscripts, shows that various forms of the *fiedel* family, psalteries, harps, shawms, drums, and even glockenspiels were in common use in Germany during the fourteenth century. And the charming miniatures of the thirteenth-century Codex of the time of Alfonso X in Spain in the library of the Escorial show that the same instruments were used there.

The music for the medieval dances was probably played on combinations of instruments that would sound to modern ears, to paraphrase Rabelais, " above the pitch, out of tune, and off the hinges." Strings and wind and brass instruments were all mixed together in a sort of neutral style of rendition. Later, in the sixteenth century, after Italian violinists had established the primacy of their instruments, a mixed orchestra of bowed instruments became the popular medium for the interpretation of dance music.

THE ORGAN

A word is necessary regarding the most popular instrument of the medieval period — the organ, the instrument that shares with the sixteenth-century lute and the viol the distinction of beginning what may be called the reign of free, independent instrumental music. The Romans used the organ in their theatrical spectacles, building it of considerable power and blowing it with compressed air. The Christians, once their antipathy was overcome, made the organ serve as an accompanimental instrument in their services from the fourth century on. In the great Gothic age of cathedral building, the organ played its part in the magnificent ritual of the Church, being at that time an instrument of several keyboards and pedals, with twenty or more sets of pipes. Amiens Cathedral, for example, had in 1429 an organ of three keyboards, with forty stops and a pedal keyboard. There were also small instruments, the *portatives* and *positives*, capable of being carried about, some of them being played and blown by the same person. The instrument was ready for its literature before composers had fully developed any idea of what we know as instrumental style. One would have thought that the variety of color to be obtained from even a few sets of pipes might have suggested more diversity in writing for the keyboard than it actually did. Except for differences in mechanical perfection, the instrument has remained practically unchanged from medieval to modern times.

The Germans, the French, and the English have been, until recent times, the most passionate lovers of the organ, and these nations have done a great deal toward achieving its perfection. Their organ lofts brought forth many of their finest musicians, both practical and theoretical, and from the sixteenth century on there gathered round the parish church and cathedral a busy, fruitful activity. This tradition of the organist as the center of music making dates back to the time of Henry de Saxonia, organist of the Chapter of Notre Dame, in the early fifteenth century. It has been for long one of the strongest and most beneficial influences in the musical life of the various nations — an influence now broken, alas, as individual music making is everywhere being weakened by the supplying of music from central founts, much in the manner of such everyday commodities as water and electricity. Neither organ nor organist is of great importance in the musical life of the present.

THE NATURE OF THE MUSIC

Wooldridge has remarked that the history of instrumental music during the Middle Ages is one of the most tantalizing problems before the student of musicology. There is, as we have just seen, sufficient evidence in the other arts that music at this time was a very lively business; the hosts of lutes, organs, flutes, and brass instruments displayed in the pictures and referred to in the literature — Chaucer alone has a long list of such references — must have had something played on them. But what? How fascinating it would be to know, for instance, what sort of music was used by that lively group depicted in the Utrecht Psalter

Photo Houvet

MUSIC (from Chartres Cathedral)

In these figures we see represented the two popular medieval traditions regarding the origin of music. There are countless examples in medieval art of representations of King David as the incarnation of music, striking bells which are suspended above him: thus the medieval artist follows the tradition of his time that Tubal, the descendant of Cain, invented music by striking resonant bodies with hammers of different weights. At Chartres, beneath each of the figures representing the arts, is seen the seated figure of a man engaged in writing or meditation; the sculptor has followed the other popular tradition of the time as to the origin of music. The figure is probably Pythagoras, to whom the "Greeks attributed this invention," in the words of a writer of the period.

and whether the evident anxiety of the pair of organists and the tremendous labor of the quartet of blowers was due to the faulty mechanisms of their instrument or to the heavy demands of the music used!

Undoubtedly most of the music employed by the players of this time was never written down but was transmitted from master to pupil, becoming somewhat modified and changed in the process. For there was not the same incentive or necessity for writing down the music played by a single instrument that there was for vocal music needed for a number of performers; and the processes of printing did not come into general use until somewhat later.

It was this unknown and unwritten music that formed the basis of the first complete compositions that enable us to see something tangible amidst the mists of the medieval instrumental music — the well-developed, completely independent instrumental works found in the fifteenth-century German organ books and the Italian and Spanish lute collections of the early sixteenth century. So the few fragments of the earlier time that have survived and have found their way to the various libraries of Europe are worth special attention.

The chief sources of information so far discovered are a fourteenth-century *chansonnier* now in the National Library in Paris, which contains a number of the *estampies* — dance tunes; the so-called *Robertsbridge Fragment* in the British Museum, containing six pieces for the organ, three of them purely instrumental, three transcriptions of motets, with the upper voices "colored" or varied in a simple way; and a few miscellaneous transcriptions of vocal works and dances. It may be said in general that these lamentably few survivors of what must have been a considerable literature show:

First, that the organ was used more during the Middle Ages than has been generally thought — it was Guillaume de Machaut who first called it the King of Instruments — and that much of the music played on it must have been vocal music taken bodily from the various settings of the Church's service. An early fifteenth-century *Liber organisatoris* defining the duties of the organist of Notre Dame, Paris, states specifically that part of such duty shall consist in playing on certain occasions the Kyrie, the Gloria, the Sequences, the Sanctus, and the Agnus Dei.

Second, that when the organists did play in what might be called instrumental style, there was very little difference between that music and what was written for the voices — perhaps the upper melodic voice might occasionally be given a little different treatment suggestive of what came to be known later as *variation*.

Third, that in the case of music played on the other instruments, either singly or in combination, no general distinction can be made. All the

The British Museum

A GOTHIC MANUSCRIPT SHOWING INSTRUMENTS OF THE PERIOD

Done by a French illuminator of the early fifteenth century, this shows a Tree of Jesse bearing various instruments in use at the time. In order from left to right these are:

Schalmei (ancestor of the oboe)
Trumpet
Busine (ancestor of the trumpet)
Harp
Rebec (ancestor of the violin)
Mandolin
Flute
Fiedel (viol)
Pair of drums
Lute
Psaltery

instruments used could seemingly be combined without regard to qualities of timbre or of sonority; and they were given the same sort of music the vocalists used. Any voice part was played by any instrument that had the requisite compass.

The Renaissance

CAUSES AND EFFECTS

By the grace of God light and dignity have been in my time restored to letters, and now I see therein such improvement that at present I would hardly be admitted to the first class of primary pupils, I who in my prime was not unjustly regarded as the wisest man of the age. . . . The whole world is full of savants, learned teachers, ample libraries, so that it seems to me that not even in the time of Plato, Cicero, or Papinian was there such faculty for study as one sees now. Now all studies are restored, the languages installed: Greek, without which it is shameful for man to call himself a scholar, Hebrew, Chaldean, Latin. These exist in elegant and exact printed books invented in my time by divine inspiration, just as, on the other hand, artillery was by diabolical suggestion.

— François Rabelais, 1532

VARIED INTERPRETATIONS

IF any proof is needed that history, like life itself, cannot be made to fit exactly into the separate periods into which we so carefully divide it in order to bring its events into something resembling order, it will be found in this epoch, the Renaissance. For this important period, stretching over an indefinite era — some historians include both the late fourteenth as well as the whole of the seventeenth century within its borders — presents a new aspect each time a different interpretation of it shifts our angle of approach. To Rabelais it was obviously important as a period devoted to the resurrection of classic learning, the development of scientific invention being a secondary and retroactive influence. To others the Renaissance has meant the period of man's renewal of interest in himself and the world he lives in, enabling him to look on life as a thing of joy in itself and not merely as a preparation for an existence to come. Many look on this epoch as one in which there took place a tremendous process of social, economic, national, and spiritual upheaval which found its most powerful outlet in the field of religious controversies. The pragmatist sees the Renaissance as the time when man began to become interested in the mechanical conception of life and in making his knowledge of natural forces conform to physical laws. Man established the fact that the earth is round and moves about the sun and so had the courage to sail in search of adventurous proof into regions before unknown. The historian of art thinks of this time as one in which man awoke to the fact that beauty was worth cultivating for its own sake and not merely as a means for serving other objects.

We have already tried to show all this, as well as the fact that the forces which reached their culminating peak of influence during the sixteenth century — the height of the Renaissance movement — had been gradually at work centuries before. So that while we speak of Renaissance ideals as having developed during the sixteenth century, in reality they were formed away back in the Middle Ages; and likewise they stretched far ahead into the future, giving promise of what was to come in the modern world in the way of literature, science, and political freedom. In the words of its most eloquent interpreter, the Renaissance was a process of transition, fusion, preparation, and fresh endeavor, which affected all phases of man's activities and which laid the foundation of much of our spiritual and mental existence today.

Among the many material explanations which are generally given for the Renaissance are such things as the fall of Constantinople to the Ottomans in 1453 and the consequent flight of her scholars to the West, bringing with them the knowledge and art of Greece and the ancient East; the voyages of discovery of Columbus, Da Gama, and Magellan; the inventions of the printing press and gunpowder. There is little question that all these were factors contributory to this great intellectual upheaval which came to a head in the sixteenth century; but, again, it is extremely difficult to distinguish between causes and effects. Did the invention by Gutenberg, for instance, or whoever it was that first used movable type for printing, come about through the increased curiosity of the Renais-

STATUE OF BARTOLOMMEO COLLEONI
General of the Venetian Republic (modeled by Verrocchio)

sance man and his desire to acquire more learning, or was it one of the reasons for his achieving individualism and liberation from the ideals of a past age? There is a simpler explanation than those usually advanced for this *volte-face* in man's thinking which, perhaps without adequate reason, and certainly without exact definiteness, we have learned to call the Renaissance.

As Sir Charles Oman has said in his interpretation of this much-discussed period (*The Sixteenth Century*), once wonder, mystery, and spiritual values are removed from the life of man, it is inevitable that he becomes a materialist. If he can no longer look on the teachings of established authority as implicitly valid and begins to realize that his own ideas and thoughts are of value and worthy of his attention, he becomes an individualist. And this is exactly what transpired in the fifteenth century. The preceding periods had created new mental outlooks for man; instead of having an essentially spiritual concept of life, a concept which demanded imaginative rather than intellectual thinking, there arose new incentives for living, such as the acquiring of worldly wisdom, material gains, and temporal power. The Renaissance tended to heap scorn on the rags of the medieval " romancer "; new dreamers arose, but their world was one of business and politics rather than of the spirit. Italy, through her fortunate geographical situation, became the center for all this tremendous activity and for the financier who made it possible. Various city-states, such as Florence and Venice, emerged and became rich and powerful; their *condottieri* of government and politics were the strong men of the time. It was a period of great vitality, strong forcefulness, hard business, and extreme cruelty; and in it arose many strange contradictions.

Freed from the leading strings of the Church, man began to look about him, peering into every corner of the universe and demanding an answer to all its riddles. In the process he spared neither prince nor pontiff and did not hesitate to question the authority of both State and Church. Learning, which in the Middle Ages had been considered as important only for churchmen, began to be cultivated for its own sake. The old classic writers had, of course, not been unknown to the school and church men of medieval Europe; but these dignitaries had read such authors as Aristotle, Pliny, Virgil, and the rest for what they could teach in the way of manners and morals. It was the discovery of the Renaissance, as Chambers has so well pointed out in *The History of Taste,* that these classics were beautiful as literature and not merely useful as moral teachings. To the medieval scholar, Cicero was a writer of essays having a moral leaning, and Virgil was famous because he was thought to have foretold the coming of Christ; to the men of the Renaissance, Cicero was again one of the great orators of all time, and Virgil was " crowned anew with the laurels of the poet." Thus was the pagan humanism of the classic civilizations revived and cultivated for its significance as a factor in human life and happiness. Beauty was worth cultivating for its own sake and not merely for what it could teach. And all the fine arts — architecture, painting, sculpture, literature, and music — were assiduously cultivated and fostered by the rich and enthusiastic patrons of the period.

Courtesy of the Bärenreiter Publishing Co.

GOTHIC FOURTEENTH-CENTURY PIETÀ

(From the Elisabethkirche in Marburg)

A PLASTIC ILLUSTRATION

No better example of this difference in spirit could possibly be found than that shown by the three pieces of sculpture illustrated here — the first from the fourteenth century, Gothic in every line and feature; the second from the transitional fifteenth century; the third from the sixteenth century, typically Renaissance in line and proportion. All have the same subject, even the same pose: Mary, the mother of Christ, holds in her lap the dead body of her Son, after its removal from the cross.

The unknown artist of the Gothic period has made his figures distressingly gaunt and angular — the body of Christ is elongated out of all proportion to the conception as a whole. But he has emphasized the religious significance of his work: the dead Christ is the Saviour of the world, who has suffered an agonizing death for its sins; and Mary is a mother sorrowing for her beloved Son and also for man in general.

Courtesy of the Johnson Art Collection, Philadelphia

FIFTEENTH–CENTURY PIETÀ by Benedetto da Majano

In Benedetto da Majano's treatment there is not so great a concern with religious ideas: the figures have more human grace and interest; they are not so symbolically powerful but for that reason are perhaps more "artistic." There can be felt here an interest in the individual, a concentration on the expression of the sculptor's conception that was not found in the earlier work. This is not to say, of course, that these had reached the state in which we find them in Michelangelo's rendering of the same subject a century later.

What an entirely different conception is Michelangelo's! The whole effect is one of graceful balance and lovely proportion, the representational significance being quite secondary. The dead body resting in the flowing luxuriance of the robe is that of a young Greek Adonis, beautiful in its lines and perfect in its modeling; the proportion of the figure of Mary is carefully arranged and nobly executed, but there is no intensity of suffering or shadow of agony in her beautiful classic countenance. Even her outstretched hand suggests the need of the sculptor for compositional

RENAISSANCE SIXTEENTH-CENTURY PIETÀ

By Michelangelo — in Rome

balance — the idea of art for art's sake — rather than any sense of emotional expressiveness. Here, modeled so that anyone who runs may read, is the real difference between the Middle Ages and the Renaissance: these sculptured figures are more eloquent than any words.

GAINS AND LOSSES

The sixteenth century frankly recognized art and learning as the outstanding symbols of its spirit of progress and expansion, of its joy in living and its faith in doing. Artists were cultivated, their worth recognized, and their talents encouraged as in no other period of the world's history. Simply to mention the names of some of the Renaissance painters, sculptors, and writers is sufficient to indicate their quality: Giotto, Fra Angelico, Botticelli, Raphael, Michelangelo, Ghiberti, Donatello, Desiderio, Boccaccio, Rabelais, Cervantes, Shakespeare.

The great fault of the Renaissance conception of art was the sharp distinction it drew between art and life, beauty and truth. In the Middle Ages there had been no difference between artisan and artist: painting and sculpture were not thought of as nobler than wood carving or cobbling, and the designers of some of the great cathedrals and churches built at the time were the artisans in actual charge of the work. During the Renaissance the artist began to be considered an individual apart: he had little connection with life itself and was principally interested in producing art, without much concern for its connection with the world outside himself. Poetry and painting, architecture and sculpture became *subjects* — to be discussed and studied and academically argued about. Quarrels between artists and scholars and humanists were common; the minutest details in form and grammar, technique and construction were discussed. In a word, learning and art became disassociated from life, something produced for the select and the elect. As Albert Guérard has said, the motto of the Renaissance scholar might well have been: "I am a Humanist, and therefore everything broadly human is distasteful to me."

Professor C. R. Morey, in his book on *Christian Art*, speaks of this point of view as one of the most important Renaissance influences and one which was not invented until the sixteenth century. Out of the ardent study of the antique past and the consideration of Greek and Roman ideals, we see arise a complete revolution in artistic thinking and practice — the emergence of the idea that there is such a thing as an absolute standard of perfection, capable of being intellectually achieved, and without any necessary relationship to practical experience. The discussion of what constitutes balance, unity, the relationship of the parts to the whole — in short an artistic ideal — occupied a great deal of the attention of the artists in the sixteenth-century Florentine Academy. And these problems were solved, not as we of today would expect, by a reference to nature, but by the interpretation of the philosophy and art of antiquity.

Literally speaking, art was largely a matter of mathematical correctness, for mathematics played an essential part in the selective principles of such great artists as Leonardo, Brunelleschi, Dürer, and Michelangelo. Alberti's comment is characteristic:

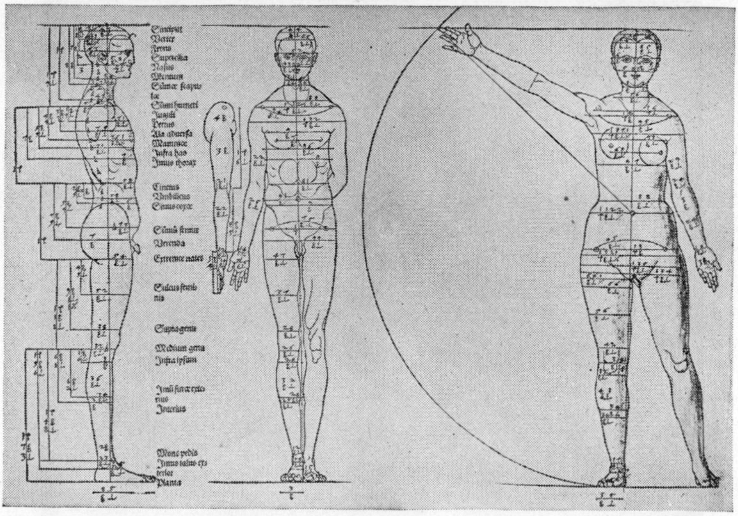

The British Museum

TWO PLATES FROM DÜRER'S "DE SYMMETRIA PARTIUM," 1532

"The several kinds of artists, though they go several ways to work, shall resemble nature and be as like the life as may be; for the bringing of which to effect, it is most evident, that by how much the more exquisitely they follow some determined rule or method, so much the fewer defects will they be guilty of, so much the fewer errors commit, and in all manner of accounts their works will succeed and come off with the greater advantage."

The systematic building up of the various features of the architectural style of the Renaissance, all of them borrowed from classic sources; the production of a great deal of statuary resembling antique models; the planning of the composition of a painting so as to use such a mathematical scheme as the so-called Hellenic triangle — all these are clear evidences of the predominance at that time of the academic point of view. Law and order, balance and proportion were all matters of taking thought; and such ideals, as Professor Morey points out, came to affect even political events, causing such things as the arbitrary partition of Italy by Charles V in 1530 and the centralization of France under the Bourbons, when, for the sake of unity and uniformity, city charters, feudal rights, and guild privileges were all abandoned.

MADONNA DEL ARPIE by A. del Sarto (1486–1531)
This is one of the most famous examples of the careful planning of a Renaissance painting according to the so-called "Hellenic triangle."

WHAT THE RENAISSANCE DID FOR MUSIC

Certain very definite achievements in music may be credited to the sixteenth century, each of them representative in a different way of these multifarious ideals of the Renaissance:

First. The continued development of the woven, contrapuntal style which had had its beginnings in the Gothic centuries to a point where it was capable of completely expressing both the humanized religious emotion of such composers as Palestrina and Victoria and the secularized sophistication of such pagan humanists as Monteverdi and Gesualdo.

Second. The cultivation of music for varied instruments and the development of styles well suited to their individual requirements. This change came about through the gradual secularization of art that occurred during the Renaissance, the mechanical conceptions which began to prevail at this time, and the passion for law and order then general. For the musical instrument is nothing but a mechanical tool, and its use necessarily imposes definite limitations and patterns according to which music can be put together.

Third. The complete breaking away from the traditions of the past in the development of harmony as we know it today, notably exemplified in the opera, a form which resulted from the desire of its originators to imitate the classic Greek drama and which led to the modern harmonic sense. By this we mean the conception of music as being the result of vertically grouped tones instead of the product of horizontally interwoven melodies. This harmonic way of thinking is based on natural physical laws, for the notes which go to make up a simple chord are the mechanically selected natural overtones of the note on which the chord is built. This was but another manifestation of the awakening Renaissance interest in the physical laws of nature.

THE RENAISSANCE IN ITALY

The Italy of the Renaissance, with its magnificent palaces, its classically ornamented buildings, its terraces and gorgeously decorated galleries, this enchanted the nobles of France, the lords of England, and the rich men of Spain and Germany.

—Albert Malet: *Nouvelle Histoire de France*

AN ARTIST OF THE RENAISSANCE

THE traveler to modern Italy is likely to look on Florence as the one city which most fully represents the life and spirit of the Renaissance. He is usually taken to the great building in the center of this lovely city, the Medici Palace, built by the most famous of all Florentine families, and is shown there, spread out on its walls, the colorful depictions of

Courtesy of The Museum of Fine Arts, Boston

LORENZO DE' MEDICI

"The representative man of his nation at a moment when political institutions were everywhere inclining to despotism, and when the spiritual life of the Italians found its noblest expression in art and literature."

— Attributed to Verrocchio

Renaissance life as painted by Gozzoli. There are three pictures supposed to represent the journey of the three kings to Bethlehem; in reality these are gorgeous depictions of life in Florence at the time of the Renaissance. They contain all the local celebrities of the period, decked out in their gay clothes, placed against a background studied from the natural surroundings of Florence, the figures being chosen from the Medicean circles. If Florence, as has so often been remarked, is the heart of the Renaissance, these Gozzoli pictures represent the heart of Florence and should be seen by all those who would understand this period in Italian history.

We have already described the changes in spirit brought about by the fourteenth and fifteenth centuries. Italy at that time was made up of a

JOURNEY OF THE THREE KINGS (First Episode) by Benozzo Gozzoli
The picture is founded on the historical meeting in Florence in 1439 of an Episcopal council for the uniting of the Eastern and Western churches. The figure of the third Magi is that of Lorenzo de' Medici.

number of small, entirely independent states, each of them maintaining a separate existence. In the north were the domains of Savoy, Milan, and Modena, all of them under the sovereignty of dukes. The rich and powerful republics of Genoa, Venice, and Florence were under the power of merchant princes of the Medici type — bankers and businessmen who had been powerful enough to seize the government of their cities and dictate their policies. In central Italy were the Papal States with their center at Rome; and in the south the kingdoms of Naples and Sicily struggled to hold their own against the more powerful republics to the north. It was the demand for splendor on the part of these various rulers, together with the attempt of each prince and tyrant to outdo the others in the magnificence of his local surroundings, that so markedly advanced the arts of architecture, painting, and sculpture at this time.

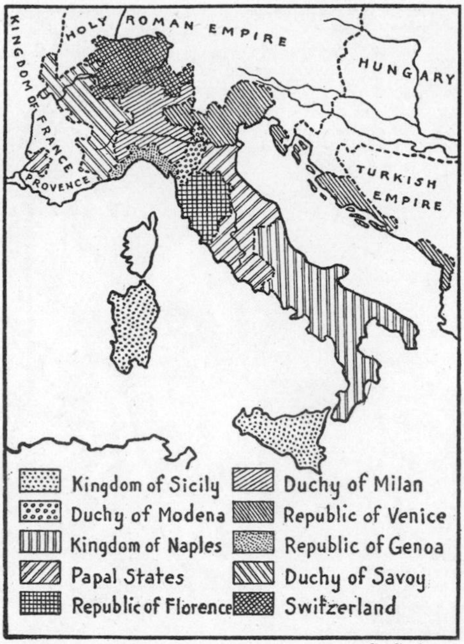

C. C. Stover

RENAISSANCE ITALY

The result was the production in enormous profusion of some of the most glowing pictures, monumental architecture, outstanding pieces of sculpture, and exciting literary works the world has ever seen in any one country or during a comparable period.

THE RESULTS IN MUSIC

In the art of music the effects were not so happy. After the striking works produced in Italy under the inspiration of the *Ars nova* — the *ballate, madrigals,* and *caccias* of which we have spoken — there came during the first part of the fifteenth century a decided slump in musical production and invention. Taught and stimulated by the Florentine writers of the *Ars nova,* the composers of England and the Netherlands took the leadership in music from Italy. When the Popes temporarily abandoned Rome in 1305 as the official residence of the Holy See and moved to Avignon in southern France, a number of local French and Netherlandish musicians were attracted there. When the primacy of Rome was later re-established, these artists came back with the Pope to Italy, with the result that during the fifteenth century the musical life of the country fell largely into the hands of foreigners. The educated and cultured classes in Italy preferred foreign music and musicians and left the cultivation of native music to the less educated, just as they did in Germany in the eighteenth century, in England during the nineteenth, and in America during the twentieth.

There is plenty of evidence, moreover, that this court and aristocratic music of fifteenth-century Italy was a vital force in the life of the time. A tour of any art gallery possessing a good collection of Italian pictures of this period will show this clearly, for the artists depicted again and again the use of musical instruments in all circles of Renaissance society. And we have the poems, together with some of the music used, from the carnivals and fetes produced by Lorenzo de' Medici: these seem to have been sung by all sorts of characters — devils, beggars, nuns, Jews, and so on — and give us a clear picture of the musical side of these elaborate entertainments. Most informing of all these sources of evidence are the records left behind by a number of contemporary writers, especially those of Teofilo Folengo, a nobleman of the period, one-time student at Bologna University and a brother of the Benedictine order; and Baldassare Castiglione, who in his famous *Il cortegiano* (*The Courtier*) depicted the ideal qualities of the gentlemen of the Renaissance.

FOLENGO ON RENAISSANCE MUSIC

In his *Maccheronei* Folengo describes many of the popular uses of music in sixteenth-century Italy; he tells of the instruments in general use, among them the shawm (oboe), the bagpipe, the rebec (the medieval ancestor of the violin), the harpsichord, and the lute. He describes the dancing in the country villages and gives the names of the dances used; he relates how his friends, while journeying about the country at night, used to sing songs in four parts, and describes in some detail the nature of the harmonies they used. The soprano or upper voice, he says, was the one to which most attention was paid, the tenor being the guide and ruler, with the alto supplying an ornamental counterpoint and the bass supporting and augmenting the whole — a description which would aptly fit a Bach chorale or a modern hymn tune. But these plain four-part harmonies used by the native Italians were in striking contrast to those used in medieval times, when the tenor was the voice which dominated the whole and the others were made to move about it. In a long panegyric on the beauties of music, Folengo names the principal composers then writing in Italy: most of them were from the north, the Netherlands or France; there was but one Italian, Costanza Festa.

MUSIC IN "IL CORTEGIANO"

Castiglione's description, written largely between 1514 and 1518, gives the attributes of the ideal courtier: he was to be a connoisseur of painting, an accomplished musician and scholar, something of a wit and a gallant, a soldier, and a statesman. Castiglione describes in detail the famous palace of the Duke of Urbino, one of the great art patrons of the era, and mentions especially the pictures and books and the collections of musical instruments. Music and dancing, according to his account, were the pastimes of every Italian court, and he is at great pains to show what may be expected of the gentleman musician; he must possess a good voice, sing well at sight, and be able to accompany himself on various solo instruments.

There is an amusing description of a lady — tradition says it was Beatrice Sforza — who, upon inviting one of her soldier friends to an evening of singing and dancing, received the reply that such frivolities were beneath his dignity; whereupon she told him in no uncertain terms that when he was not at war and the country had no need for his services, he had better oil himself and put himself away with his armor, for he could hardly become more rusty than he already was!

Later on, Castiglione employs some technical illustrations from the practices of dancing and music, showing that such allusions were readily understood by his readers. He speaks of the moving effect produced by the different styles of singing in his day and insists that there is no more "honorable or praiseworthy leisure than music as a rest from toil and a medicine for sick souls." This is especially true of the courts, he says, where, "apart from the refreshment that music brings to all, many things are done to give pleasure to the ladies, whose tender and gentle souls are easily penetrated by harmony and filled with sweetness. Therefore it is not surprising that both in ancient times and in those present, they should be inclined towards musicians and regard music as the most grateful food for the mind."

In this book of Castiglione's a reference of special interest to the historian is that in which he speaks of a solo performance which consisted of reciting poetry to the accompaniment of an instrument so as to heighten the beauty and increase the significance of the words. It has long been thought that this sort of *recitativo,* which later influenced the writers of opera, had been devised by Vincenzo Galilei, the father of the famous astronomer, in an attempt to imitate what he considered to have been the musical practices of the Greeks. But here is a reference showing that this usage was common long before Galilei's employment of it.

THE RENAISSANCE MADRIGAL AN ITALIAN DEVELOPMENT

The development of the sixteenth-century madrigal occurred in these musical circles described in such detail by Castiglione. In protest against the involved contrapuntal style of the foreigners from the Netherlands and France, the native musicians in Venice, Florence, and Rome had developed types of their own: the *frottola* (little fruit) and the *villanella,* forms which better suited their natural feeling and spirit. Although they were written for and sung by Venetian, Mantuan, and other prominent nobles of the period, they were strongly influenced by the popular dance music of the people. Little songs of graceful, amorous character, they were set for four parts (three of which were usually played on instruments) and had a prominent melody, which was placed in the soprano and followed closely the rhythm of the words to which it was set, the other parts forming a pseudo-polyphonic accompaniment. Bartolomeo Tromboncino, official musician at the important ducal court of Mantua, was the principal composer in these styles.

Courtesy of The National Gallery, London

FROTTOLE SINGERS by Roberti

It was the obviousness of these *frottole* and *villanelle* and their repetition of the same music for many verses that irked the taste of the cultured literary and musical circles of the time. In an attempt to develop these simple forms, the prominent composers of Italy, many of them church musicians from Flanders and the Netherlands, may be said to have founded the madrigal style. The new works which they developed may be looked upon as the logical elaborations of the *madrigali* of the fourteenth century (of which Landino's madrigal has been cited as an example), carried out in the manner of a period two centuries later.

Naturally these later works were richer in technical achievement because of the additional experiments which had taken place in the meantime. Using the free-flowing, melodious *frottole* as bases, composers like Willaert and Arcadelt brought to bear on them the full force of their invention and technical facility. The result was what we have come to know as the *madrigal*, a form that was originally cultivated by musicians alone and intended for an intimate circle of connoisseurs and amateurs such as gathered at the courts of the princes and in the academies of the time. It was not in any sense a *popular* form of expression: this must always be kept in mind when appraising it as an art form.

The new idea spread like wildfire in the aristocratic circles. Arcadelt's first madrigals appeared in 1539, and from that time onward for a number of years there poured out of Italy a steady stream of these works. That the same spirit animated the composers in the other countries may be seen from the table on page 305, which lists the names and dates of the principal madrigal composers in the various countries.

No better description of the characteristics of this form could be found than that given by the composer of some of the best English madrigals, Thomas Morley, in his book *A Plaine and Easie Introduction to Practicall Musicke*, written in 1597:

"The best kind of light musicke is termed Madrigal . . . a kind of musicke made upon songs and sonnets such as Petrarcha and manie Poets of our time have excelled in. . . . As for the musicke it is next unto the Motet the most artificial and to men of understanding the most delightful. If therefore you will compose in this kind you must possess yourself with an amorous humor . . . so that you must in your musicke be wavering like the wind, sometime wanton, sometime drooping, sometime grave and staide, otherwhile effeminat, you may maintaine points and revert them, use triplaes and shew the verie uttermost of your varietie, and the more varietie you shew, the better shal you please."

The sensuous delight experienced by those who wrote and sang these madrigals came through the clever manipulation of means rather than from any deep expression of feeling. From its very beginning, the form of the music was free enough as regards structure: the composer would take verses of any meter that appealed to him, usually a stanza of some five or six lines chosen from a lyric, pastoral, or amorous poem, although he sometimes set words of a grave character. Here are two examples:

"Cor mio, montre vi mire
Visibilmente mi transform' in voi;
E transformato poi
In solo sospir' l'anima spiro.

"O bellezza mortale!
O bellezza vitale!
Poi che si teste un core
Per ter inasce e per te nato morte."

"In pride of May
The fields are gay
The birds do sweetly sing;
So Nature would
That all things should
With joy begin the spring.

"Then, Lady dear,
Do not appear
In beauty like the spring;
I will dare say
The birds that day
More cheerfully will sing."

The composers dealt with such words line by line, even breaking them into phrases, thus dividing their work into definite sections. The parts were usually written for four or five voices, in both harmonic and contrapuntal style, the latter often of very involved and curious workmanship. The chief distinguishing mark of the madrigal was its marvelous rhythmic freedom, no matter how complicated the weaving of the various parts. Each voice followed the meter of the verse with absolute accuracy, sometimes in slow, sometimes in quick tempo, according to the dictates of the words. The prevailing atmosphere of the poem was caught in a sort of stylized musical paraphrase, and there were often curious attempts at what may be called word painting: "long festoons of thirds were woven about such expressions as 'chains of love'; sighs were translated by pauses and breaks in the melody; the idea of duration, of immobility, was expressed by the holding of a single voice, the others carrying their parts relentlessly. The voices rose on such words as 'heaven,' 'heights'; they fell on the words 'earth,' 'abyss,' 'hell.' The notes scattered in silvery groups round the words 'laughter,' 'joyous,' 'gay,' etc.; tears are expressed by audacious discords and unexpected modulations" (Prunières:

Monteverdi). There was a good deal of imitation between the various parts, but it was hardly ever strict in the sense of the mechanical canons and devices of the earlier church music. Everything was free, yet strongly conventional; expressive, yet severely intellectual; imaginative, yet purely artificial. The madrigals were indeed a happy compromise between pure, spontaneous utterance and calculated ingenuity. Considering their restricted field, no more perfect art form has been devised.[1]

Having invented the madrigal, the Italians achieved great distinction in writing it. All the outstanding composers, including even Palestrina, wrote in this style. As we might expect, there is a vocal flow, a directness of expression, and a dramatic intensity in these Italian madrigals that was never quite equaled by the composers of the other nations. The leading man was Luca Marenzio, who was attached to the papal chapel. Other names of the same period were Gastoldi and Donati. In the latter part of the sixteenth and the beginning years of the seventeenth century an increased dramatic force began to make itself felt in the Italian madrigals, using the harmonies and effects that were being developed in the contemporary new form of the *opera*. A number of composers arose whose works stand in strong contrast to the self-contained forms used earlier: Orazio Vecchi, principally known for his "madrigal comedy" *Amfiparnasso*, a full-fledged dramatic piece written in madrigal form, with all the speeches of the various characters given to single voices with contrapuntal accompaniment; Gesualdo, Prince of Venosa, who boldly introduced a chromaticism in his madrigals that is strangely prophetic of Wagner's dramatic use of the same device almost three hundred years later; and, above all the others, Claudio Monteverdi, one of the greatest geniuses in music.

In their audacious chromaticisms, their unexampled realization of moods, and their versatility of expression, Monteverdi's madrigals represent, to those who know them, the high-water mark of the whole movement. Almost all of them are beautiful (he wrote five books altogether),

[1] The composers of the earlier madrigals did not take a particularly subjective attitude toward emotional expression in music. Later on, the increasing humanistic tendencies of the period brought about an outlook described in the contemporary phrase as *Dare spirito vito alle parole*, "giving words living spirit by means of tone."

with a wonderfully sure feeling for effect. Especially noteworthy as representing in almost perfect form the ideals of the Renaissance is his madrigal sestina *Le lagrime d'amante al sepolcro dell' amata* (*Tears of a Lover at the Tomb of His Loved One*), a cycle of six madrigals set to a carefully constructed lot of texts based on arbitrarily designed rhyme schemes — the whole thing designed for the same sophisticated audiences as were the *Orlando Furioso* and the paintings of Botticelli.

SACRED MUSIC OF THE SIXTEENTH CENTURY

But the interest of this period was by no means confined to secular music. Perhaps in no other field did the flame of genius burn so brightly in this era of creative activity as it did in the field of sacred music. The three great names Palestrina, Di Lasso, and Victoria represent figures of pronounced individuality, their works being definitely the expression of their own personalities as well as the culmination of all the brilliant experiments of the Netherland composers; they may be said to be the real symbols of the Renaissance spirit in music. Palestrina (1525–1594) will always stand as the composer of an ideal type of church music, humanely harmonious and yet purged of all unnecessary objectiveness. Having completely mastered the technique of his predecessors in this field, he had a perfect means for the expression of those mystic, exalted ideals that are so unlike anything else in all music. While the other composers of the time were equally proficient in sacred and secular styles and wrote for both instruments and voices, Palestrina confined himself almost entirely to choral music. His manner of writing *a cappella* (that is, for voices, unaccompanied) is so pure and so completely adapted to the beauties of the human voice as a musical instrument, that it is impossible to think of his music as being rendered by any other medium. There is a peculiarly unearthly quality about it. Palestrina was not characteristic of the time in this aspect of his genius, and in listening to the melting transcience of his harmonies, we seem lifted completely beyond the confines of time and space.

It was Hegel who said that the one quality which art must possess if it is to endure is a certain vital energy in which there is present a quality of

Convent, PP. de l'Oratoire, Rome

PALESTRINA
Painting by an unknown sixteenth-century artist

universality not merely as law and maxim but operative in unison with the soul and emotions. It is just this that characterizes Palestrina's music. He seems close to us of the present, not merely because he did not hesitate to use freely that chordal, harmonic style to which our ears are accustomed, but largely because of his ability to express with unearthly beauty the universal longing for things beyond this earth that is one of the most compelling of human experiences. The environment in which he was reared and the peculiar circumstances of his life made it inevitable that most of his music should be written for the Church; and his great genius, coupled with the peculiar spiritual and expressive qualities of his music, make his works the perfect embodiment of that mystic adoration which is so essential a part of Catholic worship.

With Palestrina, as with his great Spanish contemporary, Victoria, the considerations of the Church had precedence over everything else. Embarrassed by schism and beset by heresies, the Catholic Church at this time was struggling to get her house in order and reform some of her most evident faults. In the historic series of gatherings which goes by the name of the Council of Trent (1545–1563), one of the topics for discussion was the reform of church music, which, the Church Fathers felt, had become far too elaborate and secular in style. The use of unsuitable and secular tunes as the basis for settings of the Mass scandalized the more serious-minded, and the general subordination of the text made for loss of religious significance. Palestrina's Masses — notably his *Missa Papae Marcelli* — were considered by the commission of cardinals as ideal models for illustrating the proper treatment of the liturgic text. He wrote ninety-three four-to-eight-part settings of this greatest of Christian rites, as well as over three hundred fifty motets. Most of these could well be used as choice examples of an effective, exalted church-music style, perfectly suited for giving voice to all the emotions of the faithful.

What, for instance, could be more expressive of the reproachful sorrow inherent in the words than Palestrina's setting of the *Improperia*, that part of the Church's liturgy which has been used in the Good Friday services of the Sistine Chapel for over three hundred years? Simple as this music is, uttering the bitter remonstrances of Christ to his people for having treated all his kindness with ingratitude, nothing which this composer ever did better illustrates his ability to feel keenly and express himself vividly. In direct antithesis to such brokenhearted sorrow is the spirit of exalted joy and rapt transports of the Christmas motet, *Hodie Christus natus est*. It is in such brief moments of revelation that Palestrina will best please the average listener, rather than in his longer and more involved compositions.

Yet if we would understand the intricate perfection of his music, a perfection which serves to heighten its ultimate effect, it is necessary that we study in detail such a work as his Mass *Assumpta est Maria,* one of the loveliest of all his settings. For only then can the magic of his manner of weaving themes throughout the whole fabric of the composition be fully realized. The comparison of this music with the tapestries of the period is one which cannot be resisted; for Palestrina's art is indeed the art of " some marvelous piece of needlework, of weblike pattern, gleaming with gold, silver, and soft colors, obeying the hidden law of design, but presenting an indefinite yet gorgeous whole. The ear, like the eye, endeavors to distinguish the course of one thread, only to be deflected by another. It receives no exact impression, but the vague perception it conveys to the brain is of an agreeable, harmonious whole, rising to sensations of acute pleasure. This simile, however, fails in one important aspect: no general perception of color could affect the mind so powerfully as sound or produce the same moral effect. Palestrina's music penetrates the depth of the soul, and its selflessness widens the conception of things appertaining to the spirit. More, far more than a new formula of art, it was founded on antiquity and built up on international inspiration " (Pyne: *Palestrina, His Life and Times*).

MUSIC IN VENICE

In addition to Florence and Rome, which after the restoration of the papal power became the center of the school which culminated in Palestrina, there were other Italian cities that were active in this great cultural revolution. Important among these was Venice, isolated among her salt marshes in splendid grandeur at the head of the Adriatic, her people thriving on their profitable trade with the East, her artists full of a colorful zest for life, the extravagance and love of display of her rulers household words throughout the world then known. The painting, architecture, and music that were produced in Venice during the Renaissance were a result of the love of color which so strongly predominated in Eastern art, a joy of life and love of display engendered by the luxurious gaiety and extravagance of her existence, combined with the intellectual and spiritual ideals characteristic of the Florentine and Sienese artists. Important painters who reflected this Venetian way of thinking

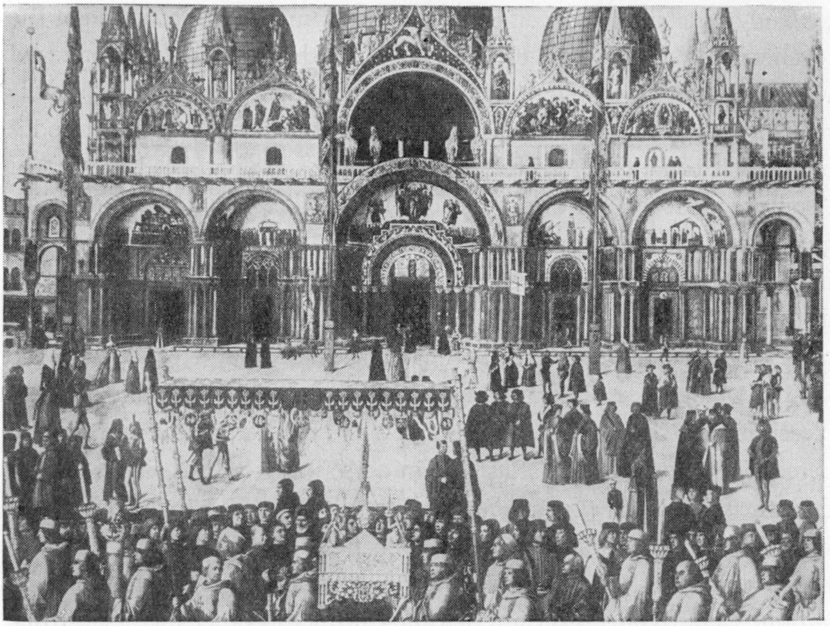

A RENAISSANCE FESTIVAL PROCESSION IN THE PIAZZA OF ST. MARK

The scene was painted by Giovanni Bellini (1426?–1516).

and living were Giovanni Bellini, Giorgione, and Titian. The rich colors, marvelous texture, strong contrasts, warm emotion, and gorgeous splendor of the works of these men may be said to be characteristically Venetian. So is the church of Santa Maria della Salute, with its sumptuous design and richly varied ornament, its superb location on the Grand Canal adding to its impressive effect. The two great names in Venetian music of this time are Andrea and Giovanni Gabrieli, uncle and nephew, both of them organists of the Church of St. Mark's, which is one of the most characteristically Venetian of all the churches of the city, a colorful symbol of the close bond between her religious and civil life. The music of Giovanni Gabrieli mirrors the luxuriance of the Venice of the doges as completely as do the paintings of Giorgione or Titian: it is rich and brilliant, yet deep and profound. Although most of it was written for use in the services of the church, it is nevertheless full of glowing hues and ardent warmth.

GIORGIONE'S "CONCERT" (c. 1510)
Here is shown one of the most famous Venetian Renaissance paintings.

In St. Mark's there happened to be two organ lofts, one in each of the side transepts, and this circumstance was of great importance in the music of the Gabrielis, for it allowed the use of two groups of musicians facing each other across a large, resonant church; and it led to the writing of music, both vocal and instrumental, that was based on combinations of differently constituted choirs of vocalists and instrumentalists. There is a great deal of antiphonal questioning and answering in this Venetian music, with opportunities for achieving that peculiar timbre which comes from music reverberating in the wide spaces of a cathedral. The Venetians are among the earliest composers to write specifically for instruments. While their general style was that of the vocal contrapuntal music of the time, and while it was the custom to play such things on instruments long before Giovanni Gabrieli's time, he was the first to indicate definitely the instruments he wished to be used in playing his compositions and to give specific directions for their interpretation.

Representative of this powerful Venetian style is the younger Gabrieli's *Sonata pian e forte* from his *Sacrae symphoniae* of 1597. This work for the first time in the history of music indicates in its score the control of tonal intensities; it is written for two "choirs," one of brass and the other of strings and brass. Dr. Sachs remarks on its lack of design, there being in it no definite melodies or carefully planned tonal web. Rather there is contrast of tone color, the balanced and contrasted ensemble of strings and brasses giving sharp and brilliant effects alternating with those that are heavy and more somber. Even in such compositions as his organ *ricercari* (a form which Gabrieli transmuted into that which we know as the *fugue*), the insistence is always on color rather than on design. A small number of pure and contrasting qualities of organ tone is used, instead of making any attempt to indulge in the overwhelming power and dazzling brilliance which later came to be definitely associated with this instrument.

We are here present at another of those progressive liberations of style that make the study of musical history interesting, if we grasp what these liberations meant to the men of their generation, and do not try to judge them by the standards of the present. We should not form the habit of judging the music of the past by the standards of today; for if we do this, much of this early music is bound to sound dull to us. We should try to use imagination and put ourselves back into the time when such music was new and exciting; we should forget all about modern music when we listen to such things as these *ricercari* of Gabrieli; rather we should try to recapture some sense of the amazement that the flying fingers and thundering pipes must have caused in those days, an amazement which probably gave utterance to the familiar words: "Well, well, whatever is the world coming to; I wonder what we shall be hearing next?"

But it is Monteverdi who stands as the greatest man of this epoch, an important link between the old and new styles of the sixteenth and seventeenth centuries; for not only did he carry the polyphonic vocal style to great heights, but he also proved himself to be the father of modern dramatic and orchestral music. He is the first composer to whom those whose experience with music has been limited to the works of the eighteenth and nineteenth centuries can listen with real pleasure and understanding. His music, in whatever style it was written, was essentially dramatic, romantic, and adventurous. Realizing that no one could go further than he had in the madrigalian style, he made, as Prunières has said, a complete *volte-face* and laid hands on the aristocratic spectacle that had been invented and laboriously carried out by his Florentine contemporaries, turning this humanistic plaything into the modern music drama. Of this, more in another chapter.

THE RENAISSANCE IN FRANCE AND THE NETHERLANDS

THE RISE OF FRANCE AS A WORLD POWER

AFTER long years of impoverishment brought on by wars with England and anarchy within her own borders, France began in the fifteenth century to try to establish herself as the dominant power of Europe. Louis XI, a royal despot if there ever was one, ruled from 1461 to 1483. In what had formerly been a decrepit monarchy he dealt a final blow to the system of medieval feudalism and, by stringent administrative reforms and an active policy of territorial acquisition, was able to put his country in condition for foreign conquests. His son, Charles VIII, by marrying Anne of Brittany and thus adding this duchy to the French Empire, continued this policy. He was the first to invade Italy, making a temporary conquest of Naples at just about the time Columbus set forth on his memorable voyage of discovery.

Charles died without leaving any male heirs and was succeeded by a distant relative of another branch of the House of Valois — Louis XII, known as *le père du peuple*. In alliance with the Spaniards, who in the sixteenth century were the great people of Europe, Louis conquered Milan and Naples, and then, in league with other powers, tried to deprive the Venetians of their holdings on the mainland of Italy. The final result of all this war and intrigue was the expulsion of the French from the Italian peninsula in 1512. This, however, did not end Italy's troubles.

Louis was succeeded by his brilliant cousin, Francis I. Reigning from 1515 to 1547, this gentleman king held the throne during the great years of the Renaissance and proved himself an ideal man for the time. He patronized all the arts, and it is pleasant to record that literature, music, sculpture, and architecture flourished mightily during his reign. The long series of Italian campaigns of his predecessors, together with his own attempts to recover and hold parts of Italy, brought France into direct and vital contact with the ideals of the Renaissance. It was Francis who made attempts to transport bodily some of the most famous of the Italian artists, bringing home with him Leonardo da Vinci, who died soon afterwards, Andrea del Sarto, who did not stay long, and others.

THE INFLUENCE OF ITALY

Long before this, however, as early as the reign of Louis VIII, Italian sculptors had come to France and had made a deep impression there. The Gothic figures of the French *imagiers* gradually forsook their peculiarities of style and Christian feeling and took on more of that ideal cast of beauty that was fostered by the Florentine study of the antique. Nowhere can this be seen so clearly as in the Church of St. Denis, Paris, already mentioned as one of the earliest Gothic structures in France and a sort of French Westminster Abbey, containing, as it does, the tombs of French kings and notables until almost the time of the Bourbons. In walking through the array of tombs in this old abbey church, we pass gradually from the Gothic world to that of the Renaissance; and this change in form corresponds to the change in thought between these two periods. The sculptors of the Middle Ages have fixed the royal figures in humble, recumbent positions, showing them pitiable in death, and surrounding them with figures of sinister *pleurants*, mourners over the royal decease. In the tombs of the sixteenth-century kings, Louis XII and Francis I, the figures are not in the least suggestive of death, but of glory and power; these beautiful sculptured figures, modeled after classic sources and placed against a background recording the exploits of the king, are not Christian but pagan. Theirs is no temporary tomb, where man awaits his final resurrection in faith and

Archives Photographiques

THE RENAISSANCE TOMB OF FRANCIS I IN THE CHURCH OF ST. DENIS, PARIS

Compare this tomb with the Gothic tomb of Philippe Pot, page 194.

hope; rather is it a triumphant monument assuring him of worldly immortality after his brief and brilliant career on earth.

So, too, with architecture and painting. The traveling artists who were so numerous in the early days of the Renaissance, the Italians invited to France by private individuals, the French artists who returned home from Italy with their luggage full of copies of Italian art — all these gradually effected such a penetration of Italian methods into northern art as to revolutionize European tastes completely. This, of course, could not have been done had not the Renaissance mind outgrown the conceptions of the Gothic era. Architects had invented the Gothic

Archives Photographiques

A FRENCH RENAISSANCE CHÂTEAU OF THE SIXTEENTH CENTURY

cathedral to suit the religious requirements of that time; the feudal castles and fortresses were built to fit the necessities of a warlike period; and the artists of the thirteenth century had a definite system of iconography by which they expressed concurrent religious beliefs. But when Christian faith had diminished so that no longer huge communal churches were necessary; when monarchical France made feudal fortresses no longer compulsory, men turned their architectonic energies into building great houses in the Italian Renaissance style, their chief aim being the creation of beauty. And the sixteenth-century painter responded to the collective taste of his time by using humanistic and classic subjects rather than religious ones, and by painting in a way that showed that beauty was worthy of cultivation in itself rather than merely as a universal language for the propagation of the faith.

Thus two styles, one the result of long tradition, the other introduced through the charm of a foreign novelty that happened to fit well the natural aptitude of the country, both benefiting by a return of national energy, flourished in France from the time of Charles VIII to that of Henry II — roughly from the latter fifteenth to the middle sixteenth century. But the new style, founded on a wider and more humane base, permeated by a spirit of law and order, gradually triumphed: rejecting all ideas of compromise, it completely eliminated the other style — sometimes with unfortunate results — severing forever the ties which had so long bound a united Christian people and its universal religious art.

MUSIC FOLLOWS THE OTHER ARTS

During this period of transition, music followed the same tendencies. We have considered the outstanding characteristics of Gothic music — the elaborate craftsmanship, the perfection of a style consisting of an ingenious and skillful weaving together of various voices, resulting in a sort of universal expression of personal concepts, and the definitely religious quality which closely associated it with the services of the Church.

Gradually there came out of Italy other ideals which led eventually to the complete secularization of the art: the substitution of instruments for voices in one or more of the woven parts; the compression into an accompaniment, capable of being played on a single lute, of the polyphonic parts of the older style (Italian lutenists had published such arrangements as early as 1508); the consequent shifting of the relationship between the parts, with the constant development of the idea of a chief melody and accompanying voices; and the gradual tendency to use more and more a chordal rather than a purely contrapuntal type of writing. This penetration of Renaissance ideals can be seen very clearly in the music of France, but it affected that of other countries as well.

During the later Middle Ages in France there developed a peculiarly nationalistic type of expression, the *chanson*, which may be said in general to correspond with the Italian madrigal. The earliest examples we have of the chanson, by Busnois and De la Rue, are as simple in structure as the Italian *frottola*, and even clearer and more concise in expression. Gradually, as the Italian influence made itself more and more felt, these compositions became more elaborate, with involved counterpoint, and often bristled with the artificial devices of the artistry of the time. The chanson of the middle of the sixteenth century was a highly sophisticated composition, set to various kinds of texts, mostly amatory. Referred to by a contemporary writer as *lascives, sales, et impudiques*, and by a modern writer as "airy, sprightly, and full of pretty babblings," these compositions are truly French in nature, having fresh, lively melodies, pleasing wit, spirited words, and piquant rhythms.

As might be expected, the chansons were mostly composed according to the old tradition of writing in several simultaneous melodic lines, each of them requiring an individual interpreter. They often showed a peculiar tendency toward tonal painting — a tendency that was later to reappear in a more elaborate form in French music. Clément Jannequin, best-known composer of the chanson, wrote several celebrated program pieces, notably the *Bataille de Marignan* (descriptive of the defeat of the Swiss by Francis I in 1515, and ending realistically with a Swiss cry of defeat, in dialect: "Everything is lost, by God!"); the *Cris de Paris*, depicting the street noises of the time; *La chasse*, in which we are present at a court hunt; and, best of all, *Le chant des oiseaux*, a piquant description of a bird concert, with naïve references to the amorous customs of the period.

Other well-known writers of the chanson were Claudin de Sermisy (his lovely *En entrant en ung Jardin* is characteristic), Claude le Jeune (*Revoici venir du printemps*), Guillaume Costeley (*Je voy des glissantes eaux*), and Charles Tessier (*Au joli bois*).

Unquestionably there were various ways of performing these works. The usual one was to assign each part to an individual voice, the whole composition thus being sung; but often some of the parts were given to instruments, the resulting effect being partly vocal and partly instrumental. We have evidence that the chansons were often played by instruments alone, with a result that must have been pleasing, for their general style is quite neutral and not dictated by any considerations of voice or instruments, either bowed or wind. Musical archaeologists have discovered in old libraries pages of chanson music with the first words of a poem at their head but with no words under the staves, thus showing that they were copies made for purely instrumental use with no thought

Courtesy of Musée Carnavalet

"GUINGUETTE" AT THE TIME OF FRANCIS I

The setting is in the environs of the Quai St. Bernard, Paris.

of vocal execution. The fifteenth-century Flemish composer Obrecht's gay chanson *Tsat een meskin* is an example of such a case.

The earlier chansons were largely polyphonic in nature, each voice being of equal importance and having individual interest. Later on, affected by the Renaissance ideal, we find many in which this purely polyphonic interest has been displaced by a melody in one of the parts, with the others serving a subordinate role. Evidently this was the sort of thing that was favored at the height of the French Renaissance under Francis I. Claudin's *En entrant en ung Jardin* was certainly sung this way, as were most of the works in Pierre Attaignant's *Trente-cinq livres contenant chansons,* published in Paris from 1538 to 1549. There is a charming picture in the Musée Carnavalet showing a *compagnie* of this period gathered in the country just outside Paris. We can imagine the three musicians of this picture playing and singing Claudin's happy song, the vocalist supplying the melody and indicating the rhythm with his hand for his accompanists, who play the other parts on flute and lute.

Such a development of new senses of vocal and instrumental relationships, as well as those between preponderant and subordinate voices, led directly to our modern ideals of harmonic music. Another factor that greatly heightened this development was the reduction of the accompaniment of these chansons to a form suitable for playing on the lute, a great number of such arrangements being made and printed in France. The first collection was issued by the celebrated printer Attaignant, who seems to have had exclusive possession of the field, in 1529; he called it *Très brève et familière introduction,* and it contained a large number of arrangements of chansons in the manner of the Italian lutenists. Twenty-five years later there appeared another under the title of *Hortes Musarum,* and again in 1571 Adrian le Roy and Robert Ballard, *imprimeurs du Roy,* issued a third. Thus in a period in which the printing of music was by no means common, there were issued in France within less than fifty years three great collections of these lute songs. With real melodies of a rich character and definitely subordinated accompanimental parts, they did much to tune man's ear to the harmonic sense of tone to which it later became so accustomed. The French musician of the later sixteenth century was thus as strong an influence in disseminating the ideals of the Italian Renaissance as were his brother artists, the sculptors, the painters, and the architects.

RELIGIOUS MUSIC OF THE RENAISSANCE

Sixteenth-century France, as anyone who knows the history of this brilliant country will remember, was far from being united in matters of religion. The latter half of this hundred years was given over to a cruel series of wars between Protestants and Catholics, in which the leaders of both parties, as well as two of the French kings, fell by the hands of assassins. It was a generation of intolerance of opinion and barbarity of action, each side striving to force its beliefs on the country as a whole; and yet this religious strife had a stimulating effect on music.

During the first part of the century the music of the established church was able to resist most of the infiltrations that had so affected the character of the chanson and the madrigal. Jean Mouton (*d.* 1522), a pupil of Josquin des Prés's, was the outstanding composer of Catholic church music at this time. He was a singer in the royal chapel choirs of both Louis XII and Francis I and was a composer who developed a virtuoso contrapuntal technique while maintaining a natural gift for simple and grand effects.

During the second half of the century, Orlando di Lasso (or Orlandus Lassus) came into his own as a composer. Born in Mons about 1530, he traveled over all civilized Europe during the course of his life and so learned to adapt himself quickly and easily to different national styles. In spite of his fluency and facility in writing, he was a composer of definite individuality, one whose brilliant achievements in both sacred and secular music are too little known. In no other composer is the influence of the Renaissance so clearly evident. He took the old Josquinian counterpoint as the basis for his writing, and on this he imposed the decorativeness of the Italian madrigal style together with its dramatic chromaticism, mixing with them a dash of Venetian passion and color. The result is irresistible. He was able to achieve a happy apposition of polyphonic and homophonic effects and expressed his strong religious beliefs with a joyous exaltation and an élan that is robust and human in comparison with the mysticism of his contemporary, Palestrina.[2] The effect of Di Lasso's music is powerful and inevitable, brilliant to the last degree; its imagination is above all the other writing of the time. If, as is so often done, we are to liken Palestrina to the tranquil Raphael, Di Lasso must be compared to Michelangelo in his heroic strength and variety of expression.

[2] Lehman Engel has made the following pertinent comparison between these two great men: "Palestrina's work was closely associated in every sense with the past, while Lassus's was greatly affected by his own present. Through it he reached out toward the future. His works are far more varied and cover a wider range than do Palestrina's, and his aesthetic and emotional approach is personal and warm in contradistinction to Palestrina's, which is remote and impersonal. Lassus often wrote 'light' music intended purely as entertainment and often wrote to texts which were bawdy and even pornographic. He set out to succeed in a world in which there was only superlative success or obscure servitude. His success was a complete one in competition with some genius and much near-genius. Viewed today Lassus's work bears the stamp of inspired greatness, and his quality of workmanship is unexcelled by any later master. He combined the skill of the Netherland craftsman with the more profound and deeper personal sentiment of the rising German art. One wonders whether the overwhelming success of his life in art was not due to rather than in spite of the unceasing hectic demands made on his talents."

© *August Reusch, Munich*

THE BAVARIAN COURT CAPELLA UNDER THE DIRECTION OF DI LASSO

(From Hans Mielich Kodex in the Staatsbibliothek, Munich)

Di Lasso sits at the clavier; around him are the players on viol and gamba, lute, zinke, bassoon, and trombone; the singers make up the background.

There are over five hundred motets for 2, 3, 4, 5, 6, 7, 8, 10, and even 12 voices in his great collection *Magnum opus musicam*. Perhaps the best example of his poetic lively style of motet writing is his *Alme Deus*, written originally to secular words. He wrote also a number of Masses and settings of psalms. Especially effective are his settings of the seven so-called "Penitential Psalms," filled as they are with the deep anguish of his soul.

Mention should be made also of Di Lasso's compatriot, Philippe de Monte (c. 1521–1603), whose work likewise showed the strong influence of his Italian predecessors. Some 38 of his Masses and 318 of his motets have come down to us. In them are again found the ideals of the earlier Flemish contrapuntal masters combined with the puissant uses of color, dramatic effectiveness, and melodic charm of the Italian writers. He was Kapellmeister to the emperor Maximilian from 1568.

FRENCH REFORMATION MUSIC

A peculiar outgrowth of the Renaissance influence in France was the production of Protestant religious music which followed the break with the established church. We shall see in our discussion of the Renaissance in Germany what a tremendous influence the Reformation had on the development of music there: Luther gave a great deal of time and attention to its cultivation for his new ritual. But the Protestant leaders in the other countries were not so artistically minded. Zwingli excluded music entirely from the services of his church, and Calvin limited it to the unisonal singing of psalms, thus, as he believed, emulating the ancient Hebrews in excluding all secular and human elements from the worship of the church. In France, where the Calvinistic movement gained considerable headway, two poets of the time — which in general was an exceedingly prolific one for French poetry — furnished metrical translations for these psalm settings favored by the Genevan reformer: Clément Marot, previously given to writings of a decidedly frivolous nature, and Théodore Béza. The musical settings were largely the work of Claude Goudimel, who during his early life had set many a Catholic Mass to music (but who gave up his life in defense of his new faith in the massacres following St. Bartholomew), as well as of Claude le Jeune, who likewise wrote a great deal of secular music.

For the actual church service these men wrote an adaptation of what was known as the *chanson mesurée,* secular songs composed according to the strict requirements of verse, their syllables being sung simultaneously by all voices. There resulted a simple sort of four-part chordal harmony, built around a melody placed in the tenor. Except for this latter fact, these Huguenot psalm settings sound very familiar to modern ears, their syllabic treatment of the words and general style being that known to generations of singers of Anglican hymns or Presbyterian psalms. These simple settings were the only ones allowed by Calvin in his church, and Goudimel and Le Jeune composed a great number of them, some of which are still to be found in our hymn books.

But even Calvinism could not entirely discourage the love of artistry that had been fostered by the current ideals of the *cinquecento.* The French Protestant composers realized that it was not enough to write music for the faithful in order to direct their minds and thoughts toward higher things. It was necessary also to furnish music which could be sung with some of the aesthetic pleasure and sense of satisfaction that was to be derived from the other arts of the time. And so they produced another type of music, using a much more elaborate style and requiring greater skill in its execution—music not to be sung in church, as Goudimel said, but for the praise of God in the home. These richly polyphonic settings seem to take on an added impulse of freedom and suggestion of artistry from their increased movement. One or another of the parts takes little flights around the voice which holds the melody. Nothing is overdone; and all is charming, simple, and seemly, as befitted the spirit of Calvinistic reform.

INSTRUMENTAL MUSIC AND DANCES

The lute music of the sixteenth century may be regarded as the first really independent instrumental music. We have observed that this instrument was very popular during this period, and it was natural that an independent type of music was developed for it alone. This was done, as we shall see, in Spain; but its use spread rapidly to every country. All Europe during the sixteenth century seemed seized with a desire to play the lute. France, with its cultivation of all the luxuries of the world, was no exception, and its lute music possesses a delicate refinement that sets it off from the rest. Attaignant published (1529) the first book of lute music, *Dix-huit basses danses,* and this was quickly followed by others, notably by John Baptiste Besard's *Thesaurus harmonicus,* containing original and arranged works by all the great lutenists of the time. This lute style reached its culmination in France in the seventeenth century, when Gaultier published a series of pieces which exhausted the instrument's possibilities, combining all the rhythmic and melodic effects of which it was capable.

In 1589 a priest in Langres, writing under the pseudonym of Thoinot Arbeau, published a celebrated treatise on dancing, the *Orchésographie,* which gave not only the description of the various steps then in vogue but likewise a notation of the different tunes to which they were danced. Many of these tunes were played on the lute, others on various sorts of brass, wood-wind, and string instruments. About the middle of the century a troupe of Italian violinists came to Paris and established themselves in the favor of the French court; this troupe came to be known later as the *vingt-quatre violons du Roy,* the most famous dance band in history. From that time, all the court dance music was played by orchestras of bowed instruments, another instance of the Italian shaping of French taste.

The most popular of these sixteenth-century dances [3] seems to have been the *basse danse,*[4] its graceful steps being danced by two people.

[3] At the present time it would seem that the oldest printed book on the dance is the copy of an anonymous treatise, *L'art et instruction de bien danser basse danse* (now in possession of the Royal College of Physicians, London), originally published by Michel Toulouze at the sign of *La corne du cerf,* Paris, probably as early as 1496. This is now issued in a modern reprint, as is another pamphlet of about the same time, *The manner of dancing of bace dances after the use of France and other places, translated out of the French in English* by Robert Coplande, the original of which is in the Bodleian Library. Both of these are of fascinating interest to students of early music and dances.

[4] The *basse danse* is supposed to owe its name to the gliding motion of the feet that was used, in contrast to the dances in which the feet were lifted from the ground. The name may suggest nothing more than its lowly origin.

Always associated with this was the *tordion,* an " after-dance " contrasting in rhythm and character and marked by leaping jumps. Another popular dance was the pavan, with its pendant galliard. " The steps of the pavan and the *basse danse* are slow and heavy, those of the galliard and *tordion,* light and graceful," says the *Orchésographie.* The *branles* were lively round dances executed by a whole ring of dancers, circling first one way around, and then the other, and gradually accelerating in speed — whence the possible derivation of our word *brawl,* which suggests the probable final culmination!

On account of her comparative later insignificance in the world of creative music, we are likely to forget France's important and significant place in the early development of the art. During the sixteenth and seventeenth centuries she was especially active in cultivating that which came to her from her meridional neighbor, impressing this music with the peculiar grace and charm — that clarity and balance that we have come to recognize as French.

THE RENAISSANCE IN SPAIN

THE PARADOXES OF SPAIN

FRIEDRICH SCHILLER, the great German poet, in his play *Don Carlos* has given an unforgettable picture of sixteenth-century Spain, the one great country of Europe which, while the others were beginning to expand under the warming spirit of the Renaissance ideal of liberty of thought and action, found itself still bound fast in the medieval chains of absolutism. At the very height of her one great period of prosperity, at a time when she might have made herself for centuries the dominating force in Europe, it was Spain's misfortune to be governed by the hand of an absolute despot who, in order to further his own bigoted ambitions, completely abolished all privileges and rights which might in any way interfere with his desires and suppressed all independence of thought by force of arms and by the malevolent processes of the Church's agency for the punishment of heresy — the Inquisition.

Courtesy of The Metropolitan Museum of Art

PHILIP II OF SPAIN

Engraved by Cornelius Visscher

With words such as these the hero in Schiller's play addresses his king, Philip II, pleading for the future which he sees possible for his land — "those rich and blooming provinces, filled with a great and decent people:

Restore us all you have deprived us of!
And generous as strong, let happiness
Flow from your horn of plenty!
    Let man's mind
Ripen in your vast empire — give us back
All you have taken from us, and become
Amidst a thousand kings, a king indeed!
Renounce the mimicry of Godlike powers
Which level us to nothing! Be in truth
An image of the Deity himself!
Never did mortal man possess so much
For purpose so divine . . . one pen stroke now,
One motion of your hand, can new create
The earth!"

This is only one of the many paradoxes of Spain, that in the face of such an opportunity for becoming the world's most powerful empire, the only thing she did was to waste her substance and break her proud spirit in a series of fanatical religious persecutions. There are many others.

A rocky peninsula set at the far western end of Europe, surrounded by wild seas and encircled by precipitous ranges of mountains, Spain has nevertheless been able to give the world some of its most valued agronomic products. Her history has no analogy to that of any other Christian nation. In one century she made herself the mistress of all Europe; hardly more than a hundred years later, through her lack of intellect and oversupply of wealth, she rapidly deteriorated into a " soulless, mortifying corpse, gloomy and self-consuming." And this she has remained ever since, unable alike to live in the past or go on to the future. A people convinced of its own superiority and strongly resistant to all innovations, the Spanish race has never been able to create either a united country or a completely indigenous art, but has borrowed from and imitated, one after another, all the schools and styles in Europe, oftentimes exaggerating their characteristics and combining their elements in such astounding ways as almost to approach caricature.[5]

THE ROOTS OF SPANISH ART

" A study of Spain will ensure the art lover at least one thing — a new leaf in the album of his experiences," begins a well-known historical sketch of Spanish architecture, sculpture, and painting. The art lover will be able to recognize all the familiarities of the Romanesque, Gothic, and Renaissance styles, but with a strange difference; for added to the characteristics of these schools as he knows them in Italy, France, and Germany are certain traits derived from the creations of the country's ancient conquerors, the Moors and the Arabs, that give them that spirit

[5] Those who have not made a close study of Spanish history are likely to forget the tremendous influences which have been exerted on the country from outside: Romans, Visigoths, Jews, Syrians, and Arabs in turn have occupied the Spanish peninsula. The conflict with the Arabs and the Moors, who first came to Spain in the eighth century, lasted over eight hundred years; and the peculiar desire for religious and racial unity which followed their withdrawal was a natural result.

which we can call "Spanish." The Arab taste exerted a strong influence on architecture, modifying the Gothic and Renaissance styles throughout the country. The native feeling for plastic art was strongly touched with it, and it was combined with Italian, French, and even German ideals in various parts of the peninsula. Spanish painting, grounded securely on an Italian-Flemish foundation, owes its peculiar genius for fiery energy and truthful realism to this distinctive blend of racial qualities.

As in the other European countries, Spanish art has been inextricably bound up with the political history of the empire. The story is quickly told, being largely one of a few powerful, and not particularly brilliant, monarchs. The sixteenth century was the great epoch of Spanish history, an epoch that opened in 1469 with the marriage of Ferdinand and Isabella and the consequent union of the kingdoms of Castile and Aragon. Thus was laid the foundation for what might have been the world's most powerful kingdom; but the expulsion of the Jews and the Moors — the two most useful and enterprising races of the country — made such an eventuality impossible, in spite of Spain's discovery of America and the consequent opening up of undreamed resources and wealth.

The outlook of the Isabelline artists was purely Gothic, as the churches, sculpture, and painting of the time show clearly enough. Mixed with this Gothic taste was a love of fantastic splendor and elaborate design which we have spoken of as derived from the Arabs. In 1516 the Hapsburg, Charles V, became emperor and reigned over Spain for a period of forty years, conquering in that time Mexico, Peru, Chile, and Tunis and extending the Spanish borders until they included a good part of the Old World as well as most of the New World. It was during this apogee of Spanish power that the ideals and principles of Italian Renaissance art began to be felt in the land: beginning with the brilliant *plateresque* sculpture and architecture, which was Gothic in form and Renaissance in detail, this Italian influence made itself felt in all parts of the country, achieving notable results in painting, literature, and music.

The cause for the rapid decline from these dizzy heights of political and material power has been suggested — the unreasoning bigotry and stupidity of an iron-handed tyrant, who tried to stay the progress of thought and the natural evolution of the ideas originating with the

THE MAIN DOORWAY OF THE COLEGIO DE SAN GREGORIO

A fine example of Spanish plateresque architecture, the college was built in Valladolid during the sixteenth century.

Renaissance. The religious controversies were bad enough; but in their wake came the destruction of the great Armada that was to have stood as the symbol of Spanish mastery of the seas, the loss of Portugal, and the insurrections at home in Catalonia. Before a century was out, the once proud empire was permanently crippled and forever doomed.

Because of this brief, dazzling flash of power and riches, her romantic history and her remarkable ethnological constituency — made up as it was of Iberians, Celts, Basques, Goths, Arabs, Moors, and Jews — Spain was able to achieve an influential position in the history of art. Not only did she produce some of its greatest men, such as Velásquez, Cervantes, and Victoria, but modern research is beginning to show that her contact with Asia during the Middle Ages was far more direct than that of any other nation and that it has profoundly influenced all European art.

SPAIN'S PLACE IN MUSIC

The first that we hear of music in Spain is in connection with dancing, which has always been one of the country's chief amusements. Martial, an early writer, described the castanetted rhythms of the dances of Cádiz as being "wild and lascivious." Dances and danceable music may be said to have constituted the dominant influence in Spanish music up to the fifteenth century; as a matter of fact, dances such as Martial described may still be seen in the mountainous regions of Andalusia in the south, their rhythms persuasively conveyed by the Moorish gypsies.

But the Moors left behind them more important evidences of a musical culture than merely rhythms. We have shown in the section on the music of the troubadours how the latest Spanish research on the subject indicates that Spain received with open arms and developed to a point of great beauty the Arabic music brought in at the time of the invasion of the Moors.[6] In the universities founded by the far-seeing Moorish princes

[6] The greatest collection of these Arabic tunes extant is that made by Alfonso the Wise at the end of the thirteenth century, *Las Cantigas*. Formerly supposed to have been influenced by the troubadours, Ribera interprets them as corresponding to the lyric and rhythmic system of the Spanish Moors and says that they were probably set down by a Moorish musician employed by Alfonso.

of Granada, musical theory was made the subject of profound study, the result being that the peculiar melodic physiognomy of this Arabic music left a profound influence on the folk music of Spain. It is difficult for modern musicians to realize what an enormous amount of this didactic literature was produced by these Spanish pedagogues, a literature that was based not on the ideas which other medieval writers had developed from their study of Greek theory, but which was entirely different, being influenced by medieval Arabic forms and enriched through practice.

This gave Spanish music from an early period a rhythmic and melodic character which it otherwise would not have possessed. Some of this literature was devoted to the plainchant, some to instrumental music, its express purpose being that of the practical training of pupils in all branches of the art. It was one of these Spanish theorists who, around 1480, conceived the idea of tempering the twelve semitones of the scale, one of the foundation stones upon which the system of modern music has been erected.[7] Another, in 1565, wrote a method for teaching the playing of keyboard instruments, giving fingering and other similar details. In 1553 Diego Ortiz, Kapellmeister to the Duke of Alba, published a course in the forming of variations over a given bass, this being the popular way of improvising music for the court dances of the time.

[7] In this connection it is necessary to remember that during the course of music's development there have been a number of varying schemes for arranging sounds into the most workable order. These have been based on differing acoustical plans adopted as the result of experiments by theorists, which reach as far back as the sixth century B.C., when the Greek Pythagoras first investigated the basic mathematical ratios between the different series of ordered sounds which came to be grouped into the modea. It became necessary to modify slightly the intervals making up the various scale patterns, because an interval whose mathematical ratio made it sound perfectly "in tune" in one scale could not be incorporated into another without sounding "out of tune." Hence arose what are known as systems of "temperament," that is, means of distributing these inaccuracies, inevitable in any system that is to allow free passage from key to key, so as least to offend the ear. Developing from the Pythagorean system, the chief types of temperament which have been adopted have been (1) "equal temperament," in which only the interval of the octave is exact, all the others being slightly inaccurate, but none so much so as to distress the average ear; (2) "mean tone temperament" (in use from about 1600 to 1800), in which a few intervals are absolutely accurate, the rest not, making it practicable to use some, but not all, keys without distress; (3) "just intonation," in which all the intervals are dead in tune, making passage from one key to another impossible. Observe the difference between these systems by listening to the records prepared by Mr. N. Lindsay Norden.

That these sixteenth-century Spanish educators in music were familiar enough with the work of their European predecessors and confreres is evident from such a treatise as that of Fernando Esteban, which includes quotations from such representative non-Spanish composers as Philippe de Vitry, Guillaume de Machaut, Dunstable, Dufay, and Ockeghem. The Spaniards studied this counterpoint assiduously and were thoroughly conversant with all the details of its craftsmanship, a fact that can be proved by a look at their works. But their background made them more interested in preserving the poetic value of their texts than were the writers of France and Italy, who did not seem particularly concerned when the meaning of the words they set became entirely lost through the intricate and involved weaving of the parts. In the Spanish *romances* and *villancicos,* the two forms most popular in the sixteenth century, the composers achieved a happy blend of the craftsmanship of the scholastics and the individual flavor and characteristic features of the popular Arabian and Moorish music. Dr. Sachs has expressed it thus: when the composers of one of these sixteenth-century works contemplated the words of a *romance* recounting the exploits of that glorious past that is undying in the memory of every Spaniard, or of a lyric *villancico* containing a poetic idea many times repeated, he seemed to forget all about the bounds imposed by strict polyphony. Fired by the spirit of the words, he created a vigorous and almost entirely independent melody that combined both aristocratic and popular elements.

Thus we have the peculiarly Spanish phenomenon of composers who, having made their bow to European tradition and having written their works in the international three-and-four part forms, lost no time in issuing versions for solo voice, with an accompaniment by a sort of guitar lute known as the *vihuela,* an instrument that was used by high society as well as by the musicians of the lower classes.

Representative composers of secular works during the golden age of Spanish music were Fuenllana, Gonzales, Vasquez (whose charming *villancico, Vos me matasteis,* can well stand as a representative example of the whole period), Pisador (who published a *Libro de musica de vihuela* in 1552), and above all the others, Antonio de Cabezon, an outstanding composer of clavier music, and Luis Milan, the greatest of all Spanish

THE LUTE PLAYER

By H. Brosamer, 1537

writers of instrumental music. Milan was the first to write specifically for the *vihuela;* his pieces in the *Libro de musica* published in 1536 are perfect examples of the virtuosity which marked this sixteenth-century instrumental style. Milan was also a poet, courtier to the Valencian sovereigns, and an outstanding performer on the lute, which, because of its suitability for outdoor use, had secured such a firm hold on Spanish affection.

THE POPULAR LUTE

The most popular of Renaissance instruments, the lute, as employed in Spain, was built like a flat, pear-shaped guitar and had six pairs of strings, tuned a fourth apart. Its tone was not very powerful but was capable of a great delicacy and sweetness of utterance. Its possibilities were limited by the mechanical difficulties of fingering, which made possible only combinations of simple polyphony and detached chords. But its sharp-cut, accented tone emphasized the rhythmic features so characteristic of dance music; thus, while tradition made it an aristocratic instrument, its practical possibilities made it a popular one.

The place which this instrument held in the life of its time[8] may be gathered from a seventeenth-century description, *A Recreative Praeledium to the Lute Part of Musick's Monument, or a Remembrancer of the Best Practical Musick both divine and civil that has ever been known to have been in the world*, by Thomas Mace, one of the clerks of Trinity College, Cambridge:

"Beloved Reader, you must know,
That Lutes could Speak ere you could so;
There has been Times when They have been
Discoursers unto King and Queen;
To Nobles and the Highest Peers;
And Free Access had to Their Ears
Familiarly; scarce pass'd a Day
They would not Hear what Lute would say:
But sure at Night, though in their Bed,
They'd Listen well what then She said.
She has Discourses so sublime,
No language yet in Any Time
Had Words sufficient to define
Her Choice Expressions so Divine
Her Matters of such High Concern
No Common Folks can It discern
'Twas ne'er intended for the Rude
And Boisterous — Churlish — Multitude;
But for Those Choice-Refined-Spirits
Which Heav'nly Rapture oft Inherits."

Milan's great lute fantasias, which he called *pavanes*, are perhaps the greatest music ever written for the instrument. Taking their general form from the Italian dance, they strongly suggest the romantic fire and earnest sincerity that are typical of the best Spanish art.

[8] This instrumental family included members of various sizes, from the large *theorbo* to the small *mandore*. The Spanish lute (*vihuela*) had a body somewhat resembling a modern guitar. It is interesting that Leonardo da Vinci, going to the court of Milan in 1482, was known as a musician as well as a painter and that he took with him at that time a silver lute of his own making, shaped like the head of a horse. Marsilio Ficino, the famous humanist scholar, according to tradition, died with his lute in his hands.

CABEZON

The beginning of the sixteenth century shows efforts on the part of the composers in all countries to experiment with instrumental contrapuntal music; but none of them can compare in actual artistic results with the Spaniards. Outstanding among the writers of clavier music was the blind musician Cabezon, whose works were collected and edited by his son, under the title *Obras de musica*. This collection, published in 1578, some years after the death of the composer whose name it bears, is one of the most significant works of Spain's golden age in music. It contains a number of pieces for *tecla* (keyboard instruments), as well as others for the harp and *vihuela*, some of them playable interchangeably on all these instruments. There are also contrapuntal pieces invented or written over liturgical melodies, variations, and *tientos* (toccatas).

"No one who seriously studies the works of Cabezon is likely to feel that any praise of him is exaggerated. To associate him with Bach signifies more than the expression of an unconsidered admiration. It points to an inner relationship that links the Spanish master more closely to the great German than perhaps to any other musician. In any event, I know of no one among the clavier and organ composers of all time who, by reason of musical spontaneity, profundity, and exalted seriousness of purpose, austerity and sublimity of thought, and — last but not least — complete contrapuntal mastery, more properly belongs in his company" (Willi Apel: *Musical Quarterly*).

MORALES AND VICTORIA

The other great names in Spanish Renaissance music are Cristobal Morales, born in Seville about 1512, and Tomás Luis de Victoria, born about 1540. Both these men wrote church music and lived their productive years during the time of the Spanish ascendancy. Their art shows little of either Gothic or Moorish influence, being strongly Renaissance in its character; yet it cannot be said that there is nothing Spanish about it. Both men were influenced by their surroundings, just as was El Greco, the Greek artist who lived in Spain and whose paintings may be said to

THE DEAD CHRIST
By El Greco

express the essence of Spanish character. All these men studied and absorbed the European technical methods of their predecessors. The point is that they were able to feel like Spaniards. No one who has heard even such a short work as Victoria's sublime motet *O vos omnes* could ever mistake his style for that of one of his Italian contemporaries, any more than he could think of El Greco's superreligious combination of asceticism and ecstasy as being anything but intensely Spanish.

Victoria felt that music should be devoted entirely to the aim and end for which it was originally intended — " the praise and glory of God "; and he carried out this ideal to such an extent that he refused altogether to write secular music. In this respect it is important to remember that the Renaissance did not have the same freeing influence in Spain that it did in the other countries of Europe. Racially conscious and integrated to an almost unbelievable degree after his long fights against the Moor and the consequent saving of Europe for the Christian religion, the sixteenth-century Spaniard felt himself a man chosen of God for the special purpose of upholding his true religion.

Consequently there could be none of the questioning of faith that occurred in the other countries, a fact which explains much of the ardor and fire of Victoria's music and of El Greco's painting. The Spanish at the time of the Renaissance still maintained the medieval conception that this world is a mere interlude between birth and a glorious, all-important afterlife. Their whole point of view regarding art and life was that of loyal allegiance to the Church, their strong, burning faith feeding their natural ardor and increasing their native intensity.

Critics speak of El Greco as a painter whose temperament was unusually sympathetic to the religious ecstasy of sixteenth-century Spain. There is a peculiar quality about his composition, an excitement and intensity about his method of depicting light, an ability to make us feel that his figures defy all natural and materialistic laws, that give his pictures their atmosphere of mysticism. "Where painting touches upon the ecstatic and the supernal," says Cheney, "El Greco is master above all others."

The same may be said regarding Victoria. In Rome, where he seems to have spent much time, he came into contact with the other great musical giants of the period; [9] but he remained true to his national feeling and continued to incorporate into his music the fiery mysticism that was so characteristic of the Spanish soul. Nothing shows this better than the Kyrie from his Mass *Orbis Factor*. In the piquant setting which he gives the words "Lord, have mercy upon us," we hear his strong personal conviction as well as his national temperament. It is as if he had been able to catch the elevated thought and devout mysticism of his contemporary, Palestrina, and infuse into them his own passionate nature. He wrote extensively in all religious forms, and his works should be much better known today than they are: only occasionally do we have opportunity

[9] This Italian influence in Victoria is exactly paralleled in the art of El Greco, which, although essentially Spanish, is based on Italian Renaissance forms.

of hearing them, even in the service music of the Church. A more intimate study would convince us that we have in the sixteenth-century Palestrina and Victoria two companion figures such as are so familiar in the eighteenth-century Bach and Handel.

THE RENAISSANCE IN ENGLAND

They have no fancy, and never are surprised into a covert or witty word . . . but they delight in strong earthy expression, not mistakable . . . This homeliness, veracity, and plain style . . . imparts into songs and ballads the smell of the earth, the breath of cattle and, like a Dutch painter, seeks a household charm, though by pails and pans.

— Emerson on the English

" THE ENGLISH, ARE THEY HUMAN? "

THE well-known paradox of the English has been well described by Dorothy Thompson in a recent commentary on the world scene: " Consider the English, a most remarkable people. Producers of cotton textiles, woolen goods, coal, chinaware, the best men's clothes and the worst women's, dealers in money, sharp traders, the ancestors of our own Yankees, who dealt in slaves and later went to war to free them. Inhabiters of rows and rows of dingy little brick villas, each with a hedge to shield him from his neighbors. Prosaic and shrewd. Noted for common sense and a philosophy glorifying self-interest. Also noted for a love of nature, a passion for poetry, and the world's largest and best production of it. By and large a dull people, with a positive dislike of intellect. Yet producing intellectual giants. Haters of war, who have indulged in as much of it as any race on earth." And, we might well add, in some respects the most unmusical people in Europe, yet one which, in the first flush of national consciousness, at the time of the Renaissance, produced some of the best music ever written. Having done so, they fell silent until the end of the nineteenth century. A strange and remarkable people who seem to the rest of the world a little mad, and yet who are always able to achieve a certain method in their madness.

Courtesy of The National Portrait Gallery, London

KING HENRY VIII — artist unknown
(Head from Holbein's portrait)

It was the sixteenth century that saw the development of England from a medieval city-state into the beginnings of a great world power. The twenty-four-year reign of Henry VII, marked as it was by careful thrift and hard toil, did much to repair the ravages of the preceding century and lay the foundation for the glories to come. Under a series of rulers remarkable for their individuality rather than for their ability — Henry VIII, a strange combination of artistic ability, intellectual shrewdness, and bestial vitality; Mary Tudor, an embittered bigot whose devotion to her Catholic faith brought the country to the brink of revolution; Elizabeth, a clear-headed, unscrupulous woman who was able to maintain herself for so long a period by " meeting the extremes around her with her own extremes of cunning and prevarication " — these hundred years form one of the greatest ages in England's glory. During them her trade and seamanship, her learning, literature, art, and music developed enormously; moreover, taking whatever she needed from the various elements of the European Renaissance, England was able at this time to produce literature, music, even a church that were peculiarly her own and that reflected her characteristics. Everything at the time tended to increase this feeling of independence and insularity in the growing empire. The development of the language, the establishment of a fleet that was able to command the mastery of the seas, the successful break with Rome and the consequent establishment of the Church of England — all contributed toward the fostering of that confident self-esteem which has remained until this day one of the country's most striking characteristics.

Shakespeare, born in 1564, only six years after the accession of Elizabeth, and therefore a typical Elizabethan, puts it thus:

" This royal throne of kings, this sceptr'd isle,
This earth of majesty, this seat of Mars,
This other Eden, demiparadise;
This fortress built by Nature for herself
Against infection and the hand of war;
This happy breed of men, this little world;
This precious stone set in the silver sea,
Which serves it in the office of a wall,
Or as a moat defensive to a house,
Against the envy of less happier lands;
This blessed plot, this earth, this realm, this England."

That this was the spirit of the era and not a mere megalomaniac embroidering of language by a poet may be gathered from a contemporary passage from the *Memoires des sages et royales Œconomies d'Estat de Henry le Grand,* written by Sully, the powerful minister of that famous French King, in the early years of the seventeenth century:

" It is certain that the English detest us with a hatred so strong and widespread that one is tempted to regard it as one of the inborn characteristics of that people. More truthfully, it is the outcome of their pride and presumption, there being no people in Europe more haughty, more disdainful, more intoxicated with the notion of their own excellence. If they are to be believed, reason and wit exist only amongst themselves; they worship all their own opinions and scorn those of other nations; nor does it ever occur to them to listen to others or to question their own. Actually this characteristic harms them more than it does us. It places them at the mercy of all their fancies. Ringed by the sea, they may be said to have acquired all its instability."

THE REAL CULTURE OF THE ENGLISH

A retrospective and perhaps more unbiased glance at the England of that period suggests that her people may have had good reason for this "pride and presumption." London, the center of the country then as now, was already a city of some three hundred thousand souls, with well-laid-out streets, an important money exchange, many permanent theaters, and a well-functioning educational system. The city was thronging with business and vibrant with pleasure; the country was becoming dotted with large and comfortable manor houses, built in a peculiar blend of Gothic and Renaissance forms; the average educational level was high: both men and women read Latin poets, studied mathematics and science, composed and sang music.

An accurate picture of the times is given by Morley in his *Plaine and Easie Introduction to Practicall Musicke,* published in 1597:

"Supper being ended and Musicke bookes, according to the custome, being brought to the table, the mistresse of the house presented me with a part, earnestly requesting me to sing; but when, after many excuses, I protested unfainedly that I could not, every one began to wonder, some whispering to others, demanding how I was brought up."

London was a center of a culture which, while it followed the general ideals of its Renaissance archetypes, became essentially national. The court and its circle read the poems of Philip Sidney, Thomas Wyatt, Edmund Spenser, and Christopher Marlowe — all of them obviously patterned after Renaissance models, yet as English in their fresh spontaneity and peculiar imagery as the Sussex downs or the chalk cliffs of Dover. The plays of Shakespeare and Marlowe, although they used the themes common to the time and sounded its general sensibilities, can hardly be thought of as being anything but English; as a sixteenth-century writer said, " The Muses would speak Shakespeare's fine-filed phrase if they would speak English." And while the influence of foreign models is strongly shown in the music of the sixteenth century, in no other art did the native craftsmen achieve such notable success in establishing a characteristic style of national expression.

ENGLISH MADRIGALS

The madrigals of the Elizabethan age, the fairest musical treasure England possesses, are copied clearly enough after Italian models,[10] both as regards their contrapuntal intricacy and their harmonic simplicity; but their composers, Morley, Wilbye, Dowland, Byrd, and the rest, were able to infuse into their compositions a certain robustness and straightforwardness, as well as a sweetness, freshness, and humor that mark them as characteristically English. Called by various names — ballet (having a strong rhythm, infectious melody, and a fa-la refrain), canzonet, song, and air — these English madrigals were sung and played during the late sixteenth and early seventeenth centuries. They were generally published in separate part books and sung by small groups of amateurs seated about a table. These singers employed a wide latitude of interpretation and presentation, often supplying missing vocal parts by means of instruments and embroidering the written melodies with various kinds of improvised ornamentations. Set by brilliant and versatile composers to a splendid lot of lyric poetry written during this golden age of English literature, it is no wonder that the madrigal in England achieved such an astounding perfection and popular success.

Characteristic examples are " Now Is the Month of Maying," a ballet by Morley; " Adieu, Sweet Amaryllis " and " Sweet Honey Sucking Bees " by Wilbye, whose sixty-five works in this form represent the madrigal at its best; " On the Plains " and " As Vesta Was from Latmos Hill

[10] Tradition has it that it was Nicholas Yonge, a singer in the choir of St. Paul's Cathedral, London, who first introduced the Italian madrigal into England. He published a collection of Italian madrigals translated into English in 1588 and again in 1597.

Descending " by Weelkes; " Hard by a Crystal Fountain " by Morley, the latter two from a collection published in honor of Queen Elizabeth and called *The Triumphs of Oriana,* in obvious imitation of an earlier Italian set of similar character; and the single work thought by many to be the loveliest of all, " The Silver Swan " by Gibbons.

ECCLESIASTICAL MUSIC

The English church music of this time was affected by the constantly changing religious complexions of the different monarchs. When Henry VIII made up his mind to have a national church of his own entirely outside the pale of the papacy, it became necessary to adopt the creed and the ritual of the Established Church to fit the needs of the national one. Christopher Tye and Thomas Tallis happened to be the leading composers at the time and so were entrusted with the task of modifying the chants and composing the " anthems " for the new rite. With Henry's son and successor, Edward VI, there came a definite Protestant reaction. Mary Tudor, daughter of Henry, who succeeded to the throne on the early death of Edward, was a Catholic and took constant opportunity of forcing her ideals on the country. With Elizabeth, her successor, came the final adoption of the thirty-nine articles of faith, which, by retaining certain Catholic rites and leaning strongly toward a moderate Protestantism, effected a typically English compromise.

These rapid and constant changes in official belief did not particularly affect the exterior lives of the composers of church music, however. Tallis was a gentleman of the Chapel Royal during the reigns of Henry VIII, Edward VI, Mary Tudor, and Elizabeth and seemed able to write Catholic motets and Protestant anthems with equal ease. Byrd, an ardent member of the Catholic Church, " withoute which I beleeve there is noe salvacon for me," as he wrote in his will, composed a great deal of music for the Anglican services; and so the authorities were content to ignore his personal beliefs. But there is no question that Byrd's best music was written for the Church in which he believed so thoroughly; for he felt that there is a " certain hidden power in the thoughts underlying the words themselves, so that as one meditates upon the sacred words and constantly and seriously considers them, the right notes, in some inexplicable fashion, suggest themselves quite spontaneously." His finest work was his great five-part Mass, which, as one English critic claims, is " without a parallel in the whole field of English church music and is only equaled by the highest flights of the greatest masters in other lands."

Before considering the instrumental music of this century in England, it will be well to add a note regarding two aspects of this sixteenth-century choral style that is not too well understood by the choirs who today are attempting to sing it. The first is that the modal influence is still strong in this sacred and secular music, but not paramount, so that a curious mixture of key feelings is characteristic. (This is apart from personal traits of the composers, such as Byrd's use of major and minor thirds in conjunction.) The other element has already been mentioned — the rhythmic freedom necessary for an adequate reproduction of this music. As the independent melodic lines were woven together, so were the meters. The performers sang from music which had each part printed on a separate line, without bars, or a bar line was put in merely to clarify some point of accent. One singer did not see the other parts; only his own was before him. This demanded much higher reading skill than in a modern part song of equal difficulty, where, if we are getting into a tangle, we can always see what the other parts are doing and have a chance to pick up our place a few bars ahead.

In general, the fitting of words and notes was far purer in madrigalian times, though there were then some differences of word stress in the language. Hence comes the chief technical difficulty in getting singers to perform madrigals really well. They have been so long tied by the leg to bar lines that, like prisoners freed, it is some time before they can enjoy their freedom.

ENGLISH RENAISSANCE MUSIC FOR INSTRUMENTS

Instrumental music was closely associated with choral music during the Renaissance, as we have seen; it was often used for accompanying the voices, the instrumentation following very closely the various vocal parts. If any of the voices happened to be missing, they were actually

Archives Photographiques

A RENAISSANCE FIVE-PART MADRIGAL

The copper engraving by "L'ouie" indicates that there were parts for voices, lute, and viola da gamba.

supplied by various instruments; thus vocal and instrumental parts were inextricably mingled, and it may be taken for granted that the same work was hardly ever performed twice in the same way.

But gradually the instruments began to live a life of their own: transcriptions of madrigals and dances were made for them; and compositions were written in which they were used to form a prelude, an interlude, or a finale to vocal works, as well as to supply the accompaniment. The lute did not seem to achieve so great a popularity in England as it did on the Continent; the viol was the instrument largely affected by "gentlemen in privat meetings." Having six strings and played on the knee rather than under the chin, viols were made in all sizes and were kept in sets or "chests" in properly appointed domestic establishments of the time. Tastes varied as to the sizes of viols that made up these chests; but there were usually six of them — two basses, two tenors, and two trebles, "all truly and proportionately suited."

It may be said in general that the music used for these families of instruments, called "consort music" (a mixed collection of instruments being known as a "broken consort"), was essentially transplanted vocal music. The favorite form of viol consort music was the fantasy, a sort of instrumental madrigal in which one instrument after another takes up part of the principal melody, all of them being engaged in making a real contrapuntal contribution to the whole. There was no attempt to provide strong contrasts between sections, as was done in the instrumental suites based on popular dance tunes; but the fantasy composers were content to work toward a cumulative climax, as did the fugue writers a century later. Indeed, it was out of the fantasy that the fugue finally evolved. Literally hundreds of these fantasies were written by the English composers of this century, the most notable being those by William Byrd, "the father of English music," and Thomas Weelkes, one of the greatest of the madrigalists. Music for the broken consort, combinations of viols, lutes, flutes, and so on, did not become popular in England until the early part of the next century, when such collections as Morley's *First Book of Consort Lessons* (1611) began to appear.

England's great contribution to the development of instrumental music was made in the type of music written for keyboard instruments. Organs and harpsichords were the favorite instruments at the court of Henry VIII, who himself was able to play well on the lute and harpsichord and sing from book at sight, as well as draw the best bow in England and joust marvelously, according to contemporary description. We get an intimate picture of the position of music in sixteenth-century England from some of the dispatches sent home by Sebastiano Giustiniani, an ambassador of the seigniory of Venice to Henry's court, and quoted in Rawdon Brown's translation *Four Years at the Court of Henry VIII*. Describing some of the May Day festivities at Greenwich Palace, the writer tells how the king went to dinner, and "by his Majesty's order, the ambassadors, and we likewise, dined in his palace, with the chief nobility of this land. After dinner the ambassadors were taken into certain chambers containing a number of organs and harpsichords and flutes and other instruments, and where the prelates and chief nobles were assembled to see the joust which was then in preparation; and in the meantime the ambassadors told some of these grandees that I was proficient on some of these instruments; so they asked me to play, and knowing that I could not refuse, I did so for a long while, both on the harpsichords and organs, and really bore myself bravely, and was listened to with great attention. . . . The prelates who were present told me that the king would certainly choose to hear me, as his Majesty practices on these instruments day and night, and that he will very much like my playing."

Later on, a friar, Dionisius Memo, who was organist of St. Mark's, Venice, came over to London; Giustiniani sent word of his visit to Venice and described his arrival "with a most excellent instrument of his, which he has brought hither with much pains and cost. I presented him in the first place to the Cardinal, telling him that when your Highness heard of his wanting to quit Venice for the purpose of coming to his Majesty, you gave him gracious leave, which you would not have done had he intended going anywhere else. His lordship chose to hear him in the presence of many lords and *virtuosi*, who were as pleased as possible with him; after which his right reverend lordship told him to go to the King, who would see him very willingly, employing many words of flattering commendation. He afterwards went to his Majesty, who, knowing he was there, sent for him immediately after dinner, and made him play before a great number of lords and all his *virtuosi*. He played not merely to the satisfaction, but to the incredible admiration and pleasure of everybody, and especially of his Majesty, who is extremely skilled in music, and of the two Queens [Catherine of Aragon and Margaret of Scotland]. My secretary was also present, who highly extolled the performance, and told the King many things in his praise as it went on, mentioning how much favor he enjoyed with your Highness and all Venice, which had been content to deprive itself for the satisfaction of his Majesty, with many other very suitable words, so that said Majesty has included him among his instrumental musicians, nay, has appointed him their chief, and says that he will write to Rome to have him unfrocked out of his monastic weeds, so that he may merely retain holy orders, and that he will make him his chaplain."

Fortunately for us a collection of organ music of this time has survived, one belonging to a master of the choir at St. Paul's, London, during the reign of Mary Tudor, daughter of Henry VIII; and so we have a good idea of what the music sounded like which these composers wrote for organ and harpsichord. There are over a hundred compositions in the collection, many of them obvious transcriptions of vocal motets and madrigals; others are manipulations of chant melodies, many of them in purely vocal style, a number based on the same tune, that associated with the vesper services for Trinity Sunday. The latter were called *In Nomine*. Wooldridge says that while no satisfactory reason has been found for the frequent choice of this cantus by so many English composers, it continued to exercise the ingenuity of practically every good writer of instrumental music in England from the time of Taverner at the beginning of the sixteenth century to that of Purcell at the end of the seventeenth.

KEYBOARD INSTRUMENTS AND THEIR MUSIC

There were two general kinds of keyboard stringed instruments in use at this time: the struck type (clavichord) and the plucked type (harpsichord, spinet, and virginal). It is impossible to determine which of these was developed first; both were in use until after the time of Bach. The principle of the clavichord is seen from the painting by Van Hemessen. The strings were struck by brass tangents placed at the end of each key. One string could serve several tangents, since they acted as does the finger on a violin string, stopping off a portion of it, the resulting pitch depending on where the string was hit. The tone of this instrument was tiny, but capable of a pleasing vibrato obtained by moving the finger on the key. Gradations of relative loudness and softness could also be obtained by regulating the force of the stroke of the fingers on the keys.

In the harpsichord the key mechanism actually plucked the string by means of a quill or a leather plectrum set in a "jack." A much louder tone was thus produced; but it was one that could not be varied, except by bringing into action an entirely different set of plectra, actuated by

Courtesy of The Worcester Museum

WOMAN PLAYING THE CLAVICHORD by Jan Van Hemessen

It has been suggested that this is a portrait of Eleanor of Portugal, sister of Emperor Charles V.

another keyboard. The virginal [11] was perhaps more popular than the harpsichord, although the exact difference between the terms is not clear. In its wide use it could be likened to the piano of today.

William Byrd (1542–1623), by far the greatest musician of the time in England, richly endowed in his ability to write both sacred and secular and both vocal and instrumental music, was the first composer in any country to develop the real potentialities of these stringed keyboard instruments. Based in general on continental models, Byrd's compositions

[11] The origin of this word is disputed: some authorities associate it with Elizabeth the Virgin Queen, who was a great player on this instrument; it may have meant simply an instrument for young ladies, an idea given color by the fact that the first music printed for the instrument in England was called *Parthenia* (*Songs for Maidens*) and had on its title page a picture of a young lady playing.

use all the forms then current, but in such a manner as to make them characteristically English. Typical of one sort is his little suite which he called *The Earl of Salisbury*, made up of two of the court dances, a pavan and a galliard, published in the first book of keyboard music ever to be printed in England — *Parthenia* or *The Maydenhead of the first musicke that ever was printed for the Virginalls, composed by three famous Masters, William Byrd, Dr. John Bull, and Orlando Gibbons, Gentilmen of his Majesties most Illustrious Chappell.*

Byrd and Bull, the latter nicknamed the " wildly whirling," wrote many sets of variations, one of the earliest purely instrumental forms which did not imitate in any sense the polyphonic vocal style of writing. There is a plausible story that this form originated with the Spanish composers and was brought to England during the time of Mary Tudor, whose husband was Philip of Spain, thus naturally bringing the two countries into very close touch with each other. These variations began with a simple tune, which was played through a number of times; only, instead of making the repetition exact, the composer or player added a few ornaments made up of passage work and instrumental figures, or he even made some changes in the tune for the pure pleasure of " falsifying the expectation of his own ear." Byrd and Bull were not content with merely mechanical variations but infused a poetic idea or program into a few of their pieces. Byrd's *The Bells* and Bull's *The King's Hunt* are good examples of this, each of them using a poetic conceit as the basis for our interest in the music, and each working up the interest in the variations until a climax is reached. Farnaby's *The New Sa-Hoo,* on the other hand, is an example of the variation form used without a poetic program; it is simply the manipulation of a well-known Dutch tune of the time.

Such short numbers as Farnaby's " A Toye," " His Dreame," and " His Rest " and Peerson's " The Fall of the Leafe " show these early English virginalists searching for expressive possibilities in the new technique they were developing for their instrument. These were early predecessors of the " piano poems " which became so popular later on and were written by hundreds of composers from Schumann to Debussy. All these works mentioned are, as we might expect, short and simple in form, for the matter of lengthy development of ideas had not yet been thought of.

Still other forms used by these early instrumental writers were the descriptive piece, such as Byrd's *The Battle*, copied from Jannequin's famous *Battle of Marignan* and attempting to produce on the instrument the same rather futile imitations of trumpets, drums, war noises, and so forth; and the *Divisions on a Ground*, consisting of a florid embellishment of a short bass tune. Norcome's *Divisions for Lute and Viol* is a good example. Byrd's *The Bells*, already mentioned, is interesting in that it is a combination of three of these early styles, for it is written over a short ground bass of two notes and is a series of nine variations, each of them vividly descriptive of the pealing of various types of bells, large and small.

It was customary to make collections of these pieces, and most of our direct knowledge of the English instrumental music of these Renaissance centuries comes from such anthologies. Some of these were in manuscript, such as *The Fitzwilliam Virginal Book* (containing, besides English compositions, arrangements of music by prominent continental composers), *Benjamin Cosyn's Virginal Book, My Lady Nevells Booke* (all of whose forty works are by Byrd); others were printed, such as the *Parthenia.* The publisher of the latter dedicated the work to Elizabeth, daughter of James I, then king, the same Elizabeth who later became the wife of the " Most High and Mighty and Magnificent Prince Frederick, Elector Palatine of the Reine," and progenitor of the present reigning house of England. This publisher begs Elizabeth to remember that if she (who was a pupil of Byrd's) will only vouchsafe her " white hands," the music " will arrive with more pleasure at ye princely ears of your Grete Fredericke."

LUTE SONGS

There remains to be said a word regarding the lute songs that were so popular in England in the palmy days of her music making, adaptations of the Spanish type of romances and *villancicos*, collections of which were published in Spain as early as 1536. Similar books appeared in England, the form reaching its height in the lute songs of John Dowland, a cosmopolitan Englishman, who traveled all over Europe making his music known. These solo songs were really madrigals of a simple type, the melody of which was capable of being sung by a solo voice, while a lute, usually played by the singer, supplied the other parts. In Dowland's collections, published in the early part of the seventeenth century, optional choral parts were provided, so that if desired the accompanying instrument or instruments could be dispensed with, and purely vocal renditions given. The lute was often reinforced by some instrument with more sustaining power, such as the viola da gamba. The lute songs were extremely popular in their day. A contemporary readily admits "prick song [contrapuntal music] to be a faire musicke, so it be done upon the booke surely and after a good sorte. But to sing to the lute is much better, because all sweetness consisteth in one alone [that is, lies in one solo part]; and singing to the lute with the dittie (methinke) is more pleasant than the rest, for it addeth to the words such a grace and strength that it is a great wonder" (Castiglione's *Il Cortegiano*). Such "singing with the dittie," moreover, greatly strengthened the growing favor of the harmonic over the polyphonic style and marked the beginning of the solo art song, a development which in time led to the masterpieces of Schubert, Schumann, and Brahms.

Thus it was that music flourished under that "Most Accomplished Prince, Henry" and his redoubtable progeny. In point of time, many of these English developments were behind those of the rest of Europe, although in the matter of keyboard music, the Elizabethan composers probably led. In general the connection between the artistic development and the economic improvement and commercial expansion of this nation that was beginning to find itself was close. Traditions of the Elizabethan school of composers — many of them great men — lasted well into the next century and doubtless would have been carried strongly into the time of Purcell had not the Puritan revolution intervened. The music of this composer, different as it was from that of Byrd, was still as characteristically English. But after him there is nothing more to be said until the end of the nineteenth century. The reasons why, in so far as music was concerned, the greater and more powerful the nation became, the poorer its art, are plain enough if we take into account the general state of culture and life of the country as a whole.

VISSCHER'S VIEW

MUSIC AN ESSENTIAL OF LIFE

It is difficult for us today to realize how general was the practice of music in Renaissance times. In Elizabethan days England was much more of a common community than she has ever been since: all classes were brought together in comparatively close contact, family and servants, patrician and plebeian, peer and commoner, city man and country dweller. The unifying social cement which held together all cultural life was music, the one thing which all people could enjoy together. As yet the common majority could read little and write less. The art of literature did not come into being in England until the end of the century, when the ability to read and write became more general, owing to the establishment of the grammar schools. But all the people knew and practiced music; the leisure time of all classes was taken up with music and dancing in those pre-novel, pre-radio days. The court had its own instrumental and vocal performers, as we have seen, king and courtier uniting to make music; the great town and country houses had their madrigals, both vocal and instrumental; the working man had his own " neat and spruce ayres, common tunes being known by the boys and working people singing in the streets, among them many excellent and well-contrived," writes Mace. " Every troublesome and laborious occupation useth musicke for solace and recreation; hence it is that manual labourers and mechanical

Courtesy of Folger Library, Washington

OF LONDON, 1616

artificers of all sorts keepe such a chaunting and singing in their shoppes — the tailor on his bulk, the shoemaker at his last, the mason at his wall, the ship boy at his oar, and the tinker at his pan."

And these classes mingled rather freely in their music making; there are many examples in the literature of the period of families playing and singing together with the servants. The traditions of the bards and minstrels were still strong enough to make a talent for music an *open sesame* to higher degrees of social rank. Fifteenth-century English poets were all of them musicians capable of singing their verses to the lute. Even in the next century, when each of these twin arts began to pursue more of an individual existence, owing to the gradual creation of a new order of readers and the growing intricacies of musical style, poems were always written by those whose lives had a musical background. "Hee who cometh with words set in delightfull proportion either accompanied with or prepared for the well inchaunting spell of Musicke" was a poet. The cultured composers of early music for instruments were in the habit of taking popular tunes of the day as themes for their pieces, as Byrd did in his *Carman's Whistle*. Everywhere music was being produced in fact as well as in fancy; England was, indeed, "a nest of singing birds."

It is hardly necessary to dwell on the unfortunate picture that follows: the outbreak of civil war; the strong social influences of Puritanism, with its general scorn for beauty and its austere days of scripture reading and psalm singing; the importation, after the monarchy had been restored, of foreign music and musicians to please and entertain the people. Gradually music was divorced from the ordinary activities of Englishmen, and these became more and more concerned with the production of material wealth; the cultivation of music drifted into the hands of specialists and professionals, many of them from other countries. As the Industrial Revolution spread its pall of dirty smoke, ugly cities, and social disintegration over the country, the men of one class no longer cared about those of another, either as to how they lived or how they amused themselves. At the height of Victorian prosperity and imperialistic megalomania, music in England was at its lowest ebb. The nest of nightingales had become a blackened ruin, silent amongst the " dark satanic mills."

THE RENAISSANCE IN GERMANY

But for him [Luther] there would have been no seventeenth century of German competition, and so no Johann Sebastian Bach; from which it follows that there would have been no Beethoven, Wagner, or Brahms. For if it is too much to say, simply and directly, that all Teutonic art music proceeds from the Lutheran chorales, it is not too much to say that all Teutonic art music proceeds from the sources which the Lutheran chorales first explored and so first made vitally and progressively " popular."

— Eva Mary Grew: *Music & Letters*, January, 1938

GERMANY'S EARLY BACKGROUND

WE have become so accustomed to thinking of Germany as one of the outstanding musical nations that it is difficult to realize that in the two centuries we have been considering — the fifteenth and the sixteenth — the art of music in this country was extremely backward in its flowering in comparison with its position in Flanders, Italy, Spain, and England. A brief glance at the country's political development will help to explain this. We have seen that art seems to flourish best under a rich, powerful, and more or less centralized form of government, but Renaissance Germany offered almost exactly the opposite conditions. If we look at a map of the Europe of 1000 A.D., two centuries after the time of Charlemagne, we find that what had been the eastern part of his great empire had become broken up into a large number of sections, each of them ruled by a duke, who was a king in all but name. By the thirteenth century, St. Louis in France had been able to weld together a real monarchy out of what had been the western part of Charlemagne's domains; but no such unification came in Germany until the nineteenth century. In a political sense there was no Germany at all during the fifteenth and sixteenth centuries, only a great number of duchies, held loosely together by a kaiser who played the rather grandiose role of Holy Roman Emperor, but who in reality, as Voltaire said, was neither holy, Roman, nor emperor. Each of these independent states and principalities differed greatly from the others, and there was little idea of co-operation or reciprocity among them.

THE LIEDER

That there were unmistakable racial bonds, however, is proved by the large number of *lieder* — contrapuntal compositions corresponding in general character to the *chansons* — that were produced at this time in all parts of Germany, especially in the south.[12] These works, with their wide range of expression from a simplc, sincere naïveté to a noble grandeur, are unmistakably German and could have been written by no other race. They filled a deep-rooted need in the people for some sort of simple, straightforward means of expressing their natural romantic feelings, and so became extremely popular. The first collection of these lieder, a manuscript known as the *Lochheimer Liederbuch,* consisting of a number of three-part arrangements, was made in the middle of the fifteenth century. Later many printed collections appeared.

[12] Strictly translated, the word *lied* means simply " song." Its use, however, is generally restricted to the German-Austrian products of the Romantic Era, from about 1780 on. These Renaissance compositions in Germany were an entirely different type of music and must not be confused with the later lieder.

Those who seek the real basis for the later pre-eminence of German music and musicians will find it here in these fifteenth-century and sixteenth-century contrapuntal songs, for they combine a deep sentiment, which arises out of the spirit of the folk, with a method of expression that is robust and strong yet surprisingly effective. The lied was based on a *cantus firmus*, usually taken from one of the old traditional folk melodies. The practice of the composers was to place this in one of the parts and weave about it other voices which, while closely matching its general style and melodic line, at the same time amplified and developed it. Instead of the rather pretentious architecture of the Italian madrigal, we find in these German polyphonic settings a new intensification and enhancement of the spirit of the simple folk song.

As was true of their more elaborate Italian and French parallels, the lieder were mainly love songs; but in such collections as that of the art-loving Nuremberg physician, Georg Forster, who from 1539 to 1556 published no fewer than five anthologies containing nearly four hundred lieder, we find occupational songs, reflective expressions of an ennobling nature, what might be called political songs, and plenty of drinking and convivial songs. Composers sprang up all over Germany: early names, among a large number of unimportant craftsmen, are Von Fulda, Stoltzer, and Finck. Gradually there was formed a sort of school of these lieder composers, centering in the imperial court of Maximilian at Innsbruck[13] and the ducal courts at Stuttgart and Munich. The important men of these groups were Heinrich Isaak (born in Holland, *c.* 1450–1517), Ludwig Senfl (*c.* 1492–1555), and Arnold Bruck (*d.* 1545).

The best way to realize the peculiar qualities of these works and how much they contain of promise for that which was to follow is to study in some detail a few characteristic examples. Good to begin with are Isaak's two songs of farewell, probably written on his taking leave of the Innsbruck court to wander afield in the world: *Zwischen Berg* (" 'Twixt mountain steep and valley deep the road runs free and wide "), vigorous, proud, and full of hope for the future; and *Innsbruck, ich muss*

[13] We possess striking records of the enlightened glories of Maximilian's court in some treatises written by his own hand, *Sir Teuerdank* and *Der Weisskunig*, as well as in Dürer's famous series of woodcuts showing various phases of the court life, including its musical forces.

THE EMPEROR MAXIMILIAN

By Burgkmair, 1508

dich lassen ("Innsbruck, I now must leave thee"), filled with a nostalgic longing for the past. Hofhaimer's sorrowful *Meins traurens ist ursach* ("The reason for my sorrow") shows the ability of these composers to use a simple, imitative polyphony to enhance the original heartfelt beauty of the German popular song. In such a setting as *Ach Elselein, liebes Elselein,* Senfl combines two well-known folk melodies in a masterly fashion.

GERMANY VERSUS ITALY

But these rather slender expressions of native composers could not hold their own against the strong tide from the south: the latter half of the sixteenth century saw a complete dominance of Italian culture in

German life. The knowledge of Italian art developed by the general practice then in vogue — of all German artists spending their apprentice years in Italy — as well as the employment of a great many foreigners, especially musicians, by the German courts, broke through the old barriers and stimulated the imitation of foreign models. The results, however, were never satisfactory. For the German masters, no matter how much they might study Italian styles, never were able to assimilate Italian ways of thinking. They might pay homage to the Renaissance ideals, but they were never able to disguise completely their essentially northern mentality.

Albrecht Dürer (1471–1528), the greatest of the German painters, is a case in point: he was pre-eminent not because of his technical methods of composition and coloring learned from the Italians but because his genius was great enough for him to express honestly and directly those conceptions which reveal the soul and atmosphere of Germany. His followers, overwhelmed by the popular influence of the Italian art of the time, were never able to advance beyond the point of copying Italian mannerisms. Falling between two stools, their work is of little importance.

What is probably the most important single example of German art of this period stands in St. Sebald's Church in Nuremberg, a city which still gives in its rows of picturesque, high-gabled houses a unique picture of a typical German Renaissance town. In the early years of the sixteenth

THE SIXTEENTH–CENTURY NUREMBERG by Dürer (1471–1528)

THE TOMB OF ST. SEBALD, NUREMBERG

century the most celebrated German artist in bronze, Peter Vischer, finished here his beautiful shrine in honor of the saint whose name the church bears. Within the architectural framework of the saint's coffin are a number of statuettes which show how strongly the native Germanism of the creator was influenced by Italian ideals. But even in a masterwork of this kind there seems to be no real amalgamation of styles: classical deities find themselves in such strange company as the twelve apostles and the four cardinal Christian virtues.

Music offers an exactly parallel case. Owing to the existence of a number of important foreign figures who sojourned in Germany, among them Orlando di Lasso, who spent the latter part of his life as court musician in Munich, and Scandello, who was master of the electoral chapel in Dresden, the Italian influences reigned supreme during the latter part of the sixteenth century in Germany. It was the fashion for the art patrons of the time to affect Italian styles; and German composers did their best to furnish what was wanted, attempting to mix certain Italian ingredients with the native products that had formerly been so much in favor.

But they were hardly more successful than the artists had been. The works of the sixteenth-century German composers who affected the Italian style, often using Italian words, were not always effectual. Hans Leo Hassler (1564–1612), who had a genuine talent, came nearest to success in his assimilation of Italian models: he was able to combine much of the characteristic German introspection and naïveté with Italian grace and swift charm. Such a simple thing as his little strophically composed *Mein G'müth ist mir verwirret, das macht ein Mägdlein zart* ("A tender maid's the cause of my confusion") is perhaps most typical of this composer, who was a worthy predecessor of Schütz and Bach. We cannot help feeling that he was most successful when he was most German, as in his *Mein Lieb will mit mir kriegen* ("My love would do me battle"). It seems, as a German historian has remarked, that during the last years of the sixteenth century the native blossoms which earlier had flowered so luxuriantly in the native soil and had given real promise for a completely native flora, dried up and withered. The Italian importations and blossoms had an easy conquest.

PAUMANN AND HIS FOLLOWERS

Some fifty years before Vischer and his sons began to erect their monument in St. Sebald's, a blind virtuoso by the name of Conrad Paumann (*d.* 1473) played the organ there. The following lines are taken from a contemporary poem and show Paumann to have been the most remarkable man in the city:

"Dass er ein Meister ob allen Meistern ist . . .	("For he is a master above all others . . .
Wollt einen Meister der Kunst man krönen	If a master of Art were to be crowned,
Er trug dann wohl eine goldne Kron'."	It would be he that deserves a golden crown.")

This remarkable man was the shining light in the German music of the time; he left behind him a large work with the formidable title *Fundamentum organisandi,* the oldest instruction book on instrumental composition in existence, containing transcriptions of church melodies, lieder, and dance tunes for the organ or clavier. (An earlier fragment for organ — the so-called Robertsbridge Fragment of the fourteenth century in the British Museum — has already been mentioned. Its main feature is the coloration of the upper voice in a manner suggestive of the later German composers, only much simpler.) The pieces in this anthology of Paumann's show very definitely the peculiar fascination which these German artists found in the decorative and ornamental aspects of Renaissance art. Just as the German architects decorated their façades with such eye-filling features as elaborate doorways, ornamented gables, carved figures, and gay friezes, without ever really assimilating the fundamental principles of Renaissance architectural design, so Paumann and the organists who followed him *kolorierten* (colored) their melodies, overlaying them with superficial ornament without affecting their organic growth.

A number of other instruction books followed, giving both theoretical and practical materials for the use of the musical amateur, who was beginning to assume an important place in German musical life. These books (the most famous of them were Virdung's *Musica getutscht,* 1511, and Schlick's *Tabulaturen . . . uff die Orgeln und Lauten*) make little distinction between music for different instruments, one of them maintaining that "what you have learnt to play on the lute, you can easily learn also on harp, psaltery, or viol." The influence of vocal music also is strong in these early instrumental books, many of the pieces being merely ornamented transcriptions of popular motets. But gradually during this period there were worked out the principles of a real instrumental style, principles most effectively used by the English composers.

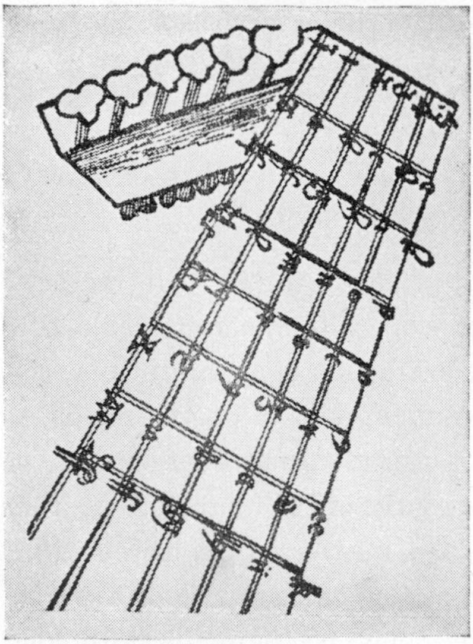

LUTE FINGER BOARD RELATED TO TABLATURE NOTATION (From *Musica getutscht*)

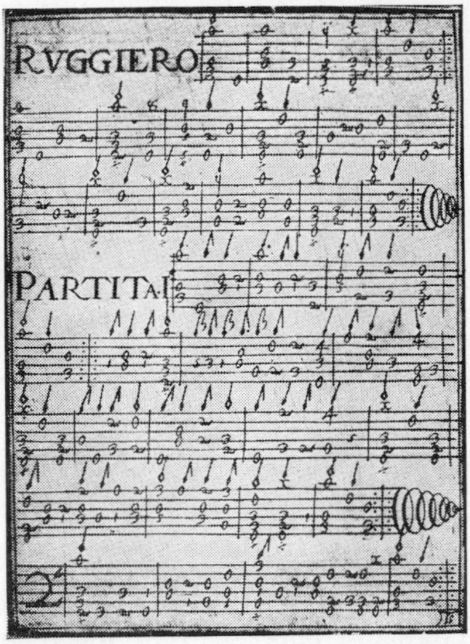

ITALIAN TABLATURE (From *Libro primo d'intavolatura di Chitarrone*)

Tablature can perhaps best be described by saying that it was a system of notation which told the player not which musical tone he was to think of, but actually just where he was to put his fingers on his instrument. The staff notation we use was originally developed for singers and defines relationships of pitch; that is, it shows the singer or player the pitch distances between the various notes represented on the staff. Tablature, on the other hand, was a purely mechanical system, showing the player, by various devices, where he was to put his fingers in order to reproduce the music that had been thought of by the composer. Many sorts of tablature have been invented: these were in use at different times and in various countries. Some of them are still employed, such as the guitar tablature of Spain, the mandolin tablature of Naples, and the ukulele tablature of America.

A page of tablature music, as can be seen from the accompanying illustrations, looks like a collection of musical staves, with numbers on the lines instead of notes: in lute music, the lines of the staff represented the strings of the instrument, the figures showing which fingers should be placed on the frets to produce the notes. The rhythm was usually indicated by note values placed above the lines.

This early instrumental music, beginning with the Robertsbridge Fragment, was written in a system of tablature notation somewhat similar to that which had been developed for the lute, where the frets on the neck of the instrument were designated by letters of the alphabet and several supplementary signs. The organ tablature (used also for other keyed instruments) was likewise written on one stave which gave the top voice in notes. The other, lower, voices were designated by letters.

Many of these German composers, in addition to writing secular and instrumental works, did a number of things for the service of the Catholic Church, which organization, in spite of internal political and sectarian strife, maintained a dominant position in the religious life of the country as a whole. Isaak, who had drunk so deeply at the well of Flemish music, was a prolific composer of Masses, and one of the most treasured examples of early music is his *Choralis constantinus*, a complete setting of the offices for the ecclesiastical year. Hofmeyer, Paminger (whom Luther called a *musico inter primos*), Hassler, Aichinger, and Jacobus Gallus (Handl) were important men of this period in this field. The last is considered by historians one of the most important figures of the whole period, often being called, not without reason, the German Palestrina.

THE REFORMATION IN GERMANY

The most important manifestation of the Renaissance spirit in Germany was, of course, the Reformation. The natural temperament and intellectual endowment of the German people made such a response to the individualistic and humanistic ideals of the period inevitable. This break from the established church had its real inception in the struggle of the spirit of man for self-expression. The historians have become fond of saying that such a change in ideals was inevitable and that the currents from which flowed the Reformation were so much older than Luther, that if he had not appeared to head such a revolt, some other reformer would have arisen. In other words, the nailing of the ninety-five theses attacking the alleged wickednesses of the Catholic Church to a door at the University of Wittenberg in 1517 by one of its professors, Dr. Martin Luther, was only the physical act which precipitated a spiritual revolution long in preparation and which the spirit of the century had made unavoidable. The results of this revolution, we are reminded, were by no means uniformly beneficial; some of them were disastrous in so far as the development of any cultural interests was concerned.

ITS EFFECTS ON MUSIC

All this may be true; but as musicians we can be thankful that it was Luther and not someone like Calvin or Knox who captained such a revolt. For out of the happy coincidence of Luther's being a musician as well as a reformer came one of the most notable contributions made by the Germans to music, the Protestant chorale. It was a cardinal point in the doctrine of Luther's dissenting sect that each individual was capable of a direct relationship with his God, a doctrine which repudiated the representative ideals of the medieval Church, which had allowed access to Christ only through the special mediation of his deputies, the clergy. And so in the worship of this Protestant body, each man had his own part to play, a part which could not be taken by another individual, be he priest or chorister.

In his evangelical ritual, therefore, Luther provided for liturgical forms that gave the congregation opportunities for direct participation in the service. Instead of merely participating in the Mass by listening to it or by having small portions of it to sing, the members of the Protestant congregations were given hymns to sing before and after the sermon, at the beginning and at the end of service. Thus the chorales, those magnificent, majestic expressions of the religious principles of the new church, came into being. In their creation, Luther played a direct part.

LUTHER AS MUSICIAN

Luther was a good musician, although seemingly without interest in any of the other arts. He regarded poetry as purely utilitarian and was entirely oblivious of the arts of form; traveling through Italy at the height of the Renaissance, he had not a single word to say about the beauty being created on all sides of him. He played both flute and lute, understood the principles of polyphony (Josquin des Prés was his special idol), and was on good terms with a number of the leading German composers of his day. So he chose wisely the hymns which his congregations were to sing: some of them originated from Gregorian chants, others from earlier sacred folk songs; some from contemporary secular melodies ("the

AN EARLY CHORALE BOOK open at Luther's tune *Ein Feste Burg*

devil has no right to all the good tunes," said Luther); a number were especially composed, some of them by the great reformer himself. It was because of his musical talents and unflagging interest that these chorales became the foundation stone of music in Germany, their style affecting all her later composers from Bach to Brahms and Wagner.

Luther was artist enough to realize that the untrained singers of the congregation could not utilize anything but the simplest music; and so, in addition to providing hymns which had a strong melodic part for the people to sing, he had polyphonic arrangements made of these chorales in the current style of the German lieder. For he felt that when " natural music is heightened and polished by art, there man first beholds and can with great wonder examine to a certain extent (for it cannot be wholly seized or understood) the great and perfect wisdom of God in his marvelous work of music, in which this is most singular and indeed astonishing that one man sings a simple tune or tenor (as musicians call it) together with which three, four, or five voices also sing, which as it were play and skip delightfully round this simple tune or tenor and wonderfully grace or adorn the said tune with manifold devices and sounds, performing as it were a heavenly dance so that those who at all understand it are moved by it, must be greatly amazed and believe that there is nothing more extraordinary in this world than such a song adorned with many voices."

In 1524 Johann Walther, Luther's friend and musical adviser, published his *Church Chorale Book* at Wittenberg, containing a number of these arrangements with the melody in the tenor part and the other voices woven about it in the fashion so quaintly described above. A later collection, the *Neue deutsche Geistliche Gesange* of Georg Rhaw, published in 1544, contained numbers by all the composers of the early Reformation period, among them Arnold Bruck, whose impressive setting of Luther's words *Aus tiefer Noth* ("In deepest need") may be taken to be representative of the deep feeling and sincere artistry of these German Protestant contrapuntal settings.

THE ARTISTRY OF THE CHORALE

Later on the tune made its way into the upper or soprano voice, and the settings became more suitable for congregational use, finally resulting in the kind of arrangements which Johann Sebastian Bach made a century later and which are among the finest things in all music. In these comparatively simple little pieces in harmonic style, with their masterly part writing, there is a wealth of poetic utterance and a strength of emotional expression that has never been surpassed. "Nothing in music is more wonderful, perhaps more surprising, than the power and grip which these chorales have over all classes of musical listeners and over the singers themselves. . . . These simple four-part compositions . . . have, in fact and in the supremest degree, a religious and mystic effect upon the hearer that cannot be analyzed or explained" (Hannam). They are Germany's outstanding contribution to Renaissance art.

A Table Showing the Most Important Madrigal Composers of the Sixteenth Century

FLEMISH	ITALIAN	FRENCH	ENGLISH	GERMAN
Willaert [14]		Jannequin		
c. 1480–1562		c. 1485–c. 1560		
Verdelot [14]		De Sermisy		
c. 1490–1560		c. 1490–1562		
Gombert	Festa			
1495–1570	c. 1495–1545			
Arcadelt [14]	A. Gabrieli			
c. 1514–c. 1570	c. 1510–1586			
De Rore [14]				Scandello [16]
1516–1565				1517–1580
De Monte [14]	Palestrina			
c. 1521–1603	1525–1594			
Di Lasso [15]		Le Jeune		
c. 1530–1594		c. 1528–1602		
	Vecchi	Costeley		
	c. 1551–1605	1531–1606		
	Marenzio		Byrd	Regnart
	c. 1553–1599		1542–1623	1540–1600
	Gastoldi		Morley	Lechner
	c. 1556–1622		1557–c. 1603	1550–1606
	Gesualdo of Venosa		Pilkington	Eccard
	c. 1560–1613		c. 1562–1638	1553–1611
	Anerio		Dowland	Hassler
	1560–1614		1563–1626	1564–1612
	Monteverdi		Bateson	
	1567–1643		1570–1630	
			Tomkins	
			1573–1656	
			Wilbye	
			1574–1638	
			Weelkes	
			c. 1575–1623	
	Frescobaldi		Gibbons	
	1583–1643		1583–1625	

[14] These men were Netherlanders who worked in Italy.
[15] Di Lasso wrote in the Italian, French, and German styles.
[16] An Italian who introduced the madrigal style to Germany.

The Overture to the Baroque

Whosoever looketh into this narrowly hardly ever finds himself twice in the same state . . . If I speak diversely of myself, it is because I see myself diversely. All contrarieties are found in me at some moment and in some fashion. Bashful, insolent; chaste, lustful; talkative, taciturn; laborious, delicate; witty, dull; melancholy, gay; lying, truthful; learned, ignorant; both liberal and avaricious and prodigal. All these things I perceive in myself in some degree according as I turn myself about.

— Montaigne (1533–1592)

THE SEVENTEENTH CENTURY IN EUROPE

Rien n'est beau que le vrai; le vrai seul est aimable.

— Boileau

Man is but a reed, the feeblest thing in nature, but he is a thinking reed. The universe need not arm itself to crush him. A vapor, a drop of water, is enough to kill him. But even if the universe should crush him, man would still be nobler than his destroyer because he knows that he dies and he knows the advantage which the universe has over him . . . All our dignity, then, consists in thought. By thought we must raise ourselves . . . Let us labor, then, to think well.

— Pascal: *Pensées*

THE EMERGENCE OF THE BAROQUE SPIRIT

AFTER such a period as the Renaissance, that of the Baroque was inevitable. The sixteenth century had opened with a feeling of joyous exultation and great hope; it closed with a period of doubt, with most of the countries of Europe torn and divided, fighting at one another's throats for existence. The Renaissance had shown impressively enough

Deutsches Museum, Berlin

A PIETÀ OF THE BAROQUE EPOCH

Compare this Pietà by an unknown wood carver of the seventeenth century with the Gothic and Renaissance Pietàs of the fourteenth, fifteenth, and sixteenth centuries shown on pages 225, 226, and 227, and the essence of the Baroque spirit will be immediately manifest.

that men could admire and practice literature, art, and music without necessarily becoming any the better for it. Never had there been greater or more enthusiastic patronage of art; yet too often the art votaries of the Renaissance were its greatest scoundrels, its most foul-minded exponents, and its most corrupt politicians. As Oman says, the employment of a skilled chisel, a facile pen or paintbrush did not necessarily make the men of the Renaissance prophets of a better age to come. The attempt which had been made to supplant the ideals of former ages with a cult of beauty worship sufficient unto itself did not turn out successfully; and a period of natural disillusionment followed. When old beliefs have been discarded, old faiths destroyed, and the new ones installed in their place have been shown to be inadequate and insufficient, there seems to be but one thing left for man to cultivate — action. The seventeenth century was a time of tremendous physical and material activity; something of its scope has been indicated in an earlier chapter. Its artists were largely concerned with a similar development, the cultivation of form, a concern which ultimately led to an overexpansion of virtuosity for its own sake. The result was the style, full of subtleties and sophistications, that we call the *Baroque*.

A possible derivation of this term is the Portuguese *barroco*, the name for the rough pearls that were so generally used as decoration in the florid jewelry of the time. The dark, luscious, rich roll of this word is most suggestive of its application in art history, for it signifies the cultivation of the extraordinary, the outlandish and fantastic, in the hope that a spiritual want will be filled. This spirit of Baroque was by no means a peculiarity of the seventeenth century, for it has occurred in art whenever a great technical facility has happened to coincide in point of time with an overabundance of emotional sensibility. The Greeks had a Baroque epoch, as did the Middle Ages; but at no period in the long history of art were these coincident characteristics so marked as in the centuries immediately following the Renaissance. These ideals gave rise during the seventeenth and eighteenth centuries to a kind of expression in painting, architecture, literature, and sculpture, as well as in music that was so exaggerated in form and so elaborated in style as to border often on the grotesque. The artist of these centuries tried to seek a means for escaping reality, not through the medium of religion, nor by worshiping beauty, nor by cultivating antiquity, as his predecessors had done, but rather by contradicting all its fundamental laws and ends.

This explains what one writer has called the endless extravagant fantasies of Baroque art. Churches were built which, through their gay, restless, vivid architecture — a style which often seems to defy all laws of symmetry and balance — attempted to dispel current doubts and atone for the age's lack of strong faith. "Forget all the uncertainties of the past," these Baroque architects seem to say; "here is not dimness and doubt, but light; here are laid out for you all the riches of heaven — golden saints, painted clouds, marble figures, displayed in a glory that never was on land or sea. Unreal? Of course these are unreal; but then, so is life, for it is nothing but a dream which leads us out and beyond the limits of finite existence."

The Louvre, Paris

THE INTERIOR OF ST. PETER'S, ROME (from a painting by Panini)

"Imaginative, surprising, and gay, richly covered with colored marbles, carvings, paintings, and gilding, the Baroque sought to attract attention by a striking and picturesque appearance. And in that it was successful" (Gardner).

The Baroque painters tried to move their disillusioned spectators in much the same way, by filling their works with sentimental appeal, gorgeous color, overtheatrical form, and dramatic intensity. The results in the case of the great men — Michelangelo, who like Beethoven bestrode two epochs, Rubens, Il Tintoretto, and El Greco — were very impressive, for these artists felt within themselves a surging power which arose from the struggle of their own against the contemporary ideals. Michelangelo's

Alte Pinakothek, Munich

THE RAPE OF THE DAUGHTERS OF LEUCIPPUS, by Rubens

art has been called the passionate thunder of a harassed mind, and so it was; but it gave us the grandiloquent impressiveness of *The Last Judgment*. Again, we owe Rubens's luminous color and abundant splendor to his desire to be as impressive as possible, a desire which was the motivating force of the whole Counter-Reformation movement of the Jesuits,[1] who tried to attract adherents to the Church through Baroque display.

[1] Their founder, Ignatius de Loyola, in his *Spiritual Exercises* definitely leads the observer to a close personal identification of himself with the sufferings of the Church's great figures, the saints and the martyrs.

MUSIC'S NEW MASTERY AMONG THE ARTS

In every age it seems to have been true that some particular art has been supreme: in the Greek and Gothic periods, it was architecture; in the Renaissance, it was painting; and we may safely say that in the Baroque it was music. The newly invented form of the opera, with its combining of music and drama and the consequent heightening of effect and sensibility, is characteristic of this period; it quickly developed a magnificence and splendor that quite put to shame later operatic performances, magnificent as they were. Instrumental music, with its promise of unlimited riches to come, largely took the place of vocal music during this era, the sonata triumphing over the cantata. The substitution of instruments for the human voice is but another evidence of the desire of the Baroque epoch for more and more exploitation of technical means and expressive possibilities; for instruments possess capabilities of color, nuance, and massive expressiveness of which voices are quite incapable.

Means were gradually developed and techniques improved, until the whole period culminated in the burst of grandeur that was Handel and the glory that was Bach. These men (Bach had another side, as we shall see), with the splendor of their technical achievements and the intensity as well as the grandiosity of their expression, try to lead us out and beyond ourselves, to make us forget the limits of ordinary existence in the magnificence of their diction and in the gorgeousness of their style, just as did the architects and painters with their golden domes and painted clouds.

THE REIGN OF REASON

But this was not the only characteristic of this paradoxical period. One of the most brilliant periods in all history, standing squarely at the crossroads between medieval and modern times, it was an age of real achievement, strong hope, and vigorous activity. During its course, man, struggling out of the mystic darkness of the Middle Ages, made new sallies into the unknown and began to discover new ways of overcoming it. Stimulated by the liberating influence of the Renaissance, he began to realize the power of his intellect and to use it in every possible field of endeavor. Whitehead has called this the century of genius, a period so rich intellectually that it has provided us with most of the mental capital upon which we have been living ever since.

No one has written a better preface to this age than did Francis Bacon, one of its greatest figures and "the most powerful mind of modern times." In his *Interpretation of Nature*, written in 1577, he said:

"If any man could succeed — not merely in bringing to light some particular invention, however useful, but in kindling in nature a luminary which would, at its first rising, shed some light on the present limits and borders of human discoveries, and which afterwards, as it rose still higher, would reveal and bring into clear view every nook and cranny of darkness — it seemed to me that such a discoverer would deserve to be called the true Extender of the Kingdom of Man over the universe, the Champion of human liberty, and the Exterminator of the necessities that now keep men in bondage."

Here, briefly and clearly stated, are the ideals of the scientific method which became the accepted manner of investigating the unknown. This method, rapidly developing during this century and the next, has finally come to be the chief vehicle for the expression of man's thought and may well be, unless directed into different paths, the means for his ultimate destruction. It was Bacon who first enunciated the principles of this scientific method of inquiry: First get facts, but get them not out of books or from former authorities or from your own consciousness, as had been done in the past, but by going to nature, "putting her on the rack and compelling her to bear witness." Such facts, while valuable in themselves, are useful because by knowing them we can deduce those forms and laws which underlay the universe.

So men like Descartes and Pascal began the study of mathematics in order to be able to reckon quantities and have an instrument for the handling of facts: the results they achieved have made possible such "triumphs" of engineering as our modern bridges, skyscrapers, and machines. Isaac Newton, one of the greatest speculative geniuses of the human race, by his creation of the differential calculus and by his experiments in physics and astronomy, created a scientific revolution. Galileo's and Kepler's researches in astronomy, Harvey's in biology, Vesalius's in anatomy, Spinoza's speculations in metaphysics — all these placed science on a new and surer foundation and made possible the developments that have since taken place.

In a word, the seventeenth century marks the triumph of the scientific mind: this established itself in every phase of human activity — politics, economics, religion, philology, and art, as well as in the natural sciences. Descartes, the French philosopher, the one man who had more to do with the forming of this spirit than anyone else and whose writings express the spirit and thought of the time more clearly than do any others, thus explains his reasons for turning to science:

"Those long chains of reasoning, simple and easy as they are, of which geometricians make use in order to arrive at the most difficult demonstrations caused me to imagine that all those things which fall under the cognizance of man might very likely be mutually related in the same fashion; and that, provided only that we abstain from receiving anything as true which is not so, and always retain the order which is necessary to deduce one conclusion from another, there can be nothing so remote that we cannot reach to it, nor so recondite that we cannot discover it."

— *Discours de la méthode*

Even the extreme absolutism of the government of the most important and influential country at this time — France — may be attributed to this attempt to relate everything in order, to provide a center from which the universe could be ruled and governed in a regular and systematic manner. Such a center was provided in King Louis XIV, with his motto *L'état, c'est moi:* which is to say, he was the sun, appointed by God and Reason, about which the whole human system should be made to revolve. If anyone thought differently at the time, he would have been considered as being unable to think clearly and rationally. The king carried out his uncontested powers of authority by means of a carefully designed and completely efficient system of administration. The whole country was ruled by a minutely graded hierarchy; taxes were relentless and heavy, and provided a seemingly never-ending source for the immense expenditures of the state. Even the business of the country was on a rationalistic basis, for Louis's minister, Colbert, devised an economic system which he called *Mercantilism*, having as its basis the idea that the wealth of a country consists in its store of gold and precious metals, and so as much of these should be brought into the country as possible, and as little taken out — a purely rational formula which has held seeming magic for economists ever since.

The aristocracy, the army, even the Church, were organized and governed with uniformity and correctness, their one purpose of existence being that of enhancing and supporting the royalty they served. Under domineering masters of strategy the king's army became the best in Europe and won most of the battles of that distracted time. The Church was made over into a Gallic National Church, an organization which did not acknowledge the power and authority of Rome except in spiritual affairs. The *Académie française* was founded in order to fix definitely the meanings and to limit the use of words, the goal being to make the language *clara et distincta* at the sacrifice, if necessary, of richness and imagery.

Even so abstract a thing as " beauty " was explained in scientific terms by these seventeenth-century rationalists. Descartes, who was fond of and wrote a great deal about music, said: " We should busy ourselves with no object about which we cannot attain a certitude equal to that of the demonstrations of arithmetic and geometry," although he did admit that the understanding, which alone is capable of perceiving truth, ought to be aided by " imagination, sense, and memory, lest perchance we omit any expedient that lies within our power."

Hence the same " reasonableness of reason " that was found throughout the rest of society governed the art of this century: its aesthetic was summed up in a trenchant line seriously at variance with modern ideals: " that which is not clear and distinct is not beautiful." Everywhere reason was the dictator of what should be written or painted or built. This was the golden age of French literature, but the ruling class, with its divinely ordered powers, imposed the laws by which this literature should be created. The great tragic dramas of Corneille and Racine were fashioned after the code of tradition, and, if we do not accept these traditions, must today seem dry and overformal. Molière, who succeeded in creating a type of comedy that has never been surpassed in any other country, and

Courtesy of The Art Institute of Chicago

SAINT JOHN ON PATMOS by Nicolas Poussin

who frankly criticized and ridiculed the foibles and weaknesses of the court in such works as *Le bourgeois gentilhomme* and *Les précieuses ridicules*, was merely the exception that proves the rule, a man greater than his time. Aside from him, the limitations settled down over all — even over great figures such as Boileau, whose maxim for poetry was the same — " Nothing is true unless it is beautiful." Poussin, the outstanding French painter of the time, was almost as much a logician as he was an artist, always associating in his pictures the intelligence of the mind with the pleasure of the eye [2]; his conception of nature was an entirely controlled and rational one. Architecture was merely an arrangement of symmetry and balance; gardens were laid out in the form of geometrical figures and planted with the aid of rulers and compasses. Everything was expected to be formal, large, grand, and noble, and, above all else, clear and rational.

[2] His artistic credo was expressed in his statement: " Beauty is at all times based upon a unity imposed upon a chaos of sense perceptions."

De Cou from Ewing Galloway, N. Y.

THE PALACE AT VERSAILLES

THE WORSHIP OF FORM

Heterogeneous as these various aspects of the century — an active, delving curiosity, a determination to know scientifically as well as to experience the world in terms of logic, and a desire to realize it as an illusion — seem to us today, they were welded together into a cultural tendency that affected all the phases of man's activity. The result which gradually manifested itself was a worship of, and delight in, form. In its various aspects — its attempt to substitute illusion for reality, its details of dress and deportment, its love of logical thinking, its correct and classic art — the Baroque was an age of formality. And nowhere is this seen more clearly than in the field of music.

The musical developments of the seventeenth century are important not because of what they produced but because of what they promised for the future. Very early in the period opera made its first appearance, one that was, as we shall see, typically Baroque in spirit, and it was this new style of composition which was invented in the opera, in which there appeared a new manner of using a distinct melody, played or sung to an accompaniment of chords, which formed the basis for the scientific and logical developments that followed. These developments were largely concerned with using as the basis for composition the chord — a group of superimposed and simultaneously sounding notes — rather than spinning music out of the weaving together of a number of intertwining melodies as had largely been done before. The seventeenth century was the time in which the chord became the accepted foundation on which music could be erected; and it was the time when the science of the relationships between these chords — what we have learned to call *harmony* — was definitely established. Of course, chords had existed long before this. We find plenty of them throughout the sixteenth-century music, and in fact as far back as the medieval *faulx bourdon;* but the study of them as blocks of tone, subordinate to and essential for the accompaniment of a melody, was a characteristic seventeenth-century phenomenon. A comparison of any music of the end of the sixteenth century — Palestrina's, for example — with that of the end of the seventeenth — such as Purcell's *Dido and Aeneas* — should make this clear and illustrate exactly what we mean.

In this new style there was something that could please the logicians and that could satisfy their need for rationalizing all things: certain given facts conditioned others, which followed inevitably. It was found that particular notes in a melody required or suggested definite chords in the accompaniment. And, what is more, these chords could be classified and arranged in order, and relationships could be established between them. Gradually it was found that two chords were used more than any others — the tonic and the dominant. These became supreme, and the scales in which they were placed, the major and the minor, were employed to the exclusion of all the others. Thus was music systematized and rationalized and made a matter of mathematical equations and diagrams. The consequences for the future are what is important here; for out of this rationalization came the whole modern harmonic system and the music of Haydn, Mozart, Beethoven, and the rest.

Another reason why this new monodic type of writing found especial favor at this time was that it fitted the general demands of the period for clarity and simplicity of expression. "That which I can clearly and distinctly perceive is true," said Descartes again and again; and this ideal of *clara et distincta perceptio* is inherent in the relationship of chords to a melody. Nothing could be simpler or in more striking contrast to the "complications and magnificent difficulties" which the early opera writers saw in the polyphonic style. Such relationships, being established as true (for them), were consequently beautiful. It was as simple as that!

Moreover, the preoccupation of the time with the problems of form in art made inevitable an interest in the perfecting of the formal foundations of music on the part of the composers of this time. The general aesthetic tendencies of the century, combined with the new uses to which the keyboard instruments were being put in playing a type of music specially adapted to their style, made necessary a kind of music possessing definite principles of internal organization, that is, form. It was during this century that German organists first wrote fugues, according to our modern conception of this type of structure, developing their principles from the earlier and freer *ricercare* and *fantasia*. Out of the rudimentary and simple harpsichord suites of the sixteenth century, Jacques Champion de Chambonnières fashioned the dance suite, a form which became very important to the writers of the next century; and his form was adopted by such contemporaries as Purcell in England and Froberger in Germany. The tremendous and sudden popularity of the violin as a performing instrument made necessary the evolution of a form of instrumental music suitable to its peculiar character. Composers developed, out of the freely contrapuntal *canzona*, pieces which they called *sonatas*. At first this term implied simply that the music was meant to be played rather than sung; but gradually it acquired more definite significance. The works of Corelli and Purcell, both seventeenth-century composers, are the first examples of this form that give satisfaction to modern ears.

It must be realized that all these multifarious activities went on more or less simultaneously. The general intellectual keenness of this age made for an amazing development of performing technique in instrumental music, a development which was closely related to the perfecting of the instruments themselves. We must always remember that the evolution of the violin and its music was contemporary with the development of the opera, both taking place against the same stimulating aesthetic and intellectual background. Hand in hand with the growth of this new style of writing went also a strengthening of the old polyphonic vitality, now transplanted to instrumental music, a strengthening which produced finally the masterpieces of Sebastian Bach.

Although the century produced only two outstanding men, Monteverdi and Purcell, it gave to music, as it did to science, many of the ideas on which we have been living ever since. It has been said of Francis Bacon that he rang the bell that called the wits together and announced that Europe had come of age. We may likewise say of his fellow countryman, Purcell, and of Monteverdi, that they proclaim, in no uncertain terms, that the age of modern music has now begun.

THE BIRTH OF OPERA

Before offering you this music of mine, I think proper to make known to you what led me to invent this new kind of vocal writing; since reason must be the beginning and source of all human doings, and he who cannot give his reason at once lays himself open to the suspicion of having worked at haphazard. Although our music was brought upon the stage by Sig. Emilio del Cavalieri, with marvelous originality, before anyone else I know of, it nevertheless pleased Signori Iacopo Corsi and Ottavio Rinuccini (in the year 1594) to have me set to music the play of Dafne, written by Sig. Ottavio Rinuccini, treating it in another manner, to show by a simple experiment of what the song of our age is capable. Wherefore, seeing that I had to do with Dramatic Poetry, and must accordingly seek, in my music, to imitate one who speaks (and doubtless no one ever yet spoke in singing), it seemed to me that the ancient Greeks and Romans (who, in the opinion of many, sang the whole of their tragedies on the stage) must have made use of a sort of music which, while surpassing the sounds of ordinary speech, fell so far short of the melody of singing as to assume the shape of something intermediate between the two. And this is why we find in their poems so large an use made of the Iambic Metre, which does not rise to the sublimity of the Hexameter, albeit it is said to overstep the bounds of ordinary speech. Therefore, abandoning every style of vocal writing known hitherto, I gave myself up wholly to contriving the sort of imitation (of speech) demanded by this poem. And, considering that the sort of vocal delivery applied by the ancients to singing, and called by them vox diastematica *(as if held in check and kept in suspense), could be somewhat accelerated, so as to hold a mean course between the slow and deliberate pace of singing and the nimble, rapid pace of speaking, and thus be made to serve my purpose (as they, too, adapted it to the reading of poems and heroic verse) by approaching the speaking voice, called by them* vox continuata*, as has also been done by our modern composers (if perhaps for another purpose); considering this, I also recognized that, in our speech, some sounds are intoned in such a way that harmony can be based upon them and that, in the course of conversation, we pass through many others which are not so intoned, until we return to one which is capable of forming a new consonance. And, having regard for the accents and modes of expression we use — in grief, rejoicing, etc. — I have made the bass move at a rate appropriate to them, now faster, now slower, according to the emotions to be expressed, and have sustained it through both dissonances and consonances* [tra le false, e tra le buone proporzioni]*, until the speaker's voice, after passing through various degrees of pitch, comes to those sounds which, being intoned in ordinary speech, facilitate the formation of a new consonance. And I have done this . . . to the end that the employment of dissonances shall diminish, or conceal that advantage of which ancient music may perhaps have had less need. And finally (though I dare not assert that this was the sort of singing done in Greek or Roman plays), I have deemed it the only sort that can be admissible in our music, by adapting itself to our speech.*

Receive it, therefore, kindly, courteous readers, and, though I may not, this time, have reached the point I thought myself able to reach (regard for novelty having been a curb on my course), accept it graciously in every way. And perhaps it will come to pass on another occasion that I shall show you something more perfect than this. Meanwhile, I shall think to have done enough if I have opened the path for the talent of others, for them to walk in my footsteps to that glory to which it has not been given to me to attain. And I hope that my use of dissonances, played and sung discreetly, yet without timidity (having pleased so many and worthy men), will not trouble you; especially in the sad and grave airs of Orfeo, Arcetro, and Dafne . . .

And may you live happy.

— From Peri's Preface to his opera *Eurydice* (Apthorp: *The Opera Past and Present*)

THE BIRTH OF A NEW ART

"So let me die.
Why must I, who have trusted in thee,
Feel the blows of such a cruel fate
And suffer so bitter a fortune?
Ah, let me perish, let me die!"

WE have only to read such words as these, voicing the lament of the unhappy Ariadne and sung by one of the characters in Monteverdi's opera of that name, written in 1608, to realize that a new spirit has come into music, one quite different from the ideals of such works as we have so far been considering. Monteverdi was able to clothe these words, filled as they are with self-pity and expressive of the utmost despair, ardent passion, and longing for death, with music which so heightens their emotional effect and emphasizes their natural intensity as to make us realize that at this point we have come to the beginnings of the modern period of music. For here is a musical setting that makes an immediate appeal to our hearts, just as it did to the hearts of the people in 1608, when, as a contemporary account puts it, "there was no one in the audience who was not greatly moved; none of the ladies present, at the singing of the beautiful 'Lament,' could withhold their tears of sympathy, so filled with vehement passion was the music, and so movingly was it sung."

In listening to this Lament of Monteverdi's, the most casual hearer will realize that its composer was not concerned with any process of weaving sounds together so as to secure the generalized, abstract type of musical beauty that we found in the madrigals. Here the musician has come to a more direct grip with life and has been able to translate his experience into music that is moving in the same sense that Beethoven's or Wagner's music is. We find that there are also clear-cut technical changes: all the involved contrapuntal feeling is gone; the accompaniment has taken on a chordal, harmonic form; there is a clearly defined difference between the vocal and the instrumental parts. In 1605, we must remember, composers like Wilbye, and even Monteverdi himself, were writing madrigals — plenty of them — of the usual sort; and here, but a few years later, there suddenly emerges an entirely new form, one filled with quite a different feeling.

The actual change from one style to the other was sudden enough; but it was made inevitable by the artistic ideals which the Renaissance had set in motion, and there were in the music of the sixteenth century many presentiments that it was coming. The discovery of the best physical means for conveying this new aspect of personal emotion and dramatic intensity in music was, like so many of the world's important discoveries, something in the way of an accident; but years before the first opera was invented in 1600, composers were striving to inject a more dramatic and expressive spirit into their music. Among them were Gesualdo of Venosa, who introduced dissonances into his madrigals in order to make them more effective, and Orazio Vecchi, who attempted what has since come to be known as a " madrigal opera " — a drama of three acts in which the entire text was set in madrigal form for five-part chorus.

In his book on *The History of Taste,* Frank Chambers has pointed out that the natural and inevitable result of the whole Renaissance movement was the emergence of the ideal of Classicism. This spirit in art was brought about through the revival of interest in the older classic civilizations and the pursuant formation of a set of principles derived from the study of these civilizations for the guidance of contemporary artists in their creative activity. Outstanding among such classic ideas was that which declared that art should attempt above all things to imitate nature. As Giovanni Lomazzo, whose *Trattato dell' Arte pittura, scultura ed architettura,* published in 1584, was a formulation of the ideals of Italian classicism, said: " All the arts have the same end, intending nothing else than to resemble things as near life as may be. An emotion represented in a picture should be able to arouse the same emotion in the beholder; a laughing picture will arouse laughter, grieving cause grief, wondering arouse wonder, etc." In brief, art should essay to imitate natural things, idealizing them, and supplying, if need be, any defects that might exist. It is easy to see why, then, with this spirit of naturalism so strongly current, the writers of the late Renaissance became impatient with the restrictions laid on them by the purely contrapuntal type of music and sought an expression that would be more direct and personal.

ITS SOURCES

The discovery of how best to do this came through a characteristically Renaissance effort to imitate the musical ideals of the ancient Greeks and to add some contribution to Italian drama that would make it comparable to what Spanish and English writers had done in that field. Along about the eighties of the sixteenth century, a group of amateur antiquarians began to investigate the manner in which the Greeks might have used music in their dramas, thinking thus to be able to increase the expressiveness of contemporary musical declamation. These men, bound together in an artistic circle, the *Camerata* — composers, singers, and instrumentalists — were thoroughly familiar with the music of their times; and they realized that it was not suitable for the purpose they had in mind. A few specimens of early Greek music were available to them, in fact, almost as many as we have today. Although none of this group could read this music, it inspired Galilei, father of the famous astronomer, to attempt an adaptation of a part of Dante's *Divine Comedy* in what he conceived might have been the Greek manner of composing dramatic music.

This pleased the fellow members of the *Camerata* so well that two of them combined to produce a whole drama with music. Rinuccini, a poet, wrote a dramatic poem, *Dafne*, that was set to music by Jacopo Peri, director of music to the Florentine court. This was produced in one of the great houses of the nobility in Florence in 1597 and was in turn so well received that its author and composer united in another similar enterprise, the writing of a *dramma per musica* on the classic Eurydice theme. It was first played on the occasion of the wedding of Maria de' Medici and Henry IV of France in 1600 and constitutes the first *opera* the music of which has come down to us, that of *Dafne* being lost.

Thus was born not only a new type of music [3] but an entirely new era. These dramatic musicians working in Florence at the beginning of the

[3] This new kind of music received several names. Sometimes it was called *Le Nuove Musiche* (The New Music), from the title of a book of songs written in this style by Caccini; sometimes it was given the title *Dramma per Musica* (Drama through Music); and Peri and Rinuccini called their work a *favola in musica* — a musical fable. The best generic term to use in describing it is *monody*, meaning that it is based on the principle of one voice accompanied, instead of many voices intertwined.

seventeenth century thought that they were reviving the glories of the Greek classic drama. What they actually did was to invent a musical form which made possible the direct expression of personal feeling on the stage, its music being a close reflection of the ideas and emotions of the text. So was the door opened leading to modern musical expression. When *Eurydice* was published, Peri wrote a detailed Preface, quoted in part on pages 320 and 321, giving the reasons for what he had tried to do, which explains, better than can any amount of description, this new kind of writing.

In reality, the idea of thus associating music with drama was neither new nor confined to the practices of the Greeks. All nations and peoples have loved the drama and from its earliest days gave music a share in its representations. Holy Mother Church soon recognized the lessons that dramatic representation of her mysteries could teach, and during the Middle Ages she produced mystery and miracle plays about the lives of her great figures, as well as moralities, teaching through the personification of Good, Evil, Covetousness, Charity, and the other qualities of man's mind. At appropriate places in these medieval dramas there were inserted suitable musical interludes to heighten the dramatic effects, such as, for example, the songs of the angels and shepherds and the touching lullaby by the mothers of the slaughtered innocents in the famous English Coventry Christmas play of the sixteenth century.

In Italy the *sacre rappresentazioni* (sacred dramas), special kinds of mystery or miracle plays, were important as direct predecessors of the opera; for at the height of their development — about the middle of the sixteenth century — they seem to have been largely sung, with few spoken lines, and had definite interludes which were given over to dancing. The special channel through which these religious dramas permeated the common, secular life of the people was the *commedia dell' arte*, with its characters of Harlequin, Pantaloon, Pulcinella, and the other figures which have survived only in rather faded pantomime and fancy-dress relics. Here the ancient Greek and Roman plays, much attenuated and liberally filled out with contemporary impromptus and gags, were made the bases of the art. These Italian comedians traveled abroad to France and England, and Shakespeare used more than one of their ideas and

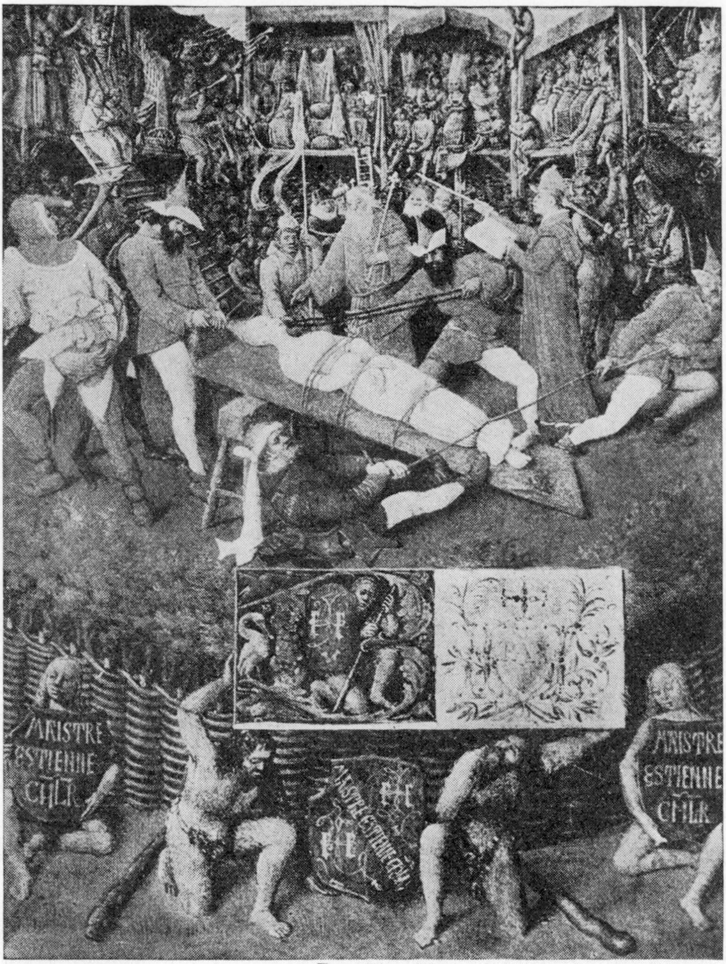

From Livre d'heures d'Estienne Chevalier, Chantilly

SCENE FROM A MEDIEVAL MYSTERY PLAY: "The Martyrdom of Apollonia"

Notice the general details: the scene, of course, is that which would constitute the "hit" of the whole play, that of the torture. In the background of the open stage upon which this is being enacted are a number of raised booths in which the other episodes would be played; to the right is Hell's Mouth, with its attendant demons, who constantly roamed about, enlivening the whole; to the left is a curtained Heaven, with its angels, waiting to receive the soul of the martyred victim. Grouped just to the right is a group of musicians with trumpets and wood-wind instruments. There is good reason to suppose that these, as well as singers, were employed in other episodes. In the center, with stick and book, stands the *regisseur*, directing the action.

brought to fresh life a number of their characters. Music was an integral part of their plays.

Still another important forerunner of the opera was that traditional Renaissance social entertainment, the masque — a combination of poetry, vocal and instrumental music, dancing, pageantry, acting, elaborate costuming and scenic decoration, the whole treating, in the most elaborate and lavish manner possible, classic and allegorical subjects. The form seems to have developed first in Italy, possibly having its origin in the huge processions put on by the Renaissance princes, consisting of long lines of men on horseback, carrying torches, wearing masks and fantastic costumes, and accompanied by musicians. It passed rapidly to France (the popular *ballet de cour,* of which no less than eighty were given during the twenty-year reign of King Henry IV, was really a masque) and reached its highest perfection and elaborateness in Elizabethan England.[4] The instrumental musicians used in these tremendous spectacles were scattered about the scenes in association with various groups of dramatic characters, a fact which may have led to the traditional grouping together of certain instrumental timbres and thus laid the foundations for later developments in the orchestra. There were both choruses and solo parts in monodic style for the voice.

There were other Italian Renaissance ingredients which had a determining influence on the final flavor of the whole: (1) the carnival songs, ribald and licentious stanzas directed at the ladies present at these festival masques, which were later toned down and treated in a dramatic fashion; (2) the choruses and dances from the pastoral dramas which,

[4] Francis Bacon has left an interesting description of the contemporary masque in his essay, *Of Masques and Triumphs:* " These things are but toys, to come amongst such serious observations. But yet, since princes will have such things, it is better they should be graced with elegancy than daubed with cost. Dancing to song is a thing of great state and pleasure. I understand it, that the song be in quire, placed aloft, and accompanied with some broken music [an accompaniment furnished by a band in which the instruments were not all of one kind]; and the ditty fitted to the device.

" Acting in song, especially in dialogues, hath an extreme good grace: I say acting, not dancing; and the voices of the dialogue would be strong and manly (a base and a tenor; no treble), and the ditty high and tragical; not nice or dainty. Several quires, placed one over against another, and taking the voice by catches, anthem-wise, give great pleasure. . . . Let the songs be loud and cheerful, and not chirpings or pulings. Let the music likewise be sharp and loud and well placed."

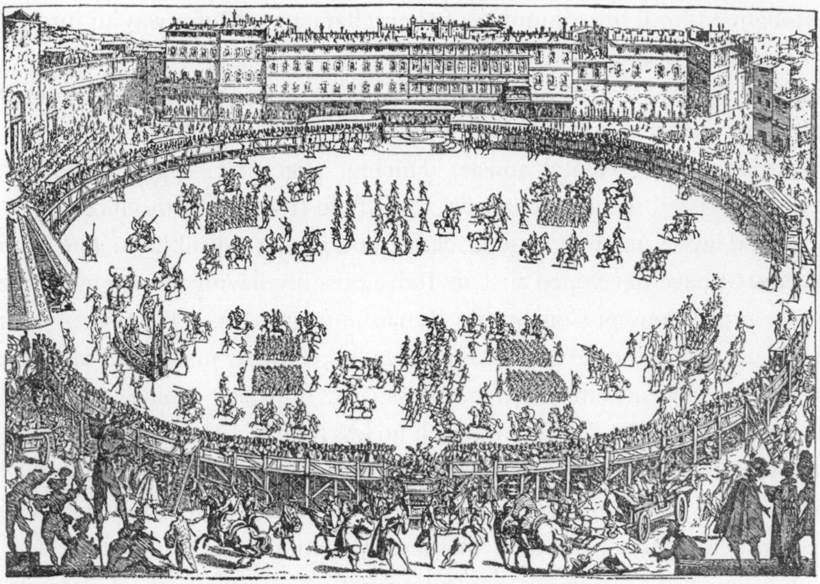

THE WARS OF LOVE

The scene represents a Renaissance spectacle produced in the Piazza di S. Croce in Florence, with text by Salvadori and music by Peri and other composers.

modeled on the classic Latin eclogues, became the delight of the fashionable sixteenth-century world; and (3) the madrigal comedies, attempts to dramatize and unify in one continuous and developed piece the short, lyric madrigal type of writing of which Vecchi's *L'Amfiparnasso* is the classic example.

There is a great deal of confusion among the writers of musical history as to just how and when all these various elements were fused into the form we know as *opera*. Some of them give great prominence to Poliziano's *Favola di Orfeo,* produced at the court of Mantua sometime between 1472 and 1483, as being an important forerunner of the form. An Italian musicologist, Tirabassi, claims that the little 34-page *Orfeo dolente* by Domenico Belli, choirmaster of the Church of San Lorenzo in Florence, is the first opera. Sometimes Peri's *Dafne* is given this honor, sometimes *Eurydice* by Peri and in part by Caccini. Such matters may well be left to the scholars; it is important for the general reader, however, to realize what a desire for novelty there was in the air at the time. As a Florentine musician put it, " The one thing everyone agreed on was that, since the music of the day was quite inadequate to the expression of the words and its development actually repugnant to the thought, means must be found in the attempt to bring music back to that of classical times, to bring out the chief melody so that the poetry should be clearly intelligible " (Soni, writing in 1640).

Once the form was started, there were problems of all sorts to be solved: how best to carry on a dialogue to music; whether to let the music be continuous or to intersperse it with speaking; what part the chorus, hitherto paramount, was to play; what sort of instruments should be used for accompaniment — this when no orchestral mold existed beyond that of the " chest of viols " and " broken consorts " of miscellaneous instruments. All these questions had to be decided; and it was, indeed, a matter of *solvitur ambulando!*

Opera, for the majority of people, has always been an exotic form. This is easily enough understood, for it is unnatural, and in its most elaborate shapes makes very heavy demands on the listener's power of attention. It is not too much to say that without a great deal of solid study, much of Wagner's work, the greatest that has ever been written in this form, must remain uncomprehended. For the mass of citizens, music is still a recreation; they always resent the idea of having to work at it, and so they will always prefer the operas which make the smallest demands. How delightful it must have been in the earliest days of opera, when everything was fresh and adventurously exciting; when the Italians, always quick in the dramatic uptake, had around them all the stimuli for such new invention: the patronage and money of the nobility, leisure and zest for experiment, and the background of Renaissance example in the other arts!

AS DRYDEN SAW OPERA

Not so many years after Peri and Rinuccini presented their first opera in Florence, the English writer John Dryden, whose experience with the stage in London gave him a particular insight into dramatic problems, wrote this description of opera:

"An opera is a poetical tale, or fiction, represented by vocal and instrumental music, adorned with scenes, machines, and dancing. The supposed persons of this musical drama are generally supernatural, as gods, and goddesses, and heroes, which at least are descended from them, and are in due time to be adopted into their number. The subject, therefore, being extended beyond the limits of human nature, admits of that sort of marvelous and surprising conduct which is rejected in other plays. Human impossibilities are to be received as they are in faith, because, where gods are introduced, a supreme power is to be understood, and second causes are out of doors . . . If the persons represented were to speak upon the stage, it would follow, of necessity, that the expressions should be lofty, figurative, and majestical, but the nature of an opera denies the frequent use of these poetical ornaments; for vocal music, though it often admits a loftiness of sound, yet always exacts an harmonious sweetness; or, to distinguish yet more justly, the recitative part of the opera requires a more masculine beauty of expression and sound; the other, which for want of a proper English word I must call the *songish* part, must abound in the softness and variety of numbers; its principal intention being to please the hearing than to gratify the understanding. It appears, indeed, preposterous at first sight, that rhyme, on any consideration, should take place of reason; but, in order to resolve the problem, this fundamental proposition must be settled, that the first inventors of any art or science, provided they have brought it to perfection, are, in reason, to give laws to it; and, according to their model, all after-undertakers are to build."

THE CHARACTERISTICS OF THE FIRST OPERA

If we examine Peri's *Eurydice* in any detail we shall find readily enough that most of the "after-undertakers" in opera used it for a model and built pretty well after its plan; all the advantages as well as the shortcomings of the later music dramas are here present in embryo. In general, the work presents a number of broad dramatic situations, with a text that gives opportunity for both histrionic incident and reflective comment. There are a number of different stage pictures to please the eye and enough stage action to hold the interest of the spectator. The ending, in defiance of the classic myth on which the text is based, is a happy one, thus establishing a license that succeeding generations of operatic writers have followed.

The music is used for heightening the dramatic expression. All music, if properly devised, can be made to intensify the expression of emotion, just as poetry does, in comparison with ordinary prose. And it has been the particular function of dramatic music ever since the *stile recitativo* or *rappresentativo* was evolved by Peri — dry and barren as it may seem today — to make it possible for the singer to re-create the emotions of his part in a more intensified form. Listen to the monologue of Orpheus from this opera, which begins *Funeste piaggie:* "Ye dismal hillsides, how sad ye are without Eurydice." The accompanying chords are primitive, to be sure; the elaborate mechanism of the preceding era has been swept away; but there is a simple poignancy of expression that was generally lacking in the more elegantly mannered music of the madrigals.

Peri's accompanying orchestra was a strange one according to modern standards — a harpsichord, a chitarrone (bass lute), a large lute, a viola da gamba, and, for special effects in certain parts of the score, three flutes. The harpsichord played the chordal accompaniments for the recitative, against a running background of gamba tone. Thus was established another custom which held for years after as to the proper rendition of accompaniment for recitative. In the score only the vocal part and the bass were written out, the players filling in the chords from a sort of abbreviated musical shorthand supplied by the composer (called *figured bass*), a method which was generally used until the time of Mozart and Beethoven. In addition to supplying the accompaniments, this orchestra (playing behind the scenes) provided a general atmospheric background for the action of the piece; for instance, Peri introduces into one of his songs short instrumental interludes for the three flutes, in an attempt to suggest the pastoral quality of the text, the flute having been the favored instrument of the Greek shepherds. Here is the direct ancestor of all the means for providing emotional color so richly developed by later operatic composers. Furthermore, there were a number of massed choruses and dances, all of them being integral parts of the dramatic action. The music for these was written in a curious mixture of a primitive attempt at harmonic effects and a use of the older madrigalian counterpoint. The principles of monodic choral construction, so effective in the later operas, had not been sufficiently worked out to be applied here with effectiveness.

ORATORIO

To the same year, 1600, belongs the first performance of what came to be known as *oratorio*, Cavalieri's *La Rappresentazione dell' Anima e del Corpo* (*The Representation of the Soul and Body*), which introduces such characters as Time, Life, Pleasure, Intellect, as well as the Soul and the Body, and employs dancing and scenery, as well as acting and singing. Its general features were almost exactly like those of Peri's opera, with simple choruses and instrumental interludes. The whole thing was, in fact, nothing but an opera on a sacred subject, performed in a church. Thus both these styles, opera and oratorio, grew from one stem, as did the ancient mystery plays and the secular dramas.[5] Later oratorio developed into a form different from these early dramatic *rappresentazione* and today is a form entirely devoid of theatrical elements. It seems decidedly to be declining in favor, after a long prosperous period, while opera, generally speaking, is holding its own. The two arose out of different manifestations and purposes, from the same instinct for drama and for the deployment of the solo voice: opera at first for the courtly circles, oratorio for the simple. It is interesting to see how their positions have been reversed.

POPULAR INFLUENCE ON OPERATIC STYLE

The emergence of opera as a popular form of entertainment (the first opera theater being opened in Venice in 1637) brought pressure on composers to please their paying patrons. Now very rarely in history have the masses, however good their upbringing, been fond of long and complex pieces of music. Generations went to the building up of a public for Wagner; and even today it is the commonest thing to hear people declare that they cannot stand his long works. An educated public for any kind of opera has to be developed slowly; and the instinct of every member of it, in the beginning, is to enjoy short patches of anything, but

[5] The word *oratorio* comes from *oratory*, the establishment in which St. Philip Neri, the founder of the Order of the Oratorians — an order of priests without vows — held his religious dramatic representations.

not to wish for either very long or very involved scenes. Great elaboration came only with the multiplication of orchestral resources and the use of the leitmotiv. But although the practice of the period up to Monteverdi had been to keep most of the pieces of music short, the possibilities of operatic freedom tempted composers to try longer flights. Here the popular taste was influential, and that taste has always shaped a great deal of the world's opera, so that the memory of nine tenths of operagoers is concerned with particular airs which can be readily carried in the memory and hummed. The supreme example of almost a whole nation's likings is that of Gilbert and Sullivan, the only operatic material for which the British people are ever likely to care much. Those clever works abound in short, crisp, aphoristic passages, in gaiety (and occasionally simple pathos), qualities which delight without putting much strain on mind or spirit or ear. Giving all due praise to these works, which have been the lifelong joy of millions, nevertheless, to most of their devotees, operas such as Mozart and Wagner wrote are almost as foreign as those of Monteverdi.

MONTEVERDI

We can say that this composer was the first to write a great opera. Bridging two epochs, he is the outstanding representative of this greatest change in style that music has ever seen. Born in Cremona in 1567, he became the chief musician at the court of Gonzaga in Mantua, whence he went to St. Mark's, Venice, where he became *maestro di cappella*. Having achieved a superb technique in the writing of the contrapuntal style, he was the ideal man to breathe the breath of life into the rather stilted and ineffectual new form of the opera. We may call him the most advanced polyphonist of the sixteenth century, for many of his works foreshadow the changes that were to come later. And he was also the first man of the seventeenth century to endow the rather arid inventions of the modernists with something of the rich heritage of the past. " In either century, the new or the old, he was undisputed master."

If we look at some of the music from this composer's opera *Orfeo*, first produced in Mantua in 1607 and readily available in modern reprints, we shall see what a genius could do in the way of dramatic, descriptive music and orchestral effects. We can see here how completely changed was Peri's dry *stilo rappresentativo*. With Monteverdi it becomes a powerful, dramatic medium, suggestive of the intonation of impassioned speech. How boldly and well this composer expressed the spirit of naturalism that was abroad in his time is readily seen in such excerpts as the Lament from *Ariadne* (already quoted), the expressive song of Orpheus when he learns of the death of Eurydice, from *Orfeo*, and the song of the Nurse, from his last opera, *Poppea*. In all these we find striking use of dissonances, a use which must have seemed extremely harsh to Monteverdi's contemporaries, if we can judge by the following diatribe of one of them:

> "These new composers believe that they have done everything when they satisfy the ear. Day and night they spend their time at their instruments, that they may try out the effects of pieces interlarded with dissonances — the fools. They never realize that these instruments betray them. They seem to be satisfied if they can produce the greatest possible tonal disturbance by bringing together altogether unrelated elements and mountainous collections of cacophonies."
>
> — Artusi

Monteverdi did not hesitate to use these dissonances, moreover, as "unprepared discords," thus firmly establishing our modern ideas of key relationships and sounding the death knell of the older modal systems of tonalities. We find him struggling also with problems of form and achieving some remarkable results in the way of working out something to take the place of the elaborate imitative devices of the earlier polyphony. Certain repetitions of phrases (as, for example, in Ariadne's Lament), suggestive of the later leitmotiv, a real distinction between narrative recitative and lyric aria, and such a strictness of invention as is evidenced in his monody *Ohime, ch'io cado*, where he makes use of a set of melodic variants over a fixed bass, are portents of the great things which followed in the next two centuries. Monteverdi provided his operas with a characteristic prelude, in which the instruments sound effectively, and his connecting instrumental *ritornellos* and *sinfonias* are a definite part of his dramatic development. To put it briefly, we have here the beginning of the evolution of modern music.

But we should not think of this composer as a mere theoretician, of interest only as an innovator. We have already quoted a contemporary account of the first performance of *Ariadne* in Mantua, an account which leaves no doubt as to Monteverdi's ability to move the people of his time. Monteverdi was one of the first geniuses in music. Finding a newly created form ready for his use, he was able to stamp his own individuality on it and make it a vital and moving thing. Nef has said that in no other period of music's history has there been such a strong urge toward directness and naturalness as in the first half of the seventeenth century. And, he adds, no modern *verismo* has been produced of the rank of Claudio Monteverdi, who may well be placed beside his contemporary, Shakespeare; just as the latter lets each of his characters use his own individual speech, so the Italian dramatist uses "demonic and raging passion as easily as grace and tender fervor."

It would be uselessly tiresome to enumerate all the composers who made contributions to the development of opera during the seventeenth century. Suffice it to say that once the opera became a more democratic institution through the opening of a number of theaters devoted to it in Italy and France, there began the modern "virtuoso" system, with its interest in singing rather than composition, its caballing impresarios, and its applauding publics. This developed first in Venice and spread from there through all Italy and into Germany, France, and far-off England.

THE DEVELOPMENT OF THE OPERA

BAROQUE OPERA IN ITALY

IT is in the operas of Cavalli (a pupil of Monteverdi's) and Cesti and in the cantatas and oratorios of Carissimi that the Baroque spirit will be first noted in music. We have seen how Monteverdi strove above all else for music that was realistic and at the same time emotionally expressive. With these later men there came a smoothing out of such intensities, a trend toward more pleasing and more brilliant melodies that would give the singer increased opportunities for the display of technique, an expression that was grandiose rather than eloquent, structurally impressive rather than movingly expressive.

INTERIOR OF THE CORTINA THEATER, VIENNA, 1667

The production is that of Cesti's *Il pomo d'oro* (from an engraving by Franz Geffels).

A well-known engraving of the time shows the interior of one of the theaters in Vienna during the performance of one of Cesti's operas, *Il pomo d'oro.*[6] Everything bespeaks the spirit of the Baroque — the splendor of the wooden interior of the building, the magnificence of the audience, the elaborateness of the stage appointments. And if we examine the music of this opera (or any other by these composers), we find a greatly increased emphasis on elaborate choral writing, both for the solo voices and for the chorus ensembles. The whole thing is designed from the viewpoint of the singer rather than from that of the composer. The vocal lines are no longer direct and simple but have developed devices that will

[6] This opera was written in 1667 in honor of the wedding of Leopold I, Emperor of Austria, mighty warrior and the founder of a magnificent operatic enterprise which was able to produce no fewer than an average of eight operas a year through a period of half a century — over four hundred new works all together.

show off the voice; and there is a distinct feeling for massed effects in the harmonic structure of the choruses. *Il pomo d'oro* and the other Baroque operas are "singer's operas." The one thing desired above all else was vocal melody and brilliance; plot and expressive truth were comparatively unimportant.

The same characteristics mark the oratorios and cantatas of Carissimi. Although he wrote no operas himself, he strongly influenced the development of the form through the manner in which he employed the chorus in his oratorios. It was natural that, except for such a man as Monteverdi, who had found the means for making madrigals dramatic, the older style of writing for chorus should be lost in the new trappings of opera. The choruses of most of the early operas are of poor quality when we compare them with the magnificent writing that preceded them. Carissimi was able to invest his oratorio choruses with much of the effectiveness of the sixteenth-century madrigals, introducing a certain amount of realistic and descriptive writing. His lively dramatic sense can be seen in his popular *Vittoria,* a song which celebrates a lover's deliverance from a bondage which in his case seems to have been grievous rather than rapturous. This delight is expressed with the most charming vivacity and in the most elegant form: Carissimi's was the truly Baroque lover.

VOCAL CHAMBER MUSIC

In addition to works for the opera theater and sacred oratory, composers of this time paid a great deal of attention to a form of music which has almost completely disappeared today — what might be called *vocal chamber music.* This consisted of short compositions for one or several solo voices and was intended for the salons and chambers of the wealthy patrons of art; but it was by no means thought to be inferior to the operas or the oratorios. Carissimi especially cultivated the cantata, thus establishing a type which later composers richly developed. These works consisted usually of a regular alternation of recitative and aria and combined a clarity of expression with a balanced symmetry of style that suggests the later string quartets.

These were especially cultivated by Alessandro Scarlatti and were extremely popular during the latter years of the seventeenth century, owing to a feeling, increased by a papal interdiction, that opera was a form of music not particularly conducive to public morality. So the wealthy patrons of the time encouraged the writing of these cantatas which, as Burney said, contain a " little drama entire, having a beginning, a middle, and an end, in which the charms of poetry are united with those of music, and the mind is amused while the ear is gratified." Typical examples are Scarlatti's *Sento nel core certo dolore* and Handel's *Mel dolce dell' oblio*.

AGOSTINO STEFFANI

The vocal duets of Steffani, like the man who wrote them, are as characteristic of the period as anything it produced. In them the recitative style, so carefully developed by Peri and his followers, completely disappears; and the melodies are written for one purpose only, that of the glorification of the human voice. The idealism of Monteverdi here succumbs to the Italian predilection for absolute beauty: Renaissance naturalism and expressiveness have changed into Baroque *bel canto*.

It is difficult to conceive of a more typical Baroque figure than Steffani: a vital and energetic individual, " honorable priest," court and chamber musician, organist, opera composer, diplomat, trusted ambassador of princes and popes, he seems to have been skilled in all forms of human behavior, honoring everything he touched. Polished, sophisticated, urbane, he was connected in various roles with the princely courts of Munich and Hanover; he became intimate with their royal families and was entrusted by them with many a delicate diplomatic mission to various European capitals. Yet he never forsook entirely his chosen career of music and somehow found time, in the midst of all this brilliant activity, to compose eighteen operas and some eighty vocal chamber-music duets. His bearing was said by one observer to have been " grave but tempered with a sweetness and affability that rendered his conversation very engaging "; no better description could be given of his music, with its aristocratic, naturally graceful, movement, and its Baroque impressiveness.

Courtesy of the Historical Museum of Munich

A SETTING FROM STEFFANI'S OPERA "SERVIO TULLIO"

The opera, produced in Munich in 1685–1686, showed this forest scene according to Baroque ideals.

THE GERMAN SPIRIT: SCHÜTZ

These new forms quickly spread to other countries, at least, to those centers wherein were musical strongholds, such as Munich and Vienna. It was the Italians who spread the gospel, and composers of other nations largely copied their style, both in opera and in vocal chamber music of the kind just mentioned — solo cantatas and duets. Naturally the German spirit worked on all these forms, but it was only in oratorio that for some time we find much marked change, the obvious reason being the difference in religion between the north and the south. Whilst Germany lost something of Italian freedom of vocal utterance, it gained much in the development of the formal side of the oratorio, a development which led, through Schütz, to Bach and his great Mass and Passions.

Heinrich Schütz, the so-called Father of German music, was born into the uneasy world of 1585, a world filled with religious strife and conflict. He spent much time abroad during his student days, coming in Italy into contact with the operatic developments in Venice and working there with Gabrieli, whose influence on his style is strongly marked. When he went back to his native land and was made director of the music at the court of the Elector of Saxony, he sent some of the royal musicians to Italy to benefit as he had done. He even put Rinuccini's libretto of *Dafne* into German for a performance at his court, probably the first operatic presentation in Germany. But opera was not then the most congenial form to the Germans, and although there were several attempts at writing native works, notably the *Frauenzimmer Gesprechspiele gesangweis auf italianische Art gesetzt* by Georg Philipp Harsdörffer in 1644, the form did not prove popular.

Schütz was concerned with sacred music; he poured forth in profusion sacred songs, motets, dramatic cantatas, psalm settings, and "dialogues" from the Scriptures — all of them vivid, colored music. In the larger works, such as his Passion settings, he gave freer declamatory rein to solo parts. Perhaps his setting of Psalm CXI (Praise Ye the Lord) is as good an example of his style as we could find. The crisp chording, the taking up of the music in one part after another, the massive effects, and the big, swelling, woven ending all suggest a lively, fresh approach to the text, a sense of pomp, color, drama, and dignity in which we can find (though this is a comparatively small example of the composer's powers) a mingling of Italian and German types of mind, with a personal grip that distinguishes the outstanding molder of style.

FRENCH OPERA AND BALLET

The French have always been a nation of intellectual individualists, jealous of their native ability and hesitant about importing the ideas of others. They were comparatively slow in taking up the *nuove musiche* of the Italians, although a number of sporadic attempts were made, usually under the patronage of politicians, to introduce the Italian opera into Paris in the first part of the century. The spontaneous combustion

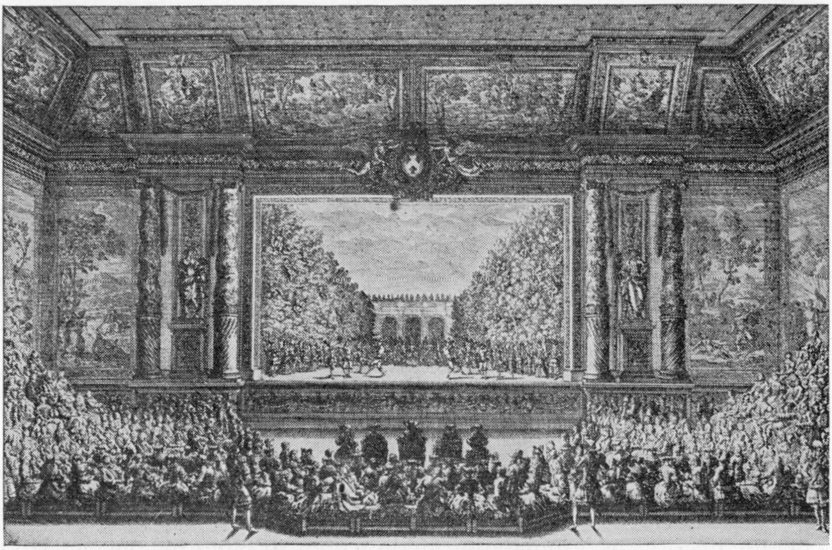

" LES FESTES DE L'AMOUR ET DE BACCHUS," by Jean Lepautre

The seventeenth-century spectacle — " a comedy with music " — was given in the theater at Versailles in 1664.

caused by the combination of Latin temperaments proved too much, however, and the Italians left in disgust at the cabals and jealousies of Paris. Probably the real difficulty behind this inability to establish early the Italian music in France was the essential differences in the artistic taste of the two countries. To the French the Italian music seemed noisily violent and unnecessarily obstreperous. Mersenne, one of the Frenchmen expressing himself at the time, said in his *Harmonie universelle*, " The Italians express passion, intellectual ideas, and spirited emotions just as intensely as they can, and with a strange violence, while we French are concerned with pleasing the ear and are anxious that our music be dominated by *sweetness*."

LULLY

Court influence was the factor which finally brought the country into the great sweep of Italian inventions. The most famous name in this connection is that of Lully or Lulli, the difference in the two spellings of his name showing that he belonged to both France and Italy. Born in Florence in 1632, he was taken to France at the age of fourteen and placed as kitchen scullion in one of the establishments of a court favorite. His natural gifts for music and dancing, combined with a native wit and a quick intelligence and an ability to write the sort of scurrilities then beloved by the French, gave him a position as a sort of musical dictator in Paris, having the sole right to produce opera in the city. He had learned how to please the French with the many ballets he wrote for various court performances. From earliest times the ballet has interested the French, whose natural predilection for dancing had led to the development of a brilliant court ballet, in which members of the royal circle eagerly joined, as early as the sixteenth century.[7]

Lully was shrewd enough to use this fondness of the French for dancing and pageantry (a fondness which can be traced through their entire operatic history) as a foundation upon which to build his operas. Most of this dance and pageant music may sound a bit dry and conventional to our ears today, but we must remember that for over a century it constituted the model for all the instrumental music of Europe.

One of Lully's happiest inspirations — truly Baroque in the full sense of the word — was the form he developed for the overtures to his operas: a pompous, regal first section, a lively, fugued second, and a slow, sustained finale to relieve the rhythmic tension and soothe the ear. In listening to such a thing as his overture to *Alceste,* it does not require an overabundance of imaginative power to hear in its strains a suggestion of the regal elegance of the Sun King's court and see him entering his loge for the beginning of the opera. This form of the Lullian overture was generally

[7] Henri Prunières in his *Le Ballet de cour avant Lully* gives an interesting account of one of these early French ballets:

"The curtain, opening, discovered a *décor* representing a forest. A curious person emerged. It was 'Messire Gobbemagne, grand gonfalonier of the Isle of Monkeys,' followed by three violins 'dressed as Turks, who danced and played.' Gobbemagne drew from the wood two torchbearing pages disguised as green snails, who did monkey tricks in cadence. Then one after the other all the violins and all the torchbearers entered the hall. The violins mounted onto their stand, and the green snails, having danced bizarrely, retired. After this burlesque prologue, the action began: the enchantress Alcine came out of the forest, sounding a lute. . . . Alcine came before the king's throne and sang verses in which she was followed by her chorus of nymphs, who took up the last verse of each rhyme."

adopted by composers of other nations and was used by them for a great many years.

In his dramatic writing, too, Lully was careful to cater to the taste of his public. Frenchmen of every age, as a noted German critic has well said, have always worshiped the spoken word in their dramatic creations, its proper accentuation, rhythmic flow, and even the timbre of its delivery. They have never been content to let it be dominated either by music or by dramatic action: for this reason much of the elaborate pantomime in French operas is accompanied by instrumental music.[8] So we find in the airs and recitatives from Lully's works a maintenance of the principles of proper declamation, rather than any attempt to provide pleasing vocal melodies such as the Italian works of the time provide. The airs are not greatly different from the recitatives, both being marked by a careful restraint and respect for declamatory values.

Even in such a comparatively melodious and expressive number as the well-known air *Bois épais* from *Amadis,* the rise and fall of the vocal line is carefully studied as regards the words. In it the delicate sensibility of French emotion, without excess or sentimentality, is readily observed: the remembrance that the somber woods bring, the thought of parting, and the impassioned desire, now that the best is gone, to taste old happinesses no more.

Other outstanding features of the Lully operas, features which stamped themselves indelibly on the national French school for years, were the prologues of gods and goddesses singing the praises of the king in massed choral manner, with all the formality of court etiquette, and the elevation of the orchestra to a place of greater importance than it had occupied in Italian works, with their special emphasis on the beauties of vocal utterance.

Lully was the great artist of his epoch in France. Together with his friend Molière (for whose *Le bourgeois gentilhomme* he wrote some of his best incidental music) he dominated the whole dramatic situation for

[8] It was the sense of logic inherent in the French which made them refuse what the English so readily accepted — the production of operas in a foreign tongue, in which the dramatic element was merely an excuse for vocal display, often of unnaturally produced voices. Lully, the Italian, was allowed to compose operas for them, but they had to be French operas, in the French language.

years. His influence was felt in every circle. The story goes that when a powerful cabinet minister of the time demanded from Lully, "How do you have the nerve to apply for a post on my committee? Did you ever do anything aside from making people happy?" the composer replied complacently, "If you could only manage that, you would do it, just as I have."

TENDENCIES IN ENGLAND: PURCELL

There remains the noting of operatic tendencies in England at this time. Dryden's remarks, published in 1685 and already quoted, would seem to indicate that the Italian craze was as strong in London as in the other European capitals. As a matter of fact, it is impossible to survey the musical history of England without large regrets. English musicians, catching fire from the art of the Italian madrigalist, as we have seen, took up the torch and made it blaze gloriously in the days of Shakespeare and Good Queen Bess, the days when foreign exploration and conquest, leading to tremendous mercantile expansion, laid the foundation stones for England's general prosperity. But war was never far away, and civil war, perhaps the most lamentable of all, threw men's minds out of gear for art. Though it is a mistake to imagine that Puritanism frowned on all music — its votaries chiefly hated elaborate church music, as well as everything connected with the theater — the middle seventeenth century was no time in which great art might be expected to flourish in England. With the Restoration, in 1660, Charles II brought foreign musicians to gratify his tastes; and it is largely owing to the fact that the prevailing standards were not of the best that Henry Purcell, the outstanding genius of these years, had not a greater effect on English music. He was unfortunate in his day and generation; and England was still more unfortunate in that he lived for so short a time — only thirty-seven years, from 1658 to 1695. One swallow does not make a summer, nor can one near-genius sufficiently influence a heedless age.

It is not to be wondered at that one side of Purcell's work shows the influence of the court, which musicians in those days were bound to flatter. By the other, deeper, side he ought to be judged; it is easy, by happening to get hold of one of his works written in his lighter style, to think him rather lacking in body. Though his life was so sadly short, he wrote harpsichord and string music in great abundance, settings of Pope and Dryden odes, church music, solo songs with fine declamatory and chromatically expressive elements in them, much music for plays, and a single opera, *Dido and Aeneas*, the latter composed for performance in a girls' school.

© *National Portrait Gallery, London*

HENRY PURCELL

This little opera, like so many early works in this form, goes back to classic mythology for its subject: the story is the well-known one from the fourth book of Virgil's *Aeneid*, to which are added certain features popular in the Restoration theater. There is a rousing chorus of witches, and the original performance was prefaced by an epilogue that was very characteristic of the time. It contained such lines as these:

> "Here, blest with innocence and peace of mind,
> Not only bred to virtue, but inclin'd;
> We flowrish, and defie all human kind."

And the bad men-around-town are repulsed with vehemence:

> "Let the vain Fop range yon vile lewd Town,
> Learn Play-house Wit, and vow 'tis all his own;
> Let him Cock, Huff, Strut, Ogle, Lye and Swear,
> How he's admired by such and such a Player;
> All's one to us, his Charms have here no power,
> Our Hearts have just the temper as before;
> Besides to show we live with strictest Rules,
> Our Nunnery-Door is charm'd to shut out Fools."

With an atmosphere such as this, together with limited forces (the soloists were probably brought in by the composer), it is hardly to be expected that Purcell could do his best work. *Dido and Aeneas* contains one great song that is universally known — Dido's Lament, sung before she takes her life: a masterpiece indeed, written, like so many of Purcell's themes, on a ground bass (that is, a short theme that is repeated all the time as the bass of the harmonies). The poignancy, the swift intense power of the music is beyond all praise. But apart from one other striking song, this opera is almost scrappy; everything is too short. We are just getting into a mood when it is broken off. There are excellent dances, Purcell's music being one of the deftest ever to set feet amoving; there are some of the too-brief strokes of witchcraft music that are more fully filled out in other works. And there is, if we can get into it, a direct, English, open-air sentiment that is likable enough. This spirit is to be found most purely in some of his other songs: "Britons, Strike Home," "I Attempt from Love's Sickness to Fly," "Nymphs and Shepherds," and a score of others, every one strongly tinctured with both a personal and a national style. Purcell learned much from both the French and the Italians and always gladly acknowledged this, with a modesty that is not the least of his admirable traits. But it is for his quality of Englishness — Shakespearean in both its freshness and subtlety, not the grosser Englishness of "John Bull" — that he stands out in memory, with something of pathos, against the poor background of his time and because of the shortness of his life.

Aside from his fine sense of drama, one of this composer's most striking features was his understanding of the voice: he is like Handel in that, though probably in nothing else. Purcell was brought up among singers in the Chapel Royal and later became organist of Westminster Abbey.

As soon as he was gone from the picture, English music took on that placidly imitative quality, that blotting-paper absorption of whatever the foreigner liked to send, that lasted until the end of the nineteenth century. It was not without a few sturdy figures — Arne and some good church composers among them — but there was little interest in the opera as far as native composers were concerned. The coming of Handel, excellent as it was for the country in his provision of an overwhelming number of outstanding operas and oratorios, smothered what little creative power the land could muster.

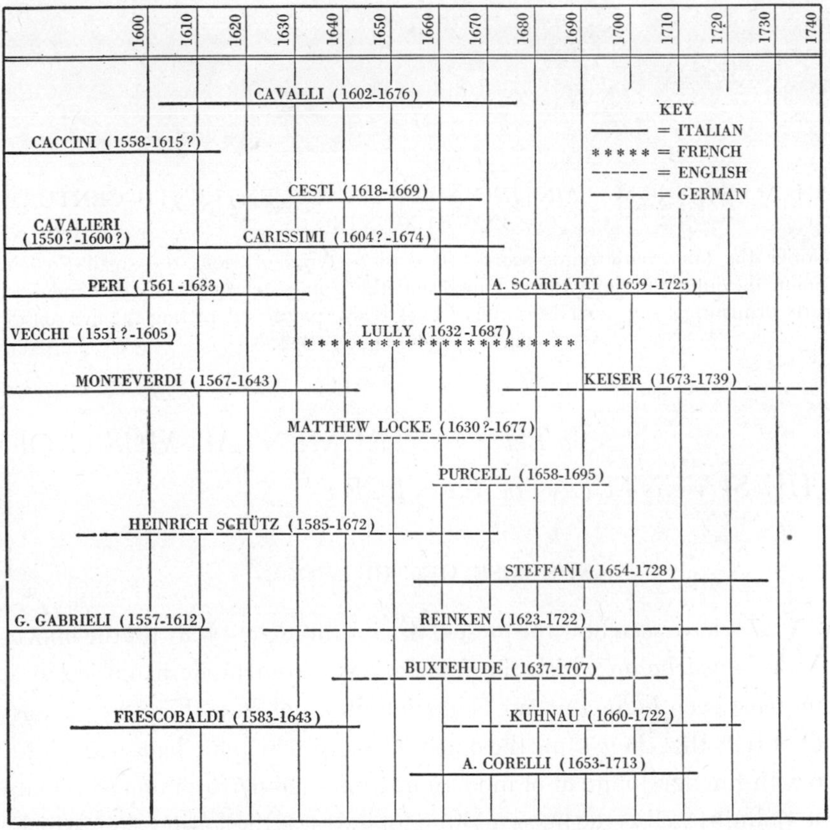

MUSICIANS OF THE EARLY BAROQUE

AN ALLEGORICAL PAINTING SHOWING SEVENTEENTH-CENTURY INSTRUMENTS

Notice the table with music scores, the various types of viols, the small French violin, the lute, the flute, the pommer, and the trombone. In the background is a party of madrigal singers. This is one of a set of five pictures depicting the five senses of man by Jan Breughel, 1620.

THE INSTRUMENTAL MUSIC OF THE SEVENTEENTH CENTURY

THE RISE OF THE VIOLIN

WE have seen how the present day is beholden to Italy for the *nuove musiche* on which the foundations of our modern musical system have been built. But our obligation does not stop there. For it was out of Italy that there came the one instrument which has had so much to do with the development of modern instrumental performing technique, the violin, as well as the music written for it. It was the Latin genius which first provided a satisfactory solution of how best to put together an aesthetically satisfying series of contrasting movements to form what was called the *sonata*.

Composers of all kinds of music have always had to mold their ideas to fit the instruments which they have had available. Of all the revolutionary changes that have taken place in the history of music, one of the most striking was that in which the royal gamba (viol) family, with its various members speaking a soft, discreet, and aristocratic language in all registers, was supplanted [9] by the bourgeois, penetrating, and agile violins. The consensus of opinion seems to be that the violin was invented in Brescia, in northern Italy; at least its type became fixed there during the latter sixteenth century and spread rapidly into all corners of Europe. We have become so used to considering the singing violin as the instrument par excellence that it is with something of a shock that we learn with what disdain these early instruments were considered. Here is a description written in Lyons, France, one of the centers of early violin manufacture in the middle of the sixteenth century:

"The violin is very much the opposite of the viol; its body is smaller, flatter, and it is much rougher in tone . . . We call viols the instrument which gentlemen, merchants, and other people of quality use for their pastime . . . The other sort is called the violin, and it is the instrument

[9] This word is used advisedly, for in reality the violins were not the successors of the viols, both families existing contemporaneously for many years, the viols being finally superseded when public rather than private performances of music became the rule, around the end of the seventeenth century. It is not generally recognized that there were so many fundamental differences between these two families, some authorities even doubting that they had a common ancestor. The most striking of these differences are:

Viol Family	*Violin Family*
Tone rather veiled, dull, slow-speaking	Tone brilliant, flexible, agile
Flat back	Convex back
Sloping shoulders	Rounded shoulders
Normally six strings with fretted finger board capable of adjustment	Four strings without fretted finger board
Light strings without tremendous tension	Strings very strong and taut
Held downwards, smaller instruments between the knees, larger ones between the legs	Held in various positions, the violins under chin
Bow stick curved outward from hairs, allowing freedom in playing chord	Bow stick curved inward, making for more delicate, brilliant effects

commonly used in playing for the dance; and this for good reason, for it is easier to tune, because the fifth is pleasanter to the ear than the fourth. It is also easier to carry, which is a very necessary matter, even in conducting a wedding or a mummery. There are found few people who make use of it except those who make their living by it as a trade."

— *Epitome musical des tons, sons et accords,* Lyon, 1556.
Quoted by Pincherle in *Musical Quarterly*

One of the principal reasons for this disdain was undoubtedly the tremendously increased sonority of which these new instruments were capable, a sonority which assaulted the ears so long accustomed to the gentle tones of the viols. Another was that the later designs and varnishes by which the Italian makers tempered the shrillness of this *barbare* and changed its tone into the warmth we know had not yet been invented. And the fact that these early violins were played by domestics "acting by the command and for the pleasure of their masters" in dancing did not improve their social status. Baltasarini de Belgiojoso and his troupe of violinists came from Italy to Paris about 1560; and although they captured the fancy of the court to such an extent that the leader changed his name to Beaujoyeulx and that of his band to the *Vingt-quatre violons du roy,* it was nearly a century later (1636) before such a eulogy as this could be written:

"Those who have heard the king's twenty-four violins admit that they have never heard anything more ravishing and more effective. Hence it seems that this instrument is, of all, the most popular for the dance, as we may observe in the ballets and on all hands elsewhere. Now the beauties and the graces that are practiced upon it are so great in number that one may prefer it to all instruments, for the strokes of the bow are so ravishing that there is no greater disappointment than not to hear it to the end. Particularly when they are intermingled with trills and with easy touches of the left hand, which compel the hearer to confess that the violin is the king of instruments." — Quoted by Pincherle

It was not until the members of the Amati family in the early days of the seventeenth century began to make their beautiful instruments, which are still so much sought after today, that the violin fulfilled its possibilities. By the time of Antonius Stradivarius (1644–1737) the art of violin making reached its climax, a climax which has never been transcended,

Library of the Paris Conservatoire

THE WORKSHOP OF AN EIGHTEENTH-CENTURY INSTRUMENT MAKER

and the instrument as we know it today began to be made in Germany, France, and England as well as in Italy.

The violin did not fully establish itself as a musical instrument with the music lovers of the time, however, until a new form somewhat commensurate with its singing and emotional qualities had been evolved. We always think of Arcangelo Corelli (1653–1713) as being the founder of modern violin music and playing; but as a matter of fact there were many other composers writing real violin music before his time, among them Legrenzi, Vitali, and Neri. But he was the outstanding figure, and so, as always happens, receives the credit of being the first all-round master of the violin, in both composition and performance. He concentrated on writing sonatas, that is, accompanied string music, for the Church, for chamber, and, perhaps we might say, for the pure delight of fiddling.

CORELLI

It was Corelli who planned the sequence of movements in the sonata, and although later practice greatly extended their scope, the germ may be found in his works. Two types of these sonatas were general: church (*sonata da chiesa*) and chamber (*sonata da camera*). These have much in common, the chief difference being the lighter mood of the latter and the stronger influence of the dance. The four standard movements are almost invariably alternately quick and slow. One of the quick ones is fugal in style, deriving directly from the old vocal music; the corresponding movement in the chamber sonata is usually in one of the dance styles. Those characteristics which we have mentioned as typical of seventeenth-century music — the use of the homophonic style, major and minor scales, and so on — are all present. Key contrast in the movements is just beginning, the third being sometimes in a different key from the others. But this now vital element was arrived at slowly, though of course key balance was present within the movements themselves.

Corelli wrote many of these sonatas for his favorite instrument, perhaps the best known being the so-called *La Folía,* a significant and very effective work which maintains an honorable place in violin literature. In France the new form helped the violin to become popular with genteel people; in England we find Purcell (as he says in the Preface to his published sonatas) imitating the Italian form. His *Golden Sonata,* written in 1695, is in reality a *sonata da chiesa* after Corelli's best manner. These works, with their alternation of polyphonic and homophonic effects and their beautifully melodious slow movements, are striking examples of how far the new music for the violin developed within a short space of time. Although we of the present are apt to find this music somewhat lacking in color and excitement, for it was not until the days of Corelli's pupils that we begin to find the crisp principles of sonata writing as we know it emerging, it is a long distance from the tentative compositions of the sixteenth century.

EARLY ORGAN MUSIC

The first composers to write for the organ music that may be said to show anything like the possibilities of which this instrument is capable were the Gabrielis in Venice. Just at the turn of the century Frescobaldi, another outstanding Italian organ composer, became popular; it is said that his fame was so great that when he played for the first time on the great organ in St. Peter's, Rome, in 1608, thirty-thousand people assembled there to hear him. He wrote a great deal of organ music, largely in the polyphonic style, as did Jan Sweelinck in Holland. The influence of the latter was particularly strong in Germany (where he was called the *deutsche Organistenmacher*), his pupils Reinken and Buxtehude imitating and developing his style and passing on his influence to the next generation, where it affected directly the music of the great Sebastian Bach himself. Pachelbel was another seventeenth-century German organist who lived and worked in the south. He was a follower of Frescobaldi and thus transmitted the Italian traditions directly to the German style. Samuel Scheidt was still another famous organist and composer of the time in Germany, where organs and organists were in special favor, owing to the poverty of the country arising from the bitter Thirty Years' War, and the consequent inability of the people to pay for chamber and operatic music. The forms which these German composers worked out for their music have remained in use ever since: the prelude and the fugue, the choral prelude, the passacaglia, the chaconne, and the toccata.

FRENCH KEYBOARD SUITES

In France a number of important organists arose, but very little of their works has survived. Chief among these was Chambonnières (c. 1602–1672), clavecinist to Louis XIV and teacher of Couperin, who left behind him not serious organ music but over a hundred pieces for the harpsichord, grouped into suites and made up chiefly of the dance tunes and rhythms of the period. These dance suites of Chambonnières's are indicative of the new interest in keyboard instruments which developed everywhere during the latter part of the seventeenth century. After the lively activity of the Renaissance composers, little attention was given to the keyboard instruments for a number of years. But as the century drew to a close, composers in France and England (where a new interest in art was awakened through the Restoration) and Germany began to give more attention to harpsichord and clavichord music and prepared the way for the great clavecinists of the eighteenth century. Italy, absorbed in her operatic developments, did not feel this impulse until later, when she produced the best clavecinist of them all, Domenico Scarlatti. In 1696 there was published in England Purcell's great *Choice Collection of Lessons for the Harpsichord or Spinet*, consisting of suites like those of Chambonnières's, made up of contrasted movements. Froberger in Germany wrote the same type of dance suite; but his music, as befitted his nationality, has a more dignified and severe aspect than the French or English suites of the time.

THE SUITE IN GENERAL

Although the music of the courtly dances was originally designed only as an accompaniment for dancing, composers found that the varied impulses of these measures made ideal material for separate instrumental use in short, contrasted movements. The generally slow character of the motions was well suited to the undeveloped instrumental technique of the time and to the limitations of the instruments. It was quickly found that single dances were not particularly striking by themselves, but when grouped according to some principle of unity and contrast, the result was artistically satisfying.

The most popular of these dance movements used in the classical suite were:

Pavan. Of Spanish-Italian origin, slow and stately, in four-time; a favorite at the court of Henry III in France and Henry VIII and Elizabeth in England.

Galliard. In rapid three-time; a gay foil to and companion of the pavan.

Courante. The name means "running." It was quick in notes but rather sedate in motion. It was first set in two-time, and later in three-time.

Saraband. Possibly of Oriental origin. Shakespeare speaks of it as "full of state and ancientry." In slow three-time, it had the second beat stressed. Movements of the arms and the whole body accompanied it.

Minuet. A three-time dance which came to the court from the countryside. Essentially requiring an elegant carriage, this dance assumed high importance by becoming one of the movements in the sonata and symphony.

Gavotte. In two-time or four-time, beginning at the half measure. It habitually followed the minuet. It was taken up by the court of Louis XIV, and kissing (later, the offering of flowers) played a part in it.

Bourrée. Similar to the gavotte, but beginning on the last quarter of the measure.

Gigue. Apparently of British countryside origin. Taken up by composers for lute and keyboard, it spread to the Continent and was chosen as the brisk finale of the suite. Usually it is in compound time, using some sort of combination of three's.

Allemande. Other names are *Alman* and *Almain*. The word means " German." This serious dance was chosen to open the classical suite.

The four cornerstones of the suite were *allemande, courante, saraband,* and *gigue*. A variety of other dances, besides those described above, will be found in various forms of the suite; and of course there is a still greater diversity of local and national dance types, reference to some of which will be found in the appropriate chapter on national music.

THE GERMAN KUHNAU

The really big man in the Germany of this century was Johann Kuhnau (1660–1722), the immediate predecessor of Bach as the cantor of St. Thomas's Church, Leipzig. At this time Germany was a beleaguered land, overrun by the armies of Sweden, France, and Spain in that last great conflict caused by the differences between Catholics and Protestants. Artistically it was completely in the hands of the Italians, for the artists from the south flooded Bavaria, Saxony, Thuringia, Austria, and even the provinces of the north: Cavalli reigned supreme in Munich, Hasse in Dresden, Vivaldi in Darmstadt, Cesti and Caldara in Vienna. German to the very core, Kuhnau struggled manfully to uphold the solemnity and the dignity of his native art against what he considered the madness of a country given over to the frivolities of the Italians, even the church adapting its dramatic, operatic style in the settings of some of its liturgical solemnities.

Kuhnau was, in the words of one of his contemporaries, " very learned in theology, jurisprudence, rhetoric, poetry, mathematics, foreign languages, and music." He knew Greek and Hebrew, could translate works from French and Italian into German, and wrote a considerable number of original works in a vigorous and forceful style, including an amusing novel pillorying the Italians and the " Italianuses " who had deserted him for the captivating lightness of the south. His contemporaries considered Kuhnau one of the great composers of the century; he was one of the earliest to set the style for the modern sonata; and his descriptive program pieces for clavichord — *Biblische Historien,* he called them — are among the few examples outside the works of the great men — Bach, Handel, and Couperin — still remembered today.

Something of the unusual nature and quiet assurance of character of this old cantor may be gained from this Preface which he wrote for some of these sonatas:

" It did not take me long to produce these: it was with me just as it is in certain countries where, thanks to the unusual heat, everything grows with such rapidity that the harvest may be reaped a month after sowing. While writing these sonatas I experienced such eagerness that without neglecting my other occupations I wrote one every day, so that this work, which I began on a Monday, was completed by the Monday of the next week. I mention this merely so that no one shall expect in them anything rare or exceptional. It is true that we are not always craving for extraordinary things; we often eat the simplest fruits of our fields with as much pleasure as the rarest and most exquisite foreign fruits, although the latter may be very costly and come from a great distance. I know there are gourmets among the amateurs of music who will accept nothing save that which comes from France or Italy — above all when fortune has permitted them to breathe the air of these countries. My fruits are at the disposal of all; those who do not find them to their taste have only to seek elsewhere. As for the critics, they will not spare them; but the venom of the ignorant is powerless to injure them more than the cool dew will harm ripened fruit."

Good old self-assured German!

One of the Biblical sonatas tells of Saul's madness and David's refreshing harp playing which cured him. There are many powerful chords, uncommon for that day, and the sudden changes of mood suggest, without extravagance, Saul's stricken mind. The best known of these sonatas is *David and Goliath's Combat;* when attempting the representation of Goliath's boasting and stamping and of David's courageous defiance, Kuhnau works on a plane which may be called the median, in which a blend of imitation and suggestion is used. When he wants to show us the flight of the Philistines, he can do nothing but scurry scalically about; and the course of the stone from David's sling has to be set down by much the same means. Here Kuhnau is attempting what is either really impracticable or superficial and obvious.

There are, however, two sections of the work in which he goes much deeper and attains something of true expressive and suggestive power. One is that which depicts the Israelites' dejection and their trust in God (each section of the work is quaintly labeled in words by the careful composer). Here the chromatic dropping background of repeated-note accompaniment is genuinely poetic; above it rises a chorale tune, the plea to God. The other moment in which Kuhnau best rises above the merely imitative level is the death of Goliath; here a weighty descending figure suggests the gradual crumpling up of the body, and another may well stand for the departing breath as the giant's life ebbs away. The end of the sonata, with its various rejoicings, takes us back to familiar dance forms of the time, and quite away from pictorialism.

In all such early program music some of the best interest lies in picking out the various planes of effect and hearing how, on the limited instruments of the time, certain things could, and others could not, be done. We must also try to decide which, of all the things attempted, are worth while and which are not. Such a responsibility is always upon us, whether we hear the bleating sheep in Richard Strauss's *Don Quixote,* for instance, or listen to some of the extremer "absolute" music of today. What is significant, and what is not?

That he was not entirely happy in his ideas is obvious when we read the lengthy Preface which Kuhnau wrote for these Biblical sonatas, trying to explain some of their inconsistencies and discrepancies. But the instrument for which he wrote them, the clavichord, was not capable of the effects he was seeking. Small in tone, with a very simple mechanism consisting of a brass or iron plate fitted vertically to the end of each key and just striking the string when the key was depressed, it could not give a tone suited to the grandiose ideas found in these dramatic programmistic tone poems of Kuhnau. This instrument was much better suited to sensitive and delicate music such as came later in the time of "sighs, tears, and tender smiles," the Rococo. But it did have an expressive quality that the harpsichord completely lacked. There were many arguments at the time as to the relative merits of these two instruments. Both Bach and Kuhnau preferred the clavichord, the latter in a letter to the famous music critic of the time, Mattheson, saying that the clavichord was the "most expressive of all keyboard instruments."

CONCERTED MUSIC

There remains a word to be said regarding the concerted instrumental music of this century. The orchestra of this period was no longer merely a miscellaneous collection of instruments, chosen without seeming reason; a conception of instrumental coloring now begins to develop, and we find combinations that coalesce somewhat along modern lines. In a desire to vary their instrumental combinations as much as possible and to use the violin for solo purposes, a type of sonata called the *concerto* was evolved. This embodied the principle of an accompanied soloist (the first concerto was written by Torelli and Albinoni in 1698 for violin and orchestra) and was later developed into the *concerto grosso*, for which several solo instruments are used against a background of strings. A fine example of the simple concerto is such a work as Vivaldi's in D major, Op. 3, No. 8; Corelli's charming *Concerto for Christmas Night* illustrates the *concerto grosso*. It employs the same general plan as his sonatas but gives pleasing opportunities for the interchange of effects between the whole orchestra and a smaller group of soloists — *tutti* and *soli*. In this case the soloists are two violinists and a cellist, and the orchestra is one of strings. The work opens with a tutti, a brief, joyous rush that is succeeded by a *grave*; then comes a lively allegro giving the soloists prominence, followed by a beautiful slow section, interrupted by a fiery allegro;

then comes a quick piece in minuet style and a section in gavotte rhythm; and at the end is a lovely poetic pastoral, serene in its inspiration and suggesting the later *Pastoral Symphony* of *The Messiah*. It seems as if, after allowing his fancy to play around the various happy aspects of Christmas, the composer put all his affection into this final evocation and salutation to the Babe. These concertos played an important part in the development of later instrumental style, Sebastian Bach and Handel both writing many works in the forms laid down here in the seventeenth century.

PURCELL'S INSTRUMENTAL GENIUS

Purcell's *Fantasias* for strings, in from three to eight parts, illustrate another aspect of the instrumental music of this time; they are, in fact, so far advanced in style as to warrant us in thinking of their composer as a modern writer, entirely able to explore the possibilities of both chromaticism and instrumental counterpoint in ways that at the time were fresh and new. These grand works possess a flexibility of key and a harmonic sheen that was achieved by no other composer of anywhere near this period — not even Bach or Handel. The best of them — there are thirteen altogether — is that " upon one note," the title implying that one note (it happens to be the fifth of the key) persists throughout the piece. The music is magnificently woven, with plenty of contrapuntal imitations between the various parts. Yet there is nothing pedantic or academic in it for modern hearers; to enjoy it today, we do not have to consider it as a museum piece. There is contrast in color and mood, the whole reaching a powerfully contrived conclusion. This is real Music of the Future, in so far as the time of its writing was concerned, and stands as one of the most remarkable things of its period. In one of his prefaces, " To the Reader," Purcell has explained that it is useless to attempt anything in the way of a description of music in words, adding that " despite all the learned encomiums that words can contrive, music commends itself best by the performance of a skillful hand." And no better illustration of this could possibly be given than his *Fantasia on One Note*.

MUSIC OF THE GUILDS

Still another aspect of seventeenth-century concerted music was the writing of compositions for the special use of various guilds and corporations of musicians. These organizations had formed an important part of the musical life of France ever since the time of the minstrels and the troubadours; they had branches in all the provinces and a central organization in Paris, where their " King of the Minstrels " or " King of the Violins " ruled over the musicians of the country, much in the fashion of a modern labor leader. These corporations had a strangle hold on the performance of music throughout the whole country; and there were many quarrels with the clavecinists, lutenists, and composers who did not willingly submit to their pretensions. The whole situation, until the suppression of the guilds in 1774, strangely resembles the labor troubles of our time.

In Germany the influence of these organizations was more beneficent: musicians in the cities and towns throughout the country united in corporations for their own benefit and protection. These " town musicians," as they were named because they were supported by the various municipalities, were called upon to furnish music for all official occasions, playing in church and in secular processions. In addition they could be hired for private use at weddings, funerals, and so forth. Even the small towns maintained groups of trombone and trumpet players — *Stadtpfeifer* — whose duties included the playing of a chorale three times a day from the steeple of the village church and the playing of a secular program daily from the tower of the *Rathaus*. This quaint custom, which survived in Germany well into the nineteenth century and may still be found there in a few isolated examples, has had much to do with the establishment of the country's musical taste and style. For out of the chorale there came certain elements in the music of Bach, Brahms, and Wagner and many an unknown composer.

Characteristic of the music played by these seventeenth-century German *Stadtpfeifer* is the collection *Fünff-stimmigte blasende Musik* of Johann Pezel, published in 1685, the year of Bach's birth. Much of this is solid and deeply felt music that forecasts the greater glories to come.

The Eighteenth Century

GENERAL BACKGROUNDS

AT THE TURN OF THE CENTURY

HE who would obtain something in the way of a general understanding of the spirit which underlay the first fifty years of the eighteenth century, the period that is usually designated as the "High Baroque," can do no better than read Sacheverell Sitwell's *Southern Baroque Art*, a study of the painting, architecture, and music of Italy and Spain in the seventeenth and eighteenth centuries. For here, in grandiose, orotund prose that is as Baroque as English can be, is set down a series of intimately detailed descriptions characteristic of this period of tremendous vitality, ardent exuberance, daring conception, and elaborate ornament.

The fact that the term *Baroque* has assumed in present-day art criticism a deprecatory meaning somewhat similar to that which was in the minds of the Renaissance worthies when they used the adjective *Gothic* to mean something crude and barbaric has often been remarked. Long-established prejudice has heaped a number of abusive appellations on the not altogether undeserving head of Baroque art, among them such expressions as *cheap, tawdry, sensational, vulgar, falsely emotional, overdramatic*. But these derogatory epithets, merited perhaps when applied to single examples and certain circumstances, are certainly unfair when given to the general characteristics of the period, for they tend to exaggerate the defects and fail altogether to suggest anything of the essential nature and underlying artistic intentions that have made this era one of the most animative and prolific in the world's history.

A few of Mr. Sitwell's pictures will give us a better understanding of some of the definable qualities of this misunderstood time. Santa Maria

DAVID DANCING BEFORE THE ARK by Sebastiano Conca

la Nuova was one of the most elaborate of the hundreds of Neapolitan churches built during the Baroque era and filled with its peculiar kind of sculpture and painting. High up on its ceiling will be found the last fresco which Sebastiano Conca, a characteristic Baroque painter, ever did. This fresco shows David dancing and playing his harp before the ark, a subject familiar enough to all the readers of the Old Testament. But certainly none of these has ever imagined such a David or such an ark as is here revealed. In a composition crowded with grandiose figures clothed in the garments of classical antiquity and filled with the magnificent architecture that we always associate with Rome in its period of greatest glory stands a crowned figure, gaily strumming a harp. Thronging the imposing stairway which forms an essential part of the scene is a sumptuous parade of magnificent figures, each of them an integral part of the design. High in the heavens float huge draperies that are filled out by the wind until they are the size of clouds, each of them bearing additional groups of spectators, while from the center burst radiant shafts of light which, streaming from the gilded heavens, glorify the ark of the covenant. The whole thing, overpowering in its picturesque richness, is about as far a cry from primitive ceremony and tribal king described in the Bible as can possibly be imagined.

Or take the scene in the Certosa di San Martino, a monastery perched high on the cliffs above Naples. A practical-minded English traveler who visited this monastery in 1779 estimated that its income, although considerably reduced, reached the annual total of some hundred fifty thousand pounds. Here in the very last year of the century, Sitwell tells us, the monks gave a party to celebrate the coming of the French to Naples; and they invited a group of distinguished guests of both sexes to a dance in the apartments of the prior. "A printed memorial of the occasion remarks that the monks, full of joy and admiration, seeing such pretty smiling women dancing among them, could not help rejoicing, more than the rest, at the coming of Liberty."

Another picture is that of the opera theater in the Viennese royal palace of Emperor Charles VI, father of Maria Theresa, and the last male Hapsburg Holy Roman Emperor, whose life span (1685–1740) is almost exactly contemporary with that of Bach. Charles was the great patron of

THE KARLSKIRCHE, VIENNA (from a hand-colored engraving of 1800)
The most renowned of Bernhard Fischer von Erlach's churches, this one was built in 1716–1739.

Bernhard Fischer von Erlach, the Baroque architect whose creations have done so much to add to the flamboyant beauties of Vienna and to make this city resemble a modern Rome. The emperor maintained in his service a whole race of Italians to whom he entrusted the task of providing the decorations, music, and actors for the impressive operatic and stage spectacles which he gave on state occasions. These Italians had evolved a system of stage decorations by means of which they could quickly erect different architectural scenes and suggest outdoor vistas of such elaborate proportions as to give the participating actors the air of immortals who had just arrived from another planet. The chief personages in these Baroque pageants, which invariably depicted scenes from pagan and Christian mythology, came on the stage as if their chariots had just dropped them near the stairways and on the avenues for a few hours and were waiting to take them away to still greater splendors.

MACHINERY FOR THE APPEARANCE OF THE GODS IN A BAROQUE OPERA
(From a contemporary sketch)

These architectural façades and arboreal boscages, made up out of units that were capable of endless combinations, were changed and inhabited by a different population of actors in each episode. It is difficult for us, in these days, when the ideals of economy are forced on every operatic stage manager, to realize the abundant luxuriance of these Baroque stage settings. No expense was spared, and no trouble was too great. Huge groups of characters were used to give impressiveness and elegance to the scene in somewhat the modern Hollywood sense. Underneath the stage there were all kinds of machines for working the clouds and manipulating the wires which produced the supernatural effects. In front, between the stage and the audience, the orchestra was ready to accompany the singers, chief among these in the present case being the great *castrato* Farinelli, for whose entrance the audience, which had talked ceaselessly through every other scene, waited breathlessly.

THE "CASTRATO," A TYPICAL BAROQUE PHENOMENON

The audience knew from past experience that there were no feats of vocal conjuring, no displays of technical skill of which this most famous of all the Baroque *castrati* was incapable. His execution, with its embroidered roulades and cascades of melody, its ability to die away like the tones of a bell or increase until it took on the dimensions of a brazen trumpet, the sweet boyish quality of his voice, rendered permanent by a cruel surgical operation, was as characteristically a Baroque phenomenon as the stage decorations, the architecture of the theater, or the dress of the audience. The most complicated passages, the seemingly impossible feats of breath control, were accomplished with the ease and elegance that is found only in the most eloquent and impassioned orator. The whole opera was interrupted from time to time so that songs, altogether extraneous to its action and plot, could be interpolated for the purpose of giving such singers opportunity for the display of their powers.

"After all the melting scenes in the opera, after the music that could have drawn tears from the eyes of a stone statue and was potent, in proportion, towards the soft and, as it were, feathery breasts of the audience, there is nothing to be surprised at in hearing of the frenetic enthusiasm with which Farinelli was greeted as the opera came to an end. He was called and recalled repeatedly, and was, in the end, persuaded to sing by himself again, while the whole theater was dead silent and as if entranced.

"This terrifying parade of his ability went from one end to the other of his powers. His lowest notes were like the roaring of flames imprisoned deep down inside the earth, and in the highest register his voice was a wind playing among the lolling bells of green leaves on every bough. He could travel from one extreme to the other without as much difficulty as you would have crossing from the hot glare of the sun into the deep shade beneath a tree, and yet this quick run from top to bottom of his voice was like the rain pelting down from its cloud on to the hard earth beneath. When he came to the end of his song, and all the bravura passages were sheathed and put away like a sword, the quiet level finish of the music came along, leading towards fields which were open to the sun and never frowned upon by storms. His singing died away on a wonderful sustained cantabile note, as if he were anxious for the audience to forget his skill and remember only the pathos and purity of his voice."

— **Sitwell: *Southern Baroque Art***

Such scenes as this were taking place in these years in every part of Europe.

Another manifestation of the richness, artificiality, and strangeness of this period is the taking of the same artist, Farinelli, to Madrid to sing before the demented King Philip, whose utter melancholy in the midst of all his Baroque tinsel and glitter nothing or nobody had been able to cure. Farinelli remained in the Spanish capital for over ten years, warding off the king's unhappiness by singing the same four songs to him every night during this time (he must have repeated them three thousand times), never again singing in public for anyone. He was made unofficial prime minister for his pains and given the title of a Knight of Calatrava, one of the highest orders of Spanish chivalry.

SPIRITUAL CHARACTERISTICS

Underlying these isolated examples of Baroque splendor and magnificence are certain spiritual characteristics which show them to be but different manifestations of a spirit that was common to the time. They all show, for instance, a tremendous and vigorous joy in life, an *élan* for existence, that could result only in a profusion of various activities. The intellectual outlook of the eighteenth century may not have been so serious as that of the seventeenth; but it was colorful, luxuriant, and magnificent, devoted to the art of making life as interesting and enjoyable as possible. There was an unbridled exuberance of spirit and an assurance of creative ability at this time which manifested itself in a seeming willingness to try anything, no matter how extravagantly fantastic or far removed it may have been from direct contact with life. And, above all, there was the overpowering desire for magnificence, shown through the exploration of every technical and expressive means possible, a magnificence which in its later Rococo manifestation has taken on a graceful refinement and aristocratic formality.

All this produced a great deal of painting, literature, and music to which the epithets already mentioned may well be applied. But it also produced, we must remember, the paintings of such men as El Greco and Rubens, the architecture of Bernini and Vanvitelli (whose palace at Caserta was considered the greatest building feat of the time), the murals of Tiepolo, the plays of Corneille and Racine, and the music of Handel and Bach. The leisure and the luxury of this period were made possible, to be sure, by the taxes and labor of an intellectually impoverished and socially degraded people; but its richly buoyant vitality of artistic conception and execution cannot be explained on such material basis alone.

THE ROCOCO SPIRIT

Everywhere throughout Europe there was much the same feeling, the same social and cultural existence, the same sort of governance; and these continued to be very much alike in all countries until disrupted by the events of the French Revolution, which brought the era to its tragic end. So the seventeenth and eighteenth centuries flow into each other without any very definite line of demarcation, just as do their two styles of art, the Baroque and the Rococo. The latter, graceful, formal, and essentially superficial, may be said to have been the art of a minority society, pretty well bored with, and yet hungry for, life, exceedingly lighthearted and thoughtless, yet sophisticated and very intelligent. It had its birth in France, where it started as a method of interior decoration, and reached its culmination in Germany, where it produced a stylized, polished art that was perfectly adapted to the demands of its time and used its materials with an ease and fluency that is almost unbelievable.

Beneath the Rococo grace and fragile beauty of such an interior as that of the Amalienburg in Munich there exists a real and profound art. The scrolls and curving lines, the gold and silver and glass ornaments, the mirrors and polished floors — all are molded by the architect Cuvillies into a whole that has character and significance. It suggests not so much superficiality as it does an extremely fluent, sophisticated artistry, an artistry that at all costs maintains a sense of illusion, determined to keep up appearances by providing a lovely, variegated shell for life, no matter what there may be beneath, worshiping the semblance rather than the soul.

ROCOCO PERFECTION — one of the rooms in the Amalienburg, Munich

And this is, after all, the real essence of the Rococo, to be found alike in the prose of Pope and Voltaire, the poetry of Collins and Milton, the paintings of Watteau, Boucher, and Lancret, the architecture of the Brothers Asam, Cuvillies, and Cotte, the sculpture of Houdon, and the music of the younger Scarlatti, Rameau, Haydn, and Mozart. Mozart's music is one of the greatest achievements in all European art history, and in its many-sidedness and great scope equals the work of any other composer. In a short lifetime of not quite thirty-six years Mozart wrote over six hundred works: there is an enormous wealth of ideas in them, a curious mixture of the silvery lightness and the dreamy fantasy of the Rococo, with an underlying depth of thought and seriousness of purpose prophetic of the Romantic Movement to come. We shall have a great deal to say about this later on, but it deserves special mention here, for while Mozart was the great outstanding figure of the Rococo period, he was a great deal more — a genius whose range of expression could not be confined to any one epoch.

SYMPTOMS OF THE CENTURY

The eighteenth century, as we look back at it now, appears as an era of magnificent order and symmetry, with its center the French court at Versailles. This longing for order was but another manifestation of the attempt to compensate in some form for the lack of a real spiritual *raison d'être*. It was expressed in various ways, none more characteristic than the appearance at about the middle of the century of Diderot's famous *Encyclopédie*, a work of great scholarship, marked by a desire to ascertain the real truth regarding the various topics presented. One of Diderot's most quoted remarks is typical of him: "The first step towards philosophy is incredulity." He carried this spirit of skepticism into all his researches, and it was this that did much toward attaining the rational order and balance for which this work has become noted.

Also symptomatic of this longing for order was Samuel Johnson's dictionary, which appeared in 1755. In the introduction to this great work, which established its author as the founder of English lexicography, Johnson voices the spirit of the times:

> "When I took the first survey of my undertaking, I found our speech copious without order, and energetic without rule: wherever I turned my view, there was perplexity to be disentangled and confusion to be regulated; choice was to be made out of boundless variety, without any established principle of selection; adulterations were to be detected, without a settled test of purity; and modes of expression to be rejected or received, without the suffrages of any writers of classical reputation or acknowledged authority.
>
> "Having therefore no assistance but from general grammar, I applied myself to the perusal of our writers; and noting whatever might be of use to ascertain or illustrate any word or phrase, accumulated in time the materials of a dictionary, which, by degrees, I reduced to method, establishing to myself, in the progress of the work, such rules as experience and analogy suggested to me; experience, which practice and observation were continually increasing; and analogy, which, though in some words obscure, was evident in others."

In music it was this century which laid the solid foundations of order on which so much of the art's later structures were built. Haydn, profiting by the long years of experiment on the part of his immediate predecessors and his contemporaries, ordained the types of form according to which symphonies and quartets have been written ever since and chose the groups which should comprise the orchestra to play these compositions. In fact, we could well adapt Johnson's words to suit Haydn's practice; for he actually had to make a choice from a boundless variety of materials available and without having much in the way of established principles of selection. He likewise reduced his materials to method; and that he chose wisely and ordered well is proved by the fact that so many composers since his time have followed in his footsteps.

It is obvious enough that there are very few critical laws which held through all these changes we have chronicled. What has seemed to be the essence of truth in one century has been felt to be utterly false in another. Practically the only rule that established its validity is that artistic fashions, like all others, are bound to change; and that change, when it does come, is likely to be violent.

Up to the eighteenth century, the close of what is usually known as the "classic period," art had been subject to definite restrictions. Subordinated to the "higher purpose" of the Church during the Middle Ages, it had freed itself from that hindrance, only to be brought heavily under the discipline of classic tradition and reason. The art of the Renaissance, the Baroque, and the Rococo was produced according to certain rules of form which had grown up largely as the result of what was considered classic taste; it was a reasoned art, standing for ideal beauty and for a portrayal of nature only when beautiful. And in addition there were the demands of a society that was supreme to be met, with its insistence on luxurious display and elegant refinement, no matter what the cost in imaginative truth. The wonder is that a period of such urbane smoothness and social refinement could produce an art that had in it so much strength and real vitality.

Cliché Vizzavona

" In the eighteenth century there were the demands of a society that was supreme to be met, with its insistence on luxurious display and elegant refinement, no matter what the cost in imaginative truth."

THE EIGHTEENTH-CENTURY OPERA

One thing I dislike is the laying too much stress upon some one voice, wch is purchased at a dear rate. Were it not as well If somewhat of that was abated & added to the rest to bring ye orchestre to a neerer equality? Many persons come to hear that single voice, who care not for all the rest, especially If it be a fair Lady; And observing ye discours of the Quallity crittiques, I found it runs most upon ye point, who sings best? and not whether ye musick be good, and wherein? and it is a sorry case to sitt by one who during a recitativo, sighs and groans at what he is to endure, before this favorite ariette, or that ballet, comes up.

And it is a fault in ye composition to overcalculate for ye prime voice, as If no other part were worth Regarding, whereupon the whole enterteinment consists of solos, and very little or no consorts of voices: where is there a chorus of 4 full voices Interwoven with ye proper consort instruments to be heard? I am sure nature affords not means for musick to be so good any other way. If they say It is not suitable to a Drama to have many sing together. The contrary of that is most apparently true; for (excepting ye comedys) wch of ye Ancient Dramatiques had not a chorus that sang what was proper to the subject? And now at last, from what I can perceiv, the Operas made In England of ye latter date, are more substantially musicall, than those wch are used notati out of Itally, wch latter have of late diverted from the Lofty style downe to the Ballad, fitt for the streets that receivs them, whereby it appears that the Italian vein is much degenerated.

— Roger North: *The Musicall Gramarian,* c. 1728

THE PROLIFIC EIGHTEENTH CENTURY

THE music of the eighteenth century is so affluent in composers and so uniform in style that in many cases it would take an expert — and even he would not always be sure — to determine whether a piece had been written by Scarlatti, Vivaldi, Telemann, Couperin, Marcello, Handel, or even Bach himself. The number of Baroque and Rococo composers is legion: in the operatic field — to mention only the leaders — there were Steffani, Pallavicino, Stradella, Provenzale, Leo, Alessandro Scarlatti, Jommelli, Traetta, Paisiello, Pergolesi, Cimarosa, Piccinni, Galuppi, Hasse, Handel, Gluck, Mozart, Naumann, Graun, Fux, Caldara, Campra, Destouches, Rameau. Some of these men busied themselves also with writing church music, and in addition there were such specialists in this field as Durante, D'Astorga, Marcello, Lotti, Padre Martini, Bach, and Haydn. And in instrumental music we find such great names as Vivaldi, Tartini, Sebastian Bach, Couperin, Domenico Scarlatti, Haydn, Mozart; as well as the minor ones of Alberti, Sammartini, Stamitz, Richter, C. P. E. Bach, Wilhelm Friedemann Bach, Johann Christian Bach, J. G. Graun, Clérambault, Marchand, Boccherini, Daquin, Leclair, Mondonville, and Mattheson. Such fecundity reminds us again of the hundreds of Baroque churches and palaces which Sitwell says are to be found in Italy alone. What other age has been so prolific?

Naturally enough, a great deal of the music of these composers sounds stilted and dated to modern ears; there is in it a quality of " patness," of having been easily written, the process of creation, once started, having gone on to its inevitable conclusion. In listening to much of this eighteenth-century music it seems as if the composers had been moved to write it by the prolific spirit of the times, rather than through any impelling desire on their part to express something. The result, as Newman has said of a certain type of Bach's works, was merely the equivalent of good, honest journalism — well enough in its way, but having little claim to the more dignified title of *literature*. But there is about the best of this Baroque music, even when it is so largely given over to that pursuit of ornamentation that was dear to the times, a largeness of conception, a vitality of expression, and a boldness of execution that, when contrasted with the oversimplification of art today, makes it seem most compelling and convincing.

ALESSANDRO SCARLATTI AS TYPICAL OPERA COMPOSER

Take, for example, some of the music of Alessandro Scarlatti (1659–1725), the biggest man in the most popular form of the time — opera. His work so gathers up all the styles and manners of his predecessors and crystallizes them into what has been spoken of for years as the standard Italian opera tradition, that it is worthy of special attention.

Characteristics of these Scarlatti operas as they were given in one of the five opera houses which flourished in eighteenth-century Naples were:

First, that the overture was written with regard for a definite form: it consisted of three contrasting sections, first an allegro, followed by an adagio, and finally a concluding allegro, this time of fugal character. This general scheme of three sections arranged in the order of *quick, slow, quick* survived long after the rest of Scarlatti's work was forgotten and later became the basis for many a composition by Haydn and Mozart.

Second, that beauty of vocal melody was the great desideratum; the dramatic plot was only an excuse — and usually a very poor one — for the music. A great deal of the dramatic action — the " dull parts which have to get on with the story of the play," as one writer expresses it — were sung in *recitativo secco*, a " dry recitative " accompanied by only an occasional chord on the harpsichord. Scarlatti used also a kind of recitative that was accompanied by stringed instruments, which fact infused a new color and emotional atmosphere into the opera. But what the audience awaited were the *arias*, set pieces for all the principal characters, introduced every so often and in a fixed order and used to express any emotion desired — joy as well as sorrow, rage as well as despair. They were designed not so much for the expression of emotional truthfulness as for providing a well-rounded form of aesthetic proportion. Scarlatti set the style of writing them in the *da capo* form, that is, with three parts, one of which was repeated after the second had been introduced, *a-b-a*. Nothing more typical of Baroque formalism could be found. Thus such an opera as *Griselda* is really nothing but a series of arias for the principals in sweet cantilena or gallant coloratura, linked together by recitatives, with no ensembles or choruses of any kind.

Third, that the *castrati* type of singing predominated. Of the six principal characters which the opera demanded, the three men — and always the hero — were artificial sopranos. This fact colored the whole nature of the work, giving it a character which fitted its unreal story and its grandiose scenic conception; for nothing natural or human would have seemed congruous. The only thing that was of interest to the audience was the singing, especially that of these instrumentalized voices.

Fourth, that the singers were expected to be something in the way of creators as well; for they never sang their arias as written and were expected to introduce embellishments of various sorts into the repetition

Courtesy of The Louvre

AN EIGHTEENTH-CENTURY DRAMATIC PRESENTATION
Leonardo Vinci's *La Contesa de Numi* (painting by Panini)

sections of their arias. The audience judged the different artists not alone by their virtuosity, but by their ability to heighten the vocal effects that had been written down by the composer. And the auditors were so trained in the niceties of vocal virtuosity that they could — and did — evaluate every point made by composer and singer. As a contemporary observer of the practice wrote:

"Among the Things worthy of consideration, the first to be taken Notice of, is the Manner in which all *Airs* divided into three parts are to be sung. In the first Part they require nothing but the simplest Ornaments, of a good Taste and few, that the Composition may remain simple, plain, and pure; in the second, they expect that to this Purity some artful Graces be added, by which the judicious may hear, that the Ability of the Singer is greater; and, in repeating the *Air*, he that does not vary it for the better, is no great Master . . .

"Without varying the *Airs* the knowledge of the Singers could never be discovered; but from the Nature and Quality of the Variations, it will easily be discerned in two of the greatest Singers which is the best."

— J. E. Galliard: *Observations on the Florid Song*, 1724

Fifth, that the voices were extraordinarily beautiful. These were the real days of great solo singing, the era of *bel canto*, and the operatic scores of the time show that all the artists, and especially the *castrati*, must have possessed a virtuosity of execution that is almost unbelievable.

Sixth, that the plots were utterly barren, dramatically speaking. The subjects of the Baroque operas were always mythological in character, and although the poets attempted to make their gods and heroes live again, they usually succeeded in making them men of their own time only, dressed up to suit the occasion and singing music quite unfitted to the character of the drama, its real purpose being the display of the singer's trills and flourishes.

Scarlatti divided his time between Rome, the capital, and Naples, which was the richest and most influential city in Italy at this time. His fluent, graceful style, together with the innovations he introduced (the "Italian overture" and the *da capo* aria) and the countless composers who imitated his writing, made him the greatest influence of the early eighteenth century. With him and his followers of the Neapolitan school, who knew so well how to treat the human voice and exploit its every possibility, vocal solo song assumed a place of importance in music that it never again equaled. Other important names in this Neapolitan group were Leonardo Vinci, a descendant of the famous artist's family, Nicola Jommelli and Tommaso Traetta, who reintroduced the chorus as an important dramatic element, and Pietro Metastasio, the famous poet who wrote so many of the best librettos of this period.

THE UNIVERSAL NEAPOLITAN STYLE

It was this Neapolitan style that spread all over Europe and made the acquirement of Italian culture a fashionable fad of the life of the time and an important influence in the development of its taste. Germany came completely under its spell: Dresden, for example, the capital of the Kingdom of Saxony, was to all intents and purposes merely an outpost of Italy during the eighteenth century. The brilliant opera in this lovely city was entirely in the hands of singers from the southern peninsula. Agents of the Saxon king went to Italy and secured there a number of paintings, notably Raphael's *Sistine Madonna,* for the royal art galleries. So many Italian stonemasons and builders were working on the churches and palaces in Dresden that a special village was created for housing them. Winckelmann, the father of modern art history, went to Italy from Dresden, and the German poet, Herder, in describing this beautiful city on the Elbe, called it a *deutsches Florenz*. So with Salzburg and Vienna in Austria. In North Germany, the few experiments made in native opera at Hamburg became entirely submerged in the stream of Baroque influence that flowed so steadily from Italy. Provincial capitals like Madrid, Lisbon, Copenhagen, and St. Petersburg set up Italian operas and staffed them with Italian artists. In Paris, where Italian architects were busy creating many of the structures that have since made the city famous, the native musical forces had finally to capitulate to the charms of the music from the south. London became a devotee of the Italian style early in the eighteenth century, try as the native artists and writers might to make it seem ridiculous and " foreign " — the greatest condemnatory epithet an Englishman can use! This from Addison's *Spectator* (March 21, 1711) is typical:

"It is my design in this paper to deliver down to posterity a faithful account of the Italian opera . . . for there is no question but that our great-grandchildren will be very curious to know the reason why their forefathers used to sit together like an audience of foreigners in their own country, and to hear whole plays acted in a language which they did not understand.

"*Arsinoë* was the first opera that gave us a taste of Italian music. The great success this opera met with alarmed the fiddlers of the town, who laid down an established rule that 'nothing is capable of being set to music that is not nonsense.'

"This maxim was no sooner received but we immediately fell to translating the Italian operas; and, as there was no danger of hurting the sense of these extraordinary pieces, our authors would often make up words of their own.

"The next step to our refinement was the introducing of Italian actors into our opera, who sung their parts in their own language, at the same time that our countrymen performed theirs in our native tongue . . . the lover frequently made his court, and gained the heart of his princess, in a language which she did not understand.

"At length the audience grew tired of understanding half the opera; and therefore to ease themselves entirely of the failure of thinking, have ordered it that the whole opera is performed in an unknown tongue."

And an early eighteenth-century poem by Ambrose Philips, dedicated to a popular Italian singer in London in 1725, leaves us in no doubt as to his views:

"Little syren of the stage,
Charmer of an idle age;
Empty warbler, breathing lyre,
Wanton gale of fond desire;
Bane of ev'ry manly heart;
Oh, too pleasing is thy strain,
Hence to southern climes again;
Tuneful mischief, vocal spell,
To this island bid farewell;
Leave us, as we ought to be,
Leave the Britons rough and free."

What could be more characteristic of the time and place of its origin?

OPERA BUFFA IN ITALY

In the midst of all this Baroque glory of the opera, there was born another, new, type of music drama, one which dealt with everyday characters rather than with classical heroes, whose music was straightforward and sincere and whose parts were given to qualified actors rather than to mere singers. This developed out of the custom the opera librettists had of introducing several comic characters toward the end of their works in order to mitigate somewhat the artificiality and unreality of their plots. From this grew the popular *opera buffa* (literally " comic opera ") which, produced for the common people, spread rapidly over all Europe.

Pergolesi's *La serva padrona,* produced in Naples in 1733, was the first of these to become popular; a charming little work for only two singing characters, it was originally intended as an intermezzo between the acts of a longer drama. There is a natural humanity and sparkling wit about this work which appealed strongly to the French, for whom it was produced in 1752, almost twenty years after its first performance in Naples. The stilted conventionalities of the grand opera, in which " grand " was too often the only operative force, had wearied the French public, and it took to this new style eagerly. In fact, Pergolesi's music captured all Europe and strongly influenced contemporary instrumental developments.

Another work in this style known today is Cimarosa's sparkling *Il matrimonio segreto* (*The Secret Wedding*). In its variety and fluidity of style, in its abundance and freshness of ideas, it stands as the most illustrious example of this important Neapolitan art form. Its overture is one of the most lively pieces of music imaginable, and the modern revivals of this work make us realize how much Mozart, and, indeed, all later music, owed to these Italian *opera buffa.* There is " good-humored laughter " here, a fresh melodic spontaneity that was absolutely *sui generis.* Princes, bishops, potentates of all sorts wanted these tunes for their own orchestras; and, since their composers could not give them exactly, they imitated the style as best they could. Pergolesi's and Cimarosa's laughing melodies were literally taken over into the new instrumental music that was being written and may thus be said to be the literal ancestors — perhaps first cousins — of some of Emanuel Bach's and Haydn's ideas.

J. PH. RAMEAU

OPERA IN FRANCE

At the same time that these influences were being felt in France, the traditions of the lofty Lully style were being kept alive there by Rameau (1683–1764); a native Frenchman, he had a wider range of expression than his noted predecessor, but kept the same insistence on the drama as the most important element in the whole. The first forty years of his life were spent in wandering about Europe, picking up ideas and working out the theories which he finally gathered into his *Traité de l'harmonie réduite a ses principes naturels*. Thus he was known as a distinguished theorist on harmonic questions long before he took up the writing of operas. But it is characteristic of the creative Frenchman, as a dramatic critic has said, that he finally arrives at the stage, no matter what his early work may have been; for the theater is the center of the intellectual life of the country. Rameau did not take up dramatic writing until well into middle life, but he succeeded remarkably in it. His ability is best seen in the stately ballets which he provided for his operas. Typically

Baroque in their brilliance, they consist of strings of dignified dances: minuets, gavottes, bourrées, rondeaus, and so on — all revealing a capacity for line drawing that is extremely effective. As is to be expected of a deep thinker on the subject of harmony, his music is notably fresh without being in the least freakish. Full of spirit, rich in variety, brilliant in color, it is typically French, a veritable incarnation of the spirit of its race.

A contemporary, Diderot, thus summarizes Rameau's lifework:

"He delivered us from the plainchant that we had been psalmodizing for over a hundred years [a slap at the French declamatory opera] . . . He presented us with a certain number of operas in which we find harmony, bits of song, disconnected ideas, clashes, soaring flights, triumphs, onslaughts, glorifications, murmurs, breathless victories, *airs de danse* that will live eternally."

IN GERMANY

In Germany, as we have said, the operatic situation was almost hopeless, in so far as native composition went. At Hamburg, in the early days of the century, there flourished for a few years an attempt at cultivating national opera. A number of composers tried their hand: Franck, Theile, Mattheson, Telemann, Keiser, and even Handel; but there was no patronage of an aristocratic and wealthy court to sustain the venture and to direct the taste. Eventually the whole thing fell through because of lack of material. Handel's success in this field came later, in the setting of London.

AND ENGLAND

Contemporary with the vogue for Italian opera which has waxed and waned in England to this day was Gay's *The Beggar's Opera*, the production of which in 1728 stimulated a number of similar ballad operas, in which the literary blades of the day took a hand, concocting fancies and satires and fitting them to old ballads and popular songs. As Henry Carey, one of the chief English composers at the turn of the century, rather bitterly remarked:

MASQUERADES AND OPERAS, BURLINGTON GATE

An engraving by Hogarth

" These handy Hirelings can, in half a Day,
Steal a new Ballad Farce from some old Play:
To mangled Scraps of many an Ancient Tune
Tagg Feetless Jingle, Jarring and Jejune.
The jaded Play'rs with equal haste rehearse,
'Till Sing Song limps to Horrid, Hobbling Verse! "

But nothing came of all this activity. Gay's little masterpiece alone survives to remind us of this popular vogue of the eighteenth-century operatic stage in England. The ballad opera, transplanted to Germany, and expanded and developed there, became the *Singspiel* of hallowed memory in the evolution of the German national style of opera.

Otherwise the Italians reigned supreme until the advent of Handel, who, as we shall see, largely continued their traditions. One of the best of Hogarth's early engravings, done in 1724, bearing the title " Masquerades and Operas," admirably satirizes the Baroque era in England with the following inscription:

"O how refin'd how elegant we're grown!
What noble Entertainments Charm the Town!
Whether to hear the Dragon's roar we go,
Or gaze supriz'd on Fawks's matchless show,
Or to the Opera's or to the Masques,
To eat up Ortelans, and empty Flasques
And rifle Pies from Shakespears clinging Page,
Good Gods! how great's the gusto of the Age."

THE GALANT INSTRUMENTALISTS

Galant — Well-bred. That which strives to please. Affable, correct in its setting and in its bearing.

— Petit Larousse

COUPERIN, THE SUPREME GALANT

FRANCE seemed to be much more willing to take up with the new Italian styles in instrumental writing than she had been to adopt the southern operatic music. François Couperin was the most famous member of a large family of organists and harpsichordists that played an important part in French musical life for over two centuries. He was born fifteen years after Corelli, and in him France contributed an outstanding figure to the development of instrumental style. The field on which Couperin entered was, however, far from a barren one, for the harpsichord, with its incisiveness of tone and its quality of impersonality, had proved very acceptable to the French temperament, and a number of composers had written music for it before Couperin's time. Such things as Geoffroy's *Tombeau en forme d'allemande,* a dramatic elegiac sort of piece in which the influence of the operatic style is strongly shown, and Dornel's little *Le pendant d'oreille* and *Le noce d'Auteuil* — fantastic, droll, and altogether charming — show the general styles of keyboard music in France at the turn of the century.

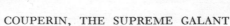

Couperin, who was called *le Grand* to distinguish him from the lesser members of his family, followed the general trend; but his art is completely French in manner and has been called the purest and most characteristic expression of the Gallic temperament in music. He wrote instrumental music, church and organ music, and a few secular vocal pieces. His vast output included four books of harpsichord pieces, containing some 230 numbers; organ works (*Pièces pour orgue consistantes en deux*

LE CONCERT DE CLAVECIN by Van Loo

Messes — 42 in all, for many years thought to be the work of his uncle); a considerable amount of religious vocal music, including motets, elevations, and *Leçons de Ténèbres;* and some very interesting chamber music for small combinations of various instruments, including four *Concerts Royaux* written as a sort of homage to his sovereign Louis XIV. In addition to all this music there appeared the famous didactic works *L'Art de toucher le clavecin* and *Régle pour l'accompagnement.*

As *Ordinaire de la Musique de la chambre du Roi* and *Organiste du Roi,* Couperin stood in high favor with his king and took part in the royal concerts for many years. In spite of his great prominence during the eighteenth century, he remains an almost unknown figure to the great majority of present-day music lovers.

It is in his keyboard music for the harpsichord that Couperin is happiest. He wrote a great deal for this instrument, his *pièces* being divided into twenty-seven *ordres*, more usually called *suites* or *partitas*. Also he completed in 1716 *L'art de toucher le clavecin*, a treatise which strongly influenced his contemporaries, even the great Bach himself, and those who followed after him. In his earlier *ordres* he adapted the dance-suite form which had been in use for nearly a century; but in the later ones, the composer took to poetic titles, such as *Les jongleurs, Le moucheron, Le tendre Nanette*, etc., a procedure which he thus naïvely explains:

"I have always had in view different incidents that guided me in their composition; hence, the titles correspond to ideas that I had. I may be excused from rendering an account of them. Nevertheless, as there are among these titles some that appear to flatter me, it is well to state that the pieces bearing them are, in a manner, portraits which, under my fingers, have sometimes taken on the guise of good likenesses and that the majority of these opportune titles are applicable rather to amiable originals that I desired to represent than to copies I made of them."

PELLUCID FORMS

The form of these harpsichord suites is simple enough: they are almost always in two parts, one starting in the tonic and moving to the related major or dominant key, the second moving back from this to the tonic. Obviously there is little key variety or surprise here; all that had to come later. Sometimes the pieces run on in brief sections to form a rondo, the form that had been so popular in France from the fifteenth century on. Indeed, we may say that the rondo and the couplet (the latter term was applied to those themes used only once, appearing between the various statements of the main theme) were a standard Couperin formula. But anyone who has heard such works of his in this form as *La favorite* or *La passacaille* will realize how powerful a thing it can become in the hands of a genius. *La favorite* is interesting as a typical classic portrayal of an objective mood — melancholy for melancholy's sake, for the beauty, poetry, and nobility and the sweet, enveloping happiness it gives, as Mme. Landowska has so well phrased it. It is interesting to compare this

Courtesy of The Metropolitan Museum of Art

MADAME FAVART, by Drouais

The pastel shades of this eighteenth-century painting exemplify the Rococo spirit.

music with such a work as Beethoven's *Sonata pathétique,* where the melancholy mood is born of actual disillusionment and made to serve a dramatic, romantic end. *La passacaille,* according to Landowska, who, above all others, should certainly know, is the " queen of harpsichord pieces." In listening to such a rendition of it as this great artist gives, we realize fully the great dignity, serious purpose, and graceful expression of which this galant eighteenth-century style is capable. If one would penetrate to the very heart of this epoch and be convinced of the beauties it contains, he could do no better than listen repeatedly to such lovely music as this. The motley procession of court figures which is depicted in *Les folies françaises,* twelve programistic pieces in variation form, is as characteristic of the century as anything Watteau or Lancret ever painted.

In all Couperin's harpsichord music, ornaments are freely employed; they were part of the technique of the time and were born of the instrument's necessity, since its tone had so little sustaining power. Though they never reached, in this older music, the level of Chopin's significance in ornamentation, these graces could be made to suggest character, as, for instance, the mordents and trills suggest the demure elegance of *Sœur Monique*. Their use sometimes becomes rather a trick, so that in *Les moissonneurs* it sounds too much as if the court had taken to the fields; but in general they are an essential part of Couperin's sustained melodic line and striking harmonies.

Couperin's fluent, exquisite style, surcharged with ornament and grace, is characteristic of the Rococo period; but his reflective, well-ordered, rationalistic spirit, his calm, straightforward bearing, his careful balance between sense and sensibility raise him above its transitory mannerisms and ensure his immortality as one of the great representatives of French genius. By virtue of his art he stands as the personification of a supremely classic age.

DOMENICO SCARLATTI

Italy, although overwhelmingly engaged in the production of operas at this time, found opportunity for writing instrumental music, too. Such men as Alessandro Scarlatti and Domenico Zipoli wrote harpsichord music that could have been played equally well on the organ, for it shows little understanding of the essential differences in the character and sonorities of these two instruments. But with Domenico Scarlatti (son of Alessandro), born the same year as Sebastian Bach, 1685, we reach forward into the sphere of virtuoso music for the harpsichord. His sonatas (*esercizi* — exercises — was his modest name for them) cover a great deal of technical ground, and some of his innovations, such as crossing the hands when playing, must have seemed amazing enough in their day.

It is perhaps a fair generalization to say that Domenico was more concerned with technical pleasures than he was with poetic expression. The name *exercise* indicates the scope of his pieces but says nothing of their exciting brilliance. He wrote over five hundred of these sonatas or sonatinas, all of them single-movement pieces of various lengths. When we use these terms in describing them, we do so in the old sense of an instrumental, as distinguished from a vocal, piece and have to forget both the Corelli sonata (suite, it really was) and the modern significance of the term. There are some signs, in these works of Domenico's, of the emergence of a clear-cut second theme as the germ of the two-subject exposition section that came in later with Haydn; but there is no attempt at development of such themes, beyond a little playing with rhythmic figures.

But if these Scarlatti works lack something of poetic significance, they have everything else — *élan*, brilliance, gaiety, lyricism, key daring, technical virtuosity, and rich loquacity. Hearing a performance of them by such an artist as Landowska or Ehlers is a thrilling experience and makes us realize, as nothing else can, what a brilliant period theirs was. Even to modern ears inured to Liszt and Beethoven, a performance of this music can be made to sound invigorating and interesting, even exciting. In freshness of invention and brilliance of execution those sonatas of Domenico Scarlatti's are the counterpart of Watteau's lighthearted grace and serene elegance.

THE FORGOTTEN GALUPPI

So little of Domenico's music, the product of a really original mind, is known today, that it is little wonder that the music of Baldassare Galuppi (1706–1785), one of the more conventional Italian composers of the time, has completely disappeared. And yet as recently as 1855 Robert Browning was able to say of the music of this composer:

" Oh Galuppi, Baldassaro, this is very sad to find!
I can hardly misconceive you; it would prove me deaf and blind;
But although I take your meaning, 'tis with such a heavy mind!

" Here you come with your old music, and here's all the good it brings.
What, they lived once thus at Venice where the merchants were the kings,
Where St. Mark's is, where the Doges used to wed the sea with rings?

"Ay, because the sea's the street there; and 'tis arched by . . . what you call
. . . Shylock's bridge with houses on it, where they kept the carnival:
I was never out of England — it's as if I saw it all."

Very likely it was this "Brave Galuppi" who first introduced the several-movement sonata to the world. Not being content with merely imitating his greater compatriot and contemporary who had brought the one-movement form to such a high state of perfection, Galuppi used several movements in his sonatas, the better to provide a more diversified range of emotion. He thus stands at the halfway point between the Scarlatti one-movement works and the fully developed sonatas of Haydn and Mozart. Some of his single movements are worthy of comparison with the greatest music produced during the period.

A rather doubtful honor goes to another Italian writer of harpsichord music, the man who is supposed to have invented the kind of inane bass writing used in so much later piano music, even in some of the best. In order to outline the harmony without providing merely chunky chordal accompaniments, Domenico Alberti inserted this kind of bass figure in his sonatas:

etc.

And ever since, this has gone by the name of the Alberti bass.

THE PRODIGIOUS TELEMANN

"A Lulli fame has won: Corelli may be praised,
But Telemann alone above all else is raised."

". . . But who is this old man, who with his nimble pen, full of a pious enthusiasm, enchants the Eternal Temple? Listen! How the waves of the sea are roaring! How the mountains cry aloud with joy and sing hymns unto the Lord! How harmonious an 'Amen' fills the devout heart with a sacred awe! How the temples tremble with the pious shout of Alleluia! Telemann, it is thou, thou, the father of sacred music . . ."

— Quoted by Rolland: *A Musical Tour through the Land of the Past*

These two lines of doggerel from an eighteenth-century "Who's Who in Music," Mattheson's *Ehrenpforte*, and the quotation from a contemporary poem reflect the universal opinion of the time as regards Georg Philipp Telemann (1681–1767). His contemporaries did not hesitate to place this "father of sacred music" on a plane that was considerably higher than that occupied by Johann Sebastian Bach; and yet today he is in every sense of the word a forgotten man!

Even Telemann's unexampled prolificacy, in which he was so characteristic of his time, has been forgotten. Rolland, in his interesting study of this old master, has estimated that in the twenty years which represent him at the height of his career, he produced 12 complete cycles of sacred music for all the Sundays and feast days of the year, 19 Passions (the librettos of which were often from his pen), 20 operas, 40 serenades, 600 miscellaneous instrumental pieces for various instruments, 700 airs, etc., etc. What a man! In addition he found time to fulfill the duties of *Kapellmeister* and cantor in Hamburg: to provide the service music for the five principal churches there; to direct the opera, a task which, Rolland reminds us, was no sinecure, for there were even more cabals and cliques than usual to render the life of an opera impressario a difficult matter; [1] to found a series of popular concerts, which have continued in Hamburg to this day; to journey to Paris, the city of his dreams, where he conducted some of his compositions; to publish the first musical journal ever to be printed in Germany; to act as correspondent to the Eisenach court, writing letters descriptive of the happenings in North Germany; and to write three autobiographies containing all the details of his busy life.

[1] An eighteenth-century French writer, M. de la Borde, has an amusing comment on this in his *Essai sur la musique*, published in Paris in 1780. As paraphrased by Burney in his History, this account says that the government of an opera is a painful and embarrassing employment. It is necessary that the director of so complicated a machine should know how to manage all the springs, remove every obstacle to their motion, gratify the taste and sometimes the caprice of the fickle public, unite in one interest a crowd of different rival talents, excite emulation without jealousy, distribute rewards with justice and delicacy, censure and punish with address, limit the unbounded demands of some by flattery, check the independence of others by apparent concessions, and try to establish in the interior government of this republic as much harmony as reigns in the orchestra. It is manifest, adds Burney, that nothing but the most subtle and artful character can hope to accomplish such Herculean labors!

Whatever our opinion may be regarding the quality of Telemann's music, there can be nothing but wonderment as to its quantity. Like Rolland, we cannot help being impressed with the "prodigious vitality of a man, who, from his tenth to his eighty-sixth year, wrote music with indefatigable joy and enthusiasm and without prejudice to a hundred other occupations!" The little of his music that is still played shows a lively, loquacious, if not very profound, personality; it possesses a Rococo graciousness rather than a Baroque impressiveness. In contradistinction to most of the chamber music of its time, Telemann's *Tafelmusik*, a collection of concertos and chamber works, dispenses with the *basso continuo*, a method of tying together the musical fabric by means of some such instrument as the harpsichord or the organ playing chords which filled in the harmonies suggested by the violoncello part. "I so contrived that the bass was a natural melody," writes Telemann, "forming, with the other parts, an appropriate harmony, which developed with each note in such a way that it seemed as though it could not be otherwise. Many sought to persuade me that I had displayed the best of my powers in these compositions." Here are the foundations of modern style.

Above everything, Telemann was a progressive; he was always attracted by the new in art and did not conceal his disdain for what he called "fossils." "One should never say to art: 'Thou shalt go no farther.' One is always going farther, and one should always go farther," he writes. He was a great student of the music of other countries — France (especially) and Poland and Italy — and through this study he introduced new ideas and fresh life into the rather stodgy German style, which, as Rolland says, was beginning to smell somewhat musty. "It would have been in danger of asphyxiation but for the great draughts of fresh air which men like Telemann let into it through the open doors of France, Poland, and Italy. . . . If we wish to understand the extraordinary blaze of music that illumined Germany from the time of Haydn, Mozart, and Beethoven, we must have some acquaintance with those who prepared this magnificent beacon; we must watch the lighting of the fire."

And nowhere can we see better that the works of the great classics are merely the logical conclusion of the whole Baroque-Rococo century than in these forgotten things of Telemann's.

The Scarlattis — father and son

Couperin-le-Grand

Telemann

COMPOSERS OF THE GALANT PERIOD

NIETZSCHE AND THE EIGHTEENTH CENTURY

In his revolt against what he considered the excesses of Wagnerian Romanticism, Nietzsche has given us an excellent description of the best music left behind by such eighteenth-century composers as the Scarlattis and Couperin. " In contrast to the Romantic disorder, that hodgepodge of tones beloved of a cultivated populace with its aspirations after the elevated, the sublime, the involved, I prefer a malicious, buoyant, fluid art, distinctly artificial, an art that coruscates like a clear flame in a cloudless sky. We know what is requisite for that: serenity, every kind of serenity, my friends! "

We need not agree entirely to realize the truth of this characterization of Rococo art at its best. Perhaps it is this element of eighteenth-century serenity that makes the greatest appeal to us of the twentieth century. However artificial and stilted, unnatural and oversophisticated the age may have been, it provided a setting out of which there came an art that, taken in its perfection, has never been surpassed.

A MUSICAL REFORMER – GLUCK

When I undertook to set the opera of Alceste *to music, I resolved to avoid all those abuses which had crept into Italian Opera through the mistaken vanity of singers and the unwise compliance of composers, and which had rendered it wearisome and ridiculous instead of being, as it once was, the grandest and most important stage of modern times. I endeavored to reduce music to its proper function — that of seconding poetry by enforcing the expression of the sentiment and the interest of the situations without interrupting the action or weakening it by superfluous ornament.*

— From Gluck's Preface to *Alceste,* translated in Forsyth: *Music and Nationalism*

TUMULT IN MID-EIGHTEENTH-CENTURY PARIS

ANY visitor to mid-eighteenth-century Paris would certainly have been conscious of a strong undercurrent of unrest that was running underneath the calm splendor and sumptuous luxury of the court life and the confident rationality of the intellectual activities of the period. The architects and the decorators, the painters and the sculptors of the time indulged the taste of the court for refuge from the pompous splendor and the Baroque grandeur of Versailles by building more intimate and luxurious structures for their life of pleasure (such as the Petit Trianon), by covering their walls with white and gold stucco molded into graceful arabesque and shell designs, by filling their rooms with huge mirrors, exquisite and graceful furniture, statues with flowing lines, and paintings with soft colors. The king gave himself largely to a life of luxury, quite oblivious of the brutal realities which made such a life possible, letting his ministers and his underlings run the government, plunging the country into unsuccessful wars and bringing it to the verge of bankruptcy. The nobility and the clergy exercised their special privileges of collecting a variety of time-honored dues from the people and of escaping, in turn, from most of the tax burden which rested so heavily on the members of "the third estate," that is, the common people. The intellectuals were following the injunction of Pope:

> "Know then thyself; presume not God to scan;
> The proper study of mankind is Man!"

These intellectuals were making further discoveries in all the branches of science. While all this was going on, reformers, among them some of the best minds of the country, were loudly and eloquently discussing the abuses and the iniquities of the time, bringing the attention of everyone concerned, through the distribution of pamphlets and circulars, to the evils and injustices of the *ancien régime*.

Economists wrote treatises on the inequalities of the system of taxation and spread them far and wide, there being no newspapers by means of which public questions could be discussed. Philosophers such as Voltaire (1694–1778), with keen wit and shrewd skill, opposed the Church, one of the most powerful forces in the country, as an institution that was inimical to the exercise of reason and so hostile to reform as to constitute a dangerous obstacle to human progress. Men like Jean Jacques Rousseau (1712–1778) applied similar talents to exposing the political wrongs of the time, boldly asking in such works as *The Social Contract* the question: "By what right does one man rule over another?" D'Alembert and

Diderot, through their great seventeen-volume *Encyclopédie*, published from 1751 to 1772, enlisted the services of the best writers of the century in increasing the interest in natural science and industry, at the same time inculcating many revolutionary ideals and inducing a general attitude of scepticism and discontent. The whole second half of the eighteenth century was given over, in the words of a famous historian, to outspoken and acrid criticism of the existing social and governmental system, a criticism which exerted a tremendous influence in bringing about the revolutions which were to follow. And, strange as it may seem to us of the present day, one of the liveliest subjects of controversy was music.

French music by this time had gone stale. For eighty years, ever since its institution under Lully, the French opera had undergone little change, its principal interest being, as we have seen, in the musical declamation of dramatic texts. The works of Lully and Rameau have been well called "tragedies in song." It seemed as if no other composer felt it permissible to write in a different style, and such a routined and constant iteration of the same ideas so irked the young intellectuals that it provoked one of them, Grimm (who afterward contributed many stirring articles to the *Encyclopédie*), to issue a pamphlet in 1752 which had as its aim the impression upon the public mind of the fact that French music was not invulnerable. In the bitter discussion which followed, Rousseau,[2]

[2] The career of this stormy Genevan philosopher was of great importance to music, directly because of the articles he wrote about music and the works he composed, and indirectly — and of even greater importance — because of his philosophic annunciation of the principles of a new humanism, principles which helped do away with the old regime in politics and found a new one — the Romantic Movement — in art.

Although not a natural musician (it was said that he went about teaching music when he could hardly play a tune), Rousseau at the age of 41 wrote a little opera *Le devin du village* (*The Village Soothsayer*) which was performed at Fontainebleau and later became popular all over France, Louis XV joining his people in singing its vivacious melodies. If anyone thinks that these jaunty Gallic tunes have lost their flavor, let him listen to Martha Angelici's rendering (in *L'Anthologie Sonore*) of the most famous of them, *J'ai perdu mon serviteur*.

Rousseau is sometimes credited with being the originator of the *melodrama*, a form of play in which the spoken voice is employed against a musical background. This idea, however, was probably used by the Greeks, and there were other eighteenth-century examples of the form before he wrote his much-discussed *Pygmalion* in 1762.

Cliché Vizzavona

THE CHEVALIER GLUCK, by Duplessis

taking up the cudgels for Grimm, did not hesitate to make the defiant statement that Italian music was better than French.

As if the gods would take a hand in this *petite guerre d'intelligence,* it so happened that it was just at this time that the Italians came to Paris with their performance of Pergolesi's *La serva padrona* which so took the fancy of the citizens. The whole town was astir: everyone took sides, the Encyclopedists being, of course, in the van as champions of the new, Italian dispensation, trying out their wings in this miniature musical tumult for the longer flights of universal revolution which came later.

His polemics include such things as the *Lettre sur la musique française,* written in 1743, and the *Dissertation sur la musique moderne,* written in 1753, and contain such remarks as "there is neither time nor melody in French music because the language is not capable of either: French song is a continuous bark, its harmony crude and suggestive of the work of a student; French airs are not airs at all, nor French recitatives worth anything. And so I conclude that the French have no music at all." They include also the articles mentioned in the text, written for the great *Encyclopédie,* the errors of which were later pointed out by Rameau, and a dictionary of music (1767) which still remains an outstanding source book for those who would study eighteenth-century music and its forms.

In the course of this tempest in a teapot — this lining up of the French style of opera, with its predilection for the drama, against the Italian, with its overdevelopment of the music — many foolish things were said and written. For the Italian opera, with its long sequences of recitative and its overinsistence on vocal virtuosity, was quite as much in need of reform as was the French.

But out of all the discussion came a realization that some sort of reformation in opera was desirable, if not inevitable, some means by which the best qualities of both styles could be kept and blended. All the great literary minds of France began to visualize the need for a different musical order, just as they did for the necessity of a new social and economic one.

Voltaire summarized this better than any of the other writers, in the conclusion of his *Mélanges littéraires*, a collection of essays published in 1761:

" It is to be hoped that some genius may arise, strong enough to convert the nation from this abuse and to impart to a stage production that has become a necessity the dignity and ethic spirit that it now lacks . . . The tide of bad taste is rising and insensibly submerging the memory of what was once the glory of the nation. Yet again I repeat: The opera must be set on a different footing, that it may no longer deserve the scorn with which it is regarded by all the nations of Europe."

— Quoted in " Gluck and the Encyclopaedists " by Julien Tiersot

THE CAREER OF GLUCK

During this period of bitter controversy and acrid philosophizing in Paris, a German-Bohemian musician in far-off Vienna was preparing himself for the role that had been so perspicaciously described by Voltaire — that of a genius able to set the opera on a different footing. Christoph Willibald Gluck, who, in the words of a contemporary, made " out of Italian and French music, out of that of every people, a music of his own, seeking in nature all the sounds of true expression, and conquering them for himself," proved to be the man for whom Paris was waiting.

Born in a little village in the forests of the Upper Palatinate, of humble parentage, Gluck passed the early years of his life in acquiring the cosmopolitan background that proved so useful for his later career. From Prague, where he had the beginnings of a musical education, he went to Vienna, and thence to Italy, where he lived for ten years and wrote a number of operas in the Italian style. Afterwards he traveled to London, then to Hamburg, Denmark, Vienna, and Prague again. Everywhere he produced new works in the best Italian manner, making no particular stir beyond that of a routined, gifted musician. After another visit to Italy, he returned to Vienna, intending to settle there, where he had married a rich Dutch lady who was able to bring him a considerable fortune. But in two years he was off again to Italy, where one of his operas created such an impression that he was knighted by the Pope, receiving, so it was said, the Order of the Golden Spur and the title *cavaliere*. Returning again to Vienna, where he had been engaged as musical director to the court, he busied himself with writing French comic operas and furnishing the music for various court functions. Such was his background, one ideally suited to the demands which were later to be made on him.

THE GREAT MAN OF VIENNA: METASTASIO

The great man in opera at that time in Vienna was Metastasio, the imperial court poet and principal writer of librettos for Italian operas, the man, according to Burney, "whose writings have probably contributed more to the perfection of vocal melody and music in general than the united efforts of all the great European composers." Brought up in the atmosphere of the Baroque opera and with the opportunity of coming into direct contact with many of its principal musical and dramatic figures, Metastasio had an ideal training for his lifework. It was said that he composed his poems sitting at the harpsichord, often outlining the melodies to which they were later set. No wonder that he became the great favorite of all the Italians of the eighteenth century; settling in Vienna, he became the spoiled darling of the whole literary and musical world.

A lover of *bel canto* and all the Italian traditions, Metastasio was too great an artist not to realize the shortcomings of the Neapolitan style; and in a letter (written, as Rolland shows, some twenty years before Gluck announced the principles which underlay his reforms of the opera, in his famous dedicatory preface to *Alceste*) Metastasio placed himself on record as favoring many of the ideas later proclaimed by Gluck: the supremacy of poetry over music, the necessary importance of the drama, the power of the right sort of music to interpret the spirit of the words. Which goes to prove that as early as 1749, and in the case of so confirmed an Italian as Metastasio, reform was in the air.

It was inevitable that Gluck and Metastasio should have come into frequent contact. Fulfilling his numerous commissions for Italian operas from various sources, Gluck had set many of Metastasio's librettos. But the calm, polite, inflexibly Baroque temperament of the poet fitted ill with the strong, audacious, revolutionary spirit of the composer, who, aware of the tendencies of the time, was becoming impatient to write in a new, more naturalistic style. And when Count Durazzo, the intendant of the Vienna opera, encouraged Gluck to break from the Metastasian ideals, and the advent of a new librettist, Calzabigi, made such a break possible, the composer wrote a series of three operas, *Orfeo*, *Alceste*, and *Paride ed Elena*, in a style which attempted to conform music with nature and reason.

RIVAL LIBRETTISTS

We need not take too seriously Calzabigi's disapproval of a fellow librettist in his description of how *Orfeo* came into being to realize that he, as "obstetrician of the new operatic reform," as Alfred Einstein calls him, was instrumental in instigating Gluck's reform:

"The then intendant of the spectacles of the imperial court, Count Durazzo, believed that Calzabigi (who had come shortly before to Vienna with some reputation as a poet) might have some opera books in his desk, and invited him to dispose of them to him. Calzabigi was obliged to accede to the request of a man of such weight. He wrote *Orfeo* . . . and chose Gluck to set it to music. Everyone in Vienna knows that the imperial poet, Metastasio, belittled Gluck, and that the feeling was mutual; for Gluck thought little of Metastasio's meticulous dramas. He was of the opinion that this high-flown poetry and these neatly manufactured characters had nothing that was great and elevated to offer to music . . . Gluck hated those meek political, philosophical, and moral views of Metastasio's, his metaphors, his garrulous little passions, his geometrically devised word plays. Gluck liked emotions captured from simple nature, mighty passions at boiling point and at the climax of their outbreak, loud theatrical tumults. The imperial poet, on the other hand, took delight in ingenious flowers of speech, which he liked to present in the form of antitheses, in amorous disputes, in academic discourses, in petty characters one and all full of lovelorn affectation. The minds of these two were diametrically opposed to each other."

— Einstein: *Gluck*

Gluck similarly attributes the chief merits of his new operatic style to his librettist, in a letter written in 1781 to the *Mercure de France*:

" I should reproach myself even more grievously if I consented to let the invention of the new style of Italian opera be attributed to me, the success of which justified the attempt: it is to M. Calzabigi that the principal merit belongs; and if my music has had some success, I think it my duty to recognize that I am beholden for it to him, since it was he who enabled me to develop the resources of my art."

— *ibid.*

Although the novelty of these new works by Calzabigi and Gluck astounded the Viennese audiences, they preferred the older style of writing and went on demanding operas conceived according to the earlier formulas. Gluck himself wrote several of them after finishing *Orfeo*, one of them to a libretto especially composed for him by Metastasio! His reform seemingly had little effect.

Nothing daunted, Gluck turned his eyes toward Paris, attracted no doubt by the demands for operatic reform which had been so strongly expressed there. After a carefully launched preparatory program, he visited Paris in 1773 and attempted to have his works accepted by the *Opéra*. The authorities, not anxious to encourage him and yet not willing to refuse him entirely, said they could not produce anything unless he undertook to write five new works for them. Gluck immediately accepted the proposal, writing as the first *Iphigénie en Aulide*, which was produced in April, 1774, and created a tremendous furore. With characteristic vivacity, Paris immediately began to take sides and form parties for and against the new music. When, in August of the same year, Gluck produced a French version of *Orfeo* — *Orphée et Eurydice* — the excitement knew no bounds. Returning to Vienna, the composer was made Imperial Court Musician by the empress, Maria Theresa.

PICCINNI (from a contemporary portrait)

GLUCK VERSUS PICCINNI

Two years later, Maria's daughter, the young French queen, Marie Antoinette, added further fuel to the Parisian flames by having a prominent Italian opera composer, Niccola Piccinni, invited to Paris and made director of a music school there. The real purpose of his coming was, however, to provoke a squabble with Gluck, so that everyone could take sides for or against the new style. And, although Gluck himself was too wise to become inveigled into any sort of direct competition with Piccinni, take sides everyone did, furiously and bitterly.

Burney thus describes this edifying spectacle:

"The almost universal cry at Paris was that he [Gluck] had recovered the dramatic Music of the ancient Greeks; that there was no other worth hearing; that he was the only musician in Europe who knew how to express the passions; these and other encomiums preparatory to his apotheosis were uttered and published in the journals and newspapers of Paris, accompanied with constant and contemptuous censures of Italian Music, when Piccinni arrived (1776). This admirable composer, the delight and pride of Naples, as Gluck of Vienna, had no sooner erected his standard in France, than all the friends of Italian Music, of Rousseau's doctrines, and of the plan, if not the language of Metastasio's dramas, inlisted in his services. A furious war broke out, all Paris was on the *qui vive*. No door was opened to a visitor, without this question being asked previous to his admission: *Monsieur! êtes vous* PICCINNISTE *ou* GLUCKISTE?[3]

"These disputes, and those of musical critics and rival artists throughout the kingdom, seem to me to have soured and diminished the pleasure arising from Music in proportion as the art has advanced to perfection."

—Burney: *General History*

This seems to have been what Gluck thought, for, after the successful production of two more operas, *Armide* and *Iphigénie en Tauride*, and the failure of another, *Echo et Narcisse*, he decided to leave Paris forever.[4] He wrote in 1780, after his return to Vienna:

"I shall hardly allow myself to be persuaded again to become the object of criticism or the praise of the French nation, for they are as changeable as red cockerels."

He spent his last seven years in Vienna, in almost complete retirement.

[3] At this time Benjamin Franklin was American ambassador at the court of Louis XVI and championed the cause of Gluck. When Marie Antoinette heard of this, she exclaimed, "What can a man whose *métier* is to place rods on buildings know of music?"

[4] Piccinni lived on in Paris long after Gluck had departed, and he later became a Professor of the Conservatoire, suffering severely in the French Revolution, as if Fate would compensate for his apparent success over a much greater rival. In all he wrote over 125 operas.

GLUCK'S REFORMS

In his Preface to the second of his revolutionary works, *Alceste*, Gluck tells us exactly what he tried to accomplish in his reform of the opera. He aimed at avoiding the abuses that the vanity of singers and the mistaken acquiescence of composers had allowed to creep into Italian opera: meaningless repetitions, improvisations by the soloists, orchestral interludes that broke up the continuity of the orchestration — all these were to be avoided. The great aim was that music, reinforcing the poetry, should not interrupt the action or draw attention to itself with foolish ornamentation. The music was to be like the light and shade, the coloring in a drawing, "which animates the figures without altering their outlines." The overture, he saw, ought to foreshadow the nature of the opera and prepare the listeners' minds. Orchestration throughout must be so chosen and deployed as to serve the emotion of the words and augment it. Recitative and air must not be so disparate. "A grand simplicity" was his aim — no parade of difficulties, no forced novelty, but the free breaking of any of the old rules if the new conception of art demanded it. It is all perfectly wise, wholesome, and, to us, obvious.

If we listen to *Orpheus*, we find not a chilly Greek myth but a simple human story. There is no subplot, no complication. Orpheus, in his grief for his dead wife Eurydice, descends to Hades to try to release her by his music. The beauty of his playing and of his singing masters the Furies — how dramatic is their first refusal! — and he is allowed to seek Eurydice in Elysium, where the chorus of Blessed Spirits is heavenly indeed. The condition is made that he must not look upon Eurydice until they are again in the world of man. His exceeding love causes him to break the rule, and Eurydice's breath departs. Here enters the one trace of older plot practice. Amor, the god of Love, takes pity on them, and, because of Orpheus's great affection, restores Eurydice to life.

In the simplicity of plot, in the use of the chorus of dark and happy spirits, in the ballet, and in its moving airs, the work is perennially affecting. The part of Orpheus, written for a male alto — here the old usage held — is now usually sung by a female, with some loss of realism. Such a work is bound, of course, to present to modern ears a good many traces of its ancestry; Gluck could not be expected to cast off all his older style: he was not aiming at novelty for its own sake. But in the closing up of the plot, in the unity of the writing, as well as in the bold individual touches (such as the snarling of Cerberus and the tensity of the writing for the Infernal chorus), together with the ageless beauty of the ballet music in the Elysian fields and the touching " I have lost my Eurydice," known to every music lover, there is a whole new world of operatic joys. The pathos of Orpheus's appeal to the shades, with its sad melisma on " woe," strikes directly at the heart. This is no languid amusement in coloratura vocalism through an unreal plot, garnished with courtly caperings by the ballet. This is the path to a new fusion of arts, a new way of spiritual pleasure in the opera house. Gluck pursued the same path with eager enthusiasm in further Greek stories made human, *Alceste, Iphigénie en Tauride,* and the rest. He added this human touch to his instrumentation as well, making the instruments reinforce the emotional effect of the words.

It was no small virtue that the subjects of his operas were so noble. Not always, before or since, has opera lived so virtuously; but the world could hardly be expected to sustain or continue such a strain of nobility and humanity. With the exception of Mozart's and Beethoven's work, the opera fell back into the trough of tradition — history shows many a similar case — until the strong tide and wild winds of Romance swept it into other seas and fresh adventures.

Gluck's attempted reforms failed in the practical sense that they had no immediate effect on opera; but they are important as marking the beginning of that spirit of naturalistic revolt, that stir in European intellectual life which led to the great Romantic literature and music of the first half of the next century. In his striving for naturalism and dramatic consistency, Gluck was able to create a world of illusion which forever closed the door to the past and its type of *castrato* court operas and was strongly suggestive of the great things that were to come. Like his contemporaries in other fields, the philosophers, the Encyclopedists, and the reformers of the eighteenth century, Gluck helped to lay the foundations for the great revolt which the inherent characteristics of the Baroque-Rococo times made inevitable.

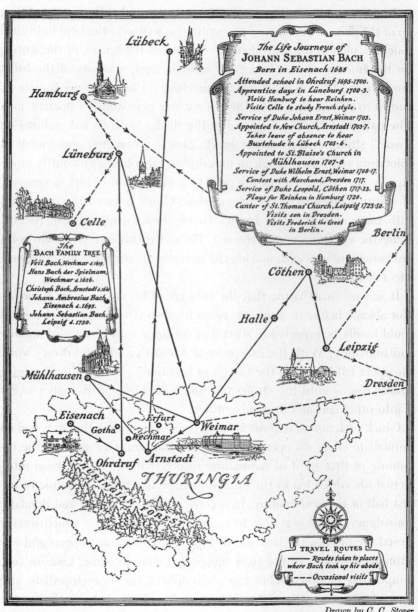

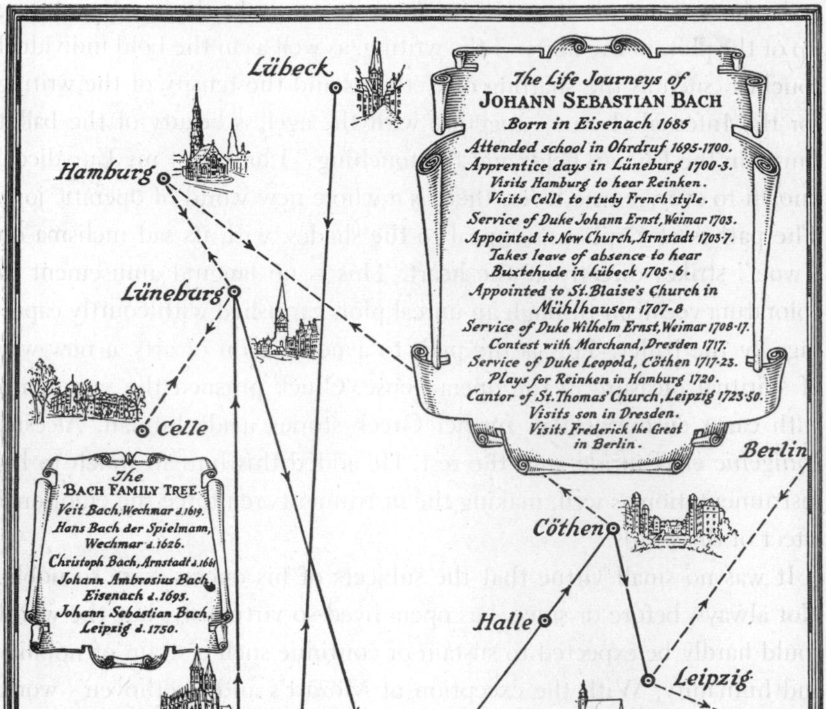
The Life Journeys of
JOHANN SEBASTIAN BACH
Born in Eisenach 1685
Attended school in Ohrdruf 1695-1700.
Apprentice days in Lüneburg 1700-3.
Visits Hamburg to hear Reinken.
Visits Celle to study French style.
Service of Duke Johann Ernst, Weimar 1703.
Appointed to New Church, Arnstadt 1703-7.
Takes leave of absence to hear
Buxtehude in Lübeck 1705-6.
Appointed to St. Blaise's Church in
Mühlhausen 1707-8
Service of Duke Wilhelm Ernst, Weimar 1708-17.
Contest with Marchand, Dresden 1717.
Service of Duke Leopold, Cöthen 1717-23.
Plays for Reinken in Hamburg 1720.
Cantor of St. Thomas' Church, Leipzig 1723-50.
Visits son in Dresden.
Visits Frederick the Great
in Berlin.
The
BACH FAMILY TREE
Veit Bach, Wechmar d. 1619.
Hans Bach der Spielmann,
Wechmar d. 1626.
Christoph Bach, Arnstadt d. 1661
Johann Ambrosius Bach,
Eisenach d. 1695.
Johann Sebastian Bach,
Leipzig d. 1750.
Lübeck
Hamburg
Lüneburg
Celle
Berlin
Cöthen
Halle
Leipzig
Dresden
Mühlhausen
Eisenach
Gotha
Erfurt
Weimar
Wechmar
Ohrdruf
Arnstadt
THURINGIA
THURINGIAN FOREST
TRAVEL ROUTES
Routes taken to places where Bach took up his abode
Occasional visits

Drawn by C. C. Stover

And There Were Giants in Those Days

There were giants in the earth in those days; and also after that, when the sons of God came in unto the daughters of men, and they bare children to them, the same became mighty men which were of old, men of renown.

— Genesis vi, 4.

THE SACRED MUSIC OF BACH

The story of that wonder man of music, Johann Sebastian Bach, is that of the innermost life of the German spirit during the darkest century of the nation's existence.

— Richard Wagner

THE TRUE BACH

" Come kindly Death, come blest repose,
Come, for my life is dreary
And I of earth am weary.
Come, for I wait for thee,
Come soon and calm thou me;
Gently mine eyelids close,
Come blest repose."

THIS song of Johann Sebastian Bach's, one of the finest things that ever came from his pen, full of strong yet tender feeling, with an almost overpowering nostalgic longing for release from all the sorrows and difficulties of life, may seem a strange introduction to the work of one of the world's greatest composers. Yet in many ways it is most characteristic. Written at the very height of his career, while he was in full possession of his genius and at a time when he was seemingly completely happy, it shows him essentially to have been a mystic in the real sense of the word — one who by contemplation and self-surrender seeks to obtain a union with his Deity. This spirit runs through all his great religious works. Perhaps in the case of no other composer is it so true that the placid, uneventful, rather prosaic life of the outer man differs so much from the intense, spiritual life of the inner man that neither seems to have any part in the other. Bach the typical man of his period, organist and *Kapellmeister* to small German courts, master in a boys' school, cantor of one of Germany's principal churches, wise teacher, father of a large family, devoted husband, is a figure well known to us. But Bach the spiritual contender, the emotional poet and tone painter, the "incorrigible Romanticist," expressing himself with an intensity that completely belies the normal course of his life, the man who in the midst of a seemingly comfortable world was inwardly dead to its realities, his mind transfixed by a subjective existence having death as its greatly to be desired goal — this man is unfamiliar to most of us. And yet it is this Bach, represented by the song *Komm, süsser Tod,* into which he breathed everything of himself that was yearning for expression, as his great biographer, Schweitzer, has said — this is the real, the essential Bach.

In spite of the fact that many still consider Bach a composer of patterned, absolute, and, if the truth is fully acknowledged, not very interesting music, this composer was really a writer of an intensely expressive and highly imaginative type. Instead of being, as is usually thought, the ideal composer of absolute music, at his best he represents the subjective ideal. Possessing an unusual depth of feeling and a deeply ingrained religious conviction, as well as a musical imagination that was coupled with unparalleled technical powers, he seemed able to transmute whatever he attempted in the way of religious expression into profound subjective beauty and universal truth that far transcends any suggestion of temporal creed or doctrinal tenet. It seems that whenever there was opportunity for blending his musical genius and his firm faith, whenever he was engaged in expressing the things which he really believed, he achieved his finest results. No matter how sentimentally outmoded the texts he set or how far removed they seem from the ideals of present-day experience, he was able to sublimate his beliefs in such a way that we get from his religious music a spiritual satisfaction and a depth of emotional experience that is afforded by the work of no other composer. So it is natural that we turn first to a consideration of this music.

In Bach we come to the culmination of one of the great epochs of the art; he represents the acme of the polyphonic grandeur and intricacy which we have been tracing from its earliest, almost instinctive, beginnings. We have seen what a world of differing spiritual and human aspirations there was in this long period of development; while it was unified, externally, by the general use of woven melodies and rhythms, the era was in reality widely diversified. Nothing more unlike than the madrigals of Monteverdi and the motets and Masses of Palestrina can be imagined, even though both composers made use of the same technical means of expression. So, too, the contrapuntal music of Bach, with its marked emotion, its very personal, Protestant feeling, is far removed from the period of the Universal Church and the mysticism of passive and helpless man in the midst of untranslatable earthly trials. The lovely setting of Josquin des Prés's *Incarnatus* which we considered in an earlier chapter and Bach's beautiful treatment of the same words in his *B Minor Mass,* both of them outstanding masterpieces of polyphonic expression, are worlds apart in meaning.

But strongly as we may feel that this direct, personal, spiritual Bach is the real Bach, we must remember that it is not, by any means, all of him. Among the many explanations that might well be given of why he must always stand as the greatest of musicians, that of his many-sidedness is perhaps the most significant. Bigness is not synonymous with greatness, as we of this century are learning only too well; but Bach was big, broad, voluminous, and great, in the deepest and highest sense. He wrote an almost unbelievable amount of music during his long, active life; and like all the great composers, there were times in his career when the mere ease of production and the perfection of the processes of composition tended to overwriting. It seems to have been as true of him as it has been of other great workers in the arts — Shakespeare, Beethoven, Rembrandt, Rubens — that the very process of bringing into the

H. D. McKinney

THE *STAMMHAUS* OF THE BACH FAMILY IN WECHMAR

A tablet on its walls has the following inscription:

"In this house lived Veit Bach around the year 1600, and after him his son Hans Bach, both of them bakers. Hans also learned music in Gotha and became a credit to that profession. Seven generations of this Bach family have given the world a hundred practicing musicians and music scholars, and in the person of Johann Sebastian Bach, one of its greatest composers, the outstanding contrapuntist and organ player of his time.

"All honor to their memory."

world any masterpieces necessitates the expenditure of a tremendous amount of creative energy, some of which is inevitably diverted into channels that are not important. The very quality of the works of these men depends to a certain degree on the quantity they produced; but in the main, Bach's music making was exceedingly profitable as well as prolific.

AN ORGANIST'S PROSAIC LIFE

The details of Bach's life are generally known. They are of particular interest in so far as they directly affected his creative output. Born in 1685, of a long line of provincial church and town musicians, in the very heart of German Protestantism, in Eisenach, Thuringia, he spent his early years in preparation for the profession which it was inevitable for him to follow. As he lost both parents at an early age, he came under the tutelage of an older organist brother, and through him and the masters at the schools he attended, coupled with the insatiable curiosity of genius, Bach received an excellent foundational training in organ, clavier, and violin playing and came into direct contact with the choral practices of the Lutheran Church of the time. His first real position was as organist in Arnstadt, a little town not far from his birthplace, from which post he absented himself shortly after being appointed, in order to go north and learn more of his profession from Buxtehude, the great organist of his time, in Lübeck. This leave of absence became so extended that the young Bach found himself in difficulty with the church authorities upon his return, the first skirmish of a perpetual war on the prerogatives of his position in which he was engaged the rest of his life. He was a strongly opinionated, hot-headed individual, thoroughly convinced of his rights and strongly determined to uphold them, even in the face of the most duly constituted authority.

From Arnstadt, Bach went to another provincial Thuringian town, Mühlhausen, where he stayed for a short time and then was called to Weimar, the little town that has become known as the German Athens, as organist of the duke's court chapel. This position can hardly be said to have been commensurate with Bach's genius, but it gave him plenty of opportunity for quiet study and composition and an organ on which to play. It was during this period at Weimar, from 1708 to 1717, that he wrote most of the great organ works for which he has become famous. His own organ was small and undistinguished, but he was in demand as a virtuoso player and recitalist, and so had opportunity for playing larger instruments. Some of his masterpieces were written for such occasions, although most of them first saw the light of day in the incongruous chapel of Duke Wilhelm's castle at Weimar. Fortunately Bach did not write for the moment. Many of his works he never heard given with anything that would seem adequate to us in the way of resources. But he seemed always to be able to hear with an inner ear and to idealize his conceptions in such a way as to make them the greatest of their kind in the literature.

Courtesy of the Erfurt Museum

THE YOUTHFUL BACH

The portrait is supposed to be that of Bach.

AT ANHALT-CÖTHEN

The middle period of Bach's life was spent in the service of another prince, Leopold of Anhalt-Cöthen. Here he was *Kapellmeister* to the court's little orchestra. And, since there was no religious duty connected with his post and no organ to play, he interested himself in the writing of a great deal of instrumental, secular music. A good violinist, he turned his attention to that instrument and wrote for it as well as for the orchestra and the clavier. Most of his works in these fields came from this period.

IN LEIPZIG

In 1723, at the age of 38, Bach was elected cantor of St. Thomas's and its associated churches in Leipzig, one of the most important musical positions in Germany at the time. He spent the rest of his life there, training the singers of the choir, teaching in the school connected with the church, writing music for the weekly services, raising his large family, and generally quarreling with the authorities — not exactly what we would call an artistic milieu. Yet out of it came, for the reasons we have already noted, his greatest works, for this was his time of abundant fruitfulness, both in quality and quantity. Nearly three hundred cantatas, a number of large choral works of the utmost importance, including the *St. Matthew Passion* and the *B Minor Mass,* as well as various instrumental compositions, flowed in a steady stream from his facile pen. He traveled more than he had ever done in his life, going as far afield as Berlin. There he visited Frederick the Great, played for him, and sent him his *Musikalisches Opfer* as a memento of the visit. His last years, happy enough as to personal affairs, were embittered by quarrels with those in authority over him. He died July 28, 1750, at the age of sixty-five.

BACH, THE GREATER AND THE LESSER

Many present-day critics are wont to divide the hundreds of compositions left us by this composer into two general classes — what might be called the Greater and the Lesser Bach. Enough has already been said here to suggest that the former group would certainly include the majority of the religious choral works, and the latter many of the instrumental secular ones. This is probably as clear a line of demarcation as is necessary. There is no doubt that the expressive side of Bach's genius is most concentratedly shown in his sacred music, the cantatas, Masses, and Passions, and in that branch of his instrumental music most closely associated with these, his organ chorale preludes and fugues. No better example could be found of these expressive works than the *B Minor Mass,* and a study of Bach might well begin and end with this tremendous composition, one of the sublime summits in the terrain of the art.

"B MINOR MASS"

It grew in musical stature and favor with its creator during Bach's forty-sixth to fifty-second years of life, from 1731 to 1737. The term *Mass* is, of course, closely associated with the ritual of the Catholic Church; but the Lutheran service had its Mass as well, keeping two sections of the original six at the time its ritual was "reformed." These two, the *Kyrie eleison* and the *Gloria*, formed the rich beginning of the main Lutheran *Gottesdienst*. But, attracted by the expressive potentialities of the full Catholic text, Bach enlarged the shorter species of the Lutheran ritual to the grandeur we know today, adding the four sections, *Credo, Sanctus, Benedictus,* and *Agnus Dei,* thus bringing the whole into formal parallelism with the Roman rite. But the spirit of the work is thoroughly Lutheran, and its form makes it impossible to use it in the Catholic service.

The additions which Bach made were taken largely from cantatas he had already composed.[1] The choral writing is commonly in five parts: for two sopranos, alto, tenor, and bass, although in the *Sanctus* and

[1] The historical origins of the various sections of the *B Minor Mass* are interesting:
The *Kyrie* and the *Gloria in excelsis* (the portions which the Lutheran and Catholic liturgies had in common) were written in 1733 and sent to Friedrich August, Duke of Saxony, together with a letter of appeal for patronage, begging "that they be received not on their merits as compositions but with your Majesty's notorious generosity." He offered these two sections of the Mass as "trifling proofs of the science I have been able to acquire in music." There is no record that Augustus ever paid them any attention whatever.
The two four-part choruses, *Gratias agimus* and *Dona pacem* are to be found, with differences, in the Rathswahl cantata of 1731.
The *Qui tollis* chorus was founded on the opening chorus of a much earlier cantata, *Schauet doch.*
The *Crucifixus* was taken direct from the cantata *Weinen, Klagen* (1724).
The *Hosanna* was adapted from a welcome song to the King of Saxony (1734).
The *Agnus Dei* used materials found in an Ascensiontide cantata, *Lobet Gott in seinen Reichen.*

The structure of this great work was erected during the mature years of Bach's life; in round figures it contains some 2300 bars, about a third of which, 638, to be exact, is borrowed material. The work was not written for any special occasion, which does not mean that it is in any sense a "patchy" work. Where Bach incorporated what he had previously said elsewhere it could have been only for the reason that he felt it adequate to the purpose of this particular composition as a whole, and that nothing new need be composed.

FIRST PAGE OF THE "CRUCIFIXUS"

in the *Hosanna* six and eight parts respectively are employed. The orchestra contains three of the specially high Bach trumpets that are no longer present in our orchestras, besides two each of flutes, oboes, and bassoons, with strings, kettledrums, and an important part for the organ, this latter indicated in the score by a figured bass. Another instrument of which Bach was fond, the *oboe d'amore*, darkly sweet, is used at times; and the hunting horn, in the tenth number, accompanying the bass soloist and joyously acclaiming the sovereignty of the Most High, is an indication of the human sensibility that is always pulsing through this work, making us remember again the use of realism of which Bach was so fond, and suggestive of the Lutheran pietism, with its overemphasis on religious sentimentalism.

The music is in twenty-four movements, comprising fifteen choruses, six solo airs (one each for soprano and tenor, two each for alto and bass), and three duets (two for soprano and alto, one for soprano and tenor). It is to be noted that Bach did not use here the operatic form of aria, that is, the regular three-part *da capo* form, since he must have realized that any mechanical repetition of a thought in a work of this kind could only weaken its significance. It is interesting to realize that, of all Bach's works, this is one which he never heard in its entirety, although he performed its first two sections with his choirs in Leipzig.

This Mass as a whole is Bach at his greatest and fullest. We hear all sides of his manifold genius, and each listener will have his favorite movement; to realize fully the master's greatness, it should be heard again and again, until it is really known by heart. This may sound like something of a heavy task, but for the right listeners it can but be a revelation of the imaginative manipulation of ideas inspired by a faith that was as natural and unquestioned as the facts of the composer's everyday existence. The student will realize in this work better than in almost any other in the history of music the truth that technique is, after all, the vital food of any composer's spirit.

This great composition was, in the fullest sense of the word, the great culmination of Bach's creative career. It achieved for his art what Beethoven intended the *Ninth Symphony* should do for his, and what Wagner planned, and did not quite carry out, in the *Niebelungen Ring*.

" ST. MATTHEW PASSION "

Next to the Mass in the depth of its feeling and the surety of its expression comes the *St. Matthew Passion*, a work that is so " intensely felt, so deeply impassioned, so poignantly dramatic, that it seems embroidered with tears and colored with flames and blood." Of the three settings of the Passion story which Bach is known to have made, this one according to the gospel of St. Matthew is by far the richest. It is a magnificently realized and very dramatic exposition of the story of Christ's suffering and death. In it the balance of emotion is beautifully attained. We find, as was also true of the Mass, that a tense situation is relieved, or a dark one lightened, by the placing of particular items in conjunction. If one of these is omitted, as is so often done in modern performances, it can be readily seen that the balance of sensitivity may be entirely spoiled. Conductors who have carefully studied Bach's directions tell us that his knowledge of effects — as regards, for instance, the placing of choirs, orchestra, and soloists — was remarkable, and that the moving power of his works as wholes is enhanced or weakened by close attention to his specific instructions. It seems to be the general opinion at the present that a small choir and orchestra, say, groups of forty singers and thirty players, gives a much more intimate and touching effect in the *St. Matthew Passion* than is possible with a very large body of musicians such as usually takes part in the Mass. The place of the multitude here is in the chorales, which were meant for all to join in as a corporate act of worship.

The general form of the Passion had been in use for over a century in the German church. Schütz was the first to apply the Italian operatic style of Monteverdi and his followers to the development of a semi-dramatic piece for use in church on Good Friday, using as text the moving words of the Passion story as contained in the various gospels. He did this so effectively and sincerely that Bach, a century later, followed closely in his footsteps; the later works use the same general apparatus — recitatives to carry on the dramatic development of the story, arias of both a dramatic and a reflective nature, choruses and chorales for the congregation — as did the earlier.

In listening to a modern production of this emotionally stirring work, one of the most affecting, indeed, in all music, the hearer will probably find it difficult to recover the point of view of the worshiper of 1729, listening to this composition under Bach's direction in St. Thomas's Church in Leipzig. Here again we find that peculiar type of religious imagery that was in vogue at the time, but which has long since passed out of style. The imagination of Bach's day did not hesitate to indulge in ecstasies that seem to us as oversentimental and having no place in religious worship. Yet, we must again insist, so great was Bach's power and so sincere his expression that these textual embarrassments furnish the basis for some of his finest music, music that lies essentially in a world quite apart from theological beliefs and which speaks to us today, more than two hundred years after it was written, with unaltered eloquence and changeless power.

USE OF LEITMOTIV

It was Bach's habit to use in all these choral works — the cantatas and the Mass, as well as the Passions — certain realistic motives to symbolize various ideas and images and emotions. Schweitzer and Pirro, who have gone into this matter more thoroughly than have any other writers, have pointed out wave motives, step motives, and motives suggestive of grief, despair, terror, felicity, and all the rest of the human emotions. The accompaniment to the ineffably beautiful *Crucifixus* in the Mass is built up over a stark, chromatic grief motive, which the composer uses again and again in similar places. In the aria in the *St. Matthew Passion* reflecting on the bitter picture of Jesus carrying the cross, Bach uses a stumbling, sinking motive to suggest the scene. In that part of the narrative where the Evangelist tells of Peter's suddenly remembering the words of Jesus: "Before the cock crow thou shalt deny me thrice," Bach uses a motive which actually imitates the cock's crowing. But it is exceedingly doubtful whether the sensitive listener of today, unless he is forewarned, would be conscious of all this elaborate naïve literalism. What matters to him is that this music is full of a great emotion which transcends time and place and communicates itself to him as forcefully as it did to the listener who sat under Bach himself. It is the marvelous tone poet and master of emotional expression that impresses us; we have forgotten the eighteenth-century cantor of a Leipzig church, writing music that was wont to indulge in the simple literalism and sentimental pieties of his period.

THE CANTATAS

Any adequate study of the cantatas would take a lifetime. Carl Philipp Emanuel, Bach's second son, said that his father had written nearly three hundred such works; of these, about two hundred have survived. Most of them were written for use in the Sunday services of the churches where Bach was in charge of the music. Each cantata, written on a theme appropriate to the day in the church calendar, occupied an important place in the *Hauptgottesdienst* or morning service. Others were written for special occasions, and a few appeared with secular words. In form they range all the way from a series of arias for solo voice, such as *Meine Seele rühmt und preist* (No. 189) to the impressive and severe eight-movement *Christ lag in Todesbanden* (No. 4), in which every movement — introductory symphony, choruses, duets, and solos — is a variation or fantasia on the chorale tune of that name. Sanford Terry, one of the best writers on Bach, had this to say of the cantatas:

"Their music reveals the deeps of his character, the high purpose to which he dedicated his genius . . . it is a faithful mirror in which the mind of its composer is revealed. The cantatas disclose the fact that his astonishing fecundity was controlled by searching and frequent pondering of the texts he set. They reveal the keenness and clarity with which he visualized Bible scenes and characters. How consistent and devotional, for instance, is his portrayal of the Saviour's gracious dignity! After hearing the several Michaelmas cantatas, who can doubt that Bach pictured Satan, not as Isaiah's Lucifer, the Day Star, the Son of the Morning, but as the malignant and cumberous Serpent of Genesis, the Great Dragon of Revelation? For always Bach depicts his rolling gait in writhing themes, which outline his motion as clearly as an etcher's pen. With what tender touches he points the scene of the Nativity! And with what poignant emotion he follows the Saviour's footsteps to Calvary!

"With truth, therefore, Schweitzer observes that the cantatas are the most reliable indicators of Bach's genius and character. For their range is so wide, they reflect him from so many angles, and express him in so many moods, that they reveal his personality no less than his art . . . Bach was one of the tenderest and most emotional of men, with the eye of a painter and the soul of a poet. But the fact is fully revealed only to those who are at the pains to translate him."

Because these works are so far removed from contemporary thought, and because, in addition, they are difficult for modern choralists to manage, we have few opportunities of hearing them today. They are still sung as part of the Bach tradition in certain of the Leipzig churches, and appear occasionally on programs of choral societies, completely out of character in this latter environment. But of all the Bach works they are least accessible for the layman.

VOICES TREATED AS INSTRUMENTS

A word may well be added here concerning Bach's treatment of the voice. Perhaps it was due to the fact that he never came into direct touch with the birthplace of the opera — Italy — or it may have been the result of his absolutely independent, forthright nature; but we never find him making any concessions to the limitations of the human voice, or writing a singer's part with the idea of giving him a grateful opportunity for technical display *à la mode italienne*. He writes a solo part for a soprano or a bass in exactly the same fashion that he would one for a violin or a cello, often using the same figures and paying scant attention to the necessity for breathing spaces, awkwardness of intervals for singing, and so on. In consequence, especially for a generation whose greatest interpretative achievements in music lie in fields other than choralism, many of Bach's arias and duets, as well as the individual parts in the choruses, seem almost impossible of adequate presentation. What Bach was interested in, of course, was the direct and pointed expression of his ideas. Whether the part which he wrote was particularly grateful for the instrument to which it was to be given or offered opportunity for virtuosity concerned him not at all. He sometimes wrote phrases which are physically difficult to sing. In consequence, we have a great deal of bad Bach playing and singing, especially the latter; and it would have been better for his reputation had Bach taken a hint or two from his contemporary, Handel, whose choral writing, although it has less expressive greatness and moving subtlety than Bach's, always lies well for the voice, and consequently makes an excellent effect.

ORGAN WORKS

The instrumental works that come closest to the great choral works in intensity of expression and poignancy of emotional speech are the organ compositions. These are touched with much the same imaginative spirit, the same dramatic intensity, and the same magnificence of style that we find in the *B Minor Mass* or in the *St. Matthew Passion*. In many of the *Chorale Preludes* — organ meditations on hymn tunes — we find just as truly as in any of the choral works Bach's spirit of yearning, of musing on man's frailty and on God's sustaining might. In their imposing magnificence, their wealth of meticulously executed detail, their magnificent rhythms and flashes of brilliant color, some of the great organ works, such as the *Fantasia and Fugue in G Minor*, are as imposing, and as truly magnificent, as anything in music.

Ernest Newman has said that for him the *Chorale Preludes* are the heart of Bach; and it is certain that they hold within them a complete world of his expressiveness. For they offered to him that sort of external stimulus which his imagination seemed to need for its richest and most fruitful release. Give him a pictorial image, or suggest a mood or present a dramatic idea, and his mind starts working immediately and gives us something that is deeply felt and beautifully expressed. The words and tunes associated with the church which he had served since his early boyhood, tunes that he had known ever since he could remember anything at all, seemed especially stimulating to him. He would take one of them, muse upon some phase of its words, and suggest its spirit in the instrumental composition that we call by the name of *chorale prelude*. Most of these are program music, pure and simple, small symphonic poems for the organ.

Take for example the prelude on the tune *Das alte Jahr vergangen ist*, one of the most terse of these works. The poetic program of this is given, not by the words associated with the hymn tune, words that express thankfulness for "help in troubles past," but in the concomitant idea suggested by the title: "The old year has passed away." He needed but these words to set him "brooding upon the pathos of things that are past, upon the sadness of all terminations, of that which is gone and irrecoverable. He remembers what an ended year must mean to all of us who know the common lot of change and frustration and regret; and sadness falls upon his spirit and overflows into music that exhales 'the very soul of sorrow,' as Ernest Newman says of it — music of a beauty and poignancy that is another world from the externality of such music as the Brandenburg Concertos" (Lawrence Gilman in *The New York Herald Tribune*).

If we look at the score we notice that the little chromatic rising motive which is heard at the beginning in the part for the left hand occurs in some part or other in almost every measure. It is this chromatic harmony — very poignantly modern, it is — that suggests the feeling of sad regret, of irreparable loss. The whole thing is a tiny dozen-measure tone poem of purest gold. Other chorale preludes suggest different types of treatment. Sometimes the tune is used as a theme against which accompanimental variants are introduced; sometimes a phrase of it becomes a subject for a fugue; sometimes it is used almost literally, line for line and harmony for harmony, as it occurred in Bach's hymnal. But almost always the music which results, while an expression of the general thought with which the chorale was concerned, is of such universal interest and expresses a beauty so far beyond the theology of Bach's day, that it will survive the "decay of creeds and even the death of faith."

There are many instances in these chorale preludes, as also in the choral works, of Bach's daring use of musical means that were far ahead of the practices of his time. For not only was he a writer whose expressiveness, grandeur of utterance, and perfection of form have never been equaled, but he was likewise one of the most daring and adventurous radicals of all musical history. The boldness of many of his progressions and chordal formations strikes home with telling power even today, when our ears have become accustomed to the harmonies of Wagner and Debussy, not to speak of the dissonances of Schönberg and his followers. There was nothing tentative or hesitant in his style; he was as sure of how to express himself as of what it was he wanted to express, and beside him some of the later composers — even the best ones — seem timid and halting. There is good reason for the veneration in which he has been held by great musicians: Beethoven, Brahms, Mendelssohn, Wagner, Franck — all studied his works carefully and thought of him as the father of all music.

THE BAROQUE BACH

In addition to the one hundred forty-three chorale preludes he left us, Bach wrote a considerable number of other works for his favorite instrument, among them a number of preludes and fugues. In these he went through a typically Baroque period, of which the showy *Toccata and Fugue in D Minor* is very characteristic. Some of the other great organ works, such as the *Fantasia and Fugue in G Minor*, are a bit freer as to style and more meaty in content. The latter, written when Bach was making a trip to Hamburg in 1720, seems to have been composed to show the organists in that city how well he could handle this style, which had always been popular in North Germany. In their part weaving, in their magnificent opulence of tone, in their bold harmonies and clever manipulation of key changes, and in their freshness of invention and freedom from pedantry, the best of these organ works stand alone. They show their composer at the top of his form, the tonal genius, rejoicing in his strength and power, and wearing his learning lightly — buoyant, confident, well-knit music. All together there are forty of these organ fugues, most of them with some sort of introductory movement, a prelude, a toccata, or a fantasia. In addition, there is a magnificent passacaglia (written on a constantly repeated theme) and fugue; some trio-sonatas, much more difficult to play well than they seem and written for the instruction of his sons in organ playing; and some miscellaneous pieces, including four transcriptions of "Vivaldi" orchestral concertos.

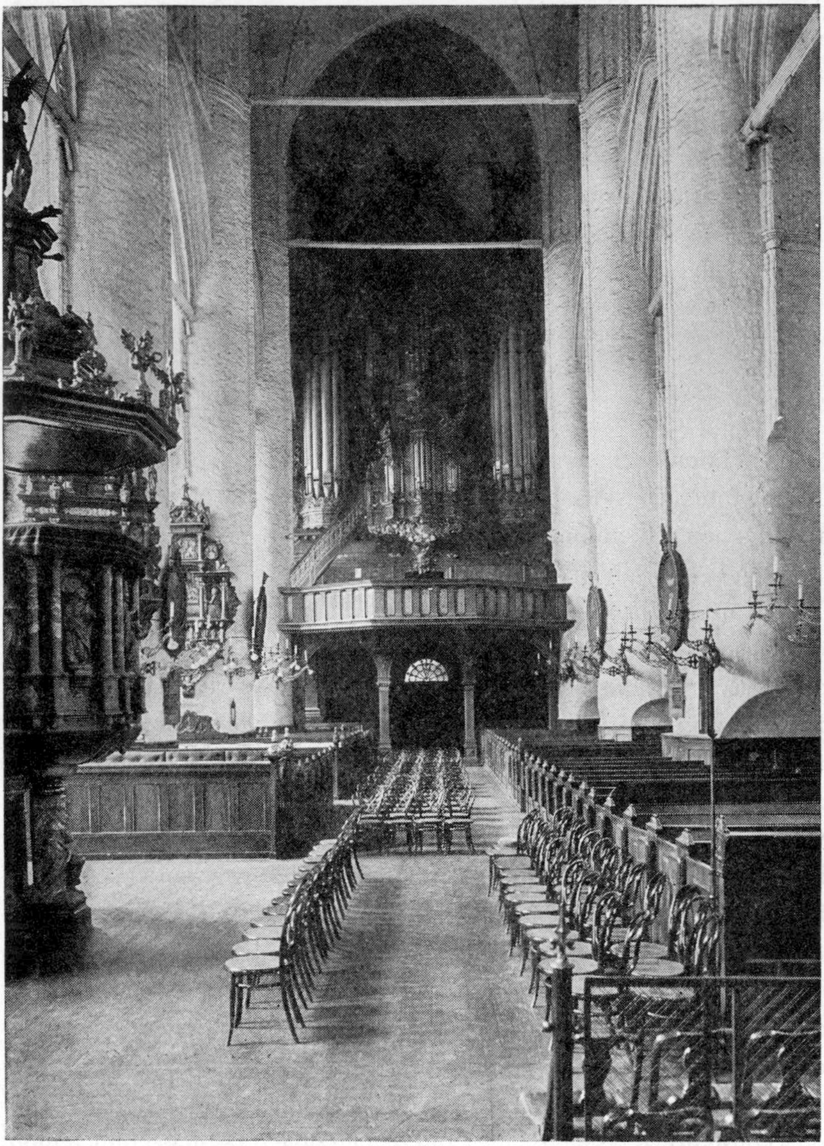

THE INTERIOR OF THE KATHARINENKIRCHE, HAMBURG
It is probable that Bach first played the *G Minor Fantasie and Fugue* here in 1720.

ORCHESTRA OR ORGAN?

There is a great deal of discussion just now as to how these organ works may best be interpreted, whether they should be played on the instrument for which they were written or should be transferred to the orchestra. It must be remembered in this connection that our organs today have tonal qualities that are quite different from the instruments of Bach's time. Although mechanically they are greatly improved, our modern organs are not well adapted to the conveyance of many-voiced music of the type of Bach's. The orchestra is the ideal instrument for this polyphonic style. Each player can readily carry on his share of the weaving, carefully blending with all the other parts and, under the direction of the conductor, molding and shaping the whole so as to give proper balance and timbre.

Harvey Grace, a well-known English critic, has expressed this well:

"Even the most enthusiastic organist must feel at times that, fine as his instrument is, it cannot do full justice to such gigantic conceptions as the 'Wedge' Prelude and Fugue, the 'great' G minor, the B minor. . . . An organ of the right ample resources is rare, save in buildings so large and resonant that, if the music is played with the power and pace it so demands, the details are lost. On the other hand, if we decide that the beauty of the polyphony must be shown, we can do so only by the adoption of a steady tempo and a quiet registration, in which case the impetus of the music is destroyed and its fire damped down. No medium but the orchestra can show to the fullest advantage all the great qualities of these works — their texture, growth, and climax. . . . Bach's organ music is immeasurably greater than its medium."

THE INTEGRITY OF TRANSCRIPTIONS

It would seem, then, that much of the music which Bach wrote for the organ achieves its true stature when heard on the orchestra; and with this in mind a number of transcriptions of this music have been made. Some of these transcriptions, when carefully done, and when they adhere to the mood and style of the original, are marvelously effective. But, and it is a big *but*, it has become the habit of certain transcribers to attempt to heighten their effects, to increase their sonorities, and to intensify their coloring to a point where the result is overpowerfully garish — modern in a way that calls attention to the virtuosity of the transcription and the playing of it, instead of centering the attention on the content of the music. This is not good Bach, exciting and novel as the music may seem at first hearing. Schweitzer has probably thought more about the music of Bach than any other man alive today, and he says that, in listening to it, it is necessary that we attain a composure and an inwardness that will bring to life something of the deep spiritual qualities which lie hidden there. Superficially brilliant, gorgeously colored, modernized orchestrations, played at a pace that makes adequate comprehension of the various lines of sound of which this music is composed absolutely impossible, will not help us attain this state of grace.

On the other hand, there should be no place in modern life for the dull, mechanical interpretations of Bach that are so often perpetrated by organists, with no attempt to achieve the necessary independence of part playing and no plasticity of phrasing to bring out the life inherent in this music.[2] An additional reason why these organ renditions of Bach's so often seem difficult to listen to is that the players usually choose some of his least interesting works. We have already intimated that this composer, great as he is, had his pedestrian moments — times when in the course of his busy life and the need for the performance of an incredible amount of routine labors, his powers of imagination and inspiration flagged and those of his invention flourished. It is these moments that organists so often blazon forth on their programs, forgetting that there is second-rate and third-rate, as well as first-rate, Bach. A great deal of this

[2] Surely there must be some happy medium between the two extremes so often heard in the interpretations of Bach — between those which, as one writer has expressed it, dress out the old cantor in a costume suitable for the Beaux Arts Ball, with all the opulence of color and slickness of playing of which the modern orchestra is capable, and the over-ascetic and dry monotony heard in other renditions. These two extremes may be heard in the records of Stokowski and Schweitzer. Neither is wholly satisfactory to an understanding listener; but as a steady diet, the latter will prove more nourishing.

inferior music, turned out with the easy facility of the journalist, rather than with the inspired imagination of the poet, with its complacently jogging rhythms and easy contrapuntal embroideries of obvious harmonic progressions, is, unfortunately, what many people know and hear as characteristic Bach. The sensitive listener turns impatiently away from this journalistic small talk of a great mind, this workmanlike but uninspired prose, this by-product of an intellect, and demands the essential and incomparable truths which he knows this composer capable of expressing. He will not willingly endure these dull performances of what Newman has called the "jigging, jogging Bach," but will endeavor to find music of this composer that appeals to his imagination, kindling into life the experiences and visions that brought it into being in the mind of Bach. For he well knows that in the use of a language of sound that possesses the "mysterious faculty of rendering thoughts with a clearness and definiteness surpassing its own natural power of expression, Bach is the greatest among the great."

THE SECULAR WORKS OF BACH

It must be by this time almost four years since your high-wellbornness favored me with a gracious reply to a letter addressed to you; and if I remember that you kindly condescended to ask for some news of my fate, this shall now most obediently be done.

My vicissitudes from youth onward are well known to you, up to the change which drew me to Cöthen as Director of Music. There I had a gracious prince who loved music as well as he knew it, at whose court I thought to close my earthly career. But it was so ordained that the said Serenissimus espoused a Bernburgish princess, whereupon it began to appear as though the musical inclinations of the said prince were to grow somewhat lukewarm, the rather because the new princess seemed to be something of an amusa.

Thus God willed that my vocation should be that of musical director and cantor at the St. Thomas School here, although I could not at first accommodate myself to the thought of being turned from a Kapellmeister into a cantor.

— From a letter of Bach's, October 28, 1730

EXPRESSIONAL RELATIONSHIP AND ORGANIZED SOUND

ONE careful student of Bach's music has made the statement that at least two thirds of the enormous quantity of music contained in the Complete Edition of the *Bach-Gesellschaft* (which represents his whole life's work) is music of an obviously expressional character, its meaning directly related to some imaginative concept through a verbal text or a poetic program of some sort. The other third may be said to be music of the absolute type, making its appeal largely through its qualities as organized sound rather than depending on expressional relationships. This is an exact reversal of the opinions that have been generally held — for Bach is almost always considered pre-eminently a composer of patterned, formal music — but it is an opinion on which such Bach experts as Schweitzer and Terry agree. As we have seen, most of this program music of Bach's — using the expression in its widest sense — was written for the church; the remaining third of his output is mostly secular in character and consists of instrumental works of various sorts: for clavier, violin, flute, cello, and orchestra. Cast in the general mold of its period, much of this music moves along with all the external qualities of some of his greater works but with little of their internal content. With the treasures of the *Well-tempered Clavichord* before us, as well as some isolated movements from the orchestral and chamber works — things which represent the very best of our composer — we can hardly say that these secular compositions as a whole are inferior to the sacred ones; but they certainly contain the least treasurable side of his genius, a great deal more of the sub-Bach than of the super-Bach.

A mere outline of these works is sufficient to indicate their general nature. There are a number of orchestral works, including the *Brandenburg Concertos;* four suites and fifteen concertos for various instruments with the accompaniment of a string orchestra and a clavier; an imposing list of things for unaccompanied instruments — six sonatas for violin alone and six for cello alone, works which require superb handling on the part of modern players, who have to cope with a different type of bow than was in use in Bach's day, if they would make them interesting. There are also compositions for instruments with clavier accompaniment, including sonatas for violin and clavier and flute and clavier; and a whole horde of works for clavier alone, including the two books of the *Well-tempered Clavichord* (forty-eight preludes and fugues in the various major and minor keys), and a number of fantasias, fugues, and suites.

BACH'S USE OF CONCERTO FORM

Of the so-called orchestral works, the six Brandenburg Concertos, written for the duke of that name, are most familiar; they are, however, not orchestral works in the modern sense but were written for a *Hofkapelle* of the type found in most of the princely establishments in the Germany of that time, a group of string players of average ability, with a few wood-wind and brass instruments added. When played by a large modern band, as is so often done, these concertos lose their true character; for the individuality and play of the various parts are completely lost in the huge swirl of orchestral tone.

These concertos derive their very form from the nature of the body for which they were written: a few gifted soloists interplaying with the remainder of the orchestra, which probably never comprised more than twenty or twenty-five men. So they sound best when played by a small body of musicians, and are really chamber-music works rather than orchestral ones. Bach's use of this form was the same as that of his contemporaries, who tried to see what could be freshly done in the way of manipulating the old principle of contrast. In these eighteenth-century concertos, besides a variety of subjects, there was brought in a variety of people to handle them. Each of the Brandenburg Concertos is scored for different instrumental combinations, the soloists being pitted against the orchestra. Contrast, argument, even conflict, these exciting new possibilities opened up. This principle had been seen at its simplest as soon as music changed from unaccompanied into accompanied singing. There was at once some other element, the instrument, that had to be reckoned with, in addition to the voice; but the latter became master, an influence which has lingered on in some of the later show concertos, where the violinist or pianist is so obviously the master of the situation.

The root of the formal conception of these compositions was the idea of the interplay of individual soloists and the orchestral body as a whole, an essentially dramatic idea, exemplified in every good stage play. Uniting or dividing, the various actors show tensions and reliefs; and they are always unequally matched in dramatic power. We know the influence of a single personality. In our day stunts and commercial publicity have twisted proportions and vulgarized values; but behind all our interest in people lies the interest in the working out of their individual personalities — the demonstration of what they are, told in what they do and what happens to them. All life is a campaign, with its ups and downs: so, too, is a concerto. This interplay of personalities is suggested musically by the manner in which the various themes are intertwined in these early concertos. The later types, with which most music lovers of today are more familiar, extensively deploy the solo part, against the much more subtle power wielded by the nineteenth-century orchestra. These later works show the full possibility of these various types of interplay in the way they use themes, in the alternation of soloist and band, and in the playing off of the various bodies in the orchestra itself. But Bach's use of the *concerto grosso*, as these early works were called, is quite typical, although we find more varied combinations in his orchestra than in other compositions of the time.

THE "OUVERTURES"

There is some confusion regarding the four works which he called *Ouvertures*. We generally give them the name of *suite*, for they comprise a set of movements of varying character, based on dance rhythms of contrasting styles. They were written for different instrumental combinations: one for wood winds and strings, one for flute and strings, and two for oboes, bassoons, trumpets, drums, and strings — the latter rather a strange orchestral *mélange*, according to modern tastes. The *B Minor Suite*, for flute and strings, is the favorite, and quite rightly so, for it has delectable parts for the soloist; it contains six movements in addition to the overture, which is itself of considerable length, written in the form which

Lully invented for his series of operas that culminated about the time Bach was born. We find that Handel, too, adopted this form of the overture, consisting of a slow prelude followed by a quick movement in fugal style, and oftentimes, as if in apology for being a bit serious and heavy, rounded off by a dance.

A SOLITARY PICTORIAL PIECE

An amusing, if not particularly important, early clavier work of Bach's is his *Capriccio on the Departure of a Beloved Brother,* written in 1704, when the nineteen-year-old boy was organist at Arnstadt and his elder brother, Johann Jakob, an oboeist, decided to forsake the quiet ways of Thuringia in order to become a military bandsman in the service of Charles XII of Sweden. This involved not only a journey, and in those days journeys were exciting enterprises, but possible dangers as a soldier; for the young king, then only twenty-two, had been a man of war ever since he was crowned at the age of fifteen, and by 1700 had defeated the Danes and was at once hurling his troops at Russia and later at Poland. So even a musician in such service was likely to smell powder; there was sufficient reason for his relatives' anxiety, and Bach put into a piece of program music an expression of their fears and their good wishes for the adventurer. Only a year or two before, Kuhnau had brought out his famous *Bible Sonatas,* landmarks in the history of pictorial suggestion in music. Bach thought that he would try his hand at the style; and the six sections of this little work show how well the young composer was able to mingle poetic suggestion and technical skill. Although he never essayed purely instrumental program music again, he seldom lost this idea of poetic suggestiveness.

In studying Bach's larger keyboard works, we must keep in mind the fact that he was much more concerned with the musical design of them than he was with the instruments on which they were to be played. In listening to some of Bach's keyboard music (apart from that for the organ), we have to remember that he thought little of whether it was to be played on the delicate, sweet clavichord, whose strings were struck by a metal " finger," or on the more powerful, potentially majestic harpsichord, with its plucked strings, two manuals (sets of keys), and various stops for giving different timbres and octave effects. It might be a valuable exercise, if one were fortunate enough to be able to hear both a clavichord and a harpsichord, to go through the set of the *Well-tempered Clavichord* preludes and fugues and decide for which each is best suited.

THE SOLUTION OF A PROBLEM

Bach had always interested himself in musical science. Composers in his day were severely hampered by the system of tuning then in general use, which, in order to avoid technicalities, placed certain keys in accurate tuning at the expense of others, which became badly out of tune and so were unhappy keys for a composer to use. It was not merely a matter of writing only in one key — the annoyance developed when the composers wished to modulate to others. Bach, ever a man of bold action and determination, advocated the system of " equal temperament," then becoming known, whereby all the twelve semitones of the octave were so adjusted that none was offensively out of tune. This made all keys available; the composer's keyboard, or clavier, was now " well-tempered " or tuned; hence the name of the set of pieces which Bach wrote to celebrate, as it were, an epoch-making decision. *Das wohltemperirtes Clavier* to Bach may have seemed simply a commonsense piece of business; for us it is the work that opened up all the wealth of later music, with its absolute freedom of key change, of which, as time went on, later composers learned how to take the most delightful advantage.

So Bach brought out, in 1722 (he was then thirty-seven), his first set of twenty-four pieces in all the major and minor keys; another set appeared later, in 1744. The two together make up what pianists know briefly as *The Forty-eight*, a work that has been well called the pianist's Old Testament, the New being the Beethoven piano sonatas. Bach wrote a prelude and a fugue for every key. Some of this first set were pieces that Bach had already composed for other purposes; some were newly written. They were done for his pleasure — sometimes to satisfy his wish to work out a piece of technique, sometimes to express a mood in a brief time.[3] The preludes, as befits their modest name, though they often contain a remarkable amount of material and science, usually work out an idea, embodied in a phrase or some musical bit of shaping that can scarcely be called a tune or a theme. There are all sorts of thoughts and moods in them; some of them are connected with their fugues only in the slightest way, as by contrast of mood.

FUGUES IN GENERAL

In studying the fugues of this remarkable collection, the listener should have a fair idea of the principles of this form, particularly of its being a structure built from a (usually) small theme, which structure grows and climaxes. Bach used a variety of fugal types. We are not to seek from him any " rules," but to gather principles, both of working out technical problems and of embodying poetic expression in fugal style. (Perhaps it may be added here, by way of definition, that the fugue *subject* is heard in turn in the several " voices " or parts — which in *The Forty-eight* means 2, 3, 4, or 5; its *countersubject* is its continuation, heard while the *subject* is being given by another voice, in the dominant, as the *answer*. Episodes carry on the action while the subject is resting from its entries, and a *stretto* occurs when an answer enters before the subject has fully ended. The whole form is treated at some length in the authors' *Discovering Music*, Chapter XXVI, where one of these fugues is outlined.) A novice, believing that the fixed rules of fugue construction should certainly be followed in such a work as the *Well-tempered Clavichord*, might well ask, on finding that some of them do not follow text-book principles, " Is not Bach wrong here? " This master of fugal construction did set forth the principles of their form in a complete and

[3] In this connection it is well to notice the inscription attached to the autographed copy of *Das wohltemperirtes Clavier* now in possession of the Berlin Library: " The well-tempered Clavier; or, Preludes and Fugues on every Tone and Semitone, with the major third Ut, Re, Mi, and minor third, Re, Mi, Fa. For the Use and Profit of Young Musicians anxious to learn, and as a Pastime for others already expert in the Art. Composed and set forth by Johann Sebastian Bach, at present Capellmeister and Director of Chamber-music at the princely Court of Anhalt-Cöthen."

scholastic way in his *Die Kunst der Fuge;* but in *The Forty-eight* we can expect as many kinds of fugal shaping as, Kipling said, there are ways of constructing tribal lays. Difference in treatment shows Bach's zest for attacking problems; and though the results are by no manner of means equal, we can find something fresh in each prelude and fugue.

FRENCH SUITES

About 1720--1722 Bach wrote some keyboard pieces, for use on either harpsichord or clavichord, for his wife, Anna Magdalena, to play, and so cultivate her skill. As might be expected, these are quite light and graceful in style and not especially severe as to content. We know them as the *French Suites,* so called because of their delicate Latin spirit, which Bach at one period took considerable pains to cultivate and which was a lightening influence on the development of his style. The title may have been given to this music by Bach's household and his friends, but it was an unofficial one. Each suite contains half a dozen or more pieces in the fashion of court dances — the foundation dances used for this type of composition in Bach's time being the flowing *allemande,* the running *courante,* the dignified, sometimes quite somber *saraband,* and the final lilting *gigue.* The fifth of these *French Suites,* for example, contains an *allemande,* a *courante,* a *saraband,* a *gavotte,* a *bourrée,* a *loure* (a dance once accompanied by bagpipes), and a *gigue.*

Any detailed enumeration of more of these instrumental works would be impossible in a book such as this.[4] The first biographer of Bach, Johann Nikolaus Forkel, writing fifty years after the composer's death, has said that one needs to be steeped in this music to appreciate the genius of its author. For, he adds, the greater the work, the closer the study demanded

[4] Mention should especially be made of the great clavier works of the Leipzig period, the so-called *Goldberg Variations,* a long and difficult set written for a count who required some sort of musical performance to relieve his sleepless hours; the six partitas (a sort of general name for *suite*); the *Italian Concerto* and the *Partita in B Minor;* the *Musikalisches Opfer* (part of which is for flute, violin, and clavier), written in an attempt to recall to the memory of Frederick the Great Bach's skill in improvisation; *The Art of Fugue,* a series of fugues and canons on a single theme, written in 1749 and published after his death by his son Carl Philip Emanuel.

for its apprehension; " the butterfly method, a sip here and there, is of little use." Unfortunately, the limitations of ordinary existence make anything but such a butterfly method almost impossible for all of us unless we happen to be musical scholars. But if our " sip here and there " has included the works mentioned in this chapter, we can be sure that we have had at least an adequate introduction to this " greatest orator poet that ever addressed the world in the language of music."

HANDEL THE MAGNIFICENT

I am emboldened, Sir, by the generous Concern You please to take in relation to my affairs, to give you an account of the Success I have met here. The Nobility did me the Honour to make amongst themselves a Subscription for 6 Nights, which did fill a Room of 600 Persons. so that I needed not sell one single Ticket at the Door and without Vanity the Performance was received with a general Approbation. Sigra. Avolio, which I brought with me from London pleases extraordinary. I have formed an other Tenor Voice which gives great satisfaction . . . and the Chorus Singers (by my Direction) do exceeding well, as for the Instruments they are really excellent. Mr. Dubourgh being at the Head of them, and the Musick sounds delightfully in this charming Room, which puts me in such spirits (and my Health being so good) that I exert my self on my Organ with more than usual success.

I opened with the Allegro, Penseroso, & Moderato, and I assure you that the Words of the Moderato are vastly admired. The Audience being composed (besides the Flower of Ladyes of Distinction and other People of the greatest quality) of so many Bishops, Deans, Heads of the Colledge, the most eminent People in the Law as the Chancellor, Auditor General, &ct. all which are very much taken with the Poetry. I cannot sufficiently express the kind treatment I receive here, but the Politeness of this generous Nation can not be unknown to You, so I left you judge of the satisfaction I enjoy, passing my time with Honour, profit and Pleasure.

—From a letter of Handel's to Charles Jennens, writer of the libretto of *The Messiah*, dated Dublin, December 29, 1741

HANDEL (from a portrait in the National Portrait Gallery, London)

AN EIGHTEENTH-CENTURY PREMIÈRE

FEBRUARY 19, 1736, was a great night for the city of London; for it marked the first performance there of a new oratorio by Mr. Handel, the German musician who had come to England in 1710 and had had the town pretty much by the ears ever since. The theater in the Haymarket, where the performance was to be given, was crowded to the doors. It seemed as if the entire *haut monde* was present, the ladies in their colossal crinolines of such enormous proportions that they had to coax them sideways through the entrance doors, the men in their brave silk coats, knee breeches, rich jabots, and lace cuffs, with glittering gold braid and silver embroideries and gala sword hanging at their side. Rumor had it that there was over four hundred fifty pounds in the house — no inconsiderable sum for those days — and that the composer, who was known to have been broken in health and distressed in mind through the failure of his Italian opera ventures and the calumnies of his many and powerful enemies, was determined to stage a comeback. His new oratorio, set to the words of the late Mr. Dryden, one-time poet laureate, was said to be a work of great genius, written at white heat, in the short space of some twenty days. And composer-producer-director Handel, who had been famous in the past for bringing great Italian opera stars to London to sing his principal parts, had found, it was said, a native young tenor of unusual ability for this occasion. And so society, which in its usual fickleness had first brilliantly supported Handel's London enterprises and then devastatingly forsaken them, was again curious and thronged his theater for the first-night performance of this new work, *Alexander's Feast.*

In some respects it was the greatest triumph of Handel's checkered career. Nothing more congenial to his typically Baroque imagination than Dryden's brilliant, coldly scintillating verse could have been found. It was Dryden, the literary dictator of England during the last quarter of the seventeenth century, who expressed himself on Handel's art as follows:

> "As from the power of sacred lays
> The spheres began to move,
> And sang the great Creator's praise
> To all the Blest above;
> So when the last and dreadful hour
> This crumbling pageant shall devour,
> The trumpet shall be heard on high,
> The dead shall live, the living die,
> And Music shall untune the sky!"

The rich grandeur of Handel's music, his usual majestic choruses, his dignified and effective recitative, the flowing, well-developed melodic lines of his solos, and the brilliance of the performance — everything combined to make the new oratorio a hit; and the large audience went into raptures, bestowing on the composer an applause "such as had seldom been heard in London," as a contemporary account put it.

HANDEL THE TYPICAL BAROQUE FIGURE

The whole incident was characteristic of the life of this musician. During the years when Bach was establishing himself as organist and composer to the little provincial court of Saxe-Weimar, Handel, already a noted figure, well-trained in the Italian operatic tradition, came to London to seek his fame and fortune. It is not often that destiny decrees the entrance on the stage of life at exactly the same moment of two men of such equal power and opposite temperament as Bach and Handel. The life of the first was provincial and circumscribed, bourgeois in its every aspect, merely the external setting for a spiritual existence of intense reality. In this respect Bach was a man of the Baroque — the world for him but a dream, his experience of it making him constantly yearn for an existence that was beyond the confines of consciousness. His way of escape was through a religion in which he firmly believed, instead of through the usual means of the time, a magic piling up of unrealities and a gorgeous succession of *divertissements*. Externally, at least, Handel was more a typical Baroque figure than Bach. Vital and forceful, his life was crowded with incident and intrigue, dramatic success following crushing failure. His very appearance was characteristic — a gigantic and corpulent figure, with enormous hands and feet and a fat, bovine face enswathed in a huge wig. (The Baroque gentleman probably cultivated corpulence as a means for heightening his outward appearance of dignity and imposing grandeur.) Handel's clothing suggested his important position in life: his velvet greatcoat embroidered with brave color, his fine shirt with beruffled collar and cuffs, his walking stick with gold knob, all proclaimed him a man about town, very much concerned with practical affairs.

Before coming to London, Handel had had a thoroughly adequate preparatory career as an operatic writer. He was connected for three years with the opera in Hamburg, a more or less rough and ready establishment producing German as well as Italian pieces. From there he went to Italy, where he visited Florence, Venice, Rome, and Naples. He produced a number of operas in the prevailing mode, some of them creating a furore even among the Italians, and came into contact with the most important musical figures of the time, Corelli, Lotti, and the Scarlattis. Returning to Germany, he was made *Kapellmeister* to the court of the Elector of Hanover. One of his first official acts after taking up his duties was to request a leave of absence so that he could go to England. Here it was that he was to spend the rest of his life, for he lived in London for over forty years.

HIS OPERAS

It was inevitable that his early experience and natural bent should lead him to the writing of operas in the Italian style, especially when the demand on the part of English society was strong for this type of music. Up to the time of Handel's arrival in London, after the brief epoch of Purcell's genius (a genius which was scarcely appreciated), music had been almost entirely in the hands of itinerant Italians. Opera, although the years have proved that it is not a plant of native growth or one of which English appetites are genuinely fond, became established in London in the middle of the seventeenth century and has flourished there intermittently ever since. One of its great periods of glory was the Handel epoch. An account from one of the first issues of that ingenious eighteenth-century predecessor of our modern gossip magazine, Addison's *Spectator*, describes something of the characteristic extravagance with which these operas were produced. The work in question may well have been *Rinaldo*, Handel's first venture in this field, brought out in 1711:

"An Opera may be allowed to be extravagantly lavish in its Decorations, as its only Design is to gratifie the Senses, and keep up an indolent Attention in the Audience. Common Sense however requires, that there should be nothing in the Scenes and Machines which may appear Childish and Absurd. [*English practicality flying in the face of Baroque imaginative splendor!*] How would the Wits of King Charles's Time have laughed, to have seen Nicolini exposed to a Tempest in Robes of Ermin, and sailing in an open Boat upon a Sea of Paste-Board? What a Field of Raillery would they have been let into, had they been entertain'd with painted Dragons spitting wild-fire, enchanted Chariots drawn by Flanders Mares, and real Cascades in artificial Land-skips? A little Skill in Criticism would inform us, that Shadows and Realities ought not to be mix'd together in the same Piece; and that Scenes, which are designed as the Representations of Nature, should be filled with Resemblances, and not with the Things themselves. If one would represent a wide Champian Country filled with Herds and Flocks, it would be ridiculous to draw the Country only upon the Scenes, and to crowd several Parts of the Stage with Sheep and Oxen. This is joining together Inconsistencies, and making the Decoration partly Real and partly Imaginary. I would recommend what I have here said, to the Directors, as well as to the Admirers, of our Modern Opera.

"As I was walking in the Streets about a Fortnight ago, I saw an ordinary Fellow carrying a Cage full of little Birds upon his Shoulder; and, as I was wondering with my self what Use he would put them to, he was met very luckily by an Acquaintance, who had the same Curiosity. Upon his asking him what he had upon his Shoulder, he told him that he had been buying Sparrows for the Opera. Sparrows for the Opera, says his Friend, licking his lips, what, are they to be roasted? No, no, says the other, they are to enter towards the end of the first act, and to fly about the Stage.

"This strange Dialogue awakened my Curiosity so far, that I immediately bought the Opera, by which means I perceived that the Sparrows were to act the part of Singing Birds in a delightful Grove though upon a nearer Enquiry I found the sparrows put the same Trick upon the audience, that Sir *Martin Mar-all* practised upon his Mistress; for, though they flew in Sight, the Musick proceeded from a consort of Flagellets and Bird-calls which had been planted behind the Scenes. At the same time I made this Discovery, I found by the Discourse of the Actors, that there were great Designs on foot for the Improvement of the Opera; that it had been proposed to break down a part of the Wall, and to surprize the Audience with a Party of an hundred Horse, and that there was actually a Project of bringing the *New-River* into the House, to be employed in Jetteaus and Water-works. This Project, as I have since heard, is postponed 'till the Summer-season; when it is thought the Coolness that proceeds from Fountains and Cascades will be more acceptable and refreshing to People of Quality. In the mean time, to find out a more agreeable Entertainment for the Winter-Season, the Opera of *Rinaldo* is filled with Thunder and Lightning Illuminations and Fireworks; which the Audience may look upon without catching Cold, and indeed without much Danger of being burnt; for there are several Engines filled with Water, and ready to play at a Minute's warning, in case any such accident should happen. However, as I have a very great Friendship for the Owner of this Theatre, I hope that he has been wise enough to insure his House before he would let this Opera be acted in it."

Handel's success as an opera writer and producer earned for him and his partners what we would consider to be large sums of money, even in these days of musical entrepreneurs. But they also aroused envy, suspicion, and hatred on the part of his rivals. He had to fight for everything he gained and make his way through cliques of court hangers-on; but in spite of failing health and great loneliness of spirit, he never lost courage. He ranks as one of the heroes of artistic strife and the fight against misfortune, along with Sir Walter Scott, Poe, and many another.

Handel wrote forty-seven of these operas, in addition to innumerable *pasticci*, dramatic odes and the like; they all seem to us of today, as Bernard Shaw has expressed it, nothing but stage concerts designed for showing off the technical skill of singers. They have set, formal stories mostly drawn from classic sources, little variety of scene, and hardly any action. What dramatic qualities they possess reside entirely in the music, all of it formalized according to the taste of the period. There is a large number of arias, each of them with its corresponding lot of recitative to carry on the dramatic development. These standardized conventions, coupled with the fact that many of the soprano airs were written for performance by *castrati*, and the tiresome repetitiousness of their style, keep the Handelian operas off the modern stage.[5] A few airs from them have

[5] Postwar Germany saw a renewal of interest in the Handelian operas, and a number of them were restaged there, with various types of modern *décor*. But such interest seems to have been but transitory, for nothing has been heard of them in more recent years. It is difficult to believe that these works can ever again become part of the operatic repertoire because of the fact that they are based on a dramatic aesthetic that is entirely foreign to modern ideals.

survived the ravages of time. It would seem, for instance, as if nothing could ever kill the hardy universality of such a thing as *Ombra mai fu.* Written for an opera called *Serse* in 1738, to very undistinguished words, it has been given every sort of setting imaginable and arranged for every sort of instrumental combination possible, from massed military bands to harp ensembles.[6] "Hear me, ye winds and waves," from *Scipione* (1726), is only slightly less well known. But for modern ears the most attractive music in the operas is contained in the dances with which they were diversified. No better exhibition of Handel's peculiar qualities can be found than the suite of dances from *Alcina,* produced in 1731, and modern arrangers and composers have not hesitated to help themselves liberally to the riches to be found throughout Handel's scores and have drawn many other orchestral suites and ballets from this source.

From 1719 to 1729 Handel composed and directed operas for the newly formed Royal Academy of Music with varying decrees of success. Rivals sprang up on all sides, the most potent of them being Bononcini, imported in 1720 as a co-director of the academy. That the public was more or less neutral in this famous artistic combat may be gathered from some of the doggerel current at the time:

"Some say, compar'd to Bononcini
That Mynheer Handel's but a Ninny;
Others aver, that he to Handel
Is scarcely fit to hold a candle:
Strange all this difference should be
Twixt Tweedle-dum and Tweedle-dee."

Yet the rivalries continued to grow. London became surfeited with the riches supplied in the way of Italian opera; and in 1729, when a new fad arose in the way of *The Beggar's Opera,* a folk piece in English, satirizing the weaknesses of the Italian style, it proved the culminating English straw which broke the Italian camel's back. The academy failed, and with it went Handel's hopes and a great deal of his money. Magnificent opportunist that he was, he immediately turned his attention to other fields of composition.

[6] A recent gramophone catalogue lists twenty-four different vocal renditions of this aria, together with thirty-nine various transcriptions!

THE ORATORIOS

From this time on, Handel devoted himself largely to the writing of oratorios,[7] although he did not give up operas entirely until 1745. In these oratorios he was able, in the words of a letter of the time, successfully to " set up against the operas. He hired all the goddesses from farces and the singers of Roast Beef from between the acts at both theaters, with a man with one note in his voice, and a girl without ever an one; and so they sing and make brave hallelujahs. And the good company encores the recitative, if it happens to have any cadence like what they call a tune " (Horace Walpole: *Letters;* written to Sir Horace Mann, February 24, 1743).

As a matter of fact, these Handelian oratorios are merely continuations of Handelian opera without staging and costuming and action; written in English, they give more attention to the chorus but treat the recitative and the aria in dramatic style, in exactly the same way as a Handel opera. They provided the composer with a popular form in which to work, and he produced them in his theaters, with the best singers and instrumentalists that he could obtain. Their librettos were taken either from classic sources — Acis and Galatea, Hercules, Judas Maccabaeus, Semele, Theodora, and so on — or from Holy Writ — Esther, Israel in Egypt, Joseph, Joshua, Samson, and the Messiah. He wrote twenty-six of them in all,

[7] Before Handel started writing his oratorios, the form did not seem to have been used at all in England. The first work to gain fame was *Esther,* written in 1720 for performance in the private chapel of the Duke of Chandos, a work which is supposed to have netted Handel some thousand pounds. It was given with scenery and costumes. Twelve years later it was revised by Gates, Master of the Chapel Royal, and presented in the Crown and Anchor tavern for the members of a musical academy. Learning of the success of this production, the Princess Royal wished to see it performed, with scenery and action, at the opera; but the Bishop of London, who had authority over the choristers of the Chapel Royal, refused to allow them to appear in a sacred work in such secular surroundings. This so incensed Handel that he prepared an official performance which he advertised as being by His Majesty's Command, with the information that " there will be no action on the stage, but the house will be fitted up in a decent manner for the audience, the Musick to be disposed after the manner of the Coronation Service " (a series of four anthems for the accession of George II). This performance was repeated a number of times, so successful was this new style and so perfectly did it fit English tastes. Thus the English concert oratorio came into being, an event which was to exert tremendous influence on British taste and life.

A HANDEL ORATORIO (from a contemporary engraving by Hogarth)

most of them frankly for money; for he sensed that this type of production, with its peculiar blend of piety and passion, possessed a hold on the English public, which has never cared much for complexity in art, for what it calls " cleverness." Handel's great success entirely overwhelmed English composition and colored the people's preferences for well over a century after his death. *The Messiah* has been the most potent force in all English music and is still to be reckoned with today.

Two characteristic oratorios are *Semele,* the libretto of which was written by Congreve, originally for operatic treatment, and adapted by

Handel in 1743, and *The Messiah,* written to a text compiled by a poor worm of a clergyman secretary to Charles Jennens, one of the rich and influential art patrons of the period.[8] *Semele* is hardly known, even in England, although it contains three of Handel's most glorious arias, "Where'er you walk," "O Sleep, why dost thou leave me?" and "Now Love, that everlasting boy." Its libretto is typical: the story of Jupiter's carrying off Semele when she is about to be married to Athamas and the device by which Juno, the affronted goddess of marriage, contrives to bring about the destruction of Semele by her lover's lightnings. Not exactly a story of absorbing interest in the twentieth century, whatever it may have been in the eighteenth. *The Messiah,* on the other hand, is one of the most popular works in all music. When it was first produced at a charity concert in Dublin in 1742, the local reviewer remarked that "words are wanting to express the exquisite Delight it afforded to the admiring crowded Audience." In so far as English-speaking audiences are concerned, it has been providing this exquisite delight ever since.

The Messiah was actually composed in three weeks, although some of it may have been in Handel's mind before. Four of the choruses he adapted, after his not uncommon fashion, from other music of his. (It may be mentioned that he extended this plan of borrowing to the works of other composers as well, a habit which seems to have been more or less common to that time. Haste had much to do with Handel's appropriations, and Professor Dent has suggested that a certain slight mental instability from which Handel at times suffered had also something to do with them.) Speed in composition was facilitated by the lightness of the orchestration, which, as we have noted, had not then attained the heights of a complex art, though the orchestra was almost complete, as we know it today, with the exception of clarinets and the extension of the brass

[8] Newman Flower, in his great book on Handel, from which several of our old prints have been taken, quotes Dr. Samuel Johnson, on being asked concerning Jennens, "Who is this conceited gentleman who lays down the law so dogmatically?" as replying:

"A vain fool crazed by his wealth, who, were he in Heaven, would criticize the Lord Almighty; who lives surrounded by all the luxuries of an Eastern potentate—verily an English 'Solyman the Magnificent'; who never walks abroad without a train of footmen at his heels, and, like Wolsey, with a scented sponge 'neath his nose, lest the breath of the vulgar herd should contaminate his sacred person."

that we owe to the nineteenth-century experimenters such as Sax. Slight accompaniments sufficed for many solos and for all the recitatives. The important duty of filling these up was given to the *continuo* player, who was usually also the conductor, since the separate function of this important modern-day specialist with the baton had not yet evolved. The *continuo* part was written as a figured bass and so could be quickly sketched in when composing. To a large extent its filling up was an art of improvisation on the part of the harpsichordist. A number of years later Mozart took it upon himself to write out additional accompaniments to this oratorio from these figured bass parts, accompaniments which are, unfortunately, out of taste with the rest and are today seldom used.

The work contains a tremendous amount of material — three broad sections, the first concerning the prophecy of the Messiah's coming, followed by the lovable Christmas music; after it a section devoted to the sufferings and the death of the Saviour, full of deeply felt sorrow; and lastly the Resurrection section, with meditations on Christ's place in the world. There are over fifty numbers all together, although the work as a whole is seldom given. It would repay close study in detail, if one would penetrate the very essence of Handel's manner of expression.

OTHER WORKS

Of all Handel's instrumental works the best known is the so-called *Water Music*, as characteristic a thing as he ever wrote. This was a set of some twenty dances and "airs," not this time arranged from vocal works. Around them arose the pleasant story that when Handel was out of favor with George I, because he had outstayed his leave from Germany when his royal master was the Elector of Hanover, his friends arranged that this music, specially composed, should be played on a barge behind the state vessel, while his Majesty was making a triumphal procession down the River Thames in 1715. Sticklers for the truth deny this, saying that the music was written in 1717, when Handel was in full favor again. No matter; a legend is a legend, and its truth or untruth need not concern us, so long as nothing important hangs on it! The music as a whole is very rarely played, the selection generally used consisting of six numbers only. Handel scored this music for piccolo, flutes, oboes, bassoons, horns, trumpets, and strings, doubtless with an ear to the carrying effect upon the water. In modern arrangements, much fuller orchestration is employed: it is always one of the difficulties of historical estimate that we can so seldom hear old music as the composer really wrote it. Even if we had his proportion of instruments as they are used today, we should have to allow for the difference in sound. For instance, the older oboes and bassoons were coarser than ours, and in a day when the proportions of the orchestra had not reached its finality, more of these instruments were used than today.

A final word can well be spoken for Handel's sonatas and concertos; he wrote nineteen so-called sonatas for solo instrument and several sets for two instruments with figured bass. In many of these definite instruments are specified, but in performance one instrument was often substituted for another. These belong to an early period of the composer's life, when, as he said, he composed with great enthusiasm, "like a very devil." Although little played, they are full of splendid broad and easy-flowing melodies, with accompaniments that are simple and strong. The effect is somewhat more openhearted than in Bach's rather more austere sonatas. The cool beauty of the slow movements is always refreshing, and the athletic motion of the allegros makes it seem the simplest thing in the world to toss off such movements. Short though they are, there is much craft in them.

His best-known concertos are those of Opus 6, *concerti grossi* in the real sense of the word, employing the usual dialogue form between a group of solo strings and the full orchestral body. There are twelve of these, minor works perhaps, but full of Handel's usual melodic charm. Here, as in so many of his other works, there is a certain ruddy strength combined with a suave grace and lovely plenitude.

THE LAST YEARS

We have seen how for over forty years Handel and London had been enemies, his life there one long series of dramatic struggles, malicious foes, and crafty friends. It is pleasant to be able to record that in the end he triumphed and became the acknowledged master of English music.[9] But at what a cost! Worn out with the exhaustive labor and feverish haste of composition, he was just ready to celebrate his triumph when a new enemy appeared, blindness. This alone, of all his troubles, seemed to bring him despair; for it meant giving up work. His last oratorio, *Jephtha*, produced in 1752, was completed with difficulty, and by 1753 he had completely lost his sight. These last years saw many triumphant revivals of works at which London had scoffed when they were first produced, revivals which brought him in a great deal of money. But best of all, they enabled him to vindicate himself. He died in April, 1759, and was buried, after a fulsome funeral at which not a note of his own music was played, in Westminster Abbey. One of the contemporary obituary notices concluded in this fashion: " He was perhaps as great a genius in music as Mr. Pope in poetry; the musical composition of the one being as expressive of the passions, as the happy versification of the other excelled in harmony " (*Scots Magazine*, April, 1759).

Such a bracketing of these two eighteenth-century masters may seem somewhat of a conceit, so different were they in many respects. But could anything be found that more fittingly describes the spirit of Handel, the great master of the Baroque, than the last stanza of Pope's " The Dying Christian to His Soul "?

> " The world recedes; it disappears!
> Heav'n opens in my eyes! my ears
> With sounds seraphic ring;
> Lend, lend your wings! I mount! I fly!
> O Grave! where is thy victory?
> O Death! where is thy sting? "

[9] It is often felt that Handel's tunes have a certain Englishness about them (like Purcell's, for example) and that his imagination received refreshing impetus from British melodic forthrightness.

Haydn and Mozart

THE EARLY ORCHESTRAL EXPERIMENTERS

THE BEGINNINGS OF MODERN ORCHESTRAL MUSIC

THE processes of ratiocination which we have described as affecting the musical output of the eighteenth century so strongly were not concerned with the opera alone. Two other great classifications of modern music, that written for the orchestra and that written for smaller, chamber-music combinations, such as the string quartet, had their beginnings in the intellectual atmosphere of this period — the conviction that reason and order should be the arbiter of art as well as the standard of personal conduct.

During the course of our chronicle we have had much to say concerning the use of instruments during the various epochs of history and have tried to show how it came about that certain of them were chosen to form the basis of the modern orchestra. Let us recapitulate briefly:

From the dawn of musical history it has been evident that man used musical instruments of all sorts, singly and in combination; but the art of grouping instruments in some sort of logical ensembles of a definite type, such as the symphony or the chamber orchestra, and the writing of music for them, is comparatively modern, dating from the eighteenth century. Earlier than this, orchestras (using this term in its generally accepted sense of an ensemble of instruments) seemingly comprised any gathering together of instruments that happened to be convenient. The Egyptian wall paintings, the accounts of the Greek historians, the medieval manuscripts, all assure us that these heterogeneous combinations would sound illogical and strange to the modern ear.

The problem of how the present ideals of orchestration slowly came to realization is one that has not been solved by modern research. Up till the end of the Middle Ages there seems to be little information available. We get hints here and there of many different types of instruments being played, but just how or when they were used together we do not know. Gottfried von Strassburg, a minnesinger thoroughly conversant with the musical traditions of his time, credits his hero Tristan with being able to play six different instruments: the *fiedel*, the hurdy-gurdy, the harp, the rotta, the lyre, and the zither; but he does not tell us whether such instruments as these were ever played in combination by the minstrels. We have mentioned the rich depiction of instruments by the artists of the late medieval period; but we cannot be certain that the instruments shown were played in a concerted fashion, even when they are so depicted by the artists.

In the fourteenth and fifteenth centuries there are historical references to orchestras, conducting, and so forth; but there was certainly no recognized standard of ensemble grouping in the various countries, and the type of music used in one place might prove quite impractical in another. When we first hear anything about what might be called an orchestra in the modern sense, we find that it was a group of mixed instruments used for accompanying vocal music and playing the same parts the singers sang. During the early Renaissance these *consorts*, as they were called, were freely used with voices, and no distinction was made between vocal and instrumental parts, nor were any indications given as to which were meant to be played and which were to be sung. Writing of this period in 1776, Hawkins said that concerts of instruments alone were a later invention, "at least there is no clear evidence of the form in which they existed." Only gradually did composers learn that it was possible to achieve with instruments certain effects that had been quite impossible with voices; this realization was the beginning of the modern orchestral style.

We have suggested several possible influences which aided this process of learning how best to group and use instruments: the use of isolated and scattered instrumental groups in the great masques and pageants, such use showing which instruments would make the best effect when played together;[1] the popular renditions of music by folk bands of nimble-witted musicians who would quickly grasp the principles of practicality in combining instruments;[2] and the use of instrumental groups in church for accompanying services.[3]

It was not until toward the end of the sixteenth century, however, that instrumental music finally succeeded in loosening the bonds that had tied it so closely to vocal music. It was the Gabrielis of Venice who showed the possibilities of ensemble instrumental music when played alone. They discovered what the historians call *dynamic antithesis,* the effectiveness of contrast between music produced by a large and a small group of instruments, or the same group playing alternately soft and loud. Then came the idea of grouping according to their tone color or timbre, together with the use of a changing group of instruments within the orchestral body in order to obtain varied effects. These were naturally conditioned by the inventive genius of the instrument makers as well as by the cogitative ability of the composers. Here are some of the outstanding items in this process of development:

One of the earliest instrumental ensembles of which we have definite record is that used by Monteverdi in his opera *Orpheus* (1607). It consisted of the following instruments: fifteen viols of three different

1 In his *Histoire littéraire, musicale, chorégraphique, pittoresque, morale, critique, facétieuse, politique et galante* of the Académie Imperiale de Musique, Castil-Blaze describes how, in a masque performed in honor of the Duke of Milan in 1489, " they changed their instruments according to the character of the music played. Each singer, each dancer, had his special orchestra which was arranged according to the sentiments intended to be expressed by his song or dance. It was an excellent plan which . . . produced a succession of trumpets, of violins with their acute tones, the arpeggios of lutes, and the soft airs of flutes and reed pipes. The orchestration of Monteverdi proves that at the time composers varied their instrumentation thus."

2 At a later date when traveling through Italy, the English historian Burney heard outside his inn at Brescia a " band of two violins, a mandolin, a French horn, a trumpet, and a violoncello — and though in the dark they played long concertos, with solo parts for the mandolin, I was surprised at the memory of these performers; in short, it was excellent street music." And in Venice he was pleased with " an excellent band of music, consisting of violins, flutes, horns, bases, and a kettledrum."

3 The German historian Michael Praetorius (1571–1621) tells about accompanying a church motet with the following orchestra: two theorbos, three lutes, two zithers, four harpsichords and spinets, seven viola da gambas, two *Querflöte*, and a bass viol; which, together with the vocal forces involved (two boy sopranos and an alto), gave a " marvelous, glorious resonance "!

sizes, two violins, two large flutes, two ordinary flutes, two oboes, two cornets (the old wooden instruments), four trumpets, five trombones, a harp, two harpsichords, two small organs, and a regal (a portable reed organ). This combination of forty instruments probably made use of all the instrumentalists available to this court composer of Mantua; but in spite of its miscellaneousness there is evident here the principle of the string choir as the foundation of the whole orchestral scheme.

If we examine the scores of such representative early seventeenth-century composers as Schütz and Lully, we find the gradual emergence of the wood-wind instruments as soloists; and by the end of the century the standard four-part string division had become universal: first violin, second violin, tenor viol (viola), violoncello doubling with the string bass, the latter sounding an octave lower.

Bach's scores show, significantly enough, that the brass had not yet become a separate choir in itself, that a keyboard instrument was still used to mix and bind the orchestral timbres, and that no standard procedure was followed in the grouping of the instruments. Strings, oboes, flutes, and clavier; strings, trumpets, and clavier; strings, oboes, flutes, and clavier; strings, oboes, flutes, trumpets, drums, and clavier—all such combinations alternate in a Bach score without apparent reason for any particular choice. Moreover, the functions and capacities of the instruments are little differentiated, strings, wood winds, and brass all playing the same kind of passages in ensemble or in succession.

Gluck was an important figure in the development of the orchestra as an instrument. For it was his constant experimentation with means for achieving dramatic expressiveness that led him to enrich the emotional color of his opera orchestra. He did not hesitate to use such instruments as the piccolo, the trombone, the harp, the bass drum, the English horn, and the clarinet; he investigated the tone-color possibilities of the viola and the violoncello; and he discarded the blend-destroying keyboard instrument, although it was often used in orchestras long after his time. His band functioned by choirs, that is, by unified groups set off from one another and used independently for color. It was this flexible and unified instrument, speaking comparatively, that was further enriched and developed by the Mannheim composers, as described below.

MUSIC FOR THE ORCHESTRA

During this time there likewise developed the idea of using a definite kind of thematic material specially suited to the means and style of the ensemble. This grew not only out of the dynamic and color-change possibilities of the orchestra, but out of the new harmonic system introduced into music at the beginning of the seventeenth century. In other words, the orchestra developed a musical vocabulary and an expressive language of its own, capable of carrying out all the possibilities which had been gradually accumulating. The chief feature of this new language was the use of instrumental *themes* as material out of which the musical structure was fashioned. No longer did vocal and dance idioms serve as the sole source of material for instrumental writers. These were transformed into definite melodic themes, which were contrasted with one another and which served as the germs out of which the whole structure logically grew.

Finally, and this was definitely the work of the composers of the eighteenth century, there came the crystallization of formulas according to which musical thought was molded, the evolution of logical schemes of construction by means of which the ideas of the composer could be best expressed. If anyone would know what the eighteenth century did for instrumental music, let him compare a Bach Brandenburg Concerto (which would be a fair exemplification of the instrumental ideals held up to this time) with a Haydn symphony. Bach and Handel at one end of the eighteenth century may be said to have been the culmination of the traditional style of writing and musical culture which grew out of the vocal, contrapuntal music of the past. Haydn and Mozart, at the other end, wrote in an entirely new style and employed entirely different means. What came between?

This was no sudden transformation, wrought, as the operatic inventions of the early seventeenth century had been, by a small group of experimenters. The whole of civilized Europe may be said to have taken part in it: the Italians, with their cyclic, three-movement overtures of light, fluent, harmonic style; the French, with their form of overture and suite and their galant manner of writing; and the Germans, with their peculiar capacity for expressing both the grave and the gay and their blend of philosophical reason and emotional expressiveness. All these factors interacted on one another directly and indirectly. The century was one of intense intellectual curiosity in so far as the musicians and artists were concerned, and the men in one country, in spite of the poor physical means of communication, were thoroughly conversant with the work of their contemporaries in the others.

THE MANNHEIMERS

There were certain centers, however, which seemed to be especially potent forces in this work of international artistic development. In so far as music was concerned, the chief of these was the orchestra maintained by an art-loving prince in the little ducal court of Mannheim, a town halfway between the centers of German and French culture. We have a good contemporary account of this musical establishment of Prince Karl Theodore at Mannheim, for in 1772 the roving Englishman in search of materials of his history of music, Dr. Charles Burney, visited it, was very much impressed by its "expensive magnificence," and wrote the following description of this experimental laboratory out of which came so many of the principles of modern orchestral writing and playing:

"I found it to be all that its fame had made me expect: power will naturally arise from a great number of hands; but the judicious use of this power, on all occasions, must be the consequence of good discipline; indeed there are more solo players and good composers in this than perhaps in any other orchestra in Europe; it is an army of generals, equally fit to plan a battle, as to fight it." (We cannot help wondering what Burney might have said of the Boston, the Philadelphia, or the London Philharmonic orchestras!)

"But it has not been merely at the Elector's great opera that instrumental music has been so much cultivated and refined, but at his concerts, where this extraordinary band has 'ample room and verge enough' to display all its powers, and to produce great effects without the impropriety of destroying the grandeur and more delicate beauties peculiar to vocal music; it was here that Stamitz . . . first surpassed the bounds of common opera overtures, which had hitherto only served in the theatre as a kind of court crier, with an 'O Yes' in order to awaken attention and bespeak silence at the entrance of the singers. Since the discovery which the genius of Stamitz first made, every effect has been tried which such an aggregate of sound can produce; it was here that *Crescendo* and *Diminuendo* had birth; and the *Piano,* which had before chiefly been used as an echo, with which it was generally synonymous, as well as the *Forte,* were found to be musical colours which had their shares as much as red or blue in painting.

"I found, however, an imperfection in this band, common to all others that I have ever yet heard, but which I was in hopes would be removed by men so attentive and so able; the defect I mean is the want of truth in the wind instruments. I know it is natural to those instruments to be out of tune, but some of that art and diligence which these great performers have manifested in vanquishing difficulties of other kinds, would surely be well employed in correcting this leaven which so sours and corrupts all harmony. This was too plainly the case tonight, with the bassoons and hautbois (oboes), which were rather too sharp at the beginning, and continued growing sharper to the end of the opera.

"My ears were unable to discover any other imperfection in the orchestra throughout the whole performance; and this imperfection is so common to orchestras in general that the censure will not be very severe upon this, or afford much matter for triumph to the performers of any other orchestra in Europe.

"The Elector, who is himself a very good performer upon the German flute, and who can, occasionally, play his part upon the violoncello, has a concert in his palace every evening when there is no public exhibition at the theatre; but when that happens, not only his own subjects, but all foreigners have admission gratis.

"The going out from the opera at Schwetzingen, during the summer, into the electoral gardens, which, in the French style, are extremely beautiful, affords one of the gayest and most splendid sights imaginable; the country here is flat and naked, and therefore would be less favorable to the free and open manner of laying out grounds in English horticulture, than to that which has been adopted.

"His electoral highness' suite at Schwetzingen during summer amounts to fifteen hundred persons, who are all lodged in this little village at his expense. To a stranger walking through the streets of Schwetzingen during summer, this place must seem inhabited only by a colony of musicians, who are constantly exercising their profession: at one house a fine player on the violin is heard; at another, a German flute; here an excellent hautbois; there a bassoon, a clarinet, a violoncello, or a concert

THE CASTLE GARDEN AT SCHWETZINGEN

It was in the midst of such idyllic surroundings as this that the modern orchestra came into existence.

of several instruments together. Music seems to be the chief and the most constant of his electoral highness' amusements; and the operas and concerts, to which all his subjects have admission, form the judgment and establish the taste for music throughout the electorate."

— Burney: *Present State of Music in Germany, Netherlands, and United Provinces*

THEIR SHAPING OF ORCHESTRAL STYLE

In the effort to "surpass the bounds of common opera overtures," Johann Stamitz (1717–1757), the founder and principal composer of this Mannheim group, and the other men who worked with him in these musical experiments — Richter, Holzbauer, Toeschi, and Wendling — discovered and practiced most of the innovations which are to be found in the Haydn quartets and symphonies and which have often been attributed to him. Briefly, these are:

First, the use of the so-called sonata form (first-movement form), a kind of constructional formula which has as its basis the use of two principal themes of differing and contrasting nature, the thematic elaboration of these in another section, and their repetition in a third.

Second, the addition of the minuet as a fourth movement to the three until then customary in the sonata, thus bringing in a new and enlivening element.

Third, the gradual dispensing with the usual *basso continuo* (already noted in one of Telemann's works), and the increasing of the importance of the melody.

Fourth, the introduction of distinctive motives or themes, rising out of the possibilities of the instrumental style.

Fifth, the use of a simple harmonic rather than an elaborate contrapuntal style.

Stamitz's *Sonata à trois parties concertantes,* Op. 1, has been called the starting point of this new movement and should be consulted by all those who would trace the beginnings of modern orchestral writing. Although it exemplifies well enough the fact that *aller Anfang ist schwer,* it still stands in many respects one of the most interesting documents in music history.

THE CONTRIBUTION OF ANOTHER BACH

Just how far these Mannheim compositions may have affected or have been affected by the work of Carl Philip Emanuel Bach, Sebastian's second son, it is impossible to say; but at any rate we find in the piano works of this composer (a contemporary of the Mannheim group), who in his day was considered the peer of his father, the same principles of thematic and melodic development that are present in the orchestral composition of Stamitz. In speaking of Emanuel Bach, Burney was moved to remark: "How he formed his style would be difficult to trace; he certainly neither inherited nor adopted it from his father who was his only master. . . . He spoke irreverently of canons, which, he said, were dry and despicable pièces of pedantry that anyone might compose who would sacrifice his time to them." Very probably the general influences of the time, together with an understanding of the work that had been done by his predecessors, led to Emanuel Bach's adopting these innovations which were being applied contemporaneously in other parts of Europe. If, for instance, we examine such a typical example of Philip Emanuel's work as his first sonata (in G major) of the *Second Collection for Connoisseurs and Amateurs,* we shall find a three-movement work in which the general form of the modern sonata, as we know it, is definitely fixed: an opening movement in sonata form, with two main themes, a development section and a recapitulation; a slow movement of song type, very suggestive of the spirit of the galant composers; and a third, a jolly finale with the general character of a rondo (one theme constantly recurring).

Although Haydn seems never to have mentioned any study that he made of the works of the Mannheim groups — he must have known them, however, for they were played everywhere and looked on as models for this kind of music — he acknowledged that one of the chief influences in his musical education had been the study of Emanuel's music; and Bach, in turn, said that Haydn was the only man who had ever really understood him. So that we may say definitely enough that the new forms and principles which we find in Haydn's sonatas, quartets, and symphonies came directly from the piano works of Carl Philip Emanuel Bach and indirectly from the compositions of the Mannheim composers and the men in other countries (such as Giovanni Sammartini and Luigi Boccherini) who were experimenting along the same lines.

After all, it is only a matter of academic interest, this tracing of Haydn's musical ancestry; the important thing to note is that in various parts of Europe ground was being broken for the great florescence that was to come at the end of the century. The men we have mentioned, although the list is by no means complete, are characteristic of this period, creating, as they did, out of its predominant tendencies, a type of expression that was at the same time brilliant and refined, charming and intelligent, with as special a care for the manner in which it was organized as for the clarity with which it was expressed. The reason why the music of Haydn and Mozart has survived while that of their immediate predecessors and contemporaries, such as Gossec and Dittersdorf, has perished, is not so much because of the superior inspiration of these two great men, as because of their ability to feel deeply and to express themselves emotionally as well as logically. Twentieth-century composers, please note!

FRANZ JOSEF HAYDN

When I think of the Divine Being, my heart is so full of joy that the notes fly off as from a spindle; and as I have a cheerful heart he will pardon me if I serve him cheerfully.

— Haydn

This memorial to Haydn's name
Consecrates this forever a sacred spot;
His muse reminds us plaintively
That the art of this great Master,
Who joins skill of craft and depth of feeling,
Was once upon a time called " modern."

— From a monument erected in Rohrau, Haydn's birthplace

THE CLASSICAL EXPERIMENTER

IT was St. Paul who said, " It is the letter that killeth but the spirit that giveth life." Haydn has been credited with being the father of the modern sonata, the string quartet, and the symphony by practically every writer on the history of music. Yet if there had been nothing more to his music than this, he would be as dead today as are the composers we have just been discussing, Johann Stamitz and Emanuel Bach. Possessing an insatiable curiosity, Haydn, through the entire course of his long life, was a constant experimenter and pioneer in his art, as quick to seize on everything that agreed with his ideals as he was to reject anything that seemed unsuited to his purpose or contrary to his spirit. But in addition to this, his music has a certain personality, a heart-warming attractiveness which shows its composer to have known life intimately and to have lived it with gusto. A formalist in art — " classicist " is the word generally used to depict his temperament — he nevertheless sensed that the important thing in music is its spiritual quality, its soul, its poignant emotion. And so his music lives today, while that of his predecessors is brought to life only occasionally for the delectation of those interested in the historical development of the art.

There is no reason why we should attempt to minimize the formal achievements of Haydn. It was he who went forward after his contemporaries, who had helped evolve the style, had finished their work of preparation. Gathering together the various experimental threads, he was the first one to weave out of them a fabric of beautiful form; and he was able also to define those instruments of expression that we have used ever since. His interest embraced every field of activity — instrumental music, church music, song, opera, and finally oratorio. He brought to all his work an inquiring and practical mind, a fertile and boundless curiosity, a real imagination, a physical vigor and well-being, and a religious contentment, which make him stand out as one of the great figures in music.

HIS ACHIEVEMENTS SUMMARIZED

It may be well to state briefly just what these formal achievements of this eighteenth-century pioneer were: a crystallization of the constructive principles of the form of the symphony and the sonata, principles which have guided and influenced the work of every composer who has used these forms since; the organization of the modern instrument which we have come to know as the orchestra, basing its foundation on a quartet of strings and increasing its dynamic and color effects by the addition of wind and percussion instruments; the establishment of a definite line

Rudolf Lesch Fine Arts, Inc.

FRANZ JOSEF HAYDN

of demarcation between chamber and orchestral types of music (these had been much the same in style before, but Haydn established the string quartet as a distinctive instrument and showed the type of music best suited to it); the production of a style of harmonic, instrumental writing that was as complete and satisfying and lent itself as well to all the demands made on it as did that of the older polyphonic vocal chorus music of the sixteenth-century writers. We are accustomed to take these all for granted and to forget that they have not always existed.

It was his complete success in all this ground-breaking labor that encouraged his friend and pupil, Mozart, to dub him affectionately "Papa Haydn." This title, given with real understanding and deep appreciation of Haydn's qualities, has taken on a rather condescending tinge of meaning through the years, suggestive of a peruked, classic formalist, whose music, charming enough, perhaps, has little significance beyond its grace of line and its appropriateness of design. It was in this sense that the nineteenth-century Romanticist, Rubinstein, liked to refer to Haydn; but it has turned out as a shrewd observer of the time said it would: Rubinstein has become great-great-grandfather Rubinstein, while Haydn is still Papa Haydn!

For Haydn was a seeker of spiritual as well as formal qualities, always striving to clarify his position and attain the height of those creative powers he knew he possessed. "Ambitious, uncompromising, energetic, patient, Haydn fought his way forward to an ideal goal not clearly seen at first, to approach it more closely, as the faithful strive to approach the object of their devotions. His unusual natural endowments favored the development of his native qualities and of his character as man and artist" (Adler: "Haydn and the Viennese Classical School"). Such qualifications do not produce stereotyped, conventional art, but vital, forceful, and personal art, no matter how polished and courteous it may be after the manner of its time.

THE WAY OF HIS LIFE

An understanding of Haydn's life helps to explain the place he came to occupy in music. He himself felt that a divine Providence, after equipping him with the proper mental and musical attributes, furnished him likewise with ideal opportunities for perfecting his genius. There was first his early training as a choir boy and café musician in Vienna, where he dug out for himself the principles he needed, largely through a study of Emanuel Bach's sonatas and Fux's theoretical treatise, *Gradus ad Parnassum;* then there was his position as director of the musical establishment at Weinzirl, a small castle in Lower Austria, followed by his later post as conductor and composer for Prince Esterhazy at the latter's sumptuous palaces in Vienna, Eisenstadt, and Esterház. This post not only gave Haydn an ideal orchestra with which to experiment, but also placed him under the necessity of having to furnish compositions for this band to play.

And Haydn was shrewd enough to value these opportunities and to make the most of them, seeing no insult in having to wear a uniform or

A SCENE FROM A HAYDN OPERA

(From a picture in possession of V. E. Pollak, Vienna)

Thirteen violins and violas, one cello, two basses, two flutes, and a bassoon constitute the orchestra for this opera staged in the opera house at Esterház. Haydn himself is at the cembalo.

to eat with the servants at Esterház; and when opportunity came later through the death of his prince, to free himself from all this eighteenth-century system of patronage and to step out in the freedom of his own personality as composer and conductor in London, he was ready and fully qualified. He was as successful then as he had been formerly, receiving his honors with due humility, and not losing, in his contact with the world's great, his common touch. Among his finest compositions are the symphonies he wrote for performance in London; he conducted them himself, sitting at the harpsichord, as was the contemporary custom. Yet, with it all, he remained a simple, sincere person. When, after writing his oratorios *The Creation* and *The Seasons*, in which critics feel that he achieved the full maturity of his power, he died, full of years and honors, his only lament was that he was just beginning to learn how to compose.

MUTUAL MOTIVATION

Mozart, Haydn's junior by twenty-four years, was strongly influenced by his works. Haydn's dates are 1732 to 1809, a life of 77 years; Mozart's, 1756 to 1791, a life of 35 years. Mozart learned, in youth, from Haydn; and Haydn, in his late quartets and particularly his last symphonies, acknowledged, with the humbleness of a great man, what Mozart's music had taught him. He refers with grief and anger to the neglect of the "inimitable works of this unique genius." Mozart dedicated some of his works to Haydn with respect and affection, for, as he said, it was from him that he learned to write quartets. To a pianist friend who had pointed out a slip of Haydn's, he said: "Put the two of us together and we shall fall far short of being a Haydn!" Then he added, "Nobody can do everything — jest and frighten, arouse laughter or move deeply — like Haydn."

These expressions of reciprocal regard go far beyond conventional phrases. Each composer knew that the other had something to give him out of a nature quite different — Mozart from his intensely dramatic, swift-rushing, operatic scintillation and his tragic power; Haydn from his inventive, philosophical, humorous mind, tinged with a certain easy-going quality, a liking for rustic flavor, and a settled sense of certainty in his career that poor, traveling Mozart never knew. Haydn had his depths as well as did Mozart, less profoundly stirred by the sense of the world's weight and the soul's tragedies, but depths nevertheless, filled with a knowledge of humanity translated into a serene expression.

Beethoven, the third great figure in the succession of the so-called school of Viennese classicism, came to Vienna at the age of twenty-one to study with Haydn, and although he expressed himself as being dissatisfied with him as a teacher (we should be tempted to say that Beethoven was always dissatisfied with humanity — with women and friends as well as with teachers!) he did not hesitate to adopt his technique of writing. Of the 245 exercises which have survived from Beethoven's study with Haydn, only 42 were corrected by the latter, who was, at the time, extremely busy. It was probably this that made Beethoven impatient rather than any deficiency in the quality of instruction received.

HAYDN'S DISTINCTIVE QUALITIES

There are qualities in Haydn's music that make him a distinctive figure for the listener of today, a figure that stands apart from the other great men of the period, even from his two great pupils. Taking into account the circumstances under which they were written, we find that over one hundred fifty symphonies of this composer — particularly the later ones written for the London impresario, Salomon — together with his eighty-three quartets, represent a freshness of vigor and a robustness of energy that is anything but typical of the scented salon atmosphere of his period. He was able to weave into his musical fabric warp and woof of both court and countryside, but there is more of the country than of the court. He loved good, straightforward, folkish tunes (perhaps his Slavic origin accounts for this) and square-cut dance rhythms, a fact which gives a fresh, open-air quality to his music and makes it seem closely akin to nature. And his style of writing was well suited to such treatment. It is in strong distinction to the music of Mozart who, although he lived the greater part of his life amidst some of the most beautiful scenery in the world, seems never to have been conscious of it or to have been affected by it in the slightest. As a composer, Haydn betrays his country origin, for he gives us a sense of contact with the soil, an elemental and unaffected simplicity that is appealing and immediate, one to which we react unconsciously.

Then, too, there is in these symphonies a distinct reflection of Haydn's personal philosophy: he did not hesitate to ascribe his scores to God's glory or to say that one of his reasons for writing music was "that the weary and worn or the man burdened with affairs might enjoy something of solace and refreshment." Coupled with this imperturbable philosophic attitude towards God and his fellow man was a certain shrewdness and practicality of nature, and a well-developed sense of humor, which colored his music and contributed to its popularity. Perhaps the fact that he had married a Xantippe of a wife helped him to take life philosophically and in his daily stride; and there is a comforting touch of demos about his work that endears it to us today and assures its outlasting a great deal of the aristocratic art of its period.

This feeling of democratic familiarity, of Jack's-as-good-as-his-neighbor spirit that we have with Haydn's music is nowhere better demonstrated than in the nicknames that have become associated with certain of his works, names that suggest something of their appeal and easy amiability. We somehow cannot imagine calling anything that Beethoven wrote, or Brahms or even Mozart, a *Dudelsack* or a *Lark* or a *Frog* quartet or a *Surprise* or a *Hen* or a *Clock* symphony! And yet these whimsical appellations seem somehow appropriate when they are applied to Haydn's compositions, even though we may not always know their meaning any more than we do that of some of the terms in Mother Goose. Something of the composer's spirit has survived in them.

CREATIVE PERIODS IN HIS LIFE

Karl Geiringer, a well-known Austrian biographer of Haydn, has divided his creative life into five periods which happen to coincide with the last five decades of the century:

First Period (1750–1760); with Count Fürnberg at his castle at Weinzirl, and later with Count Morzin

During this time Haydn wrote his first string quartets and symphonies, both of which show strongly the influence of earlier Viennese composers. His first quartets are in five-movement form and show that the composer was still affected by the old dance suites; the first two symphonies are written with a keyboard instrument included in the orchestration. To this period also belongs Haydn's earliest opera, written in the comic Viennese style, *Der neue krumme Teufel,* and one of the first of the long list of works for the Church, his *Missa brevis* in F.

Second Period (1761–1770); with Prince Paul Anton Esterhazy as his director of music at Eisenstadt, and later at Esterház

Haydn began to experiment and take his own path, aided by the rich musical resources of the Esterhazy court. Program symphonies — *Le matin, Le midi, Le soir* — were still influenced by the dance suite. His best operas were written for the Esterhazy establishment, especially *Acide e Galatea,* in the finest *opera seria* tradition, and the *opera buffa* *Lo Speziale.*

THE PLAN OF THE GROUNDS AT SCHLOSS ESTERHAZY

The layout shows the provision made for accommodating the Prince's musicians. Haydn lived here for many years.

Third Period (1771–1780); *Fourth Period* (1781–1790)

" There was no one near to confuse and torment me and so I was compelled to become original " is Haydn's own explanation of the rapid development of his genius during these years with the Esterhazys. Included in his tremendous output of this time were 5 Masses, 11 operas, music for four marionette plays, 60 symphonies, 40 string quartets, and 125 baryton compositions, since his prince was extremely fond of this bass viol and a good performer on it. A much greater depth of feeling is noticeable in these works: the composer has come under the influence of the rising Romantic Movement and does not hesitate to show it in his music.

Fifth Period (1791–1803); in Vienna and London

This is a period of supreme mastery and world recognition. The London symphonies, his best quartets, and his two oratorios were all written during this time. Six masses show his continuing interest in the music of the Church; and a warm Romanticism in all that he did shows his awareness of the times.

THE SYMPHONIES

The most rewarding beauties in Haydn's symphonies came in the last years of his life, after he had worked out the constructive principles of their form and had come into stimulating contact with Mozart. But there is much interest all along the way, ever and anon in the works he wrote at the time he was connected with Prince Esterhazy's little orchestra at Eisenstadt and Esterház, where he led, dressed in his uniform of blue coat with silver buttons, a white collar, and a pigtail wig. He served this princely family for twenty-nine years, and during this period over eighty symphonies came from his pen, including a set of six ordered by the director of the *concerts spirituels* in Paris. Most of these are no longer played by present-day conductors, but the wealth of material they contain may be realized through an occasional hearing of such things as *La poule* (the second of the Parisian set, which received its name from a peculiar " cluck " in the second theme, and which lays a prize egg in its last, fugal movement), *La reine* (Paris symphony number four, dedicated to Queen Marie Antoinette, with its happy use of a popular French tune for the theme of its second movement), and the amusing *Abschieds* (*Farewell*) *Symphony* (in which, by a clever way of ending the last movement, Haydn conveyed to his prince the desire of his orchestra to return to winter quarters in Vienna).

In 1790, Haydn went to England on the invitation of the outstanding London impresario and orchestral leader of the time. For him he produced the twelve symphonies which are known today as the Salomon symphonies. Among these, outstanding are *Mit dem Paukenschlag* (*Symphony with the Drumbeat*, also known by its English nickname, *The Surprise Symphony*), *The Clock Symphony*, the *Military Symphony*, and *Mit dem Paukenwirbel* (*Drumroll Symphony*). In all these there are certain Haydn hallmarks that can be easily recognized — such things as his long curtain-raising introductions (not inevitable, by any means, but usual), his phrase extensions, his sudden modulating jumps from key to key, and the amusing " pussyfoot " returns which he often makes to the principal theme.

A revival of interest in these Haydn symphonies,[4] particularly those written during the Esterhazy period (the years 1761 to 1790), has been recently brought about through the labors of Dr. Alfred Einstein, who has made a number of them available to orchestras through accurate editions. We are made more than ever aware, in listening to these newly published works, of Haydn's wide emotional range: grave vigor, romantic lyricism, and poetic reflection are all to be found in delectable symphonies which have for so long been forgotten.

THE QUARTETS

There are good reasons why Haydn's quartets, in so far as the modern listener is concerned, are his finest works. For one thing, the essential nature of the instrument on which they are played has not changed from Haydn's day to ours; a modern quartet uses exactly the same combination of instruments, sounding just as it did when Haydn selected it as the norm for this type of writing. And so we need not make the

[4] A recent musical statistician has estimated that out of all the symphonies of Haydn's that are regarded as authentic, only twenty are in the repertoire of our leading orchestras. This is probably a high estimate.

historical adjustment that is necessary when listening to one of his symphonies, where his orchestration is comparatively limited and somewhat slight in comparison with that to which we are accustomed. Then, too, he seemed to have put more of himself into these chamber works than he did in his compositions for orchestra. Experience had proved that the four instruments of the quartet provided the most perfect, concise, and self-contained combination possible in music; whereas further experimentation with the various orchestral timbres was always possible and he liked to try this, sometimes with rather restricting effect on his style.

A study of the Haydn string quartets is a long journey, with many pauses by the way for special refreshment, solace, and happy enjoyment. A ten-year lapse in their writing (between Op. 20, written in 1771, and Op. 33, composed in 1781) conveniently divides them into two great groups. The earlier works are naturally more experimental; the composer was searching for the most fitting manner in which to express his ideas. In them, to use the words of Edwin Evans, the modern string quartet was not only born but passed through its adolescence to a maturity. We enjoy the early ones chiefly for certain movements, such as the two universal favorites, the slow-movement serenade in Op. 3, No. 5, and the bagpipe minuet from Op. 3, No. 3.

The last group shows the influence of a stronger musical personality, that of Mozart. Having learned from Haydn how to write quartets, the younger composer in turn showed the older the possibilities of which the form was capable. Most of these later quartets are included in sets of six each, and among them are some of Haydn's most famous works, such as *The Lark*, Op. 64, No. 5; *The Horseman*, Op. 74, No. 3; and *The Emperor*, Op. 76, No. 3, this latter containing the well-known variations on the composer's own "Emperor's Hymn." But the greatest of them all are without doubt his last two works in this form, the two quartets making up Op. 77. It is a matter of personal preference as to which of these two quartets is the better; Professor Tovey calls the second Haydn's greatest instrumental composition. Both contain a depth of thought and a mastery of expression that have hardly been equaled by any other composer using this form, not even Beethoven himself.

ORATORIOS

After his return from London, where he had been much impressed by the oratorios of Handel, Haydn was moved to compose his two great works in this form. The interest in oratorio performances today has reached such a condition of insentient decrepitude that music lovers have few opportunities of hearing either *The Creation* or *The Seasons*. But a little study of their scores will show, as Bekker has said, that they are not primarily vocal works with orchestral accompaniment as the Handel oratorios are, but orchestral works completed and enhanced by chorus and soloists. Into them Haydn poured the full experiences of his long life in music, and it is here that we find his only attempts at " descriptive " writing; they are his crowning achievements in vocal music, for none of his early operas or church compositions have proved to be of importance. *The Seasons*, his last work, was finished in 1801, at just about the time Beethoven was writing his second symphony.

As it was from his English experiences that Haydn took his resolve to write oratorios, he seems to have drawn some inspiration from the English countryside for *The Seasons*; for, Ernest Newman has well said, as we listen to it, we seem to see " the cottages and cottagers and serving maids and horses and horsemen of the Morland engravings. Perhaps it is a generalized expression of the eighteenth-century way of looking at nature as something sweet and friendly in spite of its occasional discomfort." It was left to the more intense Romantics to find darker depths in Nature; for Haydn her beauties arouse gentle happiness or, as in *The Creation*, reverence, and the sense of sublimity. One strong charm of *The Seasons*, which might well be sung much oftener, for it contains some of the world's best pastoral music, is the poetry of the Scot, James Thomson — a good deal marred, alas, by Haydn's librettist. " The love of nature," says Coleridge, " seems to have led Thomson to a cheerful religion "; he would " carry his fellow men along with him into nature " (instead of fleeing to it from them, as, for example, Cowper did). Thomson and Haydn were well met, and it is worth anyone's while who is attracted by Haydn's music to go to Thomson's original poem for its quiet refreshment. Apart from its genial arias, such as " With joy the impatient husbandman," its trios with chorus, its fugal rallies, its suggestions of the sounds of nature, its hunting scene in autumn, its atmosphere of the winter fireside storytelling, there is a delightful series of open-air and domestic pictures which have never been bettered in music.

The Creation, beginning with an imaginative "representation of chaos" that looks forward to Weberian chromatic dramatics, adds high science to simple faith (to balance which boons, the librettist, vile but well-intentioned, added to and mutilated Milton's poetry). The famous depictions of the animals can be received with Haydn's own simple-hearted good will. Three archangels and the heavenly choir carry on the narrative through the six days of creation; but the work, though lengthy, is not long-winded, and it is a great pity to cut it in performance, as is usually done. In the choruses Haydn outshines Handel's humanity and perhaps equals his sublimity. Haydn is simple-minded, if you like, but his happy-hearted assurance enables him to avoid taking his belief in heaven too ponderously. Unlike the solemn philosopher who regretted that "cheerfulness would keep breaking in," he freely releases that spirit, and can find also, with few notes, a beautiful, strong feeling for the great moments of the narrative, such as the "Let there be light!" A few of the most famous of all arias are here: "With verdure clad," "Now heaven in fullest glory shone," "In native worth," and "On mighty pens majestic soars the eagle"; whilst the choruses "The heavens are telling" and "Achieved is the glorious work" have been for generations the delight of choirs.

Few experiences are more rewarding than to review Haydn's development as symphonist and master of chamber music and to close on the note of these choral works that take us back, more concentratedly, to that grand humanity, that wisdom spiced with the best of good humor, that colors so much of his work. Nothing is more likely, if approached in this spirit, to clinch our enjoyment of him as composer of some of the most cordial, refreshing music of the ages.

"IN SEARCH OF MOZART"

All my musical self-respect is based upon my keen appreciation of Mozart's works. It is still as true as it was before the Eroica Symphony *was written, that there is nothing better in art than Mozart's best. We have had Beethoven, Schubert, Mendelssohn, Schumann, Götz, and Brahms since his time: we have even had Dr. Parry, Professor Stanford, Mr. Cowen, Dr. Mackenzie, and Sir Arthur Sullivan; but the more they have left the Mozart quartet or quintet behind, the further it comes out ahead in its perfection of temper and refinement of consciousness.*

— Bernard Shaw: *Music in London*

The happiest artist is the one who furiously pursues his art without distraction from another world. It is when a man is torn between the passion of his intellect and the passion of his emotions that a crisis occurs.

— Anonymous

MOZART: THE NECESSITY FOR MATURITY OF TASTE

SOMETIME during the early years of the nineteenth century in London, Keats was moved to compose his famous "Ode on a Grecian Urn," which contains a good description of Mozart's music:

"When old age shall this generation waste,
Thou shalt remain, in midst of other woe
Than ours, a friend to man, to whom thou say'st,
'Beauty is truth, truth beauty — that is all
Ye know on earth, and all ye need to know.'"

For it is the awareness of the complete synonymity between truth and beauty in this music which constitutes its greatest appeal.

In the Preface to his huge biography of Mozart, Otto Jahn has described, tersely and effectively, the educative experience which most of the lovers of the music of this composer have undergone. He says:

"At a certain stage of our mental development, Mozart's music seemed cold and unintelligible to our restless spirit — turning to him in later years we were amazed alike at the wondrous wealth of his art and at our former insensibility to it."

Cardinal Newman has made a similar observation regarding the works of such classic authors as Homer and Horace:

"Passages, which to a boy are but rhetorical commonplaces, neither better nor worse than a hundred others, which any clever writer might supply . . . at length come home to him, when long years have passed, and he has had experience of life, and pierce him, as if he had never before known them, with their sad earnestness and vivid exactness. Then he comes to understand how it is that lines, the birth of some chance morning or evening at an Ionian festival or among the Sabine hills, have lasted generation after generation for thousands of years, with a power over the mind and a charm which the current literature of his own day, with all its obvious advantages, is utterly unable to reveal."

In so far as the great majority of individuals is concerned, the understanding of and love for such things as Mozart's music and Homer's poetry seem to be among the things in life which have to be acquired gradually and which can be fully possessed only when we are properly qualified to receive them.

We have said in the book *Discovering Music* that the education (using the word in its derivative meaning of a "leading on") of a music lover, if it takes a natural course, must necessarily go through certain definite and progressive stages. Initially we seem to be what Shaw has called "Titan fanciers," that is, we have a native, barbarous relish for everything that is big, impressive, and obvious. The reasons for this instinctive preferment of the grandiloquent over the simple and delicate are, as Nietzsche has said, lost in the domain of morals. But there is no doubt that most individuals are able early in their emotional development to enjoy the singer who can sing the highest and loudest and the composer whose muscular vigor seems to give a very definite assurance of the transport of his passion and the grandeur of his suffering.

The colorful and melancholic romance of Tchaikovsky, the vigorous dynamism of Beethoven, or the appealing transports of Wagner have meaning at the very beginning of a person's musical experience, whereas, to use Jahn's words, Mozart's music may well seem cold and unintelligible. Yet, inevitably, if the listener is sensitive enough to learn to be discriminating, as he hears more and more of this music, he will come under the spell of its tranquil perfection of style, its lyric sweetness, and its poignant depth of feeling. And he will come to realize that it is, in a sense, the *ultima thule* of musical experience, the point beyond which no progress can be made. Finally he will recognize that the calm serenity and the tranquil perfection which constitute so much of the essential beauty of this music, and which at first seemed rather obvious and naïve, are really the result of long conflict and fierce struggle.

Mozart's music is in the best sense of the word *classic*, for it represents in essence the great truths with which the mind of man is eternally concerned. And because these truths are uttered with such unbelievable ease and unparalleled euphony, they seem all the more plausible and convincing.

MUSIC VERSUS LIFE

In discussing the types of music which Bach, Handel, and Haydn wrote, we have said that they were strongly conditioned by the events of their lives. The same cannot be said of Mozart. In his case we are struck by the widely contrasting lines of his exterior and his creative life; they run, as has been often observed, in exactly contrary motion. His outward life started bravely and successfully in a number of grand tours all over Europe, displaying his powers as a *Wunderkind*; his middle years were given over to humiliating service for ungrateful patrons and underestimated labors for his family; at the end, after he had been crushed with debts and exhausted by overwork, came an early death and a pauper's grave. Creatively, his life progressed impressively in the other direction, from an early and almost unbelievable natural expressive ability to heights which represent the summits of musical composition.

It is easy to sentimentalize, as has been recently done by some of his biographers, the great injustices and the crying wrongs of Mozart's life. We see reflected in his music something of the joys and the sorrows, the humor and the gaiety, as well as the bitterness and the disillusionment, with which his life was filled. But by and large his life had only the most superficial connection with his music. His actual creative career was, as Margit Varro has so musically said, like a sustained melody

THE FOURTEEN-YEAR-OLD MOZART

(From a painting of 1770)

which, through a long and consistently maintained crescendo, came finally to its triumphant climax. Underneath this his physical life seems a modest and rather ineffectual counterpoint that, commencing on a promising note, ends in a complete silence.

THE TRAVELING PRODIGY

From his very earliest days (Mozart was born in Salzburg, January 27, 1756) this composer was plunged into a world of aristocratic patronage that was typical of the century. His father, Leopold, was fairly well known as a composer and was famous as the author of a violin method that was used all over Europe during the latter half of the eighteenth century. Wolfgang, as well as his sister Marianne, took to music as naturally as a duck to water: he was able to play the piano at three and to compose little pieces when he was five years of age. Later on, his father taught him the violin and the organ as well.

Convinced that he could exhibit his children as prodigies, Leopold took them on a tour of the fashionable world in 1762, presenting them in Munich and Vienna, and introducing them to the courts at both places with great success. This was the first of a number of similar tours which were undertaken during the next ten years, in the course of which the young Mozart was brought into contact not only with all the great court figures of the time in Vienna, Paris, London, the Hague, Florence, and Rome, but also with its outstanding musical personalities — such men as Johann Christian Bach, Rameau, Baron Grimm, Sammartini (teacher of Gluck), Farinelli (the great *castrato*), Padre Martini (Italy's grand old man of the period), Piccinni, Jommelli, Gluck, and Haydn.

It is impossible for us to realize what a tremendous influence all these different scenes, these various styles of music, must have had on this young, precocious lad with the phenomenal memory and the unbelievable powers of musicianship.[5] It has been often said that his music is the perfect blending of the Italian and German and French styles: the explanation of this fact lies in these early tours which he took under the supervision and guidance of his astute father. Given his natural endowments, perhaps greater than those of any other musician, his thorough technical training at the hand of his father, and this unusual opportunity of knowing what all the great and near-great minds of the world had said in music, he had every right to look forward, at the end of his last tour, undertaken when he was twenty-one, to an appointment that would give him his just place in an appreciative world.

[5] There are a number of stories regarding both of these. Perhaps the most impressive of them is the testimony of Schachtner, the court trumpeter at Salzburg, who said that Wolfgang's ear was so delicate that he could detect and remember to the next day a difference of half a quarter of a tone and so susceptible that he fainted the first time he heard a trumpet.

When he was in Rome in 1770 he went to the Sistine Chapel to hear Allegri's celebrated *Miserere;* when he came home after the performance, he was able to write out this entire contrapuntal composition, his copy needing only one or two corrections after he had heard the work a second time.

THE MOZART FAMILY, painted by De la Croce in 1780–1781
Mozart and his sister ("Nannerl") are at the piano, Leopold is standing, and in the background is the picture of the mother, who had died in 1778. The intimate nature of the relationships between the members of this family has been recently revealed through the publication of Emily Anderson's three-volume collection of the Mozart family letters.

This he never found, although he spent the rest of his short life looking for it. Owing to a peculiar concurrence of circumstances — his own impractical nature, his inability or disinclination to fit, as Haydn had done, into a more or less menial position as musician to one of the courts of the time, and the very fact that this whole court system upon which such patronage depended was beginning to break down of its own weight — Mozart spent most of his mature life in Vienna, eking out a precarious existence by teaching, composing, and giving concerts, and by borrowing money wherever he could. In the last ten years of this miserable physical existence, while he was exhausting himself in an effort to keep one step ahead of his creditors and give his family a fairly comfortable and reasonable life, he wrote all his great music — masterpieces that could not pay even for the meager demands he made on society. But they have secured his enduring place among the world's immortals. He died in 1791, at the age of thirty-five, when most men are just beginning to learn how to live.

HOW MOZART COMPOSED

It is in his music that we must seek to know Mozart. Of all types,[6] and covering as wide a range as Haydn's, the six hundred authentic works that we have from his pen were written in the short space of twenty years — an average of over thirty compositions a year. Contrary to his usual custom in such things, Mozart once wrote a detailed description of how he composed, a description which shows that it must have been an exceedingly rapid process. But even at that, the tremendous physical and mental energy necessary to turn out this amazing amount of sonatas, concertos, serenades, quartets, symphonies, chamber-music works, operas, and Masses — some of them among the greatest in the world — can hardly be imagined:

[6] The great Köchel catalogue, prepared by a Viennese botanist in an attempt to bring Mozart's hundreds of unnumbered works into some sort of decent order, lists the following classifications. This Köchel numeration is now universally used as a means of identifying the works of this prolific composer, the numbers referring to items in this catalogue.

Operas, 22
Church music, 60 various compositions — hymns, motets, Masses, etc.
Arias with orchestra, 54
Songs with voice and piano, 36
Choral works with orchestra, oratorio, cantatas, etc., 7
Music for several voices unaccompanied, 24 compositions, most of them canons
Miscellaneous choral works, 20
Symphonies, 52
Miscellaneous orchestral works, 96 *divertimenti*, serenades, dances, etc.
Concertos for piano and orchestra, 25
Concertos for violin and orchestra, 12
Other concertos, 14
Sonatas for organ and orchestra, 3
Sonatas for organ and strings, 14
String quintets, 5
String quartets, 24
String trios and duets, 5
Piano quartets, 2
Piano trios, 8
Miscellaneous chamber compositions, 15
Works for violin and piano, 38
Works for piano solo, 60 sonatas, variations, rondos, etc.
Works for piano four hands, 10
Works for two pianos, 2
Miscellaneous, 5 works for harmonica, mechanical organ, unspecified instruments

"When I am, as it were, completely myself, entirely alone, and of good cheer — say, traveling in a carriage, or walking after a good meal, or during the night when I cannot sleep; it is on such occasions that my ideas flow best and most abundantly. Whence and how they come, I know not; nor can I force them. Those ideas that please me I retain in memory, and am accustomed, as I have been told, to hum them to myself. If I continue in this way, it soon occurs to me how I may turn this or that morsel to account, so as to make a good dish of it, that is to say, agreeably to the rules of counterpoint, to the peculiarities of the various instruments, etc.

"All this fires my soul, and, provided I am not disturbed, my subject enlarges itself, becomes methodized and defined, and the whole, though it be long, stands almost complete and finished in my mind, so that I can survey it, like a fine picture or a beautiful statue, at a glance. Nor do I hear in my imagination the parts successively, but I hear them, as it were, all at once. What a delight this is I cannot tell! All this inventing, this producing, takes place in a pleasing lively dream. Still the actual hearing of the *tout ensemble* is after all the best. What has been produced I do not easily forget, and this is perhaps the best gift I have my Divine Maker to thank for.

"When I proceed to write down my ideas, I take out of the bag of my memory, if I may use that phrase, what has previously been collected into it the way I have mentioned. For this reason the committing to paper is done quickly enough, for everything is, as I said before, already finished; and it rarely differs on paper from what it was in my imagination. At this occupation I can therefore suffer myself to be disturbed; for whatever may be going on around me, I write, and even talk, but only of fowls and geese, or of Gretel or Bärbel or some such matters. But why my productions take from my hand that particular form and style that makes them Mozartish, and different from the works of other composers, is probably owing to the same cause which renders my nose so large or so aquiline, or, in short, makes it Mozart's, and different from those of other people. For I really do not study or aim at any originality."

— Holmes: *Life of Mozart* [7]

[7] This letter is supposed to have been written to a Baron von P. in 1789 and was first published in the *Allgemeine musikalische Zeitung* in 1815. Various Mozart biographers consider it a forgery, and Emily Anderson, in her great collection of Mozart letters, says that it is obviously spurious. The majority of Mozart's letters are so natural and non-literary in style that one is led to question the authenticity of this one. But if it was not from Mozart's hand, it must have been written by one who knew his habits well, for it is an excellent account of how he brought his music to paper.

TRACING HIS DEVELOPMENT

It is entirely possible to trace Mozart's course of development by means of representative compositions taken from the various periods of his life; and such a procedure gives an intimate and unforgettable picture of the amazing spiritual progress which this genius made as his short life unfolded itself amid exterior circumstances that were not too encouraging at its beginning and became steadily worse as it progressed.

Take, for example,[8] the *Andante* movement from the little *D Major Symphony* (K. 112), written when Wolfgang was a boy of fifteen, while he was in Milan composing a serenade for performance there; Italianate as it can be, galant in manner, its form is taut and sure. But there is little of the spirit that was to come later. While he was working on it, he sent this characteristic letter home:

"I cannot write much, firstly, because I know not what to say; secondly, because my fingers already ache from writing. . . . I am always blowing my little whistle, and no one answers."

The works of the next year, 1772, are the first, according to Wyzewa and Saint-Foix (the French writers whose authentic work on Mozart has done a great deal to re-create an interest in his music), to show the hand of a real genius. They possess something of a romantic frenzy, showing that even this young lad of sixteen, trained according to the traditions and in the midst of all the glory of the eighteenth century, was beginning to respond to the new ideas astir in the world — ideas that were later to shake it to its foundations and establish new political and humanistic ideals. Listen to the nervous first movement of the *Divertimento in F* (K. 138), or the delicious dissonances and romantic feeling of its *Andante*, and the suggestion of Wyzewa and Saint-Foix's that Mozart was suffering a touch of *Sturm und Drang* will seem reasonable enough. There is sufficient romantic feeling in this music that was probably written for the occasion of accompanying a routine function of the Salzburg court to give it a new note of passionate expressiveness. But the little *Symphony in C Major* (K. 200), written the next year, shows nothing

[8] These works are chosen partly because of their availability on phonograph records.

Courtesy of the Bärenreiter Publishing Company, Germany

THE TWENTY–ONE–YEAR–OLD MOZART
(From an oil painting of 1777 in the Liceo Musicale, Bologna)

of this adolescent striving; it is music of pure delight, written by a youth to whom the writing of music was as effortless as any of the procreative processes of nature. Mozart never seemed to have had any trouble with the form in which his thoughts were to be clothed. In these works, as in all his music, it is crystal clear and perfectly suited to its purpose.

The year after the American colonists decided, in July, 1776, that they were and " of right ought to be, free and independent " citizens of their own land, Wolfgang sounded a Declaration of Independence of his own. Realizing that he could not go on forever as a sort of court servant to the tyrannical Archbishop of Salzburg, he began to cast about for new ways of advancing himself. Knowing that the career of a piano virtuoso offered possibilities, he commenced writing concertos and other piano music in which the virtuoso elements were, for the first time, emphasized. The lovely and dramatic *E Flat Concerto* (K. 271), composed for a French player, Mlle. Jeunhomme, shows this new instinct for keyboard display admirably. It was finished just before Mozart started on the last of his great tours, the journey to Paris, undertaken when he was twenty-one. He never achieved a more genuine, heartfelt emotion than that expressed in the *Andantino* of this work; and the cadenza just before the end of it is one that was written down by the composer himself (he usually left these to be improvised by the player) and shows us exactly how he wished these accessory virtuoso elements to sound. The coruscating rondo, brilliant and inspired, is full of youthful enthusiasm; it is a fine illustration of Italian lyricism adapted to the instrumental medium.

It was on this Parisian journey that the boy, now come of age, also achieved something of independence in the matter of his family relationships. Away from his father, who had thought it prudent to remain in Salzburg, and accompanied only by his mother, Wolfgang took advantage of his freedom by falling in love, not once, but over and over again. First it was a rather naughty cousin in Augsburg, then a Mlle. Rose, daughter of Cannabich, the conductor of the famous Mannheim orchestra, "a very beautiful and charming young girl," according to his own account; she was followed by Mlle. Gustl, daughter of the Mannheim flautist Wendling, and finally by Aloysia Weber, a gay young opera singer, daughter of the impecunious prompter and copyist of the Mannheim opera.

But nothing came of it all, even the expected opportunities in Paris. A capable young musician of twenty-two was an entirely different proposition for the Paris impresarios than the sensational young seven-year-old who had visited the city fifteen years before. In spite of a few performances of his works and a great deal of running to and fro, he finally had to write his father: "I have not yet got to know anyone. . . . They know what they have to do and that is enough." His mother, alone and homesick, became ill and finally died; and Wolfgang, disappointed and regretful, left Paris to return to his old life in Salzburg, where the prince bishop received him again and made him court organist at the munificent salary of 500 florins a year.

Here he lived for two years, unhappy and unknown. But out of this period there came some of his most delectable works, among them the spontaneous and perfectly constructed *Violin Sonata in B Flat* (K. 378), a *Sinfonia Concertante* for violin and viola (K. 364) which shows how wonderfully he understood the possibilities of both these instruments, and one of the finest symphonies, the *Symphony in C Major* (K. 338), a work which is deserving of more hearings than it gets. Ghéon characterizes this little masterpiece well when he says that Mozart never wrote anything that was firmer, more flowing, or more perfectly balanced, halfway between amusement and conviction, subtlety and ardor, grace and strength. He rather heretically adds that conductors might well substitute it for one of the three later Mozart symphonies they are always giving us — the *E Flat Symphony*, the *G Minor Symphony*, and the *Jupiter Symphony*.

In March, 1781, Mozart rather suddenly received a summons from the archbishop to join him in Vienna. The young musician immediately left his detested native city, never to return, except for a visit to his father. Vienna was his home for the rest of his life — not a very appreciative one, unfortunately, for the times and circumstances did not seem right there for the encouragement of a musician of Mozart's stamp. He established himself, however, and decided, much against his father's will, to marry. The bride of his choice was none other than Constanze Weber, the sister of the singer Aloysia who had jilted him in Mannheim. In the midst of all sorts of unpleasant domestic intrigue — for the girl's mother was as anxious for the marriage as Wolfgang's father was against it [9] — and the excitement incident to writing an opera, *The Abduction*

[9] Even Ghéon suggests that Frau Weber may have taken advantage of the situation and "forced the young man to bring to light his still confused feelings in the form of a premature declaration." This is the way Mozart explained it to his father:

"Now to come to the written assurance of my honorable intentions towards the girl. You know that they have a trustee, the father being dead. Certain officious and impertinent persons must needs fill this man's ears (he knows nothing about me) with all sorts of stories about me — how there was need to beware of me — that I was perpetually with her — that I might jilt her, and that then the girl would be ruined, etc. The trustee swallowed all this — for the mother, who knows me and knows me to be honorable, let things take their course, and said nothing to him of the matter.

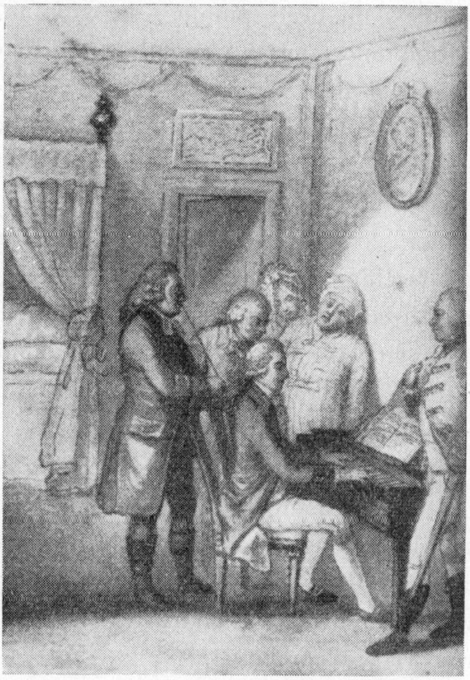

Courtesy of the Stadtmuseum, Salzburg

MOZART IN THE CIRCLE OF HIS SALZBURG FRIENDS

Colored drawing of about 1780 by Schütz

from the Seraglio, on the very eve of his marriage, Mozart took time to write a serenade for his old friends, the Haffners, in Salzburg.

For all our intercourse consisted in the fact that I lodged with them and afterwards visited the house daily. No man ever saw me with her outside the house. This gentleman filled the mother's ears with his representations till she told me of it and begged me to speak to him myself as he was to come that very day. He came. We talked — the result was that he told the mother to forbid me all intercourse with her daughter until I had settled the matter with him in writing. . . . What other course was open to me? I had either to give my written promise, or agree not to see the girl. What man who loves with truth and constancy can absent himself from his beloved? Might not the mother, might not the beloved one herself, place the most dreadful interpretation upon it? I accordingly drew up a document, promising to wed Mademoiselle Constanze Weber within the space of three years. In the unlikely event of my changing my mind she should have a claim on me of 300 florins a year. But what did the divine girl do as soon as the trustee was gone? She asked her mother for the document, and said to me, 'Dear Mozart! I need no written assurance from you — I trust your word — thus!' And she tore up the paper!" (*Letters of Mozart*, translated by Bozman)

" My heart is restless, my head spinning," he wrote to his father. . . . " How can one think and compose something worth while in such a state. What will come of it? "

What came of it was some of the most graceful music he ever wrote, full of a gaiety and delicate perfection that suggests anything but the pain of the quarrels which he was suffering at the time of its composition. (The " Haffner " *Symphony in D,* K. 385, was afterward arranged from this music.) Nothing he ever did better illustrates the complete disparity between Mozart the human individual and Mozart the artist. Overworked, distraught with alternate joy at his coming marriage and despair at his father's attitude, burdened with the thousand and one things incident to the production of an opera, he was nevertheless so little concerned with all these exterior details as to be able to write music of such quality as to prove a surprise even to himself when he came to rearrange it later. Mozart once wrote to one of his benefactors that he would like to have everything good, pure, and beautiful; and seemingly he was able to will it so in his music, no matter what the exterior circumstances under which it was composed.

He was finally able to marry and settle down, his troubles, for the time being at least, over. Some of the fire in his blood was communicated to his music. Listen to the superb *Fantasia in C Minor* for the piano [10] (K. 396), composed at this time, and so powerful as to suggest Beethoven. He had more quiet in which to work and devoted a great deal of time to studying the works of Bach and Haydn. Out of this there came the great set of six quartets, modeled after Haydn's style and using all his technical means as well as some of Bach's contrapuntal skill. The first of these was written on the last night of the first year of his marriage. The second, in D minor (K. 421), was written down (it had probably been composed in his mind long before) during the night of his wife's first confinement;

10 There are two C minor fantasias for the piano by Mozart; the one most frequently programmed is the later one, listed by Köchel as number 475. But this earlier work presents Mozart in a new light, especially as regards his piano music. While the classic style is carefully preserved throughout, there is a tremendous communication of emotional and physical power that can only be thought of as Romantic. If properly interpreted, this great fantasia is a gigantic introduction to the whole Romantic Movement in music.

yet it shows no trace whatever of these circumstances. Of all his quartets, it is perhaps the most completely detached from the concerns of this world, its spirit entirely empyrean. The last of this set of quartets, the one in C major (K. 465), is celebrated because of its dissonant introduction. A great deal has been written about this, in an attempt to explain that it must be great because it is incomprehensible. The most obvious explanation would seem to be that, for once, Mozart simply did not achieve what he intended; the harmonies of these opening measures in this quartet remain as " confused, obscure, and artificial " as they were thought to be by the critics of the time. It is merely a piece of writing that does not come off when played.

In the early part of 1785 Leopold came on to Vienna to visit his son. He wrote home to his daughter:

> " On Saturday evening we had Herr Josef Haydn and the two Barons Tindi with us, and the new quartets were played — the three new ones [K. 458, 464, 465] he has composed in addition to the ones we already know [K. 387, 421, 428]. The new ones are a little easier than the first three, indeed, but excellently written. Herr Haydn said to me, ' I tell you, calling God as witness and speaking as a man of honor, that your son is the greatest composer I know, either personally or by repute! He has taste, and, in addition, the most complete understanding of composition.' "
>
> — *Letters of Mozart*, translated by Bozman

At the end of March, Leopold returned to Salzburg. Father and son were never to meet again.

" These," Mozart once wrote during this period, " are the academies at which I have to play [he meant concerts which he must organize, for which he must sell the tickets, compose the music, and appear as soloist]:

> " Thursday, Feb. 26th, at the Galitzins
> Monday, March 1st, at Joh. Esterhazys
> Thursday, March 4th, at the Galitzins
> Friday, March 5th, at the Esterhazys
> Monday, March 8th, *idem.*
> Thursday, March 11th, at the Galitzins
> Wednesday, March 17th, my first private concert "

Not a very light schedule for one who, in addition, must teach all morning long and try to find time to devote to composition as well. But the academies were occasions for which new music must be forthcoming. During his twenty-ninth and thirtieth years Mozart was very much sought after for these fashionable affairs; and if he had been at all provident in the usual sense, he could have been much better off financially as a result. But when he had money, he liked to spend it gaily, and it was his custom to give these rich patrons everything he had without receiving very much for it. We do not know whether his audiences realized what he was giving them: probably they did not. We of a later generation are the ones who have profited by all this activity, for out of this busy period there came the piano concertos and *Figaro*.

THE PIANO CONCERTOS

The piano concertos, although they represent the essential Mozart at the very height of his powers and in the most favorable light, are, for some reason, not often played. Perhaps it is because the great concertos of the Romantic composers are so much more rewarding from the modern virtuoso's point of view, and so much easier to play. There is nothing Gargantuan about these Mozart works, nothing that can satisfy the exhibitionist; but their crisp brilliance, their graceful pianistic line standing out in clear relief against the complementary voices of the orchestra, represent such raptures of freedom and such improvisatory exaltation that the few pianists qualified to play them properly can achieve their greatest artistic triumphs with them.

It was the custom in Mozart's time for the virtuoso to improvise in public; and no one, if we can trust the witness of contemporaries, ever excelled Mozart as an improvisator. Endowed with a facile imagination, a perfect memory, a brilliant technique and an innate sense of what was beautiful, in his extemporary performances he seemed able to loose his daemonic power to the full. And in the piano concertos — this opinion is not general — he came nearer to obtaining this creative freshness and enthusiasm than in anything else he put down on paper. Of the twenty-five works in this form that he left us, twelve belong to this virtuoso period between 1782 and 1786. These twelve are not all equal in content, by any means, there being a number of very conventional movements in them; but they contain, among other wonders, the slow movement of the *A Major Concerto* (K. 414), the first and last movements of the great *D Minor Concerto* (K. 466), the whole of the *E Flat Major Concerto* (K. 482), and the ineffably beautiful *Andante* of the *A Major Concerto* (K. 488). In all these movements, one feels that a perfect balance has been achieved between piano and orchestra, the piano being at one and the same time an essential part of the ensemble, yet never overwhelming or competing with it, as so often happens in the later concertos. These works seem spontaneous and fresh, as if, as one of Mozart's contemporaries put it, they were a *game;* but we know how true was Mozart's reply to this suggestion: "Oh, I, too, had to work hard before being what I am!" Covering, as they do, all phases of the composer's life, these compositions are a fair epitome of his work.

THE NOTE OF SADNESS

Anyone who listens to Mozart's music for a time will sense an element of sadness, reverie, melancholy — call it whatever he may. In the midst of some joyous flight of melody — and no one can be more joyous than Mozart — we are suddenly conscious of this spirit of sadness. Sometimes it is no more than a passing shadow, as, for instance, the chromatic inflection of the second theme of the first movement in the *G Minor Symphony;* at other times Mozart indulges this mood at some length, as in the brooding opening measures of the *D Minor Piano Concerto* (K. 466); more often than not he gives over his whole slow movements to it, the most beautiful examples being the *Adagio* of the *G Minor Quintet* (K. 516) and the marvelous *Andante* of the *E Flat Piano Concerto* (K. 482). What is the meaning of this melancholic touch in the music of an artist who, seemingly above all others, was so vitally and joyously alive and did not hesitate to be prodigal of his life in his art?

Ghéon suggests that the answer is to be found in a letter to his father written in 1787, upon hearing of the latter's serious illness:

"... I have accustomed myself always to expect the worst in all circumstances [the psychologists would probably explain such an attitude as the source of so much of the serenity that is found in Mozart]. Since death, when we come to consider it, is the true end of life, I have made the acquaintance, for some years now, of this best and truest friend of man, so that his image no longer frightens me, but suggests, on the contrary, peace and consolation. And I thank God for giving me the opportunity ... of coming to recognize him as the key to true happiness. I never go to bed without thinking that, young as I am, I may perhaps never see another day; and yet no one who really knows me can say that I am morose or sad with my fellows! I thank my Creator every day of my life for this blessing, and wish with all my heart that I might share it with my fellow men."

— *Letters of Mozart,* translated by Bozman

And so Mozart pours out in his music this conception of death as the real end of life, its full accomplishment and final appeasement.

This sense of the immutability of the law of nature, the inevitability of death, was a source of artistic inspiration long before the author of Ecclesiastes wrote, sometime back in the pre-Christian centuries:

"For that which befalleth the sons of men befalleth the beasts; even one thing befalleth them: as the one dieth, so dieth the other ... so that a man hath no pre-eminence above a beast: for all is vanity.

"Wherefore I perceive that there is nothing better than that a man should rejoice in his own works; for that is his portion: for who shall bring him to see what shall be after him?"

Great artists have a way of universalizing such sentiments as these that are common to all men. We feel this quality of regretful reverie over the futility of human existence in the music of many a composer — in Beethoven's last quartets; in that magnificent set of four songs which marks the end of Brahms's creative career (the *Vier ernste Gesänge*), set to the words which we have quoted from Ecclesiastes; and in Mahler's *Lied von der Erde*. But nowhere has it been productive of greater beauty than in the works of Mozart; with him there is no sense of struggle and bitter renunciation such as we find in some of the works of the Romantics. Everything is tranquilly calm and peacefully resigned, happily sad, if such an expression can mean anything. And it is all pure music; there are no literary or other extra-musical associations necessary. Out of the quality of his melodies, the poignancy of his rhythms, and the coloring of his instrumentation, Mozart has been able to create an abstract type of expression that reveals to us the deepest secrets of his heart. Not to know this aspect of his music is to miss one of his most essential qualities.

THE LAST THREE SYMPHONIES

So much has been written about the last three symphonies, composed in the thirty-third summer of his life, that any attempt to elaborate on their qualities here would be repetitious. Written in quick succession — the *Symphony in E Flat* (K. 543) finished on June 26, the *Symphony in G Minor* (K. 550) on July 25, and the *Symphony in C Major* (*Jupiter*) on August 10 — it seems as if he must have realized that the candle of his life was nearly burned out. His letters of the time are full of distress and misery: "if you could and would lend me 100 florins, I should be very greatly obliged to you . . . my circumstances are such that I must absolutely get money — in whom am I to put my trust? . . . if you should perhaps be unable to lend me so large a sum, I beg of you to lend me a few hundred gulden, at least until tomorrow."

Yet there is nothing of all this in these great works which mark the apogee of his creative ability: perfectly balanced, beautifully written, they seem as if they must have been the product of Augustan leisure and plenty. The *Symphony in G Minor* is the most popular of all Mozart's works — perhaps deservedly so. In the great *Jupiter Symphony* there is more of the provenance of the Jovian attributes of lawgiving, of truth and justice royally dispersed, than of bolt-throwing or war. This work contains some of Mozart's most advanced and provocative writing, some of it definitely experimental and looking forward to the developments that were to come. It finishes with what is surely the most astonishing example of fugality since Bach.

During the remaining three years of his life, Mozart wrote very little music for the orchestra: he may have felt that he had already expressed everything he wished to say in these three great symphonies. The *Clarinet Quintet in A* (K. 581) was the only instrumental work of importance before the end; but what a work it is! As skillfully written and as full of deep feeling as anything he ever did, its melodies so fill our minds that nothing else seems to matter. All lovers of Mozart will be inclined to agree with Ghéon's statement that in this work, from the very first measure, there is nothing that seems to jar, " not a single gap, a superfluous ornament "; and yet in it there is a deep sorrow and a yearning sadness. The incomparably gay and Rococo *opera buffa, Cosi fan tutte*, and the strangely fantastic *Zauberflöte* also belong to these last years, as does the controversial *Requiem*. It is necessary to keep in mind the mixed origin of this work in listening to it — the fact that not all of it is by Mozart. Indeed his friend Süssmayr claimed the authorship of the greater part of it, with justice, in so far as the truth may be known. But the glorious opening movement with its great double fugue shows Mozart at his best, even if comparatively little of the remainder (whether Süssmayr's or Mozart's) does.

The serious illness of his wife, who, after years of struggle with poverty and the strain incident to the bringing up of a family, finally broke down in 1789, hastened Mozart's end. The last months of this short life do not make pleasant reading: his attempt to finish the *Requiem;* his utter physical collapse and cruel passing; the hurried funeral, with no music and only a few friends; the committal of the body to a grave in the paupers' section of the cemetery, with no one but the undertakers present; and the unfortunate loss of record as to where even this poor tomb is located. But he was able to leave behind him abundant witness to the fact that he had reached the highest point of civilization to which the art of music has attained.

THE CLIMACTIC FIGURE OF THE CENTURY

In concluding any consideration of Mozart's place in musical history, we need especially to emphasize one point, namely, that he stands as the culmination of the eighteenth century, its last and most perfect product, and has little to do with the nineteenth century. His music is representative of the classic spirit of his time at its best; for it seems to dwell, to use the phrase of Sainte-Beuve, at the very source and center of all existence and to be able to move, as occasion arises, in any direction. In it there is none of the exaggeration and straining of emphasis that we sometimes find in the works of later composers; it seems to have assimilated completely the styles of all music up to its time and to have made them its own; there is in it that balance and proportion that was so dear to the minds of the period. Combined with all these qualities there is a universality that makes this music unique and that needs no interpretation in terms of other composers.

Yet we often hear conductors, steeped in the traditions of the Romantic school and awed by the greatness of its figures, try to make this music speak with the accents of the nineteenth century. Too often, like Jacob of old, they try to deceive. The hands may be those of Mozart, right enough; but the voice is certainly that of Beethoven. *Feeling* does not have to be read into this music — it is there already and will be evident enough if it is left to speak for itself. But it is always feeling subordinated to something that is higher than itself. This must be recognized in any proper interpretation of Mozart.

After all, he was, as Rossini said, *the only one*. There has never been another like him; and he loses rather than gains when we try to make him other than he was.

AN OPERATIC APEX

MOZART AND HIS OPERATIC BACKGROUND

QUITE aside from their own individual qualities, the operas of Mozart deserve special consideration in any study of the history of music, for not only do they epitomize and aggrandize the tendencies which had manifested themselves in this style of writing up to their time, but they also laid the foundations for a great deal of the subsequent operatic works written in France, Italy, and Germany. Mozart's operas bring the eighteenth century to an end; they also start a new era, one which greatly influenced the Italian writers of the nineteenth century as well as the Romantic reformers, Weber and Wagner.

We have seen how Mozart left untouched no species of music current in his day: church music, concertos, symphonies, chamber music, popular *divertimenti* and serenades, piano sonatas, operas — he tried them all. But there seems to be considerable difference of opinion among the critics as to the type in which he was supreme. A noted English writer on the opera [11] says, for example, that the works in which Mozart is most intensely himself are the operas; while an equally famous German critic [12] maintains that he was originally and essentially an instrumental composer and that considerable "discrimination is indicated" in the matter of his operas. Where there is such a wide difference of opinion among the doctors, the ordinary listener may well be encouraged to form his own opinions; but however we may rank the operas of Mozart, it is well to keep always in mind that their particular quality is due not only to the fact that their composer was a man of outstanding genius, but also that he wrote just when he did — at the end of the eighteenth century.

Review the scene briefly. Back of him stands the two-century-old tradition of Italian opera, a tradition based originally on the lofty ideals of truthfulness and freedom in vocal declamation, but which, in the course of its development, had become sadly debased and was chiefly concerned with the display of the melodic possibilities of the human voice. But always, even though the Italian *opera seria* was made up largely of a long series of floridly melodic arias, it maintained a certain aristocratic and graceful elegance which was peculiar to itself and which a genius such as Mozart could stir into new life. Paralleling this serious opera was the *opera buffa* — light opera — which had arisen out of a derisive and lively parodying of the grand opera by those who felt its unnaturalness and wanted to do something to relieve it. By the time of Mozart this light opera had achieved a definite superiority over its ostentatious predecessor because of its superior wit and sense of lively dramatic development. Here was a form ready for the vitalizing hand of a composer such as Mozart, its juxtaposition of elements from the classic comedy and its plots of inevitable disguise, mistaken identity, and the rest,

11 Edward J. Dent.
12 Alfred Einstein.

with those of political and artistic parody and sentimental episodes, perfectly adapted to his naturally brilliant style.

But, most important of all was the rise of a newly developed and graciously skilled element of musical expression, the classic orchestra; capable not only of imitating the grace and elegance of contemporary singing, but also of infusing a new tenderness and emotion into music, this instrument became an outstanding feature of the period. Mozart's immediate predecessors had established the norm of its organization and had shown how to write music for it; and his own natural inclinations and early environment gave him a thorough grounding in its style. He it was who first successfully utilized this symphonic technique to give an adequate background to the vocal elements in his operas. There have been many others who have followed, but none who have surpassed him in this.

HIS OPERAS MIRRORS OF MAN

These are only the materials which Mozart found ready to his hand; they do not in themselves explain the incomparable quality of such works as *Le Nozze di Figaro* or *Don Giovanni* or *Cosi fan tutte.* His great genius lay in his ability to take these elements that we have mentioned, these conventional styles and technical resources, and, through his powers of dramatic characterization, to weld them into a truthful mirror of human conduct. With all their eighteenth-century conventions, the operas just named are filled with real characters, each of them carefully delineated musically; they have dramatic continuity and climax; they are able to portray psychological motives of considerable complexity with deftness and surety. And they do all this without violating in any sense the principles of good musical form. Mozart did not hesitate to use all the means which he inherited from his predecessors — the aria, the overture, the recitative, and so forth: he added to these certain technical achievements perfected by his immediate precursors in the way of ensemble numbers by a group of singers; and the finale, a scene which in its very confusion of having all the characters singing at once and the audience not being able to follow anything clearly enough to know just what was happening, necessitated the fall of the curtain to bring the act to any sort of reasonable conclusion.

But in using all these he was wise enough never to allow the dramatic elements to overweigh his musical necessities, as his great follower, Wagner, often does; nor did he allow the possibility of a *coup de théâtre* to overbalance his inherent sense of dramatic propriety, as the Italians Donizetti, Bellini, and even Verdi are wont to do. Without being in any sense a reformer, Mozart was able to achieve, in the words of Alfred Einstein, a miraculous harmony of profound dramatic truth and characterization with perfect musical form. It is in this that his peculiar preeminence and distinction lie.

OPERA SERIA

His operatic works fall naturally into various groups: *opera seria, opera buffa,* and the German operas. Most of the *opere serie* were written during his youth and, with their rather slavish following of the convention of the Neapolitan school — sketchy recitative, bravura arias, and so on — are hardly representative of Mozart at his best. They comprise the following operas:

La finta Semplice, written in Vienna in 1768, but not produced until 1769 in Salzburg (The idea of the composer's writing this work came from the emperor, according to Mozart's father.)

Mitridate Re di Ponto, produced in Milan under the composer's direction in 1770

Lucio Scilla, ordered for performance in Milan, 1772

Idomeneo, the first mature work, written when he was twenty-five and, unfortunately, seldom performed today (Critics are united in proclaiming this to be his best serious opera because of its fine treatment of arias and concerted pieces.)

La Clemenza di Tito, written in haste on commission for the coronation of Leopold II, King of Bohemia, at Prague in 1791 (One of Mozart's few failures, it seems to have been impossible to give this work any semblance of dramatic life.)

OPERA BUFFA

In the field of the *opera buffa* Mozart accomplished his greatest achievements, for it was this genre, so admirably cultivated by the eighteenth-century Italian dramatists, that he seemed to find most congenial. Rarely seeking heroic stature, the Italians nevertheless, better than anyone else, seem to have been able to hit off the lighter humors of the world; and they have created, time and time again, stage conventions that the world delightedly agrees to, however unlike life they may be. When the argument is not high, we can the more easily be pleased; we do not feel called upon for too critical an approach and are willing to accept the result as an amusing, satiric set of comedies, wonderfully suited to the exigencies of the stage. The leading eighteenth-century exponents of this Italian comedic spirit were Carlo Goldoni (1707–1793), who wrote many of his one hundred fifty comedies in France, where he settled as Italian master to the royal family, and Carlo Gozzi (1720–1806). Both men were natives of Venice and portrayed a comic, if somewhat conventionalized, picture of the events and life of their period; but they did more. It has been said that the one aim which steadily pervaded all Goldoni's writings, no matter what their comic or satiric qualities, was the advancement of honorable sentiments and the correction of the prevailing vices and follies of the day. In one of his plays, he says: "Nature has made us all equals, and nature has taught us that we are all made of the same clay." He contrived plots to show that the promptings of nature are virtuous and should be cultivated.

In this Goldoni was ably seconded by the popular eighteenth-century French playwright, Beaumarchais, who, in his witty and shrewd comedies *The Barber of Seville* and *The Marriage of Figaro,* gave such a convincing picture of the decadence of the nobility and reflected so patently the feeling of the common folk of the time, that the latter play was personally banned by Louis XVI. It was only after the firm and independent author had fought this royal censorship for five years that *The Marriage of Figaro* was finally allowed production at the Théâtre Français in 1784. Its tremendous success is a matter of history; and it is still played the world over.

Courtesy of Mozart Museum, Salzburg

MOZART IN 1782 (from an incompleted portrait by Lange)

"THE MARRIAGE OF FIGARO"

Little wonder then that Mozart and his rather disreputable librettist, a Venetian Jew by the name of Lorenzo da Ponte, former professor of rhetoric at Treviso and at the time the court poet of Vienna, selected Beaumarchais's popular comedy as the basis for an *opera buffa*. Da Ponte, whatever his other qualities, was a thorough man of the theater and was able to concoct a brilliant, scintillating libretto which exactly fitted Mozart's rapierlike wit and power of characterization. There is nothing of the original political allusion and universal import of the play left in the libretto: Da Ponte shifted the emphasis and has tried merely to amuse us in the Italian manner typical of the century; his plot of intrigue has no serious intentions whatever and centers upon the fickleness of a count who spends his life pursuing pretty girls, especially Susanna, the maid-in-waiting to his wife. The fact that Susanna is betrothed to Figaro, the count's valet and clever man of the world, makes for all sorts of amusing imbroglios. In the course of the opera's development, the plot becomes so involved, and there are so many subsidiary complots and cross intrigues, changes of disguise, and misinterpreted designs, that the confusion of the listener is complete, especially at the conclusion of the whole thing, where all the principal characters are wandering about in a dark garden scene, each of them misinterpreting the intentions of the others. But it does not really matter: Mozart keeps our interest throughout; everything is as light as a feather, perfect in its precision, gay as a marriage bell, completely formal and yet entrancingly human.

Without detracting in the least from the impetuous brilliance of the characteristic comedy of manners which Da Ponte had fashioned for him, Mozart brings the libretto to life through his score: the spirit, temper, and reality of the whole opera comes from the music. Staged by means of a number of short scenes, it passes before we are hardly aware of its existence. The outstanding features, as we have hinted, are the solo arias and the concerted act finales; but even the recitatives, which up to this time had been largely formal and were used merely for getting over the action and most of the talk, are made an essential part of the make-up of the whole. *The Marriage of Figaro* is the first and almost the last opera of its kind,[13] inimitable in its perfection; it will always stand, in the minds of many of Mozart's admirers, as his most characteristic work — the consummate creation of a musician who was in the same degree a dramatist.

[13] As we shall see later, Rossini's *Barber of Seville*, based likewise on Beaumarchais, is worthy to be placed alongside of *Figaro;* but there are no others.

Without going into any of the details of the involved plot of *The Marriage of Figaro*, a few instances of its method of musical characterization may be pointed out as typical of the smooth skill and utter perfection of its development. There never seems to be any quarrel between psychologist and poet, as is so often the case in operatic plots: as Ghéon says, in *Figaro* we feel that the one dissects and analyzes the human machine with a lucid coldness, while the other puts it together again and composes the proper music for it, tenderly and lovingly. The two together make the one inimitable genius — Mozart. At the very opening of the opera his power is felt, as Figaro and Susanna are chattering, not in the usual detached recitative, but in a duet which gives immediately an exact idea of their respective characters. As Susanna tells Figaro about the master's designs on her, the music shows us her nature and also tells us what Figaro thinks about this news, surprising even to him. The later arias sung by Figaro and Dr. Bartolo demonstrate by their character how Figaro resolves to outwit his master through the subtle manipulation of plots, and how Bartolo, whose chief ambition in life is to discredit Figaro, sings a different tune, one full of heavy conceit and pompous hate. The orchestral accompaniment of the first is full of lightheaded confidence; in the second it seems to urge on the villain's rage.

Cherubino's first aria (*Non so più cosa son*) shows us his adolescent ardor, as well as the doubts and hopes of young love; again the character is clearly limned, and we are able to know exactly what sort of individual this ardent page really is. With the lament of the countess for the passing of her husband's love, *Porgi amor*, the atmosphere of humorous intrigue vanishes for the moment; we hear, in the purity of the melody and in the sympathy of the harmony and the orchestration, proof of the singer's faithfulness. Indeed, we might be tempted to hate the count, did not we remember that this is, after all, artificial eighteenth-century comedy, not nineteenth-century realism. For Mozart so grips our interest and arouses our sympathy for the innocent woman as to make us forget, for a moment, that the plot demands that she should be deceived. But at the end of the opera, Mozart conveys the idea clearly enough that, though the count seems humbled and subdued, he will hardly remain faithful to his wife for more than a day or two at a time.

The artless love song which Cherubino sings to please the countess, *Voi che sapete,* is perhaps the aria most widely sung apart from the opera. In it he describes what love is like; immediately we are in its spirit of the tender, genuine, dewy-fresh feeling of adolescence, widely different from the music of the countess. Such a concerted piece as the exacting sextet of the third act, *Riconosci in questo amplesso,* in which the truth about Figaro's parentage is discovered, shows Mozart's manner of treating ensembles: there is a great deal of lively orchestral commentary, with the voices swiftly carrying on the business of the plot and the motion of the whole quickened thereby.

So it goes throughout the opera — arias, duets, and concerted pieces dovetailed together with astonishing skill and limned with flashing brilliance. A first-class performance of *Figaro* (unfortunately they are few, these days!) leaves us breathless at the radiance, the lightness of touch, the éclat with which everything is carried off. We come away wondering, as someone has said, whether it was the music that produced the action, or the action the music: for the dialogue has been completely music, and the music itself is the dialogue.

"DON GIOVANNI"

There has been a great deal of critical discussion as to whether or not Mozart's second great opera written in conjunction with Da Ponte, *Don Giovanni,* is a comic opera; and this in spite of the fact that the librettist definitely designated his work as a *dramma giacosa,* and that it was so considered by Mozart in composing the music. For this grand opera, in addition to its play of comedy, calls for certain depictions of tenderness, jealousy, and pride that are not to be found in *Figaro.* Mozart's genius again being equal to the task, the music of *Don Giovanni* has an intensity of expression and a dramatic amplitude that is hardly to be expected in the earlier work. Moreover, the nature of the subject demands a certain theatrical sense for the spectacular, which naturally takes it out of the more intimate and stylized atmosphere of the comedy of manners.

Time has probably been too benevolent to this libretto: because of Mozart's music, it has come to be considered a classic and so is usually treated by theater managers with undue solemnity and reverence; scholarly studies and monographs have been written about it [14] as if it were one of the great works of the musico-dramatic stage. As a matter of fact, in spite of its threatening, melodramatic Statue, its frequent denunciations of the conduct of its libertine hero, its spectacular representation of his ultimate fate, it is a not overconvincing record of its famous protagonist's progress through a series of merry pursuits of women to his inevitable doom in Hell, largely "lifted" from an earlier *capriccio drammatico* by the Italian librettist Bertati. Indeed, if it had been written in more modern times, it is almost certain that Mozart's adventurous librettist would have found himself involved in charges of plagiarism, so close is the resemblance between Da Ponte's libretto and its earlier model.

And the ironically delectable episode at the very end of the work, a closing sextet sung after Don Giovanni has traversed, in a cloud of theatrical smoke, the trap-door way to Hades, gives the whole thing away and tells us what composer and librettist thought of their conglomeration of comedy and melodrama. So we need not take *Don Giovanni* too reverently: if it were not for the superb quality of Mozart's music, it would have, long before this, gone the way of its numerous prototypes.

Because of its many-sided characterizations, most connoisseurs consider *Don Giovanni* to be Mozart's outstanding work, some enthusiasts maintaining it to be the greatest and most perfectly co-ordinated opera ever written. Don Giovanni, the carefree, full-blooded, crafty libertine to whom life is merely a grand philandering adventure; his sly, lecherous confederate, Leporello; their feminine victims, Donna Anna, the daughter of Il Commendatore, virtuous and outraged; Donna Elvira, a grandam whose love Giovanni has scorned; Zerlina, charming, naïve, simple, the most desirable of them all; Il Commendatore, who loses his life at the very beginning of the opera as he attempts to defend his daughter's honor from Giovanni's wily attack; Don Ottavio, Anna's lover, whom she constantly (and, if the truth be told, rather tiresomely) beseeches to avenge

[14] The latest and one of the best is by Paul Stefan, published by the Reichner Verlag of Vienna.

the death of her father; Masetto, Zerlina's betrothed, a suspicious peasant resentful of the insults he must stand from his predatory superiors; and the awful, avenging Statue of the Commendatore, which finally achieves Giovanni's downfall: for all these Mozart has written characteristic music, his method of treatment being similar to that of *Figaro*. Arias, duets, and swiftly moving concerted numbers are connected by rapid-fire recitatives containing much of the life-giving dramatic elements. Mozart gives a great deal of his character delineation to his orchestral accompaniment, described by a contemporary as containing an " overpowering number of notes "; to which the composer retorted, " Just as many as are required." The vocal parts make consummate demands on the singers for fluent finesse of style, rapid singing, apt phrasing, ability to set forth long, lyric lines, fine focused tone, and consistent clarity of utterance — demands that are unfortunately difficult of fulfillment today. So, because of these inherent difficulties of production, *Don Giovanni* remains for most of the present generation a classic sort of museum piece, instead of being the warm-blooded, melodramatic, and very human work its creators intended.

" COSI FAN TUTTE "

The third of Mozart's great comic operas, *Cosi fan tutte*, was written in 1789, only two years before his death. In some ways the most characteristic of all his works, representing the very quintessence of his bravura style at its lightest and wittiest, this opera was for many years thought to be inferior and second-rate. But recent restudy has given a better perspective, and we are coming to realize that, like the others, this little eighteenth-century comedy is a unique masterpiece, exquisite and dainty, fragile and witty, sophisticated and cynical. Its story, again by Da Ponte, is simple enough: two young officers, in a rash moment of boastfulness, decide that they will try the constancy of their loves, and, with the aid of a cynical philosopher and a willing servant, dupe the girls by pretending to go off to the wars. Returning in disguise, they pay court, each to the other's woman, with such ardor and charm that, although at first refused, they are finally accepted as lovers. Then comes the denouement —

" The artifice and refinement of the Rococo palace of Hellbrunn," near Salzburg the return of the officers as their real selves, dismay, and final forgiveness; so it will always be: *cosi fan tutte* — " all women are like that."

Here is a perfect example of eighteenth-century *opera buffa,* with its sham and farce, its utter childishness and brilliant raillery. Ghéon well likens it to the artifice and refinement of the Rococo palace and gardens at Hellbrunn, near Mozart's birthplace, built by one of the prince bishops of Salzburg for the delectation of his inamorata. " The very refinement, harmony, and unexpectedness of all the sham fishes and singing birds, sham stalactites and automatons, the collection of grottoes and fountains, give one something of the same pleasure as certain works of Mozart — in particular *Cosi fan tutte*. Perhaps Mozart did not push artificiality quite so far, but he used nature rather as did the architect, building out of authentic pebbles and shells — authentic human emotion — a world at once real and sham, somewhat mechanical and yet alive, enchanted with its beauty and yet laughing at itself because it sees the ridiculousness of its narcissism. The scenes of *Cosi fan tutte* are like a succession of these fountains and grottoes. The duets and trios affect a symmetry that neither *Don Giovanni* nor *Figaro* possesses to the same degree. Less characterized, the voices are more content merely to satisfy the ear " (*In Search of Mozart*).

Looked at in this light, this last *opera buffa* must always be one of Mozart's most delectable works.

THE GERMAN OPERAS

The two German operas — *Die Entführung aus dem Serail* and *Die Zauberflöte* — are of more importance historically than they are artistically. *The Seraglio*, as the first is usually called in English, was written in 1782, the first German opera to be composed by an outstanding man; with its spoken dialogue, its bourgeois plot, and its Philistine wit, it derives straight from the Viennese operetta. And although Mozart wrote some delightful music for it, it remains such a jumble of styles and so strongly lacks an imaginative dramatic urge as to warrant its almost complete oblivion outside the borders of Germany.

The Magic Flute, written to order to a preposterous and confusing libretto by a practical showman of the time — one Schikaneder — and produced only a month before Mozart's death in 1791, must always remain more or less of a mystery for the average listener. Mozart, crippled with financial and domestic worries, weakened by illness, and wearied by his fight for liberty of expression, no longer seemed to possess either moral or physical strength to impose his demands on the librettist; and so he accepted a subject which, although it may have originally had some value as a fairy extravaganza, became so bogged in mystery and symbolism, so utterly preposterous in its dramatic development, so thoroughly bad from the viewpoint of decent workmanship, as to make impossible any such successful synthesis as had been achieved in the other operas.

Which is not to say that it does not contain some beautiful and overpowering music, music that has a new strength and which sounds a truly German note in its symbolic solemnity and its romantic intensity. According to no less an authority than Wagner, this opera "laid the foundations and exhausted the possibilities of German opera," which is putting it rather strongly in view of the works he was later to compose! Another German critic has said that with this one work Mozart gained for German opera a position comparable to that held in the drama by Schiller and Goethe — an affirmation that a non-German would certainly question. But anyone can easily recognize in listening to this debatable masterpiece that, whatever its merits or demerits, it did open the mysterious door to a new age, as Dent has said. For with it, the first great work composed for the common man in the street instead of for the prince or the aristocrat in his palace, there begins a long, rich line of fantastic, legendary, romantic operas, a line which reaches from Weber to Wagner, and beyond to Debussy and Strauss and even Berg.

Which is, after all, perhaps distinction enough!

Music Becomes More Personal

THE ROMANTIC IDEAL IN ART

Hinaus ins Freie!

— Goethe: *Faust*

CLASSIC VERSUS ROMANTIC: HOW THE DEBATE BEGAN

IF either Haydn or Mozart had been asked, by an eighteenth-century counterpart of that ubiquitous individual known in the twentieth as the "inquiring reporter," for an opinion regarding the classic style in music he probably would not have known what the reporter was talking about. And yet, as we said in the last chapter, the music of these composers has come to be considered representative of that style, so objective is its spirit, so universal its appeal, and so almost ideally proportioned its structure.

It was not until well into the nineteenth century that people began to talk about the difference between Romanticism and Classicism and to discuss their qualities and characteristics, their advantages and shortcomings. In 1830, Goethe published this statement in his *Conversations with Eckermann:*

"The divisions of poetry into Classic and Romantic, which today is so general throughout the world and which has caused so much argument and discord, comes originally from Schiller and me. It was my principle always to work objectively in poetry: Schiller's to write subjectively. He thought that his way was right, and in order to defend himself wrote an *Essay on Simple and Sentimental Poetry*. Little by little, the idea spread throughout the whole world. Everybody is talking of Romanticism and Classicism. Fifty years ago nobody gave the matter a thought."

Photograph courtesy of Bruckmann, Munich

LISZT AT THE PIANO, SURROUNDED BY HIS FELLOW ROMANTICISTS

At his feet sits the Countess d'Agoult; in the chairs are Alexandre Dumas and George Sand; standing are Victor Hugo and Rossini. The painting is one by Danhauser.

There may be some disagreement among scholars as to the validity of Goethe's claim of being the first to differentiate between Romanticism and Classicism in art; but there can be no question as to the truth of his statement that since his time there has been a great deal of talking and writing — perhaps too much — about these labels which have been more or less arbitrarily fastened not only on poetry, but on all the arts. Yet with all this discussion, no one has ever fixed clearly the meaning of these " worn, smudged, and ambiguous words " or defined exactly the differences between them.

ETYMOLOGICAL ROOTS

Lucas, in his book *The Decline and Fall of the Romantic Ideal,* tells us that the first metaphorical use of the Latin word *classis* (meaning originally a " host," and applied to that class of Roman citizens who could afford the most heavily armed military hosts: all the others were *infra classem*) was that of Aulus Gellius, who distinguished a *classicus scriptor* from a *prolitarius*. And this connotation of *standard*, of belonging to the best class, especially if it was associated somehow with the civilizations of Greece and Rome, has remained with the word ever since. It was thus that the artists of the Renaissance thought of *classical*, and when the word was inserted into the English language, it was applied to anything that was thought to conform to the standards of classic antiquity.

The pedigree of *Romantic* is somewhat more complicated. The first Latin usage referred to a vernacular language introduced by barbarian invaders, which by the eighth century had taken its place alongside the official Latin. It was called the *lingua Romanica*. Thus the old French, and then the Provençal and the Spanish, and finally all the Latin vernaculars, came to be thought of as Romance languages, and the literature composed in them — made up of fictitious and fantastic stories in both verse and prose — was called *Romantic literature*. It was this meaning of the fictitious, unreal, fantastic, of the strange and fairy-tale-like that became gradually attached to a type of literature (and consequently other arts), as well as the temperaments associated with producing it and the forms which resulted therefrom. So that in a general sense the epithet *Romantic*, which began with meaning, in the seventeenth century, a lying sort of tale, assumed during the eighteenth the connotation of strange, unusual, fantastic, and was attached to such things, as Lucas observes, as "Gothic ruins, wild landscapes, and other delightful mixtures of terror and sublimity."

PRESENT-DAY APPLICATIONS

In all our present-day usages of these terms there persist definite traces of these etymological meanings. We designate as classic such things as the Parthenon, the poetry of Sophocles or Horace, the prose of Demosthenes, not merely because they were produced by the Greek and Roman cultures, but also for the reason that they represent something standard, unique, ideal, that seems to stand somehow at the very source and center of all existence (to use Sainte-Beuve's phrase again), their natural freedom of form, their sense of balance and proportion, their sanity and reality, their peculiar blending of idealism and actuality representing a norm by which all other things of their class may well be judged. In the same sense we speak of the poetry of Milton, the plays of Racine, the sculpture of Michelangelo, the music of Mozart as classic, although these represent cultural civilizations that are far removed from those of Greco-Roman times.

Likewise, in the older usage the term *Romantic* suggests anything that is out of the ordinary, highly imaginative, free and unrestrained, overpowering and remote — in a sense, attributes that are opposed to reason, balance, and calmness of spirit. Thus *The Rime of the Ancient Mariner, The Arabian Nights, Macbeth, The Afternoon of a Faun* can be thought of as Romantic, although they come from widely separated epochs in the world's creative history.

MISTAKEN USAGES

A number of unfortunate connotations have arisen from the wrong application of these etymological differences between Classic and Romantic. A common distinction often made is that in which Classicism, because of its particular associations, is considered as an appeal to reason, while Romanticism is described as being an appeal to the emotions. In a sense this is true, of course; but there is no such clear-cut difference between these terms. For it is easy enough to show that the supreme examples of both literature and music (the two arts which are most strongly affected by such differences) have at the same time form and balance which appeal to the intellect and those vast sweeps of emotion and devouring passion which traverse all human life. A great deal of the art which is strongly Romantic has also the control, balance, and reason which we think of as characteristically classic — the poetry of Schiller and the symphonies of Beethoven, for example. And anything more truly and destructively passionate than the hate of Electra and Clytemnestra or the overpowering terror of the final act of *Don Giovanni* can hardly be imagined!

Another distinction that is often made is that between the element of personal freedom and the rights of the individual — characteristics of Romanticism strongly emphasized, as we shall see, at the beginning of the nineteenth century — and the necessity which Classicism imposes of submerging such individualism in the interest of securing a perfect balance of the whole: in a word, of achieving general excellence rather than particular uniqueness. But the notes of individuality and freedom are strongly sounded in many a so-called classic: the despair of Molière's *Misanthrope* is individual; and the feeling that rises, sometimes poignantly, sometimes lyrically, out of so much of the music of Bach is very personal. On the other hand, some of the best Romantic art, such as the poetry of Coleridge (*The Rime of the Ancient Mariner* is one of the greatest of sermons on absorption in self) and Keats and the music of Brahms can hardly be said to be egocentrically personal.

There have been many other such distinctions. Goethe made the very sweeping statement that if a work is thoroughly good, it is bound to be classical; for " Romanticism," he assures us, " is disease; Classicism, health." Which leads us to speculate as to just how he managed to justify certain aspects of his *Faust*. A contemporary, Stendhal, confuses the issue still further by saying that Romanticism, at any time, is that art which is contemporary; Classicism is that which was produced yesterday. Thus all good art would be first Romantic and then Classic. According to such a theory, Haydn's style was Romantic in his day, just as was Stravinsky's to those who first heard it in the early years of the twentieth century; whereas, both the *Surprise Symphony* and the *Sacre du printemps* are now to be considered classics, belonging as they do to the past.

Plausible theories have also been worked out which show the whole history of Occidental art to have been a succession of three phases: a preclassic or symbolic stage, characterized by primitivism and the struggle to acquire technical facility; a classic stage, marked by an absolutely homogeneous unity of content and form; and a Romantic stage, an overdeveloped aspect of this perfect state, with emphasis laid on personal expression of feeling and new methods of saying old things, ending finally in incoherence and decadence.[1]

[1] These theories are discussed thoroughly in Sorokin's *Fluctuation of Forms of Art*.

Probably the greatest of all these sources of confusion, however, is that which mixes the aesthetic-critical meaning with the historical application of these terms. The French, with characteristic logic, have avoided this difficulty by having two words to use for *Romantic:* they use *Romanesque* to designate that attitude towards life and art that we have just been discussing, while they confine their use of *Romantique* to that great historical movement which took place at the end of the eighteenth and the beginning of the nineteenth century and which has come to be known in English as the Romantic Movement.

THE SPRINGS OF THE ROMANTIC SPIRIT

We have spoken of the gradual rise and spread of a new spirit in life and art at this time; at the risk of being somewhat pedantic, we can show the general nature of this spirit best by means of a brief summary of the sources from which it sprang and the results which it finally achieved.

The feeling arose that the common man up until this time had had little opportunity for real freedom of thought in any political, religious, or social sense. In essence, this was, of course, a revolt which had been made inevitable by the extremes of the autocratic governments then to be found in both Church and State.

The empirical and practical philosophy of Francis Bacon, as well as the necessity of having to prove everything clearly and mathematically before it could be accepted as true, arising from the philosophy of Descartes, made for a constant elevation of the reason at the cost of the imagination and led inevitably to an oversmugness and stuffiness of conception that could but stifle man's real originality and independence of thought.

The general conventions and artificialities that were to be found throughout the entire social structure created *l'honnête homme,* the individual whose personal existence was entirely subordinated to the general good of society. The conduct of such a correct, restrained and elegant creature was ruled by a sense of decorum, of never offending what were accepted as the canons of good taste. It was society that set up the standards of thought and action during the seventeenth and eighteenth centuries, and any individual who did not conform to these standards was condemned.

The process of imitating and copying classic models had become common in all the arts. Its initiation during the Renaissance had at first been tremendously energizing because of the renewing of contact with the great minds of the past; but this had gradually deteriorated by the seventeenth century into a " grandeur of generality " that attached more importance to the manner in which an idea was expressed than to the idea itself. A pseudo-classicism was the result, which, instead of achieving the perfection, balance, and reasonable self-control that are the real attributes of the classic spirit, served rather to limit the creator's means to doing that which had been sanctioned by tradition and approved by convention.

It was factors such as these which created the spirit of revolt epitomized in the cry of Goethe's Faust which heads this chapter: *Hinaus ins Freie!* — Away from all this and out into the open — a spirit of revolt which a continued acceptance of tradition and routine made unavoidable. This was the cry that was taken up by such leaders of the thought of the time as Rousseau and Schiller and Byron and which became so much a part of the people's philosophy as to change the whole political and cultural tone of Europe. It is this that the French have called *Romantique*.

Although we may never be able to define satisfactorily such a spirit, it is not difficult to see what it led to: a new understanding of and interest in the common people — the natural, unsophisticated type of humanity which dwelt in village cottages rather than in lordly halls. It pointed the way to the open country and the possibility of contemplating the beauties and terrors of nature as a means of relief from the burdensome routines of society; it suggested another convenient flight from the realities of the present by means of the consideration of times that were past and places that were distant; it insisted upon the importance, above all else, of exalting man's natural impulses and emotions — of a dedication of oneself " to unpath'd waters and undream'd shores " — with none of the confining restrictions of eighteenth-century rationalism; it tended to cultivate the picturesque and colorful, the strange and eccentric at the expense of the accepted and usual; it emphasized the principle of invention rather than that of imitation, of creating anew rather than merely following the models of the past; and, finally, it led man to look upon his artistic creations more in the light of a language of the emotions than as a means for the conveyance of ideas.

Here are the causes for the rise of that great thrust that we have come to know as the Romantic Movement, as well as some of its main tendencies. In general it was an aesthetic rather than a political movement, although some of the principles which underlay it were at the root of such political phenomena as the American Revolution and the French Revolution. It likewise caused something of a revolution in religious thought, in some places separating the Church and the State, abolishing the prerogatives which the former had held for so long; in others it aroused the conviction that religion was not merely a matter of external creeds and formal organization, but one primarily concerned with the hearts and lives of men.

Eighteenth-century intellectuals and moralists had been sure that their age was the most advanced and "enlightened" the world had ever seen — with the possible exception of classic antiquity — and that the human reason, if given free scope, would be able to banish all ignorance and superstition and initiate a glorious era of reasoned progress. But it did not work out that way: the terrible horrors of the French Revolution and the Napoleonic Wars brought about severe disillusionment and led the clergymen and moralists of the latter part of the century to question the validity of the viewpoint of their predecessors. Was reason enough to guide man and show him the way to his highest destiny? Had not feeling and sentiment been neglected at the expense of logic? Was not the great medieval age of faith much better off than the much vaunted and supersophisticated age of reason? Was not the vision of progress more concerned with the kingdom of man than with the realm of reason? The attempt to provide adequate answers to questions such as these led directly to the thinking which ushered in the Romantic Movement. It was this thinking that produced and reinforced reactionary movements in religion, politics, morals, and social life, without frustrating, however, the general trend of intellectual progress.

Courtesy of The Louvre, Paris

THE OATH OF THE HORATIANS by David

The painting is a characteristic classic of the eighteenth century.

ROMANTICISM AS A FORCE IN ART

But it was as a revolution in art that Romanticism is important. Rousseau, its first great figure, a writer and a musician as well as a philosopher, stood firmly on the principle that man's emotions and instincts should be the guiding motives of his conduct. He thus opposed the principle of decorum and was insistent that in order to get back to natural instincts it was necessary to throw off the restraints and artificialities of society. His arguments attracted many followers, among them Victor Hugo and George Sand, and produced some vigorous and picturesque writing, especially in the field of poetry. And, it is only fair to add, his ramshackle thinking led to some of the unfortunate excesses which marked the whole movement. In the drama, where classic convention had exerted almost a strangle hold, this revolutionary spirit led to extravagances of all sorts.

Courtesy of The Louvre, Paris

ROMANTICISM IN PAINTING AND POETRY

Delacroix: *The Wreck of "Don Juan,"* after Byron's *Don Juan*, Canto II

" 'Twas twilight, and the sunless day went down
Over the waste of waters; like a veil,
Which, if withdrawn, would but disclose the frown
Of one whose hate is masked but to assail.
Thus to their hopeless eyes the night was shown,
And grimly darkled o'er the faces pale,
And the dim desolate deep: twelve days had Fear
Been their familiar, and now Death was here. . . .

" At half-past eight o'clock, booms, hencoops, spars,
And all things, for a chance, had been cast loose
That still could keep afloat the struggling tars,
For yet they strove, although of no great use:
There was no light in heaven but a few stars,
The boats put off o'ercrowded with their crews;
She gave a heel, and then a lurch to port,
And, going down head foremost — sunk, in short.

" Then rose from sea to sky the wild farewell —
Then shrieked the timid, and stood still the brave —
Then some leaped overboard with dreadful yell,
As eager to anticipate their grave; . . ."

In painting, Romanticism had been a potent force even as far back as the beginning of the seventeenth century, when Caravaggio, the brilliant Italian individualist, flung his challenge in the face of Renaissance Classicism. Later men like Salvator Rosa, Richard Wilson, and Francesco Guardi kept alive the same spirit; and the "official" Classicism of the school of David and his followers in nineteenth-century France assured a Romantic outbreak there. These men, in an attempt to rebel against the Rococo graces and charms of painters like Fragonard, Watteau, and Boucher, reverted completely to Greco-Roman styles and topics. Géricault and Delacroix, the latter one of the most fervid of all the Romantics, embodied in their works the passion and turbulence of the new school, together with its disregard for convention and its emphasis on individual emotion. No better understanding of the fundamental differences between the Classicism of the eighteenth and the Romanticism of the nineteenth century could be gained than that to be obtained through a comparison of such pictures as David's *Oath of the Horatians* and Delacroix's *The Wreck of "Don Juan."*

The influence of Romanticism was by no means confined to France. It spread to other countries where it had varying and lasting effects: in England its force was mostly felt in poetry. One of its earliest manifestations was the arousing of a love of folklore and poetry in all countries, a love which had sadly lapsed during the classic insistence on cultivation and refinement. Bishop Percy's famous collection of folk legends,[2] *Reliques of Ancient English Poetry,* published in 1765, and the *Ossian* of James Macpherson, an epic made up of pretended translations of poems from a third-century Scottish bard and published in 1761–1765, were the first tangible results of this new ideal in poetry. These were copied

[2] One of the most famous of these anonymous ballads is that of "Edward"; it has been the inspiration for several important pieces of Romantic music. Here are the opening stanzas:

"Why does your brand sae drop wi' blude,
Edward, Edward?
Why does your brand sae drop wi' blude,
And why sae sad gang ye, O?"
"O I hae kill'd my hawk sae gude,
Mither, mither;
O I hae kill'd my hawk sae gude,
And I had nae mair but he, O."

"Your hawk's blude was never sae red,
Edward, Edward;
"Your hawk's blude was never sae red,
My dear son, I tell thee, O."
"O I hae kill'd my red-roan steed,
Mither, mither;
O I hae kill'd my red-roan steed,
That erst was sae fair and free, O."

and translated into other languages, especially the German, and had a strong influence on the development of the Romantic spirit in literature.

This spirit is to be felt in the works of all the poets who lived and wrote at the turn of the century — Wordsworth, with his portrayal of the way nature affects a " heart that watches and receives "; Coleridge, with his " strange power of speech "; Byron, with his spirit of hot revolt and insistence upon the rights of personal freedom; Shelley, and his hatred of tyranny and his vision of what man might become " between the cradle and the grave."

In Germany Romanticism produced the period of *Sturm und Drang*, perhaps the most extraordinary of all the outbursts caused by its ebullience. The two leading figures of this *Sturm und Drang* were Goethe and Schiller: we have seen how it was their discussions of the principles of poetic writing that led to the first distinctions that were made between the classic and Romantic spirits. Goethe was really a pioneering leader of his generation in science and philosophy, and though in literature he stood as a protagonist of classic form, his influence upon Schiller and the other artists of the time was that of a stimulatingly bold individualist. It was the genius of these two men that raised the Romantic Movement to its greatest heights in so far as literature is concerned and produced some of the world's masterpieces in that field.

It is the very nature of such a spirit as Romanticism, however, to go to extremes, and it was these extremes that led a people as childlike and as imaginative as the Germans to an overexaggeration of literary fancy and symbolism that often bordered on the ridiculous. This can be seen clearly enough in the works of E. T. A. Hoffmann, who was an excellent musician as well as a facile writer,[3] and Jean Paul Richter, one of the idols of the composer Robert Schumann. One page of Hoffmann's fantastic

[3] The following, written in 1810, shows Hoffmann's real understanding of both these fields, as well as something of his style:

" The instrumental compositions of Haydn, Mozart, and Beethoven breathe the same romantic spirit, a spirit which comes from a deep understanding of the essential property of music.

" Haydn conceives romantically that which is human in man; he is, therefore, more comprehensible to the majority. Mozart is able to grasp the superhuman, that which dwells in the imagination. Beethoven is able to stir within us fear, horror, terror, grief, and to awaken that endless longing which is the very essence of Romanticism."

TWO YOUTHS OBSERVING THE MOON by Caspar David Friedrich (1820)

A German critic has defined Romanticism as that which appeals primarily and very strongly to the imagination and the emotions and which stresses the fantastic and emotional at the expense of the rational and normal. No better example of Romanticism in German painting and poetry could be given than this picture of Friedrich's or the little stanza by Ludwig Tieck:

" Mondbeglänzte Zaubernacht,	Magic night of moonlight,
Die den Sinn gefangen halt,	Holding all our senses captive
Wundervolle Märchenwelt,	World of wondrous fairy tales
Steig' auf in der alten Pracht."	Come again, with your old power.

Kreisleriana or Jean Paul's *Thorn, Fruit, and Flower Pieces* will show how strained was their struggle to bridge the gap which they felt to exist between the " real " and the " ideal." Music to them was the perfect art because it could best do this through the very nature of its abstractness, its immense infinitude, and its eternal quest of something that seems always to elude man. Jean Paul, addressing Music, said: " Thou speakest of things which all my endless life I have never found and never shall find."

LINKS BETWEEN LITERATURE AND MUSIC

And so these writers, together with their followers, tried to reduce all the other arts to the terms of music. For them the colors of flowers sang, their forms resounded; music died away like a " stream of blue light." And Hoffmann confesses that after he had heard a great deal of music, " there takes place in me a confusion of colors, sounds, and perfumes; it is as though they all sprang up mysteriously together from some ray of light and then united to form a marvelous concert."

Hoffmann and Richter represent the connecting links between Romantic authorship and Romantic musical composition: it was through them that the literary ideals of the movement diffused into music. Schumann was a great disciple of theirs and did not hesitate to copy their style and imitate their imagery in both words and music.

MUSIC'S NEW VITALITY

It may be said that the Romantic Movement in music was inspirited rather than inspired by that in literature; its greatest figure — Beethoven — arose quite independently of its direct line of influence, although he incorporated, as we shall see, the best of its ideals with those he received from the classic world of Haydn and Mozart. The real musical Romanticists are marked by the same characteristics as their brethren in the other arts; but music as a cultural factor in the history of the world received greater benefit from Romanticism than did any of the other arts.[4] The piano pieces of Schumann and Chopin, the symphonies of Brahms, the operas of Wagner, the tone poems of Strauss — all of them characteristically Romantic works — are greater than most of the things produced as a result of the Romantic spirit in literature, painting, or sculpture, because music is in essence a Romantic art, allowing infinite reaches of the composer's imagination and stirring within the hearer responses that he is able to feel strongly but not to express definitely.

[4] Some would add " with the possible exception of literature." But great as was the effect of Romanticism on literature it never produced a trio of authors of the stature of Beethoven, Brahms, and Wagner.

All the musical Romantics show a higher degree of nervous intensity than do their classic predecessors; their melodies soar more fervidly, their stresses are more pointed: they live, generally, at a higher degree of pressure. The great widening of operatic scope after Mozart gave these composers one main outlet for their Romantic tendencies; the influence of the development of instrumental music was another outlet. The new piano had expressive possibilities that were denied Bach and even Mozart; the orchestra was coming into its own as an expressive medium, though we have to remember with sympathy the weaknesses of the performers which Beethoven had to put up with. In general it may be said that the freeing of imagination and personality at this time went along with the freeing of instrumental technique and potentialities.

HISTORICALLY SPEAKING

It is in its historic sense that Romanticism must be judged; as a principle it is firmly established in art. There is no question but that the thinking of its founder — Rousseau — is responsible for certain of the over-sentimentalized social and political doctrines which have been carried over into the modern world. Like any violent reaction, necessary and wholesome in itself, Romanticism went completely out of bounds: the freeing of the individual's emotion and the intensifying of his imagination which had been its original aims degenerated into something which resembled mere frenzy, with a corresponding loss of a sense of balance and control.

This led the taste of the first third of the twentieth century to swing away from the whole idea; the intelligentsia of recent years have not hesitated to deprecate it roundly: the practice of " in dreams beholding the Hebrides " has not been overpopular. Irving Babbitt has written a set of books designed to emphasize the need of discipline in modern life as a means of protecting ourselves against the various forms of naturalistic excesses that were set in motion by the Rousseau philosophy. Yet if we seek the true values, the strengths as well as the weaknesses of Romanticism, we must conclude that the former outweigh the latter, certainly in so far as music is concerned.

The remaining pages of this chapter will show that without Romanticism's impelling spirit of freedom, its insistence upon the right of the individual to express his emotions in his music — to make it an interpretation of life, responding to all the impulses of its period — we would of necessity have to relinquish some of the greatest joys of our art. And there are not many of us who would care to contemplate the history of music minus the works of such composers as Beethoven, Brahms, and Wagner!

The great secret of Romantic power in music was that it could be experienced by so many different temperaments and through such various musical mediums: Beethoven with his orchestra and choir singing of the brotherhood of man and the fatherhood of God; Schumann flowing over with love songs in the year of his marriage; Weber delighting in the Germanic horrors of his Wolf's Glen; Berlioz dreaming of the thousands of performers necessary to carry out the grandiosity of his imagination; Wagner spinning his wondrous tales of gods and men and destiny; Brahms speaking alike with the Jovian accents of Olympus and with a tender sweetness that recognizes the futility of all man's existence here on earth; Strauss, with his vivid imagination and genial humor, depicting the foibles and weaknesses of humanity.

IMPULSE AND IDEA

It is curious that the juggling of these two terms, "Classic" and "Romantic," has never ceased since Goethe and Schiller started it a hundred years ago; and in this juggling most of the misconceptions of which we have spoken are constantly reappearing. As a matter of fact, in the widest sense all art must be both Classic and Romantic. There have been but two special powers, as Taine has well said, that have moved mankind — *impulse* and *idea*, which is but another way of saying the *emotions* and the *intellect*, *Classicism* and *Romanticism*. These have been present through the whole development of art — when the early Church was struggling to utilize artistic expression in painting, sculpture, and music as its medium for the impersonal communication of its beliefs; during the Middle Ages; during the time of the Renaissance; in the rationalistic centuries. Even today, when strong attempts are being made to eliminate emotional quality from music and painting and literature, they are active and always will be. It is this fusion which rises above the transient and the incidental in the perfection of the greatest art.

BEETHOVEN THE LIBERATOR

In him, emotion is conciliated with reason.
— Édouard Herriot

THE RIGHT MAN AT THE RIGHT TIME

"WE will have to admit that, in the history of music, there rules a daemon — that things seem to come to pass according to some higher plan." In commenting upon the dramatic incidents and mysterious developments that have taken place in the course of music history, Alfred Einstein, a painstaking scholar and an objective observer, has not hesitated to offer this subjective explanation of them. And he calls attention to the career of Beethoven as a good illustration of this point.

He could hardly have chosen a more felicitous example, for there can be little question that Beethoven owes his outstanding position in music history to the fact that he was a man of great talent who happened to be born at exactly the right time. It was Goethe who remarked that the matter of genius was largely a matter of luck: "When I was eighteen," he said, "Germany was eighteen, too; a man could accomplish something then — I am glad I began when I did and not today, when the demands are so much greater." In the case of Beethoven, it was not only Germany but the whole of Europe that was eighteen when he was: the entire political and intellectual fabric of the last years of the eighteenth century afforded exactly the sort of background that was best suited to the development of his particular genius.

In all circles — political, intellectual, social, scientific, as well as artistic — there was a demand for greater freedom of thought and wider range of action, together with a strong swing away from the generally accepted modes of life and conduct. Rousseau became famous overnight by giving the answer he did to the question announced for competition by the Academy of Dijon as to whether the progress of the sciences and arts had corrupted or purified society: "There is no doubt but that man was being ruined by the pressure of a corrupt society." Voltaire, through his nimble wit and unbounded energy, fought a one-man revolution against the superstition and corruption of the ruling and cultivated classes. Goethe and Schiller flaunted aloft their colorful banners proclaiming the right of man to complete intellectual and imaginative freedom. Everywhere there stirred a new conception of the status of the kingdom of man and fresh visions of the possibility of its progress.

Into the very midst of this teeming period was interjected a temperament ideally fitted by nature to take full advantage of its characteristics: Beethoven's life span, from 1770 to 1827, comes at the very height of this revolution in thought and reaction against reason. And, although he died three years before Goethe published his famous statement claiming that it was an argument between the two poets that was responsible for defining the essential differences between Classicism and Romanticism, his work shows more clearly than does that of any other artist just what these differences were. By nature an individualist of the most pronounced type — "there is only one Beethoven," he was always to insist — he possessed other qualities that made him unique. Sincere almost to the point of crudity, he was absolutely disdainful of all shams and artificialities; his was a highly sensitive and passionate nature, but it was coupled with an active and logical mind, one that was actuated by incessant intellectual curiosities; [5] the victim of some of the most cruel blows ever dealt to

[5] Kuno Francke, in his book *The Social Forces in German Literature*, has this to say of Klopstock, Beethoven's favorite poet; in reading it, we realize well enough why the liberal-minded composer was so strongly attracted to, and influenced by, the Romantic poet:

"Klopstock was a true liberator. He was the first among modern German poets to draw his inspiration from the depth of a heart beating for all humanity. He was the first among them greater than his works. By putting the stamp of his own wonderful personality upon everything he did or wrote — by lifting himself, his friends, the objects of his love and veneration, into the sphere of extraordinary spiritual experiences — he raised the ideals of his age to a higher pitch; and although his memory has been dimmed through the greater men who came after him, the note struck by him still vibrates in the finest chords of the life of today."

man by fate, he nevertheless believed in the necessity for human suffering and the value of spiritual courage.

Beethoven was linked by all his youthful training, as well as by his inherent intellectual sanity and balance, to the traditions of the past; yet his intense ardor and need for liberty of expression pushed him on into the freedom of that present in which he was fortunate enough to live. (It is hardly necessary to point out that such an intense individualism would have been impossible of expression had Beethoven been born fifty years earlier.) He was forced by the circumstances of his career, by such facts as his never having married and his becoming completely deaf in the later years of his life, into an isolation from the world that made inevitable a constant and organic spiritual development such as has taken place in no other artist. And it was this spiritual development which was the motive for all his great music, an influence that finally led him to attempt expression of states of consciousness beyond the ordinary experiences of man.

Even in such matters as that of the freedom from patronage which the times made possible, Beethoven was fortunate. For he could never have lived under the rather humiliating circumstances which Haydn and Mozart took more or less for granted; his independent nature demanded economic and spiritual freedom, and these luckily were possible because of the spirit of the times. It seems as if never before or since have the characteristics of a composer fitted so well the background of the period in which he lived; nor has any period provided a composer with such stimulating surroundings in which to develop the peculiar characteristics of his genius. Whether we attempt to explain this in terms of daemonic control or resort to the more pedestrian but scientific recognition of the flowering of a temperament as due to accidents of circumstance and period, Beethoven's place in historical time must always seem a fortunate one. For he stood at the crossroads between the old and the new in music, on the great summit between the Classic and the Romantic, where he could look back reminiscently on the calm and pleasant spirit of the one, as well as forward into the exciting vistas of the other. Ideally fitted by nature for his place in the world, Beethoven took full advantage of all his endowments.

THREE-PERIOD BIOGRAPHIES

The three-period biographical treatment of great careers has long become commonplace — the division of lives into distinct periods of preparation, fulfillment, and retrospection. In the first of these the biographer is wont to show the youthful enthusiasms of his subject and to describe him as one girding up his loins and preparing himself, by whatever means are suited to his purpose, for the race that is set before him. The second period occupies the mature years of discretion and is usually considered the most representative, the works produced in it bearing the truest characteristics of their creator's genius. The third is marked by the philosophic resignation so well phrased by St. Paul — "I have fought a good fight, I have finished my course, henceforth . . ."

Such a division is a natural enough one for Beethoven's life, but with this important distinction: with him there was no suggestion (as, for instance, with Haydn) of a retrospective awaiting of the end, his great work done. The compositions which came out of the last years of Beethoven's life — the five great string quartets and the *Ninth Symphony* — are the result of an inner development of such intensity as to make them the most spiritual creations of his whole life. In every sense of the word, we can say that Beethoven's was a career that was in process of flowering until its very end.

THE EARLY YEARS

The only idea of development in Beethoven's life that is tenable is in the spiritual sense of the word: exteriorly, he developed very little, and the consequences were of small importance to his career; interiorly, no man has ever made more of himself. He was a descendant of a Flemish family of some standing musically: his grandfather, also named Ludwig, a bass singer in the cathedral at Liége, came to Bonn, a little electoral city on the Rhine just below Cologne, and established himself there as *kürfürstlicher Hofmusiker*, chief court musician, in 1733. Grandfather Beethoven directed not only the chapel services of Clemens August the

Elector, but also all the court concerts, balls, banquet music, and so forth, and he sang important roles in the electoral opera. In addition, in order to eke out his miserly official salary, he was a wine merchant; altogether, he was a man of real parts, for whom his grandson had deep respect.

Johann Beethoven, Ludwig's second son, father of the composer, was likewise a court musician, but with a difference. Not only did he possess mediocre talent, but he was brutal and domineering and drank to excess. In all truth we may say that his only purpose in existence was that

BEETHOVEN'S GRANDFATHER

of serving as the necessary connecting link between grandfather and grandson. It was the mother of this family, a woman of humble position but great integrity, who was its stabilizing influence; and it is to her and to the old Flemish grandfather that we trace most of Beethoven's qualities of mind and character.

As throughout his later life, the events of Beethoven's early years in Bonn can be considered only as calamitous from the viewpoint of ordinary existence; if we consider them as factors in his spiritual development, they can be regarded as most opportune. With the hope of his becoming another Mozart, Beethoven's father required him, under the constant threat of punishment, to secure as complete a musical education as the Elector's court afforded. At the age of twelve young Ludwig occupied several positions of importance in the local musical world, among them that of court organist and cembalist in the theater. His family life was thoroughly unhappy, and only the care and devotion of his mother made it bearable; due to his father's love of drink, the family was in dire poverty most of the time, kept together only through the financial help of the young musician.

At sixteen he made a swift and futile visit to Vienna in the hope of bettering his position through lessons from Mozart; he had to hurry back to Bonn in order to see his mother before she died. The following excerpt from a letter written at the time shows his state of mind:

"I found my mother still alive but in the most deplorable state; the disease was consumption, and about seven weeks ago, after much pain and suffering, she died. She was such a good, lovable mother, my best friend. Oh! who was happier than I when I could still say the sweet word, Mother. And it was heard! — but to whom may I now address it? . . . I have passed very few pleasant hours since my arrival here, having during the whole time suffered from asthma, which may, I fear, develop into consumption; to this is added melancholy — almost as great an evil as my malady itself."

Two years later Ludwig had to petition the Elector to give him the official living for the family, so incompetent had his father become. When in 1792 he decided to seek his fortunes in the great musical center of the time, Vienna, he had acquired not only a practical experience in music that gave him the quiet self-confidence that was so well proportioned to his native individuality and power, but he had also experienced an unusual degree of suffering which helped him to a sensitive understanding of his fellow men. His fatherland had likewise made an important, if unconscious, contribution to his genius. The Rhinelanders have always been noted for their warm sympathy and keen understanding of life: Herriot quotes Maurice Barrès's description of them, "mindful of the hazards that haunt their vigils, these good people grow compassionate in a truly human way, are moved together with the stricken, and never become accessories to forces loosed in nature and man." It was qualities such as these that helped shape Beethoven's character and which later entered into his music.

IN VIENNA

While hardly the brilliant center of society which it later became, Vienna during the last years of the eighteenth century and the early years of the nineteenth was a city addicted to music, the arts, and the theater; in spite of a serious background, its people knew how to enjoy life. The common meeting ground of north and south, east and west, the city was famous for its life of pleasurable intrigues, delightful manners, correct and intelligent civility, and taste for the good things in life and art. In such a milieu Beethoven quickly made himself known; he secured entrance into the homes of the aristocracy and the wealthy through his unusual prowess as a pianist and improvisator. He sought lessons from one after another of the famous teachers of the day — Haydn, Albrechtsberger, and Salieri — just to be certain that they had nothing to teach him; but, though his personal contacts with his great predecessors was unfortunate, he did not hesitate to study their scores and learn from what they had done. Speaking of Haydn, Beethoven said: "He gave me lessons, but I learned nothing from him." From the vantage point of the years, we know better: listening to Haydn's *C Major Sonata* for the piano proves such a statement ridiculous.

But the important thing, the thing which gave him the courage he needed to go ahead, was the fact that he soon found out that he could "pass all the tests" and stand completely on his own feet. So heady was this feeling of superiority that he wrote at the time: "*Power* is the morality of those who stand out from their fellows, and it is also mine." This sense of power, of brooking no interference, is first felt in his *Trio in C Minor*, Op. 1, No. 3, written and performed soon after his coming to Vienna. The first movement of this work, full of premonitions of his later style, so perturbed Haydn, who was present at its initial presentation, that the sixty-year-old master advised its suppression. Beethoven took the suggestion so ill that he gave vent to the statement quoted above and thought that Haydn was jealous of him and determined to be his enemy. It never seemed to enter his head that there might be some truth in Haydn's statement that he had been too rebellious in his shattering of tradition; to him, this was simply a blow — the more powerful because it was the first — in a cause which he was to make peculiarly his own.

To this period of youthful vigor belong a number of important works. "I live in the midst of music," he writes; "scarcely is one thing finished before I commence another. As I am writing now, I often do two or three thing at one time." Among these were such outstanding items as the piano sonata in C sharp minor, *Quasi una fantasia*, Op. 27, No. 2, dedicated to a young pupil, Giulietta Guicciardi, daughter of a court councilor, with whom the impressionable, warm-blooded musician thought he was in love; the *Sonata pathétique*, Op. 13, dedicated to Prince Lichnowsky, one of the wealthy music patrons in Vienna at the time, at whose morning musicales Beethoven often played; and the three works which go to make up Op. 10, probably written versions of some of his innumerable improvisations.

It was during this time that he wrote his first two symphonies and the set of six quartets which comprise Op. 18, works that are closely modeled after the older style of his predecessors but which also contain many of the marked individualities such as this composer later developed. The structure of the first symphony is exactly like that used by Haydn fifty years earlier: a four-movement form in which the general scheme of the first movement is that of a conflict based on two opposing themes; a meditative, ingratiating slow movement; followed by a graceful, dancelike third section, which in turn paves the way for a fourth movement bringing the whole to a rapid and vigorous close. Beethoven was wise enough to realize that such a carefully rationalized and perfectly integrated structure could be made to serve his own ends.

In these first two symphonies and the quartets of Op. 18, he completely assimilated these forms, and so it is inevitable that these works remind us of Haydn and Mozart. But the writing of them gave Beethoven such complete mastery over structural details as to enable him later to make his technique serve his spiritual purpose: like every great creative artist, he did not hesitate to follow in the footsteps of his predecessors in order to learn how to strike out a path for himself.

To this early period belongs well over half of the set of thirty-two Beethoven piano sonatas which have come to be known as the New Testament of the pianist's Bible. Best known among these are the *Sonata pathétique*, Op. 13 (a name given this work by its publisher because "nothing so powerful and so full of tragic passion had been dreamt of in piano music" — a statement needing a great deal of qualifying, in view of Mozart's works); the *Sonata in A Flat Major*, dedicated to Prince Lichnowsky, Op. 26; the second of the *Fantasia Sonatas*, Op. 27, No. 2, called everywhere the *Moonlight Sonata*; and the lovely work in D major that is usually called the *Pastoral Sonata*, Op. 28.

In these works Beethoven did not follow any set method of formal procedure but was content to let his compositions, sometimes written in three movements, sometimes in four, express his strongly felt and contrasted moods. One has a suspicion while listening to some of them that their composer attempted, even in these early works, to transcend the natural boundaries of pianistic possibilities; in the later sonatas, there can be little doubt about it!

THE SECOND GREAT PERIOD

The so-called "Heiligenstadt Will," written in the autumn of 1802 in a little village on the outskirts of Vienna and one of the most revealing documents ever given by an artist to the world, marks the beginning of his second great period. It shows the thirty-two-year-old composer in an entirely new mood; no longer consciously defiant — his spirit has become subdued because of his unfortunate and incurable deafness — he seems ready to abandon the struggle, only to find that his creative power is indestructible and that his suffering gives him courage and strength to go on. During these first years of the new century, Beethoven was learning for himself what it means to be a hero: instead of allowing his infirmity to annihilate him, he realized that he must face it: "I will take Fate by the throat — it shall not bend me completely to its will"; and he found how to make his troubles serve as a spiritual stimulus for his music.

Courtesy of Reiffenstein Company, Vienna

ONE OF THE BEETHOVEN HOUSES IN HEILIGENSTADT

It was here, in 1802, that Beethoven wrote the famous testament, one of the most important documents in his life.

For my brothers Carl and — Beethoven

" O ye men who think or say that I am malevolent, stubborn or misanthropic, how greatly do ye wrong me, you who do not know the secret causes of my seeming, from childhood my heart and mind were disposed to the gentle feelings of good will, I was ever eager to accomplish great deeds, but reflect now that for 6 years I have been in a hopeless case, aggravated by senseless physicians, cheated year after year in the hope of improvement, finally compelled to face the prospect of a *lasting malady* (whose cure will take years, or, perhaps, be impossible), born with an ardent and lively temperament, even susceptible to the diversions of society, I was compelled early to isolate myself, to live in loneliness, when I at times tried to forget all this, O how harshly was I repulsed by the doubly sad experience of my bad hearing, and yet it was impossible for me to say to men speak louder, shout, for I am deaf. Ah how could I possibly admit an infirmity in the one sense which should have been more perfect in me than in others, a sense which I once possessed in highest perfection such as few surely in my profession enjoy or ever could have enjoyed — O I cannot do it, therefore forgive me when you see me draw back when I would gladly mingle with you. . . .

" Only art it was that withheld me, ah it seemed impossible to leave the world until I had produced all that I felt called upon to produce, and so I endured this wretched existence — truly wretched, an excitable body which a sudden change can throw into the worst state — Patience — it is said I must now choose for my guide, I have done so, I hope my determination will remain firm to endure until it pleases the inexorable parcae to break the thread, perhaps I shall get better, perhaps not, I am prepared. . . ."

From The Heiligenstadt Testament

THE "EROICA SYMPHONY"

Certainly it is this idea of spiritual conflict which lies at the basis of the *Eroica Symphony* (Op. 55), the first outstanding work of his second period. Exteriorly its generating force was the concept of Napoleon, whom Beethoven thought of as a savior of mankind and an exemplar of what the human will could accomplish; and he finished this great work and wrote his dedication of it with this concept in mind. It was only transitorily, however, that Napoleon satisfied his demands as a hero protagonist; Beethoven did not hesitate to erase his dedication upon hearing that Napoleon had proclaimed himself emperor: he exclaimed, "He is just like any other man, ready to tread the rights of man under his feet and serve nothing but his own ambition." *To the memory of a great man* was the dedication substituted for the one originally meant for the backsliding tyrant: the great man was Beethoven himself, although he may not consciously have meant it so. For the music is but a protraction, through a medium of which he was now complete master, of the spiritual experiences which he so pitifully tried to convey to his brothers in the "Heiligenstadt Will."

Sullivan, in his book *Beethoven, His Spiritual Development*, shows this more clearly than has anyone else: how Beethoven in the first movement of the *Eroica* expressed everything he knew of courage and defiance of fate; this is followed by the black despair of the second movement, cast in the form of a funeral march; in turn there comes another indomitable rush of creative energy in the marvelous scherzo — "Oh! life is so beautiful — to live it a thousand times," he said at the time; and the last movement is based on a theme which we know from appearances of it in other works to have been associated in his mind with Prometheus, the Greek legendary hero who defied the gods and devoted his energies to benefiting humanity. The poetic idea as well as the life cycle was thus complete: first defiant courage, then utter and hopeless suffering and despair, this leading to a realization of the indestructibility of the creative force and the final liberation of Promethean strength which pushed him toward new heights of achievement. "Never before in music has so important, manifold, and completely coherent an experience been communicated."

In imbuing music with this personal, poetic meaning, Beethoven did not need to resort to any distorted structure; as a whole, this symphony keeps the traditional Haydn form, each movement being formulated in a manner that is well suited to its imaginative meaning. The first retains the conventional sonata structure, but the form is so shaped by the imagination as to make it almost a new entity, perhaps the greatest single movement in all symphonic literature. The idea of the funeral march was a novel one, but through it Beethoven was able to link his own personal suffering with the more objective human experience of death and the bitterness of the grave. The scherzo is an entirely new form, one based on the older minuet of Haydn but possessed of a spirit of such daemonic energy that we recognize it as the most characteristic of all the Beethoven innovations. By finally using a complex variation form,[6] Beethoven seems to suggest, according to Sullivan, the variety of achievement that was open to his tremendous energy, an explanation that for many satisfactorily disposes of the difficulties which critics have found in this movement.

In orchestrating this work, Beethoven did not hesitate to enlarge the bounds of his orchestral expression in order to develop fully the poetic significance of his ideas. There are many "irregularities" in his writing for the orchestra — he employs tone combinations with an ear to what they convey emotionally rather than to their sensuous appeal; he uses color as a means of expressing symbolically what he wants to say and

[6] The variation form, which has been a favorite with composers and improvisators ever since the sixteenth century, when the writers of virginal music used it so freely, seemed to have been especially attractive to Beethoven. His works, from the earliest period, are replete with variations of all sorts — melodic, rhythmic, and harmonic, especially the last. With him it may be said that the variation became really a thematic development rather than the usual repetition in various guises of the same idea.

In addition to his separately published works in this form (some 29 altogether, the most important of which are perhaps the 32 *Variations in C Minor* and the 33 *Variations on a Waltz Theme of Diabelli*, both for piano), a number of individual movements from various larger works are in variation form. Numbered among these are the slow movements of the Third, Fifth, Seventh, and Ninth symphonies; the last movements of the Third and the Ninth contain also variations, as do the piano sonatas Op. 26, 14, No. 2, 109, and 111; the quartets in E and A major, Op. 124 and 132; and the *Kreutzer Sonata* for violin and piano, Op. 47.

employs a wide scale of dynamics in order to manifest his feelings. Here, as in everything else he did, he was absolutely individual, unlike anyone before or since.

CONCRETE THOUGHT EXPRESSED IN MUSIC

No one else has ever so definitely associated thought with music in the way that Beethoven did; for in his music he universalized conceptions awakened by the stirring events of the time — such concepts as liberty and heroism — as well as the more personal experiences of life. Which is not to say that he wrote program music. It was a peculiar quality of his imagination that enabled it to fuse great thoughts with musical expression — to put into sonata, symphony, and string quartet such abstract ideas as those connected with liberty, equality, heroism, and struggle. And this expression is so definite that, if we possess any imagination at all, we can share Beethoven's mind. These concepts are so great as to revalue for us not only all music but all life, all emotion, and all thought, as Ernest Newman has said. " In every artist there is a touch of audacity without which genius is inconceivable," according to Goethe. Beethoven's audacity was in his attempt to combine concrete thought with abstract expression; he accomplished it so successfully as to enhance both, without transcending the natural limits of either. He stands as the supreme combination of the classic and Romantic spirits, " dominating both periods as a superior creator who increased the forces of the past by drawing on the still unreleased powers of the future," as Bekker has said in one of the best books yet written on Beethoven's life.

The works that he produced during these years of maturity are proof enough of the fact that this concept of heroism was constantly in his mind: the motto of the Third and Fifth symphonies, the Fourth and Fifth piano concertos, the *Rasoumovsky Quartets*, and the opera *Fidelio* might be set down as *per ardua ad victoriam*. There were relaxations, of course. Not even such a spirit as Beethoven's can live constantly on the heights, and we know from his letters that while he was busy with these great works, he refreshed himself by others of a different character. The Fourth and Sixth symphonies are lovely recuperative pauses after the heroic demands of the Third and the Fifth. He wrote some program music — such things as the *Battle Symphony* (*Wellington's Victory*), a work for which he had a strange liking, and which, when it was first produced, caused a greater sensation than all his other symphonies put together — and the *Leonore Overture No. 3.*[7] Besides, there was necessary a great deal of composition for the sake of keeping body and soul together, of "wandering about," as he himself put it, in the mountains, clefts, and valleys with a piece of music paper, writing down things for the sake of bread and money; "for to such a pitch have I brought it in this all-powerful land of the Phaecians that to gain time for a big work I must always first smear a lot for money." So we have an outpouring of lieder, variations, dances, and so forth, works which can hardly be said to constitute any very important contribution either to musical literature or to their composer's reputation.

EVENTS AND ADVENTURES

There are many events in this part of Beethoven's life that are of fascinating interest to the lovers of his music. We can only hint at a few. Although he was granted an annuity of four thousand florins by some of his important patrons and friends so that he might "procure the necessities of life and follow his extraordinany talent and genius," these years were darkened by the fact that he was virtually a prisoner part of the time because of the occupation of his beloved Vienna by Napoleon and the French armies. Out of his tragic despair at this turn of events came such things as the sonata Op. 81a,[8] *Das Lebewohl, Die Abwesenheit, und Das Wiedersehen,* whose manuscript bears the notation: "Farewell, Vienna, May 4, 1809, the day of the departure of the venerated Archduke Rudolph"; the *Harp Quartet,* Op. 74, full of a feverish excitement; and the Overture to *Egmont,* that hero of Goethe's who maintained his proud

[7] Although written as an overture to the opera *Fidelio,* this is in reality a symphonic poem.

[8] Other piano sonatas belonging to this middle period are the *Appassionata,* Op. 57, a title for once entirely justified by the tragic tone of the work as a whole; and the so-called *Hammerklavier Sonata in B flat,* Op. 106, consisting of four tremendous movements, the last of which is a three-voice fugue.

bearing in the midst of all perils, "as if no sovereign's hand could ever reach him."

In 1810 Beethoven is supposed to have renounced his hopes of marrying Therese von Brunswick, the cousin of the Guicciardi, to whom he is thought to have been engaged for some years and to whom he may well have written those three famous letters to his "Unknown Beloved." There were plenty of other feminine entanglements: with young Bettina Brentano, that exuberant friend of Goethe's, a highly romantic individual who liked to "throw herself with a sort of mania on men noted for their power of intellect and gnaw at all of them, and finally to throw their bones to the dogs," according to a contemporary description. We need not take too seriously Bettina's dramatic accounts of her relations with Beethoven, in view of her mania for celebrities. After her, the master's thoughts turned toward Theresa Malfatti, the niece of one of his doctors; tradition has it that he proposed to her and was refused. Then came his infatuation for Amalie Sebald, a singer with a lovely voice, whom he met at the Bohemian spa, Töplitz.

All these amorous adventures show Beethoven to have been inclined toward love and marriage and domesticity. "Love alone — yes, love only can give you a happier life — O God — let me — let me finally find one who will strengthen me in virtue — who will be lawfully mine," he prays in his journal. Yet at the time he wrote this fervent prayer he must have realized that his deafness made such a union difficult, if not completely impossible; and his instinct probably showed him that his loneliness and solitude were necessary if he was to develop his creative powers to their utmost. However hard his life may have been for him, it is fortunate for us that he did not attempt to cheat his destiny.

Such works as his Seventh and Eighth symphonies, written in 1812, show that he had finally come to take struggle and conflict in life for granted and to enjoy his triumph over them. The second of these works is quite short, and neither one possesses the epic grandeur and tremendous force that we generally associate with Beethoven. A number of writers (among them Rolland) feel that the Seventh, even more than the Sixth, is the *Pastoral Symphony*; while he was writing this work, Beethoven entered this prayer of thankfulness in his diary: "Almighty God, how blessed I am in thy works; every tree speaks through thee. O God, what glory there is in the woodlands and on the heights there is peace, peace to serve him." The lovely second movement, full of sadness, does not so much suggest personal as universal grief; the third and fourth movements possess a whirlwind, reckless ecstasy that is unlike anything else in the composer's output, except perhaps parts of the *Eighth Symphony*, where he is likewise completely unrestrained and happy. Sullivan thinks that if Beethoven had been able to marry and enter fully into the warm humanity of the world which he felt all about him, we should have had quite a different type of writing during his last years.

THE LAST YEARS

But it was not to be. From this year of the Seventh and Eighth symphonies, a year which stands as a high-water mark in his career in so far as fame and worldly success is concerned, Beethoven sank gradually into misfortune. His finances became more and more involved because of personal and family difficulties; his body, never very strong or healthy, became more and more racked with disease; his deafness increased, making his isolation from the world complete, his only contact with it being through conversation books in which he wrote his thoughts and desires; he was deserted by a fickle public which began to favor a more brilliant and facile star — Rossini. " What has become of loyalty and faith in Austria? " he scrawls in one of the conversation books. Many of his old friends had passed on, and he was denied their companionship; his nephew Karl, who had been entrusted to his care and on whom he lavished a wealth of affection, proved to be a worthless rascal who took every opportunity to deceive his deaf uncle. Beethoven sought consolation in philosophy, in literature, in nature: " no man loves the country more than I; for forests, trees, and rocks re-echo that for which mankind longs." He became a familiar figure in the lovely little villages of the Wienerwald, Baden, Mödling, and Heiligenstadt, wandering through the Helental and Brühl valleys and climbing the slopes of the Kalenberg and the Leopoldsberg. He lived in unattractive quarters: his rooms were always in disorder, piled high with books and papers. He was often

MÖDLING

THE KALENBERG

THE LEOPOLDSBERG

"Through terraces of vines, the way wound up the mountainside to the great green shady beechwood, which, in its cathedral-like stillness and silence, seemed endless. To Schubert's landscape belonged, too, the path on which Beethoven had composed his idyll, *The Pastoral Symphony*, and the vineyards, meadows, and valleys round the Kalenberg and the Schafberg, where the little dreamy wine villages in spring are pink with peach blossom."

—Karl Kobald: *Franz Schubert and His Times*, translated by Marshall obliged to do his own cooking and showed increasing petulance and despondency. " I am only an *infelice,*" he once insisted when a visitor flattered him, and this visitor has described the indefinable sadness which overshadowed every feature, especially the eyes, which shone out from under the heavy brows, piercing him through and through.

THE "NINTH SYMPHONY"

From the last years — 1823 to 1827 — there came those problematic works, the last quartets and the *Ninth Symphony,* works which many of the admirers of the earlier Beethoven have not hesitated to describe as "difficult." The *Ninth Symphony,* which adds a chorus of voices to the usual symphonic instruments in order to express the grandeur of thought that was surging through its composer's mind, has nothing in it of human frailties or weaknesses. It is, in J. W. N. Sullivan's felicitous phrase, a revelation of existence as seen from the vantage point of a higher consciousness. In this music, Beethoven expressed the philosophy of his English contemporary, the poet-painter-mystic Blake: "He who sees the infinite in all things sees God. If the windows of perception were cleansed, everything would appear to man as it is, infinite. For man has closed himself up."

The first movement of this symphony, with its mysterious beginning — "and the earth was without form and void, and God said 'Let there be light' "; the stupendous strength and sweeping universality of the third movement; the scherzo, wherein the composer, like Blake again, sets the morning stars singing together; and the last, with its frantic pronouncement of the ideals expressed in Schiller's "Ode to Joy," all speak with an almost superhuman power. As Olin Downes has said, if puny instruments and puny man-made sounds can ever mirror cosmos, they do so here. The sketches for this work cover a number of years and show how slowly but surely the idea grew in its creator's mind. First played at a concert in May, 1824, this work today, when properly interpreted, is still overpowering in the grandeur of its feeling and seems more than ever before as if it had been carved with great strokes out of living granite.

CONTEMPORARY PENCIL DRAWING OF BEETHOVEN

The sketch shows him as " he was accustomed in his late years to leap and run rather than walk."

THE DIFFICULT QUARTETS

In writing of the *Ninth Symphony* a contemporary asked, " On whom will the mission of surpassing these unattainable limits devolve? " The answer is, of course, on Beethoven himself. For in the five quartets written during the last years of his life, 1824–1826, he seems to be a man entirely loosed from the bondages of this world, one gazing into the mysterious reaches of eternity. Anyone listening to these quartets can but be bewildered; he is undergoing some sort of spiritual experience unlike any other he may have known, and yet the means for communicating this experience are so different that it is difficult to realize just what is going on. The physical aspect of such music as that of the *Quartet in C Sharp Minor*, Op. 131, for instance, is unlike anything else ever written. We may or we may not feel that this work contains the profoundest and most valuable experience ever conveyed by an artist; but the fact that Beethoven demands almost impossible interpretative clairvoyance from his players (and, one might add, from his listeners, too) does not make this music easy to apprehend. It may be music of another world, as some have claimed; but, unfortunately, it has to be played in this. And the roughness of intonation which inevitably seems the result when this quartet is played can but offend the musical consciousness of many listeners, making this, and its brothers, "monsters of chamber music," as an unsympathetic critic has called them.

But we must listen beyond this. "I write for myself," said Beethoven at the time, and it is in a similar transfigured mood that we should try to listen. For here is

> "The prophetic soul of the wide world
> Dreaming on things to come."

Such a viewpoint has little need for sensuous beauty.

PREMONITION OF THE END

"If only I were in good health. My weakness often reaches the point of exhaustion. It is art alone that gives intimation of a hope for a higher life." Phrases such as these abound in the conversation books of Beethoven's last years. Suffering from an incurable disease, he knew well enough that his end was approaching. If anyone does not believe this, let him listen to the poignant lento movement from his last complete work, *Quartet in F Major,* Op. 135, a "sweet song of quiet and peace," as he himself described it. It is hardly necessary to detail the sad events of the last days of March, 1827. Beethoven was in utmost poverty and in the most abject surroundings, his funds so depleted that he had to economize on food, as his disciple Schindler tells us. Although resigned to death, he struggled against it until the very last. For he realized that as long as he had consciousness, he might be able to deliver himself of some of the ideas he had in him. The saddest words he spoke during these days were those which told of a whole sketched symphony lying in his desk, as well as a new overture and other things waiting to be completed. For eight days his body struggled against final disintegration; the agony must have been fearful before he died on March 26, between five and six in the afternoon, while a storm raged over the city. At his bedside there was only one faithful friend.

The death mask, made a few hours after his passing, shows tragically enough what suffering, struggle, and disappointment the years had brought; and yet, in spite of its agonizing anguish, this tragic memento of a great man breathes a spirit of resignation. From first to last his life had been one of constant development, and the very end marks the highest stage of all — that of complete submission to his fate and of final resignation to whatever was to come. In looking at this gruesome *Totenmaske* we cannot help feeling that Beethoven, like Paul, knew what a crown of glory the future held.

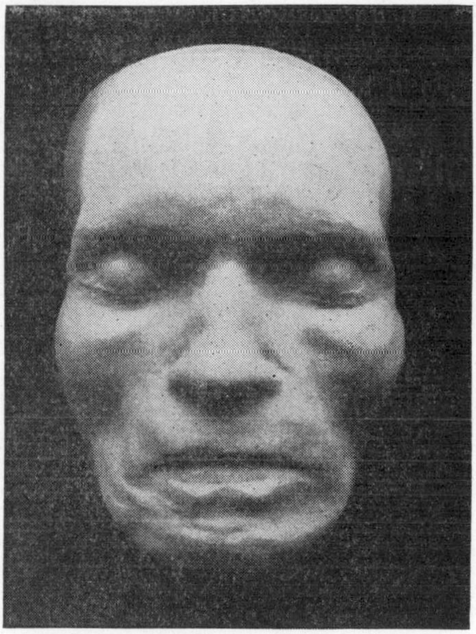

BEETHOVEN'S DEATH MASK

The Early Romantic Composers and Their Problems

SCHUBERT, THE LYRIC POET

I was a brother among many brothers and sisters. Our father and our mother were good people. I was bound to them all by deepest love. Once upon a time our father led us to a banquet, and this gave the brothers great joy. I alone was sad. Then my father came to me and bade me partake of the precious delicacies. But I could not, wherefore my father, angered, banished me from his sight. I turned my steps away, with a heart full of limitless love for those who despised it, and wandered into a distant land. Years passed whilst the greatest pain and the greatest love divided my soul. Then came news of my mother's death. I hastened to her side, and my father, softened by his sorrow, did not bar my way. There I saw her body. Tears flowed from my eyes. Like the dear old past, in which she bade us live as she had lived, I saw her lie.

And we followed her body in mourning and the bier sank into the earth. From this time on I stayed at home again. Then, once again, my father led me into his favorite garden. He asked me if it pleased me. But the garden was repugnant to me and I dared not speak. Angered, he asked me a second time whether the garden pleased me. I said no, shaking with fear. Then my father beat me and I fled. And for the second time I turned my steps away, with a heart full of limitless love for those who disdained it. I wandered once again into distant climes. Songs I sang then, for long, long years. When I wanted to sing of love, it turned to pain. And when I wanted to sing of pain, it turned to love.

And so love and pain divided my soul.

And once I received news of a pious maiden who had just died. A ring was drawn about her grave, in which many youths and old men walked in eternity, as if blessed. They spoke softly, not to wake the maiden. Heavenly thoughts seemed always to burst from the maiden's grave, like bright sparks which caused a soft murmur. I, too, longed to walk with them. Only a miracle, said the people, led into the circle. But with measured step, deep meditation and steadfast faith, with my eyes lowered, I walked into the circle, which vibrated with a wondrous, lovely sound; and I felt the blessedness of eternity as though it were compressed into one single moment. My father, too, I saw, reconciled and loving. He closed me in his arms and wept. But I wept even more.

My Dream, Allegorical Autobiography by Franz Schubert, July 3, 1822
— Translated by César Saerchinger in *The Musical Courier*

INTIMATIONS OF BEAUTY

"A LOVER of music and color, he beheld a vision of the very mind of music, and while within its trance, he composed a symphony upon the very soul of color. 'Come to my earthly paradise,' he seems to say, 'to a land where the air is always balmy and the forest ever green, where life is but a pastime and music the only labor. Come to my golden land and feast upon beauty, where the richness of tones that thrilled you for a moment shall be your portion all the day long; and the dreams you once yearned to fold shall soothe you into forgetting that there is any such thing as passion or any such thing as pain.'

"This is the land of Make-believe, eternally young and willfully fantastic with the spirit of romantic comedy. And in the last analysis, this land was the dream of this artist's short life — the goal of his aesthetic inspiration. He found for the strange, sweet spirit that had haunted his every conception a pictorial symbol as exquisite as the dream of life itself from which he never wished to wake. His single pervading spirit was made up of a mingling of a love of humanity, a poet's fondness of dreamy moods detached from an indifferent world, and an artist's passion for color, for light and shade. There are no jarring notes — the taste is always exquisite, the colors harmonious, the drawing arbitrary but emotionally expressive.

"Other men before him had looked to the many-sided, many-colored life about them for their representations, but never with a thought of making light, color, and form symbolically expressive of personal emotions. When in looking at a beautiful thing our pleasure is for the first time stimulated less by our interest in the object itself than by our impression of its beauty, we have passed from the merely receptive to the appreciative stage of observation. Our eyes mean something to the world because the visible world means something to us. We have developed creative consciousness. We have begun to discriminate.

"The significant thing about this man is that his influence seems to represent in the history of art just what the awakening to beauty means in the life of the individual. The romantic idyll which he introduced, and which served his lifelong purpose of self-expression, brought about a new epoch in music."

Many a one who has gone through the exciting experience of learning that a thing which is beautiful can mean something to him because it has beauty and not because it has some other connotations will perhaps remember that it was the *Unfinished Symphony* or one of the *Impromptus* or a song of Schubert's that first awakened him to the fact that such beauty existed in music. In listening to one of these compositions we are carried away not because of any such personal power as Beethoven was able to inject into his music, nor because of the clarity and ease of expression and the exquisite grace or tender sadness that is to be found in Mozart, nor because of such religious significance as we find in many of Bach's works. We love Schubert not only because, as was said above, the materials of art — melody (such as no one else has ever written), harmony, color, and form — are used as symbols expressive of personal emotion, but because they are used in such a way as to give concrete proof that pure beauty can exist in the tonal world and is worth cultivating for its own sake. It is a peculiar combination of deeply felt emotion and complete aesthetic satisfaction that makes Schubert's music unique.

A PARALLEL FROM ANOTHER ART

Lovers of this music may perhaps wonder why they have not come upon this apt description of its peculiar qualities and of the place of its composer in music history. The reason for this is that the author, Duncan Phillips, was writing, not about Schubert, but about an artist who lived some three hundred years before him and who worked in an entirely different medium — Giorgione of Castelfranco, one of the great painters of the Renaissance. We have quoted almost verbatim, the only words changed being those relating to the artist's name and the character of his art. The great similarity in the characteristics of these two men living so far apart in point of time has been commented upon before;

Courtesy of The Louvre, Paris

THE PASTORAL SYMPHONY by Giorgione

but we have never seen such convincing proof of it as is given in Mr. Phillips's article as he goes on to say:

" Before him . . . the oil medium had been introduced, and the scenes of scriptural story, the formulas of the faith, the saintliness of the saints, had been depicted in colored pictures for the instruction of the people and the glory of the Popes. Before him in the works of such inspired dreamers and such masters of light and shade and line as Da Vinci and Botticelli, the principles of pictorial art had been molded. But Giorgione was the first not merely to revive the aesthetic spirit of the ancient Greeks, who had sought beauty for its own sake, but also to understand that the glorious possibility of art was to devote itself to an intensely personal expression. He aspired to no vast abstract beauty, but to detect, by means of the individual consciousness, the myriad concrete proofs that the world is beautiful; that there is beauty in the variable expression of the human face, in the trees and hills of home, in the lights of morning and the shadows of afternoon, in color and character, in music and old memories, in the evanescent moods of every passing hour."

All this, too, may be paraphrased so as to apply to Schubert. Before him, too, the principles and expressive mediums of his art had been perfected and great works of abstract beauty and tremendous scope had been wrought. But in listening to most of his music we are conscious not only that he was a composer aware of the possibilities of an art devoted to an intensely personal expression, but also that he was content that this expression should offer musical proofs of the beauty that is in the world. This beauty lies in the naïve simplicity of his utterance, the magic turning of his melodies, the glowing shifts of his tone colors, the graceful plasticity of his orchestration. He is as different from his great predecessors as Giorgione was from his: his music is that of a simple, kindly, loving man who knew little of this world other than that it was beautiful (and that because it was beautiful, there was much sadness in it), and who was able to sing this beauty in such seraphic strains as to make us eager pilgrims to his land of Make-believe, wanting to visit it again and again.

Looking at such pictures as Giorgione's *The Tempest* or *The Pastoral Symphony* gives us the same sort of experience that we get in listening to the *Unfinished Symphony:* both artists were lyricists, the one painting his lyrics, the other drawing them from the depths of some instrument; both held the gift of easy persuasion as a flower holds its perfume and with the same lack of concern as to impulse; both showed the most exquisite feeling in their expression, but neither had any need for story or program for his works; both knew instinctively how to organize materials without making us conscious of the process. Rossetti has described Giorgione's Venetian pastoral as "life touching lips with immortality"; and no better phrase could be coined for describing the essential nature of Schubert's music.

A MISAPPREHENDED COMPOSER

Because of the peculiar character of his music, Schubert has been the victim of misunderstanding. Through the misguided adulations of his sincere admirers, he has come down to us a pathetically oversentimentalized figure, completely baffled by the world and supremely unhappy in his life. The first of his biographers, Sir George Grove, pictured him as a man " born in the lowest ranks and moving in the society of his own class," with little cultural background, interested in nothing but his carefree, Bohemian existence. He described him as a provincial, untaught, intuitive genius who prodigally wasted his divine melodies on the desert air of *biedermeier* [1] Vienna and died, poverty-stricken, exhausted by his life of neglect and want, just as he was about to receive for the first time proper academic instruction in music. And this general pattern has been followed by most writers since; the real facts place this greatest Romanticist in music in a different light.

Like most of his fellow composers, including Haydn, Beethoven, Mozart, Liszt, and Wagner, Schubert was born a man of the people, the son of a hard-working, honest, and God-fearing schoolmaster in one of the Viennese suburbs. This father, like all good Austrian schoolmasters, knew music and initiated Franz and his two elder brothers into some of its mysteries through the beneficent means of a household quartet and a chamber orchestra. Family quartet parties among the German peoples seem to have occupied as important a place in the regime of daily life as family prayers did among the Calvinistic Protestants; both are symptomatic and explain much. At least these family musical gatherings gave young Schubert a knowledge of the symphonies and quartets of Haydn and Mozart, as well as an opportunity to play his own first efforts at composing.

HIS LIFE

At twelve Franz, who in addition to being a violinist and a pianist, possessed a good soprano voice, entered the Imperial Court Choir School, where he so astonished the teachers with his ability in playing, singing, and writing music, that they gave up trying to teach him anything new, saying that he already knew everything by instinct. But they did give him a good general education, a far better one than either Mozart or Beethoven or Brahms ever received; and his class reports in the subjects taught —

[1] A term popularly used in Vienna to characterize the homely, bourgeois spirit of the typical middle-class citizen.

Latin, Greek, mathematics, history, and natural science — show that instead of being the dullard usually pictured, he was one of the highest in his class. His education was so good, in fact, that he was able to assist his father in teaching his school, and for three years, from the age of seventeen to twenty, Franz was actually engaged in the drudgery of teaching the parish youngsters of Lichtenthal their A B C's. Not a very congenial task, certainly, but one which gave him time for further study in music and practice in composition.

From this period comes an extract from his diary, which shows clearly the sensitive and understanding nature of this young musician:

June 15, 1816 — "a brilliant, beautiful day, the memory of which will remain with me for my whole life. From distant space echo still within me the magic tones of Mozart's music. How wonderfully powerful and yet gentle and soft, played in Schlesinger's masterly style, penetrating deeply into my heart. No time or circumstance can efface these beautiful sounds from my memory, sounds which will everlastingly affect our inner existence. Oh! Mozart, how many and endless are the impressions of a brighter and better life that you have imprinted on our souls! This quartet is certainly one of his finest works; I felt that I, too, must contribute something, and so played some of Beethoven's variations and sang my settings of Goethe's *Rastlose Liebe* and Schiller's *Amalia*. Although I can congratulate myself on *Amalia* being a success, I can't deny that Goethe's poetic genius had the lion's share of the applause."
— *Franz Schubert and His Times* by Karl Kobald; translated by Beatrice Marshall

These were not the only songs he wrote during this time. Many of his most famous ballads, lieder, and lyrics date from this early period and were written before Schubert was nineteen.[2] Among these are *Heidenröslein, An Mignon, Gretchen am Spinnrade, Der Wanderer*, and, above

[2] Because Schubert is usually spoken of as the first great writer of art songs, it must not be thought that he invented the form. Other German composers who wrote self-contained songs were Hassler, Bach, Gluck, Mozart, Beethoven, and Weber; but none of these gave more than momentary attention to the lied. Beethoven is said to have remarked, "Songs I do not like to write!" and Mozart achieved results representative of his genius in only one song, *Das Veilchen*.

The boy Schubert was strongly influenced by some of his immediate predecessors and older contemporaries, notably by Carl Friedrich Zelter (1758–1832), a well-known Berlin musician of the time; by Johann Rudolf Zumsteeg (1760–1802), whose narrative and dramatic ballads were especially admired by the young composer; and by Johann Friedrich Reichardt (1752–1814), court conductor of Frederick the Great.

all the others, *Erlkönig*. An acquaintance has left a vivid account of the writing of the last, one of his finest songs, which is so characteristic of his method of composing that it is worth quoting in full:

"One afternoon I went with Mayrhofer to see Schubert, who at that time was living at his father's house. We found him with a glowing face reading the *Erlkönig* aloud from a book. With the book in his hand, he walked up and down several times. Suddenly he seated himself at the table and in the shortest possible time, as quickly as it could be written down, the magnificent ballad was committed to paper. We ran with it, as Schubert at that time had no piano, to the choir school, and there the same evening the *Erlkönig* was sung and hailed with enthusiasm."

Two symphonies out of this boyish period are the charming ones in B flat, usually listed as No. 2 and 5, written during Schubert's eighteenth and nineteenth years. Mozart's influence is evident, but the music is real Schubert, perfect in its continuity and consistent in its inspiration.[3] Soon after writing it, Franz gave up his teaching drudgery to spend the rest of his life — the unbelievably short space of eleven years — with his friends, a group of young intellectual men about town, artists, littérateurs, and art amateurs. It was these Bohemian intimates of Schubert's who filled his short life from this point on. Many of them were sons of the well to do, who, tired of the stiffness of ancestral respectability, decided to go it on their own and devote their time to the arts. Prominent in this group were the poets Mayrhofer and Bauernfeld, the artists Schwind and Kupelwieser, the composers Hüttenbrenner and Lachner, and the actor Schober. Carefree, impecunious, and "wild" (at least according to the Victorian judgment of Sir George Grove), loving their wine, women, and song with true Viennese gusto, these men had interests that were far better calculated to further Schubert's native genius than those of the professional musicians and the aristocratic gentry with whom Beethoven, Mozart, and Haydn associated. Schubert realized this instinctively, and was glad to live out his life in their happy circle.

[3] These works are excellent refutations of the statement so often made that Schubert never had any real musical "education." As competent a critic as Tovey remarks that no student in a musical conservatory ever produced better models of form than these early successful works of Schubert's, and that "no academic criticism has yet been framed that can pick holes in this little *Symphony in B Flat* (No. 5)."

SCHUBERT IN THE COMPANY OF HIS FRIENDS IN GRINZING

In the background of this sketch by Schubert's friend, Schwind, can be seen the Kalenberg and the Leopoldsberg.

"The son of the Lichtenthaler schoolmaster, whom life treated generally in such a stepmotherly fashion, was in his element when, on balmy spring or summer evenings, he sat dreaming over a glass of wine in a garden full of the scent of pinks, lavender, and briar roses in Grinzing, Nussdorf, Dornbach, or Salmannsdorf. From near and far sounded the sob of fiddles and tinkling guitars; Viennese folk music in rhythmical three-four time. And Schubert, born of the people and grown up in their midst, felt as if he heard his own voice speaking to him. He would sit quietly there meditating, and, lifted on the wings of wine, would spin new melodies."

—*Franz Schubert and His Times* by Karl Kobald; translated by Beatrice Marshall

His existence was far from being that of an indolent Bohemian, however. This group of young musical and literary enthusiasts, together with their friends and followers, came to be called the *Schubertianer* and their meetings, *Schubertiads*, for it was the genial spirit and lovely music of the modest, reserved composer which proved the dominant force in their gatherings. Working hard at their art by day — the great mass of music which Schubert wrote during these eleven years is hardly believable — these friends met at different houses and on various country excursions for fun as well as for serious discussions, beauty, wit, sentiment, and art being blended under the most fortunate circumstances possible. We have many accounts of Schubert's interest in these affairs — of his sitting at the piano for hours and playing music which appealed to the taste of *biedermeier* Vienna; of his composing piano duets for the delectation of eager amateurs. As one of his friends described him at the time, he was " serious, profound, speaking of art and poetry, of his youth, of friends and other prominent people, of the relations of ideals to life."

And constantly writing, writing. By no means unknown nor neglected in his native city, for there were over a hundred performances of his works there during his lifetime, he was unable to manage his affairs as did his contemporary Beethoven and so never received much publicity or actual money from his compositions. (We must remember that it was not customary for composers of his time to free-lance as he tried to do; even Beethoven, the outstanding celebrity of the period, had to depend largely on patronage and help from the aristocracy. So Schubert, who was by no means worldly wise, was unfortunately exploited.) Nevertheless he kept on, setting an extremely high standard for himself, always striving to equal, without in any sense copying, the work of his ideal, Beethoven. Surely the saddest fact in Schubert's life was that he never heard his mature orchestral works performed at all, in spite of which he conscientiously kept on composing. Only a few years before his death he wrote to one of his friends that he had " tried his hand at two quartets and an octet with the hope of blazing the way to a grand symphony." It was thus that a composer who had already written the two movements of the *Unfinished Symphony* tried to answer the question which he himself raised after hearing some of Beethoven's music: " Who can hope to do anything after him? "

NEW DEPTHS

There is no doubt that the works of his last year show a change of attitude on Schubert's part; the *C Major Quintet*, the *C Major Symphony*, the *Schwanengesang*, the last three piano sonatas, all have in them an added note of poignant suffering, as if their composer had undergone some tremendous emotional experience. A victim of a serious disease, did he perhaps sense his oncoming end? At any rate, there is something in this music beyond the pure quality of sensuous beauty in which he had earlier delighted; it seems to have been written by a man, as someone has said, who had looked into Hell and was newly seeing God. But even here we can hardly think of him as discontented. Any man possessed of such an inexhaustible flow of music which welled up out of his consciousness as freely as a spring of water out of the earth could not be really unhappy. There is no discrepancy between his life and his music; both possessed an indescribable sense of well-being, a simple naïveté and sweetness, as well as a deep inwardness which brings all these other qualities into relief.

SCHUBERT'S QUALITIES

It would be an injustice to think of this composer as being only a superb melodist. His genius as a harmonist, chiefly in the matter of modulations where he achieved color and charm that have never been equaled, and as an orchestrater of unusual ability (especially when we consider the fact that he never had a chance to try out his effects on the orchestra) have been somewhat overshadowed by his superb lyricism. In the best of his work, his form is indissolubly linked with the material; yet in nearly everything he did there is a certain amount of diffuseness, due perhaps to his habit of rarely reshaping his ideas. But no matter how much he lapses, there is always present in his important music a certain sublimity, as Tovey has said, which marks it out from anything else ever written.

His masterpieces are, without question, his more than six hundred songs; [4] his two great symphonies (the *Symphony in B Minor* and the *Symphony in C Major*); a few piano sonatas, notably the three written

[4] Schubert's pre-eminence in this form is so marked that we are inclined to forget his great contemporary Carl Loewe (1796–1869), who created a new genre in song, the so-called *ballad*, a vividly descriptive dramatic work usually set to a historical text. Outstanding examples of these are Loewe's *Edward*, *Archibald Douglas*, and *Prinz Eugen*. Although not so well known as Schubert's setting, Loewe's *Erlkönig* is a magnificent song.

in 1828 (in C minor, A, and B flat); the *Death and the Maiden Quartet*; the two trios for piano, cello, and violin, Op. 99 and 100; the string quintets, Op. 114 (*Forellen*), with double bass and piano; and Op. 163, with two cellos. On a somewhat lower plane, but lovely and fresh and characteristic, are the *Moments Musicals*, the *Waltzes*, the lyric piano pieces and the incidental music to *Rosamunde*. In addition there are such *pièces d'occasion* as the Masses, sacred and secular choruses, male-voice music, four-hand piano pieces, etc.

And having these, we should be content. On his death Schubert was mourned as having left behind him a "rich possession, but even fairer hopes." One of his most ardent admirers calls his early death in 1828, at the very moment when his genius arrived at full maturity, the "direst calamity which has yet befallen the world of music." Who knows? Perhaps a wise Providence removed this gloriously inspired, naïve musician from the field of his labors while his native freshness was still unimpaired. We can but look with trepidation on the fact that, at the time of his death, this greatest of all lyricists, this Giorgione of music, showed curious, unconscious strivings toward ends which might well have proved to be beyond his reach. Or that, only a few months before he died, he had made arrangements to study with a professor of counterpoint — he, the composer of some of the most spontaneously conceived contrapuntal effects in all music.

At any rate, we are more fortunate in one way than he: we have the constant opportunity of hearing the glorious heritage which he left behind. It was not until long after his death that his compositions began to be widely played; as George Eliot has put it,

> "Schubert, too, wrote for silence; half his work
> Lay like a frozen Rhine till summer came
> And warmed the grass above him."

But she hastens to add,

> "even so,
> His music lives now with a mighty youth."

MENDELSSOHN AND SCHUMANN

When we want to be made unhappy we can turn to others. It is well in these agitated modern days to be able to point to one perfectly balanced nature . . . at once manly and refined, clever and pure, brilliant and solid. For the enjoyment of such shining heights of goodness we may well forgo for once the depths of misery and sorrow.

— From Sir George Grove's typical Victorian estimate of Mendelssohn

. *And so it is throughout human life — the goal we have attained is no longer a goal, and we yearn and strive and aim ever higher and higher, until the eyes close in death and the storm-tossed body and soul lie slumbering in the grave.*

— Schumann to his mother, 1828

A LUXURIANT DECADE

THERE was something essentially romantic about the way in which nature, at the beginning of the nineteenth century, provided composers to carry on after the deaths of Beethoven and Schubert; for no less than seven outstanding men were born between the years of 1803 and 1813. Of these, two became outstanding leaders in the development of certain phases of the Romantic movement — Berlioz and Liszt; two — Schumann and Mendelssohn — were ardent heralds of its poetic-musical ideals; one — Chopin — developed into the greatest composer of piano music in the history of the art; the sixth — Wagner — whose development of opera into the music drama marked the culmination of the whole Romantic movement, turned out to be one of the great figures of the world; and Verdi, the last, paralleled in Italian dramatic art the triumphant success of Wagner in Germany.

MENDELSSOHN AND SCHUMANN

Antipodal in most respects, Mendelssohn and Schumann may nevertheless be considered together. Both were North Germans, the one born in Hamburg in 1809, the son of a wealthy Jewish banker; the other born

MENDELSSOHN

in 1810, into a cultivated, literary family of Saxony. Mendelssohn's first name was Felix, a good choice for one who seems to have known little but happiness in his life; rich, versatile in the best sense of the word (for he could paint, sketch, swim, write, and conduct almost as easily as he could compose), he matured early, passing easily from one triumph to another and becoming, in the latter years of his life, the outstanding musical figure of his day. Robert Schumann, on the other hand, decided on music as a career only after long struggle and grave doubts, and acquired his technical equipment (never really adequate) for composing only after years of difficult experiment. A man of real gifts and ardent temperament, he was a leader in various fields of activity, bringing his career to an untimely close by placing too great a strain on his emotional and creative powers. But his struggling gave him a great advantage over his more facile and objective contemporary. Mendelssohn had no need for curbing or restraining himself, and so his music is as lacking in conflict and deep feeling as was his life.

FELIX THE HAPPY

The favored son of a cultured family able to indulge his every wish, Mendelssohn was given the proper training and stimulation for the development of his precocious talent. He made his debut as a pianist when he was nine years old and produced during his eleventh year over fifty compositions of various types. He achieved perfection in the orchestral overture which he wrote for a performance of Shakespeare's *A Midsummer Night's Dream* when he was seventeen, and this scurrying, elfin work remains, in many ways, the best thing he ever did. In his twentieth year he conducted a performance of Bach's *St. Matthew Passion,* which was probably the most notable event in his career; for it gave an initial impulse to the study of the music of that forgotten master, the effects of which are still manifest. A number of journeys followed, to England (many of them), where he became a determining factor in the musical life of that country, to all parts of Germany, to Scotland, to Italy, to Austria. In 1835 he was called to direct the famous Leipzig Gewandhaus Orchestra and became the first of the great virtuoso orchestral conductors. This career was likewise of epoch-making importance, for in infusing new life into a rather mediocre orchestra he established the modern traditions of orchestral playing and interpretation.

During all these activities he devoted much time to writing music, his interest covering every field of composition. He finished four symphonies, of which the best is certainly *The Italian;* a number of concert overtures — if one would know this composer at his glowing, romantic height, let him listen to the *Fingal's Cave* overture; a violin concerto that has become the classic of its genre; a great deal of chamber music, of which the scherzos are inimitable and could have been written by no one else; an enormous amount of piano music, most of which has gone into discard, except the *Songs without Words,* short works having neat craftsmanship if little individuality; and a great deal of church and oratorio music, notably *St. Paul* and *Elijah.*

In all this music there are qualities which correspond to those we commonly label Victorian. A prolongation of the rather inhibiting nineteenth-century elegance, it is refined, clear-cut, carefully formed, more or less superficial, always under gentlemanly control. But it lacks, unfortunately, any deep conviction or moving quality. Mendelssohn was a great lover of Handel and Bach, and his music has a certain natural classic restraint and careful balance; but he was at his best when embodying his Romantic tendencies for gentle nature painting and tenderly expressed longing. It may be said that his outstanding characteristic was his marvelous technical proficiency. His idiom, while not great, was individual and beautifully clear, but it was submerged in the violent torrents which came later.

SCHUMANN, THE STRIVING ROMANTIC

In a study of the Romantic Movement, the French aesthetician Basch has made the following striking statement:

> "Romanticism minted new values and raised a hero on its buckler. The Romantic hero, instead of treading life's path with the assured step of the classic hero, advances along it, groping his way, faltering, and staggering. Between himself and reality he sees an abyss which he is neither capable nor desirous of filling. With all his energies reinforced by the desperate consciousness of the uselessness of his effort, he strives toward those heights whose attainment has been forbidden, toward an infinity, a point beyond, which, owing to a contradiction he does not ignore, yet against which he cannot defend himself, he avidly seeks in the finite world here below. Hence, in his case, throughout his spiritual organism, there is a fundamental disharmony, a continuous dissonance which his morbid pride insists is superior to banal harmonies and flat consonances. Hence, in his whole physical constitution, there is a morbid fracture, yet one which he carries not as a blemish, but as a distinction and a pre-excellence."
>
> —Quoted by Julien Tiersot in "Music and the Centenary of Romanticism"

M. Basch sees in Robert Schumann (1810–1856) the very incarnation of this spirit of Romanticism. He says that in order to understand him properly we must realize that it is his interior life that explains both the form and the content of his music. There is a feeling of "romantic disharmony," of "continuous dissonance" running all through Schumann's life like a leitmotiv, and all his music was born of it.

CLARA AND ROBERT SCHUMANN

From the very first Schumann was subject to doubt and strain as to whether or not he should confine his talents to music. His boyhood enthusiasms had led him to accept without reservation the romantic poetry of Byron, E.T.A. Hoffmann, and Jean Paul Richter, heady stuff for one of his natural predilections. And all through his life he showed the inborn gifts of a writer; through these he was able to found and edit a magazine which quickly proved itself one of the most potent artistic influences in Germany, opposed to all the shallow and retrograde tendencies of the time. He matriculated at two German universities as a law student, only gradually shifting his interest to music and not being sure as to whether his desire was to become a composer or a virtuoso pianist. When an accident to his hand, brought about by his own overenthusiasm for practice, decided the matter, he experimented with one branch of composition after another. For several years (up until his Op. 23) he wrote only piano music; then, after the happy consummation of his long suit for the hand of Clara Wieck, whom he married in 1840, he devoted his time to composing songs; after that he took up, in turn, chamber music, symphonies, and finally choral works, thinking of nothing else the while.

In almost every case this disharmony of spirit proved fatal to continued success in these various branches of composition. His first attempts were the most spontaneous. Nothing he ever did surpassed his early piano things, the *Papillons* or the *Fantasiestücke*, the *Carnaval* or the *Kinderscenen;* the songs in the first two volumes, set to the romantic utterances of Heine and Eichendorff; the first and most spontaneous of his four symphonies, expressing the springtide happiness of his early marriage; [5] or his only successful great choral work, *Das Paradies und die Peri*. In all these we find exuberant and rapturous utterance, an alternation of minute images, quick changes of mood, a hovering between concentrated passion and lovely lyricism, over-seriousness and pointed humor, mysterious poetic fantasy and graceful, obvious charm. The music is the counterpart, we are perfectly aware, of Jean Paul's fantastic poetry and Hoffmann's imaginative fancy; but, although it is clothed in a richly expressive and highly wrought style, there is in it a looseness of construction, a struggling toward an infinity beyond the composer's reach, that makes us painfully cognizant of its technical shortcomings.

Schumann as a creator of miniatures (the only successful wholes he ever composed are his songs and short piano numbers) did not possess the genius to pattern these units into consistently developed large works. His long compositions are mosaics made up of a number of closely set miniatures rather than organically wrought edifices; and so there is a great deal of repetition and monotony, of whimsical change and apparent lack of direction. His most regretful mannerism is a devotion to square-cut, even-measure phrases which, after taking off hopefully, flop down

[5] In writing to a composer who was about to perform this symphony, Schumann said:

"Could you infuse into your orchestra in the performance a sort of longing for the spring, which I had chiefly in mind when I wrote in February, 1841? The first entrance of trumpets, this I should like to have sounded as though it were from high above, like unto a call to awakening; and then I should like reading between the lines, in the rest of the Introduction, how everywhere it begins to grow green, how a butterfly takes wing; and, in the Allegro, how little by little all things come about that in any way belong to spring. True, these are fantastic thoughts, which came to me after my work was finished; only, I tell you this about the Finale, that I thought of it as the good-by of spring."

Nothing has ever stated the Romanticist's approach to music more clearly or more revealingly than this letter.

to earth again with maddening regularity.[6] He was never able to master the mysteries of orchestration; tragedy was latent in this element of his technical equipment from the very start, Tovey assures us. And his symphonic works have to be most carefully treated to make them sound at all plausible. Somehow we cannot help wishing that the good qualities of these two men could have been blended — Mendelssohn's exquisite instinct for form and orchestration with Schumann's depth of feeling and poetic imagery. Then — but what is the use of imagining?

Yet no one in his right mind, musically speaking, would be willing to dispense with Schumann's romantic, impetuous music; and if his compositions were somehow to be removed from the repertoire of the pianists, their lot would indeed be desperate! He was able to introduce a breath of fresh air into an atmosphere which had threatened to become static. His harmonic originality, encouraged by his intimate sympathy with Chopin's pianistic innovations, and his melodic intensity both deserve special mention in any study of the music of this period. In some respects Schumann was a conservative pedant, as his writings[7] show only too well; in others he was surprisingly liberal in his opinions. "Nothing is wrong which sounds right," he is supposed to have said; and, although he was not able to persuade himself that Wagner's music ever could sound right, he did not hesitate to introduce refreshing harmonies and even structural innovations into his writing.

Witness, for example, his fine *A Minor Piano Concerto* which, although unfortunately played too much, remains one of the great works in this particular form. It shows Schumann in his very best estate — warm, ardent, poetic, at times "dreaming with the pedal down," at times fiery with imaginative zeal; yet it is excellently constructed and stands as one of Romanticism's best monuments.

The same factor of essential disharmony continued to manifest itself during the later years of Schumann's life. After his outburst of concentrated composing, he tried conservatory teaching, concert tours with

[6] To be sure, Schumann often atones for these monotonous phrases by giving them an unusually effective harmonic development; but we can never get completely away from the wish that he had not become so tightly bound rhythmically.

[7] Collected in two volumes, *Music and Musicians: Essays and Criticisms;* translated, edited, and annotated by Fanny R. Ritter. New York: Schuberth, 1877.

his wife (who was a famous pianist), giving private lessons, directing singing and orchestral societies; in none of these activities was he outstandingly successful. Yet he kept on with the struggle toward that infinity from which, as Basch says, he could not defend himself, writing a great deal of music and occasionally equaling his early power (for example, in the superb piano quintet and the piano concerto). The end was inevitable; the morbid fracture which Basch feels in the physical constitution of the typical Romanticist became in Schumann's case acute. In 1854 the mental disorder which had been developing for many years reached a climax, and he spent his last years in an insane asylum, completely mad.

It is but natural that in as essentially a realistic age as ours Schumann's subjective Romanticism should not be fully appreciated nor his originality and significance realized. We can but feel in these days of reappraisal of the Romantic Movement that he is an overrated composer; but there is no need for indulging in that practice which the English picturesquely describe as " throwing out the baby with the bath water." Music, especially piano music, would be a great deal poorer without Schumann's picturesque and fervid utterances; and just because he was, perhaps, overzealous in his proclaiming of the poetic-musical ideals of his era is no reason why we should forswear the genuine enjoyment he can give us.

BERLIOZ THE UNPREDICTABLE

With all his efforts to go stark mad, he never once succeeds.

— Mendelssohn

A SUPERSENSITIVE ROMANTIC

THÉOPHILE GAUTIER, the poet, novelist, raconteur, and journalist whose life span (1811–1872) coincided generally with that of the Romantic Movement in France, in his *Histoire du romantisme* passes in review all the contemporary poets, painters, pundits, historians, and so on, and comes to the conclusion that the spirit of the whole movement was incarnated in a trio consisting of a poet, a painter, and a musician — Victor Hugo, Eugène Delacroix, and Hector Berlioz.

Anyone reading the remarkable autobiography left behind by Berlioz [8] must come to the conclusion that if an artist ever reflected perfectly the conditions of the epoch in which he lived, he was that artist. Born in 1803 in a little village near Grenoble in the south of France, he was a typical child of his age, an age described by one of its own geniuses as an "ardent generation, pale, nervous, conceived by restless mothers in the intervals between battles — of exalted, suffering souls, enrapt in morbid dreams, whose heads were bowed in tears." His youth was passed in a world that was largely in French hands; for the forces of the French Revolution, embodied in the person of Napoleon, covered at that time all Europe from Russia to Spain. Berlioz grew up in an atmosphere of intoxicating struggle, continuous, straining warfare, cruel triumph, and utter, final disaster. No wonder the sensitive lad, wandering in the sunny fields of his native Dauphiné, his mind extremely receptive to early impressions, was driven to indulging in solitary reveries or to seeking comfort in the study of Latin poets or the contemporary Romantics. A precocious, high-strung, overimaginative individual, he exhibited at an early age all the characteristics for which he later became famous: he fell so violently in love with a girl seven years his senior that the passion never left him all the rest of his life, although he did not see her again until the loneliness of old age forced him to seek her out and engage in a correspondence so violent as to frighten her and force her to the conviction that he must be insane!

HIS EARLY CAREER IN PARIS

Berlioz showed his individuality in his early student days in Paris, where he had been sent by his father, a country doctor, to study medicine. After a short experience in the dissecting rooms of the medical

[8] The accuracy of this work is not to be trusted, for Berlioz had the artistic instinct for lying which makes a good storyteller. Tovey says that as for accepting any of his own statements about his life or his works one would be wiser to "hang a dog on the evidence of Benvenuto Cellini, supported by Captain Gulliver and Cyrano de Bergerac!"

HECTOR BERLIOZ

school, the young student announced definitely that he was through with medicine for good and that music was to be his profession. The reasons for his choice seem to have been no more than a rather scanty knowledge of harmony and an ability to play the flageolet and the guitar! His parents threatened to cut off his income, but they could not shake his determination. Settling down in Paris, he took up his musical studies with frantic enthusiasm, quarreling constantly with his teachers, railing against all academic methods of instruction, violently inimical to the " soulless Italian music " with which he felt himself surrounded. He soaked himself in the works of Shakespeare, a passion which was inflamed by his falling in love with an actress who played the parts of Ophelia and Juliet; he read Goethe's *Faust* and took it for his inspiration; and, above all, he discovered the symphonies of Beethoven, the form of which showed him the path he must follow as he started on his own adventurous career.

A contemporary gives this picture of him at this period in his life: "a young man trembling with passion, and a head of hair — such a head of hair! It looked like an immense umbrella, projecting like a movable awning over the beak of a bird of prey. It was both comical and diabolical at the same time, something like the edge of a cliff, giving one vertigo."

THE "FANTASTIC SYMPHONY"

Maintaining himself by the sheer nimbleness of his wits and showing a courage that can only be called heroic, Berlioz struggled to secure the necessary technique for expressing the wild thoughts and emotions that were surging through him. His first essay at composition was a Mass with orchestral accompaniment, performed at the Church of St. Roch in 1825. This proved so unintelligible, both to executants and hearers, that he was laughed at for years in Paris. Nothing daunted, he kept on, writing, out of the intensity and misery of his unrequited passion for the Shakespearean actress (who later yielded and became his wife), a *Symphonie fantastique*, an audacious piece of program music in five movements, to which he appended the following statement as to its meaning:

"A young musician of unhealthy nature and endowed with vivid imagination [he knew himself, certainly] has poisoned himself with opium in a paroxysm of lovesick despair. The narcotic dose he had taken was too weak to cause death, but it has thrown him into a long sleep accompanied by the most extraordinary visions. In this condition his sensations, his feelings, and his memory find utterance in his sick brain in the form of musical imagery. Even the Beloved One takes the form of a melody in his mind, like a fixed idea which is ever returning and which he hears everywhere."

THE HEIGHT OF HIS CAREER

In the year in which this was first performed, 1830, fortune smiled on Berlioz to the extent of his having a cantata accepted by the jury appointed to award the *Prix de Rome*. This gave him an opportunity to study and work in Italy for three years; eighteen months was all he could stand, however, and in 1832 he was again in Paris, adding to his labors as composer those of a music critic, the latter made necessary through his marriage in 1833. He did brilliant journalistic work for years on several of the Paris papers and wrote in addition such works as the symphonies *Harold en Italie, Roméo et Juliette*, and the *Carnaval romain* overture, all of which were well received by the public. This was the height of his career; after 1840 his health became impaired through overwork and emotional exhaustion, and he seemed no longer capable of the flights of genius contained in his earlier compositions. (That popular and fantastic work, *La damnation de Faust*, may be excepted.) His operas *Benvenuto Cellini, Béatrice et Bénédict*, and *Les Troyens* seemed to be only successes *d'estime*, although the latter brought him in enough cash to enable him, in 1864, to resign his position as newspaper critic, with the following characteristic outburst:

" At last, after thirty years' bondage, I am free! No more *feuilletons* to write, no more commonplaces to excuse, no more mediocrities to praise, no more indignation to suppress; no more lies, no more comedies, no more mean compromises. I am free! I never need again set foot in a lyric theater, nor speak of nor listen to, nor even laugh at, the queer medley of music produced there. *Gloria in excelsis Deo, et in terra pax hominibus bonae voluntatis!* "

Concert tours in England, Austria, Germany, and Russia brought him a certain amount of material and artistic success. For some reason or other, perhaps because of his fiery temperament, he seemed to be able to achieve greater recognition and better understanding abroad than he did at home. The French never gave him the honor he coveted, a professorship in the *Conservatoire*, although they elected him a member of the *Académie* and gave him the cross of the Legion of Honor. The evening of his life was darkened by the failure of *Les Troyens*,[9] and he spent his last few years wandering about Europe, a broken, disillusioned, disappointed man. He died on March 9, 1869. Few persons, Sitwell observes, can have been more pleased with oblivion.

[9] Few have opportunity for hearing such a work these days; but Tovey, after hearing a concert performance of it, proclaims *Les Troyens* one of the " most gigantic and convincing masterpieces of music drama."

PURSUING BEETHOVEN'S FREEDOM

At the very beginning of his career Berlioz announced: " I have taken up music at the point where Beethoven left off " — an audacious enough statement, in all conscience. But there is more truth in it than meets the eye. We have already shown that Beethoven's great symphonies owe their place in music not only to their purely musical qualities but also to the fact that they were the first symphonies ever written which fuse poetic ideas with musical expression. Without in any sense rejecting the classic forms left by Haydn and Mozart, Beethoven put a new spiritual content into them, a content which has revalued for us all life as well as all music. We feel Beethoven's presence in such works as his *Pastoral* (*Sixth*) *Symphony;* we share his mind in the Third and the Ninth. Into all these he put innovations which help reveal his individuality and carry his thoughts, at the same time striving to liberate the form from disabling and outgrown tradition.

It was along these lines that Berlioz tried to carry on, as Tiersot has so well shown in his article on Berlioz.[10] It was no accident that caused the *Symphonie fantastique* to be conceived the day after Berlioz had first heard Beethoven's *Pastoral Symphony;* for, in spite of its macabre realism and its wealth of program details, this work is really but an elaboration of Beethoven's programmatic symphony. The first movement is constructed according to the usual symphonic procedure of having two themes stated in contrast, followed by their development and reprise. The second is obviously an adaptation of a dance rhythm, this time a waltz instead of the minuet which Haydn used. The scene in the country is fashioned after the spirit of Beethoven's brook; its difference in effect is due to the difference of the nature of the two men. And we should not object to a " March to the Scaffold " on the part of one composer, if we allow a " Funeral March " or a descriptive " Storm " on the part of another.

The important thing to realize is that, in striving to develop his music along the lines laid down by Beethoven, Berlioz evolved an entirely new type of expression — what came later to be known as the *symphonic*

[10] " Music and the Centenary of Romanticism," *Musical Quarterly*, April, 1929.

poem — created an entirely new set of orchestral sonorities, and established a new technique in writing for the orchestral instruments, which has remained the standard ever since. It is not always easy to realize these things as we listen to such a work as the *Symphonie fantastique*, for there is so much in it that seems tentative and awkward to ears that have grown accustomed to the later music it made possible — the works of Wagner, Strauss, Stravinsky, and so forth. But if we keep in mind the fact that Berlioz wrote his masterpiece only seven years after Beethoven composed his last symphony, the position of this work in the history of music will be evident enough.

TALENT, TECHNIQUE, AND GENIUS

There are two reasons, however, why Berlioz could never succeed as a composer in anything like the sense that Beethoven did. First, his musical talent was, comparatively speaking, an inferior one. Although fertile in ideas, he never seemed able to co-ordinate them or bring them to their full conclusions. His melodies seem fragmentary, and his harmonies often forced and unnatural. The torrent of his imagination stood too often in the way of his technical achievement, with the result that much of his music is merely bizarre and eccentric. Second, his was too rationalistic a spirit, too exterior a nature, as Tiersot has said, to keep music within its proper bounds as an art, particularly when he attempted opera, the form par excellence of French Romantic outpourings. He was a relentless cultivator of program music, the first composer to devote his careful attention to this style of writing; and his intense Romanticism often led him into impossible situations. He seems at his best in the expression of the macabre, the grotesque, or the tremendous — tempers not well adapted to the production of music. We can hardly take seriously such a thing as his *Requiem*, which he considered to be one of the best of his works, a Romantic evocation of the terrors of the Judgment Day, requiring a tremendous chorus, five orchestras with groups of trumpets stationed to the north, south, east, and west, sounding out the fearful melody that was to bring the dead from their tombs.

DEVELOPING THE LEITMOTIV

In order to tie together the various incidents of his program symphonies, Berlioz invented an *idée fixe*, or central theme running through all the sections, an invention which contained the germ of the leading motive idea developed later by Wagner. He wrote his *Roméo et Juliette* symphony in order that he might depict feelings other than his own, suggesting, by means of characteristic themes, the actions of the characters and even their dialogue. Out of this there came Wagner's symphonic dramas, a fact which the latter himself acknowledged when he dedicated the score of *Tristan und Isolde* to the "great and dear composer of *Roméo et Juliette*, by the grateful composer of *Tristan und Isolde*." In order to clarify and systematize the results which he obtained in his studies in orchestration, Berlioz wrote his famous *Traité d'instrumentation*, a book which has long held its place as the masterwork of its kind, a work from which his successors learned many of their secrets.

For these innovations and inventions Berlioz will be remembered. But whether he was one of the great composers of the world, unjustly neglected and completely misunderstood, as maintained by a select group today, is questionable. The very fact that he was an innovator of such supreme importance would lead us to doubt it; for in music, as in life, the inventor is seldom the one able to carry his ideas to their logical conclusion. It was Grillparzer who said that Berlioz was a genius without talent — an accurate statement; for it took men with more musical talent than he possessed to make his ideas work. He may have been able, in the words of a contemporary, to lead composers away from "the old forms of composition and to engage their heated fancies upon elegies, hymns, serenades, convent prayers, witch scenes, fishermen's songs, and such picturesquely christened caprices, where the name is oftentimes the most characteristic feature of the work"; but it took others to fill in his vast pictures, to make the striking physiognomy that he gave to music a lasting feature of the art. The very intensity of his attitude makes us distrust him:

"When I hear certain pieces of music, my vital forces seem at first to be doubled. I feel a delicious pleasure, in which reason has no part;

A CARICATURE OF BERLIOZ IN 1846

the habit of analysis comes afterwards to give birth to admiration; the emotion, increasing in proportion to the energy or the grandeur of the ideas of the composer, soon produces a strange agitation in the circulation of the blood; tears, which generally indicate the end of the paroxysm, often indicate only a progressive state of it, leading to something still more intense. In this case I have spasmodic contractions of the muscles, a trembling in all my limbs, a complete torpor of the feet and the hands, a partial paralysis of the nerves of sight and hearing; I no longer see, I scarcely hear; vertigo . . . a semiswoon."

— *Memoirs of Hector Berlioz*

No wonder he died despairing that anything that he had done would live; for how could he be aware that the future would realize his genius because of the works of those whom it inspired?

CHOPIN AND PIANO MUSIC

For us Polish musicians Chopin is an everlasting reality, an active power which exercises direct and spontaneous influence on the evolution of Polish music. It is evident that in all our musical past it is the work of Chopin which has the incontestable Polish style in the deepest and noblest meaning of the word. Under this aspect Chopin represents for us not only the symbol of the genuine greatness of Polish music, but, even more than that, he remains our master, who, by his wonderful art, solved the essential problem of every great art — how to attain in one's work the perfect expression of a profoundly and universally human dignity, without sacrificing one's innate traits and national originality.

— Szymanowski in the article on him in *The International Cyclopedia of Music and Musicians*

CHOPIN THE ENIGMATIC

IN Chopin (1810–1849) we have something of an enigma — not in the music, but in the man; we never can discover just what manner of person he was. It is easy enough to survey briefly the outward events of this composer's life: he was born in Poland, the son of a native Polish woman and a Frenchman living in Warsaw, and received his early training at the hands of foreign musicians resident in the Polish capital. Not by any means a precocious youth, he had become by 1829 a composer and player of sufficient ability to merit the following review of his Vienna concert:

"From the outset Chopin took a place in the front rank of masters. The perfect delicacy of his touch, his indescribable mechanical dexterity, the melancholy tints in his style of shading, and the rare clearness of his delivery, are, in him, qualities which bear the stamp of genius. He must be regarded as one of the most remarkable meteors blazing on the musical horizon."

Settling in Paris, Chopin became a favorite not merely with the society set but with the artists as well — men like Liszt, Meyerbeer, Bellini, Balzac, Heine, Victor Hugo — to whose circle he was welcomed as a valuable member. He concentrated his attention on the piano, teaching pupils

Culver Service

GEORGE SAND

drawn from the French and Polish nobility and playing frequently in the fashionable *salons*. Only occasionally would he give a public concert for the elite (he always had a great aversion to public appearances), playing his own works almost exclusively. In spite of the fact that everyone who heard him play seemed to be deeply impressed that no one else was able to make his music sound as he did, his compositions became the rage with both critics and public.

THE SAND EPISODE

Schumann began an article on Chopin's music with the significant phrase: " Hats off, gentlemen! A genius! " and said that Chopin was the boldest and proudest poetic spirit of the time. At the very height of his career, about 1836, Chopin became the object of almost fanatical admiration on the part of his Parisian admirers. Then began the affair with Mme. Dudevant (George Sand), a popular and rather coarse-grained romantic writer of the time, whose house at Nohant, some hundred fifty miles from Paris, was a gathering place for the leading writers, painters, and other artists of the day. Sand's interest in Chopin was probably, as has so often been pointed out, a case of *maternité amoureuse;* hers was the dominating personality, and Chopin accepted her attentions with the same disregard of moral considerations that marked all his actions. His long association with Sand gave Chopin an intimate contact, however, with the leaders of the Romantic Movement in France. He never came so definitely under its spell as did Liszt and Berlioz, for his was essentially a lyric gift; and the pictorial, dramatic approach to music, so common with other composers, was entirely foreign and incomprehensible to him.

Courtesy of the Musée Carnavalet, Paris

A FAN PAINTED BY GEORGE SAND IN 1837

Liszt is on his knees before Sand; Delacroix is shown as a shepherd and Chopin as a bird.

In 1838 Chopin exhibited the first symptoms of tuberculosis, the malady which was to carry him off; and in an effort to better his health, he and Sand spent the ensuing winter on the island of Majorca in the Mediterranean. This proved a thoroughly disagreeable and disillusioning experience for the sensitive musician, and later the two separated. Chopin, enfeebled by his tragic disease, spent the remaining years of his life giving concerts and accepting invitations to play as far afield as England and Scotland. Early in 1849 he returned to Paris, where he died a few months later. He was given an imposing funeral and an impressive burial in Père Lachaise cemetery among the great.

THE SUPREME MASTER OF THE SMALL FORM

It is difficult to reconcile this rather prosaic life of an *homme du monde* with the quality of Chopin's output and its predominantly *spirituel*, rather melancholy character. The only explanation necessary, perhaps, is that the artist does not need, in order to evoke moods, to experience them in the immediate present of real life. Much of his pleasure in his work comes from solving problems of style, of mood evocation, of craftsmanship in structure. Chopin found his world of satisfaction in expressing himself mostly in small forms and on one instrument. He wrote chiefly one-movement, largely one-idea'd piano pieces to which he gave the names of waltzes, mazurkas, études, impromptus, and so forth, according to their style and mood. In them he created a new world of technique and expression. Rarely are there any clues as to their meaning; they are simply intense, concentrated, lyric outpourings in terms ideally suited to the instrument for which they were created.

Chopin in these works freed the piano from the traditional influences which had largely shaped its development up to his time; and in this sense he was the first master of real piano music. This music, as someone has said, breathes the piano spirit, incarnates the piano soul, revels in the tone peculiar to the instrument, even turning its essential handicap — a lack of real sustaining power — to its own account, and establishes a style that has no tonal or technical resemblance to the orchestral effects of Beethoven or Liszt.

The fact that his natural tendencies led Chopin to choose the small, lyric forms for his expression does not mean that the results he achieved are to be thought of as inferior. Within the limits he chose, his music is highly organized, even though many of his pieces, in their broad outline, work out as simple three-part (A–B–A) form. But there is more to them than this — a rhythmic organization of singular perfection, harmonic originality that has hardly been surpassed [11] and yet is never eccentric, and the exploration, in pure beauty, of every pianistic resource, without a trace of the commonplaceness, vulgarity, or overemphasis that so often mars the works of his contemporaries. Liszt, a generous admirer of other men's art, said that Chopin's genius was "imperious, fantastic, and impulsive," and that he was truly himself only when he had "cut adrift from all bondage and floated on at his own wild will, swayed by the ever-undulating influences of his own mobile nature."

A POET OF THE PIANO

Contemporary descriptions of Chopin's appearance give the exact picture that we might expect from much of his music: an aristocratic bearing and manner, clear-cut features, a high forehead, a thin, slight form — an individual bordering dangerously on the *genre précieux*. His playing was evidently flawlessly accurate and exceedingly brilliant but very small

[11] It is difficult for us today, a hundred years after Chopin first used his "bewildering harmonies," to realize how novel they were. Even his earliest works bear marks of great harmonic distinction and give us a sense of hearing something entirely new and fresh. For example, nothing like the opening measures of his Op. 6, No. 1 had been written before. He intermingled dissonances and consonances in a startling fashion and often evolved the most entrancing effects by decorating simple triads and seventh chords, the added tones throwing a veil of dissonance over the fundamental harmonies. By studying the effects made possible by the use of the new "damper pedal" (Liszt is authority for the statement that no master of the piano indicated the use of the pedal as frequently as did Chopin) introduced by the piano makers at this time, Chopin became aware of the beauties afforded by the introduction of the upper overtones against a resonant fundamental chord. This led to the use of even more complex and colorful harmonies, which, however, he managed in such a way as not to disrupt the melodic outline and the essential euphony of the whole. Many modern listeners feel that Chopin's outstanding contribution to music was this unique and original harmonic construction; it is certain that it influenced such composers as Schumann, Liszt, Wagner, and Grieg.

Courtesy of The Louvre, Paris

CHOPIN — painting by Delacroix

scaled tonally; he made a great deal of use of the " peculiar yieldingness in tempo " that is called *rubato,* a characteristic which fits his music well. Over everything there breathed a spirit of restless melancholy, derived from the prevalent *mal du siècle* and intensified by the background of depression that was prevalent in his native country, crushed under the overwhelming tyranny of Russia.

This explains the sudden outbursts of terrific power and fiery mettle which occur in some of Chopin's works — the polonaises, for instance; the deep color and invigorating character of the mazurkas; the thunder and surge of such a work as the *Ballade in G Minor;* and the deep-seated, brooding melancholy of the *Funeral March* and the enigmatic autumnal flight as of leaves in the night wind to be found in the last movement of the *Sonata in B Flat Minor*. But always in these, as in Chopin's other works, there is logic — the perfect shaping of formal means to expressive ends, whether he is enjoying the contrasting of moods as in the nocturnes, solving a problem of style as in the *Barcarolle*, or displaying a series of brief poetic panoramas of tone in the preludes.

It has become so customary to think of Chopin as a composer of small forms that we are apt to neglect his great mastery of the principles of formal organization. This is to be seen in countless of the smaller works, but it is particularly evident in the longer pieces — the études and parts of the sonatas. In the latter he even maintains much of the classic formal outlines; but there is always present a spirit of organic development, even when he saw fit to adapt his means to the particular end he had in view. No matter how much he might cut himself adrift from bondage, to repeat Liszt's phrase, we can feel the essential element of organization in his music, that principle which some writers have called the "sonata principle." He was as ingenious a formalist as he was a harmonist.

CHOPIN AND THE ROMANTIC MOVEMENT

Although it was distinct from the more rugged and introspective Romanticism of the German composers Beethoven, Brahms, and so on, Chopin's contribution to the whole Romantic Movement was, as Mr. Locke has suggested, a very important one. He was never a radical in the Berliozian sense or an intellectual *curieux* as was Liszt, whose interest in the music of other men interfered strongly with his own development; but Chopin's intensely personal lyrics are imperishable testimonials to the validity of the whole movement. Matthew Arnold's words on Heine could well be adapted to him:

"The comfort of coming to a man of genius, who finds in verse his freest and most perfect expression, whose voyage over the deep of poetry destiny makes smooth! The magic of Heine's form is incomparable; he employs this form with the most exquisite lightness and ease, and yet it has at the same time the inborn fullness, pathos, and old-world charm of all true forms of popular poetry. Thus in Heine's poetry one perpetually blends the impression of French modernism and clearness with that of German sentiment and fullness."

LISZT: A SOUL DIVIDED AGAINST ITSELF

"Der freundlichste der Freunde"

— From a contemporary description of Liszt

JEKYLL AND HYDE

TO Liszt, Chopin's great contemporary, the piano was quite another instrument, one to be exploited for its own rather showy sake. The first of the great piano virtuosos, Liszt thought of the instrument in orchestral terms, both tonally and technically, and he tried to achieve on this essentially monochromatic instrument results that might suggest the rich sonority and color blend of the orchestra. Of course he did not succeed; but in pursuing this particular ambition he developed a method of writing which resulted in a great deal of flashy, overshowy music that is hardly representative of his real artistic stature. The essential Liszt is to be found elsewhere than in the purple passages and grandiloquent periods of so much of his piano music; but in this, as in everything else in his life, Liszt was a heart divided, a soul knowing the tawdry from the true but always harkening after the cheap applause that the one so easily brings while yet aspiring to the truth that is its own reward. The appellation so often given him, the Dr. Jekyll and Mr. Hyde of music, is a good one.

THE BASIS OF LISZT'S STYLE

To understand fully the reasons for Liszt's piano style we must go back to still another picturesque figure of the Romantic Movement, to the dark, sardonic Paganini, the great Italian violin virtuoso who, during the early part of the nineteenth century, set Europe by the ears with his transcendental playing.[12] This unbelievable figure, who was thought by even

[12] A contemporary critic thus describes Paganini's appearance on the stage:

"A sallow, haggard, ungraceful specter, with his instrument clutched rather than held in his lean clawlike fingers: you would as soon expect melody from a sepulcher. A few seconds elapse, the burst of applause subsides, and a change comes over the

THE YOUNG LISZT

He was the most romantic figure of all the musicians.

sane-minded people to have been taught to play by the Devil, caused everywhere what can only be described as consternation by the performances he gave, not only of the pieces in the classic violin repertoire, but also of the new and curious type of pieces which he developed for his instrument. This music, as described by Sitwell,[13] was a new invention, comparable to the enlargement in the scope of poetry brought about by the Romantic writers: "all the romantic properties, mutterings of thunder, beating of rain, howling of wind, were there; and the human passions, anger, jealousy, daemonic laughter, could be imputed."

---

musician, so sudden that you are already tempted to believe him a sorcerer. His figure grows erect, his attitude commanding, his features stern and thoughtful.

"He commenced with a soft, streamy note of celestial quality, and with three or four whips of his bow elicited points of sound that mounted to the third heaven and as bright as the stars. A scream of astonishment and delight burst from the audience. . . . During these effects a book caught on fire on one of the desks and burnt for some time, unobserved by the musicians, who could neither see nor hear, though repeatedly called to by the audience, anything but the feats of this wonderful performance."

[13] In his book on Liszt. In order to get the real character of this remarkable individual, Sitwell's whole description should be read.

Victoria and Albert Museum

PAGANINI and the Royal Philharmonic Orchestra, by Daniel Maclise

Liszt heard this extraordinary musician play when the latter came to Paris to give his first concert there in March, 1831. Paganini was then fifty years old, Liszt twenty; but the impact of the older man on the younger was of such terrific force that it changed the whole course of Liszt's life. For technical possibilities were revealed to the eager, impressionable youth such as he had never even dreamed of; and the potentialities of showmanship were disclosed to a nature only too prone to take advantage of them. Liszt has been called a combination of great actor and Hindu fakir; Paganini was his prototype in this.

PIANO MUSIC

For the next seventeen years the world rang with the fame of the great virtuoso Liszt, the "Paganini of the piano." An apt phrase, but not one which conveys the whole truth: for to his fabulous technical achievements, which he modeled after those of Paganini, Liszt added a conception of the function and art of the interpreter which was unique at the time. While he did not deny himself the glory of dazzling the public as a virtuoso player, Liszt developed a high-minded conception of the interpreter as one who should strive to reveal the composer's inmost self — another manifestation of his dual nature. According to all the contemporary accounts, his playing "defied description in words." Would that the phonograph had been invented so that we might compare his playing with that of our modern virtuosos!

From this concert period comes a great deal of piano music obviously designed for the programs which he played on his triumphal tours about Europe. Much of this was actually written down and published after Liszt's retirement from the concert platform, but it was his long experience as a dazzler of the public which inspired its composition. In most of these piano pieces, nobility and showmanship go together: his showiness is at its best when sentiment is not involved, in such things as *La campanella*, the amazing variations, or some of his fantasias on operatic airs or his transcriptions of instrumental pieces. (In passing, it may be said that Liszt was an insatiable "arranger" for the piano, the world's most astonishing practitioner of that subtly difficult art.) But when he becomes concerned with such sentimental maunderings as those in the *Liebesträume* he is wearisome. The best of his piano works are certain numbers in the *Années de pèlerinage* (*Years of Pilgrimage*), especially the *fantaisie-sonata* on Victor Hugo's poem, *D'après une lecture de Dante;* and the dramatic, black-cloaked, romantic *B Minor Sonata.*

AT WEIMAR

In 1848, dissatisfied with his place in the musical firmament, Liszt accepted the position of court *Kapellmeister* at the little ducal court of Weimar in order to acquire some practical knowledge of the orchestra and how to write for it. His ambition was to become known as a composer and not merely as a virtuoso. His previous experience had given him no opportunity for acquiring such knowledge, and he welcomed this appointment in a quiet little backwater, a place quite out of the musical maelstrom in which he had lived so long. He went to Weimar, as he said,

" to conquer the theater of my thought, as I have done for my personality as an artist." His duties at the theater,[14] where he at first produced the usual repertoire pieces of the time, occupied only part of his energy; the rest he gave over to his studies as a composer.

Trusting to others, especially his clever young secretary Raff, to show him how to score for the orchestra, he set out to master the problems of orchestral and choral writing. Raff evidently had no illusions as to Liszt's technique in composing, for he writes to a friend in 1849 that he feels it is high time Liszt " stopped using the piano as if it were the orchestra, and the orchestra as a piano, time he realized that counterpoint was one of the most useful elements in music, and that he was making a stone heap out of the formal edifice bequeathed by the past — sometimes spinning out a song to the lengths of 19 pages, while at others he had no idea as to where he could find material enough." These were the days when Liszt showed his real mettle, when he, the *grand homme* of music, did not disdain to receive instruction in his own field from an unknown but capable secretary.

THE PRINCESS AND WAGNER

Fate was not content that Liszt should simply settle for a time in Weimar, learn his job as composer and conductor, and then move out again into the concert world in which he had been so active. Two strong personalities entered his life, and again changed its course: the Princess Wittgenstein, with whom, in 1847, he had begun what he thought was to be but another of the agreeable amorous adventures with which he beguiled himself; and Richard Wagner, then an exiled, thwarted composer whose opera *Tannhäuser* Liszt had produced in 1849, and who in April, 1850, made this direct appeal to Liszt regarding the first performance of his *Lohengrin:*

[14] In his efforts to show that Liszt was not much of a conductor, Ernest Newman, in his monumental biography of Wagner (Vol. II) quotes Hiller's criticism: "The unanimous opinion was that he [Liszt] is not fit to wield the baton, at any rate in music on a large scale. It is not merely that, in general, he does not mark the beat in the simplest way established by the great masters, but that by his Baroque animation he continually, and sometimes dangerously, causes the orchestra to vacillate."

Courtesy of the Opera Museum, Paris

LE GALOP CHROMATIQUE executed by the Devil of Harmony, 1843
The original is a colored cartoon of Liszt by an unknown contemporary artist.

"You are the only man to whom I would address this request. To no one but you would I entrust the creation of my opera; but to you I deliver it unconditionally, joyfully, calmly. Produce it where you will, even if it is only in Weimar."

And produce it Liszt did, in August, 1850, thereby putting both himself and Weimar on the musical map!

It was the princess, who had left her Russian husband to be with Liszt in Weimar, who confirmed him in the determination to become known as a composer in the large, orchestral forms. During his stay at Weimar he evolved a new form of orchestral composition to which he gave the name *symphonic poem.* Although based on a poetic program, these works use a constructive scheme of real musical worth, ingeniously transforming their main themes according to the necessities of the program: this was Liszt's own invention, based on Berlioz's model, and he wrote some of his best music in carrying out the idea. Among his twelve symphonic poems, the best are no longer played: it is Liszt's fate to be usually represented on modern orchestral programs by but one of these works, *Les préludes,* which, because of its paucity of material, is not too effective.

The great *Faust* and *Dante* symphonies belong also to this period, the first being Liszt at his very best. The whole huge conception in three character sketches, Faust, Gretchen, and Mephistopheles, is a thoroughly musical and strongly poetic one and deserves a more frequent hearing. Liszt's great tragedy as a composer was the fact that so many of the ideas and ideals which he helped develop have been expressed so much more forcefully and more clearly by the greater genius of his followers that his own originality and power have been almost completely eclipsed or at least thrust pretty well into the background.

The relationship of Wagner and Liszt was a close and complex one, each man reacting strongly on the other. Wagner, with the leechlike tenacity for which he was famous, fastened himself on the more noted and richer man, accepting all the financial and spiritual aid which Liszt was generous enough to give him, and all the time crying for more. "Your friendship—if you could only understand how much it means to me," runs an early letter. "I have no other wish than to live near you always. It is not Paris or London; it is you who can best bring out whatever may still be in me." Provided, the insinuation is, that he is sent some more money! "If you want to do me a kindness, send me money so that I can get away." "I am sorry to say, in the language of this sweet nineteenth century, that means send as much money as you possibly can." So runs the story, through letter after letter; and Liszt, the most kindhearted and most generous of men, responded, not to Wagner alone, but to all artists who appealed to him for help.

On the other hand, it was Wagner's music, particularly his opera *Lohengrin,* which opened Liszt's mind to the possibilities of the music of the future, and his whole contact with Wagner was a refreshing and stimulating, if extremely trying, experience. He gradually began to glimpse what the younger composer was striving to do and tried in every way possible to help Wagner develop his ideals of the music drama. Unfortunately neither Weimar nor Germany as a whole was ready for the things Wagner had in mind. In 1859 Liszt became so completely disgusted with the provincialism of Weimar as to leave it for Rome, where he spent many of the remaining years of his life, seeking consolation in religion, even receiving minor orders in the Roman Church.

Courtesy of the Lisztmuseum, Weimar

LISZT'S MUSIC ROOMS IN WEIMAR

"It is so delicious in that room of his! It was all furnished and put in order for him by the Grand Duchess herself. The walls are pale gray, with a gilded border running round the room, or rather two rooms, which are divided, but not separated, by crimson curtains. The furniture is crimson and everything is so *comfortable*. . . . A splendid grand piano stands in one window (he received a new one every year). The other window is always wide open and looks out on the park. . . . His writing table is beautifully fitted up with things that all match. Everything is in bronze; inkstand, paperweight, matchbox, etc., and there is always a lighted candle standing on it by which he and the gentlemen can light their cigars."

— Amy Fay: *Music Study in Germany*

THE LATER YEARS

In 1869 he emerged from this retirement and returned for part of each year to Weimar, where he lived simply in a little cottage and gave lessons to the pupils who flocked to him from all parts of the world. Thereafter he divided his life largely between Rome, Weimar, and Budapest, where he had been made president of the Hungarian Academy of Music; he traveled almost incessantly, giving his help wherever he thought it might be needed. A few piano compositions date from this last period, notably the *Mephisto Waltzes*. In 1886 he celebrated his seventy-fifth birthday by a triumphant grand tour, visiting London and Paris and playing for his admirers. Shortly after the finish of this trip, he went to Bayreuth, where his daughter, who had married Wagner, was striving to develop the great festivals devoted to her husband's music. He caught cold after one of the performances of *Tristan* and died on July 31 of that year.

Opinion will always vary as to the artistic value of Liszt's contribution to music; the character of a great deal of his work makes its excessive repetition almost insufferable. But his significance in history is clear. Locke, in the book *Music and the Romantic Movement in France*, shows just what this is. More than any other Liszt established the poetic basis of program music and showed how thematic development in this style could be carried out. He turned away, as Beethoven and Berlioz had done before him, from the conception of art for art's sake to the theory of art as an interpretation of life. And this is what he tried to make his music. His powers were not sufficient for him fully to achieve his ideals, and he had many faults in common with the other Romantic artists. But his name will always be among the great names of music, the very first, as Sitwell has said, to come to mind when its nobler virtues are spoken of.

Wagner—His Predecessors and Contemporaries

ITALIAN OPERA OF THE NINETEENTH CENTURY

Hush! the curtain rises.

Observe that very beautiful scene, how admirably those pillars are painted!

So well, that one almost fancies them real.

That is C., whom you will admire as much for her superior style of acting as the wonderful powers of her voice.

Those are indeed enchanting sounds; and how pleasing and modest in her manners!

Do you understand Italian?

Just enough to know what is going forward.

When the first act of the opera is over, you will be entertained with a short pantomime intermixed with dances.

This is the divertissement: the bill mentions a new dancer who is to dance a hornpipe in it.

The Prince of Wales is just come into his box: he speaks to the Duchess of L.

Between the acts amuse yourself by looking around this brilliant company.

How graceful these two dancers are!

You will see presently V. and A. who will much more surprise you.

Is it possible?

Judge for yourself; there they are.

I could not have imagined that art could have been carried so far.

We may, I think, fairly infer that it now has reached its utmost degree of perfection.

Indeed I think so. This evening's amusement has far surpassed every thing I expected.

—Rev. Thomas Vivier: *French and English Dialogues upon Several Subjects; Exclusively Adapted for the Use of Young Ladies,* 1814

DIFFERENCES IN THE NATIONAL STYLES

NO better starting point for a discussion of nineteenth-century opera could be found than one which shows the great differences which exist in national styles of humor as they are exemplified in the dramatic works of the various countries. For these differences had a great deal to do with the development of opera at the time. It was the distinctive quality of the old Italian high comedy, even when used by a German composer such as Mozart, which set the tone for early nineteenth-century opera. We have already had something to say about the origins and eighteenth-century traditions of this Italian comic genre. Before describing how it affected the operatic writing of the new century, we may well turn aside briefly and consider something of the comedic traditions of the other countries.

The French, who feel that they alone have been the true guardians of this spirit of comedy through the years, are much less personal and human than are the dramatic comedians of Italy and Germany. They have always had a leaning toward the satiric brand of comedy, one largely freed from sympathetic or human reactions. In the words of one historian of the theater, they like to place life on the rack and watch the result from a viewpoint that is impersonal and aloof, their sense of comedy arising out of the ability to ridicule the foibles and to describe the weaknesses of human nature. In this field of "detached comedy" their great seventeenth-century playwright, Molière, was a supreme master, and his feeling for satire and burlesque has strongly impregnated the French operatic stage down to the present day.

The eighteenth-century German *Singspiel* was a simple folk play consisting of spoken dialogue with musical numbers interspersed from time to time; it came out of the secularized medieval plays of a comic nature and possessed a rather broad and elementary sense of humor, bordering on buffoonery. These naïve folk works were not able to withstand the growing demand of the public for the more sophisticated Italian and French productions, and they became submerged in the advance of *opera buffa* and the operetta. The Anglo-Saxons have never had a national style of comic opera: not even their much-vaunted Gilbert and

Sullivan is native; for most of its fun lies in the dialogue, and Sullivan's Englishness was only a minor element in his style, which drew largely on Mozart and on the French and Italian light operas for a great deal of its inspiration. *The Beggar's Opera,* a sort of English *Singspiel,* written some two hundred years ago, could have established a national style; but, like its German counterparts, it went down under the onslaught of the foreign invaders. The reasons for this precipitate retreat are obvious enough when we hear some of the works of Dibdin and Arne which followed *The Beggar's Opera.* These works were simply collections of the ruddy, vigorous sort of tunes which England has turned out by the thousands during the course of the centuries; they have almost no dramatic value whatever.

THE ITALIAN SPIRIT

It was in the comic genre that the Italian spirit worked most effectively; it was scarcely at all successful in the tragic. The exceptions stand out so prominently as to establish the validity of such a statement. What, for example, did Donizetti make of Sir Walter Scott's tragedy of Lucy, the Bride of Lammermoor? Scarcely anything but a remarkable mad scene, lasting perhaps twenty minutes, in which the prima donna takes the stage and the drama flies out the window; while the same composer's masterpiece of comedy, *Don Pasquale,* has hardly any rival. It may have been this necessity for the predominance of leading vocal stars that dashed Italian hopes for tragic greatness in opera; but whatever the reasons, the limitations of the stage or the vanity of singers, it must be admitted that the amusing Italian operas written during the late eighteenth and early nineteenth centuries constitute a type that has never been equaled.

THE RIDDLE OF ROSSINI

Who were the chief composers of this kind of opera? In addition to Mozart, there was Cimarosa, whose *Il matrimonio segreto* (1792) was in its day considered better than anything Mozart wrote; even today its

ROSSINI

frothy champagne can give great pleasure, although it is hardly to be mentioned in the same breath with the more heady draughts of Mozart. It was Cimarosa who served as a model for Rossini (1792–1868), a composer of much finer caliber and one whom Beethoven declared supreme in his particular field. Rossini's great masterpiece, *The Barber of Seville*, written in 1816, is in the true line of French-Italian comedy. Founded on the same plot as Mozart's *Marriage of Figaro*, it is worthy to stand beside that work in its clever characterizations, its patter songs, its verve and sparkling wit, its warm and sympathetic orchestration. The overture to this charming work sets the stage to perfection for the artificial comedy which follows in the best traditions of *opera buffa;* the famous patter song *Largo al factotum* has been the model for scores of others, including most of Sir Arthur Sullivan's; and the rest of the opera, because of its genial caprices and amusing situations, must always remain a favorite with the general public. Another of Rossini's comedies was *La Cenerentola* (*Cinderella*), written immediately after *The Barber of Seville;* it has much of that opera's verve but nothing like so witty and sparkling a plot. This glittering, impudent work occupied Rossini for some three and a half weeks; the *Barber* took two!

Other operas by which this composer was well known in his day were *Tancredi, Semiramide* (Venice, 1823), *Moïse* (Paris, 1827), and above all the grand opera, *William Tell* (1829), in which Rossini showed his ability to satisfy the requirements of the Parisians. A strong, powerful work, with plenty of musical scene painting and luscious melodies, *William Tell* demands singers of exceptional ability — for our generation, at least — and so is seldom heard. Its highly seasoned overture remains a favorite number in the repertoire of provincial bands.

Rossini was known far beyond the borders of Italy. In 1822 he visited Vienna, where his operas were produced with tremendous success. It is easy enough to trace the influence of his particular brand of melodic inspiration in the works of the German composers of the time — Weber, Schubert, and even Beethoven; and he, in turn, picked up from them many an idea as to orchestration and symphonic style. He developed so personal a mannerism of orchestral writing as to become known as *Signor Crescendo,* because of his method of working up excitement. At the very height of his career, at a time when he was one of the most popular composers in Europe, he suddenly retired and wrote very little for the remaining forty years of his life, thus providing music researchers with one of the most curious problems in the history of the art.

Werfel attributes this retirement to a "veiled neurasthenia." It may be that, beneath the surface, he did not feel his success to be complete; that his rather cynical arrogance, which probably hid an excessive sensitiveness, turned to pique, and this combined with a strain of natural laziness to bring about his long silence. Chorley, the English critic, shrewdly believed that Rossini may have expected people to beleaguer him for more works; they did not, and his chagrin developed into obstinate refusal to write any music at all. In Italy he had been king; when he removed to Paris, he found himself in the cross currents of official cliquism. Wagner, when similarly beset, fought like a demon; Rossini, a lesser man who was often in ill health, was no fighter. Whatever the reasons may have been, *William Tell* marks at once the height and the end of his career.

DONIZETTI AND BELLINI

At the beginning of the second quarter of the century, Paris took Vienna's place as the center of European musical activity. One of the chief reasons for this was that, no matter what the political or economic situation of France might be, whether she had an emperor, a king, or a republic, the government supported the opera as a matter of national pride. And naturally this well-supported institution became the goal of all composers, Italian as well as French. Paris was then, as she has remained since, the international center of the artistic and intellectual activities of the Continent. So, although we find that the outstanding writers of operatic music of the period were born and trained in Italy, they almost invariably deserted the Italian for the French scene.

Two of these early nineteenth-century Italians are still remembered, although most of their works are more honored by breach than by performance — Donizetti (1797–1848) and Bellini (1801–1835). It seems obvious enough today that both these men wrote too hastily and without careful enough preparation to give their works any great staying power; but in their time, they were the rulers of the smart Parisian *monde*. In addition to comedies, they composed a number of nationalistic-romantic works, after the manner of the Byron-Scott school, whose influence was making itself felt in Italy as elsewhere. These happened to chime in well at the time with national aspirations; and so many a patriotic libretto was used, no matter what its national setting might be, the better to minister at the altar of Italian freedom.

We find such characteristic Bellini titles as these, expressive of either the patriotic or the melodramatic-romantic sentiments of the literary spirit of the age: *The Pirate*, *The Capulets and the Montagues* (that is, *Romeo and Juliet*), *Norma* (*The Druid Priestess*), *The Puritans*. Bellini did not live long enough to produce an imposing list of works; but Donizetti in his fifty-one years turned out an astonishing number of operas — some sixty-seven in all! This fact alone suggests to us that we can hardly expect anything but the slightest of construction in these works, although it is well to remember that there are other kinds of operatic quality than that to be found in the long-gestated music dramas of

Wagner. Some of Donizetti's titles are: *Alfred the Great, The Castle of Kenilworth, Elizabeth at Kenilworth, Lucy of Lammermoor* (*Lucia di Lammermoor*), based on Scott's romantic novels, *Anne Boleyn, Hugo, Count of Paris, Tasso, Mary Stuart,* and the already mentioned *Don Pasquale,* which Ernest Newman says has no rival in Italian comedy except perhaps Rossini's *Barber*. Here is a galaxy of romantic and historical people; not, it need hardly be said, a galaxy of portraits, but rather of dramatic figures given over to the stage conventions of opera. The great majority of these works do not now hold the stage, even in Italy; but in such works as do persist, we can trace the whole range of Italian powers in melodrama, and, above all, in comedic style.

Donizetti's melodramatic works were popular in a day when the drama was in rather dire straits; his librettos for the Paris opera, by the prolific Frenchman, Scribe,[1] are after a too-familiar pattern. But we have to consider these works, as indeed we must consider all of their time, in the light of the fact that the dramatic output of the first half of the century was exceedingly feeble (these were the days of Hugo and Dumas and Bulwer-Lytton) and with the understanding that to the Italians of that day opera meant almost nothing but singing. The audiences were remarkably exigent in that regard and remarkably careless about almost everything else. In particular, the orchestral parts are often extremely thin and the plots the merest novelettish cliché. Even when a good novel is adapted for the opera, the dramatic result is almost always deplorable, unity and proportion being sacrificed to musical high spots.

Take as an example such a plot of Donizetti's as *The Elixir of Love* (*L'Elisir d'amore*), an opera remembered now by but one air, *Una furtiva lagrima,* a favorite of Caruso's. In it a quack doctor sells a pretended love potion to a peasant, so that he may be able to win a wealthy bride from a soldier. When the peasant turns out to be wealthy, the maid relents, finding that, after all, she does love him. The love complications in such comedic works as *Don Pasquale,* however, do not require any test of logic. We have only to regard them with the eye that

[1] No artist has been more felicitously named; for Scribe wrote over a hundred opera librettos in the course of his life for different composers, including Auber, Meyerbeer, Boieldieu, and Halévy.

the amused observer Goldoni (1707–1793) employed when, following Molière, he fashioned his comedies of character, observing and delineating social oddities with a deft touch. If Donizetti and his fellows could have kept always to the level of the best Goldoni comedy, they would have built more securely. But it is useless to judge these operas from too elevated a dramatic standpoint; most of our pleasure in them comes from noting the manipulation of familiar characters and properties and marking how much passion the composers could infuse into threadbare sentiments and commonplace situations.

Such single airs of Donizetti's as have survived represent some of his best skill; for example, the *Spirito gentil* from *La favorita,* the sad farewell to worldly affairs of the hero who loved the king's mistress. In Caruso's record of this, we find much of the attraction of this kind of opera in the easy overcoming of vocal difficulties. Now that we no longer have singers who can do these arias in the grand manner, they lose most of their appeal. Of another kind is the " Mad Scene " from *Lucia,* where all manner of florid decoration surrounds themes of this extended *scena,* which is one of the greatest vocal tests for any soprano. But the inherent touching quality of Scott's drama here has power to make us forget some of the staginess: the heroine, believing her lover false, marries another man, and the lover, coming back, thinks, in turn, that she has been false to him. Under this great grief Lucy's mind deserts her; and the special pathos of the mad scene, which lifts it out of the ordinary, consists in her delusion that all her troubles are over and that she is to marry her beloved. The expression of her joy, though in decorative terms now outmoded, has a certain simple appeal for the sympathetic hearer; and there is no doubt that Donizetti found here a language that is both tuneful and emotionally apt. It is, however, in light comedy of the quick-riposte kind, such as we find in *Don Pasquale,* that his Italianate art shines most gaily.

Of Bellini's operas, almost the only one revived of late years is *Norma;* but *La sonnambula* (*The Sleepwalker*) made in its day the reputations of both Jenny Lind and Patti. Here the sentiment is, for us, rather heavy, but it is worth while to observe the delicacy of its expression in such an air as *Sovra il sen;* and a good example of pathetic expression is the sleep-walking air, *Ah, non credea*. In *Norma* there is the famous prayer *Casta diva* ("Chaste Queen of Heaven"), sung by the heroine, the Druid Priestess, one of the most taxing bits of vocal music ever written. There is some danger in judging any of these now rarely heard composers by single extracts: if, for instance, we were to judge Bellini by the duet in *The Puritans* in which the two gentlemen swear fidelity to their cause ("Sound the Trumpet"), we should probably find him heavy-handed, even clumsy. This is far from the truth; for most of Bellini's melodies have a grace, a tenderness, and a charm that make them distinctive. If his instrumentative and harmonic constructive gifts had been on a par with his melodic ability, he would have loomed as a much greater figure in the history of opera.

The influence of Italian opera upon the likings and the habits of both the English and the Americans is well worth marking, for it explains much that has been slow in the development of music in these two countries; a devotion to opera of the Italianate type on the part of society gave the plain man few opportunities to hear any other kind of music. It is in fact impossible to understand the development of music in Europe without realizing the force of middle-class convention, a force which was molded, in turn, by upper-class social leaders, royal patronage, and idolatry of the foreigner. It was all these that made the Italian opera popular in European countries, especially in England. And anyone reading the history of music in the United States during the nineteenth century will realize that to most of the people who had opportunities for hearing it music meant the Italian opera.

VERDI

With Giuseppe Verdi (1813–1901) we come to one of the grand old men of music in whom all musicians can delight. He was in essence a simple peasant, but he developed types of skill that no other Italian musician ever possessed. He was happy in a long life which gave him time to write twenty-seven operas, and most marvelous in the use he made of his later years, at a time when most men would have been content to rest on their laurels.

Verdi was born in a small hamlet in the north of Italy, where his father was the local innkeeper; as a young boy he showed signs of musical sensitiveness although he displayed no marvelous talent. He received his first musical instruction from the local organist, whose post he eventually inherited. Through the interest of a prosperous local merchant, Verdi was taken to Busseto, a small city in the vicinity of which he lived most of his life, and given lessons by the cathedral organist and director of the local orchestral society. This worthy musician, a good teacher and something of a composer, recognized the boy's aptitude and soon delegated some of his duties at the cathedral and at the Philharmonic Society to his fifteen-year-old protégé.

As soon as Verdi had achieved something of a local reputation, it was decided that he must go to Milan, where in 1822 he applied for entrance to the *Conservatorio*. Because he was eighteen years old (the age of admission to this famous music school was between nine and fourteen, and the pupils were supposed to leave when twenty), he was refused admittance; he settled down to study privately with Lavigna, the *maestro al cembalo* of the Milan opera. This study gave him a good grounding in the works of the Italian masters, especially Palestrina and Marcello; his public career as a composer may be said to have begun with the opera *Oberto, Conte di San Bonifacio*, undertaken at the suggestion of Masini, the director of one of the minor Milan theaters. Verdi took three years to finish this work, which was finally produced, not at the comparatively obscure theater for which it was intended, but at La Scala (1839), one of the greatest of Italian opera houses. The performance can hardly be called a success. "There is much in this opera," wrote a contemporary critic, "in common with the style of Bellini, above all an abundant, perhaps too abundant, wealth of melody. But where the words demand energy and passion the vocal line is often languid and monotonous." This is in strong contrast to the later Verdi, who is often criticized for being too violent and intense.

In this work and in those which followed it — *Un giorno di regno* (1840, a complete failure), *Nabucodonosor* (1841, the work which laid the foundation for his later success and fortune, for it made its composer the fad of the times), *I Lombardi* (1843, an even greater success, due

Casa di Riposo per Musicisti, Milan

VERDI

(From a painting by Giovanni Boldini)

partly to the attempt which the Church made to suppress it), and *Ernani* (1844) — Verdi followed the operatic fashions of the time, adding to his natural gifts for melody and strong dramatic characterizations a special patriotic touch which greatly strengthened works otherwise not particularly remarkable.

Between 1844 and 1851, the year which saw the production of the opera *Rigoletto*, Verdi's first enduring success, nine operas were written, an average of more than one a year. This composer never thought of himself other than as a man earning his living by providing good salable products, which in his case happened to be operas rather than oranges or orchids; but his inborn sense of truthfulness and his feelings as an artist were never overshadowed by his native shrewdness and business ability. Always he sought self-development and gradually achieved a composing technique that carried him to the greatest heights ever achieved in Italian opera.

From the viewpoint of today it is hard to agree with the critic of 1851 who said that the orchestration of *Rigoletto* was " remarkable, marvelous, the orchestra speaking and weeping alternately and arousing every passion." The works of these middle days of the '50's, *Rigoletto, Il Trovatore, La Traviata,* still hold the stage because of their simplicity and the energy of their melodies, their naïve dramatic truthfulness, and their innate psychological integrity. In spite of plots which today seem ridiculous — as one writer has remarked, it is doubtful whether anyone in the audience at a performance of *Il Trovatore* has a clear idea of what is happening in the last act — the concentrated and carefully developed emotional excitement of these works makes its effect and carries the audience along with torrential force.

Many of the twenty-seven operas that Verdi wrote were failures; but he never faltered, and in the end he learned to use the orchestra, particularly the wood winds, with a great deal of skill. One of Verdi's greatest assets, as well as a serious handicap, was the fact that throughout his whole life he was uninfluenced by his contemporaries. In a letter to a friend, written in 1875, he said:

> " I am unable to say what will emerge from the present musical ferment. Some want to specialize in melody like Bellini, others in harmony like Meyerbeer. I am not in favor of either. I should like a young man, when he begins to write, never to think about being a melodist or a futurist or any other of the devils created by this kind of pedantry. Melody and harmony should only be means to make music in the hands of the artist. If the day ever comes when we cease to talk of melody or harmony; of Italian or German schools; of past or future, etc., etc. — then perhaps the kingdom of art will be established.
>
> " Another calamity of the present time is that all the works of these young men are the products of *fear.* Everybody is excessively self-conscious in his writing and, when these young men sit down to compose, their predominant idea is to avoid antagonizing the public and to enter into the good graces of the critics.
>
> " You tell me that my success is due to a fusion of the two schools. *I never give either of them a thought . . .*"
>
> —Quoted in Toye: *Giuseppe Verdi*

It is this strong self-reliance that gave the works of Verdi's middle years a certain lack of flexibility.

After the highly productive years he could afford to take more time in writing; he composed but seven operas in thirty years. *La forza del destino* (1862) marks a transition point in his career and points the way to the later and much more elaborate style of *Aïda,* written in 1871 for the khedive of Egypt. It was not until *Othello,* however, written when he was 74, that Verdi came into his own. Set to a book which his musico-poetic friend and adviser, Boito, took from Shakespeare, this score may be said to represent the logical climax of the Italian operatic style, a style which always gives the stage precedence over the orchestral pit, which relies on the power of vocal melody rather than on orchestral resource to intensify mood and provide climax, and which looks upon the vocal ensemble not as a hindrance to dramatic development but as an opportunity to give expression at one and the same time to the various and often different sentiments of the singing actors on the stage. In its conception and execution *Othello* is magnificent theater, and, as a modern critic has said in reviewing a revival of this work, there has seldom if ever occurred in the musical theater such a happy welding together of movement, incident, and speech or such a sublimation of all three in inspired song.

When he was eighty, Verdi gave to the world his *Falstaff,* in which he seems to be once more striking out on a new line altogether, although the roots can be found in his earlier works. But what a difference between root and full-grown tree! *Falstaff* has a quicksilver speed and sheen: never has so rich a comedic spirit been embodied in music. Here sparkles the quintessence of Shakespearean sport and humor. Hearing a first-class performance of this opera — such a one as Toscanini has given at La Scala — leaves one breathless. There is no room here for the prima donna's spreading periods or for the hero's holding up of the dramatic action; everything is teamwork and rapierlike play, with a few moments of extended song. But how every flash of melody and turn of orchestration tells!

It used to be thought necessary to point out the strong Wagnerian influences in these later Verdi works. The example of Wagner may have stimulated Verdi's imagination, but there is not a trace of the Wagnerian conception of opera to be found in the Italian composer's style. Wagner thought of the opera fundamentally as a philosophic and symphonic conception, to be treated when necessary in a non-theatrical style. Dent has put it well in saying that often we see the Wagnerian characters only dimly through a rich orchestral haze. With Verdi, as with the long line of his Italian forebears, the opera was above everything else a vehicle for the vital projection of the drama: the characters stand in front of the orchestra, which provides them, at least in his late works, with a suitable and effective accompaniment. Accepting the conventional operatic procedures as those best adapted to his style, Verdi used them in such a way as to come close to providing the lyric theater with its most ideally balanced and integrated scores.

PUCCINI

Reviewing the activities of the post-Verdian Italian composers of opera provides little matter for great excitement. One name stands out above all the others — Puccini, who ranks in the great succession of openly sentimental, tune-making, voice-loving Italian melodramatists. His operas lack real integral development, but the way they pile up is often wonderfully rousing. Every move on the stage tells, for this composer had a perfect theatrical sense; and his stories and librettos were ideally designed for an end steadily held in view from the moment of the opera's first conception. His treatment of ideas has the not-too-common merit of adapting a style that is always recognizable as his to a plot that may be laid in any country or in any time. However critical we may be, we feel that it would be a disgruntled listener who, coming away from *La Bohème,* did not feel thoroughly satisfied with its Frenchness; from *Tosca,* with its Italianness; from *Madam Butterfly,* with its Japanese atmosphere; or from *Turandot* with its *chinoiserie.* Perhaps the fact that *The Girl of the Golden West* has not held the boards anything like so well as those other works is due to Puccini's failure to evoke anything resembling the wild-West, Buffalo-Bill atmosphere which the libretto

GIACOMO PUCCINI

demands. But his sense of the stage, as a generalized quality, and of particular atmosphere in varying works, together with his directness, his cutting superfluities, and his skill in placing his big scenes, his high lights, and the inevitable throb of his climaxes must be recognized by the student of opera.

Mr. Newman finds, as the central element in Puccini, " a self-pity that tried to heal itself of its wounds by lavishing pity upon others." This element did not crystallize until late in his life; and it is not impossible to find in Puccini's work, together with this self-pity, a certain personal hardness and curious cruelty. It is not always easy to distinguish between what is core, edible pulp, and rind, nor to separate the moving elements in the composer as a man and as an artist. We may note, in passing, that Puccini immensely admired Wagner, whom he knew to be an infinitely greater artist than himself or the rest of the men of his time. If, as someone has neatly said, he is so often to be found writing in Italics, it was partly because he had found that this was the individual way that fitted his mind and heart and realized that Germanics would be a misfit, and partly because he shrewdly knew that for success on the post-Wagnerian stage, effects must be swift, brief, cumulative, and shorn of undergrowth — shorn, even, of the philosophy that his latest work makes us think he was growing into. He had the born dramatist's eye for situations, curtains, big scenes; and, taking the long perspective of nineteenth-century opera, where, outside Verdi, could any similar vividness in this special respect be found? Though most operagoers have always thought infinitely more about the singers and their tunes than about anything else, there is in Puccini's works, marked or unmarked, the additional excitement of this big-scene element; there is also his special skill in delineating heroines, and women characters in general (more distinctively than men), a quality appealing additionally to the women in his audiences in an era of novel reading and the rise of the cinema.

It may be found that musicians are not so susceptible to some of the qualities in Puccini's music that delight the layman. They complain that so many of his tunes bear a family likeness; but what other element so much pleases the lovers of popular tunes, who, if they were presented with a different idiom in each, would never get them by heart and would therefore never like any of them? It is no small measure of Puccini's skill that he was able to hold the interest of millions in his tunes; if they had been too much alike, he could not have done so.[2]

Those whooping, soaring tunes, always carefully calculated for climax and vocal capacity, with the violins playing in octaves with them, prove irritating to some music lovers, yet are the very epitome of the sensuous machinery of Puccini's skill. The number of his different ways of attack is surprisingly limited, but his use of them is so skillful that the great majority of people like his music immensely and never complain of its being monotonous.

[2] Some day it might be profitable (musically, if not financially) to delve into the foundations of success in popular music. One of them is undoubtedly the art of reminding simple people of things they know and like, without being too reminiscent; but the degree to which reminiscence can be carried in such levels of musical art is very much greater than that which more experienced hearers will stand. On this score alone we can expect some difference between musicians and laymen in the estimate of composers like Puccini.

The curious and rather sad thing about him is that, just as he seemed about to take a new turning, he died. His new way would hardly have been as wonderful as that of Verdi in *Falstaff*, but his posthumous *Turandot* (and, to a similar extent, *Gianni Schicchi*, which more nearly adopts the standpoint of the *Falstaff* writing) seems to promise fresh pleasures for opera lovers, whether they happen to be devotees of Puccini's or not. And all such fresh pleasures in music need to be cultivated: there are not too many of them!

LESSER ITALIANS

Outside Verdi and Puccini, the tale of the late-nineteenth-century Italian opera composers is thin enough. But it would be ungrateful to pass by *Cav.* and *Pag.* (the familiar abbreviations of the two short operas, *Cavalleria rusticana* and *Pagliacci*, which have formed such a staple diet for opera lovers ever since they were written) without a word of appreciation, if only for their exciting effect on any who were fortunate enough to hear them in their heyday — the nineties.

It is interesting to compare a Puccini aria (such as *Vissi d'arte*) with a favorite from Mascagni's *Cavalleria* — the *Voi lo sapete*, for example. In the latter we have again manifest the Italian poignance, in a scene wherein the deserted maiden sings of her love for the man who has betrayed her and whom another girl has attracted. There is little to choose in the sentimental coloring, but a wider comparison of the two composers would show the superior resource and musicianship of Puccini. It is not, perhaps, easy to convince *Cavalleria* lovers of the difference because so many of them were brought up on the music in youth; such early loves are apt to be lasting, whatever the quality of their object. A clever critic suggested that the reason Mascagni has been liked best when at his worst is that only then is he most truly himself — sure of himself, unassailed by doubt, unmoved by any impulse (as Puccini was moved) to experiment and to probe wider worlds of feeling. Mascagni has never lacked flashes of the true imaginative spark; but the whole man was never able to catch fire from them. That was his tragedy. At one time he was called the true successor of Verdi; but since *Cavalleria*, written when Mascagni was twenty-six (it won a prize in an operatic-writing contest), not one of a dozen or more other operas of his has caught the easy ear of the public.

Leoncavallo (1858–1919) is another one-work man about whom there is no more to say than Mascagni; less, indeed, for his scope was slighter. Both these composers were caught up in the *verismo* craze of the time — a theory that operas and plays increase their artistic value through the depiction of the ugly and vulgar as well as the good and beautiful — stemming from the great success of Bizet's *Carmen* in France. The famous Prologue from Leoncavallo's *Pagliacci* is a happy enough idea dramatically, though its sentiment is pure humbug — that the sighs and tears from the other side of the footlights are real.

Montemezzi (*b.* 1875) is scarcely known save by one opera, *The Love of Three Kings*, in which the absence of a distinctive style is largely compensated for by a keen stage sense of melodrama. It has an ingratiating effect of summarizing certain of the most attractive Wagnerian and Puccinian qualities but is not in any sense a great work. The days of Italian operatic greatness are seemingly over — for the present, at least.

FRENCH OPERA OF THE NINETEENTH CENTURY

Music may be looked upon as a sort of thermometer that registers the degree of sensibility of the different peoples, according to the climate in which they live.

— Grétry: *Mémoires*, 1789

We love so many things in France that we do not really love music.

— Debussy

VARIOUS TYPES OF FRENCH OPERA

WE have seen how avidly, at the time of Rameau, the French took to the popular tuneful comic operas which the Italians imported into Paris. Under the aegis of such composers as Duni (an Italian),

Monsigny, and Dalayrac, they set about creating a school of comic opera of their own. In the *opéra comique* the connecting dialogue was always spoken, whereas the Italian *opera buffa* kept to the traditional recitative. Later on, at the beginning of the nineteenth century, the spirit of seriousness and revolutionary earnestness gave a new turn to *opéra comique*, a concern with grave and solemn subjects. For operas of the comic genre the term *opéra bouffe* was employed. And in distinction to both there evolved the *grand opéra*, embodying everything the term implies — florid vocalism, plenty of spectacle, and as much opportunity as possible for the ballet that was so beloved by the French. The grand opera was in its way as typical of the stateliness and grandeur of the autocratic state as were the other artistic manifestations of the spirit of the time — the Empire furniture and architecture.

André Ernest Grétry (1741–1813) and Étienne Nicolas Méhul (1763–1817) may be mentioned as typical writers of this *opéra comique* with a serious turn; both wrote a large number of works for the Paris stage. But the great man of the time was Cherubini (1760–1842), who stands as a curious link between the world of Gluck, Mozart, and Beethoven and the Romantic-dramatic world of the nineteenth century. If we are to believe Berlioz, Cherubini was a tiresome pedant; but of all opinions in the world, those of Berlioz must be taken with a generous helping of salt, for he lived in a difficult time and fitted in with few, which fact made him the powerful figure he was and one of heaven's rare gifts to French music.

CHERUBINI THE CLASSIC-ROMANTIC

Cherubini is usually considered as a follower of Gluck, but without his humanism; and of Mozart, without his humor and finesse. Yet a modern hearing of his symphony, commissioned by the London Philharmonic Society in 1815, shows him a man not dependent on anyone, one who was able to infuse immense spirit and dramatic sense into his writing. The one thing lacking — an element that is necessary to permanence — is the presence of big ideas. The music is spun along, not merely spun out, with remarkable verve; but one soon begins to long

A PERFORMANCE AT THE OPÉRA COMIQUE IN PARIS ABOUT 1780
(From a contemporary aquarelle now in the Opera Museum, Paris)

for something of real significance, the significance that can come only out of real depth of feeling. And that Cherubini simply did not have. Memories of his music are likely to center on one of the overtures to his operas — that to *The Water Carrier*, perhaps, or *Les Abencérages* or *Anacréon*. In these his classical leanings may be readily recognized and enjoyed, for his southern blood (he was born in Florence and did not come to Paris until 1788) tinges them interestingly. There is no doubt that Cherubini had skill and knew well how to direct it; but in the light of the Romantic school which followed him, his music is apt to sound thin and formal.

Paris had recovered too quickly from the spirit of Gluck's early reforms; it was in the midst of the throes of revolution; and there was plenty of competition for operatic recognition on the part of Méhul, Grétry, and Gossec. So we find Cherubini turning his attention to more serious affairs. He wrote a number of Masses, some of the best of them when he was nearly eighty. He wrote also some chamber music, though it is not so warm and sparkling as the best of his operatic writing, and he composed that odd symphony, which stands alone. Finally, in 1822, he became director of the Paris Conservatoire, giving new life and éclat to that illustrious school.

Recent attempts at reviving Cherubini's religious music do not give much promise that it will come back into regular use. It is here that his pedantry shows up most prominently, and all his scholarly devices fail to hide the fact that pertinent ideas do not flow generously or follow easily. A half-dozen operatic overtures really show this composer at his best: their brevity gives sufficient scope to his best qualities, and they do not continue long enough to show up his fatal defects.

BERLIOZ, BOIELDIEU, AND AUBER

Something of the dynamic influence of Berlioz has been suggested in another chapter; his operas had little success with the public. The best known of them, *Benvenuto Cellini* and *Beatrice and Benedict*, are occasionally revived by the French in a spirit of reverence. But they have, in spite of Berlioz's essential theatricalism in life, little dramatic value. The French have never seemed able to grasp the spirit of melodrama in opera as did the Germans; and so there is no influence in France similar to that of Weber in Germany, with all due respect to Berlioz's classically inspired, daemonic art. Boieldieu (1775–1834) is sufficiently remembered by an overture or two, that to *La dame blanche* being the most popular. His operas, however, are little but song *scenas*, put together, for the most part, against a mildly thrillerlike background. Auber (1782–1871), one of the longest-lived of composers, was able to make the best of two worlds, those of comic and grand opera. In his two score of operas he frolicked with the greatest of French ease, address, and versatility, and yet with a certain timidity, which was partly temperamental and partly the result of not developing his structural sense. In his *La muette de Portici* (also known as *Masaniello*) he was able to dig deeper. This work came out at a time (1828) when revolution was again in the air and deals with the Neapolitan patriot who led his people against Spanish tyranny. A performance of this work in Brussels in 1830 proved to be the torch which set fire to the revolution there against the Dutch. It may be noted that Verdi was, similarly, a rallying center in the fight for Italian freedom. These are strange surroundings for music, these stirrings amidst the destinies of nations!

So Auber, though he never thrilled before or again to the immediate excitement of social or political incentives, kept on in a sort of romantic playboy fashion, scarcely knowing whither the new Romantic spirit might lead, and too often allowing it to be overlaid with the cheapness of the penny thriller.

MEYERBEER THE MAGNILOQUENT

In this place we must also remember Meyerbeer, who, though treated at more length elsewhere, comes into the French scene as yet another of those composers of mixed origin who played a striking part in the development of French art, having been lured to Paris by the brilliant success possible there. One writer on the history of opera thinks that the opera house in Paris (built in 1861–1875), so familiar to every visitor to that *ville de lumière,* might well have been designed as Meyerbeer's monument, so masterfully heavy is its construction and so oppressive its wealth of ornament.

With this mention of Meyerbeer's Paris activities, we pass on to a consideration of what must be described, if we are to keep any sense of world-wide perspective, as comparatively small fry. Yet we need to beware, when considering nineteenth-century opera, of letting our minds be too fully occupied with the activities of the two really great figures, Verdi and Wagner, and failing to realize the essential qualities of the lesser men, Gounod, Massenet, Saint-Saëns, Bizet, and the rest. Their characteristic quality, be it personal or national, can be detected only by hearing a great deal of their music, and that is difficult, even in Paris. Halévy (1799–1862), for instance, is remembered solely by *La Juive,* an opera whose libretto was written for Rossini and rejected by him. In this work, the last opera in which Caruso appeared (in 1920), it is easy to see how the racial remembrance of persecution and sorrow has moved its Jewish composer. But in the rest of his operas, Halévy shows very little sense of stage character and depth of dramatic feeling; besides, the deceptive attraction of that great luminary, Meyerbeer, seems to have been impossible to resist.

A SENTIMENTALIZED " FAUST "

What need be said of Gounod (1818–1893)? Since his great charm lay in a certain sensuousness, it is easy to abuse him, especially when we realize how he maltreated Goethe's *Faust* and Shakespeare's *Romeo and Juliet.* And yet for years after its first production (in 1859) *Faust* was a musical favorite in all countries,[3] with its stirring scenes, its melodiously gilded music, its Romantic plot, and its gay, lively ballet music. In general, it may be said of Gounod, as it was of Sullivan, the English operetta composer, that he was " too much at ease in Zion " — his effects were too

[3] A noted American critic, punning on the term given by Wagner to the special theater which he had built for the production of his operas, the *Festspielhaus,* dubbed the Metropolitan Opera in New York the *Faustspielhouse.*

easily and too cheaply achieved. The ballet music is often heard; but, in most of the modern productions of *Faust*, how trivial is the dancing! We, who have been brought up on Diaghilev and the later *ballets russes*, not to speak of the modern abstractionists, are apt to forget the important place which the ballet held in French opera; and we must hear and see with different apparatus, if we can, the nineteenth-century French opera ballets, which seem to tend to kill what little dramatic reality we can find in these works.

Gounod is a combination of delicate sensuousness, entirely charming melody, and mild melodrama. Infinitely the greatest of these is his melody. Remembering that he was the composer of one of the world's most famous operas, let us enjoy this melody without too much sniffing and pass on to other French talents.

A PARODIZING BOULEVARDIER

Offenbach (1819–1880) is not easy to classify. He was a child of Jewish parents, and his great versatility probably came from a familiar and often-to-be-admired racial characteristic: he loved to do everything in a big way. This, a characteristic of the Paris of his day, the Second Empire, was fully appreciated; yet when a law was passed forbidding more than four characters on the scene at one time, as a form of protection for bigger enterprises, Offenbach could make the operetta form a huge success. He was a witty parodist: the Greek legends, so nobly treated by men like Gluck, were to him subjects for skits and jest; and he treated many of them in such clever works as *Orphée aux enfers* (1858) and *La belle Hélène* (1864). Romanticism, that movement of liberalism, took on this humorous aspect in the French taste of the '50's and '60's; and Offenbach could throw together two or three of these extravagant and parodying works in a year.

Yet his *Tales of Hoffmann*, a posthumous work, reveals a deeper power. This was revised and partly orchestrated by Guiraud; but its composer knew that it was his masterpiece, and there remains the question whether, if he had begun earlier to dig deeper, he might not have produced more of such works. Speculation is idle: enough that his inven-

OFFENBACH

tions have delighted millions and that his art has been well assimilated by many a composer since. We English-speaking peoples are most conscious of it in the works of Sullivan.

A GENIUS AND SOME TALENTS

Bizet (1838–1875) is remarkable in that, after writing a number of operas that were not notable successes but which stand musical scrutiny exceedingly well, he wrote one at the very end of his life, *Carmen*, that has remained one of the most popular of all operas, for it is as full of drama as his other works were short of it. It seems as if this composer's exquisite taste in the spinning of light harmonic webs was not sufficient to assure success until he came to the one subject which fired his imagination — that of the highly temperamental and irresistibly charming Spanish

GEORGES BIZET

cigarette girl, Carmen. This is one of the happiest "accidents" in the whole history of opera; for this work, produced only three months before Bizet's untimely death, remains an unalloyed delight as well for the unsophisticated listener as for the jaded musician.

Hardly ever has a composer of real worth become so completely obscured by his work as Bizet. His correspondence, published a number of years ago, does not in any sense reveal the sort of man we should expect from hearing such a work as *Carmen*. Instead of a lively, independent musical liberal, we find an industrious, gifted, careful musician who thought of his profession only as a means for acquiring honors and making money.

He early received recognition for his undoubted gifts, and in 1857, before he was 19, he was given the *Prix de Rome*, which was the highest official honor that France could bestow on a young composer. Several works came out of his study in Rome: *Don Procopio*, to an Italian libretto, and *La guzla de l'emir,* the latter destroyed after it had been accepted at the Opéra Comique. But his later operas, *Les pêcheurs de perles* (*The Pearl Fishers*), 1863, and *La jolie fille de Perth* (*The Fair Maid of Firth*), 1867, each received eighteen performances during his lifetime, despite the fact that they show but little originality of melody, harmony, or orchestration. Bizet then undertook three more works for the French theater, leaving them all unfinished in order to work at his one-act *opéra comique, Djamileh,* which was berated by the critics because of its Wagnerian tendencies.

In spite of this long list of failures and half-completed attempts at writing operas, another theater manager asked Bizet for a score, this time for incidental music to a play by Daudet, *L'Arlésienne*. Although in its original form this music was a failure, the composer later presented it without the drama and achieved considerable success with it. In this music (usually heard in two orchestral suites), redolent of the south, Bizet for the first time let himself go and wrote as he actually felt, without consideration for effects. The result is music beloved by all who have heard it and thought by some to be better music than that in *Carmen*.

Notwithstanding the fact that Bizet's librettists destroyed much of the original strength of Mérimée's story on which *Carmen* is based and that Bizet himself had no thought of achieving authentic Spanish atmosphere in it, he was able to provide such unsual harmonies, modulations, and orchestral color as to make his opera a great success. As someone has well said, it is the spirit of dramatic fervor and the musical quality of this work which triumphed over its obvious weaknesses. It was the first of a long succession of *verismo* operas, works which emphasize sordid and brutal subjects rather than the usual noble, inspiring, or humorous ones.

A statement that throws a great deal of light on French taste is the one, taken from a French history of music, to the effect that the "musician who really ruled the theater between the years 1880 and 1910" was J. Massenet (1842–1912). Possessed of a certain delicacy of sentiment and lightness of craftsmanship, these works of Massenet's — *Hérodiade* (based on the story of St. John the Baptist and Salome), *Thaïs, Manon, Werther* (bowdlerized Goethe), and *Le jongleur de Notre Dame* —

seem hardly more to us today than musical rose water and glycerin — glutinous masses of sweet sentimentality faintly perfumed with the odor of romance. His teacher, Ambroise Thomas (1811–1896), is of even lesser import, though he is remembered for his setting of Goethe's *Mignon*.

It can hardly be maintained, in reality, that either literary or musical taste was on a very high level in nineteenth-century France, in spite of the fact that it was the only country which officially patronized literature through supporting an academy of literary artists. It was Scribe, the facile librettist and playwright, who set the standards; he was able between the years 1820 and 1850 to "create a play frame so perfectly articulated, so facilely constructed, that any sort of sentimental stuff could be tacked on it and made plausible. His was the supreme triumph of mechanics over dramatic content. Even while innocent of any of the larger virtues of the dramatist — he knew nothing of character drawing and little of dramatic grip in the profound sense — he made hundreds of plays that pleased untold audiences. He mastered theatrical device, filled his pieces with obvious type figures, pathetic incidents, skillful ravelings and unravelings, clever sayings, happy endings, etc., and developed a formula for theatrical effectiveness" (Cheney: *The Theatre*).[4] In brief, he gave the people what they wanted, a smooth article and a sweet concoction. And it was this taste which created the demand in French dramas and librettos throughout most of the century.

It was a long time before genius or poetry or incisive characterization came into the music drama, in Germany in Wagner and in France, in a smaller way, in Debussy. It was one of the strange moves of fate that enabled Debussy, whose music is hardly dramatic at all, to write the only French opera that can genuinely be called a masterpiece — *Pelléas et Mélisande*. But this did not come until 1902. Before then it must be allowed that, with a mild outburst into "realism," as when Bruneau set Zola's *Attack on the Mill* or when Bizet wrote *Carmen* or when Charpentier used his charming lyrical gifts in setting *Louise* at the end of the century, there is little but melodramatic Romanticism of a weak sort in any

[4] "It is said that Heine on his deathbed, when his breath was failing, was asked if he could hiss; and his answer was: 'No, not even a play of Scribe's'" (Cheney).

French opera of the period, with the possible exception of two by Chabrier (1841–1894), whose *Gwendoline* and *Le roi malgré lui* show definite Wagnerian tendencies.

Saint-Saëns (1835–1921), a curious mixture of Classicism and sentimentality, wrote, daringly, upon the Biblical story of Samson and Delilah, a theme which so shocked the English that they refused to allow this work, which was highly popular elsewhere — first produced by Liszt at Weimar in 1877 — on their operatic stages until 1909! Saint-Saëns carried French (and Jewish) versatility to its extreme; he did not hesitate to attempt all manner of things; but only *Samson et Dalila* has kept the boards. Edouard Lalo (1823–1892), in his *Le roi d'Ys*, treated an exotic subject with imaginative delicacy.

As early as 1830 Halévy made a ballet of *Manon Lescaut*, one of the sentimental tales by the Abbé Prévost that several composers (including Puccini, Auber, and Massenet) delighted to set. There have been a number of other French ballet composers: everyone knows Delibes's charming *Coppélia* music, brought out at the time of the Franco-Prussian War; and the ballet suites of Luigini (a Frenchman in spite of his name) have been done to death on every conceivable occasion.

Dukas, who has so long been thought of merely as the composer of the witty tone poem, *L'apprenti sorcier*, wrote a delightful opera, *Ariane et Barbe Bleue*, a setting of a Maeterlinck fantasy with a decidedly Wagnerian tincture. The operas of Fauré (1845–1924) are almost as unknown outside Paris as are his other distinguished works. *Penelope* (1913) is one of his few contributions to the lyric stage, but his music to the play *Shylock* is well worth hearing, and that for *Pelléas et Mélisande* forms an interesting study in comparison with Debussy's. Vincent d'Indy (1851–1931) is another neglected French composer. He was a follower of Franck, and his *La Légende de Saint-Christophe* (1920), a kind of combined oratorio and opera, contains some delectable music, while such extracts from *Fervaal* as can ordinarily be heard reveal a great talent. No résumé of French operatic activities, however brief, would be complete without mention of André Messager (1853–1929), writer of a great number of melodious operettas which had a phenomenal success in France and England.

There seems to be only one conclusion possible after surveying France's contributions to the operatic form: although there was a great deal of activity, very little that is worth while came of it, and that, although many of the decisive moves in the development of this form were made in Paris, the French have contributed few first-rate operas to the international repertoire. It seems that the capacity of this people lies more in writing music for plays than in producing indissoluble music and drama. A striking proof of this is the lack of any great demand today on the part of the world's outstanding opera houses, such as Covent Garden, London, and the Metropolitan in New York, for performances of French works. These establishments have their Italian wings and their German wings, but the French departments have slowly degenerated into a state of innocuous desuetude. An occasional *Faust* or *Carmen* is offered as a vehicle for some star; but of the rest there is hardly a sign. They seem to have disappeared completely beneath a flood of Wagner, Verdi, Mozart, Puccini, and the like. Whether the future will make any change in such a decisive verdict remains to be seen.

GERMAN OPERA OF THE NINETEENTH CENTURY

ROOTS OF GERMAN OPERA

THE roots of nineteenth-century German opera, the roots out of which there came the rich fruit of the Romantic operas of Weber and the music dramas of Wagner, will be found in the native *Singspiel* [5] and its poor but attractive relative, the *Zauberposse* (the fairy pantomime). Spurred on by the great successes of the *opéra comique* and the *opera buffa* in other countries, German composers made a number of attempts during the eighteenth century to create something that would be a real national opera. Anton Schweitzer set the German poet Wieland's

[5] The first German *Singspiel*, a play with songs written after the manner of the English *Beggar's Opera*, was produced in Leipzig in 1752 with the title *Der Teufel ist los* (*The Devil's to Pay*). There followed a whole series of these works written by Hiller (1728–1804), which attained great success.

Alceste to music in 1773, and a worthy Mannheim *Kapellmeister* by the nonmusical name of Ignaz Holzbauer made a setting of a German historical play, *Günther von Schwarzburg,* in 1776. But these efforts proved to be without natural life, stillborn imitations of Italian opera performed in the German language. They lacked the warming influence of the Romantic spirit that was soon to spread over the whole country and prove such a stimulus to German artists; and they unfortunately did not have the inspiring example of Mozart and his *Don Giovanni* and *Die Zauberflöte* or of Beethoven and his mighty muse to aid them in their enterprise. All these influences helped to mold the form and to shape the substance of the German national opera when it finally arrived. Even Beethoven's opera *Fidelio,* in spite of the composer's evident distaste for the form and his inexperience in handling voices, showed how powerfully affecting the Romantic spirit in opera might be when directed by a great mind.

ITS BIRTH WITH WEBER

The actual birth of German opera may be said to date from the time of Weber (1786–1826), a musico-dramatist whose style from the beginning of his work was an individual one and not a mere imitation of those who had preceded him. His opera *Der Freischütz* is a perfect expression in music of the spirit of the legends and fireside tales of daemonic power and romantic human prowess, of love stories and darkling fate, that had been so happily injected into German literature by the Romantic Movement. *Sturm und Drang* mingled with Classicism in Germany without mutually destructive effects: Schiller and Goethe, Herder and Richter wrought powerfully but not internecinely, as have so many literary figures in other lands. The German spirit of these early years of the nineteenth century could say, with Whitman of a later age, "I am large; I contain multitudes."

We have seen how Romanticism came to Germany about 1800. Politics, inevitably, became mingled with literature, but the various phases of the Romantic spirit had ample depth of earth in the national temperament, and some of them cast strong roots clear back to the Middle Ages.

The Revolution of 1848, a revolution which flamed over the greater part of Europe, broke up many associations and uprooted many fine growths as well as some which by then had become weak and cumbersome. And in the latter part of the century the national spirit became increasingly tinctured with the philosophies of other countries. We can say again (as of Beethoven) that one of the happiest facts about Weber's short career was the fact that he was the right man at the right time, a time when the national consciousness was ready to flower in a natural way, without those wasteful defiances and war cries which so often accompany new ideas.

THE GERMANY OF NATURE AND LEGEND

It is the natural genius of the German forests, with their mysterious songs and tales, that we find predominant in Weber's music. He understood and could depict simple, homely things. His style struck fire immediately, for it was folky in its speech and friendly in its feeling. Even hostile critics have had to admit a certain "inevitable beer-gardeny obviousness." He had not the all-powerful grasp of a Wagner, nor the rapid-fire skill of a Mozart. The end of *Der Freischütz* is hurried and unspacious; so, for that matter, is the end of most of the Italian and French operas of the time. But no dramatic stroke, no passage of however few chords, misses its mark; Weber was as accurate a harmonic shooter as was the bedeviled hero of his opera.

His every overture forms an almost complete synopsis of the story which follows: vividly before us parade hero and villain, as well as the minor characters. The overture to *Der Freischütz,* for instance, contains four or five leading themes, besides sufficient serenity of melodic beauty and urgency of rhythm to please anyone who might prefer to know nothing of the drama lest such knowledge take the edge off his musical appetite. Weber's apt harmonies light up a scene as with a flame: that is, if we are able to hear them with pre-Wagnerian ears! His uses of the brass are surprisingly advanced for his time, and his broad, flowing tunes could hardly be bettered, while in the overtures there is little waste of time or material in getting from theme to theme.

The heroine's air in *Der Freischütz* (*Leise, leise*), sung by Agatha as she is waiting in the moonlight for her lover, is typical of Weber's writing. The tenderness of the opening is exquisite, and there is something attractively simple-hearted about the curves of the melody; they are so full of feeling without being sentimental. It is in his hunting and drinking songs that Weber strikes one of the familiar and folky notes which give his operas such wide appeal, both to the simple and the skilled. There is an obvious parentage to many of the ideas in Wagner's early opera, *The Flying Dutchman*, a parentage to be sought in Weber's melodic flights and his orchestral intensity. Wagner first heard *Der Freischütz* when he was but eight; and five years after that Weber was dead. Notable among the heritages Weber left to his great successor was an effective and consistent use of recurring musical ideas at dramatically significant points in the development of the drama, a device which Wagner was later to employ so startlingly.

This is especially to be noted in *Euryanthe*, the work which in Weber's own mind represented his best attempt to establish a German grand opera as the equivalent of the Italian *opera seria*. *Euryanthe*, in Weber's words, is to be considered as a " dramatic essay which counts upon the collaboration of all the sister arts for its effects and is ineffectual if deprived of their assistance." Unfortunately it is burdened with such a foolish libretto as to make it almost impossible of enjoyment to a present-day listener, however sympathetic he may be to Weber's ideals in writing it. " To make excisions within so organic a whole as this grand opera is impossible, if the composer has thoroughly thought out his work," continues Weber. Here in essence is the theory which Wagner was to use later in developing his music dramas. As a noted German critic has put it, in *Euryanthe* the seed was planted from which the whole form of the music drama was to grow; and Wagner did more than perform an act of piety when he began his career as a conductor in Dresden with a performance of this opera.

Weber's attempt to capture national feelings and enthusiasms must not be forgotten in a summary of his qualities; for this was an aspect of his Romanticism which added spice to his style. He was able, largely through his handling of the orchestra, to give a characteristic color to each of his works: *Der Freischütz* is, of course, darkly mysterious with the atmosphere of the German forests; *Euryanthe* is gallantly chivalrous with the chivalry of medieval times; *Oberon* and *Turandot* (the latter being incidental music which he wrote for Schiller's play) paint in fantastic colors the daintiness of fairyland and the glory of the East.

FORETELLING WAGNER

In everything he did Weber was feeling his way toward the synthesis that was afterwards achieved by Wagner. The later composer had a greater sense of balance as well as a much stronger grasp of his materials; but it was Weber, so little taught but so admirably inspired, who moved German opera into a position from which Wagner could later build. This was his greatest glory, although he would certainly deserve a place in music's hall of fame for his own inimitable qualities.[6]

MEYERBEER

Giacomo Meyerbeer, born Jakob Liebmann Beer (1791–1864), has been abused about as much as any composer in the world, partly with reason, and partly, unjustly. It has been said of him that he " wrote only for effect " and would hang about the stage, listening to remarks from all sorts of people, and altering his music accordingly. But such expedients had the good quality of working; they made Meyerbeer what he was, a master of effects for effect's sake. And there have been plenty of artists in other spheres who, in their time, were regarded as great, and whom time has found out. So why pick particularly on Meyerbeer? He was no fool and did not trust to merely a few overpowering moments for his effects; he took plenty of care about all his moments. If he did not have

[6] We might well add here that in addition to Weber's contributions to operatic development, he was important as the forerunner of the Romantic composers of small piano pieces of independent form — the *Klavierstücke*, as the Germans call them. His use of this style led directly to the piano pieces of Schubert, Schumann, Chopin, Liszt, and a host of minor figures. He is considered also one of the pioneers in the writing of music for *Männergesangvereine* (men's song societies).

sufficient ideas to fill them all according to modern standards, he was at least able to make a definite impression on his contemporaries, who were struck with his bold shaping of drama and his ceaseless activity in diversifying his expression.

One of the best reasons for his success was the fact that he happened to fit the mind of his day extremely well, the day after the revolutionary turmoils in France, when the new urges and demands of the common man were being more and more considered. Meyerbeer was able to dramatize common problems, and so he seized the imagination of the public. After a precocious career in Italy and Germany, he came to Paris in 1826 and made a brilliant hit with his *Robert le diable*, a furious melodrama in which the lost souls of nuns were given over to evil. He followed this up with other spectacular and novel subjects: the great explorer, Vasco da Gama, in *L'Africaine*; history brought to life and made larger than life in *Les Huguenots*, which treats of the struggle of Catholics and Huguenots in France; the Anabaptist uprising of the sixteenth century, and its great figure John of Leyden, in *Le prophète*. He made sure that his novelties would catch the ear of his time; and he also took care that the best casts of prima donnas should grace them: Jenny Lind, for example, making her first appearance in *Robert*, in 1847.

For all these works Meyerbeer wrote music of power which sometimes rose to heights of real grandeur. Such a thing as the "Blessing of the Swords" from *The Huguenots*, for instance, is terrific; there is no other word for it. But he was not able to sustain such a mood; he was incessantly changing his style to catch the public ear, with the result that his operas lack consistency and spontaneity. They seem forced, overpompous, and grandiose to us today; yet they made Meyerbeer the man of the hour in Paris in the thirties, just as Weber had been the man for the decade before in Germany. Even a slight acquaintance with such a career as his should teach us not to trust present appearances. How easy it is to reckon a Meyerbeer the equal of a Weber, or even, if he chime with the mood of the time, as greater! The whole lifework of such a spectacular figure should prove clearly enough that things are not always what they seem and that a facile temporary success may prove to be the best and surest passport to oblivion.

CONTEMPORARIES

A whole host of German opera writers contemporary with Jakob Beer has been accurately, if not very elegantly, described as "small beers." There was Marschner (1795–1861), who was perhaps more of Weber's lineage, since he manifested an ardent interest in the doings of the devil. His *Hans Heiling* is full of the supernatural Romanticism of the period and so has great interest for Germans but not much for anyone else. Marschner's greatest misfortune was to live too long. Before he had written his last opera, Wagner was on the scene with his *Rienzi* and *The Flying Dutchman*, and the lesser man was soon lost in the excitement engendered by these powerful works.

Then there was Flotow (1812–1883) — almost exactly contemporary with Wagner. Even the shortest extract from his one-time popular *Martha* shows the grace of this composer's talent. His invention, however, was by no means equal to his ability for writing tunes, and so he has not survived. Nicolai had such a very short life (1810–1849) that we can well deplore the loss of a man who could achieve the Shakespearean sparkle of *The Merry Wives of Windsor*, a work which he wrote but a few months before his end. Lortzing (1801–1851) had the good fortune to be brought up amid stage surroundings and to be an operatic singer himself. His fortunes were as changeable as his skill was limited. But he had a certain sense of good-humored fun, and his *Czar und Zimmermann* (*Czar and Carpenter*), telling of the adventures of Peter the Great of Russia, has survived (at least in Germany) because of these simple humors, while serious works by the score have died. Perhaps, as much as anything, the lighter works of these composers survived because (as Professor Dent has suggested) they speak an international language and contain so many bits of music by the admired classical writers.[7]

Peter Cornelius (1824–1874) is better known by his songs and choruses than by operas; but there is one, *The Barber of Bagdad*, which is still remembered kindly. The composer was a nephew of a well-known German painter and grew up in an artistic milieu. He was a great friend and

7 Perhaps we like them for the same reason that the man enjoyed *Hamlet* — because it contained, he found, so many well-known quotations!

disciple of Wagner's and did most of his work in the circle of the Wagnerians. Having a stronger sense of style than most of his contemporaries, he was not entirely swamped by the tremendous vigor of the great figure of his epoch. He was a quiet soul, fervent, generous, and simple. His music deserves more recognition than it has ever received; but his gift was more lyric than dramatic, and he was wise to confine it to those subjects which gave him the right feeling of freedom.

It is fitting that we add here, because of the contemporary popularity of one of his operas, the name of another operatic composer who is little known today—Karl Goldmark (1830–1915). *Die Königen von Saba,* first produced in Vienna in 1875, became known the world over; Goldmark spent ten years in writing it, lavishing on its glowing score his natural warmth of expression and love of Oriental color. He wrote in addition six other operas, besides a great deal of orchestral music.

His nephew, Rubin Goldmark (1872–1936), became a well-known figure in American music: a pupil of Dvořák's, he wrote considerable orchestral music, but was best known for his influence as a teacher. For over thirty years he taught in New York, where many of the younger generation of American composers studied with him, among them Aaron Copland and George Gershwin.

AN ISOLATED FIGURE: HUMPERDINCK

One other German opera composer, this time of the post-Wagnerian period, deserves special mention here: Engelbert Humperdinck, born in 1854. (Richard Strauss, the greatest of all German opera composers since Wagner, is dealt with in a separate chapter.) Humperdinck is known for two operas—his charming, heart-on-sleeve *Hänsel und Gretel,* still a good draw for lovers of sentiment, and *Die Königskinder.* It is perhaps unfair to complain that Humperdinck was so often nearly Wagnerian, and then not quite: he did well to keep so much of his own soul in that day. While he lacked the forging power of the greater man, he never wrote an ugly or a careless page. There is ample beauty in his music, much more than one might expect from his busy life as critic and professor. Criticism never seemed to sour him, and his music sounds anything but

JOHANN STRAUSS WITH HIS ORCHESTRA IN THE VOLKSGARTEN, VIENNA

(Drawing by F. Kaliwoda in the Historical Museum, Vienna)

academic. The happy display of German toys in *Hänsel* is never vulgar, for Humperdinck had good taste as well as a lively imagination, gifts sometimes denied to Germans. In *Die Königskinder* he seems to be seeking deeper and trying to build more boldly; and sometimes in it he comes very near to a great nobility of feeling that is not readily found in the work of that day. But it is high promise, usually, rather than complete fulfillment. One can but feel drawn to this rather lonely figure of the Wagnerian epoch.

It would be ungracious to forget here those great providers of the Viennese gaieties of the century, the Johann Strausses, father and son, as well as the lesser composers, Von Suppé and Millöcker. Johann Strauss the elder was made conductor of the court balls of Vienna in 1845. His son established his own reputation first through a series of summer concerts in St. Petersburg from 1855 to 1865. From 1870 on he wrote mainly operettas: merely to catalogue his and his father's works would be an immense task. Everyone should hear young Johann's *Die Fledermaus* as it is sung by his compatriots, not as it is done by heavy-handed Anglo-Saxons; it belongs to the gay Viennese life of the period which paralleled

Courtesy of the British Museum

PLATE FROM THOMAS WILSON'S "DESCRIPTION OF GERMAN AND FRENCH WALTZING," 1816

The waltz began with the march, partners standing side by side with arms held in the position shown in Figure 1, or, alternatively, Figure 2. Soon the dancers began the slow waltz, Figures 3 and 4; the more lively *sauteuse* followed, with jumping steps, Figures 5, 6, and 7. Then came the *jetté*, in which the couples whirled about in quick tempo in the position shown in Figure 8; and Figure 9 shows the final pose.

that of mid-century Paris, when so many minor composers flourished there, and represents the Offenbach operetta as seen and heard through another volatile nation's eyes and ears. But Strauss the younger was a much better musician than was Offenbach, and his waltzes [8] and operettas have never been surpassed.

[8] The waltz first appeared as a prominent dance somewhere about the end of the eighteenth century, its vogue being particularly pronounced during the 1820's and 1830's. It seems to have descended from the old German *Ländler* and to have had a special fascination for the Viennese, who, Beethoven complained toward the end of his life, were waltz mad. Chopin, too, found that people would rather attend the astonishingly numerous balls than his recitals. A distinguishing feature of the dance was the various posturings of the arms, which freedom of gesture excited violent comment from many onlookers of the period, who complained of "the undue freedom with which the ladies were treated, and the obliging manner in which the freedom was returned by the females" (Burney).

RICHARD WAGNER AND THE MUSIC DRAMA

THE IMPOSSIBILITY OF SAYING ANYTHING NEW

ERNEST NEWMAN, the English music critic who has written so extensively on the subject of Richard Wagner and his music, somewhere remarks that three figures of the nineteenth century have been the subject of a more extensive literature than any other figures in the whole range of human history. These three men are Napoleon Bonaparte, Abraham Lincoln, and Richard Wagner. Consequently anyone intending to write, no matter how briefly, on Wagner and his place in the history of music, must approach the subject with considerable hesitation. There are not many so fortunate as Lawrence Gilman, late critic of the *New York Herald Tribune*, who, in the preface to his book on this composer, says something to the effect that one must stand forever dumb before the vastness and imposing majesty of Wagner's music, and then proceeds to write one of the most eloquently persuasive books ever published on the Wagnerian music dramas.

There is nothing new that can be said at this late date about Wagner. His great works, *The Ring of the Nibelung, Tristan and Isolde,* and *The Mastersingers,* are capable of refuting any arguments that may be brought against them and their place in the literature of music. Not that they are perfect works or works in which it is not easy to find serious defects. But, nevertheless, we are gradually coming to realize, after long years of argument and debate, that they are worthy of being included in the register of man's greatest achievements, along with such other " imperfect works " as the sagas of the primitive peoples — *The Iliad* and *The Odyssey, The Kalevala* and *The Nibelungenlied;* the great plays of the Grecian dramatists; and the works of Shakespeare. And any account of the role which music has played in the revelation of the human spirit would be hopelessly inadequate without some detailed reference to them.

WAGNER'S PLACE IN HISTORY

It is not difficult to summarize briefly Wagner's position in history: to say that, inspired more or less by what he considered to be the ideals of the Greek dramatists, he envisioned a sort of superart in which the separate arts of music, drama, the dance, and painting were to be combined. And that for the carrying out of these ideals, he had to invent a new type of musical language, one which was made up of short themes (*Leitmotive* or leading themes, he called them), each of them representative of ideas and personages in the operatic story; and that in doing so he achieved the reform of opera which had been attempted at various times and by various composers ever since the Italians made it an instrument for vocal display rather than a means for conveying emotions.

But there is more to the subject than this. Otherwise it would never have been possible for Gilman to express the opinion that *The Ring of the Nibelung,* that enormous conglomeration of loose ends, contradictory motives, and unbelievable magic, was not only the hugest thing ever attempted by one creative mind, but that it is also, in the ultimate sense of the word, the greatest. The thing that explains Wagner, that gives him an unparalleled place in art history, is the fact that he was able to make all the multifarious activities of his tremendously alert mind — all his dramatic theories, his elaborate philosophic beliefs, his theatrical plots — the excuse for some of the most vital and deeply moving music ever written. He himself claimed — and very probably believed — that in opera poetry and drama and the arts of the stage should have an equal rank with music. But, fortunately for us, he had more than the courage of these convictions: using Beethoven's symphonies as models, logically developing in the music which he wrote for the stage the same principles which the earlier composer had employed in his works for the orchestra, Wagner achieved effects which transcended all his ideals.

With Wagner, in spite of his carefully elaborated theories, the stage drama was merely the outward form for shaping the musical ideas he had in mind, just as the sonata, the rondo, and the other traditional forms had conditioned the inspiration of Mozart and Beethoven. The drama, working itself out on the stage, was the means for instigating the music which accompanies it in the pit. And the modern researches of German critics, especially those of Alfred Lorenz, show conclusively enough [9] that the structural principles of architectural form underlie all Wagner's mature music and that it is as "formal" as are the symphonies of Beethoven.

It is the music, not the play, that is the important thing in Wagner. Contrary to general opinion, the drama with him was really nothing but a guide to the dramatic development which is constantly taking place in the music. Since he happened to be a less-talented dramatist and poet than he was a composer (unlike most opera composers, he himself constructed all the librettos for his operas) his works contain a good deal of second-rate and third-rate drama, as well as a considerable amount of poetry that, to put it mildly, is little better than literary doggerel. But this is of minor importance in comparison with the fact that he was a first-rate musician and one, moreover, that was deeply moved by the contemplation of the innate tragedy of man's existence, a tragedy which inspired most of his plots for the stage. The real difference between his music and that of Bach and Beethoven lies not so much in its structure as in the fact that, unlike them, Wagner was essentially a man of the theater and so depended on the dramatic stage for the instigation of his musical ideas.[10] A brief glimpse of his life history will explain this.

[9] See Lorenz's monumental four-part work, *The Secrets of Form in Richard Wagner.*

[10] Both Bach and Beethoven, as we have seen, depended somewhat on exterior associations for their inspiration, Bach being strongly moved by a world of visual images and Beethoven by idealistic concepts.

A COMPLEX, BAFFLING CHARACTER

It is because Wagner's character was so complex, so baffling and contradictory in many of its aspects, in brief, because he was so outstanding, considered simply as a human phenomenon, that a study of his biography is particularly interesting and rewarding. There is little wonder that in the hundred twenty-odd years since his birth all sorts of biographies have appeared, in an attempt to explain his extraordinary career, some of them written by men who have had little musical experience or background. A detailed examination of such a crowded life as his is beyond the scope of a chapter such as this; but there are certain elements in his personality and events in his life that had a direct influence on the nature of his music. These should be considered.

His love for and dependence on the theater go back to his earliest days. He was reared in a stage atmosphere: his family, its members typical German *bourgeoisie* of that period, was keenly interested in the theatrical life of Leipzig, where Wagner was born in 1813. His stepfather (some of Wagner's biographers, including the careful Newman, lean to the belief that he may have been his real father),[11] Ludwig Geyer, was an actor and a playwright and a considerable figure on the German stage of that time. Others of his family, including a brother, a sister, and a niece, made distinguished careers for themselves in drama. Indeed, Johanna Wagner, the niece, became one of the best-known operatic singers of her generation and was of considerably more importance in the eyes of the world of that time than was Richard. In his autobiography, Wagner tells us:

"What particularly attracted me to the theater — by which I mean the stage itself, the rooms behind the scenes, and the dressing rooms — was not so much the desire for entertainment and distraction, as it is with the theatrical public of the present day, but the provocative delight of

[11] The appendix to the second volume of Newman's monumental *Life of Richard Wagner* gives a good summary of the arguments which lend credence to the idea that Geyer was Wagner's father. It also shows the probability of Wagner's mother being, not the daughter of a humble baker, as has been supposed, but the natural daughter of one of the ducal family of Weimar, Prince Constantine, a brother of Karl August, the Grand Duke who did so much to help Goethe. If this is true, it would go far towards explaining Wagner's genius.

being in an element that opposed to the impressions of everyday life an absolutely different world, one that was purely fantastic, and with a touch of horror in its spell. Thus to me a stage setting, even a wing representing merely a bush, or a costume, or even a characteristic part of one, seemed to have come from another world, to have a sort of ghostly interest, and I felt that the contact with it must be a lever to lift me from the commonplace reality of the routine of daily life to that enchanting demon world."

Could anything be more revealing as to the real source of his mature inspiration? His whole afterlife was occupied in some sort of connection with the footlights, from the early posts as opera conductor in such provincial towns as Würzburg and Königsberg, where he learned the practical details of his profession, to the climax of his career at Bayreuth, where he built his own theater and superintended the production of his own works.

WAGNER AS ROMANTICIST

Of all composers of this epoch, Wagner may be said to exemplify most completely the Romantic spirit. We have shown how the revolution in aesthetic ideals which marked the last part of the eighteenth century was coincident with, and partly the result of, the social and political ferments preceding the American and French revolutions; and how one of the artistic results of this rise of democratic idealism was the rediscovery of that huge reservoir of folk poetry which the classicists, in their scholastic refinement, had taken the trouble to forget. It was this Romanticism, revived in the literary productions of the men of the latter part of the eighteenth century — Percy in England, Macpherson in Scotland, Herder and Goethe in Germany [12] — which affected so strongly the aesthetic atmosphere of Wagner's day. When this was combined with the spirit of

[12] As we have seen, Percy's *Reliques of Ancient English Poetry* (1765) rescued a large number of old English folk songs and ballads from oblivion; Macpherson's so-called Ossianic poems, probably largely translations into the vernacular of many of the bardic legends of the Celtic race, were published 1761–1765. Herder's *Voices of the Folk in Song* (1779), called the first international anthology of folk literature in the modern world, based most of its material on Percy. These, together with Goethe's great *Faust*, were striking manifestations of the rediscovery of the power of emotion to be found in the legends of the people.

THE TWENTY-EIGHT-YEAR-OLD WAGNER OF THE PARIS YEARS

The earliest known picture of the composer, this is a pencil drawing by Kietz.

revolutionary ardor that was then so strongly alive, it produced an environment that proved impossible for one of Wagner's eager and impetuous temperament to resist.

This explains Wagner's absorption in the great legends from out of the Germanic past, the *Nibelungenlied*, the *Tannhäuserlied*, and the *Heldenbuch*, works which the new Romantic interest in folk poetry had brought forth from their long isolation in libraries. And so we find that all his mature works, with the exception of *Rienzi*, were drawn from folk sources, their dramatic outlines being evolved in his mind very early in his career. It explains also Wagner's dissatisfaction with being considered merely a Romantic artist and the necessity he felt for action when the opportunity arose. He became embroiled in an abortive attempt at revolt against the crown of Saxony in 1848 to such an extent that for the most critical period of his life he was banished from his own land.

In fact at this time it must have seemed that the years comprising the first half of Wagner's life had been given over to futile attempts at getting himself established; now, viewing them so long after the event, they seem necessary for what was to come later. His career as conductor, begun in 1833, had ended ignominiously enough seven years later in a precipitate flight from his creditors — the first of the many financial crises which marked his life. Settling in Paris in a vain attempt to capture the interest of that great center of operatic activity with his *Rienzi* (a work boldly written in the Meyerbeerian manner, beating even that lavish, pretentious composer at his own game),[13] he suffered real poverty and kept himself alive only by the most menial hack work. In addition to finishing *Rienzi*, Wagner also wrote a new opera during his two and a half years in Paris, *Der fliegende Holländer*, an opera in the Romantic tradition of Marschner and Weber and far removed from the tawdry cosmopolitanism of Meyerbeer. This was the first of his works to be consistently bound together by connecting themes, a practice he was to develop later at such great length.

Called back in 1842 to his native Saxony for the first production of *Rienzi* in Dresden, he settled down in that art-loving city for a number of years. During this period he not only supervised and produced operas at the theater, but he conducted choral societies and symphonic concerts, thus gradually acquiring that intimate knowledge of Beethoven that was later to change his whole style. He also spent considerable time in the literary research that was to give him materials for all his later works, with the exception of *Tristan and Isolde*. And he likewise found time to compose two further operas, *Tannhäuser* and *Lohengrin*. The first of these, although dangerously near to Meyerbeerian commonplaceness at times, shows distinct uses of the chromatic idiom which was later to become so prominent a feature of his musical style, while the second shows the composer's new leanings toward a continuous dramatico-musical texture, without depending entirely on the use of the old Italian tradition of a succession of recitatives, arias, duos, large concerted numbers, and so on.

[13] It is interesting to observe how much of the later Wagner is foreshadowed in this early work, which as a whole is cheap and meretricious. Those who have a knowledge of the characteristics of Wagner's mature style will recognize readily enough many of these in embryo in *Rienzi*, particularly in its overture.

WILHELMINE SCHRÖDER–DEVRIENT AND JOSEF TICHATSCHEK
These two played Venus and Tannhäuser in the première performance of *Tannhäuser*, October 19, 1845, in Dresden. (The drawing is by Tischbein.)

But Wagner's new musical and dramatic ideals proved to be too radical for the tradition-loving Dresdeners, who had been brought up for many generations on a diet of the good old Italian style. *Rienzi, The Flying Dutchman*, and *Tannhäuser* were incorporated into the Dresden repertoire, but *Lohengrin* was declined; and this, together with Wagner's demands that the musical forces in Dresden be reorganized, his natural "leftist" tendencies, his ardent enthusiasms for what he considered the rights of man, and his actual participation in open rebellion, led the Saxon authorities to banish him from all the German states as a dangerous rebel. He was obliged to flee to Switzerland, by way of Weimar and Paris, and to settle down there for thirteen years. It was in the autumn of 1849 that Wagner decided to settle down in Zurich; the amnesty which opened the way for a return to Saxony was not granted until 1862.

THEORY

It was during this time that Wagner worked out, both in theory and in practice, his ideals of the *Wort-Ton-Drama,* that fusion of words, music, and action in opera which was to play such an important role in the development of his musical style. During the first few years in Switzerland he wrote no music at all. He had come to a distinct impasse. So far, the pursuit of his new ideals had brought him nothing but failure, artistic misunderstanding, and banishment from a country which he was trying to save. Here, in his new environment, he had time to work out rationally in his own mind the ideas which up to this time had been pursued mainly by instinct. This he did by means of a long series of prose works — *Art and Revolution, Opera and Drama, The Art Work of the Future* — works which, although they contain the essence of his theories, make rather heavy reading today.

We know now that these prose works were in reality the result of Wagner's attempt at this time in his life to find himself, to justify intellectually what he felt to be true. They contain many statements which do not agree with the principles he put into actual practice; for it was only natural, as Newman has observed, that in Wagner's convulsive efforts to restore to the drama the rights which had been filched from it in ordinary opera, he was led to many eager overstatements. It is by observing what he did rather than what he said that we can come to a real conclusion as to his ideals.

PRACTICE

The importance of these theoretical works lies in the fact that they cleared Wagner's mind for the music which was to follow them. In his earlier Dresden days he had written a libretto for an opera to be called *Siegfried's Death,* taking his material from the *Nibelungenlied.* When he came to work over this later, he found it to be unsatisfactory in that it did not make intelligible the motives which lay back of the actions of the two main characters, Siegfried and Brünnhilde. Thus he was forced to write another libretto dealing with the youth of Siegfried, the hero of the Nibelungen story, and then another to explain the history of Brünnhilde's former existence, and still a fourth to show how the curse arose which provided the motivation for the whole drama. Thus there came into existence the text of the tetralogy, *Der Ring des Nibelungen*, comprising the four operas, *Das Rheingold, Die Walküre, Siegfried*, and *Götterdämmerung* (*Twilight of the Gods*). Wagner started to compose the music for this in 1853; four years later, after finishing the music for *Das Rheingold, Die Walküre*, and part of *Siegfried*, he began to feel the drag of the stupendous task and the necessity for some sort of relief from it.

This took the form of a new work, along entirely different lines, one which we have come to know was gradually shaping itself in his mind as far back as the time when he was working on the composition of the first act of *Siegfried*. The possibility of sometime writing an opera on the legend of *Tristan and Isolde* had occurred to him as early as 1854; but it needed some such stimulus as now arose [14] to bring the idea to fruition. The Wagner archives in Bayreuth, where so many of the numerous letters and documents relating to his career have been carefully preserved, have published a letter which shows that while Wagner was working at *Siegfried*, he found that he had unexpectedly "dropped into *Tristan*." "For the present," he continues,[15] "this consists of music without words," adding the fact that he will probably compose most of the verse before he attempts the music. "But today, Tristan interrupts with a melody [here he quotes a four measure phrase which he later employed in the opera] that keeps spinning itself in my mind, if I would let it, so that I can think of nothing else the whole day."

14 In addition to the relief from the tremendous labor of *The Ring*, Wagner's romantic attachment to Frau Wesendonck, the wife of one of his wealthy benefactors, undoubtedly fostered this new idea.

15 This is of special significance in that it shows how wrong is the opinion generally held that it was Wagner's invariable procedure to write down first a verbal drama and then to find musical expression for it. Enough sketches have survived to show that long before the composer had put down a word of the Tristan poem, he was working out the central idea of the drama — that of the lover's great passion — in music. This shows how closely the two sides of his invention, the poetic and the musical, were united, sometimes the one furnishing the initial impulse for his work, sometimes the other.

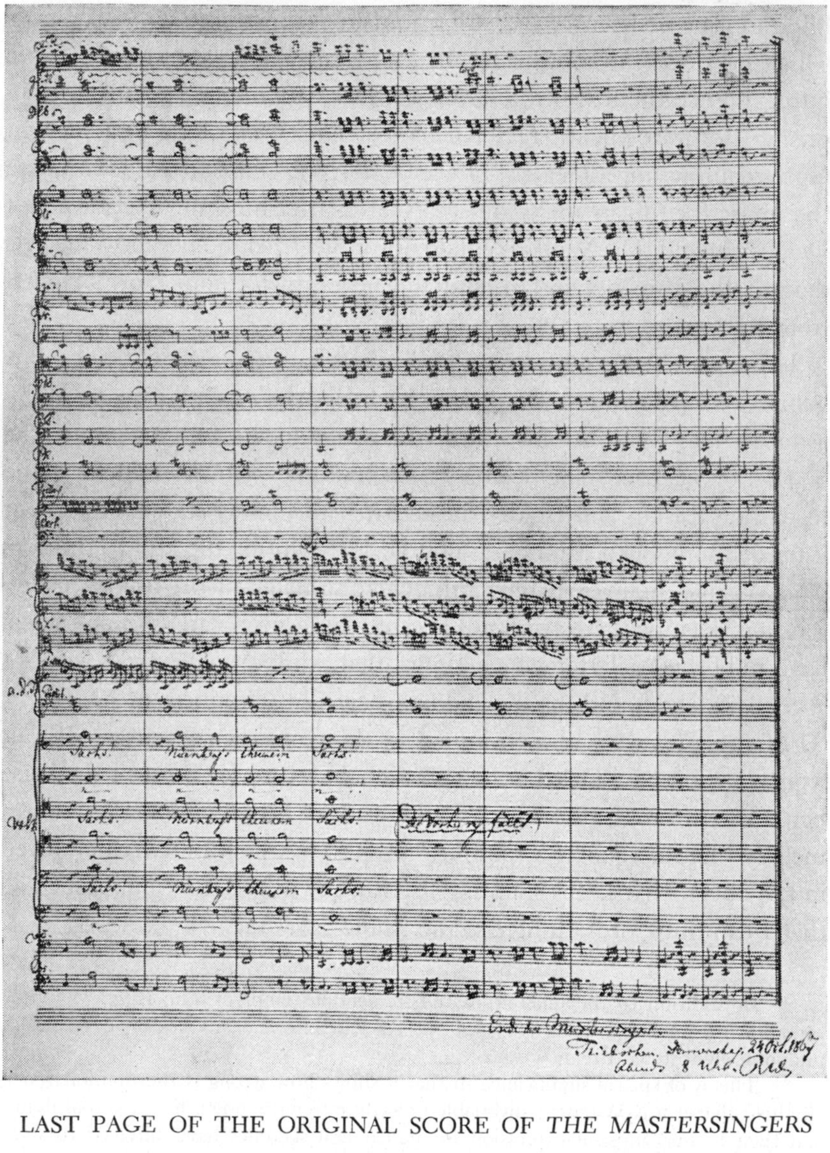

LAST PAGE OF THE ORIGINAL SCORE OF *THE MASTERSINGERS*

This tremendous work was begun in Biebrich in 1862 and finished in Triebschen in 1867. It was first performed in Munich in June, 1868, under the direction of Hans von Bülow. Wagner's calligraphy was always as clear as this.

This struggle between two moods, that of Siegfried's youthful joy in life and that of the necessary renunciation of life and love which was then filling his mind, went on for some time. While he was engaged in the physical task of writing the instrumentation of the second act of *Siegfried,* he was being unconsciously drawn towards the writing of *Tristan and Isolde.* Finally, as he says in another letter, having brought Siegfried into the forest where he was to fight the dragon, the impulse could no longer be resisted, and work was broken off with the intention of putting to paper the Tristan poem, only to find that the earlier hero could not be so summarily dismissed. And so Wagner had to go back to *Siegfried* to finish the second act, all the time being tortured with the idea of Tristan. Finally, the act being complete, he sank himself into the somber mood and fatalistic philosophy of *Tristan,* a work which was to prove the " most volcanic outburst of emotion that life can hold in store."

Before taking up his task of finishing the musical composition of *The Ring,* Wagner turned his attention to *The Mastersingers* (*Die Meistersinger*), a work which, in the universality of its sympathy and extent of its action, stands at the opposite pole from *Tristan and Isolde.* " My real self," he wrote as he worked on this score, " is roaming the streets of Nuremberg and mixing with somewhat blunt, square-cornered folk." The whole opera is a marvelous re-creation of life in that most charming of medieval German cities, " with its thousand gable ends, its ancient customs, its processions of guilds, its watchman with horn and lantern, calling the hour, its freshness and quaint loveliness by day, and its sweetness on soft summer nights." And yet, through all the admirable characterizations, the exact portraitures, and the warm humor of this work, we are aware of a depth of compassion and a warmth of human understanding that is to be found in none of his other works. Here Wagner is at his greatest; in listening to this music, we can only agree with his own estimate of *Die Meistersinger:* " it is a really wonderful work — one must have been in Paradise in order to find one's way to the heart of such a subject."

When in 1869 Wagner resumed work on the score of *Siegfried,* he brought to bear all the experience gained from writing *Tristan* and *The Mastersingers;* and so it is hardly surprising that even an amateur can sense the subtler handling of material and the surer technical resource that are to be found in the last act of this work. Which is fortunate, for in no other single act of his operas did he set himself a more difficult task or one harder to bring off musically. Nowhere else does Wagner show himself to better advantage as a polyphonist, weaving, as he does here with superb ease and matchless beauty, an orchestral fabric of unexampled splendor out of a few pertinent dramatic motto themes. The last act of *Siegfried* shows Wagner the musico-dramatist at the height of his powers. From the technical viewpoint he never wrote anything finer.

Twilight of the Gods (*Götterdämmerung*), for reasons we have already stated, is what Gilman has called a kind of sublime operatic half-breed. Most of the music belongs to the composer's most mature period; it was written in the five years from 1869 to 1874, during Wagner's fifty-sixth to sixty-first years, more than twenty-five years after he had sketched its original libretto. In the meantime had come all his elaborate theories as to the necessity of creating an operatic medium compounded equally of word language and tone language and stage pictures,[16] as well as the actual writing of *Das Rheingold, Die Walküre, Siegfried, Tristan und Isolde,* and *Die Meistersinger*. Is there any wonder that Wagner could not make a successful whole out of this grand-heroic-opera text, a text that was first conceived as a separate unit and which yet had to be made to serve as the dramatic final member for his great tetralogy?

No single work of his is such an inconsistent hodgepodge of dramatic ideas or departs more completely from his carefully developed theories as to the necessity for dramatic and musical unity in opera.[17] In *Götterdämmerung* can be found most of the old-fashioned Italian operatic conventions against which Wagner so bitterly railed in his prose works, including the chorus in full panoply on the stage, a duet in which two of the principals swear blood brotherhood, a vengeful trio of conspirators, and a full-throated death lament for the hero tenor. And yet the

[16] The student who does not care to plow through the verbosity of Wagner's prose will find an excellent summary of *Oper und Drama* in Abraham's book, *A Hundred Years of Music*.

[17] As a matter of cold fact, the only work which comes within a stone's throw of completely carrying out these ideals is *Das Rheingold;* and in many ways, this remains Wagner's least interesting opera!

musician Wagner overrode this badly patched text and its dramatic contradictions and anachronisms and gave us some music that perhaps comes nearer to consistently attaining what we speak of as the " grand style " than any other ever written.

Taking most of his thematic material from the earlier operas of *The Ring,*[18] Wagner developed and transmuted it in a way that fits exactly the dark brooding mood of the drama and wove out of these themes a score that for expressiveness and eloquence has hardly been equaled. The whole orchestral fabric seems continuous and inexhaustible; the leitmotivs are no longer merely extended vocal melodies with dramatic significance; they are, as Newman has pointed out, real instrumental germ ideas which are developed completely, symphonically speaking. Even the voice parts are hardly needed: whereas it would be impossible to make the tissue of *Das Rheingold* intelligible without the voices, Newman adds, the orchestral part of *Götterdämmerung* could flow on with hardly a break if the vocal parts were omitted altogether. Wagner comes in this work into his full stature as a symphonist; and the grandeur of his ideas, together with his astonishing development of them, make us realize, with Gilman, that for " range of utterance, for intensity of vision, for triumphant completeness of statement, Wagner remains unparalleled."

Parsifal, finished in 1879 and first given at the theater which Wagner finally succeeded in building for the special performance of his works, has always meant different things to different people. To some it stands as a sort of sacred symbol of a religious ideal; to others it is simply an old legend not too skillfully retold; there are those who see in it only a deceptive and somewhat shoddy theatricalism. Nietzsche, Wagner's one-time friend, found it " much too religious "; the liberal-minded American critic, James Huneker, thought it hardly fit for stage reproduction; and yet Newman calls it the " purest spiritual aspiration the human soul has found voice for." There is something to be said for all these viewpoints.

[18] One of the earlier commentators on Wagner's operas computed the number of original themes in the various *Ring* operas as follows: *Das Rheingold,* 35; *Die Walküre,* 22; *Siegfried,* 20; and *Götterdämmerung,* 13.

But, as always with the mature Wagner, we can forget all about the non-musical aspects of *Parsifal* and look for its real significance and importance in the music. Because it was written during the evening of the master's life, it is easy enough to infer that this music shows Wagner's invention to have been on the wane. Nothing is further from the truth; although not so consistent in style or so unflagging in invention as the music of *Tristan and Isolde* or *The Mastersingers*, there are pages — dozens of them — in this score which transcend anything else Wagner ever penned. For one who, no matter what his religious beliefs, has pondered the constantly renewed wonder of the coming of spring, the Good Friday music of the third act of *Parsifal*, with its deeply felt awe and exalted mystery, must always remain among the art's greatest treasures. In the grave and poignant beauty of this music Wagner spoke a language that was entirely new for him, one which, after all the multitudinous and varied accents to which he has accustomed us, shows him to be, of all musicians, the most universal. For here is a profound compassion and understanding that is as far from the intense eroticism of *Tristan and Isolde* as it is from the warm humanity of *The Mastersingers* or the epic grandeur of *Twilight of the Gods*.

No more fitting climax to this tempestuous life could be imagined than the best of the music of *Parsifal;* it is as if the old master, at the end of his career, would show us, as Gilman has expressed it, that after all, the innermost secret of loveliness must always be its benison of profound appeasement.

Such a record of achievement — the composition of eleven operas, several of them containing as great music as has ever been written, in a period of forty years — is impressive enough under any circumstance. But when considered in the light of Wagner's lifelong struggle against economic difficulties and his inability to secure anything like adequate recognition for his works until the later years of his life, it seems almost unbelievable. In all the annals of the artists' struggle against life, no career stands out more nobly than does Wagner's. He had, as someone has remarked, a disconcerting way of leaping from peak to peak of his development, like some inspired Apollonian goat, that did not make for the popularity of his music in so far as the majority of his contemporaries

WAGNER WITH HIS FAMILY AND FRIENDS

The group is seen at Bayreuth in the later years of Wagner's life.

was concerned. As soon as one work was finished, sometimes even before, he was away on another tack, often one that was entirely different; and so it was difficult for the public, as well as for his interpreters, to follow him.

The Meyerbeerian vulgarities of *Rienzi* were poor preparation for the qualities of *The Flying Dutchman:* consequently, this latter opera was thought to be "ghastly pallid" when it was first produced in January, 1843. Newman speaks of its reception as being a "cold douche" for Wagner; but this was but the beginning of a long series of such experiences for him. By the time he finally succeeded in persuading his friend

Liszt to produce *Lohengrin* in Weimar (August, 1850) he was already engaged on the tremendous project of *The Ring*, which was unlike anything he had written up to that time. A disconcerting genius such as this could hardly expect anything in the way of adequate financial returns from his works[19] during his lifetime. And when we add to this the fact that Wagner was by nature a spendthrift and one who believed that the world owed him a living — a good one at that — so that he did not hesitate to call on his friends for all the money they would give him; and that, having gotten it, he spent it recklessly and oftentimes needlessly; and that his independence of character and rashness of judgment, as well as his repellent personality, led to his banishment from the one country which might have given him aid during his most needy years, we can get some idea of the trying conditions under which these operas were written.

Wagner's career, as we look back on it, seems a rather ignominious series of retreats from creditors and government officials; yet in the midst of all his temporal troubles his faith in his mission in the world never faltered. Time and time again he was almost beaten by circumstances; but, fortunately for us, aid always arrived in time to revive his spirit and enable him to go ahead with his life. The amount of physical courage and indomitable energy necessary to carry on a creative career under such circumstances is impossible to realize. But in trying to estimate it, we must not forget our great debt to those who came to Wagner's aid during these dark years: Liszt, who gave him large sums of money from time to time, as well as a great deal of artistic encouragement; Cosima, Liszt's daughter, who married Wagner in 1870 and provided the domestic tranquillity that was needed so that he could finish his work; Ludwig II, young king of Bavaria, who at the time of Wagner's deepest despair, invited him to live in Munich and provided opportunities there for the first performances of both *Tristan* and *The Mastersingers*, as well as later, through the granting of a credit of 300,000 marks from the royal

19 As an illustration of how little Wagner received from the publication of his operas, the leading publishers of that time, Breitkopf and Härtel, in 1858 paid him 200 louis d'ors (some $800) for the score of *Tristan and Isolde*, with a promise of another hundred in case of an " extraordinary success." And this was at a time when Wagner's name was beginning to be well known.

THE WAGNER FESTSPIELHAUS IN BAYREUTH

The contemporary drawing shows the building as it was decorated for the first Festspiel, 1876.

treasury, making possible the opening of Wagner's ideal *Festspielhaus* in Bayreuth.[20]

But our insistence on Wagner's pre-eminence as a musician should not be misinterpreted to mean that his contributions to other fields of artistic activity were insignificant. His was an avid mind, one that reached out naturally into all phases of intellectual expression. His prose writings contain a great deal of what Newman has called " subtle aesthetic thinking," thinking which has had considerable effect on later generations. But, owing to the fact that most of the translations of these prose writings and of the letters which have appeared have been confused, colorless, and tasteless, the English-speaking peoples have unfortunately gained a distorted view of their significance.[21] Newman, who speaks with more authority on this subject than anyone else now living, not only because of

20 Even today, more than sixty years after its dedication in 1876, this theater, with its carefully planned auditorium (after Wagner's plans), its superb acoustics, and its established traditions, remains the world's best place to hear the Wagnerian dramas as they were meant to be heard.

21 See Newman's article in the 1938 *Bayreuther Festspielführer*.

ONE OF THE MANY WAGNER CARICATURES

Wagner is presented as the Musician-of-the-Future (1869).

his intimate and detailed knowledge of Wagneriana but also on account of his linguistic abilities, tells us that the greatest contribution that could be made toward an intelligent understanding, on the part of the English-speaking peoples, of all that Wagner was as man and artist and thinker would be a new translation of his letters and prose works.

WAGNER, THE CULMINATION OF AN EPOCH

In these writings Wagner laid a great deal of stress on his work as the "Music of the Future"; as a matter of fact, it was really the culmination of the past, especially the immediate past. In him there were brought to consummation, in one tremendous mechanism, the constructive principles which Beethoven developed in his symphonies; the nationalistic feelings and love of nature which had been introduced into music by Weber; the operatic effectiveness of Meyerbeer; the orchestral virtuosity of Berlioz; and all the literary and artistic Romanticism of his century. Out of these there came that magnificent composite which, for lack of a better term, we call Wagner's *tone language,* a language which, in the richness of its orchestral palette, the elaborate working out of its themes, the power of its dramatic speech, the perfection of its technical achievements, the amazing universality of its thought, the sumptuous beauty of its style, and the epic grandeur of its utterance, has not been equaled. So great was the spell which it cast on succeeding generations that no real successor to Wagner has ever appeared.

Which is not to say, of course, that Wagner had no real significance as a musical pioneer. Although from our modern point of view the Music of the Future appears to have been so firmly rooted in the past, its harmonic content (with the constant insistence upon dissonances that are for the most part unresolved) was such as to accustom the ears of later generations to the fact that such dissonance can be both beautiful and effective. Thus the way was opened for the use of even greater quantities of dissonance, and the path prepared for the complete break with tonality which came around the turn of the century. It is certainly not too much to claim that Wagner is the most important link in the long chain which stretches between the early attempts of the nineteenth century to revolt against the accepted ideals of tonality, and the twentieth-century composers, Schönberg and Berg.

Over fifty years have passed since Wagner's death in 1883; yet his pre-eminence seems more firmly established than ever. And this in spite of the bitter attacks made on his music by the modernists, who, of course, have no use for what they term his Romantic excesses; and the fact that he has been unwittingly made a backdrop-designer for latter-day political heroics in Germany.[22] In all the countries where music is cultivated,

22 A favorite quotation of the Nazi Germany of 1938: "I am the German individual; I am the German soul. If you would seek the incomparable magic of my work, you will find it in the fact that it is German" (Richard Wagner).

his works are outstanding favorites; it is very easy to see why: for he, above all other composers, has made music a language capable of expressing human emotions directly and forcefully, instead of merely reflecting them indirectly. And this language, with its unique blend of "heroic strength and sensuous loveliness, its encompassing nobility and its epic grandeur," was fortunate in having been addressed to a public capable of understanding it, and which, through unparalleled opportunities of hearing, has come to love it. Speaking broadly, we may say that the whole Romantic Movement paved the way for, and made possible the success of, Wagner.

But time goes on, and tastes change; the reason Wagner's music will probably endure is that it meets so successfully that supreme test of all art, the ability to take some great and individual human theme — love, pity, desire, greed, grief — and treat it so that it has universal significance and expresses supreme truth. In this respect, Wagner is one with Michelangelo and Shakespeare; which is, after all, a fair enough portent for the future.

The Later Romantics

JOHANNES THE GREAT

Strength, honesty, and sympathy — these have been the qualities which have carried the message of Brahms to the whole world.

— W. J. Henderson: *New York Sun*

A COMPOSER LONG MISUNDERSTOOD

IN the year 1900 the people of Boston, who like to pride themselves on living in the Athens of America, built a proud new home for the great symphony orchestra which one of their wealthy citizens had developed for their musical enlightenment. In describing this new symphony hall, a paragraphist in one of the town's most important papers added to his description of the building a quip to the effect that the architects had forgotten to provide one thing — to add to each of the numerous and handsomely designed *Exit* signs over the various doors the line

In Case of Brahms!

Five or six years before this Bernard Shaw, who started his writing career in the role of a music critic and who put into these early critiques written for the London *World* some of the most searching and trenchant things that have ever been said about music, perpetrated this fatuity:

" To me it seems quite obvious that the real Brahms is nothing more than a sentimental voluptuary with a wonderful ear. For respectability's sake he adopts the forms academically supposed to be proper to great composers . . . but you have only to compare his symphonies and quintets with those of Beethoven and Mozart to become conscious that he is the most wanton [1] of composers . . . and that when his ambition

[1] The *Oxford Dictionary* gives the following definitions for this: " sportive, playful, capricious, irresponsible, luxuriant, wild, motiveless, random, serving no purpose "!

JOHANNES BRAHMS

leads him to turn his industry in any other direction, his charm does not turn with it and he becomes the most superficial and irrelevant of formalists."

A more sympathetic but anxious American critic of the same period, W. J. Henderson, felt called upon to warn his readers that a man is not "necessarily a mere formalist because he clings to the old-fashioned sonata form. Brahms's compositions show a completeness of architectonic detail, superimposed upon a symmetrical and organic development, such as are to be found in those of no other symphonist except Beethoven. Why deny the late Viennese master depth of feeling because he fashioned the expression of that feeling with all the force of a gigantic musical intellect? Brahms's music grows slowly in public favor because it is not easy for the careless hearer to grasp its inner spirit. But it is not true that to be real music demands a Swinburnian diction. Some day, I think, if not soon [this was written in 1898, a year after the composer's death], the world will see how profoundly representative of his nation and his time Brahms was, and he will be hailed, as Milton was, an organ voice of his country.

The irresistible seriousness of Germany has never spoken with more convincing accent than in the music of Brahms. There is a feeling in this music which is far removed from any possibility of a purely sensuous embodiment. It may take time for the entire musical world to come under the spell of this austere utterance, but Brahms had the happiness of knowing ere he died that wherever music was cultivated, his individuality had at least made itself known."

These echoes from the last decade of the past century make rather strange reading today when Brahms is firmly ensconced in the circle of the gods along with Bach, Beethoven, and others. Why the doubt and hesitation and misunderstanding of the nineties—this feeling that Brahms (and to a large extent Bach as well, if we read the criticisms of the time aright) was an "inaccessible intellectual," a "recluse of the mind who dwelt in solitude, wrapped in speculations beyond the ken of common souls"?

THE REASONS

The answer is a simple one. Suddenly in the midst of the swirling vortex of Romanticism, in the period when music exuded personality, flamed with passion (Wagner's great works were just becoming known), and glowed with poetry, there appeared this serious, sober-hued artist who insisted on the necessity for restraint in expression and who, instead of composing in the admired free forms of the Romanticists, revived the vigorous sonata form of the classicists. And, because he insisted on form and careful intellectual manipulation in his writing, he was thought to have abjured imagination and forsaken feeling.

Today it is possible to realize the error of such a theory. But to contemporaries Brahms was not a figure to fire the imagination: there is little question that his placid, rather sedentary, life favored the legend of his dullness, his heaviness in orchestration, his stodginess in thought. And his rugged simplicity of character, his essentially intellectual method of developing his genius, his hatred of all easy methods of attaining popularity made his own path difficult. It was only after coming to realize the great depth of feeling that is in his music and the lofty method of his communicating it that his fellows began to realize that "here was a truly great man, great in his elementary nature, great in his almost Biblical manner of expression." And this conviction, once attained, has grown so steadily that today we are in danger of taking his uniqueness and individuality too much for granted.

It is easy enough to be wise after the fact. But if those who so completely misunderstood Brahms had only turned to such an early work as his now famous song, *Liebestreu* (*O versenk' dein Leid, mein Kind*) from his Op. 3, written when he was twenty, they would have found plenty of evidence which refutes their charges of coldness and intellectuality. In this short work there is present the essential essence of Brahms's style, for it is compelling in its emotional force and indescribably poignant in its feeling; and it is constructed with that extraordinary mastery of form which was thought by his critics to be the evidence of his concentration on structure, to the neglect of emotional content. Henderson has pointed out the fact that this one work is an unanswerable demonstration of the error of such a theory: "Brahms felt to the bottom of his soul; he had the human sympathy and the divine imagination which enabled him to publish his conceptions in perfected form."

BRAHMS'S PLACE IN MUSIC

No better summary of this composer's place in music could be desired; it can be applied to all his great works:[2] the four symphonies — the

[2] As was the case with every other composer, Brahms was not always on the heights; sometimes his imagination failed him and he had recourse to padding. His critics were not entirely wrong: there is considerable of what can only be called extraneous matter in some of his works, especially in the earlier chamber music. The following list of his compositions will show how wide a field he cultivated and how busy he was during his creative years:

Orchestral works: 9, including 4 symphonies, 2 overtures, 1 set of variations
Vocal music: 33 chorus and quartet compositions, including the *Deutsches Requiem*
Vocal music: 365 songs and duets
Chamber music: 24 quartets, quintets, trios, etc.
Concertos: 4
Piano works: 15 solo numbers and sets, excluding studies and exercises; 8 collections of duet music for piano
Organ works: 3, including 2 sets of chorale preludes

BRAHMS'S WORKROOM IN VIENNA, 1872 (etching by Schmutzer)

Nothing illustrates better the essentially simple and human quality of Brahms's life than this intimate glimpse of the room in which he worked, taken from a contemporary etching.

majestic, exultant, but somber first, the lovely, lyric, and warmly idyllic second, the alternatingly passionate and serenely contemplative third, and the austere fourth; the two great piano concertos, in reality symphonies with a richly interwoven piano part added to their gorgeous orchestral fabric; the mysterious and deeply felt *Requiem;* the beautifully written songs, which someone has called the most confidential communications of a solitary and almost abnormally sensitive soul ever written. In his piano works, while he provides a great deal of matter demanding the highest technical dexterity on the part of the executant, he avoids the " shimmering superficiality " so often written into music of this kind; his compositions for piano solo range from the graceful and lilting Hungarian dances and waltzes to the warmly expressed *Sonata in F Minor* and *Sonata in F Sharp Minor*, both of them monuments of his genius.

A North German in every fiber of his being, Brahms was born in Hamburg in 1833. The son of a poor local musician, he was brought up under circumstances which must have proved revolting to him and which may have accounted for some of his later personal eccentricities. After years of careful preparation, some of them given over to concert tours with the Hungarian violinist Reményi, some spent in quiet retirement at the little court of Detmold, absorbing the works of the classic masters, Brahms settled in Vienna in 1872 and spent the rest of his life in the congenial atmosphere of that warm-blooded, lively city. Thus his later music shows a peculiar combination of hereditary North German traits and environmental South German ones, of a natural, impulsive Romantic temperament molded by industrious and eager study of his great predecessors.

In his life, as in his music, Brahms was interested in the universal side of human nature rather than in its personal, eccentric aspect; and because he usually showed a gruff exterior, assumed partly to cover up his extremely sensitive nature and partly to ward off snobbish flattery, he was thought gauche and crude. His intimates were men and women of direct, unassuming nature; it made no difference whether they were of high or humble estate. He had no use for society and spent a great deal of time avoiding it after he had become one of the great men of Vienna.

It is impossible to think of his being anything but a religious man — none other could have written the *Requiem* or the *Four Serious Songs*, the latter his last compositions and his final self-revelation. But he was, nevertheless, a fatalist, gazing with warm eyes at the beauties of this world while realizing their essential futility. Because he recognized in Bach a kindred spirit, he turned to him as to a great god: all his life he worshiped at this shrine, and his music, both in its solid structure and its expression of profound thought and deep emotion, gained thereby.

Although he spurned many of the outer graces of life, Brahms was a man of real culture; he read widely and thought deeply during the quiet days of his rather lonely life. A contemporary describes him as shunning all hackneyed and worn-out texts when seeking materials for songs, adding the statement that "very few persons are as little given to favoring the ordinary as he is." It is because of this fastidiousness of taste and the simple strength of his character that Brahms is a good mentor. Which is not to say that he was by any means at all times the solemn classicist. There was in him a strain of wilder Romanticism that is not always sufficiently appreciated. It comes out in the first piano concerto and can be found as late as the clarinet quintet, Op. 115, where the impassioned feeling in part of the slow movement is a remarkable outburst made more significant by the contrast with the coda, in which we may perhaps hear resignation of spirit. Alfred Einstein has spoken of "the paradise of melodic purity out of which sprang his waltzes, his Hungarian dances and gypsy songs, and his folk-song arrangements." In the quintet we may all join Brahms; and it is a happy discovery for many that Brahms had his lighter side. The works mentioned above have, for many a music lover, served as a door of introduction to the master's storehouse; thus having entered, the neophyte need never glance fearfully at that other door labeled "In Case of Brahms."

In the universal delight in the dance, Brahms joins the early Strausses (the Johanns) and the late expert (Richard), with a host of composers of the eighteenth and nineteenth centuries, including even Mozart and Beethoven and ranging clear through to Tchaikovsky and his successors. In the three sets of piano waltzes (the Op. 39 and the older and the newer *Liebeslieder* series, the last two having vocal parts also), Brahms affectionately framed in miniature the best of German sentiment in this long-cherished form.

These traits diversify and round out a nature gloriously lavish and lyrical. As Basil de Sélincourt has said, even the epic with him was lyrical. He represents, this thoughtful writer adds, one of the inevitable stages of reflection on the artistically religious standpoint that art is indistinguishable from the pure essence of the good. "Bach's is still the attitude of cosmic union; his inspiration is direct; it is as if the voice of the Creator were flowing through him. Beethoven is aware of cleavage; he is a Titan of revolt, a Prometheus affirming the divine and drawing its fires from heaven. The spirit of Brahms is a spirit of atonement and reconciliation; tragedy is recognized and accepted; and now the purely human longings and raptures revive; a passion of luxuriant beauty, mingling joy and pain, flows through his music" (London *Observer*).

Sélincourt goes on to speak of Brahms's assurance of truth, of his sublime regal aloofness, while living a hearty, commonplace life, enjoying his beer and sausages. In the realm of feeling he is king: "for common men, feeling is action and memory of action; for him, feeling and memories of feeling clustered where he alone could enact them, in his imperious forms of sound."

HUGO WOLF AND STYLES IN SONG

To think of his songs one by one is to see defiling before the eyes a veritable pageant of humanity.

— Ernest Newman

THE LIED, A CHARACTERISTIC GERMAN FORM

THE German word *lied* literally translated means simply " song "; to the music lover, however, it has come to have a special significance because of its association with a particular kind of song developed by the Austro-German masters. In Italy one of man's most cherished possessions has always been a beautiful singing voice, and Italian composers have written most naturally and spontaneously when composing vocal music; so we expect Italian songs to emphasize melodies constructed for the display of beautiful voices. In France, where art is more a matter of fastidious discrimination and good vocal material is not so abundant, songs are more adroit and cleverly sophisticated than spontaneous. In Germany, owing to a number of causes, among them the innate dramatic sense of the people and their capacity for deep feeling, songs have developed into a sort of miniature music drama in which text, tune, and accompaniment play co-equal roles. The expression of the proper dramatic mood or the general philosophical concept contained in the words is as important to the lieder composer (and the lieder singer, as well) as the attainment of a beautiful melodic line or the provision of a suitable accompanimental background which has dropped any suggestion of the classic figured bass and which elaborates every possible harmonic detail.

It was Schubert who first evolved the lied as a definite musical form, although some furtive experiments in this field had been made by composers before his time, notably by Mozart and Beethoven. When at eighteen Schubert wrote his famous *Gretchen am Spinnrade* and *Erlkönig*, the lied was born. Listen to these songs interpreted by a master singer, and the characteristics we have mentioned will immediately become evident: the breadth and expressive quality of the accompaniments, often suggesting elements of tone painting; the eloquence of the musical constituents, the melody and harmony; and the union of all these to form a mood picture which conveys the very heart of the text. So it is with such songs of Schumann's as *Im wunderschönen Monat Mai*, *Frühlingsnacht*, and *Du bist wie eine Blume*; or Brahms's *Feldeinsamkeit*, *Von ewiger Liebe*, or, perhaps the most poignant of all, *O Tod, wie bitter bist du* from his *Vier ernste Gesänge*. A study of any of these will give an insight into the whole nature and purpose of the lied.

THE STYLES OF ITS COMPOSERS

Each of the outstanding lieder composers made his own distinctive contribution to the form. Schubert's was that of lovely melody, a melody which fits the mood of the text exactly. Schumann, being a pianist, emphasizes the accompaniment, without undue neglect of the vocal line; in general his songs are more powerful and suggestive but not nearly so spontaneous as Schubert's. Brahms favored the strophic form as the most suitable relation between melody and accompaniment, but his striking individuality and his insistence on formal finish are to be found in every song he wrote. It remained for Hugo Wolf (1860–1903), a composer who concentrated on the writing of songs as Chopin had on piano compositions, to bring to the lied some of the principles of the Wagnerian music drama. Which is to say that Wolf used a dramatic instrumental score for the basis of his songs, a score which vividly characterizes and powerfully portrays the thoughts and moods of the words, making use of definite motives as thematic material, and above this superimposes a vocal line which makes no pretense of melodic continuity but rather aims at a faithful rendition of the words.

WOLF'S MASTERY

Wagner was Wolf's god: both masters proceeded to their work from an identical standpoint, that of making music the perfect expression of poetic ideas. But Wolf also based his writing solidly on the work of his predecessors in Romantic song writing and, coming last, was able to avail himself of all their achievements. We find in the Wolf songs, quite a few of them written at white heat, sometimes as many as three in a day, the final consummation of the process of gradual evolution that was started by Schubert and reinforced and made more dramatic by Wagner.

One of the greatest of Wolf's songs, *Prometheus,* from the Goethe cycle, shows his genius at its best, as well as his close affinity with Wagner. It was written in one of those intense outbursts of inspiration and creative energy, outbursts which were followed by periods of complete sterility and utter despair. A favorite method of working was that of composing cycles of songs from the works of various poets — Mörike, Kleist, Eichendorff, Goethe; he also set translations of poems from Italian and Spanish sources, works which comprise the *Spanisches Liederbuch* and the *Italienisches Liederbuch.* A feature of all Wolf songs is their carefully composed piano accompaniment, sometimes so elaborate as to overshadow the vocal part. The composer also orchestrated some twenty of his total output of two hundred sixty songs.

Forced by practical necessity to undertake the uncongenial work of a Viennese newspaper critic, Wolf made many influential enemies during his lifetime through his powerfully expressed articles on some contemporary musicians, notably Brahms. These men were able to prevent the appreciation of his genius, and his works never attained during his lifetime the popularity which was their due, in spite of the valiant efforts of several societies formed for the express purpose of spreading a knowledge of his style. But after his premature death in an insane asylum, his name became famous throughout the musical world as the great master of German lied, one whose range of expression was as remarkable as its intensity of utterance. Characteristic examples of his songs are *Anakreons Grab, Auf einer Wanderung,* the three *Harfenspieler* from Goethe, *Gesang Weylas,* and *Verborgenheit.*

RICHARD STRAUSS

The talent which was once a genius

— Ernest Newman

TWO PARALLEL CAREERS

SUCH a table as the one below is striking proof of the cynic's statement that nothing in the world of art changes so quickly as taste. We have here a paralleling of the chief works of two great contemporary composers living at the turn of the twentieth century, Richard Strauss and Jean Sibelius: at the time when Strauss (born in Munich in 1864) was startling the world by the brilliance of his genius and by his anarchistic tendencies (as they were then considered) to destroy all beauty and form in the kingdom of tone, Sibelius (born in Tavastehus, Finland, in 1865) was rather tentatively beginning the long list of symphonic works which were later to make him famous.

STRAUSS	SIBELIUS
Don Juan, 1889	
Tod und Verklärung, 1890	
Till Eulenspiegel, 1895	*En Saga*, 1892
Also sprach Zarathustra, 1896	*The Swan of Tuonela*, 1893
Don Quixote, 1898	*First Symphony*, 1898
Ein Heldenleben, 1899	*Second Symphony*, 1901
Symphonia domestica, 1904	*Violin Concerto*, 1903
Salome, 1905	*Pohjola's Daughter*, 1906
	Third Symphony, 1907
Elektra, 1909	*String Quartet*, 1909
Der Rosenkavalier, 1911	*Fourth Symphony*, 1911
Alpine Symphony, 1915	*Fifth Symphony*, 1915
Die Frau ohne Schatten, 1919	*Sixth Symphony*, 1923
Die ägyptische Helena, 1928	*Seventh Symphony*, 1924
Arabella, 1929	
Die schweigsame Frau, 1935	
Daphne, 1938	
Der Friedenstag, 1938	

Staatliche Gemäldegalerie, Berlin

RICHARD STRAUSS
(From a painting by Max Liebermann)

One of the most characteristic works of each — the opera *Der Rosenkavalier* and the *Fourth Symphony*—was produced in the same year, 1911: at that time Strauss was looked upon as "unquestionably the dominating figure in music, the only possible successor to Wagner and Brahms" (to quote a critique of the time), while Sibelius was not very widely known outside Finland, and not too well known there. At the present time the German writer is considered an almost negligible figure in so far as his current writing is concerned; his best works have long been numbered among the classics of the Romantic Movement, for they represent the utmost utterance of which the school was capable; in spite of manifest weaknesses and unfortunate lapses from good taste, they are works indisputably streaked with greatness. Sibelius, on the other hand, has suddenly become one of the great men of the hour, his symphonies now being extremely popular with a public which once considered them the "ravings of a madman," he himself a figure rather foolishly proclaimed by some of his disciples as the greatest symphonic writer since Beethoven.

PROGRESS IN REVERSE

Strauss has had a unique career in that it has been a completely topsy-turvy one: he was greatest in his early works and is feeblest in his latest. When the young and quite unknown twenty-three-year-old third *Kapellmeister* of the Royal Opera in Munich wrote the scores of his two symphonic poems *Don Juan* and *Tod und Verklärung,* he was a genius: the sixty-five-year-old world-renowned composer of *The Egyptian Helen, Arabella,* and *Daphne* has become a musically facile but absolutely sterile composer, still master of his craftsmanship, but with nothing to say.

STRAUSS'S EARLY POWER

There can be little doubt about the phenomenal genius of these early works. Before he wrote them, Strauss had been largely occupied in training himself for the brilliant career opening before him. Born into a musical family of Munich, he started his composing career in the classic vein, writing a symphony, a wind-instrument serenade, and a violin concerto while he was still in his teens. Coming into contact with an ardent disciple and propagandist of the Liszt brand of Romanticism — one Alexander Ritter — Strauss abandoned these earlier tendencies and entered wholeheartedly into the folds of the new program-music school. Several important conducting posts gave him a thorough mastery of the orchestra and of how to write for it, and this, combined with his native genius, enabled him to produce effects which up to his time had hardly been dreamed of. If this seems overstatement, listen to the terrific gusts of hot-blooded passion which sweep through *Don Juan,* or the mysterious, intense brooding, the understanding comprehension of *Tod und*

Verklärung, the sparkling wit and devilish roguery of *Till Eulenspiegel:* these are new things in music, and important ones. Superb, consummate craftsmanship is in all these works, and a colossal energy which comes only when young men of genius and vivid imagination are working at white heat.

In these program pieces Strauss was able to realize the ideal form of the symphonic poem envisaged by Liszt. He found in this an opportunity to display his brilliant qualities at their best: an inimitable sense of orchestral color, coupled with an ability to use it; a searing intensity of expression, a universal emotionality; extraordinary powers of characterization. At the time these works were first produced, the great topic of discussion at all the musical *conversazioni* was Strauss's bold harmonic innovations and terrific dissonantal experiments; today no one would think of even suggesting these as a conversational topic, for they have long been accepted as a matter of musical course and have become a part of every composer's expressive technique.

THE BEGINNING OF DECLINE

It is *Also sprach Zarathustra*, a musical realization of the Nietzschean superman, a tremendous, daring attempt which is only partly successful, that marks, according to most critics, the beginning of the composer's decline in power. Scored for an enormous orchestral force, this work contains some of Strauss's most notable pages — particularly those at the beginning, the so-called sunrise music — pages which, according to as sober a critic as Philip Hale, suggest the "portals of eternity swinging slowly asunder." But there are, too, stretches of aimless, commonplace music and a striving for bombastic, sensational effect.

These tendencies become still more apparent in the tone poems which followed *Also sprach Zarathustra — Don Quixote, Ein Heldenleben,* and the *Symphonia domestica*. The first of these, a musical portrait of the immortal hero of Cervantes's tale and his faithful henchman, is done with a sad whimsicality that suits its subject thoroughly; but it is marred in spots by overrealistic imitations, of sheep bleating, windmills whirring, and the like. But this is not so bad as the meaningless verbosity of *Ein Heldenleben,* an attempt to describe the exploits, ideals, and life battles of a hero who is only too obviously Strauss himself: there are many pages in this long score that have the old inspired touch, but these are buried in shamelessly padded passages and trivialities that are hard to condone. It seems as if Strauss, in the words of Gilman, after he has created some beautiful or heroic tonal image, can never resist the temptation of the gamin to deface it by scrawling a bad joke or an obscenity somewhere on its surface.

A NEW LOW

Dedicated to Frau Strauss, the *Symphonia domestica* depicts definite scenes in the Strauss ménage, with Papa and Mamma bickering and pleading over the upbringing of their offspring, the whole ending in true German fashion with Papa Strauss realistically banging on the brass and announcing that he is the master and will do as he sees fit! Its appalling poverty of imagination marks a new low in Strauss's works, a low from which he never recovered: for from that time onward his symphonic compositions retrocede with uniform regularity.

The best of these tone poems can stand superbly on their own feet as music pure and simple; nevertheless, Strauss has insisted on associating them all with programs. When he first gave them to the world, it was the composer's practice to announce officially that he wished them to be taken as absolute music rather than as the elaboration of the specific details of a schematic program; then would follow, by one means or another, the issuing of information as to the ideas which were in the composer's mind when he wrote the music and with which the audience had to familiarize itself if it was to comprehend the full significance and completely grasp the inner meaning of the composer's score. Time and time again this happened, until the peppery admirer of Strauss, Ernest Newman, was moved to protest: "with each new work, there is the same tomfoolery — one can use no milder word to describe proceedings that no doubt have a rude kind of German humor but which strike other people as more than silly."

THE OPERAS

The composer's operatic career has followed similar lines. *Salome*, written after the failure of the *Domestic Symphony*, although it is based on an erotic, horrible subject, can be described only as a masterpiece. The libretto is an adaption of Oscar Wilde's play treating of the scorned love of the pagan Judean princess for Jokanaan the Prophet. This work marks a definite descent from the exalted heights occupied by the Wagnerian gods and heroes; but it is a marvelous score, full of sensuous imagery, tremendous energy, blazing inspiration, and real originality, the music being perfectly fitted to the drama and becoming an integral part of its malevolent atmosphere. Strauss, who could be a real innovator, achieves some startlingly original effects: the cacophonous polytonal chorus of the quarreling Jewish rabbis; the pagan apostrophe of the scorned princess to the severed head of the prophet; the terrible detestation at the very end of the opera — all these seem inevitable and unforgettable.

THE SCANDALS OF "SALOME" AND "ELEKTRA"

The moral decadence of this libretto, together with the cacophonous music and the "vulgar" instrumentation, caused tremendous opposition to this score on the part of musicians as well as the general public. So much water has flowed under the tonal bridges since its première in 1905 that it seems today a harmless enough work, from both moral and musical points of view. In fact, as a reviewer remarked after a recent revival of this work, there is a beauty and a freshness and a force to *Salome* that suggest the glories of pristine Romanticism.

The scandal of *Salome* had not entirely subsided when Strauss stirred up another with his *Elektra*. This time the Greek classics were drawn upon for the libretto, and a terrific, tense, and overwrought score was the result. There is little about this opera which suggests the universal significance of its classic prototype: Strauss's music rants and raves, shrieks and postures until all concerned, singers as well as auditors, are reduced to a state of emotional exhaustion. There are great moments, as in most of the Strauss scores, but the composer writes so continuously "at the top of his voice" that they are not easily heard.

"DER ROSENKAVALIER"

Realizing, perhaps, that he had reached the final sensation in opera, Strauss next turned his attention to a comic subject in the eighteenth-century Rococo vein — *Der Rosenkavalier*; an avowed admirer of Mozart, he achieved in this artificial Viennese comedy his greatest operatic success. Glowing with color, the orchestration of *Der Rosenkavalier* is masterful throughout: the moods alternate from wistful tenderness to boisterous rowdyism, from captivating charm to ridiculous horseplay. Everywhere there is melody, ingratiating, incessant, exuberant melody, whether expressed in captivating waltzes or in facile arias. Full of life, this music of *Der Rosenkavalier* bespeaks supreme mastery of craftsmanship: it seems like a glorious outburst before the final denouement.

Everything after this colorful work is witness to the composer's progressive dissolution. *Ariadne auf Naxos, Josefs Legende* and *Schlagobers* (these two attempts at writing ballet music), *Die Frau ohne Schatten, Intermezzo, The Egyptian Helen, Arabella,* and *Daphne* contain little but technical achievements: in them Strauss seems to have fallen a victim to his society and the utter demoralization which it experienced in the decades of the new century. Whether it is his personal tragedy or whether it is due to the general miasma of the age, his later works lack all the old freshness and spontaneity. As one writer has well put it, as he has grown older, Strauss's heart has seemed to cease feeling, and only his mind has functioned with its former power.

THE SONGS

This composer's songs show the same pathetic retrogression of creative power: a few of them written in the flush of his youthful genius — *Allerseelen, Morgen, Traum durch die Dämmerung, Zueignung* — are among our finest lieder; they depict straightforward, honest expressions of emotions deeply felt. But the songs which follow, written during the *Zarathustra-Quixote-Heldenleben* periods, show the same tendencies as the orchestral and operatic works: the sensitive tone poet is less and less in evidence, and the slick, obvious, often heavy-handed sentimentalist comes more and more to the fore.

Strauss's great tragedy is that he was born too late and has lived too long. Essentially he is of the Romantic era, and the cynical *Mechanismus* of the modern age has cooled his ardor and stilled his magic. Without realizing it consciously, he metamorphosed from a passionate, turbulent, inspired genius into a tired, placid, but, unfortunately, still indefatigable talent.[3] It is said that the latter-day Strauss remarked after hearing one of his early works that he wondered how he could have composed such a thing. Perhaps he too has envied those young geniuses, Schubert and Mozart, whom the gods took from their labors while they were at the very zenith of their powers. For they may have been more fortunate than they knew!

CÉSAR FRANCK AND MUSICAL MYSTICISM

A man of shining genius, loyal of heart and strong of soul, who seemed to have known the angels.

— One of his pupils

The affirmation of incompetence pushed to dogmatic lengths.

— Gounod on Franck's symphony

A BELGO-FRENCH COMPOSER

CÉSAR FRANCK (1822–1890), though born in Belgium, is usually accounted a French composer, one of the few refreshingly original talents which that country developed in the late nineteenth century. After Berlioz, France fell upon thin times, in which neither the mingled

[3] Up to the time of writing, Strauss's latest works are his operas *Der Friedenstag* (*The Day of Peace*), produced in July, 1938, and *Daphne*, given its première in October of the same year. Both seem as undistinguished as the other recent works from his pen.

Classicism and sentimentalism of Saint-Saëns nor the theatrical and melodramatic operas of Gounod gave her a place in the front rank of the world's musical work. Chopin may perhaps be accounted partly French, but only by adoption; Franck's whole working life was spent in Paris after his entering the Conservatoire there in 1837. His was a quiet and uneventful career: to most of his associates he was nothing more than a worthy organist and professor. Much of his time was spent conscientiously in giving music lessons to those who were not too anxious to receive instruction. Sundays always found him in his beloved organ loft at Saint Clothilde, where for nearly forty years he performed his duties as an ardent church musician and a devout Christian. These tasks comprised his whole existence until, one day in 1890, while going about such business, he was injured in a street accident, and died — as he certainly would have wished to die — in harness.

By profession he was a church organist, and his music has become greatly beloved by his confreres, for he gave them a few of the finest things in their rather limited repertoire. There was something about his mind and, above all, his heart, a combination of simplicity and mysticism, which appeals strongly to church musicians, less strongly, perhaps, to those outside that circle. In addition to his organ works, Franck left an indelible impression on two other fields, those of the orchestra and of chamber music. He left behind no great amount of music; much of the best of it was written in his late years. As a rule, he composed but one work in each of the large forms: one symphony, one piano concerto, one string quartet, one quintet, one violin sonata, and a handful of tone poems and piano and organ pieces. These are all precious to the lover of choice, inward things, for they are informed by a wonderful harmonic sense that alone would mark out Franck as a pioneer, one of the distinctive men of a great century. The pioneer is not necessarily a great composer: often he simply suggests new ways of looking at things, while others, many of them smaller men, work them out. It was Franck's good fortune to be able, in his modest corner of life, to work out himself so many of his new ideas that he stands alone, as easily recognizable as Berlioz or Delius; and this in spite of there having arisen a small school of his pupils, men like D'Indy and Chausson, who employed much of his personal idiom.

HIS INDIVIDUAL STYLE

In addition to his peculiar harmonic style, the chromaticism of which, once recognized, can never be mistaken, Franck developed what has come to be known as the "cyclic" form. In essence this consists in the use of one or more themes whose development (in varied shapes) in several movements of a large work is a unifying feature of the whole. Liszt's use of "motto" themes had exhibited this element of construction, usually in a rather obvious manner, his thematic metamorphosis rarely being subtle although often broadly effective. Franck's use of such themes is as pervasive mood-influences, rather than simply as labels. The quintet is an excellent example of the employment of this device, as is the composer's most popular work, the *Symphony in D Minor.*

THE SYMPHONY

The first thing that is noticed about this symphony is the fact that it has been so strongly influenced by the composer's organ style: the sustained quality of its orchestration does not always make for greatest effectiveness, while its often rather rambling improvisatory character is better adapted to the organ loft than the concert hall. But it has its great moments, not all of them as "mystical" as its disciples have tried to make them out. Included in its utterances are some sentimentalities which dangerously suggest the *boulevardier* rather than the religious mystic, and these are unfortunate enough to cheapen the essential nobility of the whole. In 1889, when this work was first heard, it would have been surprising if Franck's sense of chromaticism had not been influenced by Wagner; but he is never bogged, as another organist symphonist, Bruckner, so often was, by failure to trim his own peculiarly, sometimes clumsily, cut sails to the Wagnerian winds that carried him so powerfully on. At its first performance, the symphony was received with ridicule by the authorities and with cold indifference by the public. When his friends asked for his opinion, Franck answered happily, "Oh, it sounded well, just as I thought it would."

Courtesy of The Louvre, Paris

CÉSAR FRANCK (from the painting by Rougier, 1888)
He is seated at his organ in the Church of St. Clothilde.

HIS STRENGTH AND WEAKNESS

There are here, as in most of the Franck works, certain little melodic tricks which some regard as weaknesses: the way he has, for instance, of making a melody center upon the third of the key. And his combination of naïveté with a sort of innocent bombast offends the taste of others who think that Franck has too palpable a design upon our emotions; such people are apt to associate signs of high aspirations with low cunning, a judgment which does not hold in Franck's case. The majority of music lovers are content to bask in the sunshine of experience that this composer's music affords; in a certain sense he is narrow and limited in his feeling, but narrow-channeled waters are often found to run deep, and there is in their flowing a concentration of power that bears us strongly along.

Franck's best works are probably the three great organ *Chorals* (the name implies only that their thematic bases are melodies of a religious cast), especially the one in A minor (No. 3). This, one of the last things he wrote, opens rhapsodically and has a glorious development perfectly suited to its medium. By no means all those who have heard the symphony, and perhaps some of the piano works,[4] realize the riches contained in these organ and chamber-music compositions. Wherever we listen in Franck, we have the revelation of a nature at once open and noble, innocent and yet informed, together with a manifestation of subtle craftsmanship. He wrote a great deal of church music of a rather hackneyed character, most of which had better be ignored; but in his large-scale works originality of a rare order is backed by an elevated intimacy, a brooding sense of otherworldliness that does not often become weak or vague. These are qualities which tend to strengthen the listener's spirit while it exalts and renews it.

THE VIENNESE TWINS – BRUCKNER AND MAHLER

Not until we know them well are we in a position to reject their music.
— Pitts Sanborn

A VIENNESE MASTER

ANY visitor to the Vienna of 1880, when the Austrian capital was in the heyday of its glory and the center of European interest in music, might have noticed wandering about the streets a peculiarly square-cut figure in black clothes of an obvious country style, with a broad-brimmed soft hat covering a shaggy, rugged head. This was Anton Bruckner, the simple, sincere, modest professor of organ, harmony, and

[4] Of the sixteen works which Franck wrote for the piano, only two, the *Prélude, Choral et Fugue* (1884) and the *Prélude, Aria et Finale*, are often played. In addition to the symphony, he wrote six other works for orchestra that are hardly ever heard, with the exception of the delightful *Variations symphoniques* for piano and orchestra.

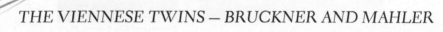

counterpoint at the conservatory and lecturer in music at the university. If the visitor had been curious enough to follow this rustic-looking man to his modest rooms on the top floor of a house in the Schottenring, one of the city's busiest thoroughfares, he would have found, according to contemporary accounts, a severe-looking apartment meagerly furnished with a worn piano, an armchair, and a chest of drawers on which would be found some open scores and a wooden crucifix.

But our suppositious visitor would hardly be aware of these external surroundings; for it is most likely that his interest would be centered in the striking personality of a young musician who was so often to be found in the apartments of Professor Bruckner — a pale, intense, and extremely dynamic young Jewish student of the conservatory and the university, Bruckner's private pupil and friend, Gustav Mahler. The names of these two figures of the twilight of Austrian Romanticism have become inextricably linked together, and with good reason: for never were two composers more closely akin spiritually. Both were Austrians born in the provinces and thrown together in the cosmopolitan crucible of the late nineteenth-century Vienna; both were intense, almost fanatical worshipers at the shrine of Wagner; both were natural Romantics, with a desire to carry on the traditions and grandeurs of the master's orchestral style, and yet possessed of a peculiar naïveté of spirit which made such expression difficult, if not almost impossible, for them; both were essentially saints and mystics as well as men of inordinate ambitions and unfortunately uneven capacities when it came to composing. All of which is to say that both wrote a number of huge, sprawling, eclectic works which do not hesitate to storm the highest heavens or plumb the lowest depths; which are of excessive length and intense earnestness; and which contain passages of almost unbelievable banality alongside some of great beauty and tremendous power. It is impossible to come to any just estimate of these scores, unlike anything else in music and speaking so personal a language, unless the hearer can see life as did their composers. As the doubters have so often remarked, it is difficult after hearing a Bruckner or a Mahler symphony to decide whether one has been hearing good stuff in spite of some bad moments or some poor stuff that has its good moments!

Stadtische Sammlungen, Vienna

ANTON BRUCKNER
(Painting by Bératon)

Bruckner came of an Upper-Austrian family of schoolteachers; he had planned to follow the family traditions, but his natural talent for music stood in the way, and as a boy of twelve he entered the great monastery of St. Florian to study music. Largely self-taught, he became a master of counterpoint and an expert organist, at first in the monastery chapel, later in the Cathedral of Linz. The middle years of his life were spent in Vienna, where most of his composing was done and where he slowly made his way against the prejudices and the partisanships of the anti-Wagnerians.

Like Beethoven, Bruckner wrote nine symphonies; but the similarity ends there. His genial melodic vein is typically Austrian and suggests his compatriot, Schubert. There was nothing of Beethoven's architectural genius about the organist composer, for although the general outlines of his huge forms can be seen easily enough, his structures are too artless and too discursive to be effective. He is liable to wander leisurely all around an idea, instead of tackling it directly. Perhaps the organ loft had too strong an influence on his style, giving it its peculiarly heavy, rambling, improvisatory character. His last wish was that he be buried beneath the organ which he had played so long at St. Florian; some cynics have maintained that he was buried under this instrument long before he was dead. But there is the simple devotion and unquestioning faith of a true Christian in his music. It was his misfortune that he was not more prolific in ideas and had to spin those he did possess to so great length. Symphonies that last an hour and a quarter are doomed to be declared, by the unconverted, " too long ": nobody else in the world needs such a time to unfold his designs.

The Third, Fourth, and Seventh are the best known and most often played of the Bruckner symphonies; but in hearing them we are not certain that we hear what the composer finally intended, for various individuals revised Bruckner's works unmercifully with the avowed intent of making him appear as the great Wagnerian successor. Bruckner seems to have been so impractical or so pitiably weak as to appear absolutely helpless in the matter, although there are some who claim that he consented to many of the alterations and shortenings made in his scores.[5]

At best there is much to enjoy in the music of this Catholic mystic who liked to describe himself as a wanderer whom a summit attracts and compels. " But I do not go direct," he adds. " I find many alluring paths which, however they may retard, do not obstruct my objective." Unfortunately, one cannot be too sure; but if we are patient, we may get something of the satisfaction that a large section of the German and Austrian public seems to derive from these Gargantuan works.

[5] William Glock, writing of the Bruckner Festival at Linz in 1936, says: " It appears that we have been hearing the symphonies of Ferdinand Löwe and not of Bruckner. On comparing the Bruckner ' original ' of the *Fourth Symphony* with that previously published, one must be suspicious as to Bruckner's responsibility for many of those weaknesses that have been described so consistently by English critics. The famous ' pauses ' are by no means all authentic, nor the dynamic indications, nor the distracting changes of tempo; in the well-known score of the Fourth there are eleven important changes of tempo in the first movement; in the original, none at all. In addition, the ' original ' scoring is totally different, and, in the *Fourth Symphony*, at least, invariably more sensitive. Even modulations have been altered in the accepted edition, and certain passages rewritten so as to become unrecognizable. This is a situation unparalleled in musical history " (London *Observer*).

MAHLER, A MORE COMPLEX CHARACTER

Mahler's was a much more complex character: a Jew, with all the intensity of emotion and psychic sensibility of which that race is capable, he had a divided spirit, one which alternately believed and doubted, which possessed lofty and noble ideals, often attempting to comprehend the whole of our universe, and yet one which did not hesitate to employ almost unbelievably childish naïvetés. At heart this composer was a simple and believing infant, yet in actual life he was what one writer has called an eternal Old Testament prophet, "restlessly pursuing the problems of life and death in order outwardly to confirm his inner faith." Even his friends did not fully understand him: as a man, especially in his capacity as conductor and opera director, he seems to have been hard, violent, hot-tempered; as an interpretative artist he was often as tender and sweet and simple as a child.

He held during his stormily active career a number of posts as *Kapellmeister* — at Kassel, Prague, Leipzig, Pest, Hamburg, and, finally, in 1897, at the court opera in Vienna. During his ten years in this last position he had ample time to prove his extraordinary ability as organizer and conductor, and the institution flourished as it never had before and never has since. His popularity in this musical city was unusual, in spite of the fanatic and ruthless vehemence with which he pursued his artistic ideals and the unfortunate brusqueness with which he expressed himself when dealing with his fellows. In 1907 he resigned in Vienna and went to New York, where he became the principal conductor of the Metropolitan Opera, and later, of the Philharmonic Orchestra, which organization he completely reformed at a fatal cost in nervous and physical energy. In 1911 he broke down and was compelled to return to Vienna, where he died in May.

Not content with the universal acclaim paid him everywhere as a great director and conductor, Mahler sought distinction also as a creative artist. He wrote nine symphonies (this number seems to have fascinated composers), as well as several important song cycles for voices and orchestra. These tremendous works can be called symphonies only by courtesy, for they have nothing in them suggestive of the classic

MAHLER
(After a painting by Fritz Erler)

forms, not even in the number or arrangement of their movements. As in Bruckner's works, there is in these Mahler symphonies music of exalted and unparalleled beauty; but it is often contiguous to passages that are banal and oversentimental. Perhaps it was because he so often strove in these works to render manifest certain psychical conceptions that seem impossible of expression, even in music, that Mahler fell short. When he did keep within the natural confines of his art, as in the magnificent *Das Lied von der Erde* (by far his finest work), he wrote as heart-searching music as has ever been put to paper.

There is no question that his ardent spirit and controversial temperament tried to do too much — to revolutionize the great opera theaters and symphonic organizations of his time, as well as to leave posterity music that would honor his name. In everything he wrote there can be felt a fever of nervous excitement and exhaustive tension: he worked

A PAGE FROM THE SCORE OF MAHLER'S EIGHTH SYMPHONY—THE "SYMPHONY OF A THOUSAND"

at white heat and his music consequently suffered. His was a peculiarly personal way of expressing himself with the orchestra, a way that was powerful, dynamic, and unconventional and which was the result of long years of practical experience with this instrument. Nevertheless he seemed to be at his best when writing for the voice, a fact that may have been the result of his long career as an opera director. His *Second Symphony* — the so-called *Resurrection Symphony* — culminates in a huge vocal chorus; in the *Eighth Symphony* he tries to express the essential contradictions of his nature through the means of a double chorus of mixed voices, a boys' choir and a number of soloists, in addition to an enormous orchestra. His song cycles, *Kindertotenlieder* and *Das Lied von der Erde*, are as true symphonies as anything else he wrote; it is said that superstition kept him from calling the latter his ninth symphony.

This work, composed after Mahler's strong spirit had been broken through his strenuous efforts to conquer the universe, has been well called a voice from the grave, a profoundly moving testament, and one of the most affecting utterances in all music. He wrote this cycle for tenor and contralto with orchestra during the last years of his life, at a time when he knew his days were numbered. Bruno Walter has described the composer's mood at the time:

"Just as in nature, twilight is followed by the brightness of the sunset glow, so the world, after the initial sinking of his vitality, now lay before him in the dimming light of an inevitable farewell.

"The 'dear Earth,' whose song he had written, looked so beautiful to him in that light that everything he thought or uttered was mysteriously permeated with a feeling of surprise at the new charm of the old life. I shall never be able to forget his expression when he told me how, on the occasion of a country visit in Moravia, he had found the world to be more beautiful than ever before, and what a peculiarly fervent happiness he had derived from the smell of the soil arising from the fields. In the background of his conversation there was now a constant spiritual upheaval, his mind ever striving . . . to take flight from his manifold intellectual themes to problems of a metaphysical nature — only now the urge and agitation were more intense. I am tempted to compare this restlessness of the soul with the excitement preceding a journey, a condition which only occasionally yielded to a touching repose when, in our conversations, we would make plans for the future."

Set to words adapted from the Chinese poets, *Das Lied von der Erde* is music that is solitary, haunting, unique, the work of a man upon whom darkness has fallen; there is nothing in all music quite like the effect of the end of its closing movement, with the contralto mysteriously but tranquilly repeating the one word *ewig* . . . *ewig* (" eternal . . . eternal "). Properly interpreted, this seems not only the farewell of an estranged spirit to an alien world, but likewise the end of the ardent, impulsive, lovely, but doomed, Romantic spirit.

HIS PLACE IN THE FUTURE

The future of Mahler's music is uncertain. In the world-turned-anti-Romantic of the past decades there is no question but that it has fared badly; there is also no question but that a reaction will come in favor of Romanticism. The particular difficulty of this specific manifestation of its spirit is that for its effect it depends so largely upon an interpreter imbued with the same intuitive and almost psychic spirit that inspired its creation. In the hands of a conductor like Bruno Walter, the composer's great disciple, this music is safe: we can almost be persuaded that it is the work of a genius. When interpreted by others, it can sound merely platitudinous and sentimental, a fact which can never make for the sort of universal admiration given to such composers as Brahms, Wagner, or even Tchaikovsky. In spite of the rather numerous performances given Mahler's music in recent years, it can hardly be said that interest in it is on the increase.

Perhaps Newman has summed it up as well as anyone: Mahler's music has too many faults to be designated a success; but if it is a failure, it is a noble one. The composer's grasp may not have been equal to his span, but the span itself commands our admiration; if somewhat flawed, he is still a genius.

A LONE NORTHERNER — SIBELIUS

It is impossible to define religion — least of all in words. Perhaps music is a mirror.

The thing that has pleased me most is that I have been able to reject. The greatest labor I have expended, perhaps, was on works that have never been completed.

On the whole, one is merely a tool. This wonderful logic — let us call it God — that governs a work of art is the forcing power.

— Sibelius

A CURIOUS SITUATION

WE have remarked the rather sudden and, in some ways, inexplicable rise of Sibelius to fame, a rise so spectacular that it has caused many of his most ardent admirers and propagandists to re-examine their opinions regarding this composer, on the assumption that the moment an artist begins to be popular one should entertain suspicions of him. So we have the rather surprising spectacle of a great composer, almost entirely unknown and unrecognized at the time he was writing his best works, later rising to somewhat dangerous heights of popularity through the propagandizing of enthusiasts and becoming suspect even by his friends. All of which does not concern Sibelius in the least: for in a world almost entirely given over to self-advancement through advertisement, he has kept himself isolated from the mob and composed as he saw fit, regardless of the world and its opinions.

In spite of all the attempts which have been made, it is impossible to fasten any definite label on Sibelius. When he first became known to the English-speaking world, he was introduced as a barbarian from an uncouth, half-civilized land, a sort of churlish invader from the north, a "spare, knotted barbarian from the world of the sagas . . . one who might have been comrade to pelted warriors who fought with clubs and hammers, who might have beaten out a rude music by black smoking hearthsides." [6]

[6] An actual quotation from an article on the composer by Paul Rosenfeld, an American critic.

Such nonsense has been pretty well dissipated by a better knowledge of the facts: Finland has proved itself to be one of the most civilized of nations, having advanced even to a state of civilization which recognizes international obligations as binding and which believes that national resources are as worth spending on subsidies to artists as on building warships. And Sibelius turns out to be an urbane, quiet individual of the country-gentleman type, born into a cultivated, musical family and living a sane, normal, and, for the most part, happy life.

NATIONALISM OVERSTRESSED

Another label which has been fastened on Sibelius is that of nationalist: "it was with the sanction of a people that Sibelius came to his task," writes one of his apologists.[7] In the recent Finnish biography of the composer by Ekman, a work which may be taken as authoritative, the statement is made that the boy who was later to become Finland's most famous citizen was of mixed extraction, with as much Swedish as Finnish blood, and that environment and conviction rather than descent gave his life its individual character. It was really not until well along in his life, as Ekman points out, that Sibelius had an opportunity of hearing the Finnish folk tunes on which he is supposed to have based his music.

Sibelius himself confirms this:

> "The language of sound that I had employed in *Kullervo* (an early symphonic poem) was considered to give such thorough and true expression of Finnish scenery and the soul of the Finnish people that many were unable to explain it in any other way than that I had made direct use of folk melodies, especially the accents of runic song, in my work. The genuinely Finnish tone could, however, not have been achieved in this way for the simple reason that at the time the work was composed I was not acquainted with my supposed model."
>
> — Ekman: *Jean Sibelius*

There is, of course, in all Sibelius's best music a suggestion of the racial instincts and traditions of the country in which he was born: the great

[7] Rosenfeld again.

national epic, the *Kalevala*, absorbed his interest continuously, as he tells us, and its tales of heroism, its wild, colorful idylls and scenes of fantastic tragedy inspired him to write some of his greatest music, including the tone poems *En Saga* and *Kullervo*, the *Lemminkainen* legends, *The Swan of Tuonela*, and *Pohjola's Daughter*. But to put all these into a neat pile and label it " Finnish " is to miss completely the fresh, inspired, and entirely incalculable genius of this composer.

QUALITIES OF SIBELIUS'S GREATNESS

Sibelius's greatness lies in his peculiar fusion of manner and matter, of nationalism and personality, as well as in his persistent experimentation with, and constant re-creation of, symphonic form. Each one of his seven symphonies achieves results that are quite different from those of the others. Sibelius is not the only composer to change his style and attack art from many sides; but this variability of style is in many writers — Stravinsky, for instance — only a confession of weakness, of having so exhausted their material that they must run about, seeking new. With Sibelius it has been a triumphant demonstration of a freshness of imagination that has persisted throughout his whole creative career.

In the very first measures of the *First Symphony*, written 1898–1899, we are aware that an entirely new voice is speaking, one whose accents are worth consideration. And throughout all the others — the richly variegated and strongly contrasted Second, the joyous Third and Fifth, full of the health and vigor of the high hills, the introspective, imaginative, and unprecedently concentrated Fourth, the rhapsodic and darkly mysterious Sixth, the one-movemented Seventh — we are conscious of unique imaginative freshness and constantly varied formal methods. It is difficult to realize that the First, Fourth, and Seventh symphonies could have been written by the same man, and yet impossible to think otherwise. They all hang together by a logic of their own,[8] yet none of them in any sense but the most general follow traditional methods.

[8] This is a favorite phrase of Ernest Newman's, one of the most active of the Sibelius supporters.

Davart

SIBELIUS

They are all the result of a striking original mind, one which does everything in its own way: we cannot account for the *First Symphony* in terms of anything that preceded it, and it is impossible to think that the Seventh will leave any posterity whatsoever.

THE COMPLETE INDIVIDUALIST

The one thing which places Sibelius head and shoulders above his contemporaries is the fact that he has concerned himself so largely with the content of what he was saying rather than merely with the manner of its delivery. Being a man of real individuality, with a vivid imagination and a sensitive reaction to his environment, he has something definite to say. And so it has not been necessary for him to adopt unusual devices — polytonality, atonality, and all the rest — to attract through their novelty and cover up an essential paucity of thought. He has not been ashamed to put feeling into his music, unaffected, deep feeling, nor to give it direct connection with life. No matter how unusual or different his expression may be, we do not feel that it suggests the composings of court councilors or the dissertations of doctors, to use his own phrases. Repeated hearings clear up the feeling of strangeness which is inevitable when listening to his works for the first time, and everything in these works seems to fall logically into proper place. So there is reason to suppose that his best works, the symphonies and some of the tone poems, will outlast their own popularity.

Like any other composer, Sibelius has his characteristic traits. One of the most striking and exciting factors in his music is its unexpectedness. It is impossible to forecast the shape into which he will run a symphony. Sometimes he has pursued the extreme concentration of a one-movement work, as in the Seventh, sometimes the extreme restraint and withdrawn communing of the Fourth; again, we have works (naturally enough, in the earlier stages) which here and there remind us of the procedure of Liszt, Borodin, or Tchaikovsky, but which bring a new luster to old practices. It is possible to say that a new work is likely to contain certain characteristic fashions of building, one of the most fundamental of these being his habit of not exposing a theme in full until late in a movement — treating bits of it, hinting, suggesting, and, we may think, at times hiding, until its presentation comes with a splendid panoply of irresistible vigor. There are smaller traits, just as characteristic, such as his liking for a busy, exciting, opening section by the strings, his abruptly breaking off a train of thought and starting another — yet without the effect of disjunction that might be feared. Then there is his remarkable orchestration. Open almost any score at any page, and you find strange-looking and strange-sounding combinations, each carrying the conviction that the idea was born thus in its creator's brain, clothed in its orchestral dress, and only thus is it to be expressed.

LAPSES

There are lapses: now and again a movement does not seem to fit its context, does not build fully into the nature of a work as a whole. Sibelius seems at moments to be rather too easily pleased with a theme and so repeats it almost *ad absurdum;* there are family resemblances in his figures and themes that seem more than a little casual. Like César Franck, Sibelius lacks a certain versatility of human contact: his music is often strongly introspective. It is always filled with a spirit that is as individual as it is deeply felt. Yet in no sense can this music be thought of as modern; it is one of the last great expressions of the Romantic ideal, realized by a personality of unusual interest. How few of his major works fail to exhilarate and to satisfy both our logical and our spiritual sense! One does not always come from hearing this music with a sense of ease; but one cannot fail to be braced and stimulated by curiosity, as well as by a feeling of keen interest in this lone composer's strikingly personal way of carving out his big ideas.

A DIVERSITY OF WORKS

Concurrently with the symphonies, Sibelius produced a great mass of other music, most of it written for prolific consumption. There are the brilliant potboilers, *Finlandia* and *Valse triste:* because of its patriotic character, the former was prohibited in the land of its birth during the years of unrest under the Russian regime; the latter was originally written as incidental music for a Finnish drama. Both these works have become exceptionally popular; while they are certainly not Sibelius at his best, they are not so cheap as they are often made by interpreters. Then there is a surprising amount of piano music, none of it significant: this medium seems to have been uncongenial, and Sibelius appears to have reserved his least important ideas for it. There is a great deal of what the Germans call *Kapellmeister* music — well-written, uninspired things, some of them for choruses, incidental dramatic music, and so on. Then there are the songs, a few of them based on the character of the ancient runes; they are of supreme importance. But the majority are simply rather superior types of drawing-room songs with, in their general build, a Straussian or a Moussorgskian derivation. Sibelius seems wisely to have kept his independent thoughts for his great works; we can really know him only through his orchestral compositions.

IS HIS POPULARITY PERMANENT?

A few years ago the English composer and critic, Constant Lambert, wrote a study of the decline which has overtaken the art of music since the time of Debussy. In this brilliant book (*Music Ho!*) the only composer spoken of with genuine admiration is Sibelius, whom Lambert calls the most important symphonic writer since Beethoven and the only one since that nineteenth-century giant who has definitely advanced what is, after all, the most complete formal expression of the music spirit. Whether we can agree with such a sweeping statement or not depends upon our outlook: there are many who think that Sibelius has been the victim of those who wish him well and that in reality he is an inferior composer, magnified beyond his deserts because, in an age of small men, he happens to be of middle stature.

Only time can tell. But in the meantime we can admire the inspiring example of a man who, in a peculiarly disjointed and feeble time, when most of his contemporaries were floundering about in fulsome attempts to be original through spectacular means, followed the dictates of his own artistic conscience and never subserved any but the highest aims; who in a period of Boeotian smallness has dared live his life in the grand style. It is from sources such as this that great music comes.

THE TWILIGHT OF THE ROMANTICS

Man must abide
His going hence, even as his coming hither:
Ripeness in all.

— Shakespeare

A SUNSET GLOW

WE should not let our judgment of an artist or a group of artists be too strongly influenced by the fact that they can be described as *fin de siècle:* it is a natural tendency to conclude that the artistic products of such men necessarily represent a definite tailing off from the great line. We must always remember that the assumption that there are certain logical aesthetic trends which tend to produce certain types of artists is only a convenient device for the clarifying of art history; the records show that time and time again such periods have waxed and waned, that fashions in art have come and gone, while great works have continuously been produced, despite the conditionings of such periods and trends.

Nevertheless, the fact that such late Romantics as Elgar, Bax, MacDowell, D'Indy, and the rest spent their creative careers in a world which had largely outgrown its original enthusiasms for the Romanticism they professed had a decided effect on their work. For it is difficult for an artist to develop his personality fully in an environment that is not completely congenial, one from which he cannot readily extract the materials he needs for the weaving of his own personal artistic patterns. He is likely under such circumstances to grow somewhat self-conscious, to tend toward mannerisms that are suggestive of inhibitions and restraints on his natural spontaneity.

ELGAR: THE ENIGMATIC ENGLISHMAN

Elgar (1857–1934) is a good example of this. The most outstanding of a group of composers who around the 1890's were engaged in attempting to revive something of the past glories of English music, he seemed to have been conscious his whole life long that, as he expressed it, " nobody really wanted his music." Born in a musically meager period and country, he had to struggle through all the early part of his life against the lack of proper social background, an important factor in the musical life of the England of his day. He did not attend any of the official academies and so was not " in the swim "; the son of a provincial parish organist, he had to make his own way through merit alone. Naturally enough, he did not seem to make much headway, at least to outward view, for many years; engaged in a number of rather unimportant posts, he was really preparing himself so that when, after a few smaller works for chorus, he finally got a hearing (in 1899) for the set of orchestral variations to which he gave the name *Enigma,* his place as the outstanding composer of England was assured.

From then on his success was complete; work after work followed, for both chorus and orchestra. Among the most important of these were the oratorio *The Dream of Gerontius* (considered by many of his admirers to be his best work) in 1900, the *First Symphony* (1908), the *Violin Concerto* (1910), the *Second Symphony* in 1911, and a great symphonic study, *Falstaff,* in 1913. He was showered with honors and degrees, made a member of many foreign academies, knighted (later made a baronet) and given the jealously guarded Order of Merit; he was invited to France and the United States to conduct his works. And yet through all these years of outward success, in spite of all the honors which a repentant world seemed anxious to bestow, it is impossible not to feel in Elgar's works a certain sense of frustration, as if he was unconsciously being inhibited from expressing his full self as a composer. This resulted in definite mannerisms: a peculiar resort to an insistent series of harmonic and melodic sequences; tremendous bursts of nervous energy which often culminated in a sort of self-conscious swagger that was quite foreign to a nature so calm and controlled; and, most dangerous of all, a verbose loquacity that tended to weaken his naturally warm musical language.

Perhaps it is these persistent idiosyncrasies, perhaps it is a certain sense of Englishness that appeals to his countrymen but which is not fully communicated to others; whatever the reason, Elgar's music has not attained any widespread popularity outside England. Its occasional performance in other countries seems only to emphasize the peculiar isolation of this composer who has so much to recommend him; for there is in his music a philosophic mellowness, a warm depth of feeling, and a pride in workmanship which is not unworthy of the country that produced Shakespeare.

HIS MASTERPIECE

Nowhere can this be better felt than in the *Enigma Variations,* the particular riddle of which is twofold: part of it remains a secret even yet, after the composer's death; part of it soon became known. The secret part concerns a theme which, the composer said, was never heard, but "went with" his variation theme and all the variations — a remarkable claim, surely, since the variations are so very diverse. What that theme is, nobody knows: one of the composer's friends suggested that it might be a Mrs. Harris of a theme, as substantial as Sairey Gamp's friend, so often heard of and never seen; or "theme" may not necessarily mean music: it might be a topic, a pervading idea; the point is not important. The other, more interesting, enigma lay in the composer's suggesting, in each of his thirteen variations, the character of some friend, and, in the finale, something of his own aspirations and hopes. We were not told until later the identity of these people: there is the gracious gentleness of Elgar's wife (in No. 1); the determined, brusque country gentleman of No. 4; the seascape in No. 13, written in remembrance of a friend who was on the ocean; the miniature "thriller" in No. 11, which is about a dog that fell into the river. All are remarkably varied sound portraits and backgrounds, illuminated by a vivid imagination and a superb orchestral power.

Apart from the *Enigma Variations,* scarcely anything of Elgar's is played outside the land of his birth. In spite of many orchestral beauties and a famous cadenza, in which one well-known English critic has felt that there is "something Greek, something of Elysium," the *Violin Concerto* rather sharply reveals to foreigners those elements in Elgar's music that have brought about its quick depreciation: the involved style (shown to perfection in the concerto's introduction), the use of themes that sound rather sentimental (an American writer has called them "Belgravian" [9]), and the use of a formal structure that is elaborate without affording the average listener sufficient sense of either balance or contrast.

It is qualities such as these that have brought about the neglect of Elgar's music in countries that have not been willing to overlook them as the English have done; which is a pity, for he has some great strengths — a certain nobility of thought and a vitality of imagination that are sorely needed in a world such as ours, and which are sadly lacking in so much of the music of his contemporaries.

[9] According to the *Oxford Dictionary,* "Of, suited to, Belgravia, fashionable London district."

A NEGLECTED FRENCH CRAFTSMAN

Of Vincent d'Indy (1851–1931), the French contemporary of Elgar, it is easy to say "Oh, the disciple of Franck"; but there was much more to him than that. He was a real individual with a distinctive personality, besides being the heir of ages of French logic, wit, and grace. An aristocrat and a theorist, an ardent expositor of cyclical form, and an idolater of his master Franck, he could be dry, but never for long. The *Symphony on a Mountain Song* of his native Cévennes brings out his genial qualities; and in the symphonic variations, *Istar*, how admirable is the dramatic and musical shaping that follows the story of this choregraphic poem (written in 1896 and first danced in 1912) wherein the goddess Istar, daughter of Sin, must, to free her young lover, the Son of Life, pass through seven doors, at each of which a demon robs her of some adornment. The music suggests the ordeal, and the ingenuity of the composer's idea is that only at the end, when the last veil is removed, do we hear his melody in its simplicity; here is a new idea in variations — proceeding from the complex to the simple. It is presented in a setting attractively Oriental, yet not conventionally so, and it has the best French qualities of style.

D'Indy has written a great deal more music than most of us get to hear: he is a composer worth cultivating, for the touch of his natural austerity is not chilling, and the warmth of his romance not enervating. It would be difficult indeed to think of a better soil for the right balancing of the characteristics he possesses than that of France: its best music has the individual bouquet of its best wines.

THE EBULLIENT CHABRIER

A different aspect of French character is seen in Chabrier, already mentioned in the section on French opera, whose zest and glowing ardor hold many attractions. He is widely known by a few compositions in which gusto and good humor are hardly matched by formal balance. His *España*, a Spanish rhapsody on original themes, reflected a new

FAURÉ

tendency in music — an enthusiasm for things Spanish which was to be cultivated frequently during the next generation. A lyric sense and a pointed humor and exuberance mark Chabrier as one of the Good Companions of music, whose acquaintance will brighten the life and cheer the heart of any listener.

FAURÉ: A FOUNTAINHEAD

Another French composer of the time who, like D'Indy, is very much overneglected, is Gabriel Fauré (1845–1924). If a few of his songs are familiar, his very considerable output of chamber music has but rarely been given the place it deserves in the art of this period. It has happened to more than one listener that first impressions of Fauré have to be revised, to the composer's advantage, on rehearings. There is in his music a curious deceptive simplicity and fluency, something that suggests a French Brahms without the bite of the great German. There is, too, a classic strain that is not the least of the sound qualities of the best French music of his day. He exercised considerable influence, both by his works and as a teacher, on other French composers, including Maurice Ravel and Roger-Ducasse.

In his incidental music to *Shylock,* adapted from Shakespeare, we can find a light French nationalistic touch, besides a wider evocative power and a free-running comedy spirit that is not easily matched outside France. The composer's peculiarly alert, natty style here is in perfect keeping with the Shakespearean comedy, and, combined with a touch of philosophy, it makes a winning French blend. One of his strongest works is his *Requiem,* written in 1887. Florent Schmitt has defined Fauré's qualities as "clarity, restraint, suppleness," qualities which should make his music more congenial to the Anglo-Saxon temperament than are those of some other foreign natures — Mahler's, for instance.

SAINT-SAËNS, THE ECLECTIC

More appealing, although a much smaller man, was the prolific Saint-Saëns (1835–1921), whose operatic talent we have already discussed. It is impossible not to give in to his jollities even when, as in his lively fourth piano concerto, they seem to be an almost ridiculous mixture of church, theater, circus, and schoolroom. The best element of this composer's style is his classical bent, although it is rather odd at times to hear him introduce some fuguing as if he had suddenly remembered that the classics' turn was due. But all that he wrote was turned out with so innocent a pleasure and so bustling an activity that one cannot be too severe: he never goes deep, but he skims gaily. He was at his best in such program works as *Phaeton* and *Le rouet d'Omphale,* which show his logical, point-to-point mind working out musical problems with admirable lucidity and sufficient heat, but no real light on anything below the surface. Their philosophy is milk-drawn; their Classicism, a shade heavy.

Almost every type of music was written by this extremely prolific (too prolific) composer; but the most of his numerous operas, symphonic works, and cantatas are of slight import. We must remember, however, that Saint-Saëns was a pioneer and did much to make French music acceptable abroad. His skill and ingenuity are undoubted; and if he sometimes annoys serious listeners, he is greatly beloved by those who seek easier satisfaction. He represents, in a simple, wholesome way, what Anglo-Saxons think of as being "typically French" rather than what Frenchmen mean by such a phrase; very few of the finer, more quintessential qualities of French art are to be found in his music.

INHERITORS OF THE FRANCK TRADITION

The school of Franck included, besides D'Indy, a number of others who worked happily in the Romantic vein. Chausson (1855–1899), a wealthy art lover whose life was cut short by an accident, is one of these, of gracious, gentle, lyrical gifts. He is generally known by but a single work, the *Poème* for violin and orchestra; but to enjoy the best of him one should hear also his symphony and his piano quartet.

Henri Duparc (1848–1933) is another lyrical singer who was, in a different way, the victim of sad circumstance, for before he was forty a breakdown in health prevented his continuing to compose. Thus he is remembered by a mere handful of pieces, mostly songs. Such concert-room favorites as *L'invitation au voyage* and *Extase* assure us that Franck had good reason for considering Duparc one of the very best of his pupils. We can but name Charles Bordes (1863–1909) and Guy Ropartz (*b.* 1864), on both of whom folk song (respectively Basque and Breton) exercised a charming influence, and the short-lived Guillaume Lekeu (1870–1894), whose emotion is often movingly somber. Lekeu is best known by his violin sonata.

FAURÉ'S DESCENDANTS

The influence of Fauré was, in its different way, as beneficial as that of Franck. Fauré, who has been described by a French critic as "remaining refractory towards the virulent microbe of Romanticism" (meaning, chiefly, Wagnerianism), nevertheless left his mark not only in his own work but on such pupils as Koechlin, Roger-Ducasse, and Schmitt; the last named (perhaps the most notable of them) has taken paths that are widely different from his master's. He is noted in a later chapter on the impressionists and their successors. Koechlin (*b.* 1867), a lover of polyphony, inclines towards advanced harmonic thought of a German cast while maintaining a lyrical impulse. If, for Anglo-Saxon ears, much of his music seems to live with rather thin, small ideas, we should always remind ourselves of the difficulty that Anglo-Saxon and Latin have in fully enjoying the most characteristic qualities and essential traits of each other's music.

Paul Dukas (1865–1935) is, for most of us, almost a one-work composer. His humorous orchestral scherzo, *L'apprenti sorcier* (after Goethe), which describes the mishaps of a young would-be wizard, has delighted the world since 1897. His greatest work came a decade later; the opera *Ariane et Barbe Bleue* (after which Dukas composed very little) was written in close collaboration with the poet Maeterlinck. The earlier work was healthily influenced by Wagner and Debussy. Dukas spoke in a more personal vein in *Ariane*, the orchestration of which has been well described as "prismatic and sensuous," and the music in general as rather refining and embellishing the effects of its period and uniting with the text in uncommon integrity, rather than creating any new significance.

THE ITALIANS

Italian non-operatic composers have been fairly divided into the categories of Romantic-impressionists and modernists, with a few markedly wholehearted Romantics, such as Sinigaglia (*b.* 1868), who makes his music gay with the folk colors of Piedmont and whose bustling overture to Goldoni's play *Le baruffe chiozzotte* is a great favorite; and equally wholehearted impressionists like Respighi, of whom we shall say a word in the chapter on that branch of art.

The little band of really modernistically minded composers, among whom Casella, Malipiero, and Pizzetti are eminent, does not exclude from its purview the tenets of impressionism (Malipiero, for instance, has written much music of that type); but these composers are perhaps most conveniently considered in our later chapter on the most recent tendencies. This band in Italy is small, which is natural enough when we remember the tremendous strength and length of the Italian operatic tradition and the country's very slight interest in any other kind of composition during the nineteenth century. In a land where opera was so long looked on as both bread and circus and where melody was considered the breath of life, it is but natural that modernist opera, or any kind of modernism, should not find its most congenial home.

A composer of Italian extraction who sought to make the best of both Romantic and modernist worlds was Busoni (1866–1924). But he was partly German: indeed, he had greater affinity with that country. Perhaps his most notable late work was an opera in a new style, *Dr. Faust*. He was a piano virtuoso as well as a composer, and probably some of the unsatisfied longings he strikingly expressed in the written word were the result of a career thus divided. He could be amazingly brilliant in his composition, and again immensely solid and contrapuntal, yet free and wide-ranging — a modernist, nevertheless not an absolute iconoclast. His was a remarkable personality, exceptionally self-analytical, and possibly thereby partly frustrated. Essentially a big composer, yet too uncertain of direction to be a great one, he was in many ways a typical figure of (as some would say) an age of excessive cerebration, still not lacking the joy that we associate with past days when composers had fewer doubts.

THE COSMOPOLITAN JEW, BLOCH

One other composer, perhaps destined to leave a considerable mark on his age, may be mentioned here, since his humane and richly expressive art keeps him in the Romantic succession in spite of his using a sharper-edged tool oftener than many before him: this is Ernest Bloch (*b.* 1880 in Switzerland), a Jew who concentrates with subtly evocative power the Old Testament spirit of impassioned faith and sorrows. Even outside that wide range he is a man of real worth, splendidly earnest, finely equipped technically. His is one of the most impressive musical minds of our age. His best works, the *Schelomo Rhapsody*, the *Israel Symphony*, and the *Trois Poèmes juifs*, were inspired by Hebrew lore.

BAX: A CELTIC MYSTIC

The works of Arnold Bax (*b.* 1883) may well be included here because he, perhaps most purely of his generation, holds by the Romantic spirit, however strongly he laces it with later rhythmical and harmonic pungencies. His Irish spirit brings out singing themes, with sometimes a folky curve to them; but he is not one of the full-bodied folk followers, so many of whom have been bogged by will-o'-the-wisp leadership in this field. Bax has produced several symphonies in swift succession, all of them showing his striking tendency toward a proliferation of harmonic richness, almost, it may be felt, to the excess of decorative quality, affectionate and natural though it seems to be. This mannerism springs, perhaps, from his Celtic temperament, but it does not make for directness of appeal. Though his later works have not, on the whole, sustained the early hopes which had been held for this composer, Bax is a man of notable powers, and nothing he writes is insignificant. Like so many of his fellows, he seems caught between the ages — a Romantic not entirely at ease with the old romance nor entirely happy with the new.

One other British composer is worth mentioning here, if for no other reason than that he has made a grim recovery from what had seemed like a disabling sickness — that wartime and postwar debility that afflicted so many young composers and for a time stultified any powers they might have possessed, and produced the era of Bright Young People. Arthur Bliss (*b.* 1891) seemed at one time as if he were going the way of the rest, albeit with a somewhat superior wit; but since the war he has strengthened his art and, by introducing a new tincture into it, has made many new friends for such works as his oboe quintet, the suite of choral pieces known by the title *Lie Strewn the White Flocks*, and the ballet music, *Checkmate*.

THE ROMANTIC SIDE OF SCHÖNBERG

In the German-speaking countries one of the most important post-Wagnerian Romantics was Arnold Schönberg; but after a number of years of bright sailing in clear Romantic waters, he seems to have run into the fog banks of theory, to put the matter simply. Before he wrote the new treatise on harmony in 1911, in which his extremist, cerebral style first took full shape, he had composed two large works in the earlier manner, *Verklärte Nacht* and *Gurrelieder*, both of which show the scope of his imagination and the quality of his genius. In these he pushed chromaticism to extremes but did not, as later, throw the old tonal systems completely overboard. Much has been written, by this composer and others, about his new system of harmony; we shall discuss this in another place, under the heading of "The Modern Revolt: Realism." Here it will be necessary only to suggest that the Romantic Schönberg is as well worth consideration as the revolutionary one.

Verklärte Nacht has a poetic background: that of a woman who, yearning for love, yields to a stranger and then meets the man she really loves. As she walks with him through the dark forest, they talk together; he encourages and cheers her, assuring her that the warmth of their love will glorify the child that is to come. The music suggests, in richest Romantic style, the atmosphere of the calm, glorious night, the confession, with its high emotion and deep regret, the comfort of the man's voice, rising to passion in the end, and then the peace-conferring night again. *Gurrelieder* shows some of those signs of megalomania that have weakened so many of the later German Romantic compositions: it demands extremely large orchestral resources (including some heavy iron chains), five soloists, three male choirs, an eight-part mixed choir. A setting of verses by the Danish poet Jacobsen, this ballad cycle is much more than a Wagnerian debauch; it shows the best of its composer's individuality (he was not thirty when he wrote a good part of it) and what he might have accomplished if he had gone on in the same way. It should have been acknowledged as much a landmark in its own way as Stravinsky's *Rite* was, a few years later. For, although in it Schönberg strove to "break through the barriers of a bygone aesthetic," to use his own words, this music is a natural growth from that of the late Wagner and owes nothing, as so very much of the German music at the turn of the century did, to Strauss. It is this quality of a real, new growth from the Wagnerian stem that makes the *Gurrelieder* so striking; the eleven years that were given to its composition brought Schönberg's creative powers to their apogee.

MAX REGER

One other German Romantic should be noted here: Max Reger (1873–1916), a classic at heart, prolific and profuse, too facile, and yet a composer who was often powerful in his manipulation of contrapuntal webs. Though he ranks as a Romantic, he was rarely sentimental, even in his songs, which, with his stimulating organ pieces, are among his best works. Verbosity was Reger's besetting sin: Ernest Newman cuttingly speaks of his music making as a process that resembles "spawning rather than composing." But in the midst of much massive facility there come touches of a real master; the unfortunate thing is that these happy moments are not frequent enough, compared with the long arid stretches which separate them. His most characteristic works are a set of *Variations on a Theme from Mozart*, the *Romantic Suite*, and the *Böcklin Suite*.

THE AMERICAN SCENE: EDWARD MAC DOWELL

The American composer Edward MacDowell (1861–1908) will best be remembered by the small piano pieces that give a romantic picture of old American scenes, rather than by the larger piano concertos and symphonic poems by which he set great store. MacDowell's originality, welcome as it seems to have been in his day, was scarcely strong enough to surmount the influences of his training in Germany; [10] there is much of Liszt in his concertos, together with a little of that Celtic touch which was one of the freshening qualities of his musical make-up. There is something endearing in the forthrightness of this composer's big, energetic movements, as well as in the little cameos of old days — Puritan times, Indian ways, and the like. MacDowell's life was cut short by a brain affection, and he had but a score or so of actively creative years.

What America needed in his day was a larger body of composers with some of his adventurous traits, however mild they seem to us today, men who could translate something of the spirit of the New World into

[10] MacDowell studied in Germany under Joseph Raff, a disciple of Mendelssohn and Liszt, and a prolific composer of music in all styles, now remembered by one small piano piece, *La fileuse*.

EDWARD MAC DOWELL, AN AMERICAN ROMANTIC

sound. MacDowell sought to do, and did in a small way, what Whitman accomplished in a large way for growing-up America; but by the eighties much of the freshness was gone. It was not so easy to catch inspiration, even for a composer wise enough, as MacDowell was, to try to isolate himself from the general background and work in a log cabin in the New England woods. Again the sense of frustration cannot be avoided, a frustration that was inevitable when we consider the country's composition. Perhaps the MacDowell attitude of mind can never be recaptured; perhaps we ought not to seek it. But the musing, the meditation, the fervor — what will take their place? Can great art be created without them?

Nationalism in Art

NATIONALISM – THE MOVEMENT IN GENERAL

My young friend had a hatred for the nineteenth century which was a mania. At times I heard him even say that he would like to destroy all music of the world from 1750 to 1900. "We have been surfeited with Romanticism," he would cry: "Beethoven's grim frown, Schumann's sentimentality, Brahms's pompousness have destroyed the pure outline of an art that was dying when Mozart was born . . . Thank God the moderns are working in the right direction and creating a music from the soil of their own country."

— Walter Starkie: *Raggle-Taggle*

IT has been said by a historian of that period that at the beginning of the sixteenth century Europe was to all intents and purposes a unified commonwealth, its members associated through the bond of religion: for the four hundred years prior to 1500, Christendom can be thought of as comprising all Europe, and all Europe was Christendom. Gradually there was a lessening of the power of that traditional hierarchy which maintained itself for so long under the title of Holy Roman Empire, and an increase of that of the local princes and kings throughout the various parts of Europe. Thus there came into being a number of political divisions — huge empires, active city-states, and petty principalities — based on common language and traditions or centering about the figure of some absolutist prince or king. Inspired by various social and economic forces, such as the development of the vernacular literatures or the rivalries of commercial expansion, a new kind of political ideal possessed Europe by the end of the sixteenth century, an ideal which threatened to supersede completely the traditions which had been left behind by feudalism: there came into being a series of strong monarchies, each of them

Archives Photographiques

ROMANTIC NATIONALISM IN SCULPTURE

La Patrie by Rude

possessed by a sense of its own integration and looking to its own particular existence. This was the background against which the spirit of nationalism grew strong.

Yet even as late as the end of the eighteenth century the great mass of the inhabitants of these different political divisions which had grown up throughout Europe possessed very little of what we have come to know as the nationalistic spirit. That is, they were not acutely and sensitively conscious of their nationality; they thought of themselves as members of some parish, rather than as belonging to some great national unit. Even up to the time of the Revolution, the French Empire, then the predominant force in Europe, was rather loosely organized; it was made up of various peoples, each of them — Normans, Bretons, Provençals, and so on — proud and jealous of its own characteristics, and it took the hard labor and careful thought of Louis XIV to transform his country from a group of semifeudal principalities into anything that resembled a completely centralized state. Germany was a collection of large and small states of miscellaneous types, with but little feeling of centralized and national power, until the advent of Bismarck. And it required a great deal of propaganda and persuasion on the part of its nationalists to goad Italy into unification. The ideals of national patriotism had long possessed the imagination of the different countries; but it was not until the nineteenth century that the spirit of nationalism as we know it burst upon the European consciousness. Then came the deluge!

A PERIOD OF INTENSE NATIONALIZATION

The era of the Second French Empire (1852–1870) was the period of great national aspiration throughout Europe. Louis Napoleon (afterward Emperor Napoleon III) was the leading spirit in the movement; not only was this attitude of mind congenial to him, but he found it useful to play upon the growing desire for nationalism on the part of the smaller European powers in order to maintain his own position in France. It was this policy which was responsible for the military and moral aid he gave to the Italians, the Rumanians, the Greeks, and others.

Germany secured her unification and established herself as a world power under Bismarck in 1871. In 1874 the Swiss cantons adopted a federal constitution which emphasized the democratic character of their nation. A united Italy came into being, built around the national state of Sardinia, through the efforts of a liberal premier, Cavour, and the group of novelists, playwrights, and poets who contributed so strikingly to Italy's great nineteenth-century revival — the *risorgimento*. The first national Italian parliament met in 1860, and the liberal-minded Victor Emmanuel, until then king of Sardinia, became *Vittorio Emanuele Re d'Italia*. The independence of Belgium had been guaranteed by the great powers of Europe as early as 1839. Rumanian demands for unification under a single ruler were granted in 1862; a Greek national state was ordained in 1863; and even such countries as Poland, Finland, and Bohemia, which were still under the domination and oppression of large empires, felt a new breath of nationalistic life.

THE STIMULUS OF THE ARTS

It is beyond the scope of such a work as this to try to account for all the many political, military, educational, and economic agencies which helped bring about such a surge of nationalism in the nineteenth century. But it is important to note that among these various forces the role of art was a conspicuous one; for, at this time, as so often happened in history, it was the cultural influences which preceded and paved the way for the political ones. The literary interest that was aroused in the different countries by the Romantic Movement, through its delving into folklore and its going back to the sources of the various languages for tales of romance and adventure, had a great deal to do with the inculcation of a national feeling of self-consciousness. The very fact that the writers of a country could found a national literature on the historic achievements of the nation's past or on the eulogies of its possible future made for nationalistic satisfaction. As Goethe said, " There is a peculiarly comforting feeling throughout a whole nation when someone succeeds in calling up its history in a really effective and sympathetic way. Then the nation is able to rejoice in the ancestral virtues and smile at the ancestral failings, feeling that it had long since overcome them." And the realization that composers could write music infused with the very spirit of a people and founded on the tunes known to everyone helped instill a pride of nation and a sense of destiny that made of fullest effect the "purposeful currents of propaganda" set in motion by the leader of the thought of the time. We may say, then, that the general trend of artistic thought started by the Romantic Movement helped to arouse the spirit of nationalism during the middle years of the nineteenth century and to stir up the various assertions of unity that were so marked a feature of the time.

NATIONALISM AS A FACTOR IN ART

But, whatever we may think of nationalism as a factor in world history — and a great deal of our modern distress, including the greatest war in the history of the world, can be laid directly at its door — the question we have to ask is whether or not this outcropping of the national spirit was a beneficent factor in art. The answer must be a positive one; for, in contrast to the spirit of medieval and Renaissance universality, the individual locality was able to contribute a nationalistic vividness and color, a quality of new-found charm and direct realism, to the art of Europe that we could ill afford to lose.

In writing music that would make a direct appeal to the people of their own countries, Moussorgsky, Dvořák, Smetana, Grieg, and Rimsky-Korsakoff heightened its appeal to the music lovers of other nations, for it always seems as if man is greatly intrigued by the greenness of the pastures over the fence. The best proof of this fact is the immediate effect on the unsophisticated listener made by works such as Rimsky-Korsakoff's *Scheherazade*, Dvořák's *New World Symphony*, and Grieg's piano pieces. Even those who have heard a great deal of music are enthralled by the gorgeous color of Moussorgsky's opera *Boris Godunov* and amused by the piquant and native humor of Smetana's *The Bartered Bride* and held by the atmospheric charm of Falla's orchestral suite, *Nights in the Gardens of Spain*.

Pushkin's tragedy, *Boris Godunov*, on which Moussorgsky based his great folk opera, together with his epics dealing with the spirit of Russian nationalism; Gogol's series of sketches of Russian provincial life; Turgenev's treatment of the abuses in Russian society and of the revolutionary spirit, even at this time prevalent in the country; Dostoevski's idealization of the peasant in such books as *Crime and Punishment* and *The Brothers Karamazov* — all these helped awaken the zestful interest of the world in that great and unfortunate empire. Mickiewicz, an intense Polish patriot and a national poet of his country during the nineteenth century, romantically singing Poland's medieval greatness as well as her natural beauty, stirred the sympathies of liberals throughout all Europe against the wrongs of an oppressed nation. In Germany the question was posed by some of her philosophers: " If England and France can have a real national literature, why cannot we? " It was with the deliberate and self-conscious intention of achieving such a national literature that Lessing wrote his drama *Minna von Barnhelm;* Herder devoted his considerable talent to the study of folklore; Goethe's early genius manifested itself in *Götz von Berlichingen;* Schiller completed his *Wallenstein;* Uhland copied the medieval ballads and folk poetry; and Heine wrote his lovely German lyrics. Likewise in Italy one of her most ardent patriots, Manzoni, produced the greatest novel of the century, *I promessi sposi.* These are only the greater lights: everywhere, in all the various languages, men of lesser talent were writing plays, poems, and novels about the common people of the time in their own lands, often going back to the old days of medievalism for local color and stirring up interest in the glorious future which they envisioned ahead.

Painting, sculpture, and architecture, too, felt the same influence. Painters turned to historical scenes and took for their subjects figures from out the glorious past of their countries. Meissonier in France, Von Kaulbach in Germany, and Vereshchagin in Russia filled their canvases with minutely detailed scenes of battle and public ceremony; these were eagerly bought to fill the great rooms of governmental buildings and royal palaces in all the European countries. Imaginative geniuses such as Corot and Millet painted the beauties of their native landscapes and the simple scenes in the life of their country; caricaturists such as Daumier in France and Cruikshank in England arose to delineate the characteristics of their countrymen as well as to portray their weaknesses and foibles. Sculptors like François Rude composed dramatic groups exalting the glories of nationalistic spirit; others, less talented, filled the streets of the great cities with pedestrian and equestrian statues of national heroes and figures in their country's history. The architects of the different lands, although they used various styles, some of them reviving the Gothic, others adapting the classic Renaissance manner, considered their art a definite expression of national life. And the great capitals of Europe, Vienna, Paris, and Munich, vied with one another in expressing the wealth and the grandeur of their heroic past in terms of the magnificence of their buildings.

ITS PLACE IN MUSIC

One of the strongest incentives to the foundation of a nationalist style in music was the desire of the composers of the nations outside Germany to break away from the stifling effects of her musical predominance, which was universally accepted by the middle of the nineteenth century. Everything written in Europe, outside the French and Italian operas, was colored by the influence of the German giants, Haydn, Mozart, Beethoven, Schubert, and Schumann. And in order to preserve their own individualities and save their creative souls, it was natural that the composers of Bohemia, Scandinavia, Russia, and the other countries should turn their vision inward and, aided and abetted by the strong nationalistic currents then prevalent in all phases of political and cultural life, compose music of predominantly national appeal. Not only did these composers use the folk songs and dances of their various countries, but they also consciously tried to catch in their harmonies and their orchestration certain qualities which they felt to be indigenous to their soil.

We shall see how successful some of them were. This nationalistic outcropping was only one phase of the Romantic Movement, and by no means its most important one; but it provided a stimulus for the writing of some very spontaneous and appealing music, most of it of compara-

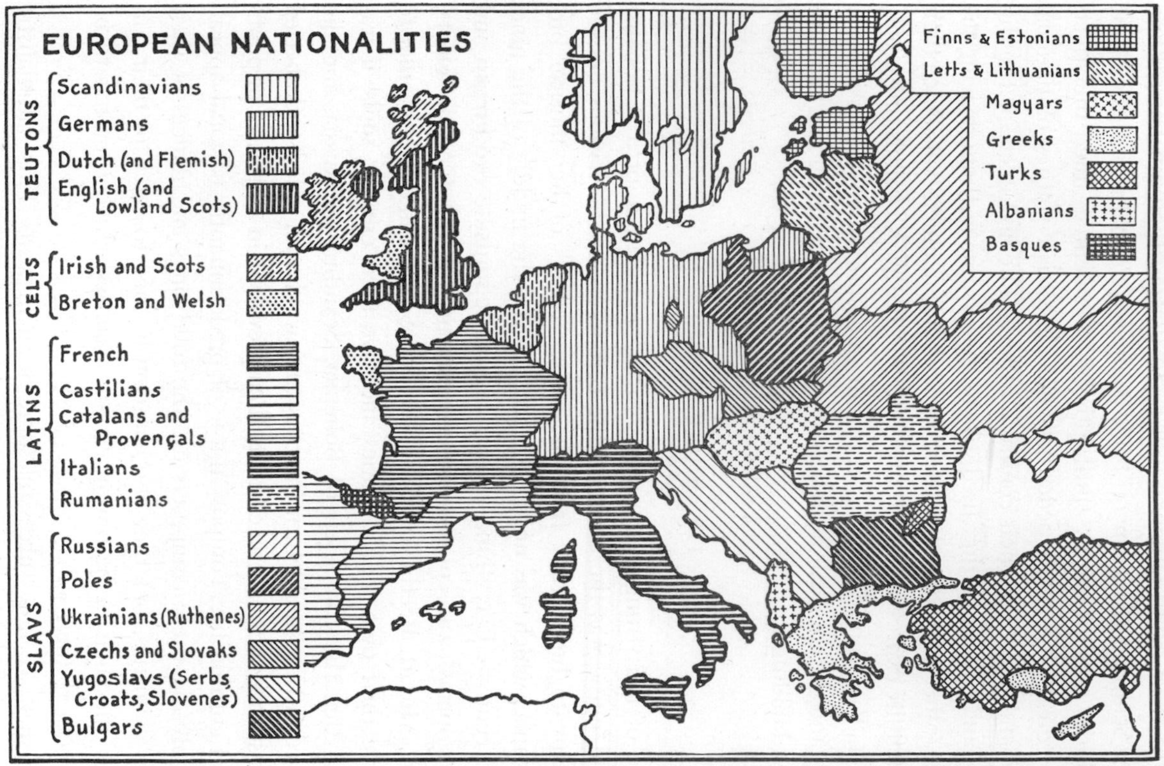

Adapted from Hayes: A Political and Cultural History of Modern Europe, Volume I

THE BEGINNING OF NATIONALISM — EUROPE IN THE SIXTEENTH CENTURY tively limited scope and rather miniature style. The greatest difficulty with all the nationalists was that they were likely to become so absorbed in making their work individual and true to the spirit of the parish pump that they forgot some of the underlying principles which might have made it more universally comprehensible — such verities as unity, balance, and coherence, for example. The great Germans whose influence the nationalists of other countries were so anxious to escape were somehow able to express ideals which we can definitely recognize as German in a manner that emphasizes their universal content rather than their nationalistic manner of speech. And so we go back to these Germans again and again, while even the best nationalistic music will not hold up under repeated hearings.

And what is more, not all attempted nationalism comes off. Consider how many fine composers have been Jews and how few have expressed anything worth while about Jewry in their music. Some of them, admittedly, have striven too hard for a cosmopolitanism to care about trying to express their racial spirit; others have tried to express it and have produced only a weak distillation. Only Ernest Bloch seems to have been able to incarnate in his music the nationalistic spirit of Jewry — the Jewry of the Old Testament and the cry of all oppressed people.

Then, too, there is a certain awkward self-consciousness about a great deal of nationalistic music. Where a composer could be as spontaneous and as free as Grieg and Dvořák often were, nationalism was a beneficent influence; but too much self-conscious striving is the enemy of the creative artist, just as is too much restraint and tension the enemy of all good interpretation. And such dogged adoption of the spirit and mannerisms of folk song as is found in the Vaughan Williams school of English nationalism could but lead into a cul-de-sac of repetitious mediocrity.

THE CLIMAX OF THE MOVEMENT

The peak of the great period of Romantic nationalism in art came somewhere around the middle of the century. While political and economic nationalism has gone on increasing (until today the nations are marked off from one another, by all kinds of arbitrary and artificial devices, more sharply than ever before in the history of the world), it has been the general tendency of the artists of the twentieth century to learn to speak a more universal language. We shall see later how all the important artistic issues developed in the different countries at the turn of the century — impressionism, realism, absolutism, and the rest — were quickly taken up by the artists of the other lands. No composers have been so widely copied and (even if vainly) imitated in their own time as Debussy and Stravinsky. In walking through an exhibit of modern art, we cannot help noticing the influence of such men as Gauguin, Cézanne, Picasso, and Matisse. And functionalism in architecture, originally an American concept, has been most advantageously developed in Europe.

The early decades of the twentieth century saw the development of what might well be called an international style in all the arts. Art works of all kinds showed the same tendencies: they were less individual, less violent in expression; they were animated neither by personal force nor by national spirit. Artists became so largely concerned with learning to speak this international language correctly that they neglected other aspects of their expression. All showed a strong leaning toward abstraction; the era of Romantic nationalism was forgotten. The passing of such a stimulating and impelling influence as nationalism (individual giants such as Sibelius and Rivera excepted) is, nevertheless, a topic for fruitful speculation. Was it brought about perhaps by the fact that, once the liberalizing surge had passed, the attractions were largely those of novelty, romance, and simplicity? These, important as they are in adding color and charm to art, can never constitute its principal source of inspiration; for the creative energy of any great spirit must derive its sustenance from the wider horizons of our common humanity, and it is only the lesser men who could make cults of these inferior values. But it is a great pity if life has become so jarringly complex and worried that we can no longer have time for the engaging qualities of Romantic nationalism; in the midst of all the strife and disillusionment of the present, we may well turn to them again for refreshment and enjoyment.

THE RUSSIANS

. . . All the wild froth of the Russian soul and the Russian nerves — and a bloody spume from the heart's abyss it often is rather than froth — spills over and wastes itself in a mad frenzy . . .

— John Cowper Powys: *Enjoyment of Literature*

RUSSIAN NATIONALISM

LYING midway between Europe and Asia, the West and the East, Russia is a fascinating study, both in its history and in its art. Its original inhabitants were Slavs, but there were so many repeated invasions by the Scandinavians from the west and the Mongols from the east and south, that little progress was made toward the establishment of a nation until the sixteenth century. It was Ivan the Great, chieftain of one of the largest principalities in the country, who drove out the Mongols, united the various tribal units, and established dominion over a territory which reached from the arctic to the Urals. He was the first of a long line of absolutist monarchs that were to rule Russia; it was his grandson, Ivan the Terrible, who took unto himself the title of "Czar of all the Russias," a custom which was followed by all his successors. In passing, it may be noted that it was this Ivan who later was taken as the subject of one of Rimsky-Korsakoff's operas, and that it was Boris Godunov, subject of the novelist Pushkin's epic and Moussorgsky's opera, who was appointed to help Ivan's son, Feodor, to rule. The Russian nationalists had at hand plenty of colorful events in the long history of their country.

During the Middle Ages Russia was strongly influenced by the civilization of the great Byzantine Empire to the southeast, an empire that was the medieval inheritor of the Greco-Roman traditions. The Ivans, when they founded their kingdom, considered themselves the direct successors of the Byzantine emperors and so took the title of "Head of the Orthodox Greek Church." This eastern, ecclesiastical influence was to continue as an important factor in the country's culture long after Russia had joined the family of European nations during the reign of Peter the Great in the eighteenth century.

The period between Ivan the Terrible and Peter the Great, nearly two centuries, was marked by a gradual expansion of the country into Asia, an expansion which was carried on largely by peasants and Cossacks, adventurous frontiersmen who led the vanguard of this territorial penetration and carried the influence of the established church and the czar clear to the plains of eastern Asia. This enlarged Russia was essentially Oriental in character, its customs and habits being Asian rather than European; and so all its people, even its czars and its nobles, for generation after generation were looked upon as barbarians by the rest of Christendom.

It was Peter the Great who made the contact with Europe: the story of his reign is well known, how he gained power by revolutionizing Russian society and establishing a numerous nobility out of the army and those devoted to his person. These nobles he placed in complete domination over the great mass of the people, who were reduced to a state of serfdom not far removed from slavery. Frustrated in some of his political objectives, Peter acquired a passion for introducing into Russia the crafts and sciences of western Europe, even though he realized his people were not ready to receive them; he used every possible means to open the door for European cultural and commercial penetration of his backward land. Catherine the Great, who died in 1796, extended the territories of the empire and made Russia a power in the world; her general policies followed the trend which Peter had established: between them, these two monarchs set the peculiar pattern of Russian civilization which lasted into the twentieth century, when it was finally overthrown by the Bolsheviks.

CHANGES IN STYLE

A nation with so many and such confused elements in its history naturally suffered many changes in the style of its art. In so far as architecture and painting are concerned, the golden age of Russia was the fifteenth century, when artists copied more or less closely the work of Byzantium and produced some real masterpieces in a national style, such as the Kremlin or the Cathedral of the Assumption in Moscow. During

RUSSIAN WEDDING PROCESSION by Kandinsky

the period of European penetration — the seventeenth and eighteenth centuries — the prevalent styles of France and Italy were copied and imitated. Peter the Great laid out the new capital city, St. Petersburg, which he built in the western marshes of the Neva, in the classic style of France rather than after the more congenial Byzantine glories of Moscow. He built extensive and palatial structures in the classic modes of Europe and so for a great many years turned Russian taste against all native and national effort in art.

During the seventeenth century no secular music existed in Russia other than the songs of the people; and the influence of the pseudo-European culture imposed by Peter was so strong all through the eighteenth century that the only music which flourished was the imported art of the Italian and French operatic composers. This exotic development, centered in St. Petersburg and Moscow, had no influence whatever on the lives of the people.

In literature the taste of the first part of the eighteenth century was French, followed later, as in the other countries, by a swing toward the Romantic style. It was not until the Russian writers of the early nineteenth century, stimulated by the rise of a distinctly nationalistic mode

Photograph by "Anthony"

SCENE FROM STRAVINSKY'S BALLET *PETROUCHKA*

of expression in other lands, began to turn their attention to the history of their own people that anything distinctive or important was produced. As long as the Russian artist, far removed from the centers of European culture, tried to imitate the models of France, Germany, and Italy and abjured his native background, he remained sterile. But once Pushkin, who had started writing poetry in imitation of the European Romantics, began to immerse himself in the colorful past of Russia and to study native poetry, he was able to produce such works of brilliant imagery and impassioned expression as *Russlan and Ludmilla* and *Boris Godunov*. Other outstanding writers followed — Gogol (1809–1852), Turgenev (1818–1883), and Dostoevski (1821–1881) — who used folk themes and did not hesitate to discuss the abuses under which the common people suffered. It seemed as if it was not until these artists had established contact with their native soil and found beauty in the spirit of their own people that they were able to assimilate the great traditions of European culture and produce works that are comparable with those written in other lands. Nineteenth-century Russian literature is a unique admixture, produced by a combination of western-European influences, Byzantine thought, native strength, and a peculiar preoccupation with the sorrows and sadnesses of humanity's common lot.

THE RISE OF TWO SCHOOLS

This century saw also the rise of a definite Russian school of composers. These divided themselves into two groups: first, those who built their nationalistic ideals on the basis of European foundations and believed that it was only a thorough knowledge of what had been written by the composers of the past that could give the Russian nationalist the power to speak his own language eloquently; and second, those who broke completely with European traditions and attempted to go to the people for inspiration and guidance. The amateur Glinka was the initiator of this latter movement: he was followed by Dargomijsky and the talented circle of dilettanti, Balakirev, Borodin, Rimsky-Korsakoff, Moussorgsky, and Cui. These two circles never met; both made important contributions to Russian music, giving it, together with the parallel developments in literature, a place among the most important manifestations of the nationalistic spirit of the nineteenth century.

THE COSMOPOLITES

"I often begin to write with the intention of using one or another popular Russian song. Sometimes, as in the finale to the *Fourth Symphony*, this comes of itself, quite unexpectedly. As to the Russian element in general in my music — the relation to the popular songs in melody and harmony — I grew up in a peaceful spot, saturated from earliest childhood with the miraculous beauty of Russian popular song, so that I love to the point of passion every expression of the Russian spirit. In short, I am Russian through and through."

— Bowen and Von Meck: *Beloved Friend*

This was the attitude of Tchaikovsky (1840–1893), the greatest of all the Russians, toward his own nationalism. Posterity, however, hardly bears him out; for we are able to realize today that this most popular of all the Muscovites was a cosmopolitan rather than a national composer: his music, although strongly colored with Russian temperament, shows definite German influences and is never far out of touch with French *esprit*. With the exception of Rimsky-Korsakoff, he was, moreover, the only real craftsman in the whole lot, having been thoroughly trained under the aegis of Anton Rubinstein, the founder of the St. Petersburg Conservatory and the outstanding pianist of Europe at the time. Since Tchaikovsky placed high value on the necessity for training and hard work as factors in musical composition, he was disclaimed by the amateur talents of the *Kutchka* (that band of five friends of Russian nationalism — Balakirev, Cui, Borodin, Moussorgsky, and Rimsky-Korsakoff) and looked upon as a traitor to real Russian music.

TCHAIKOVSKY

Of all the composers in the world, it is difficult to think of one with a more direct appeal to a large number of people than Tchaikovsky: his music needs no explaining. He described composition as being a lyric process of soul confession, pouring itself out through the medium of sound just as the lyric poet pours himself out in verse; and these confessions have been such as to make a wide appeal to all sorts and conditions of men. At first Tchaikovsky was looked upon as a Russian barbarian by those outside the country, but the latter years of the nineteenth century saw the whole world at his feet. It is only in recent years that his popular domination of the symphonic literature has been challenged by others. Today he, like so many of the Romantics, has lost caste: his emotional outbursts have taken on a threadbare, heart-on-sleeve aspect. He has become " popular " in the most derogatory sense, musicians admitting his ability as a craftsman while deploring his over-emotionalism, sometimes rising to hysteria, and his lush Romanticism.

As a matter of fact, only when we place Tchaikovsky against his proper background are we able to come to anything like a fair estimate of his music. He was a peculiar amalgam of individual characteristics: he was a Russian, first of all, an arch Romanticist living at the very zenith of that epoch; he possessed an unusually sensitive temperament, one which was tragically unsuited to normal living and which cast a dark shadow over his life, often making it almost intolerable; finally, he was driven by a strong creative urge that gave him no rest and which ensured a constant growth in artistic stature to the very end of his life.

A TYPICAL RUSSIAN

In their art the Russians have never been content with mere statement: they must always exaggerate. And it was his Russian spirit that gave Tchaikovsky his emotionally blanketed locution and his peculiar alternation of melancholy and almost hysterical gaiety, grief and joy, shade and light. In this sense he was, as Stravinsky has remarked, " the most Russian of us all." The whole idea of suffering and expiation, of tremendous emotional struggle and tragic consequence which so strongly flavors many of his works was, moreover, part and parcel of the thinking of his time: he may be well thought of as the apotheosis of the Romantic Movement; this coincidence of Tchaikovsky's being a Russian and a Romanticist accounts for his strong popular appeal. The dark tragedy of his personality is explained by the letters he wrote to his rich patron, Mme. Nadejda von Meck, whom he was careful never to meet although she gave him liberal financial and spiritual support through the most difficult part of his life. His letters explain also why some of his music — perhaps the most potent of it — was a necessary " casting out of a demon, an exorcism by the major art of expression." The fact that he was a thorough craftsman, driven by a healthy love of creation, gave us so much of that which is cheerful and effective in his music, perhaps three quarters of the whole. We are too often merely conscious of the over-emotional Tchaikovsky and are liable to forget the composer of the *Casse-noisette Suite*, the *G Major Suite*, the *Romeo and Juliet* fantasia, the early symphonies.

HIS WIDE RANGE

His was an astonishingly wide range of expression — from near-genius, through cheerful mediocrity, to utter banality — with a compellingly attractive sincerity and directness from which we cannot escape. He wrote six symphonies, of which only three — the Fourth, the Fifth, and the Sixth — survive; these are peculiarly uneven. They contain some of his finest moments which, while hardly comparable with the best of Beethoven and Brahms, are nevertheless inspired and tremendously moving; and there are others which are dreadfully weak and trite. There are few listeners, even today when it has become hackneyed through overplaying, who are not greatly moved by a performance of the *Sixth Symphony,* if it is interpreted with dignity and sincerity. But there are parts of the Fourth and the Fifth which certainly contain some of the noisiest and most banal music ever written by a great composer. The overture fantasia *Romeo and Juliet,* composed in Tchaikovsky's twenty-ninth year (1869) and dedicated to Balakirev, is great in a real Shakespearean sense. Another composition of the same sort, *Francesca da Rimini,* is effective after the Lisztian manner, with perhaps too much of a striving after effect for effect's sake. The *Casse-noisette* (*Nutcracker*) *Suite,* the orchestral *Suite in G,* the *Capriccio Italien,* and the *Serenade for Strings* are brilliant examples of their type. The *Piano Concerto in B Flat Minor* is full-blooded, lusty, strenuous in a rather vulgar way, but still appealing. Such notoriously purple patches as the *Marche slave* and the *Ouverture solennelle 1812* were never taken seriously by their composer, who admitted to the latter's being "very showy and without artistic merit because I wrote without warmth and love."

Tchaikovsky's eight operas have not held their places in the repertoire; the best of them is *Eugen Onégin,* in which his talent for lyric expression of the Italianate order is given full scope. His was not a dramatic temperament in the theatrical sense, and although he knew well enough, as his letters show, what an opera demands, he did not have theatrical qualities sufficient to sustain interest for very long. Most of the songs show very little individuality: in them he merely says things that Schumann and the other German Romantics have said much more effectively.

Tchaikovsky merits neither the undue adulation with which he was received at the turn of the century nor the rather sniffing condescension with which he is greeted today. He outlived completely the extreme spirit of Russian nationalism, if, indeed, he ever believed in it strongly. And although his music may not express the soul of Russia, it was inspired by the Russian spirit and shaped by Russian consciousness; the result, since Tchaikovsky was more of a genius than most of his nationalistic confreres, may well be of greater permanence than the utterances of the nationalists.

ANTON RUBINSTEIN

We need but mention the other great cosmopolite of Tchaikovsky's day, Anton Rubinstein; although he had great aspirations as a composer and wrote a great deal of music, including symphonies and operas, none of it possessed real originality. Those who would sample its quality may listen to the omnipresent *Kamennoi-Ostrow*. And since Tchaikovsky only Glazunov (1865–1936) stands out in any real relief as a cosmopolitan Russian: he possessed something of Tchaikovsky's blend of instrumental coloring and classic build, without any of his fiery near-genius.

THE RUSSIAN "KUTCHKA"

The group known as the Big Five or *Kutchka* looked upon Michael Glinka (1803–1857) as their prophet patriarch. A rich nobleman, he possessed, according to Tchaikovsky, a colossal talent, which suffered, however, through his unwillingness to subject himself to regular and thorough training. He worked as a dilettante, whenever the mood came, and in this, as in the general characteristics of his music, he set the style for the group of nationalists who followed. Not only did Glinka and his fellow nationalists incorporate the spirit (and often actual melodies) of Russian folk tunes [1] into their music, but they relied on dramatic intensity and natural feeling to take the place of constructive principles. How effective such a procedure could be may be judged from Glinka's *Kamarinskaya*, an orchestral fantasy on Russian folk songs, perhaps the

[1] Perhaps more than is the case with any other people, the Russians have preserved individuality of expression in their folk songs and dances: folk art of all kinds in Russia is very much alive today, in spite of the colossal regimentation now in force there. A number of features characterize Russian folk and dance tunes and make them sound unusual to Occidental ears: the use of short, two-measure phrases and sharply defined, animated rhythms; a tonality suggestive of the music of the Greek church; an affinity of style and coloring with the tunes of other Slav countries, together with their love of extravagance, their bravado of expression, and their gift for improvisation. As might be expected in so huge a land, the dances are of widely varying types, many of them making use of wild steps and vigorous motions. The best-known peasant dance is the *gopak*, which, starting in a tranquil, melancholy fashion, ends in a tremendous outburst of primitive vitality.

most strikingly original thing he ever wrote. " All of us," admits Tchaikovsky, " the moment we need Russian dance tunes, borrow *Kamarinskaya's* contrapuntal and harmonic designs quite openly. In this one short work Glinka succeeded in concentrating that which the smaller men have accomplished only through heroic effort."

GLINKA'S PATRIOTIC OPERAS

But when it came to longer works, a procedure such as this did not suffice. Glinka's two operas, in spite of some original beauties, are strikingly uneven and tiresomely repetitious mixtures of Italianate tradition and folkish development. The first, *A Life for the Czar* (1836), was based on a strong nationalistic libretto dealing with the historic enmity of the Russians and the Poles; the second, *Russlan and Ludmilla* (1842), while it has less of the folk element, emphasizes the Eastern, Oriental element which permeates so much of Russian art. While there is a great deal of picturesque color in these works, there is also an unfortunate amount of conventionality: the years have more than justified Tchaikovsky's judgment: " We are proud of Glinka, but we must admit that he did not fulfill the task his genius put upon him."

DARGOMIJSKY

Dargomijsky (1813–1869), the other composer who was the inspiration of the *Kutchka,* tried to rationalize the operatic setting of words; he wrote one opera, *Roussalka* (*The Water Witch*), in which he tried to incorporate his principles of careful regard for the integrity of the text. But it is of little importance, aside from the fact that it gave more than one hint to Moussorgsky, and so, in turn, to Debussy, when it came time for him to write his *Pelléas et Mélisande.* A later work, *The Stone Guest,* left in an incomplete form by the composer and finished by his friends, Cui and Rimsky-Korsakoff, became known as the Bible of the Russian school. In addition to his operas, Dargomijsky wrote a great number of songs.

BALAKIREV

It was Mily Balakirev (1836–1910) who founded the famous Russian Five and who was for years the most active spirit in the establishment of a significant Russian school. He and his associates, basing their ideals on the parallel movement in literature, wished to free Russian music from all "foreign influence and to make it an art for Russians alone, employing the Russian language only where words were necessary." They turned to the native folk song for their sources and were sincere in their desire to throw off all the traditions of Italian, French, and, especially, German music, which they felt had enslaved Russian art so long. Meeting at one another's houses in St. Petersburg, they would often spend the whole night talking, as only Russians can talk, about inspiration, talent, the abominations of rules, the advantages of antiprofessionalism, what constituted Russian art — time which Tchaikovsky thought [2] might better have been spent in learning something of the fundamentals of composition. There is no doubt that the group possessed talent, although Balakirev, its leading personality, never made much of his gifts: he is known today almost entirely by his Oriental fantasy for the piano, *Islamey*, and his orchestral tone poems, *Russia* and *Thamar*, the latter used for a Diaghilev ballet.

BORODIN

Borodin (1834–1887), a professor of chemistry in the Academy of Medicine, was one of the few Russian nationalists who attempted the writing of symphonies. The sense of design, not necessarily of classic German design, but form in any keen sense, was woefully lacking in all these Russians; even Tchaikovsky realized his weakness in this respect. And the three Borodin symphonies, written at intervals when because of sickness the composer could steal some time from his busy professional life, suffer in this respect. For a listener familiar with the great German works in this field, these symphonies are apt to pall because so little happens,

[2] In spite of his lush Romanticism, Tchaikovsky had a good deal of the professor in him.

and the orchestration is bound to seem awkward. But they, as do Borodin's quartets, possess many colorful moments and plaintive melodic touches, exciting enough in themselves. The tone poem *In the Steppes of Central Asia* depicts the passing of a caravan in the sandy wastes; it is a small thing, but colored to perfection. His opera *Prince Igor,* left in an unfinished state at his death and completed and edited by Rimsky-Korsakoff and Glazunov, is effective largely because of the generous measure of ballet which it contains.

Like so many of its kin among the Russian operas (most of the nationalists wrote them), *Prince Igor* carries conviction because of its composer's enthusiasm and interest in incident, rather than because of any inherent balance and proportion. It was fortunate that Borodin was happiest on the stage; his thoughts flowed freely there, and he never seems at a loss as to what he wanted to do. Since its barbaric thrills come off well, this opera holds the boards.

MOUSSORGSKY

Moussorgsky (1839–1881) was by far the most original of the Five: in his short life, which drink and drugs cut off when he was little more than forty, he produced not only the greatest of Russian music dramas but likewise a few individual works which may well stand as representative of the very best music his nation has produced. *Boris Godunov,* written in 1874, completes the cycle started by Glinka's *A Life for the Czar* forty years before. Its portrayal of rough humors, dissolute monks, the terrors of conscience and remorse, the remarkable part it gives to the chorus of people, its sense of strange, wild history (which, in spite of many diversions, nevertheless seems inevitable and irrevocable) all make it a work apart, something unlike any other opera ever written, and one possessed of a compelling and fascinating attraction. Based on Pushkin's great story, its libretto deals with the early days of Russian history and the ruthless Boris, who, arriving at supreme power, killed all those who stood in his path — an uneasy career which led to final remorse and tragic death; this text gave Moussorgsky full opportunity to show his great dramatic sense, and the results are overpowering.

Moussorgsky worked at *Boris* most of his life, making two versions of it, one in 1868 and another in 1872; these were afterward altered, revised, and reorchestrated by his friend Rimsky-Korsakoff, in an attempt to "correct" some of the composer's crudenesses and heighten some of his dramatic effects. This Rimsky-Korsakoff edition is the one generally used in theaters; but since the original Moussorgsky edition was published in 1928, one of the burning aesthetic questions has been, "Which of the two is the more effective?" It is a question of little moment: Rimsky-Korsakoff was a thoroughly effective man of the theater and one of the most brilliant orchestraters in the whole history of music; he unquestionably deleted some of Moussorgsky's Russianism, but he left the work as a whole more practical and more effective.

Khovantchina, a later opera, has not been successful. Its history of religious dissension drags heavily; the play does not hold together even so well as does *Boris*, out of which whole sections have been carved at various times without affecting its dramatic continuity, so loosely is it woven together. The music of *Khovantchina* is happiest when it is most frankly pictorial; otherwise it has little interest.

Other well-known Moussorgsky works are the popular piano pieces *Pictures at an Exhibition*, which a number of men have orchestrated, Ravel's arrangement being by far the best; and the two interesting song cycles, *Songs and Dances of Death* and *Sunless*. These latter vary in quality: some of them are superb, with a singular blend of powerful imagination and experience, digging deep into human hopes and fears ("Field Marshal Death" is a good example); others are quite characterless.

Being a member of a small landholding family, Moussorgsky grew up amid folk legends; above everything else he liked to emphasize his simple birth and lack of musical training, boasting that his genius was the richer because it had never been tamed. Later in life, he deepened; but he was always quite satisfied with his intuitive way of expression. It seemed as though he was born to be at once a fire-eating realistic pioneer and a rather simple-minded employer of the national idiom; he had a direct lyrical sense which it is worth while trying to separate from his realism when estimating his place in music history. He was frequently inspired, but he was not a great builder,[3] and his originality often led him into blind alleys; we ought to be able to enjoy his music without deifying it or him.

CUI

César Cui (1835–1918) was of French descent, an expert on fortification by profession. When he had time to write music, he composed rather coquettish and meticulous pieces, most of them of small scale, entirely forgotten today. His influence was of more importance as a critic than as a composer.

RIMSKY-KORSAKOFF

Rimsky-Korsakoff (1844–1908) was the only composer of the *Kutchka* to secure a thorough musical education, thereby proving himself a renegade to the ideals of its founding. By profession he was a naval engineer, and he acquired, in his trips through the East, a love of Oriental color and rhythm that stood him in good stead later on. When he was thirty and had already attracted considerable attention as a composer, he decided that he could go no further without more knowledge of musical theory; so he went to Tchaikovsky, then a professor in the Moscow Conservatory, for guidance. Thorough study and enormous industry made him an orchestral craftsman and a composer of several works of some importance, outstanding among them being that " gorgeous and unfailing Russian picture book in tone," *Scheherazade*. His operas are seldom heard outside Russia, although *Le coq d'or*, a symbolic fairy tale, has been played both in England and in America. Everyone can yield with real delight to the spell of its queen's song, or to " The Song of India " from the opera *Sadko*; but in general these works depend too much on color and do not give enough of the real Russian spirit to satisfy the foreigner for long.

[3] Cecil Gray has quoted Tchaikovsky as saying that this is an essential Russian characteristic: " there is a profound lacuna in our intellectual organization — the capacity for logical thinking, the spirit of method, and the feeling for continuity are entirely lacking in us."

In addition to being a composer, Rimsky-Korsakoff was an excellent teacher: Stravinsky and Respighi were among his pupils, and his treatise on orchestration has become a standard text the world over. A cultivated man, he possessed real literary gifts, and his charming autobiography, *My Musical Life*, is a good picture, impressive because of its honesty, of the whole Russian movement.

They were a fascinating company, these members of the *Kutchka*, stimulating to one another, with enormous pluck and self-confidence but little first-rate criticism (not even from themselves), and curiously child-like in many ways. They were typical products of their age, the like of which we shall hardly see again, representing one of the many aspects which the Romantic Movement assumed as it matured and developed during the course of the century.

SCRIABIN

Scriabin (1872–1915), with his aspiring harmonic system, wrote symphonies with tone-poem titles — *Poem of Fire, Poem of Ecstasy*, and so on — and created a stir with some excellent piano pieces based on Chopin's technique and his own harmonic system. But there was too much system and not enough solidity to them; their Wagnerian-Chopinian-Lisztian elements were not very happily assimilated, and, though their composer was original enough, his mannerisms soon tire the ear.

LATER RUSSIANS

Sergei Rachmaninoff (1873–1943) tried, and failed, like so many fine artists, to make the best of the two worlds of virtuoso performer and composer; very few men have succeeded equally well in both. While Rachmaninoff can hardly be called merely an echo of Tchaikovsky — for his darker, stronger elements have a pull of their own — there is little originality in his music. Yet he wrote a considerable number of things for the piano and the orchestra, to the obvious delight of a great number of people.

It is impossible to list all the very numerous Russian composers of either the older, Tchaikovskyan, or the newer, modernist, persuasion. Among the former may be placed Medtner (*b.* 1879), who, soundly based on Brahms rather than on Tchaikovsky, has worked both in the larger classical forms and in a kind of short piano piece he calls the " Fairy Tale." Liadov (1855–1914) also wrote for the orchestra pieces based on Russian legends. Taneiev (1856–1915) chose, for the most part, the less picturesque paths of chamber music: he was also a theorist of note. Arensky (1861–1906) follows closely in Tchaikovsky's footsteps, notably with a popular set of variations on a tune by the older composer. Gretchaninov (*b.* 1864), although he wrote in the larger forms, including the operatic, is best known by a few of his songs and some stunning settings for the service of the Russian Church. Ippolitov-Ivanov (1859–1935) worked for some time at Tiflis, studying Caucasian music, and put into some orchestral sketches his impressions of this particular brand of Russian Orientalism. There are two Tcherepnins, Nicolai the father (*b.* 1873), and Alexander the son (*b.* 1899). The father has been characterized as having impressionist and mystical sympathies, and the son as being influenced by Prokofiev (*b.* 1891), a composer who early indulged a taste for musical cynicism and a humor that may be hearty but is rarely genial. Prokofiev's opera *The Love for Three Oranges* and his later piano concertos show his best qualities, for he has much more solid qualities that his rather freakish, mechanistic early works indicated.[4] Miaskovsky (*b.* 1881) is a prolific symphonist, having up to the time of this writing composed seventeen symphonies, most of them long and elaborate and handling the Tchaikovsky tradition without undue warmth.

It is difficult to say much that is cheering about the later works composed under the influence of the New Russia. Dmitri Shostakovich (*b.* 1906) is the best known, internationally, of the Soviet Russian composers; he made an excellent start with a symphony of real power, written when he was 19, and an opera, *Lady Macbeth of Mzensk*, whose low-life realism shows flashes of real genius mixed with foolish skits and stretches

[4] The catalogue of Prokofiev's works includes four symphonies, together with a number of other works for orchestra; eight concertos; five piano sonatas, as well as a number of separate piano pieces; and five chamber-music compositions.

of noisy violence. These earlier works contain such a mixture of styles that it is not easy to foretell what may follow.

In 1936 he ran afoul of the government, objection being made in the authoritative paper *Pravda* to his " radical " style and the oversimplification of his treatment. His *Fourth Symphony* having been prohibited because of its " leftist," modernistic tendencies, Shostakovich returned in his Fifth (first performed in November, 1937) to the Romantic style of his *First Symphony*. This symphonic work seems to show more of Mahler's influence than that of the postwar modernists and has made a definite impression wherever it has been played. In this work the composer seems to have largely forsaken his earlier expressed belief that " music cannot help having a political basis — an idea that the *bourgeoisie* are slow to comprehend." No longer does he forgo thematic development as being bourgeois theory; there is a melodic charm and dramatic intensity in this symphony that augurs well for its success. What the future holds for the fortunes of this talented composer is impossible to prophesy.

The latest of the Russian nationalists to achieve an international reputation is Igor Markevich (*b.* 1912). Diaghilev, who commissioned a work from him, is said to have heard in his music the " quickening of a new generation which militates against the misconceptions of late years." Certainly one of the most individual of contemporary writers, Markevich has aroused considerable enthusiasm in France, where one of the principal critics has remarked that it must of necessity be a long time before the full richness and worth of this composer's work is realized.

The strange, sad figure of the present-day Stravinsky is discussed in another place. As for the rest of the composers in Russia, they are no more Russian in spirit than is the modern art of any other land: everything seems to have blended into a sort of bleakly acrid international style without any great local — or indeed, personal — significance.

THE CZECHS AND THE POLES

It has been said by travelers that the Bohemian nobility keep musicians in their houses; but, in keeping servants, it is impossible to do otherwise, as all the children of the peasants and tradespeople, in every town and village throughout the kingdom of Bohemia, are taught music at the common reading schools.

— Burney (1772)

NATIONALISM IN BOHEMIA

ONE of the first countries to achieve national independence in music was Bohemia, a division of the Austrian Empire that has since been known as Czechoslovakia. Peopled mainly by a race of Slavs — the Czechs — which had a distinctive language and literature, and, for many centuries, its own kings, Bohemia was traditionally a part of the Holy Roman Empire. Thus, although the national feeling of her people was strong, the country early became inextricably concerned with German affairs and permeated with strong Germanic influences; and when in 1526, panic-stricken because the Turks were at her gates, she elected a Hapsburg as king, she automatically became part of the Austrian domains and remained a dependent state for almost three centuries. The nationalism that centers in legends and folk tales of the country's heroes had ample opportunity to develop; for the Czechs, a " small island in a large German sea," as someone called them, continued to struggle bitterly against the Hapsburg influence all through their years of humiliation and fostered a store of patriotic fables and folk heroes to help bolster their desire for independence — independence won in 1919, lost in 1939.

SMETANA

When, in the general literary and Romantic stir of the early nineteenth century, these old folk tales and ancient elegiacs were unearthed and the middle classes began to realize their significance, the stage was set for the appearance of a national genius. Smetana (1824–1884) was the first to celebrate in music the peculiar virtues and prowess of Bohemian (as distinct from German or Austrian) natures and aspirations. His operas and his set of six symphonic poems linked under the name of *My Fatherland* create the very spirit and atmosphere of Bohemia. One of these latter, *Vltava (The Moldau)*, is a most successful example of objective pictorialism in music, tracing as it does, with eloquent orchestral description, the course of the country's largest river.

The one operatic work of Smetana's that is known the world over is his colorful comedy *The Bartered Bride:* charming and attractive as it is, this opera is by no means his finest. Travelers who have been fortunate enough to hear it in Prague or in one of the other Bohemian theaters at Bratislava or Brno, give the palm to *Libussa*, an opera which a widely traveled critic has called " one of the most majestic creations ever conceived for the lyric theater." *Dalibor*, the third of Smetana's operas, is characteristically national in that it is based on the life of a fifteenth-century Bohemian warrior who kept the realms of King Wladislaw in constant turmoil; like all Smetana's works it contains music that is wonderfully rich and vital, with a real flavor of the soil.

DVOŘÁK

Anton Dvořák (1841–1904) was perhaps a greater man, whose principal field of activity was orchestral and chamber music. An intuitive composer of the Schubert type, he suffered somewhat from the overadulation of foreigners, who were too easily satisfied with the local colors which he provided in such profusion. There is an engaging simplicity in Dvořák which led him (with, perhaps, something of peasant shrewdness) to push the folk motive sometimes beyond judiciousness. Too often he was satisfied with ideas that are inferior; even in his mature chamber music (his quartet, Op. 105, is a good example), which, aside from the *New World Symphony*, represents him at his best, there are exasperating cheapnesses, especially in the matter of melodies.

Nevertheless, no composer is a more genial companion. Brahms influenced Dvořák and secured recognition for his spirited *Slavonic Dances*,

Ed. "Manes," Prague

ANTON DVOŘÁK
(Lithograph by Max Švabinský)

originally written as piano duets and lavishly employing Bohemian mannerisms both in melody and in rhythm.[5] Together with a certain amiable diffuseness, Dvořák's work is distinguished by real creative genius and marked by a wonderfully intimate and endearing sentiment, as well as by a strong intensity of feeling. He wrote a number of symphonies, although the *New World*, composed while he was in temporary residence in the United States, in an attempt to show American composers how they might cultivate their art through folk channels, is almost the only one often heard. His nine operas are not performed outside Bohemia,

[5] The first of these dances to become familiar to outsiders was the polka, remarkably popular in the forties of the last century (when it was comparatively new even to its native land). The works of Smetana and Dvořák have familiarized us with the furiant, with its frequently changing rhythm, whose name suggests its character; the redowa, of mazurka type; and the dumka, a title remembered in a chamber work by Dvořák (*Dumky Trio*). The dumka, alternating between hectic gaiety and sadness, is actually an imported dance, native to South Russia.

since they are local and slight in subject and comparatively weak in development.

Like the instinctive instrument that he was, Dvořák responded to almost any influence that was going; but it was the response of a highly individual nature, tasting here and there, and never for a moment copying or needing to copy. His own nature was too full and too fresh to need anything more than a few contacts with good models; for the rest, shrewdness, immensely hard work, simple dignity, and nationalist enthusiasm were sufficient, because he had the touch of near-genius that transmutes all into art. Without it no amount of painstaking nationalism signifies anything; it becomes simply peddling parochialism, wearisome because so near to childishness.

Since his day very few Czechs have made a great stir outside their own country. Perhaps the best known so far is Janáček (1854–1928), who delved deeper than Dvořák into folk music but never met with wide recognition because he swung to the side of a fairly mild extremism in harmony. His opera *Jenufa* has had success in Germany as well as in Czechoslovakia; it carries speech rhythm to the highest limit, dispenses with set numbers, and uses, in a new way, leading themes, each for its own scene. Janáček is perhaps the best example of the opposite pole to Dvořák in that he took little pains to write music that was comprehensible outside his own country. He kept to his peculiarly naïve style, writing with an exuberance that to foreigners appears childish and making no concessions to a possible market and its demands for "tunefulness."

OTHER CZECHS

Other Czech composers are Suk (1874–1935), a man whose music seemed to rush into the sands of overcomplexity and to overindulge in the same sort of ultramodernism that spoiled much of Janáček's work; and Kovařovic (1862–1920), whose way was of the simpler Dvořák type. Hába (*b.* 1893) is known for his use of quarter tones, intervals less than a semitone; in listening to his music it is sometimes difficult to know whether the players are sounding what he has written or whether they are merely playing out of tune. Most of the recent Czech composers whose music is heard at all today belong to the experimental school of modernism; as if to show that a native composer can still write good tunes and full-blooded, lusty music, Weinberger (*b.* 1896) has contributed the best comic grand opera in the modern repertoire, *Schwanda, the Bagpipe Player,* a work which deserves more success than it so far has achieved outside its native land.

POLISH NATIONALISM

The name of Poland runs like a colorful thread through all European history: peopled by a fiery and turbulently independent race of Slavs who were akin to the Russians and the Czechs, this country freed herself from the Holy Roman Empire during the fourteenth century. Situated between Germany and Russia, with the Slovaks and the Magyars on the south, Poland has always been one of the danger spots of Europe; at the crossroads of Europe, she has been frequently overrun by her covetous neighbors. Her last struggle for freedom failed in 1939.

In 1386 a union of Poland and Lithuania made a strong military country, which, however, was not able to maintain its individuality against the designs of the envious monarchs to the west and south. Frederick the Great of Prussia and Maria Theresa of Austria between them made the first partition of the country in 1772; others followed in 1793 and 1795. But a number of patriots, by means of uprisings and revolutions, kept alive the spirit of nationalism, until in 1863 they were finally overwhelmed by Russia, and the country was made a province of that great empire. The inevitable miseries and gallantries entailed in such a series of wars, especially when the people involved are as excitable and as impressionable as the Poles, are the very stuff on which the spirit of Romanticism thrives.

NATIONAL MUSIC

As in other lands, the popular dances have reflected national character and aspirations. The polonaise has for hundreds of years been the greatest expression of courtly ceremonial and patriotic fervor. From the sixteenth century, when Henry of Anjou was made king of Poland, the polonaise was used to introduce court balls and other occasions of ceremony, and by the eighteenth century it had become a part of every national festivity. Even the popular poetry was modeled on the rhythm of the dance.

Liszt, in his life of Chopin, describes the method of dancing the polonaise. The host opens the ball by choosing a partner and heading with her an elaborate parade around all the rooms of the house and all the garden paths. On returning to the ballroom, the host's partner is claimed by another man, and a corresponding shuffle of partners takes place all around. This goes on all through the evening, each leader trying to outdo his predecessors in the invention of steps and gestures indicative of the pride, courage, and gallantry of the Polish nation.

The dance found its way tentatively into the classical suite, but it has been far more brilliantly celebrated in the music of Chopin, as has its companion the mazurka, which has been described as the feminine counterpart of the masculine polonaise. Both are in three-time: the mazurka's gait is the gentler, its first pulse being divided into two, often unequally (three quarters and one quarter); the polonaise has a stronger, springing effect in its subdivision of all three pulses, the first into a half and two quarters, the others into halves.

ITS FLOWERING IN CHOPIN

It was Liszt who first pointed out that Poland's national characteristics were epitomized in Chopin's polonaises: "Although Chopin was born too late and left his native land too early to be initiated into the original character of the polonaise as a national dance, he was able to supplement what others imparted to him in regard to it by his own imagination and nationality." The best of these works — such things as the C sharp minor and the E flat minor, Op. 26; the A major and the C minor of Op. 40; and the *Fantaisie polonaise*, Op. 61 — must always stand as Poland's greatest music. Their dark tempestuous despair, alternating with pages of rarest poetic beauty, make them like cannon buried amongst flowers, as Schumann put it; those who would realize the power of Poland's spell should listen to these works played by a Polish artist such as Paderewski or Arthur Rubinstein.

The nationalism of Paderewski (*b.* 1860) is of a rather mild type, which may seem strange in view of the fact that he had the unique honor of becoming the chief power in his country's late renaissance: a Polish symphony and a fantasia do little more than exploit, in acceptable terms of general romance, a few native airs.

SZYMANOWSKI

The only other composer who has raised high hopes for this country's music was Szymanowski (1883–1937), although he can scarcely be claimed as a single-minded nationalist because of his combining so many different textures and trends. An offshoot of the Debussyian school, his strikingly individual use of certain harmonic colors gives his music a strange, shimmering, ethereal quality. His string quartet, Op. 56, No. 2, is as good an example of his odd assortment of characteristics as anything he wrote, its first movement being perhaps the best example of his style, with its ghostly yearnings and strong introspection. The second movement shows French, mid-European, and Russian influences of the day; the third has Brahmsian breadth, one of the elements in this composer which might have proved a stabilizing and broadening influence if it had been more cultivated. But the harmonic terms throughout seem shallow. Szymanowski is an oddly disappointing composer from any point of view, whether that of the older-fashioned musician or of the modernist. But it is impossible to make a decided judgment, since the end of his career came in a generation so little sure of its path as his was.

It seems reasonable, then, to make the statement that Polish nationalism has not made much of an effect on the general world of music. But it is obviously impossible now to write the history of today; a hundred years hence some of the men we have mentioned here and elsewhere may be entirely unknown: others, perhaps some we have not even named, may be well known, as having contrived, in the welter of this twentieth century, to make the best of nationalism and internationalism.

THE SCANDINAVIANS

SCANDINAVIAN NATIONALISM

DURING the Middle Ages the people who constitute those nations we call Scandinavian — Denmark, Norway, and Sweden — were among the most powerful and adventurous in all Europe. Through their vigorous business and colonizing enterprise, they penetrated the lands lying south along the Baltic and even settled as far away from home as England, France, and southern Italy; they occupied Iceland and Greenland, seized Finland, and entered Russia. Fundamentally a Germanic people, the Scandinavians had many common racial characteristics, although their languages have always been divided by certain dialectical differences. All through their history they have kept more or less together: theirs have not been the intense struggles and rivalries that have marked the growth of the other European countries, although they have engaged in plenty of good, hard fighting at one time or another. Lutheran in religion since the sixteenth century, fundamentally agricultural or commercially minded, these people do not seem at first blush to constitute a type from which we could expect a national art of importance. Yet they have a splendid artistic tradition going away back to the time of the Norsemen and have produced some of the most characteristic and interesting artists in the whole field of nationalism: Hans Christian Andersen, on whose fairy tales the whole world has been reared; Björnson and Ibsen, humble-born writers of a peasant nation — Norway; Grieg, whose engaging, simple-hearted piano pieces and songs have made his name known the world over; Anders Zorn, the painter and etcher of Swedish scenes; and, in our own generation, Selma Lagerlöf, the Swedish novelist.

GRIEG THE BELOVED

When Scandinavian music is mentioned, one name comes to everyone's mind, that of Edvard Grieg, born in Bergen in 1843. He came to maturity at the same time as the great figures in Norwegian literature,

EDVARD GRIEG
(From a painting by Elif Peterssen, Oslo Museum)

Björnson and Ibsen, and contributed quite as much to the international repute of his country as did they. Educated in Germany, he determined early in his career that his music would strive to embody the spirit as well as the rhythms and melodies of his beloved land; he succeeded so well in his aim that he became known, in addition, as one of the most original composers of his time. Aside from his *Piano Concerto,* a great favorite, and his violin and piano sonatas, his work was composed mostly of miniatures — chiefly short piano things. In these he was particularly happy, for his was an inventive rather than a constructive genius; such things as his *Wedding Day at Troldhaugen* and the *Norwegian Dances* pose no problems, but they are lyrically fresh and unconventionally attractive. To realize how fully his music fits the spirit of his people, one must see a performance by a Norwegian cast of the Ibsen drama, *Peer Gynt,* for which he furnished the incidental music: the arts of Grieg and Ibsen in many of the scenes of this great masterwork come recognizably from the same folk fount.

OTHER NORWEGIANS

In addition to Grieg, Norway has given us a great deal of most acceptable music of folk-song cast, both in songs and in symphonies; operas appear to be few. Svendsen (1840–1911) was partly national, partly cosmopolitan: both his *Carnival in Paris* and his *Norwegian Artists' Carnival* are well known. Sinding (1856–1941) stands high in the Grieg succession, with a very prolific output, including that hardy perennial, *The Rustle of Spring*. His contemporary, Börgstrom (*b*. 1864), has written some symphonic poems, notably one on the subject treated by Ibsen in his play *John Gabriel Borkman*. Others who may be coming men are D. M. Johansen (*b*. 1888), who is said to use impressionistic technique in a newer national, "primitive" way; Arvid Kleven (*b*. 1901); and L. I. Jensen (*b*. 1904) — the latter two of modern tendencies. In general, however, the proximity of German culture has tended to preserve very strongly the Romantic trend in Norwegian music.

SWEDEN

There is less of interest to report here, since Sweden has not produced a composer so readily enjoyed by the plain man as Grieg the Norwegian; the novelist's art has not lacked at least two world figures, Strindberg and Lagerlöf. It may be, for reasons that are not often clear, that one country produces its greatest artists in some particular direction; there may also be cycles in these things — great poets at one period; later, great scientists. Sweden possessed a considerable number of the latter in the nineteenth century, but her music, in which the German influence largely predominates, has not been exciting.

It was Gustavus III, called the King of Song, who gave the first impetus to Swedish national music. In the century after him, the nineteenth, the study of folk song was pursued by Häffner; Geijer was a poet as well as a historian; and Berwald (1796–1868) is probably the only Swedish composer of the older school whose work became known at all in his own country. Berwald's was a personality by no means entirely swamped by German Romanticism, but there was little chance in his

H. D. McKinney

MODERN SWEDISH ARCHITECTURE

The Town Hall, Stockholm

day for any art but that of the Germans to make headway, and so he was not widely known, even in his own country. In passing, it may well be noted that Sweden's fame at this time was carried abroad rather by singers than by composers: there are few people who have not heard music lovers of the past generation rhapsodizing about the lovely singing of Jenny Lind, the Swedish nightingale, and Christine Nilsson.

Other composers of the mid-nineteenth century are Lindblad, a song writer, and Wennerberg and Landblad, writers of church and choral music. Hallström attempted opera, while the name of Söderman is well known to almost every choralist. Kurt Atterberg (*b.* 1887), engineer and critic, as well as composer, has become known chiefly because he was the winner in a contest that was foolishly instituted a few years ago to finish Schubert's *Unfinished Symphony*; his contribution honored neither Schubert nor himself. In addition he has written several symphonies and operas, showing varied if not entirely co-ordinated talents. G. Nyström is said to glance back to Grieg's straightforward simplicity and melodic charm, and possess, in addition, something of French impressionistic style, with a dash of the piquant sauce that so often is used today — Stravinsky's best. But Swedish composers in general seem to have been content to let the majority of modernisms in music go by, though they have shown themselves anxious to use them in the other arts.

DENMARK

We have a less clear idea of the essence of the Danish national spirit than we do of the Norwegian. Most music lovers could probably name but one Danish composer, Gade (1817–1890), who, founding his work on folk songs, achieved a sort of Scandinavianism that seemed effeminate to Grieg, so tinctured was it with the elements of Germanism. Other important names among the Danish composers are Laub (*b.* 1852), who has carefully studied folk and dance songs; Eduard Lassen (1830–1904); Carl Nielsen (1865–1931), who wrote in all the larger forms; and Paul Klenau (*b.* 1883), a composer of sensitive, lyrical music. In general, Danish musicians, like their fellow artists in other fields, have taken their color and inspiration from the lands which so closely hem in their little country. The representative national opera is *Elverhöi*, written in 1828 by Friedrich Kuhlau (1786–1832), a native German. The great cultural center of Denmark is Copenhagen, whose operatic and concert life has greatly stimulated national development.

FINLAND

Ethnologically the Finns are a people entirely distinct from the Scandinavians; but their history has been so closely bound up with that of Sweden that they are often considered as Scandinavian. Finland was part of the independent national state of Sweden instituted in the sixteenth century under the renowned Gustavus Vasa; in the nineteenth century the country was allocated to Russia as a result of the Napoleonic Wars, an arrangement that became extremely unpopular with the people and which helped make for a strong feeling of nationalism throughout the land. It was not until the end of the World War that the Finns were able to see the consummation of their dream of centuries — the establishment of an independent country, which took place in 1919.

As might be expected from their close connection with the two peoples, the folk songs of Finland show both Russian and Swedish characteristics. There is a prevailing melancholy to most of them, with frequent outbursts of fantastic and demonic power, a characteristic which is prevalent in Russian music. In addition to this folk-music background and the strong spirit of nationalism engendered by a political past that was full of oppression, the composers of Finland have been greatly influenced by their national folk epic, the *Kalevala*. This set of poems, which until the last century existed only in the memory of the peasants, was collected and set down by ardent nationalists and has strongly affected the spirit of both literature and music. No less a figure than Sibelius has called this great Finnish saga of early gods and wild nature an "heirloom from the distant land of runes and magicians, coming from the solitudes of the boundless forests, full of yearning and mystery." Here is a typical passage, describing the bringing of fire into the world of man:

"Therefore was the night unending,
And for long was utter darkness,
Night in Kalevala for ever,
And in Väinölä's fair dwellings,
Likewise in the heavens was darkness,
Darkness round the seat of Ukko.
Life without the fire was weary,
And without the light a burden,
Unto all mankind 'twas dismal,
And to Ukko's self 'twas dismal.
Ukko, then of Gods the highest,
In the air the great Creator,
Now began to feel most strangely,
And he pondered and reflected,
What strange thing the moon had darkened,
How the sun had been obstructed,
That the moon would shine no longer,
And the sun had ceased his shining.
Then he stepped to cloudland's borders,
On the borders of the heavens,
Wearing now his pale blue stockings,
With the heels of varied colour,
And he went the moon to seek for,
And he went to find the sunlight,
Yet he could not find the moonlight,
Nor the sun could he discover.
In the air a light struck Ukko,
And a flame did Ukko kindle,
From his flaming sword he struck it,
Sparks he struck from off the sword-blade,
From his nails he struck the fire,
From his limbs he made it crackle,
High above aloft in Heaven,
On the starry plains of heaven.
When the fire had thus been kindled,
Then he took the spark of fire,
In his golden purse he thrust it,
Placed it in his silver casket,
And he bade the maiden rock it,
Told the maid of air to rock it,

That a new moon might be fashioned,
And a new sun be constructed.
  On the long cloud's edge she sat her,
On the air-marge sat the maiden,
There it was she rocked the fire,
There she rocked the glowing brightness,
In a golden cradle rocked it,
With a silver cord she rocked it.
  Then the silver props were shaken,
Rocked about the golden cradle,
Moved the clouds and creaked the heavens,
And the props of heaven were swaying,
With the rocking of the fire,
And the rocking of the brightness.
  Thus the maid the fire was rocking,
And she rocked the fire to brightness,
With her fingers moved the fire,
With her hands the fire she tended,
And the stupid maiden dropped it,
Dropped the flame the stupid maiden,
From her hands the fire dropped downward,
From the fingers of its guardian.
  Then the sky was cleft asunder,
All the air was filled with windows,
Burst asunder by the fire-sparks,
As the red drop quick descended,
And a gap gleamed forth in heaven,
As it through the clouds dropped downward,
Through nine heavens the drop descended,
Through six spangled vaults of heaven."

— Translated by W. F. Kirby

Sibelius, the great man in Finland's art, has gone directly to the *Kalevala* for inspiration for a number of his orchestral works — *The Swan of Tuonela, Tapiola, Pohjola's Daughter*. And his popular folk rune, *Finlandia*, wonderfully expresses all that we have tried to suggest as characteristic of the soul of this people — the melancholy yet spirited melodies and rhythms of their folk music, their love of scene and legend, the humiliation of their long captivity.

Courtesy of Steinway & Sons, New York

THE SPIRIT OF FINLAND
(From a painting by Helck)

In addition to Sibelius, who has been discussed elsewhere, two or three other Finnish composers have become well known: Järnefelt (like many another, familiar through one or two of his small pieces rather than through his larger works), Merikanto, and, a little later, Palmgren and Melartin. The younger men include the short-lived Kuula, Kilpinen (*b.* 1892), and Klami. Palmgren's piano concerto, *The River*, is a good example of his talent, which does not run to both strength and length but seems happiest in brief impressions of nature and in a general Romanticism which has been compared with that of Mendelssohn's best. He is not so strong a nationalist, however, as was Kuula, who loved to explore the imaginative riches of the *Kalevala* legends.

On the whole, the Scandinavian countries in the last forty years or so have hardly fulfilled the promise and the early hopes that were aroused by the advent of so individual a composer as Grieg. The emergence of such a figure as Sibelius must, of course, be accounted sufficient glory for a century or more; but he stands alone. The others we have mentioned, although we have few opportunities of hearing their music, are known sufficiently for us to realize that if any outstanding genius dwelt among them, we should have been aware of it long before this.

THE SPANIARDS

FOLK MUSIC, THE BASIC MUSIC OF SPAIN

WHEN J. B. Trend, who has written a great deal about Spanish music and art, says in an article in *Grove's Dictionary of Music and Musicians* that " to the majority of people in Spain the only serious music is folk song," he is speaking not of peasants, but of educated people. It is this fact that explains the small number of composers whom modern Spain has produced; for the public attitude is bound to influence the interest in serious art, although it may not entirely direct it. The chief weakness of nationalism in Spain is that those composers who have arisen have not availed themselves of their great historic past, of such music as that of Victoria, for instance, whom we have already discussed.

In Russia, as we have seen, the mistake was in refusing to learn from the past of other nations. Always, nationalism in music, as in its political and social aspects, seems to tend toward shortsightedness or some other form of narrowness. Yet in itself it is a fruitful thing.

We have seen, in examples from various lands, the reaction of church music on profane music, of aristocratic troubadour art on the music of the people, of nationalism on the spirit of internationalism, and so on. But in all discussions of Spanish music there is a factor of special importance, one on which there has been a great deal of discussion among the experts — the authenticity of its sources. Those who pretend to know say, for example, that the music of Falla is purer in its evocation of the true Andalusian spirit than is that of Albeniz. These discussions may well be left to the experts, for music lovers in general can enjoy the sense of the dance and the sound of guitars, drums, castanets, and tambourines heard in so much of this music, together with the rich ornamentation that so attracts northern ears and the springing rhythms that set the feet astir.

There is an old Spanish tale of a court of morals that may well indicate what our attitude towards this music should be. Apparently the seemliness of one of the Spanish dances was being tried; a demonstration was decided upon, in order that justice might be done. Some gypsy dancers were called in: they had not been at work many moments before the learned judges and other sobersides began to twitch in sympathy, and finally they threw off wigs and gowns and joined in the dance!

SPANISH DANCES

R. Johnstone in his history of dancing has said that Andalusia, the province in the southernmost part of Spain where a large proportion of the inhabitants are descendants of the Moors, is the classic home of the dance. Whether this be true or not, there can be little question that much of the beauty and languorous expressiveness for which Spanish folk music has become famous can be traced to the Orient, together with many of the cadences and ornaments employed so profusely in this music

Courtesy of The Hispanic Society of America

A MODERN SPANISH DANCE — THE ARAGONNESE JOTA

(Painting by Joaquín Sorolla y Bastida)

and the instruments — mandolin, guitar, tambourine, and castanets — used to accompany it.

The classic sixteenth-century and seventeenth-century Spanish dance was the *chaconne*, a slow dance with three beats in a measure, framed on a ground bass; it was taken over later by the classic composers of the eighteenth century, who used its characteristic features with striking success. Popular eighteenth-century dances were the fandango, the bolero, and the seguidilla, the latter the most general of all Spanish dances, each province having its own particular version. The fandango starts in slow time and is danced by a single couple, the speed increasing as the dance proceeds. Every so often stops are introduced, the dancers remaining motionless and sometimes singing short *coplas* appropriate to the moment — a feature to be found in the other Spanish dances. The successful performance of a good stop and an expressive pose is greeted by the onlookers with the cry *Bien parada!*

The bolero, with its insistent rhythm of  seems to have been strongly influenced by other dances — the saraband, the chaconne, and the polonaise; it has been brought vividly to the attention of modern listeners by Ravel's stirring orchestral version.

"The ardent melody, at once voluptuous and melancholy, the rapid clank of castanets, the melting enthusiasm of the dancers, the suppliant looks and gestures of the partners, the languorous grace and elegance of the impassioned movements — all give to the picture of the seguidilla an irresistible attraction," according to Baron Duvillier. In this dance the *bien parada* is very important; the dancers "stand motionless and, as it were, petrified, in the position in which they are surprised by the certain final notes of the air. Those who manage to do this gracefully are applauded with repeated cries of *Bien parada! Bien parada!*" The *coplas* interpolated in the seguidillas are usually improvised by local poets to suit the particular situation.

Another well-known Spanish dance is the jota (hō′tä), the national dance of the province of Aragon in the north. Often included in religious ceremonials, the interpolated *coplas* are then of religious character, usually celebrating the birth of our Lord; when the jota is used in secular fashion, the *coplas* deal with that universal subject, love, often in a cynical fashion. Evelyn Porter, in her interesting description of Spanish dances, quotes a typical *copla:*

"On Monday I fall in love; on Tuesday I acknowledge it; on Wednesday I propose; Thursday I am accepted; on Friday jealousy is aroused; on Saturday and Sunday I start looking for a new love."

Other Spanish dances, developed later, are the habanera, which takes its name from its native city of Havana and is used so effectively by Bizet in his *Carmen;* the tango, adapted by the Spaniards from their colonial compatriots in South America; and the farruca, of Andalusian gypsy origin, declared by Morales, one of the outstanding authorities on Spanish music, to be the most musical of all the national dances.

The most widely known songs come from the mountainous districts of Andalusia: the traditional Andalusian *canto hondo* is serious, somber, even tragic. The word *flamenco* is the modern and best-known term for this type of song, with its strange intervals of less than a semitone, its repeated notes, short compass, and ornaments for special significance at high moments.

As in Russia, the works that have turned twentieth-century attention to Spain have been written almost entirely by composers of the last century. Eximeno (1729–1808) was perhaps the first to insist that Spanish folk music should be the basis of composition. Pedrell (1841–1922) devoted much of his skill to finding out what the real folk music was, once he had realized that Eximeno's basis for selection was too narrow. As part of his attempt to show that nationalism must be built on the solid foundation of the past, Pedrell edited a new edition of Victoria's works.

INTERNATIONALLY KNOWN COMPOSERS

Pedrell's logical and successful follower has been Manuel de Falla (*b.* 1876), whose range is considerably broader than that of Albeniz (1860–1909) or Granados (1867–1916). Because Albeniz lived mostly out of Spain, he was able to popularize the spicy rhythms and unfamiliar melodies of his native land in all the European countries. Falla has worked more at home, organizing folk festivals and seeking out authentic sources; he has gradually gained esteem as the leader of modern Spanish music and the preserver of the most faithful forms of its folk art. By employing certain elements of French impressionistic technique (as in his tone poem *Nights in the Gardens of Spain*), he has gained wide acceptance for his music outside his own country. In distinction to most of

ISAAC ALBENIZ

ENRIQUE GRANADOS

MANUEL DE FALLA

the other Spanish composers, Falla has written a number of operas and stage works: *La vida breve*, popular in many countries; *El amor brujo*, a ballet in which mystic lore and gypsy wizardry play a part; and *The Three-cornered Hat*, a ballet of humorous gallantry and fascinating piquancy.

There is something aristocratic about Falla's music; musicians are attracted to it because of its fine taste, its purity and grace; ordinary listeners like it because of its color and rhythm. This composer has made his aim fine art rather than mere nationalism and so has done more than any other single individual to make a place for modern Spanish music: for his work can stand squarely on its merits as music — exciting, interesting, constructive — without having to beg acceptance on merely nationalistic grounds. And his ideals have enabled him to avoid the danger which besets all nationalistic expression, that of getting into a "quaint-patois" alley; Spanish music, once the idiom has become familiar, is apt to become monotonous, and Falla has been wise to avoid such a pitfall.

While Spanish composers have not been very strongly influenced by the literature of their country, they have been affected by the influences of its scenery, its native costumes and the moods and the lives of its people. The paintings of Francisco de Goya y Lucientes (1746–1828) aroused Granados to attempt to depict in music what that artist had so freshly and powerfully portrayed on canvas. He wrote an opera, *Goyescas*, based on a set of piano pieces inspired by the Goya paintings and tapestries; Albeniz's suites for the piano, *Iberia* and *Catalonia*, contain abundant naturalistic suggestions (as well as some extraordinarily fine piano writing); and Falla's *Nights in the Gardens of Spain* is a re-creation of the scenery as well as the soul of his land. Turina (*b.* 1882) has followed in the footsteps of these composers and is internationally known by at least one work, his gay orchestral *Procesión del rocio*. Bretón (1850–1923) was an operatic writer in popular favor at home.

There has been a great deal of effective cross-pollination between the arts of Spain and France: both Debussy and Ravel wrote music that is redolent of the beauties of the country to the south — such things as *Soirée dans Grenade* and the orchestral suites *Iberia* and *Rapsodie espagnole*. And Goya's vivid canvases showed Delacroix his way and anticipated the discoveries of the impressionists. Yet another national affinity may be noted — that between the music of the Spaniards and the music of the Russians. Glinka, the first of the Russian nationalists, made a lengthy stay in France and Spain after he had absorbed something of the Italian operatic style. And we have as the result such pleasant souvenirs as his *Jota Aragonesa* and the *Night in Madrid*, both of them rather typical applications of the nationalist ideas to the life of a foreign country.

MODERN TENDENCIES

Of late there have been two definite currents in musical Spain: the one setting toward international expression — a sort of cosmopolitan superficiality without much real conviction; the other toward a pure nationalism which does not consider Albeniz and Granados to have been Spanish enough. It is significant, perhaps, that the composers of both these narrower schools have not found their way in public favor as Albeniz, Granados, and Falla have done. Of the younger men, we hear a little about Halffter and Guridi, on one side or the other; perhaps Joaquin Nin carries on a happy medium as well as anyone. It remains to be seen what will be the artistic outcome of the lamentable civil war in Spain; probably, as is the case with the majority of wars in history, it will be nothing but a calamity to art as it has been to life and hopes in every other direction.

THE HUNGARIANS AND THE RUMANIANS

THE BACKGROUND OF HISTORY

"HAD a sweetheart, mourned her loss long years and years,
Thought her dead, and every day gave her my tears.
Now I find her 'neath another's roof and shield;
But, no matter; more was lost at Mohács field."

Thus runs one of the oldest and most popular of Hungarian songs; the reference is to the battle of Mohács in 1526, through which Hungary lost its independence and its opportunity of maintaining itself as a major European power. During the Middle Ages, the Hungarian kings, beginning with Stephen the Great in the eleventh century, had, by their brilliant ability and strong military prowess, been able to form a monarchy of such an extent that it compared favorably with the vast kingdoms of England and France. Their subjects, the Magyars, were a homogenous people originally descended from Asiatic nomads and possessed of a fierce spirit of national pride; especially was this true of the ruling nobles, as strong and self-sufficient a group as was to be found in all Europe. When on the battlefield of Mohács the Turkish sultan Suleiman II, who had advanced into Europe in the hopes of seizing the territories of the Holy Roman Empire, met the Hungarian army and killed the Magyar king as well as the flower of Hungarian chivalry, the blow to the national pride was overwhelming. At the very time the nationalism of the other European countries was being fostered, that of the Magyars was lost completely. Divided into three subject states in 1547, Hungary for over a century and a half possessed not even a semblance of national unity.

But the spirit of nationalism, as we have seen, thrives on adversity: during this long period of national captivity, the Magyars became more desirous than ever of attaining their independence. In 1699, after sixteen long years of struggle, the Turks were finally driven out; but the country, instead of achieving its freedom, became united with the dominions of the Austrian Hapsburgs. Time and time again during the next century the spirit of nationalistic revolt flared up, only to be ruthlessly crushed by such reactionary conservatives in Vienna as Metternich and Schwarzenberg. Finally in 1867, taking advantage of a temporary accentuation of the spirit of liberalism within the Austrian empire, the Magyar patriots were able to elevate their country into a constituent part of the Hapsburg monarchy: the dual monarchy of Austria-Hungary was formed, in which the kingdom of Hungary was a separate entity, with its own constitution and parliament, and the flaming spirit of the Magyars was finally appeased.

DOUBTS AS TO AUTHENTICITY

Whoever has visited the gay capital of Hungary, Budapest, feels that he has become intimately acquainted with the folk music of the country. For on every side he hears the gay melodies and infectious rhythms which he recognizes as being those which Liszt used in his *Hungarian Rhapsodies* and Brahms in his *Hungarian Dances*. A native Hungarian, Liszt spent a considerable part of his varied career in Budapest and became tremendously interested in the folk music of this country, making a special study of and writing a book on the gypsies and their music. Brahms came to know these fascinating tunes through his long association as a young man with the Hungarian violinist, Reményi; and he, like Liszt, made rich capital of their natural appeal.

BARTÓK AND KODÁLY

Modern research, however, has shown that these two misguided Romantics were mistaken in their choice of material representative of the Hungarian spirit. The Liszt-Brahms themes are now considered by investigators as being nothing but cheap examples of a type of popular amusement music that is really not Magyar in spirit. Béla Bartók (*b.* 1881), Zoltán Kodály (*b.* 1882), and other scientific researchers have gone about Hungary and the adjacent countries, collecting thousands of folk tunes which they regard as distinctively Hungarian. The two composers have used these tunes as the basis for a national musical idiom which they feel stems from the very roots of their national culture. Bartók has written several orchestral suites, a piano concerto, an opera, and a number of folk-song settings. Kodály is, in general, a somewhat more ingratiating composer: his suite from the opera *Háry János*, about a preposterous national figure, genial liar, and general humbug, has become known outside Hungary, as has his *Psalmus hungaricus*, a striking choral work in modernistic manner, in which the nationalist influence is suggested by direct and swift, even fiery, response to the words, rather than by mere use of folk themes.

The serious musician naturally has a high regard for scientific research in the field of his art; it is entirely to the good that Bartók and Kodály and the rest have searched out the real from the false folk tunes in Hungary. We cannot help raising the question, however, as to whether the modernistic treatment which these men have given this material is entirely consistent with its essential nature. There are plenty of critics who assert that such modernism is merely a reversion to the primitive; and some aspects of it certainly seem so — the extremely percussive piano usage of Bartók's, for instance. The play of modern primitivism on material that is really primitive is likely to produce something unusual and exciting; much can be argued as to values: whether the old gets fair-enough play when the new is mixed with it and whether the old really retains much meaning when treated with modern dissonances. But if the new mixture (it can hardly be called a blend) is sampled for its own sake, without too much preoccupation with these nice discriminations, it can be enjoyed as a heady, if not a particularly hearty, brew. Bartók and his confreres do not over-esteem sentiment: the "heart," in their philosophy, plays but a small part in art.

DOHNÁNYI

One other Hungarian composer of the present day should be named — Dohnányi (*b.* 1877). His folk-influenced music is nothing like so extensive as that of the rest, nor has he applied himself to the subject with their intensity (one might perhaps say fanaticism). His *Ruralia hungarica Suite* represents more the type of folkiness which most people find palatable; his powers as a composer are admirable, and so the result is refreshing. To a certain Brahmsian background he adds delightful skill in key manipulation, a sense of humor, and a particular adroitness in the use of variations, which he has introduced into many of his works. There are few composers whose works may be more readily recommended to music lovers who appreciate craftsmanship and yet do not greatly care for idioms which go beyond the end of the nineteenth century. Dohnányi's second quartet, Op. 15, the F sharp minor *Suite for Orchestra,* Op. 19, and the humorous *Variations on a Nursery Song* for piano and orchestra are all familiar and give a good idea of this composer's sterling musicianship and good companionship.

THE RUMANIAN ENESCO

In the neighboring country of Rumania one composer stands out above all others: Enesco (*b.* 1881), partly because he is also a well-known violinist and conductor, familiar to concertgoers in both England and America. His *Rumanian Rhapsodies* are distinctly colored with a nationalistic spirit, although their idiom is much more accessible than Bartók's. In Rumania the same complaint has been made about the gypsies' deforming of the real folk music in contributing, not original ideas, but their own decorative flamboyance to material of which they do not understand the real nature. Enesco has been fortunate in being able to combine a feeling for nationalism with fresh ideas as to craftsmanship, thus making the result acceptable to the average listener. In order to encourage the development of Rumanian music, he has established a national prize for works by young composers of the country. Golestan (*b.* 1876) may be considered the founder of the Rumanian school. Younger members, born in the '90's or early 1900's, are Andrico, Dragoi, Mihalovici, Ragalski, and Perlea.

THE ENGLISH TRADITION

FOLK MUSIC'S VARIED APPEALS

ONE of the chief charms of the best folk music is its rather wayward appeal. Who knows what primitive spring, away down in our nature, is touched by some little wildness of melodic phrase, some emotional cadence or rhythmic bite? In a land such as the United States, to which so many nations have contributed strength and individuality, it would seem that these elements should make a particularly strong appeal. The English tradition in folk music has taken strong root in the New

World, as anyone who has heard the songs from the Appalachian Mountains can testify; and, of course, the whole subject of folk music has received a great deal of attention in the European countries, especially England.

VAUGHAN WILLIAMS, AN ENGLISH HIERARCH

A considerable school of English folk composers arose during the latter part of the nineteenth century, headed by Vaughan Williams (*b.* 1872), a composer to whom the folk idiom (above all, its modality) seems a most natural speech. For a generation Vaughan Williams has been writing works that are broadly based on this element as well as on the Tudor atmosphere that has permeated so much of the best English church music. This composer's striking individuality is clearly shown in such works as his *London* and *Pastoral* symphonies, particularly the latter, and the charming song cycle *On Wenlock Edge,* set to poems from A. E. Housman's *Shropshire Lad,* a work which in itself is as poetic an evocation of the English spirit as has ever been put on paper. Vaughan Williams has not hesitated to carry folk idioms even into the field of opera, achieving considerable success in his bustling score *Hugh the Drover*. This work is not " grand " opera in any sense; but it has sufficient affinity with the conventional form to use, on a smaller scale, the extended duet of hero and heroine which has been the high point of so many operas of the past and which has proved acceptable down to the very present.[6]

Vaughan Williams attracted a number of followers, a few of whom attained independent strength; the strongest personality among these was Philip Heseltine (1894–1930), a composer of satiric and keenly medieval tendencies, who wrote under the name of " Peter Warlock " and whose songs show a truly original and fastidious talent. E. J. Moeran (*b.* 1894), of whom we shall speak elsewhere, was another composer of definite

[6] In striking contrast to his hitherto consistent style, Vaughan Williams, in a recent piano concerto and a symphony in F minor, broke fresh ground, using a type of speech much more akin to that of his German contemporaries and suggesting that he has become involved in a new world of highly personalized *Sturm und Drang*.

individuality in the folk-song school. A man whose nature has remained mysterious to many was Gustav Holst (1874–1934), who, while maintaining a close affinity to Vaughan Williams in his fondness for medievalism and folk music, struck out a path for himself. His *Planets Suite* shows as well as anything he wrote the range and personality of his style; but in his later works there is to be felt an increasing ruggedness, even a forbidding tinge — a withdrawnness that is not easy to penetrate and which has not increased general recognition of this composer's worth.

AN OVERDUE RENAISSANCE

Since our subject is nationalism, and not merely folkism, we must remember other English composers who, largely outside the folk and medieval influence, produced good work: men like Elgar (1857–1934), of whom we have spoken elsewhere and who stands as the acknowledged head of English composition during the last generation. Other men of that generation were Sir Alexander Mackenzie (1847–1935), Sir Charles Stanford (1852–1924), and Sir Hubert Parry (1848–1918) who, with Sir Arthur Sullivan (1842–1900), stood for the classic values in Victorian England; each contributed a freshening spirit, according to his nature, that did much to bring Britain out of the doldrums in which she had so gently rocked since the time of Purcell. These men, in any extended account of English music, would deserve fuller treatment than we can give them here; but we mention them briefly, while appreciating the heavy task they faced and the spirit with which they produced music that, though naturally based on their own classic training, did attempt to seek out something of the essential "English spirit." Other men of this time were J. B. McEwen (*b.* 1868), a Lowland Scot who trod his native heath with springing step and whose music combines a philosophic introspection with French impressionism; and John Ireland (*b.* 1879), a strong Romantic. We have treated the music of Delius (1862–1934) at length in another place; but we must mention here his essential Englishness in expressing the nostalgia, the sweet, yet not sentimental, evocative power of the English countryside.

Bantock (*b.* 1868) is an eclectic who has ranged the world for impressions, yet has never found the nature of the Vaughan Williams style attractive. Ethel Smyth (1858–1944) was a composer whose music roamed widely and whose style (in the opera *The Wreckers*, for example) is apt to be patchy; yet she had plenty of virility, humor, and intensity, as is shown in her inimitable books of reminiscences, *Impressions That Remained*, *Streaks of Life*, and *A Final Burning of Boats*. Rutland Boughton (*b.* 1878) has written operas and choral works based on Celtic and Arthurian legends: his *The Immortal Hour* proved to be one of the most popular operas ever written in England.

The British love for choral singing (but not for opera) gave to these composers of the English Renaissance some of their best opportunities, and a great deal of the reputation of most of them was made in that way. But this meant a limitation of their chance of becoming known abroad, partly because of the obvious difficulty of language, and partly because few Continental nations have taken to choralism as strongly as the British people. The composers who found congenial the Elgarian tincture of mysticism or the broad national tunefulness which irradiates the music of Purcell made reputations that are higher in England than elsewhere.

The most notable gap in modern British music seems to arise from the paucity of composers born between about 1870 and 1890. Among those of the '80's very few stand out. Bax (*b.* 1883) is by far the most notable. The losses of the Great War but partly account for the shortage, though one or two of the men who were killed had already shown that they had something to say which England would have been glad to hear — men like George Butterworth and Ernest Farrar and Ivor Gurney (who, mentally injured, lingered until 1937); these were composers of the quiet sort, musing on friendly English scenes, mostly stirred, to some extent, by Vaughan Williams's passion for the countryside. But in general it would appear that the fading of the Romantic impulse had washed some of the life or faith out of one generation of composers.

We can but mention a few of those who, being of the generation born around the '90's, have shown some clear direction and strong impulses. E. J. Moeran, though of Irish descent, has found most of his inspiration in the English scene. His music glows with a gentle warmth. The *Songs of Springtime* are as good an example as any of English music that is native without being naïve (that besetting sin of the folk-song school, in which simple-mindedness is apt to overlay and spoil simplicity, a virtue which is not so easy to maintain as some of its members seem to think).

Arthur Benjamin (*b.* 1893) is an Australian who has written large-scale orchestral and pianoforte works combining real brilliance with solid craftsmanship, tinged at times with Elgarian feeling. He is one of those who do not follow too closely the Continental models of the hour, as is the habit of too many. His *Piano Concerto* lives in an exhilaration that is by no means merely superficial.

Constant Lambert (*b.* 1905) has brought into the concert world a sense of high-spirited ballet; his *Rio Grande* (poem by S. Sitwell) has great affinity with modern dance music, and another large-scale work, *Summer's Last Will and Testament,* makes clear the cosmopolitan versatility, rather than any deep-rooted individual convictions, of this active, but perhaps too self-dispersing, composer-conductor-critic.

The youngest English hope, Edward Benjamin Britten (*b.* 1913), has written some choral works which, behind a fashionable façade of nervous brilliance, allow his real talent to peep through. He has not yet highly fulfilled his early promise, but it seems in these days that every plant that has any roots at all is to be cherished.

All the many and sometimes obscure traits of character that mark the British nature have been expressed in some form or other in the music of the last half century. The strain is not exhausted, but the lure of modernism, together with something of the general postwar affliction of overcleverness, has tended to thin out the blood. The most hopeful sign that there is still some vitality left is to be found in the work of William Walton (*b.* 1902), who, basing his writing firmly on old foundations and freely using modern devices with a definite sense of direction, has achieved two works of real quality — a viola concerto (1929) and a symphony (1935). These have moved so shrewd a critic as Tovey to say that " there are no limits to what may be expected of this tone poet."

IS THERE A GERMAN NATIONALISM?

As a people made up of the most extraordinary mixing and mingling of races, perhaps even with a preponderance of the pre-Aryan element, as the " people of the center " in every sense of the term, the Germans are more intangible, more ample, more contradictory, more unknown, more incalculable, more surprising, and even more terrifying than other people are to themselves: — they escape definition and are therefore alone the despair of the French. It is characteristic of the Germans that the question, " What is German? " never dies out among them.

— Nietzsche: *Beyond Good and Evil*

An anecdote about the Englishman, the German, the Frenchman, and the Russian, who agreed to write in one brief extemporaneous sentence the definition of their respective nations, presents the German character. According to the story, the Englishman wrote, " I am "; the Frenchman, " I love "; the Russian repented, " I sin." When the German's turn came to read out his definition of himself, he asked to be excused so that he might take a walk and " think it over."

— Demiashkevich: *The National Mind*

A SPIRIT DIVIDED AGAINST ITSELF

THE title of this section brings us face to face with a basic question which no book that attempts to follow the working of the human spirit in music can possibly neglect, however difficult it may be to provide anything like a real analysis of the creative spirit of that nation which, above all others, has produced an abundance of the purest musical genius. The difficulties of this question are perhaps best epitomized by a comparison of the great Germany of the past with that of the spirit-frightening Germany of today, a comparison which always makes us wonder whether they can possibly be reconciled.

The quotations cited from Nietzsche and Demiashkevich suggest a duality or, perhaps better, a plurality in the German spirit which accounts for the violent contradictions in German life and method: Demiashkevich defines this conflict as being between the two souls which Goethe discerned as lodging side by side in the German breast — that of " totalitarianism " and that of " infinitism." On the one hand there is the passion for wholeness and unity which causes this people to sink all considerations in the pursuit of a worldly, practical end; on the other, there is the mystical, self-communing aspiration for the infinite, for divine truth and absorption in a higher sphere of being. In trying to explain the course of German history through the years, Demiashkevich propounds the theory that there has always been an alternation, with corresponding spiritual failing or progress, of these two opposed elements.

Further, he points out what we all readily realize, that the German temperament is basically of the Dionysian order as opposed to the Apollonian — that it is essentially of the mystical, metaphysical, prophet-seeking type and has few of the precise, rationalistic, analytic tendencies represented in the French character. In art, the Apollonian spirit may be said to be represented by sculpture, architecture, painting; the Dionysian, by music. It is no accident that the French have produced some of the greatest painting and architecture of the world; the Germans, the greatest music.

PHASES OF GERMAN HISTORY

When the Germans first appear on the stage of history they do so under the urge of a totalitarian impetus, as savage warriors who, in the fourth and fifth centuries, overran the Roman Empire; this caused them to drive forward in an irresistible conquest of all Europe, a drive which was succeeded by a quiescent epoch — from the sixth to the ninth century — of infinitism. During this time their native qualities made them easy proselytes to the gospel of Christianity, and the whole period is marked by outstanding developments in art and good living.

Then followed a revival of the totalitarian spirit at the expense of infinitism: during the period of the tenth to the thirteenth century there were further drives for the conquest of the southern and eastern parts of Europe, drives which culminated in the Holy Roman Empire of the German Nation of Otto I (what modern Germans call *das erste Reich*). Then, Demiashkevich points out, came another great epoch of infinitism from the fourteenth to the seventeenth century which reached its zenith in the terrible religious wars of the sixteenth and seventeenth centuries. The latter, although they took the physical form of armed conflicts between German Protestants and Catholics, were in reality expressions of the national longing for the infinite, of a desire to attain a suitable triumph for eternal religious truth. During this time Germany was weak politically and militarily; but she contributed mightily to the artistic, philosophical, and scientific progress of the world. Madame de Staël, a sympathetic French observer of the German scene, puts it in this fashion:

"This division of Germany, fatal to her political force, was nevertheless very favorable to all the efforts of genius and imagination. In matters of literary and metaphysical opinion, there was a sort of gentle anarchy, which allowed to every man the complete development of his own individual manner of perception."

Then, slowly at first, commencing with the efforts of Frederick the Great, there started a new totalitarian drive for world supremacy, a drive which is but reaching its zenith today. But before it received its greatest impetus from Bismarck, the founder of *das zweite Reich*, there ensued the greatest *Blütezeit* (literally, "flowering time") the nation has ever seen. The best qualities of German infinitism seemed to come to fruition during this period when the nation was in process of development: this was the time of the most significant literary Romanticists, Goethe and Schiller, of the hosts of Romantic musicians, Beethoven, Schubert, Schumann, Wagner, Strauss, and the rest; when the German artists soared in search of a "supernational, infinite truth and beauty," which they found revealed to them in the beauties of nature, the principles of religion, and, above all else, the struggles and aspirations of mankind.

GERMAN MUSIC UNIVERSAL RATHER THAN NATIONAL

It has been these elements of infinitism so strongly present in the German's character that have made his art universal rather than merely national. Nothing could be more purely German than the music of Bach or Beethoven or Wagner or Brahms; and yet the essential characteristics of these great spirits — all of them Men spelled with a capital *M*, to borrow Napoleon's phrase describing Goethe — appeal to the world at large. The longing of the German spirit for a communion with nature, and its adoration for, and realization of, the beauty that is in the world, to be found so strongly in the music of Beethoven and Brahms, are understood everywhere. The universal yearning for the infinite, the ardent desire for the realization of spiritual truth that we sense in the music of Bach, makes this provincial Thuringian organist the most international of all composers. Romanticism, with its native mysticism, its personal probings and aspirations, was essentially a German movement[7] — a "Dionysian revolt against the domination of the French rationalistic enlightenment and triumph associated with the names of Voltaire and Diderot." The typically Romantic figures of Schumann, Wagner, and Strauss could have come out of only a nation such as the German; and yet German music is as popular in Paris, New York, or London as it is in Berlin or Munich.

It must be recognized, of course, that any such attempt as we have made to define the German nature and to apply such definition to the course of the country's musical history cannot be considered a complete, exclusive explanation; for too many factors of a socio-political nature are involved to allow one easy account to explain any nation's art. It is a commonplace of history that the existence of so many small, independent states in the Germany of the eighteenth and early nineteenth centuries greatly fostered the development of the nation's music, opening up posts for executive musicians and composers that otherwise would not have existed. But it is exceedingly dangerous to make the statement, as one English writer has recently suggested, that Germany's preeminence in music over the other nations "probably lies largely in the greater opportunity she offered." Such leadership and superiority are better explained by the duality of German nature than by the mere accident of political growth; but it is weak oversimplification which accounts for the greatness of a nation's art through any specific cause. All that we can

[7] It was Louis Spohr, the German violinist, composer, and conductor, who conducted what has come to be known as the first music festival to be given in Germany, at Frankenhausen in 1809. His music, neither very profound nor personal, is nevertheless very characteristic of the early German Romantic style, with its excessive chromatic progressions and modulations.

be sure of is the fact that there seems to be something in the make-up or working of the German mind which accounts for the creative, universally appealing musical triumphs of the past and the almost complete sterility of the present.

WHAT OF THE PRESENT?

It seems wise, however, not to press too closely the explanation of totalitarianism as accounting for the present weakness of German music. For this weakness seems to arise from a lack of faith that cannot be accounted for by any socio-political upthrusts. It is shared by other countries that still maintain a democratic system, which is entirely opposed to the totalitarianism now so rampant in Germany; and it does not appear that these countries have taken all the color of their musical thinking from German art, as so many of them did in the eighteenth and nineteenth centuries. Of the two broadest influences of disruption, one — Schönberg's — is German; but the other — Stravinsky's — is Russian. It may be that there are now in progress world movements in art which cannot yet be analyzed with any reasonable degree of certainty.

The recognition of this duality of the German mind appears useful, however, in trying to estimate what nationalism has meant to that people's art — something quite different from the more easily understood and rather self-conscious nationalisms of the various European countries whose music, in the freeing years of the nineteenth century, so attracted the world. That there is an essential conflict between totalitarianism and infinitism in German music is evident enough. How far this strife may even now be affecting music, we know not; nor do we know when German art may swing back — suddenly or gradually — to its infinitism phase. The signs and portents of its doing so will be awaited by us all, remembering how glorious have been the achievements of the past. It is surely not merely wishful thinking that makes us believe that such a return is inevitable.

The Modern Revolt: Realism

A COMPREHENSIVE MANIFESTO

"WE must uphold the ideal of a great and scientific literature, which, free from all and every classicism and pedantocracy, will magnify the most recent discoveries, the new intoxication of speed, and the celestial life of aviators. Our poetry is poetry which essentially and totally rebels against all used forms: the tracks of verse must be torn up and the bridges of things already said must be blasted and the locomotives of our inspiration must be started toward the coming, toward the boundless fields of the New and the Future! Better a splendid disaster than a monstrous race daily rerun! We have put up too long with the station masters of poetry, the conductors of scanning, and the punctual timetables of prosody!"

In its spirit of revolt against the past, its tremendously dynamic quality of expression, its reflection of the outward life surrounding the artist, this manifesto, issued by a young Italian poet in 1909, represents for the most of us that spirit in art which we have come to recognize as *modern*. In the strictly definable sense, all art has at some time or other been modern, for it belonged to whatever present produced it. But in a general sense we have come to consider the creative art produced since 1880, roughly speaking, as belonging to a different class and representing a different spirit from that which had flourished before. This twentieth-century modernism has had many different phases; but no matter what its way of expression, subjective or emotional, impressionistic or expressionistic, abstract or poetic, it has developed from the same general backgrounds. A brief survey of the political, economic, and philosophical conditions of the century which produced it will show why its appearance was inevitable.

THE INDUSTRIAL REVOLUTION

The first half of the nineteenth century was a vigorous, enterprising era, largely given over to the rapid and universal development of the tremendous industrial revolution which had been brought about through the invention of machines to supplement or take the place of human labor. England was the home of this new concept, for it was there that the steam engine was first applied to the textile, transportation, and mining industries, with such spectacular success that the idea spread over all Europe, completely revolutionizing man's method of living and habits of thinking, and transforming a predominately agricultural society into one that became overwhelmingly industrial and capitalistic. This is hardly the place to trace the steps by which this gradual evolution took place: the substitution of mass production for the former small-scale, private industries; the migration of the population of the various lands from country to city and from farm to factory; the development of the power of capitalists who provided the financial backing for all these industrial developments; the sharp distinction which grew up between the wage-earning, laboring class, the white-collar, shopkeeping, semi-intellectual middle class, and the shrewd, exploiting, capitalistic upper class. But it is important to understand something of this economic background if we are to account adequately for the spiritual effects which followed.

ITS EFFECTS ON THE SPIRIT

The results of this mounting industrialization of mankind seemed salutary enough during the first two quarters of the century: not so completely tied to his factories and railways as to forget that there were other things in life, man began to sense a definite feeling of political and economic liberation as the Industrial Revolution spread over the face of Europe. As the common individual came more and more into prominence, the parliamentarians and the leaders of thought in the various countries, as well as the industrialists and the capitalists, began to take steps for the improvement of his condition in life: a wave of nationalistic feeling swept over Europe, as we have seen, liberalizing in its influence and stimulating in its reforms. The general artistic aspect of these years was still one of romance: humanity had not yet become so absorbed in the prose of its ledgers or the routine of its company reports as to forgo entirely fancy and imagination. "Feeling" was still fashionable, perhaps for no other reason than that it afforded some relief from the demands of the new world of machinery and materialism; the Romantic Movement was still powerful and able to enrich the cultural heritage of man by means of some outstanding contributions to both music and literature.

But as the spirit of materialism became more and more intensified during the second half of the century, this liberalistic spirit waned or became greatly modified: the result was a wave of crass mercantilism which absorbed the attention of the most of the world's thought and the growth of an imperialistic militarism which set the various countries of Europe so strongly against one another as to make the Great War of 1914 unavoidable. Everywhere there was exalted the importance of the materialistic life which the age of machines had made possible. The intellectuals of the world gave themselves over to the pursuit of natural science in order to improve still further the practical conditions of living. There was a similar shift of emphasis in all phases of man's intellectual activities: in philosophy, from the spiritual to the materialistic; in social conditions, from the individualistic to the socialistic; in religion, from traditionalism and authority to modernism and humanism; in art, from Romanticism to realism.

THE TEEMING NINETEENTH CENTURY

Some idea of the force of these impacts upon the older ways of thought and action may be gained from a mere enumeration of the most outstanding of these developments of the latter years of the century. The output of coal and iron increased in unbelievable proportions in all the industrial nations — Great Britain, Germany, France, and the United States; following the perfection of new processes for the manufacture of steel rails, the railways extended their network of lines throughout all Europe and the United States, and even over most of Asia. (In the United States alone, the mileage increased from about 30,000 at the middle of the century to about 200,000 at the end.) Steamship lines were developed to cover the seven seas, mostly under the aegis of the merchants and the parliamentarians of England, so as to connect the members of Britain's far-flung empire. The cotton, wool, linen, and silk industries became completely mechanized and new textile factories were established, not only in Britain, which for years had held the premier position in the field, but likewise in Germany, Russia, France, Italy, Austria, Spain, the United States, Japan, and even China. New processes for the artificial manufacture of textiles were developed, and chemists showed how synthetic dyes could make these textiles more readily marketable. A number of new inventions affected man's existence: some of them were destructive — the machine gun, the rifle, the submarine, dynamite; others tended to increase his comfort — central heaters, refrigerators, typewriters, bicycles, cheap paper made from wood pulp, the sewing machine, concrete buildings, sanitary plumbing, electric lighting and power developments, telephones, moving pictures and portable cameras, internal-combustion engines.

In all this material progress practical scientists played a great part; but work was being done also in the more abstract "pure" scientific fields. The conviction became general that it was *science* that would ultimately make for man's complete happiness by giving him a knowledge of the world in which he lives. Lagrange and Laplace made valuable contributions to the available knowledge of mathematics and astronomy; Leverrier, Joule, Helmholtz, Thomson, and Kelvin did the same in the field of physics. Fresnel and Foucault established the wave theory of light; Ampère, Ohm, and Faraday made noteworthy developments in the control of electrical phenomena, as did Hertz and Thomson. The latter, together with the Dutchman Lorentz, formulated the basic concepts of the electron theory. Röntgen discovered the X ray, and the Curies, radium. Significant work was done in chemistry by Dalton, Avogadro, Mendelyeev. Though the practical use of asepsis by Lister had already paved the way for modern surgical procedure, it was Pasteur who explained the essential nature of bacteria and thus revolutionized medical science: his inoculations against certain diseases were followed by the achievements of Rudolf Virchow in the field of preventive medicine and the development of the science of bacteriology under Robert Koch.

Lamarck, Cuvier, Humboldt, and Agassiz added greatly to the knowledge of botany and zoology. Lyell in 1830 laid the foundations of modern geology, and Cuvier built upon these later to establish the science of paleontology. In the midst of this new vision of the origin of the world, discoveries as to the nature of prehistoric life led Darwin to promulgate his theory of organic evolution in 1859, and others, including Huxley and Haeckel, to elaborate and popularize it. The foundations for the study of psychology as a physical science were laid by Wundt in 1872 and were built upon by James, Binet, and others.

It was natural that all these developments in business and invention, pure and applied science, would have a tremendous influence on philosophic and religious trends of thought. Evolutionary biology and geology, the social sciences, psychology, archaeology, anthropology, all seemed to point toward the fact that the origin of man and the development of his mind and behavior were purely physiological processes, having nothing to do with religious or spiritual influences. Philosophers arose who justified these new concepts, as well as the materialism and the greed, the competition and the brutality of the period, together with the grasping for their share of material prosperity by the underprivileged classes: Huxley, for whom there was no world of the spirit, no such entity as the soul; Haeckel, according to whom matter was everything, spirit, nothing; Spencer, who attributed the progress of organic and inorganic objects to natural evolution, a struggle for existence during the course of which it was the fittest who survived.

Such men as Schopenhauer and Nietzsche, feeling that there was nothing but the animal in man and that all his actions derived from such realistic conceptions as appetite and will, pronounced a philosophy of pessimism which was able to excuse the most blatant attacks of the industrialists and statesmen — supermen, they called them — on what had been commonly considered the conventional rights of the individual. Auguste

Comte conceived a new science based on the assembly of facts alone, which had as its goal the reorganization of all the existing systems of mankind; this he called *sociology:* it had great influences on later thinking through its evolution of programs for the bettering of humanity, based, not on theory and reasoning, but on the laws and trends shown by the collecting of historical, economic, and political facts relating to the activities of individuals and groups which had hitherto been considered irrelevant.

Another powerful influence of the times was the rise of what was called *scientific socialism,* a doctrine that was fostered by Karl Marx and his associate, Friedrich Engels. This came from the desire of these leaders to improve the condition of the classes oppressed by the increasing concentration of capitalism through the economic order which had been ushered in by the Industrial Revolution. Socialism advocated a class struggle between the proletariat (the laboring classes) and the capitalists, a struggle which would wipe out all the existing bourgeois institutions and substitute a form of government in which all production and distribution should be social rather than private.

Every tendency of the time thus pointed towards scientific and material progress and away from the older allegiances to religion and the other refuges of the spirit which man had developed for his solace and comfort. Although some held loyally to the older traditions of the past, many of the leaders in religious thought felt that these were anachronistic to the spirit of this age of progress and science. All sorts of liberalizing and modernistic influences came into play in an attempt to reconcile Christianity with this new spirit. Encouraged by the philosophic materialism of the writers, there developed among all sects a tendency to dissent radically from the historic doctrines of religion, with a consequent increase in the rejection of all religious beliefs entirely. In the face of these bludgeonings of industrialism and materialism, this general liberalizing of thought, Marxian socialism, scientific discoveries, and new theories, it became increasingly difficult for any sizable group of people to maintain any faith at all — that is, any belief in the intangible. In its place there came to be substituted a comfortable, material, and often completely selfish satisfaction in various kinds of scientific, mechanical, and social progress.

Cliché Vizzavona

LAKE GENEVA by Courbet

THE RISE OF REALISM

The machine and its attendant philosophics have affected art in many different ways, the most direct being through spelling the doom of handicrafts the world over. Another has been the fostering of a cult of *realism* — the reverence for things which can be realistically depicted — a type of art which has little to do with man's aspirations or idealizations but which rather emphasizes the pragmatism rampant in the contemporary world. The realists, whether writers, painters, or musicians, did not hesitate to use the ugly for the stuff of their art; they often felt that it suited their purposes better than that which was beautiful. This spirit flourished more strongly in literature than in the other arts; but its influence was felt in painting and sculpture and, a bit later — around the turn of the century — in music and architecture.

IN LITERATURE

The list of realist authors is legion. In France, Flaubert (whose *Madame Bovary*, published in 1857, is looked upon as the first great realistic novel), Daudet, De Maupassant, Zola (a radical politician as well as artist), Bourget, and above all the others, Anatole France, poured out a series of works dealing with humanity in its veristic aspects, some of them somber and sodden in character, others witty and sardonic. In England, George Meredith and Thomas Hardy concerned themselves with the pitiful and realistic struggle of people for existence; Henry James studied the leisured classes of two continents — people on a different, but no less realistic, plane; Bernard Shaw, in a brilliant series of plays, essays, and novels, set forth a personal version of the current philosophy; H. G. Wells combined the marvels of science with a study of social problems; Samuel Butler's sceptical *Way of All Flesh* carried the realistic concept to its ultimate conclusion, for it made no attempt to take seriously either life or death.

In Norway the dramas of Björnson and Ibsen, in Germany the stories and plays of Sudermann and the plays of Hauptmann, in Italy the novels and plays of Pirandello, taught a progressive and intense — often grim — objectivity. The works of Russia's realistic writers were especially effective, owing to the political struggle inherent in their background for so many years: Tolstoy, Chekhov, Gorky took delight in showing what a miserably weak cog in the machinery of Russian life the common man was, and portrayed with pessimistic realism the inevitable futility of his existence.

IN PAINTING

Political change, economic thought, and scientific discovery likewise played their part in the development of the spirit of realism in the painting of the period. Even in the earlier half of the century, when painters still thought of themselves as belonging to the classic or Romantic schools, there existed a strong tendency toward painstakingly portraying things as they are. Such men as David and Ingres in France, together with their lesser compatriots, Greuze and Le Brun, painted literal,

Courtesy of The Metropolitan Museum of Art

GOD SPARE US SUCH BITTER FORTUNE
A drawing by Goya

correct, pleasing pictures of a sort designed to suit the bourgeois taste of the new classes of art patrons which arose out of the Industrial Revolution: men made rich through their own efforts, manufacturers and merchant princes who liked to spend money on art that represented things with which they were familiar and yet that they felt to be cleverly composed. The Romantics, Delacroix and Géricault, in spite of their overtheatricalness and exaggerated emotional expression, represented nature and natural objects in a thoroughly realistic manner. Courbet, whom critics thought to confound by calling him a realist and who accepted the challenge by posting on his studio door the sign *G. Courbet, Realist,* brought a cameralike eye to bear on all sorts of subjects, often mixing with it a vivid creative imagination. Corot, with his lovely, vaporous landscapes; Goya the Spaniard, who painted and etched the most telling exposé of war's horrors the world has ever seen, as well as portraits which were candid enough to show the sitter as he actually was; Daumier, with his swift, telling technique, withering irony, and amazingly forceful method of expression; Toulouse-Lautrec, who injected the bitterness of his private life into the pictures of Parisian scenes which he painted; Degas and Manet, who brought an element of design into their essentially factual way of looking at things — these are the great names in realistic painting. Lesser men followed the same tendencies and became even more popular: Morland, Wilkie, and Landseer in England and Millet in France.

IMPRESSIONISM, REALISM'S LAST FLING

Finally there arose the school of *impressionists* — men like Monet, Sisley, Pissarro, Seurat, and Renoir — whose pictures were the result of a sincere attempt on their part to make an even more exact, natural recording of nature than their predecessors had done. Impressionism is, as has often been said, the last phase of realism, the final fling of the artists who tried to reproduce on their canvases what they felt nature revealed to their eye. Its exponents called to their help some of the new discoveries which science had made, discoveries which showed the phenomenon we know as color resulting from the breaking up of light waves: in order to gain the greatest possible realism in this respect, these impressionists, instead of mixing their colors on a palette, broke them up into tiny smears placed on the canvas in close juxtaposition, leaving the mixing and the blending of them to the eye of the beholder. This made the color seem much more alive and gave a fresh, open-air quality to their work which was in pleasing contrast to the older studio technique. Thus the whole problem of painting came to be bound up largely with but the one idea, the realistic rendering of light and color; forms were dissolved into color patches, patterns became unconventional and largely accidental, subject did not matter. The most familiar, commonplace objects became material for pictures — washwomen, bridges, factories, open-air scenes from everyday life, the sea — all painted as visual *impressions* caught under certain light conditions. One writer has rather wittily described this type of painting as reality dissolved in a luminous fog.

But if we can accept this impressionism for what it is — "an exalted poetry of nature expressed through light and color" — a new world of beauty is revealed to our eyes. All the men concerned with this movement possessed definite personalities and produced individual results: Monet is supreme in his rendering of the play of light and color over nature; Seurat, with his technique of pointillism, the use of minute, evenly spread dots of color, exalted the episodes of everyday life; Renoir, the greatest of them all, painted joyous, buoyant pictures which made use of impressionistic color in an architectural sense. Musicians are specially interested in these artists because of their direct effect on the works of Debussy and his followers.

SYMBOLISM

A parallel movement in literature was called *symbolism,* which was first established as a theory and illustrated in poetry by Stéphane Mallarmé. His ideal was the result of the success achieved by the painters: "to name an object is to sacrifice three quarters of the enjoyment which comes from the pleasure of guessing bit by bit. To suggest, that is our dream." And he and his followers, Verlaine, Rimbaud, Maeterlinck, Swinburne, and Yeats, wrote delicate, tenuous verse that is frankly sensuous in sound and suggestive rather than exact in its meaning. Words were used much as the colors of the impressionists, as symbols evocative because of their sound and certain subconscious sensations, rather than as means for conveying ideas: the central thought contained in a passage was of less importance than what one was led to read between the lines. The *opus magnum* of symbolism was Mallarmé's famous *L'après-midi d'un faune*. It was this masterpiece of vague loveliness and poetic imagination that inspired Debussy, as we shall see, to attempt to transfer to tone the symbolism which he felt the poet had tried to convey through words.

Archives Photographiques

THE TRIUMPH OF THE REPUBLIC

Dalou's statue is in the Place de la Nation, Paris.

REALISM IN THE OTHER ARTS

Sculpture and architecture reflected some of the same tendencies of realistic expression, although not so strongly. The natural realism of Dalou's *Triumph of the Republic* was widely copied by sculptors everywhere. Rodin (1840–1917), the great man of the time in sculpture, essayed all sorts of symbolic subjects by means of an individual way of expression that was a peculiar combination of imaginative mysticism and brute strength. Imagination of a high order was also infused by the American, Saint-Gaudens, into his realistic conceptions; and the Belgian, Meunier, saw in the ordinary workman engaged in his everyday task of earning a living an aesthetic subject of highest value. Architecture became eclectic in character, in an attempt to combine practicality with tradition; but there was a decided swing toward functionalism — that is, the adapting of form to the necessities of function and environment — an idea which the present day has made so largely its own.

Music did not show the effects of the current trend in the same way as its sister arts. Through all the rush of this realistic era most musicians continued to see visions and dream dreams. Composers as imaginative as Elgar, Delius, and Sibelius made great contributions to their art during this period; but they did so largely by isolating themselves completely from the world, Elgar by retiring behind the gruff exterior of a conventional Englishman, Delius by losing himself in the quiet isolation of a provincial French village, and Sibelius by remaining in the lonely wastes of Finland. There were, of course, definite realistic trends, illustrated best by the works with which Richard Strauss startled a bewildered world: the sensational operas *Salome* and *Elektra* and such tone poems as *Also sprach Zarathustra, Tod und Verklärung, Ein Heldenleben,* and the *Symphonia domestica.* Debussy's orchestral poems *L'après-midi d'un faune* and *La mer* and his now rarely heard opera *Pelléas et Mélisande* may be said to have been the direct results of impressionism. That these are perhaps the most successful incarnations of the spirit of this whole period is due to the indefinite nature of the art they represent, rather than to any difference in the ideals of the artists who created them. In the literal sense, they are the first great modern works in music.

The Musical Impressionists

IMPRESSIONISM IN GENERAL

DEBUSSY: THE INCARNATION OF IMPRESSIONISM

IN the preceding chapter we have shown something of the materialistic, philosophic, scientific, and realistic backgrounds which made modern art inevitable. In music, the summation of these tendencies came in the person of Claude Debussy (1862–1918), who devoted his life to answering the question he boldly put to his generation: "Is it not our duty to find the symphonic formula which fits our time, one which progress, daring, and modern victory demand? The century of airplanes has a right to its own music."

There are two aspects from which to view Debussy's position as one of the great men of art; it is difficult to decide which is the more important. First, he was the creator of some of the most sensitively conceived, poetically original music ever written — music which showed that the principles and ideals of the impressionists and the symbolists could be carried out even more successfully in a transient and impalpable art than in one in which the creator's vision must of necessity be fixed on canvas or paper. And second, he was one of music's great liberators from the shackles of traditions that had become outworn, the initiator of new and hitherto undreamed-of possibilities. If genius has ever given wings to music and sent it soaring up to heights to which it could not have risen otherwise, Carl Engel says, it did so through the liberating influences which Debussy introduced. His aim, like that of all the great liberators in art, differed materially from that of his predecessors; to reach it, he had to find new ways. Quite aside from the fact that they are outstanding

SUMMER by Claude Monet

and, if contemporary opinion provides any criterion, lasting works of art, *L'après-midi d'un faune* and *Pelléas et Mélisande* opened up such new visions and suggested such new horizons that it is impossible to see just what the end will be. Debussy was the first of the new moderns in music, and, so far at least, he is the greatest.

UNITIES IN THE ARTS

Any thought of this composer brings up the subject of the impressionist school in music, of which he was the most distinguished member. We have already shown that, in painting, this school, which has provided us with so many tenuous, atmospherically vague expressions, was in theory the result of an attempt on the part of the artists to be even more exact and scientific in their renderings of nature. When they came to put their theories into practice, however, the impressionists gave us pictures that, in their color lyricism, their evanescent beauties, their soft-focus loveliness, approach the suggestiveness of music and poetry. In producing such pictures as Pissarro's *Early Morning,* Monet's *Summer,* or Renoir's *The Canoeists' Breakfast,* the artists may or may not have been consciously aware of trying to make their subject matter brilliant and alive through their use of " broken color." But the person who looks at these pictures gets far more than an effect of lovely color and light: he receives somehow a suggestion, an impression, of the feeling which the artist experienced as he painted them. There is in these pictures a peculiar sense of unreality, a tendency to present illusion rather than fact, to draw as near as possible to pure sensation and emotion, without any of the usual trappings and mechanics of art.

It is little wonder that these Parisian painters of the 1880's stimulated their contemporaries in poetry and music to follow their ideals; for this style of impressionistic [1] expression suits the arts of poetry and music

[1] The term *impressionist* was first applied in derision to one of Monet's canvases.

Courtesy of The Phillips Memorial Gallery, Washington

THE CANOEISTS' BREAKFAST by Renoir

even better than it does that of painting. Out of the heated aesthetic discussions of the Paris of those days there came two movements which closely paralleled that of the painters — symbolist poetry, with its attempt, in the words of its leading exponent, to " evoke in a deliberate shadow the unmentioned object by illusive words "; and impressionistic music, with its attempt to provide " colored hearing " and " orchestral verse." Thrown together in the maelstrom of artistic controversy that rocked Paris at the time, artists like Verlaine, Mallarmé, Debussy, Manet, Pissarro strongly affected one another's opinions and shaped one another's conduct. Debussy intended at one time to take up painting as his profession and so was naturally disposed to see in the new technique of the impressionists ideas which could be transferred to music; he placed his chords, for instance, in close and unusual successions, much as his fellow artists laid their colors on canvas; and he did not hesitate to proclaim that his music could depict " various experiences and special effects of light."

THE SCHOOL OF MUSICAL IMPRESSIONISM

There is as definite a school of musical impressionism as there is of painting. Its leading figures did not always follow Debussy's lead in technical procedure, but they incorporated in their music the same general tendencies. Debussy, Delius, Ravel, Falla and the rest were primarily absorbed in the possibilities of color as an expressive medium; they looked on the communication of feeling as one of the most important elements in their music; and they were content to let the form of their work grow naturally out of its materials. So we are justified in calling them *impressionists* and in thinking of their compositions as characteristic manifestations of the general artistic tendencies of their time.

Strictly speaking, the term *color* belongs purely to the visual arts, where its use is in connection with the sensations produced on the eye by rays of decomposed light. But we have borrowed the term freely for the other arts: we speak of color in music, for example, in attempting to describe aural sensations produced by such specific factors as the *timbre* or tone quality which results from certain instruments; or the result of the management of key relationships within the course of a composition; or the particular manner in which a composer chooses and arranges his harmonies. In poetry *color* is used to refer to the choice of exact words and fit phrases which the poet makes in order to create a certain illusion. Can anyone deny the color that is inherent in Edward Rowland Sill's description of a tropical morning at sea?

" Off to the East the steady sun track
Golden meshes fill —
Webs of fire, that lace and tangle,
Never a moment still,

" Liquid palms but clap together,
Fountains, flowerlike, grow —
Limpid bells on stems of silver —
Out of a slope of snow.

" Sea depths, blue as the blue of violets —
Blue as a summer sky,
When you blink at its arch sprung over
Where in the grass you lie.

" Dimly an orange bit of rainbow
Burns where the low west clears,
Broken in air, like a passionate promise
Born of a moment's tears. . . ."

It is hardly necessary to suggest that the use of color in painting has been one of that art's chief glories from its earliest beginnings. It is not until we come to the impressionist composers, however, that we fully realize how important an agent this can be in music: the cool, lovely, and yet brightly tinted hues of Debussy, the blaze of glorious ambient color with which Ravel invests his orchestra in such a work as his second *Daphnis et Chloé* suite, the melting and shifting of Delius's peculiarly shaped color masses — all these were new elements in music, elements which have established themselves so firmly in our affections that we would never willingly forgo them.

THE COMMUNICATION OF FEELING

"How can music ever be a mere intellectual speculation or a series of curious combinations of sound that can be classified like the articles in a grocer's shop? Music is an outburst of the soul; it is addressed and should appeal instantly to the soul of the listener. It is not experimental analysis like chemistry." This characteristic remark of Delius's may be said to be representative of the attitude of the whole impressionistic school as to the importance of communicating feeling in art. Monet's lovely picture *Summer* holds us spellbound not merely because of its light nuances or its color harmonies: we immediately react to it because it communicates to us that indescribable feeling of radiant fulfillment and peaceful contentedness associated with midsummer, a happiness that is mixed with a sense of nostalgia and regret, for

> "June is short
> And we must joy in it and dance and sing
> And from her bounty draw her rosy worth."

It is the communication of just such feeling that we get in Delius's wonderful tone poem *In a Summer Garden;* Debussy makes us feel the fleeting emotions of the drowsy faun in his *L'après-midi d'un faune* and the intoxicating fragrance of the summer night in his *Iberia;* in his *Nuages* he shares with us his melancholy in watching the undying aspect of the sky and the "slow passage of clouds dissolving in a gray agony tinted with white." There is nothing descriptive about this music; it simply strives to evoke in the listener's mind something of the feeling which its creator experienced in writing it. And when the composer possesses as sensitive an imagination and as sure a technique as Debussy or Delius, the result is unforgettable.

The symbolists tried to do the same thing with words, putting them together in such harmonious combinations as would suggest to the reader, as one of their principal apologists has put it, a mood or condition which is not actually mentioned in the text but was nevertheless paramount in the poet's mind at the moment of conception. The reader of Mallarmé or Verlaine in the original French will be able to testify to their success.

Even to those unacquainted with the language, such lines as the following from the opening of *L'après-midi d'un faune* are evocative of emotion:

> " Ces nymphes, je les veux perpétuer.
> Si clair,
> Leur incarnat léger, qu'il voltige dans l'air
> Assoupi de sommeils touffus.
> Aimai-je un rêve?
> Mon doute, amas de nuit ancienne, s'achève
> En maint rameau subtil, qui, demeuré les vrais
> Bois mêmes, prouve, hélas! que bien seul je m'offrais
> Pour triomphe la faute idéale des roses."

FORM EVOLVED FROM FEELING

Because of their absorption in other things, the impressionists have often been accused, sometimes quite unjustly, of a neglect of form. They had little to do with structure in the ordinary formal sense — with repetition and arrangement of details, subjects and developments, fillings and passage work, and the rest of the paraphernalia. The shape of their works was bred rather out of the nature and sequence of the ideas they were attempting to express — their form arose naturally out of their materials. We cannot say that Henley's poem *Margaritae sorori* lacks form simply because it does not follow classic practice; it is the nature and force of the thinking which evolves its perfectly congruent shape and which gives it form in the true sense of the word:

> " A late lark twitters from the quiet skies;
> And from the west,
> Where the sun, his day's work ended,
> Lingers as in content,
> There falls on the old, gray city
> An influence luminous and serene,
> A shining peace.
> The smoke ascends
> In a rosy-and-golden haze. The spires
> Shine, and are changed. In the valley
> Shadows rise. The lark sings on. The sun,

Closing his benediction,
Sinks, and the darkening air
Thrills with a sense of the triumphing night —
Night with her train of stars
And her great gift of sleep.

"So be my passing!
My task accomplished and the long day done,
My wages taken, and in my heart
Some late lark singing,
Let me be gathered to the quiet west,
The sundown splendid and serene,
Death."

Sometimes — very often — this method of expression yields little more than a sort of sensuous loveliness; but the real masters — Renoir, Delius, Debussy, Mallarmé — provide their works with actual structural skeletons, even though they may not be orthodox ones. To say that *L'après-midi* or *Sea Drift* or *Le déjeuner des canotiers* lacks form is to display complete ignorance of the meaning of the term. For these works, rhapsodic though they are, are knit together with surety and freedom of technique, their shape and articulation, like that of the poem of Henley's, evolving from the inside instead of being the result of standardized schemes applied exteriorly.

AFTER IMPRESSIONISM, WHAT?

With the passing of the impressionists — the very characteristics of this school made its long continuance impossible — there has died a corresponding quality in art which the world will be a long time in regaining: for it seems that the beauty, imagination, and emotion which the impressionists demanded have ceased to exist. There have come inevitable, necessary changes — painters like Cézanne, with his penchant for turning impressionism into something solid and durable, Van Gogh and Gauguin, colorists and patternists, together with Braque, Picasso, Matisse, and the latest sensations in surrealism and abstractionism; intellectualism has penetrated music, its tenets loudly proclaimed by those who see in the current, frivolous pseudo-science which passes for the name of art the hope of great things to come.

It may well be, as the modernists insist, that we are living in an hour which presages the dawn of a new art; but those who have grown to love the music and the painting and the literature of the past cannot help thinking that the present hour is a somewhat cold and chilly one. Ernest Newman, a critic who has spent a lifetime amidst the masterpieces of music, has said that those who have been drunk with the beauty and the glory of the sunset of civilization as we have come to know it will have to find their consolation in the melting shapes of these last great representatives of that old, dead world. And so we turn to the music of Debussy.

DEBUSSY, HIGH PRIEST OF IMPRESSIONISM

I think there should be nothing but illusion. The contemplation of objects, the fleeting image of the daydreams they excite — these are the song; the Parnassians take the thing as a whole and show it to you; hence they are wanting in mystery; they deprive the mind of that delicious joy of believing that it is creating.

— Mallarmé

DEBUSSY AMONG THE ARTISTS

LONG before regular tours were organized to display the famous night life of Paris, an evening visitor to the *Chat Noir*, one of the Montmartre resorts most frequented by artists and musicians during the 1890's, would probably have had pointed out to him a heavy-set, feline-mannered individual, with a long, black, batlike cape and a huge felt hat that was too small for his peculiarly shaped, domical head, contentedly seated before a small round table in a prominent corner of the café. Beside him and sharing the Welsh rabbit and English ale which he was so obviously enjoying, there would very likely have been a strongly built, blond feminine companion with staring, bright green eyes.

DEBUSSY
(A contemporary etching)

If our visitor had lingered on to watch developments, as one does naturally in Paris, he would have seen other Parisian artists and writers and musicians come up to the little table to exchange jokes and stories with the couple, evidently well-known figures in the locale, or to relate the latest developments of some neighborhood *scandale*.

Had our visitor happened in at another of the Montmartre gathering places of 1895, the *Brasserie Pousset*, on another night, the same dark-set, black-bearded, cowboy-hat-crowned individual might have been seen at a table in one of the dark recesses of the café, his black beard and curly hair being almost indistinguishable in the haze of smoke set up by the cigarettes of his belligerently arguing companions. If the visitor were curious enough to listen to the conversation of this intimate group, he might have been strangely puzzled by the shop talk which flowed about the table, phrases about music, poetry, and painting being more or less indiscriminately mixed with shafts of dry wit and sardonic humor.

This *grand noir* of the *Brasserie Pousset*, the *Chat Noir*, the *Chez Weber*, the *Reynolds Bar*, and other similar night resorts of the last decade of last century was Claude Debussy, *musicien français*, as he called himself, winner of the *Prix de Rome*, and composer of some very strange-sounding music which was unlike anything that had been written in the past or that was being written at the time. This music included a string quartet which had pretty well scandalized the chamber-music devotees of the era and an orchestral piece, *L'après-midi d'un faune*, which had been brought to a first hearing in 1894. Since Debussy was a typical Parisian, there was nothing unusual in his spending his free hours in these places where his fellow artists loved to forgather: his conduct was always decorous and, although it was obvious that he loved company, he had the reputation of being very much of a solitary, giving over his days entirely to composing music in a little flat in the *Rue de Londres* which he shared with his Gaby-of-the-green-eyes.

HIS EARLY DAYS

His career up to this point had been interesting enough, but not particularly unusual or suggestive of the place he was to occupy in the history of music. Born in 1862 in the old summer-residence town of French royalty on the Seine only a few miles from Paris, Saint-Germain-en-Laye, Debussy was the son of a poor tradesman, who destined the boy for the navy although he had aspirations for becoming a painter. Without possessing any marked musical talent other than a perverse tendency to experiment at the piano with unusual chords, he entered that formidable stronghold of musical tradition, the Paris Conservatoire, in 1873. Here he met with some success in his classes in piano playing, although his revolt against the accepted conventions of academic instruction did not make his school life particularly easy.

After a short break in this period of formal instruction, during which time he was attached to the household of Tchaikovsky's rich patroness, Mme. von Meck, in the capacity of private pianist, he resumed his studies, coming under the influence of a capable and understanding teacher of composition, Guiraud, who, while condoning and even encouraging his nonconformist tendencies, advised him to wait until he was out of the Conservatoire before applying them to composition.

By rather sullenly obeying instructions and composing, in so far as he could, according to traditional convention, Debussy was awarded in 1884 the *Prix de Rome*, that objective of all French art students, for his cantata *L'enfant prodigue*; this entitled him to a period of study and retirement at the French Academy in Rome. Although he did not take full advantage of this privilege, Debussy used the time he did spend abroad in the preparation of two new works in which he felt that he could go ahead with his original ideas. "As there are no precedents, I must create anew," he wrote at the time.

HIS SPRINGTIME FLOWERING

The first of these *envois* which he sent back to his sponsors at home was the orchestral suite *Printemps*, a work which may be said to mark the beginning of Debussy's career as a musical revolutionist. Tame enough to ears that are accustomed to his innovations, this early suite was fiercely denounced by the government officials and was refused performance. In it Debussy tried, as he said, to provide a humanistic rather than a programistic description of spring, one in which he could express the gradual blossoming of the joy in living from miserable beginnings in nature. Those who would trace the composer's career as an innovator must begin with *Printemps*; in it will be found, expressed rather tentatively to be sure, the ideas which later led to *L'après-midi* and *Pelléas*.

The official critics again found Debussy "courting the unusual" in his second *envoi*, a setting of Rossetti's poem *The Blessed Damozel*, and they warned him against seeking color effects at the expense of line and form; in fact, they did not hesitate to employ the term *impressionist* in their reports on these early works and advised the composer to eschew his systematic vagueness and dreamy atmosphere, since they felt that these could lead only to confusion. Which, of course, but added fuel to the flames, making Debussy more determined than ever to pursue his own way.

INFLUENCES

Biographers have given a great deal of attention to the influences which helped shape Debussy's revolutionary ideals. Two visits to Bayreuth fastened on him the spell of the old magician, Klingsor, as he called Wagner, and there are many purple Wagnerian patches in these early works, try as Debussy might to rid himself of them. Somewhere around 1894 he discovered Moussorgsky and recognized in him a real kindred spirit. Massenet, whose music he found to be "vibrant with thrills, transports, and would-be eternal embraces," and Grieg, the northerner with the individual harmonic gift, helped him find himself; as did the eccentric, Eric Satie, the composer of the *Pieces in the Shape of a Pear* and *Airs to Make You Run*. Possessed of so unusually sensitive an ear that he was said to have been able to recognize instantly the overtones of bells, trumpets, and other instruments, Debussy obtained new vistas of possibilities through hearing the exotic music and native instruments that were brought from the Far East to the Paris World's Fair of 1889–1890. His close association with the symbolist poets and the impressionist painters and his absorption of many of their spiritual and technical ideas have already been described. The character of the artistic milieu in which he lived during these years gave direction to his whole career.

IDEALS

But all these would have been of little avail if Debussy had not been an artist as well as an innovator. The sources of his peculiar style of writing may be traced, but his manner of using them was his own. Feeling that Wagner's tremendous, exhausting grip on music had led it into "sterile and pernicious ways" which exaggerated almost to a point of caricature the ideals of development and repetition left by Beethoven, Debussy announced boldly that he would strive to achieve a kind of music "free from motives and themes, founded in reality on a single continuous theme which nothing would interrupt and which would never return upon itself. There will be development that is logical, compact, and deductive, rather than mere restatements of the same characteristic themes with hasty and superfluous 'filling in.' Such development will not be merely professional, the sort of rhetoric which is the result of academic training, but will have universal and essential psychic connotation" [2] (Oscar Thompson: *Debussy, Man and Artist*).

FULFILLMENT

These ideals came to fulfillment in the tone poem *L'après-midi d'un faune* (1894), planned at first as the prelude to a triptych based on Mallarmé's poem of the same name; the other two numbers, an *Interlude* and a *Paraphrase*, were never written. There can be little question that this work is Debussy's masterpiece; for it is music that is so individual and so free from the ordinary and accepted conventions of composition, and yet so poetically suggestive and intensely evocative, that the very fact of its composition still seems today one of the great miracles of music. Even more suggestive in mood, passionate in utterance, and colorful in expression than the poem which suggested its composition, it nevertheless reveals the composer's consummate craftsmanship and the masterful logic of his theoretical reasoning. At the time it was written, nothing exactly like it had existed before; and nothing finer has been written since.

HIS SOLITARY OPERA

Closely associated with this work and marking the summit of Debussy's career stands the opera *Pelléas et Mélisande*, based, with the author's permission, on Maeterlinck's shadowy and symbolic play. Written more or less in protest against the grandiose tyranny of Wagner's music dramas, in which, according to Debussy, the music so arrogantly predominates, this opera is an almost perfect materialization of its composer's theories concerning musical works for the stage: that the music should live the lives and work out the destinies of the protagonists in

[2] Taken from a verbal description of Debussy's arguments during a symposium of the symbolists at Pierre Louys's home, described in Fontainas's *Mes souvenirs du symbolisme*.

the drama, beginning where speech fails, "expressing the inexpressible, appearing as if from shadowy regions to which she returns from time to time." [3]

Coming upon Maeterlinck's play in the summer of 1892, Debussy seems to have been inspired by a single reading of it, but it took ten years to get his inspiration on paper. First produced at the Opéra Comique in 1902, *Pelléas et Mélisande* established its composer's place as the leading man of the time; yet it was five years before this work was heard outside France. Because of its ineffectiveness as pure stage material, this opera will probably always be limited in its appeal; but it must remain as one of the great landmarks in dramatic music. For no opera has ever been written in which the text is so naturally declaimed or in which the spiritual background of the drama is so beautifully developed by the orchestra. In every sense it is the antithesis of Wagner: its constant restraint and lack of emotional climaxes give it a peculiar sense of mysticism, however, that, profound and sincere as it is, is poorly suited to the requirements of the stage. This, coupled with the fact that there is little of sustained melodic interest in either the vocal or the orchestral score, and the rather fugitive character of the music make it a work for the chosen few. But what a world of lovelinesss there is in it for them!

THE NOCTURNES

During the time of its maturation, Debussy produced his set of three *Nocturnes* — *Nuages, Fêtes,* and *Sirènes* — for orchestra, in which his impressionistic, painterlike tendencies were perfectly illustrated. The title has a decorative rather than a musical implication, Debussy insisted: he was not concerned with the structural form of the nocturne, but rather with what the word suggests in the way of "diversified impressions and special lights." If a choice had to be made as to which single work of Debussy's contains his most individual, personal expression, it might well fall on *Nuages*. Both the peculiar quality of its harmonies and the characteristics of its orchestration suggest the effects

[3] Quoted from Debussy's own words.

sought by the impressionist painters through their use of vibrations of color and light; only in Debussy's case the imaginative concept is so sensitive and the possibilities of the medium so limitless that this work must be put down (with the possible exception of *L'après-midi d'un faune*) as the crowning glory of the impressionist movement.

THE LAST YEARS

Most critics will agree that after *Pelléas* there is little advance in Debussy's style; rather perhaps a decline, for the composer seems in this later writing to try to carry his medium beyond its natural limits, making it more definite in line and color, more robust, and, therefore, less individual. Belonging to this period is the set of three symphonic sketches, *La mer*, the composer's most extended orchestral work, full of gorgeous tonal images suggestive of the varied aspects of the ocean. But the tautening of structure, the increase in complexity of texture, the leaning toward more orthodox expression evidenced throughout the three integrated sections of this work, do not seem to fit the composer's individuality so finely as do his earlier things.

THE PIANO WORKS

Almost all Debussy's best piano music was written during this latter period of his life, after he was forty. As a whole it can hardly be said that his piano works achieve the peculiar quality of his orchestral compositions; yet he wrote some of the most idiomatic music ever penned for this instrument, which, because of its essential characteristics, is so well adapted to the impressionistic medium. The best of these establish suggestive moods rather than attempt pictorial description: the little *Clair de lune, Jardins sous la pluie, L'ile joyeuse, Reflets dans l'eau, La cathédrale engloutie*. The last, one of a set of *Préludes*, is probably Debussy's most popular piano work, largely because of its visualized program. It is in this respect different from most of the other *Préludes*, which, because of their attempts to record the composer's delicate auditory, visual, and even olfactory sensations in terms that are so well suited to the piano, seem to Ernest Newman to be Debussy's most original works, containing developments which have proved of the utmost importance for the future of music. But most listeners will prefer the orchestral works.

THE SONGS

The fifty songs that Debussy wrote cover all periods of his life from his fourteenth year on; they can never be very popular outside the French-speaking countries because of the unusually close association between their texts and their musical settings: if the listener is to realize the hidden beauties of the one, he must be able to understand the other. As much depends on the listener as on the performer or the composer: to those who know the texts, Debussy's music will furnish unending delight; for those who cannot realize the patrician beauties and fastidious fantasies of the French words, these songs must remain largely a closed book. It is of interest to note that the composer seems to have settled into his stride more quickly in his songs than in any of his other works and that his peculiar ability to image an unreal world is found in some of his earliest work in this genre: *Mandoline, Paysage sentimental, Harmonie du soir, Les cloches, Le rêve.*

CHAMBER MUSIC

Although Debussy's individual style of composition — providing the listener with fleeting impressions, colorful mosaics, charming sketches, rather than with material which is repeated and developed — is not suited to chamber music, he made one notable essay in this field — the early *String Quartet*, written in 1893. To lovers of the real Debussy this work seems to fall between two stools: for, although it employs some of the traditional devices of counterpoint and development indigenous to the classic chamber-music style, it does not do so in a masterful way. And in attempting to imitate the procedures usual to this type of writing, Debussy found little opportunity for employing the characteristics which we have come to recognize as his. It is rather significant, perhaps, that in his later days, when the fire of his inspiration had died down, Debussy turned again to chamber music, a form of writing in which ingenuity of invention can often take the place of spontaneity of imagination. His three sonatas *pour divers instruments*, published 1915–1917, suggest that the one-time rebel has become more or less a conventionalist and that an unfortunate striving for effect has been substituted for his former limpidity of expression. Vallas, in his life of the composer, calls these compositions Debussy's last will and testament; this is true, for they are the work of one who has fought his fight and finished his course and who, brooding on the past, awaits the end.

HIS NEW TECHNIQUE

Debussy might have taken for his device that of one of his famous compatriots: *Après moi le déluge*. It was his ideas of revolt against the harmonic conventions accepted by all composers from Bach to Wagner that opened the door to the reforms that have come into music since his time. More than any other composer he thought of music as a series of harmonic progressions, everything beginning and ending with the chord; and the fundamental principle of his revolt was that of escape from the chordal combinations that were usual within a given key. He did not try to destroy tonality as his successors have done, for his compositions have a general key center which determines their course; but he did not hesitate to introduce chords that are unrelated according to the older harmonic system and entirely foreign to the key. It was in this way that he achieved so much of his vagueness and impressionism.

Before his time the foundation of all music was consonance, with dissonances freely and often purposely introduced; his harmonic ideals led to dissonance's being regarded as an end in itself and not merely as a means for setting off and emphasizing consonances. He used all sorts of dissonant chords freely — sevenths, ninths, elevenths, and so on — without any idea of resolving them according to the demands of the academicians. Chords to him were complete units capable of employment in any combination or succession, consecutive fifths, fourths, seconds, sevenths, or whatever " forbidden " series the composer's fancy might dictate. He loved to run constituent members of chords in parallel lines, much like the practice of the old medieval masters of organum. And he delighted in enhancing the color richness of his fabric by establishing a definite chordal bass and then festooning it with all sorts of unusual and entirely unorthodox chords. By technical means such as these, Debussy strove, as he put it, to " rid music of that legacy of clumsy, falsely interposed traditions under whose weight the art seemed likely to succumb."

Another important item in his repertoire of effects was the use of unusual scales: the pentatonic or five-toned scale in which the shortest step is the whole tone, found in so much primitive music; the seven-note church modes — Phrygian, Dorian, and so on; and the so-called whole-tone scale, consisting of six whole tones. The unusual sound of so much of Debussy's music has led to the belief that he used these exotic scales more frequently than was actually the case; like all great artists he knew the value and necessity for restraint, and when he did introduce an exceptional scale or chords based on it, it was always with a certain definite effect in mind.

In order to achieve the vague, half-uttered impressions that so attracted him, Debussy avoided the cadences which are usual in music as the devil avoids holy water; likewise any long-drawn, definite melodic utterances were carefully eschewed. And to secure rhythmic freedom, there are elaborate and carefully considered alternations of bar values in many of his compositions — in *L'après-midi d'un faune* they fluctuate between 9/8, 6/8, 12/8, 3/4, and 4/4 — as well as between various conflicting and cross rhythms. We have mentioned his detestation of the usual devices of composition — sonata form, development, variations, and so forth; to him " discipline was to be sought in freedom and not in the outworn philosophies fit only for the feeble-minded." [4] His natural painter's instinct taught him to outline his form in much the same way that a painter frames his picture. Think of the number of his music

[4] His own words.

forms that are the result of visual images: *L'après-midi*, the *Nocturnes*, *La mer*, *Images*, *Iberia*, *L'île joyeuse*, *Jardins sous la pluie*, and many more; in all of them Debussy builds up his form just as a painter does within the natural boundaries and limitations of his picture.

THE GREAT ARTIST-REFORMER

The advent of this painter-poet-musician-reformer provided an ideal answer to that cry heard in all the aesthetic discussions on music during the closing years of the nineteenth century: " After Wagner, what? " For we may say of Debussy, the musical revolutionist, as it has been said of certain other figures in history, that if he had not existed, it would have been necessary to invent him. After the tremendous struggles of the Romanticists and the overpowering Teutonic exuberances of Wagner, music needed some strong antidote if it was to continue any kind of healthy existence. And this is what Debussy's inquiring mind, intrepid insurgent tendencies, sensitive musical ear, cool, unclouded imagination, aristocratic Gallicism, and forward-looking vision provided.

If he had possessed no qualities other than these, Debussy would still have been one of the great milestones which mark the process of musical development. But he had in addition those indefinable qualities which go to make up the supreme artist — surety of vision, clarity of expression, universality of feeling; and so we look upon him as one of the significant figures in music, the composer of works which, while they mark the beginnings of modern ideals, also happen to be among the greatest masterpieces of the art. Already Debussy the Revolutionary has become Debussy the Classic, and the works he bequeathed to posterity have joined that assemblage which for so long has withstood the onset of modernism throughout the ages. For the average listener *L'après-midi d'un faune* is as classic a work as Beethoven's *Eroica Symphony* or Brahms's *First Symphony*.

RAVEL

In art, nothing is left to chance.
— Ravel

RAVEL THE CLASSICIST

HISTORIANS of the art of painting are fond of quoting Cézanne, the leading figure of that art during the post-impressionist period, to the effect that he wished to make of impressionism an art that was " solid and durable, like that of the museum masters." The same ideal may be said to have inspired the composer Maurice Ravel (1875–1937), Debussy's contemporary and logical successor, although he may not have been consciously aware of striving to live up to it.

Courtesy of The Metropolitan Museum of Art

L'ESTAQUE by Cézanne

This is one of the many studies Cézanne made of this subject. Compare it with the picture by Poussin, the founder of the French classic school, on page 316, and it will be obvious how Cézanne tried, as he said, to combine the principles of impressionism with the " solid and durable ideals of the museum painters."

Twenty-five years ago the names of the radicals Debussy and Ravel were linked on musicians' tongues in much the same way as those of Bach and Handel or Haydn and Mozart; but it has become increasingly clear that, although the younger man seemed to employ the general compositional technique of his older colleague, fundamentally he was quite a different type of individual — a Conservative and a Classicist, with little of Debussy's desire for reform and hardly any of his warm, sensuous, human qualities. A hearing of almost any typical Ravel work — the second *Daphnis et Chloé* suite (1910), the *String Quartet* (1903) or the *Piano Concerto* (1932) — will reveal the truth of this to even the casual listener.

Ravel was a Classicist not only in his use of rigid formal devices, such as that of sonata form, but in such general tendencies as his aristocracy of taste, his clarity of expression, and his frugality of means. Like Debussy, he had a fondness for archaic things, especially the music of his compatriots, the early clavecinists; but in echoing the spirit of things past, he did so by having recourse to a world of imagination that is generally outside our visible one, in which human emotions are not present but attributed to mystic or legendary figures. In this sense, too, he was a Classic, one who saw the world from an impersonal, mystic viewpoint, entirely different from Debussy's eminently sensuous outlook. It was natural for Ravel, therefore, to limn his melodies and rhythms clearly and to make them an integral and component part of his structure, in contradistinction to the practice of his predecessor.

A CONSCIOUS DEVELOPMENT OF SELF

Ravel possessed neither the richness of nature nor the depth of feeling of Debussy, and his natural creative gift was less spontaneous. It was only by dint of tremendous energy and constant industry that he made himself a distinguished artist; his was a fastidious method of creation, that of a careful and conscious search for just the right and the most significant expression: his whole art, as one of his friends said, consisted in the rejection of the useless. "Bare essentials must ever have been for him his constant main article of faith; but these were no poor and beggarly phantoms, for he was keenly alive to the phenomenon of the world; his imagination discerned its mysteries — a world re-echoing with harmonies, colored with soft and fanciful tints." [5] It is because of this discarding of all superfluities that some critics think his work may stand the shocks of time better than that of some of his contemporaries.

There is little to record of Ravel's life: it was as artificial, sophisticated, and aloof as his art. Born in a small town in Basses-Pyrénées near the Spanish border, a fact which gave a definite Spanish color to many of his works, the young Ravel entered the Paris Conservatoire in 1889; after three futile attempts to win the *Prix de Rome*, he was refused permission to enter the contest a fourth time. This precipitated a public scandal [6] in which all musical Paris took his part against the unjust judges concerned, thus placing his name on the lips of everyone. After he had attained some note as a composer, Ravel withdrew from the hectic, contentious life of the capital and lived for many years a solitary, almost monastically ascetic life in a little hillside country town not many miles from Paris. He never married, and spent his whole life for his art; visitors have described him as devoting spare time to the cultivation of exotic plants and the raising of Siamese cats. A thoroughly cultivated denizen of sophisticated society, he was nevertheless a strange, solitary individual, almost completely unknown even to his associates.

He did not hesitate to select what he found most suitable for the development of his style from the works of his French predecessors — Fauré, Chabrier, Satie, and, above all, Debussy; [7] when it came to orchestration, an art in which he was consummate master,[8] he chose Rimsky-Korsakoff as his mentor. By the time he was twenty-eight he had, through

[5] Jean-Aubry in *The Chesterian*, January, 1938.

[6] Dubois, the principal of the Conservatoire, was so severely criticized and attacked from all sides that he had to resign in favor of Fauré, who had been one of Ravel's strongest champions in this teapot tempest. This all took place in 1905.

[7] It is said that in Ravel's last illness he asked that *L'après-midi d'un faune* be played for him.

[8] A contemporary critic quite justly describes the second *Daphnis et Chloé* suite as the most brilliant and exciting score for sheer orchestral effect in the literature of present-day music.

hard work and careful selection, achieved his own natural manner of speech: witness the *Jeux d'eau,* that most glamorous of impressionistic piano pieces; the set of three poems for voice and orchestra — *Scheherazade;* and the *String Quartet.* Afterwards there was nothing for him to do but improve this style through more industry and fastidious selection.

HIS WORKS

In 1907 there appeared the *Spanish Rhapsody,* the first of Ravel's works to draw attention to his mastery of orchestration; then came the *Mother Goose* set of five children's pieces, written as a suite for piano duet in 1908 and afterwards orchestrated by the composer (1912); the *Daphnis et Chloé* music was written originally for performance as a ballet in 1910 and then arranged for concert performance in two orchestral suites, the second of which will probably prove to be Ravel's masterpiece, so warm and human is its glow, so unearthly its shimmer of orchestral color, so fresh and vivid its sense of life; *L'heure espagnole,* a witty and sardonic musical comedy, was produced in 1911; the suite originally composed as a set of piano pieces (in 1914–1917) and later orchestrated, *Le tombeau de Couperin,* pays devoted respect to the spirit of the precise and ordered classicism of the eighteenth century; *La valse* is a brilliant postwar caricature on themes of Straussian flavor; a piano trio appeared in 1916; the concerto for piano and orchestra (not to be confused with another concerto for the left hand, which Ravel composed for the one-armed pianist, Wittgenstein), not finished until 1931, was a composition which particularly pleased its composer, for he felt that he had been able to pour his thought " into the exact world he dreamed of "; finally, in 1928, came the incredible *Bolero,* written on commission as a ballet, a *tour de force* of rhythmic monotony and orchestral brilliance which, as one Frenchman has wittily pointed out, invalidates the gastronomic aphorism so often heard in his country to the effect that the sauce will excuse the fish by rending the fish to nothing and making the sauce everything. These works show a progressive enfeeblement of the pure fancy shown in Ravel's early works.

RAVEL AT THE HEIGHT OF HIS CAREER

During the last years of his life, nature seemed intent on destroying by slow degrees the artistic triumph she had so meticulously raised over a long period: an insidious, progressive illness made musical composition impossible. He died in a Paris hospital after a vain attempt to save his life through a serious operation.

To those attracted to art that is precise, sophisticated, symmetrical, Ravel's music will always appeal; for these attributes gradually took precedence over the impressionistic style that is so evident in his earlier works. Almost more than any other composer, he is able, through one means or another, to delight his listeners — by his wit and humor, his dexterous manipulation of colors and sonorities, his varied use of dance forms.[9] Rosenfeld's characterization of him is a just one: "amusing yet artistically upright"; in this he upholds the best traditions of his race.

[9] One critic has taken the trouble to count the number of dance forms with which Ravel occupied himself: there are thirteen of them — minuet, pavan, furlana, tambourin, gigue, rigadoon, rondo, habanera, malagueña, waltz, tango, fox trot, and bolero!

DELIUS, THE END OF A CHAPTER

Music is an outburst of the soul; it is addressed and should appeal instantly to the soul of the listener.

— Delius

TWO GENERAL CATEGORIES

IT seems natural to divide the art which has come into being during the course of the centuries into great, opposing categories. There is, for example, that type which is associated with other values — religion, morals, idealism, philosophy, and so on — that art which may be called, in general terms, spiritual, since its main objective is that of upholding a world of eternal and supersensual values. In contrast there is the art that has been created for art's sake, sensate art, with its main purpose that of providing sensuous pleasure. Then there is that distinction which can be made between art that is, on the one hand, planned, clear-cut, rationally calculated, conceived primarily in an intellectual, unemotional sense, and to which some sort of intellectual approach seems essential; and that which is, on the other hand, essentially spontaneous, intuitive, emotional, symbolic, warmly human, and naturally appealing. Various terms have been given to these opposing categories in an attempt to describe their differences: the first has been called Greek, Apollonian, Classic; the second, Gothic, Dionysian, Romantic. But whatever the name given, the investigators of the phenomena of art dynamics, as well as the historians of the various arts, have not failed to note the existence of such strongly marked divisions, together with the fact that there has been some sort of rhythm in their appearances during the course of art history.

In between, of course, there are all sorts of admixtures and gradations, some of them combining a greater proportion of the characteristics of the one category, others employing more of the other. There can be no question that the greatest artists, men such as Michelangelo, Shakespeare, Mozart, and Beethoven, to mention but a few, have intuitively kept a careful balance between these two qualities. Such a work as the Sistine

Chapel mural of Michelangelo's, bringing as it does all the world's glory, as well as the joy and tribulations of man, into one carefully achieved expression, is an almost unbelievable combination of these opposing tendencies. The lesser men, however, have instinctively leaned toward one or the other pole of these trends, according to their natural endowments.

For instance, there are the meticulously created phrases of such English poets as Denham and Waller of the seventeenth century, or their greater successors in the next, Dryden and Pope, for whom, as one of them has expressed it:

> "True ease comes from art, not chance,
> As those move easiest who have learned to dance."

Or there is the sensuous beauty of Verlaine's natural poetry, which comes perhaps as near being pure feeling as the art of literature has provided; or the intuitive mysticism of such men as William Blake and Francis Thompson, with their sense of rapturous revelation that has little concern with reason. The seventeenth-century Poussin, whose hard, carefully composed painting became the foundation upon which the whole structure of French classic tradition was reared, stands in strong contrast to the tempestuous force and the intuitive, fanatic power of the later Van Gogh, who seemed to have the ability to transmute emotion directly into paint. That these tendencies are sometimes concomitant can be shown easily enough by a comparison of the cool, sophisticated, mannered, consciously manipulated art of Ravel with that of his fellow impressionist and contemporary, Frederick Delius, for whom life and art were almost entirely matters of feeling.

DELIUS, THE INTUITIVE ARTIST

Perhaps no artist, whatever his medium, has ever succeeded quite so perfectly as has Delius in achieving the ideals of those to whom art is essentially an intuitive, emotional, dynamic expression. No one else, not even Debussy, has made his art so completely suggestive of sensations and emotions without the necessity of the intervention of thought or judgment, has allowed the ear so completely to "devour the brain." Delius named one of his earlier pieces *Over the Hills and Far Away:* no more suggestive title could possibly be found for music such as his; for with its first measures we are immediately transported out of our usual selves into a land of faery fancy that has no counterpart on this earth, which has in fact never existed except in man's imagination. What matters with Delius is not technically calculated effect; rather does he strive for illusions, and so almost more than any of his generation he should be called an impressionist.

There are technical reasons for his being classified under this insignia of his period: in listening to such typical works as his *On Hearing the First Cuckoo in Spring, The Walk to the Paradise Garden,* or *In a Summer Garden,* we are strongly reminded of Debussy — and also Grieg and Wagner, perhaps. But Delius's is impressionism with a difference: for somehow he was able to make the musical idiom used by his contemporaries (he was born in 1863, only a year after Debussy) his own personal expression to a remarkable degree. Except in superficial details such as the use of some Griegian harmonies, Wagnerian chromaticisms, and impressionistic chordal and rhythmic usages, his style is as individual as that of any other composer who ever wrote. Once its essence is understood, its exquisite washes of color realized, it can never be mistaken for that of another composer.

But the thing which makes this peculiarly emotional medium of Delius's so effective is the spiritual nature that was back of it, a nature like that of no other in music. Delius was an ardent lover of beauty, as many a composer had been before him; but to him beauty was something that was not only connected with the world about him: it was rather to be found in contemplation after an event, in regarding that which is left to man after the show of life has passed on. One of his biographers speaks of the "wind as from a far country" that blows through all his most characteristic scores. It is this nostalgic longing for something that is unattainable, that has never existed, combined with a poignant tenderness that is sometimes almost unbearable, that makes the music of this composer unique. If one would experience this to the utmost, let him listen to the setting with which Delius has invested

H. D. McKinney

THE OLD BRIDGE AT GREZ-SUR-LOING

Delius lived in the small village on the southern border of the Fontainebleau forest for many years and wrote most of his music there. Grez was a resort for artists, and this bridge, which adjoined Delius's garden, was the subject of many a well-known painting by men such as Corot, Edward Munch, and Carl Larson.

the words of Whitman in his cantata *Sea Drift*, words which are almost autobiographical in so far as Delius is concerned:

> "Oh troubled reflection in the sea!
> Oh throat, oh throbbing heart!
> And I singing uselessly, uselessly all the night.
> Oh past! Oh happy life! Oh songs of joy!
> In the air, in the woods, over fields."

We may intuitively claim this music as an expression of our own souls, or we may never be able to realize its peculiar beauty; but we shall have to admit that it is unlike anything else in the history of the art — a still, small voice, perhaps, but an absolutely unique one.

Delius has often been called a nationalist, and his music cited as representative of the English spirit. Of German parentage, he was born in

England, but he spent some of the most determinative years of his life in the lonely isolation of a Florida orange plantation, lived for some years in Germany, where he studied at the Leipzig Conservatory, and spent the most vigorous creative period of his life in a little French village on the borders of the Fontainebleau forest, Grez-sur-Loing. He may therefore be reckoned a cosmopolitan composer. Eric Fenby, the latest of his biographers, who saw more of Delius during the last tragic years of the composer's life at Grez than did any other musician, says that to him Delius's music is more suggestive of France than of England.

A LATE DEVELOPMENT

Fenby's account, vividly and interestingly presented, shows us a character that is strangely at odds with the dream-laden music we have come to know. Delius's youth must have been a wild, reckless one, spent in many of the great cities of the earth, and with a number of violent love affairs. The young musician's father, a prosperous Yorkshire woolen merchant, bought his son an orange grove in Florida, in the hope that he might find himself there and settle down to a business career. It was not until Delius met and married the Scandinavian artist Jelka Rosen that he fully matured; he retired into a life of seclusion at Grez, a life in which everything and everyone were subservient to the chief business of his music. The aloofness and detachment of this isolated existence seemed to have been necessary before he could achieve the qualities of his individual style: the works which were written before his orchestral tone poem, *Paris: The Song of a Great City* (1899), give hardly a hint of what was to come during the next six years. Suddenly, after a long, plodding development during which he heard very little music other than his own, guided almost entirely by instinct, Delius seemed to discover himself. Fenby quotes him as saying that "it was a long, long time before I understood what I wanted to say, and then it came to me all at once"; and then adds that no composer, with the possible exception of Verdi, was so unlearned in the academic technique of his art.

From 1900 until the time he became paralyzed in 1922, there flowed from him a steady stream of music, some of it his most characteristic and individual. To mention only the best-known works, the following were written during this period: the opera *A Village Romeo and Juliet*; the orchestral variations on an American Negro theme, *Appalachia*; the cantatas to words by Whitman, *Sea Drift*, and the *Songs of Sunset*; the orchestral rhapsody, *Brigg Fair*, and the fantasy for orchestra, *In a Summer Garden*, these two showing his style at its very best; *A Mass of Life*, a curiously vigorous and provocative work, set to words from Nietzsche's *Also sprach Zarathustra*, which lays before us the progress of man from time to eternity and incidentally gives us insight into Delius's philosophy of life. Later, after the terrible catastrophes of paralysis and blindness had rendered his existence seemingly useless, he had still the determination to go on composing, dictating his ideas to his young friend, Fenby; between them, they finished some earlier sketches, and wrote the *Songs of Farewell*.

THE END OF ROMANTICISM

There seem to be no half measures about this music: if one leans naturally toward the Romantic type of art, he likes it the moment it is first heard; if one's tastes are instinctively classic, the sound of it will be immediately and forever distasteful. As so many critics have remarked, Delius can never be an acquired taste; the listener cannot grow into him as he does into Mozart or Brahms. Because of its peculiar sense of detachment and its fine-grained expressiveness, Delius's music is extremely difficult to interpret successfully. Not only must its interpreter be enamored of its spirit and feel its peculiar spell; he must likewise have consummate technical skill — that art which conceals art — sufficient to hold together its delicate, tenuous fabric and imbue it with life. The interpreter's task is not simplified by the fact that until Delius found out how to dispense with the classical forms and shape his thoughts perfectly according to their emotional demands, he was liable to show only too clearly his lack of formal training. As so often heard, this music may sound meandering and dull; but when played under the direction of a conductor such as Sir Thomas Beecham, it will always be for those who can respond to its magic some of the most beautiful ever written. For them, even though they may belong, as did Fenby, to the materialistic postwar generation which knows little of the world of which Delius sang, the passing of this unique figure marks the end of a chapter in music. These works, charged as they are with the sadness of a transitory and evanescent world, give the listener a peculiar sense of finality: for it seems as if with them the spirit of Romance has passed from the world.

THE AFTERMATH

THE DIFFERENCE BETWEEN GERMAN AND FRENCH ART

ONE noted German critic has said of Debussy's music that in it there is no passion, no deep feeling, and no real emotional expression; rather, it is hardly more than "suggestive sound" observed with an almost unrivaled refinement. "His is an altogether sensuous art, without any marked moral quality, without religious feeling or metaphysical overtones."

Nothing shows better the line of complete and seemingly unbridgeable demarcation that exists between the thought of the German and of the French people. In the art of the one, style or manner of expression has come about as the result of an overwhelming emotional impulse and all its attendant moral, religious, and metaphysical implications. Beethoven's symphonies and Wagner's music dramas are really the revelation of the German soul and mind: the fact that they are colossal works of art simply means that the native genius of these composers was able to forge out of the molten surge of their emotions the structure best fitted to contain them. In all French art at its best, on the other hand, emotional implication comes as the result of a superb building of style. Berlioz and Debussy are two good cases in point. The Romanticism of the first was bounded by the composer's conceptions of what could be done with the orchestra; of Debussy, by the suggestive new manipulation of sound colors. But to deny the reality or validity of such emotion is to show oneself insensitive to most essential qualities of these composers.

DEBUSSY'S INFLUENCE

It need hardly be said that such a pronouncedly German view of Debussy is by no means universal; no other single composer in the history of music, with the possible exception of Wagner, ever gave such a completely fresh and stimulating turn to the music of his time. Just as the influence of his confreres, the French impressionistic painters, made an indelible impression on all art produced since their day, so Debussy's technique and style reached out into all countries and influenced, in one way or another, almost every composer of prominence. Moreover, by disregarding aesthetic conventions and compromises, Debussy acted as a liberator of the music of his country from the spell of German domination and restored its direct line of connection with the masters of the eighteenth century. In France his style became quickly modified by other elements, notably those to which a growing intellectualism gave substance and encouragement.

SOME OTHER FRENCH IMPRESSIONISTS

French art has always been, of all national styles, the most nearly eclectic; for Paris since the days of the early universities has been the great cosmopolitan city of the world, absorbing into her life, as into her art, ideas and ideals from all the world. But because Paris is the brain of France as well as the capital of the world, these elements have been subjected to the test of French logic and their validity judged by a very exacting critical standard. So we do not expect to find either staleness or overemphasis on any one aspect prevalent for any long period in Parisian art. Both Florent Schmitt (*b.* 1870) and Albert Roussel (1869–1937) were in the best sense of the word French *eclectics*, strongly influenced by Chabrier, Fauré, and, above all others, Debussy. Schmitt's music has likewise a note of German magniloquence that is not very common in the French art of his period. This, as well as his strong dependence on Debussyan technique, is shown in his vivid orchestral *Tragédie de Salomé*, written for performance with mimed dancing. Because of its unusual harmonic intensity and dramatic use of the orchestra, this work takes rank as one of the most important post-Debussyan scores, second only to Ravel's *Daphnis et Chloé* as the vital product of the French imaginative style.

Although Roussel received his training under D'Indy's influence in the *Schola Cantorum,* he early developed a taste for the mysterious and exotic, achieving in the end a sharp-pointed, personal style quite at variance with his earlier writings. His best-known works are the three *Evocations* and a symphony written in 1922.

Jacques Ibert (*b.* 1890) is another of the French composers who early in the century came under the Debussyan spirit; he was inspired also by Ravel's precision of thought (a characteristic which may be said to underlie all the best French art) and has written some effective music, notably *Escales,* a work which is touched with subtle impressionistic color as well as good humor and wit.

IMPRESSIONISTS IN OTHER COUNTRIES

There were some Italian writers of orchestral music who followed in the footsteps of their French impressionistic colleagues; the most whole-hearted of these was Respighi (1879–1936), whose series of glowing tone poems, *The Fountains of Rome, The Pines of Rome,* and so on, employ a brilliant, even vulgar, orchestral technique based largely on that of Rimsky-Korsakoff. His adaptation of some Rossini pieces for the Russian ballet *La boutique fantasque* (1919) brought him before a new, delighted public.

A few individual composers in other countries stand out because of their devotion to impressionistic ideals: notably Cyril Scott (*b.* 1879) in England, who wrote a number of slight piano pieces à la Debussy, as well as works in larger forms which did not deviate from the same style; and Charles Griffes (1884–1920) in America, whose promising career was cut off by an untimely early death. But in general the younger men were turning more and more from Debussyan impressionism toward the veristic triumphs being achieved in Paris by Stravinsky during the first decade of the new century.

THE PROBLEMATIC PRESENT

The Twentieth Century

THE AESTHETICS OF PRESENT-DAY ART

Brahms is a putrefying corpse, Beethoven a mummy, Schumann a homesick dog howling at the moon, and Elgar is paralyzed under the effects of the poison gas of Brahms and Wagner.

— Diaghilev (1872–1929)

AN ORTHODOX VIEW

"MODERNIST art to the layman seems transcendental: it is in fact the most materialistic art in the history of mankind. It springs from experimental study and analysis of nature, not from dreaming or fabrication. There is less imagination about it than about any of the schools preceding it. If a Picasso shows a flame of fancy, he juggles with the most inane and childish facts that he has seen and observed, not with allegorical conceptions or abstract philosophical musings or even historical personages. The modernists are of the earth, earthy, and in the same boat with the modern scientists."

This quotation, taken from the memoirs of a British artist, C. R. W. Nevinson, R.B.A., gives what may be called the orthodox artist's view of modern art. Phrased for quite another purpose, that of attacking what the writer feels to be a false conception of art, it offers striking proof of the validity of the argument on which this book is based. For if such a thesis is correct — that all the significant achievements in art have arisen out of the cultural conditions of the various historical epochs and have been shaped by their prevailing aesthetic and social ideals — we can expect from the period in which we live only the type of art described by Mr. Nevinson.

We are conscious enough that we do exist in an age of distrust, uncertainty, dissatisfaction, and disillusionment, an age almost entirely given over to technical experiments and developments that have resulted in a chaos of overorganization and an almost barbaric indifference to the individual as a human being. But nevertheless, somehow or other we have expected the artists to carry on as they did in the past, producing literature, painting, and music that springs, in Nevinson's phrase, from dreaming or fabrication. And when they do not, but show themselves of the same mettle as their brothers who have preceded them, in that they strive to embody in their art the intellectual, social, and economic ideals of their time, we are apt to misunderstand them and give vent to such diatribes as that quoted above.

SEEKING NEW WORLDS

The whole of modern art is an interesting and strangely misconceived phenomenon; it is likely to be looked on as a separate entity, something which has developed quite by itself, whereas it is simply a manifestation of a general historical trend. A just perception of the period in which any generation lives is notably difficult for that generation to achieve, and the present is no exception. But we are gradually coming to realize that, broadly speaking, the first quarter of the twentieth century is one of those periods in history when the spirit of mankind realizes that what has been done in the past is not sufficient and that a new wisdom and a new beauty must be sought elsewhere. During these years the book of one epoch — call it whatever we may, "Romantic," "Industrial," or merely "Nineteenth Century" — has been slowly closing, and that of another, opening. And what seems today so chaotic, tentative, and experimental in the life about us is probably an attempt, unco-ordinated but nevertheless positive, toward such a new and quite different world.

It is hardly necessary to point out the changes which are everywhere taking place in the economic, social, and moral phases of our life: a book of this kind is not the place to attempt their description. But we can suggest that they represent signs of a new era; whether or not a better one than the last, only time can tell: it is certain that it will be a different one. We have definitely passed over the ridge of one great epoch and are beginning to traverse the slopes of another; and in no single phase of activity has this feeling of consummation and fresh endeavor been so marked as in the arts.

A CULTURE-WEARY ART

Even before the turn of the century it became clear enough that, in the industrialized countries at least, there was little life left in the conventions of art. A clever writer on the works produced during this period has called them examples of a "culture-weary" art. This is an exceedingly apt description, for after the tremendous surges of the eighteenth and nineteenth centuries, the rich outpouring of the Baroque, Rococo, and Romantic periods, with the latter culminating in its phase of impressionism, a time of scepticism and exhaustion would seem to have been inevitable. The clear vision and strong faith in materialistic developments and scientific progress which marked the nineteenth century had its echo in the vital and vigorous art of the time: the works of men like Byron, Browning, Thackeray, Liszt, Wagner, Strauss — to mention but a few — could have come only out of a period when nature seemed completely delivered into the hands of man, when God was in his heaven and all was right with the world. Even the works of such impressionistic rebels against the materialism of the latter part of the century as Manet, Renoir, and Sisley carried on the century's ideals to their inevitable conclusion, for they tried to gain their illusions by merely changing the perspective and supplying atmosphere by the scientific analysis of color. We have seen how, in trying to answer the burning question of his day — "After Wagner, what?" — Debussy really carried the processes of Romantic decline to their logical end: *Pelléas et Mélisande* is in reality a *Tristan und Isolde* written with a more modern technique and in a style which replaces all its intense passion and burning eloquence by an even more Romantic (because never fully uttered) emotion.

ESSENCE RATHER THAN APPEARANCE

The men living at the turn of the century began to question the naturalistic and positivistic world which had seemed so permanent and final to their fathers; indeed, the very scientific researches of this materialistic generation provided one of the strongest causes for its downfall. Around 1910 a demand arose for some sort of attempt at an explanation of all these scientific phenomena which had accumulated, such as the breaking up of the atom, the evolution of new ideas concerning time and space, the results of research by means of the X ray and the microscope; something that would fit them together into a comprehensive conception of the world that was not based merely on outward appearances. As a result man began to turn away from nature's external aspects in an attempt to conceive and understand what lay behind them: to him the essence of things became of greater importance than their appearance; creative minds tried to make of art some sort of dream vision freed from materialistic and physical appearances.

THE EXPRESSIONISTS

Thus the so-called school of *expressionists* arose, a group of thinkers who attempted to get behind natural appearances in order to track down the causative phenomena which they felt to underlie visible things. Added to this was a dissatisfaction with the world as they saw it and a realization of the catastrophes inherent in its social impacts, together with a revolt against nineteenth-century falseness of morality and narrowness of opinion.

We have already noted the outstanding artists of this period. Among them was Cézanne, who spent almost his whole long career in an attempt to show that nature was not what she seemed when photographed by the camera lens, but was something which, after having been absorbed by the artist's eye, could be projected through his soul. He sought to find the form behind the content, the sphere behind a peach or an apple, the cone behind a pine tree, without, however, denying that peaches

Cliché Vizzavona

CONTES BARBARES, by Paul Gauguin, 1902

Kröller-Müller Foundation, Hoenderlo, Netherlands

THE SOWER — Arles — by Vincent van Gogh

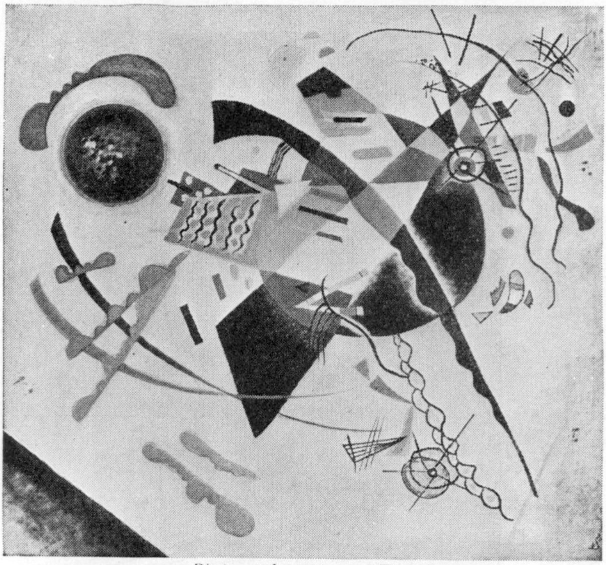

Photograph courtesy of The Museum of Modern Art

ABSTRACTION IN PAINTING

The Blue Circle, by Vassily Kandinsky
(Collection of Miss Katherine Dreier, New York)

or apples or pine trees were valid subjects for art. He believed also that the values of a landscape or a group of objects could best be represented on canvas through the manipulation of what he called "planes" — an intermingling of close and distant perspectives — and that these could be suggested to the eye by means of color sensations.

Van Gogh, another leader of the time, was able to get beneath the surface appearances and fix in vivid and startling color the wild ecstasies of his soul and the fire of his vision. Never has there been a better example of an artist to whom tradition meant little. As a discerning critic has said, Van Gogh's chief concern was that of spreading his curiously intense personality on canvas. Gauguin left a successful career as a member of civilized society and went to the South Seas in order to try to get a fuller understanding of nature and man in their primitive aspects. And Stravinsky the musician sought, at least in his earlier works, to penetrate the mask of nature and depict man in his pre-civilized and sophisticated estate.

Courtesy of The Brooklyn Museum

ABSTRACTION IN SCULPTURE

Recumbent Figure, by Sava Botzaris

THE ABSTRACTIONISTS IN GENERAL

Once these artists decided that they must be concerned with other than natural appearances, they did not hesitate to adopt methods of technique quite at variance with older practices, if in so doing they could secure the results they sought. And all sorts of groups and schools arose, most of them centering about the work of one or two leaders. The two unifying principles of these groups seemed to be their desire to express what they perceived with their minds rather than what they merely saw with their eyes or heard with their ears, and to abandon such ideas of the past as had come to be banal through their overuse during a period of centuries. These *abstractionists* were indeed culture-weary artists, trying to create a new objectivity, light, and form out of the chaos wrought by their abandoning of old ideals, to fashion a pure aesthetic reality that has a consistency entirely divorced from ordinary life. Lewisohn calls it *plastic license* and likens it to the writing of Gertrude Stein.

Courtesy of Lyonel Feininger

CHURCH IN THE MARKET PLACE, HALLE, 1930, by Feininger
(Moritzburg Museum, Halle)

CUBISTS

In painting, the *cubists* tried to carry forward Cézanne's methods of breaking natural forms into planes and building definite designs with them. They attempted to form a new kind of space relationship by "creating instead of imitating," [1] and so rejected all the accepted rules of construction, perspective, and the rest, moving around an object they attempted to depict, so as to show several points of vision at the same time. The synthetic results they achieved are familiar enough in the pictures of Picasso, Braque, Marc, and Feininger.

Futurism, an Italian movement launched after the birth of cubism in France, made a novel attempt to "dramatize simultaneously the

[1] This quotation is from the writings of an exponent of the school.

Photograph courtesy of The Museum of Modern Art

CUBISM — *The Painter and His Model,* by Pablo Picasso
(Private collection, New York)

diverse movements and aspects of an object." [2] One of the best of these is Picasso's picture which, by breaking up a violin into its component parts, expresses the texture of its wood, inside and out.

DADAISTS

Both these movements came before the World War. A third, *Dadaism,* was a humorous and largely futilitarian gesture against the useless sacrifices of the War years; [3] it tried, by assuming a mood of utter nihilism, to upset the whole artistic applecart, as one critic has well said. All sorts of absurdities were perpetrated, not only in painting but in music and

[2] This quotation is from the writings of an exponent of the school.

[3] Someone has called Dadaism an aesthetic protest on a social basis, in the guise of a cabaret attitude.

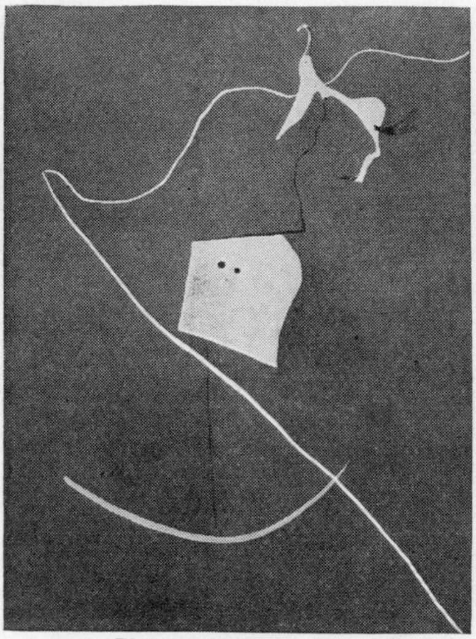

Photograph courtesy of The Museum of Modern Art

SURREALISM — *The Horse* by Joan Miro
(Collection of Mrs. Charles Russell, Jr., New York)

literature as well: thermometers, clockwork, scraps of rubbish, and pieces of newspaper were glued onto abstract paintings. But Dadaism took itself so frivolously that it laughed itself to death, fortunately.

NEO-PLASTICISTS

Neo-plasticism decided that art was a matter of simplified designs of rectangles, horizontal and perpendicular lines; it is one of the forms of pure abstraction, in which the artist makes no attempt to attain natural forms. *Purism*, on the other hand, is one of the near-abstract isms, transforming objects into abstract or nearly abstract forms.

SURREALISTS

Inspired by postwar developments, especially the doctrines of the Viennese psychologist, Dr. Freud, as to our subconscious existence, was *surrealism*, which, like so many of these painting movements, has strongly

Courtesy of Sam Lewisohn

GIRL'S HEAD by Georges Rouault
(From the Lewisohn collection)

affected the other arts. Painting in bright colors, with careful attention to detail, men like Salvador Dali draw their motives from dream-consciousness and work them out in terms of nightmares. Miro, another important surrealist, abjures natural forms and seeks to be as largely interested in design as in dreams. Klee, the German exponent of this school, tries to combine in his pictures the ideas of psychoanalysis and those received from our knowledge of primitive man; they can be understood, his apologists insist, only by a consciousness which embraces the successive worlds of the past and the vast heritage of all that has gone before. Which is something of an order!

These are only some of the various attempts made by modern artists to rebuild the scheme of things, so rudely shattered to bits during the last years of the nineteenth century and the first of the twentieth century. Not all these artists have been concerned with the generalities of abstraction and the attempt simply to mirror the chaos of the spirit of the times. There have been others who have tried to transform society by directing their shafts against the horrors of machinery and civilization,

THE DANCE, oil, 1909–1910, by Henri Matisse
(Collection of Walter P. Chrysler, Jr., New York)

" Expression for me is not to be found in the passion which blazes forth from a face or is made evident by some violent gesture. It is in the whole disposition of my picture — everything plays its part. Composition is the art of arranging, in a decorative manner, the various elements at the painter's disposal for the expression of his feelings."

— Matisse

combining the new technique with vital social criticism. These are the men of *verismo*, of the *Neue Sächlichkeit*, of *realism*. Painters like Max Beckmann, Dix, Grosz, and Georges Rouault have carried on the traditions of the great Daumier and Goya in presenting in their works a terrifying reflection of the desolation and decay of our age, a reflection which is the more effective because it employs modernistic techniques.

A MODERNISTIC CREDO

Perhaps never before in history have the ideals of a single art so dominated the aesthetic outlook of a whole period; ever since the time of the impressionists painting seems to have been the one vital art capable of striking out on new paths for itself, and the theories and arguments of the painters of the *école de Paris* have exercised a tremendous influence on modern literature, architecture, sculpture, and even music. Gradually there has arisen for all the arts a sort of general modernistic credo as to ideals and purposes, a credo that has been largely dictated by these Parisian painters and has been given provocative form by their literary ally, Jean Cocteau. Briefly stated, its ideals are these:

1. The rejection of what is called " subjective emotion " as a basis for art, the idea that " feeling " or personal experience has a place in art (This went so far in extreme cases, as in some of Picasso's paintings and Stravinsky's music, as to bar emotion of any kind.)

2. The abhorrence of what may be called " rhetoric," that is, the doing of a thing supremely well for the joy arising out of that doing; and a consequent demand for simplicity, terseness, and brutality of expression

3. The abjurance of frank, literal, and even " programmatic " representation and the insistence that art is a mere matter of representing abstract patterns, something that exists as an absolute thing in itself rather than as a means for transmuting experiences or feelings, suggesting ideas, or picturing definite objects (Schönberg, one of the leading exponents of this ideal in music, rejoiced in 1912 over the " signs that even other arts which are apparently more closely connected with matters of theme are reaching a point where they will overcome their faith in the supreme power of the understanding and the consciousness . . . ; those who ask for a text or thematic content will soon have asked their last.")

A COUNTERREACTION

All these obviously were simply reactions against the ideals of Romanticism and the metaphysical outlook which had been fastened on the world during the nineteenth century. It is likewise obvious that although the idea of pausing and taking stock was a wholesome one — for only through such means can any progress be made in art — the reaction against Romanticism was too severe.

It is significant that there has already been some reaction, in turn, against the severity of this absolutist philosophy. Artists in all fields are again favoring literary motives, no doubt due, in part, to the inevitable pull on their minds of the new ideologies that permeate every other sphere of life today. For example, the Czech woman composer, Viteslava

Kapralova, describes her *Military Symphonietta,* produced in 1928, as " not an appeal for war but an appeal for a conscious defensive attitude, mobilizing psychical feelings and enthusiasm for the preservation of national independence." Another composer seeks, so he says, " to acknowledge and greet the ideals of the generation to which he belongs, a new order founded on values of universal significance." Others see in their art a means of commenting on social problems or depicting spiritual conflict.

THREE SIMULTANEOUS STRATA OF THOUGHT

All these aesthetic problems which now seem so confusing would be greatly simplified if it were possible to confine the processes of artistic development in watertight compartments and not have them interflow, as do all other changes in mankind's mental and spiritual make-up. Our perception of even the essential nature (not to speak of the values) of these phases of art is obscured by the fact that at any given time at least three strata of activity are being worked simultaneously.

There are the best of the older practitioners, who continue to use their familiar technique, sometimes with fresh intimations of old beauty; there is a smaller class of art workers who have found, or are in process of finding, some equation between the old and the new technique, perhaps not much more than an accommodation, or something in the nature of a not very stable compound which is likely to resolve into its disparate constituents; and the class of out-and-out extremists, who, in intention at least, have thrown over all the old methods and ideals.

We have given ample illustrations of these conditions during our survey of history, although it is natural that the changes of the past appear to us much less like upheavals than those in the midst of which we live and which we must attempt to understand. If we could see with the eyes and hear with the ears of the people of three centuries ago, it is certain that we should experience much the same sense of bewilderment, or even of frustration, that many feel today. Around about 1600, for example, polyphony was declining, and the individualistic freedom of the voice was arising, though not for the first time (we remember troubadour minstrelsy), but the change was certainly more drastic. It is possible, with a little use of the imagination, to conceive the attitude of those to whom polyphony was the natural language of music and the new operatic pretensions a mere vanity — the wrong-track perverseness of froward fantasists.

We appear to be passing through a like period at present. This is said without any attempt, for the moment, to judge values: those of the revolution three centuries ago may comfortably be estimated, for it is easy to be wise so long after the event. But yet we do not argue that all judgment on the art of today should be suspended; that way lies the negation of progress, which, after all, is determined as much by the artists' education of the public as it is by the public's choice among the offerings of the artists.

All that it seems worth while to urge is that such revolution, more or less violent and prolonged, is no new factor in art. The period of its prolongation may be influenced by the general conditions of the world; so that, whilst former artistic changes of a major kind appear to have come about in a few years, and with the minimum of destructiveness, the present artistic ferments in the wild world we know should not be expected to settle into stability in one generation.

AN EMBARRASSMENT OF MEANS

If we think around present-day problems as widely as possible, we shall note factors and symptoms which complicate them and tend to make us more sympathetic toward artists in every sphere of work. Leaving aside the intricate problems of the other arts and concentrating on those in which we are particularly interested, we cannot help realizing how the nineteenth century opened up a dazzling array of new means and connotations — the fertilizing of music by poetry and the interrelation of the arts in general; the intoxicating increase in the powers of the orchestra, the supreme means of musical expression; the rise of so many multicolored nationalisms, all capable of exciting representation; the marvelous subtlety of chromatic harmony developing through Chopin, Wagner, and

Debussy. Any one of these elements would open the gates of a new heaven to a composer; the combination of them all was overpowering. In truth, this was a new golden age of opportunity, with the riches of which the listener of today is still surfeited. It is little wonder that he finds it difficult to attune ear and spirit to the starker, more sparely athletic and ascetic offerings of the new age — one whose art he cannot be blamed for reckoning, in most part, of a leaden, rather than a golden, hue. It seems clear that some transmuting process of time must be awaited before the gold standard can be reattained.

TECHNICAL USAGES OF THE NEW MUSIC

Before attempting anything in the way of a description of these developments as they affect music, we may well inquire just what technical changes have taken place in the art as the result of these new ideals. We have intimated, in the section on Debussy, what the logical end of his new harmonic and melodic usages must be — a complete abolition of the agelong antithesis between consonance and dissonance. It is this trend which so completely revolutionized modern practice and resulted in the evolution of what have come to be known as *polytonality* and *atonality*. The practice of polytonality can be noted first in Stravinsky's scores, though it had appeared tentatively long before his time (for example, at the very end of Strauss's *Zarathustra*). It consists in the simultaneous use of more than one key at a time, as for example in *Petrouchka*, where the opening chords of the scene in Petrouchka's apartment use certain elements from both the keys of C and F sharp major. *Atonality* literally means "no key"; in practice, it appears to imply the removal of any feeling of the dominance of tonality and is best exemplified in the music of Schönberg and his disciple, Berg. In addition to these, certain new tenets concerning the make-up of melody and demands for far-reaching reforms in rhythmic and formal devices have arisen, but these are much more vague in theory and practice than the new harmonic dictates. The attempt at rhythmic atheism has on the whole opened up a vista thus far disappointing, in that the extreme complication brought about by the use of elaborateness in many parts at once results in a dulling of piquances which the more spacious and leisurely combinations enabled one to apprehend easily and enjoy thoroughly.[4]

THE DIFFICULTY OF HEARING ATONALLY

Perhaps the chief technical factor which stands in the way of immediate understanding or enjoyment (for one can understand without being able to enjoy) is the absence of fixed key centers, always previously a kind of solar comfort to the musical universe. Atonality and polytonality have been supported by an imposing body of theory, which is supposed to show that the whole movement is a logical one, merely pushing forward tonal bounds once presumed fixed forever. The chief difficulty, both for composers and for listeners, when the bounds are thrown down in all directions at once — key, harmony, rhythm, melody, form — is found to be that however logical the process of unified advance may seem, the composers are unable to use all the new-shaped elements at once, and the listeners appear to be unable to take in more than one or two

[4] It is interesting to see what Ernest Bloch, one of the best thinkers on the subject of music, has to say regarding atonality:

"I am convinced that the theory of atonalism in itself is an anomaly where genuine music is concerned — a theory, frankly, as impractical as it is fundamentally stupid. To imply that a twelve-tone scale is a collection of intervals with no natural gravitation toward tonal centers, and that this complete neutralization of melodic laws will have a creative result, is to emasculate musical thought and render it completely fruitless.

"That new methods of expressing eternal principles are certain to arise and irresistibly to develop is a thing so obvious that to dwell upon it would be a truism. But nothing is more emblematic of the destructive agencies involved in a machine age, which as yet has formulated no adequate morality, than this attempt to write counterpoint as if melody too were an emanation of machines, as lifeless and will-less as they, and as completely isolated from all that concerns human nature. Indeed I do not think that a really vigorous society could have been so taken with this theory and its theoretical possibilities as ours has been — especially in Europe. The same tolerance of compromise, avoidance of difficult issues which eventually must be faced from the standpoint of basic necessities, such as the will to live, to breathe, to act with impulse and freedom — this palsy affects the peoples of the world, and reveals itself in the companion manifestation of their decadent and unvocal music."

— *The New York Times*

of them at a time. Thus, between the new combinations of inabilities, the old communication between artist and public, that never before broadly failed, has for the most part broken down completely, so that it would be idle to deny that for ninety per cent of the faithful public who call themselves " music lovers " the new developments mean nothing: the music reaches neither intellect nor heart.

Now, we should beware of too dogmatic an insistence on the latter element, in its simplest meaning. In order to understand the position of modernism with full sympathy, it is well to remember the immensely flamboyant, full-flavored, perhaps overgrown, nineteenth century, in which every form of Romanticism grew large and lush, so that even the meanest-brained or least aesthetically cultured listener could wallow (a word not spared by modernists). That is not to argue that the lushness of Romance was all a mistake; it is merely to realize the mind of the modernist as he contemplates that Gargantuan century of emotional release, and to agree, with him, that " it can never happen again." What, then, is to happen instead? There comes the parting of the ways between the bulk of modernist composers and the bulk of the public; but it would be a pity to assume that the former are the servants and the latter necessarily the masters. He would be rash who should presume that the public, or any slice of it, is ever likely to be all-wise, a satisfactory giver or guardian of the laws of art.

A SIMULTANEOUS ADVANCE ON ALL FRONTS

What the listener may well do is to realize the immense difficulty of composers' advancing triumphantly on so many fronts at once, and to seek for the signs of fruitful evolution rather than those of fretful revolution. There are two considerations which seem as likely as any to be useful guides in such a search: first, that great composers of the past never sought to make radical changes in many departments of their art; and second, that the most revolutionary composers have never been recognized in after-ages as the greatest. Monteverdi was a greater innovator than Bach, but who would claim him as an equally grand composer?

His innovations were necessary and enthusiastically to be welcomed; but the law of artistic life seems to decree that the composer cannot have it both ways: he must either risk his life in strong revolution or work it out in more peaceful and much gentler evolutions. In an age impatient of laws, whether those of nature, art, or man, it is salutary to seek those which time appears to have demonstrated as valid. This is certainly one of them.

There are far too many possibilities in the suggested revolutions of modernism to be worked out in a generation or, perhaps, even in a century. Composers who seek to wield all the new weapons at once are likely to become entangled, and so fail in communication, the operative end of their striving. If there were any sound assurance which of the elements — whether the new harmony, melody, rhythm, or form — was the best on which to concentrate, the artistic situation would be clarified, and the probability of establishing sure communication between artist and public would be far brighter. But no one knows which path should be chosen; and even those who seek one path are likely to fail, because they cannot solve the problem of equating newness in that path with a more conservative procedure, based on the usages of the past, in the others.

It was altogether too rash for the early leaders in this transition art to assert that any element whatever in the older musical cosmos had been exhausted or worked out. In various periods some one element that had reached its zenith has been temporarily dropped; but not forever. Madrigalian complexity (which, it should be remembered, was as much rhythmic as melodic, in the windings of polyphony), having come to its glorious height, was replaced by fresh elements which promised, and provided, new worlds for composers to conquer. Bach, in the process of the years, raised another peak of polyphony, while caring little for the orchestral delights which his successors were to explore and glorify. Where is that polyphony now? As magnificent and as fresh as ever, in Bach's music. But, considered as an element in modernism, has it any value? Judging from present practice alone, with modern harmonic connotations, very little; but who shall say that another great development in polyphony is impossible? Our difficulty is, on the one hand, to forget Palestrinian or Bachian methods, and, on the other, to cast the imagination forward to some new synthesis of polyphony with harmony, as yet unrealized.

Thus ever present is the problem of *selection*, a conscious responsibility for the composer, which was never, apparently, a shackle to the men of old times, but is too rarely solved by those of today. While the latter are faced by an enormously greater complexity of possible materials, they have (at least most of them) no dominating, driving force which would keep them, single-minded, on an irresistible course. The cynic will observe, " What it really boils down to is that there is a shortage of geniuses "; to that we must assent. But it would not be fair to assume that this whole problem could be settled by a genius, unless we define that too-loosely-used word very closely.

What is wanted is not genius alone — which is always rare in every age and art — but a greater sense of direction in the minds of artists in general; and it is perhaps unreasonable to expect any sudden upthrust of such a spirit, just as it is to envision a sudden conversion of the world mind to the basic qualities which, all free men agree, alone promise the continuance of a civilized life.

THE IMPACT OF STRAVINSKY

Then felt I like some watcher of the skies
When a new planet swims into his ken;
Or like stout Cortes when with eagle eyes
He star'd at the Pacific — and all his men
Look'd at each other with a wild surmise.

— Keats: " On First Looking into Chapman's Homer "

A NEW INDIVIDUALITY DEVELOPS

THERE is an immense gap in communication which is mentally felt by listeners when they compare their understanding of composers of the last century — of, say, Brahms and Wagner — with that of the modernists. We have shown the reasons for this gap and have explained

STRAVINSKY
(From a drawing by Picasso)

why the new art must remain difficult, at least until our eyes and ears and minds become better acclimated. There is one composer, Igor Stravinsky, who serves as an admirable bridge between these two territories, for he began, with exciting freshness, in the tradition of Russian pictorial nationalism, and it was not until his later years that he finally arrived, full-armed, in the camp of the moderns. In between are all sorts of varied and interesting combinations of the two styles.

Born in 1882, Stravinsky received most of his training under Rimsky-Korsakoff, and it is natural that his early works should fall into his master's modes of thought. When he was twenty-three he wrote a symphony which makes use of some folk-song material much in the Rimsky-Borodin-Glazunov tradition. A work written a few years later, *Fireworks*, adds suggestions of yet another influence, that of Dukas and his *L'apprenti sorcier*. But it was not until the ballet *The Firebird*, written in 1910, that Stravinsky's own individuality began to crystallize out of all these influences working so strongly on his impressible mind. There are still two ghosts which hover over the pages of this score, and pretty solid ghosts, too — those of Rimsky-Korsakoff and Debussy; and the music set to the various scenes of this Russian fairy tale changes abruptly from old to new and back again. But certain characteristics of the idiom we have come to know as Stravinsky's are here apparent, especially the arrangement of rhythms into ingenious patterns and the use of constantly clashing chord members and chord combinations.

TWO LONELY MASTERPIECES

His next two works, also written for the Russian Ballet, *Petrouchka* in 1912 and *Le sacre du printemps* (*The Rite of Spring*) in 1913, carry these tendencies to a logical and very effective climax. In addition, they make striking use of that device which earlier composers had hinted at and which later became almost a mannerism with Stravinsky — that simultaneous use of several tonalities, which we have described in another place. There are also clever manipulations (after Debussy's habit) of the running of constituent chord members in parallel lines, an elaboration of the practice of the ancient organum.

But these two works are much more than mere adaptations and developments of the work of other composers: they have a very definite physiognomy of their own and are the first unified works of art to be evolved from the experiments in the new style. In fact, they remain strangely isolated and lonely masterpieces. Both of them deal, in a characteristic Russian manner, with fantastic subjects beyond ordinary experience. The puppet Petrouchka looks at life with the detached observation of the cynic and shows the comedic existence which the man-machine leads in a largely disinterested world. *The Rite of Spring* suggests the primitive worship of our ancient ancestors and attempts to project the mind of twentieth-century man back into the dark, unexplored realms of prehistory. It raises to a higher power than any other music ever written that nervous excitement and emotional tension through rhythm which so many followers of Stravinsky have tried in vain to imitate. Its dependence on rhythmic pattern complexity suggests the feats of savages in remembering elaborate drum patterns and using them for the communication of excitement. This remarkable tour de force and veristic triumph has become an accepted classic. It is not difficult to imagine the tremendous enthusiasm it aroused at the time of its first production in Paris, just before the War of 1914–1918.

INFERTILE EXPERIMENTS

The Rite of Spring represents Stravinsky at the height of his powers; in it he seems to have said everything vital he had to say, and in his later works he reminds us of Richard Strauss's decline, in his almost entirely consistent progressive deterioration of imaginative control. Since Stravinsky lived in the midst of the exciting and stimulating argumentative artistic milieu of Paris, it was natural that he should be caught up in the sweep of the new absolutist currents then surging so strongly there. His autobiography shows how he became more and more indoctrinated with the theories of his literary and painter friends and how they strongly affected his aims in composition. This, coupled with the fact that after the War he was completely cut off from any connection with his native Russia, which up to that time had been a vital factor in his work, gives his later music a tentative, experimental character that is quite in opposition to his earlier trend.

He has experimented with one thing after another — new dramatic forms, different types of unusual instrumentation, the invocation of the spirits of older composers and periods, among them Bach, Tchaikovsky, Pergolesi, and Handel; he has turned to the lapidary art of the Greeks as well as to the jazz of America, without producing a single work, in a quarter century, that has held its place in the repertory of ballet, orchestral, or chamber music. Nor have other composers been able to enter into the land discovered by this musical Moses; they have copied his rhythms but missed his runes, imitated his dissonances, and provided thereby not stimulation but merely distraction, displeasure, or utter boredom.

Never has there been so great a disappointment in music. The fires that flared up with such fierce promise when fed with the broken fagots of the older style have, in *The Wedding, The Tale of the Soldier, Oedipus Rex, Symphonies of Wind Instruments* (in which the composer strives to dispense with emotional impressions altogether), and in most of his other post-*Rite* works, died down to a feeble glow; and in his latest ballet, *The Card Table,* we find merely the cold ashes of technique. It would seem that once Stravinsky had emancipated himself from the past, he had no further interest in life; it may be, as some critics insist, that the advance in technical progress made through his modernistic experiments has been worth the effort. But his early admirers would readily trade all these neoclassic miscegenations for one stunning work of the caliber of *Petrouchka* or *The Rite.*

LATER DEVELOPMENTS IN FRANCE

We have told, in the section entitled "The Aftermath," how the new spirit of Stravinskyan revolt was fomented in France by the Parisian artists gathering in the congenial prewar atmosphere of boulevard, café, and studio. There were groupings and regroupings (rather as in French politics); the so-called Group of Six (Auric, Durey, Honegger, Milhaud, Poulenc, and Tailleferre, the last a woman composer) was much discussed; but it showed less unanimity in group motivation than did the Russian "Five," and only Poulenc, Milhaud, and Honegger emerged as personalities, the first remaining a deft manipulator of tiny, mostly humorous or satirical, ideas, and the second (*b.* 1892), as an often freakish manipulator of polytonality in stage works (including the ballet *Le train bleu* and a sacred representation, *L'annonce faite à Marie,* which shows Milhaud in a more solid, more rewarding vein).

Honegger (*b.* 1892, of Swiss origin) seems to have got free, more surely than the rest, from this defiant, *épater le bourgeois* spirit that marred so much work of this time. Though he does not often soothe the ear so sweetly as in his *Pastorale d'Été,* he has produced in the difficult choral sphere one work at least, *Le roi David,* which, though unequal in style and values, decorates suggestively if scrappily the somewhat dilapidated mansion of oratorio. His *Horace Victorieux* has some of the clear-cut strength of the best French classical spirit.

FRANCIS POULENC

ARTHUR HONEGGER

DARIUS MILHAUD

For the rest, France has continued to produce "sixth parts" of composers rather than "Sixes" — a host of craftsmen who are adding their useful bricks to the modernistic city, without any very obvious town planning; whose contributions have not so far allowed them to shine out as much more than respectable artisans. Prominent members of this latest *jeune France* group are Olivier Messaien, Ives Baudrier, Daniel Lesur, André Jolivet, and Jean Françaix, all of them well-equipped and hard-working musicians. The last named is already represented by several large-scale instrumental works.

ITALIAN CONTEMPORARIES

The little band of modernist Italian composers more or less influenced by Stravinsky — they are few, for reasons connected with the dominance of opera, which we have already suggested — includes Casella (*b.* 1883), Malipiero (*b.* 1882), and Pizzetti (*b.* 1880). These all have an air of rather aristocratic detachment, as might be expected in a land so little excited about purely orchestral music. Their modernism is chiefly notable in their nonoperatic works; Pizzetti may be looked on as a lonely pathmaker in a conception of opera far removed from the lush splendors of Puccini with his high-light arias. Pizzetti makes more use of the chorus, fastidiously binds libretto and music, seeks continuity instead of broken-up sections, and spices his harmony, without attempting to shock. He is an eclectic whose music is always sure in its formal shaping and apt to be austere in idiom, though the Romantic spirit shines out, as in his *Trio* (1925).

Malipiero, who is interested in the development of a vigorous Italian style, finds even subtler effects, seeking for a modern interpretation of the spirit of the earliest operas and sometimes so finely drawing his music that it becomes thin and less congenial than Pizzetti's. Though when, as all Italians must, he "drops into melody," as Dickens's Mr. Wegg did into poetry, one easily remembers the influence of that last of the great operatic line, Puccini; but Malipiero does not always, alas, imitate him at his best. Malipiero has not found it easy, either, to reconcile the impressionistic style (works in this vein are *Impressions of Spring* and the song cycle *The Italian Seasons*) with modernism; and, as he lacks the gusto of a Respighi, his work has not endeared him to a very large public.

Casella is a learned man who has never quite succeeded in giving a convincing personal trend to his cleverness. A touch of humor is welcome; Casella's wit is quite famous, but his music obstinately fails to turn up in general orchestral programs. In humor perhaps the *Serenade* for violin, cello, clarinet, bassoon, and trumpet stands as high as anything; and there are some piquant ballets (*The Jar*, for example). The *Serenade* is the sort of music that brings the composer nearest to the hearer who is rather shy of modernism but is willing to put away his memories of Mozartean or Tchaikovskyan serenading. Casella's weaker side — his odd assortment of style and impulses — is shown in his violin concerto.

SCHÖNBERG AND HIS SCHOOL

When one observes well, things gradually become obscure. One begins to realize that one is not destined only not to guess the future (only to delineate it!) but also, to forget the past, already set forth. One wins a feeling of the most faithful carrying out of one's duty when, although wishing otherwise, one does not do what appeared holy in the past and begins quietly to rejoice over one's blindness with seeing eyes.

— Schönberg, translated by J. D. Bohm

THE GREAT MAN OF MODERN MUSIC

THE great name in modernism, in so far as music is concerned, is that of Arnold Schönberg (*b.* 1874), who, more than any other single composer, even Stravinsky, has succeeded in evolving a set of theories to explain the intellectual elements which had crept into the new neoclassic style. A man of strong Romantic tendencies, he possessed likewise an exceptional mind; he felt that in his *Verklärte Nacht*, *Gurrelieder*, and *Pelléas et Mélisande* he had developed the chromatic style of Wagner to the furthest point possible. He had to

Acme Newspictures, Inc.

ARNOLD SCHÖNBERG

strike out, as one of his biographers [5] says, in an entirely new direction, which, he decided, must be that of classic construction through the employment of strict forms.

And so there followed, after the earlier works, a series belonging to what is called his middle period, devoted completely to ingenious and intricate disciplining of his style along these new lines; he used small instrumental forces — the string quartet and the chamber orchestra — in place of the huge apparatus demanded by his *Gurrelieder*; [6] he tried

[5] Egon Wellesz: *Arnold Schönberg*. Leipzig, 1921; London, 1925.

[6] This work may be said to represent the "grand finale" of the whole Wagnerian, post-Romantic era; it was first performed, with great success, in Vienna in 1913, and calls for five solo singers, three four-part male choruses, one eight-part mixed chorus, a narrator, and an orchestra of four flutes, four piccolos, three oboes, two English horns, three clarinets in A, two E-flat clarinets, two bass clarinets, three bassoons and two contra bassoons, ten horns, four Wagner tubas, six trumpets and one bass trum-

to telescope the classical four-movement architectural scheme into one single movement (the *D Minor Quartet*, 1905, and the *Kammersinfonie*, 1906) and to develop his thematic structure somewhat along Franckian lines by transforming and varying, with a fiendishly involved technique, a few generating themes. Later on, in his second quartet, in F sharp minor (1908), he added a voice part in the manner of Mahler, and arrived, in the last movement, at an almost completely atonal expression, abjuring everything resembling what had hitherto been considered a melody.

SCHÖNBERG'S MIDDLE PERIOD

The works of 1909 to 1913 — the three piano pieces of Op. 11; the five orchestral pieces, Op. 16; the six little piano pieces, Op. 19; and *Die glückliche Hand* (*The Lucky Hand*), a concentrated musical drama written just before the war, at a time when Stravinsky was finishing *The Rite of Spring* — show Schönberg coming to final grips with the intricate problems of his slowly developing "expressionistic" style.[7] They are progressively more intense in their negation of Romanticism and their discarding of the formal principles derived from fixed tonality; gradually their composer is settling into his highly concentrated neoclassic idiom. A very suggestive side light on this period of Schönberg's life is the fact that for several years previous to the time he started to write his *Treatise on Harmony*, a work in which his theories are carefully set down in textbook fashion, he practiced the art of painting, an art in which there was, in the circles of the so-called Expressionist School, plenty of opportunity for the discussion of those neoclassic, anti-Romantic ideals which were favored by the composer.

---

pet, one alto trombone, four tenor trombones, one bass trombone, one contra-bass trombone, one contra-bass tuba, six kettledrums, one tenor drum, one side drum, one bass drum, cymbals, one triangle, one glockenspiel, one tam-tam, one xylophone, one rattle, some large iron chains, four harps, one celesta, and an enlarged body of strings. No wonder it is seldom performed!

[7] This term has been generally adopted to signify art which strives to express inner experience rather than impressions of the outer world. It was first adopted by a group of painters about 1912.

He was a close friend of the painter Vassily Kandinsky, one of the editors of a review which had as its policy the clarification of the absolutist philosophy of art; and he said that the inspiration for certain of his orchestral works first came to him as visual impressions in form and color. Thus the painters' abandonment of the representation of fixed objects had its parallel in Schönberg's rejection of the older principles of tonality. But unfortunately it was his personal and temperamental inclination to rely with an inflexibly Germanic stolidity on his painfully and self-consciously evolved theories. It is this influence, artistically so deadly, that hangs like a pall over all his later music.

A STILL NEWER DEVICE

The work which marks the end of Schönberg's experimental middle period is *Pierrot Lunaire*, a set of twenty-one songs, each of them differently orchestrated and possessing a different structural form; the scoring is for reciting (blended speaking-singing) voice, piano, flute, piccolo, clarinet, bass clarinet, violin, viola, and cello. In this he created a work which in form, content, and style exceeded anything he had done up to that time. For the first time this experimental music seems to come to life and not be merely the embodiment of the composer's theories. And in it we have a hint, in the incessant repetition of certain main themes, of the means he finally adopted in trying to solve the problem of giving some sort of unity and coherence to a type of writing broken loose from its former moorings.

This device is that of basing each piece, not on a repeated theme, but on what he called a *Tonreihe* — an arrangement in some arbitrary order of the twelve notes of the chromatic scale. These note patterns could be inverted and both the original and the inverted forms reversed, thus giving four variants of each pattern. In this device the composer's mechanistic, intellectualized, non-Romantic style is carried to its ultimate conclusion: the compositions written in this latest period, their closely woven, contrapuntal parts based on these *Tonreihen* (the four orchestral pieces, Op. 22; the five piano pieces, Op. 23; and the *Serenade*,

Op. 24), are, even more than their forebears, "paper" music, their intricacies and dissonances being established intellectually and incapable of being appreciated by the normal ear.

SCHÖNBERG'S PRESENT-DAY POSITION

There can be little doubt that Schönberg is a great man — far greater because of his inquiring mind than because of the music it has produced. But his theories seem to have resulted in a world of meaning which the average music lover, no matter how keen-eared he may be, cannot enter. There is no clue whatever for him in the shoots of tone and bits of color of the later Schönberg works. He cannot help feeling that the music is being made, on paper, with immense mathematical labor; but what does it mean? The composer, with all his explanations, does not succeed in telling us, beyond saying that the "reality or meaning of music has nothing to do with its sentiments, its expression, its sonority, its performance or atmosphere: the one thing that matters is the proportion between the sounds — something one feels rather than understands."

Yes, but if the mass of linear counterpoint (that is, counterpoint without any harmonic association to stabilize it and make it intelligible), atonal tone groups, manipulated architectural forms, and cruel jabs of orchestral color — if all these are so complicated and overelaborate that we cannot apperceive them — what value have they in such an art of communication as music? Finding more and more subtle proportions may be an absorbing pursuit for the composer, but it does not help the listener grasp the content of his thought.

There are many who sincerely admire Schönberg for his courage, even though they cannot accept his music. On the first page of his treatise stands the quotation: "The laws of Nature manifested in a man of genius are but the laws of the men of the future." Which statement, of course, has been proved true again and again; but whether Schönberg is the man of genius, and his laws the laws of nature, only time can decide. Up to the present, there seems to be considerable doubt on the part of a large number of people.

A MORE HUMANE PUPIL

Schönberg has had some notable pupils and disciples — Berg, Von Webern, Wellesz, Křenek, and others; but only one, Berg (who died in 1936, just over fifty years old), seems to have strengthened, for average consumption, some of the traits of his master with a keener sense of recognizable form and human feeling. He allowed himself a much greater degree of impassioned utterance than most of his contemporaries; and it is this element, perhaps as much as anything, that makes us wish he had lived longer so that he might have leavened the whole modernist mentality with a much-needed humanity. His best-known work is his opera *Wozzeck*, a grim, realistic work in fifteen scenes, each of which is in a different form — suite, rhapsody, passacaglia, march, and so on. The remarkable twist which he gives to this work by his formal scheme is an instance of ingenuity in the combination of elements that might seem incompatible. We have mentioned, as one of the modernist's problems, that of thinking and using freshly the various elements of melody, harmony, rhythm, and form. Berg does not seek to invent new forms but to employ old ones in the new setting of opera.

For his libretto Berg went to Büchner, one of the typical poets of the early nineteenth century, when many of the wilder Romantic spirits found part of their fulfillment in more or less revolutionary activities, social and artistic. The choice of a subject involving cruelty and degradation shows Berg to be closely linked with the veristic spirit of the late nineteenth century (as, for instance, in Zola), but in an intensified form, characteristic of twentieth-century heartlessness.

In yet another operatic work, *Lulu*, the scoring of which he did not live to complete, Berg seems to have deserted the road marked out by Schönberg and to have made a definite compromise with tonality, modifying his twelve-tone system. His last work, a violin concerto, shows him still more successfully escaping from the Schönberg theories in that he is able to combine his twelve-note system [8] with such Romantic material as a folk song and a Bach chorale.

[8] The *Tonreihe* used here is: G, B flat, D, F sharp, A, C, E, G sharp, B, C sharp, E flat, and F.

Berg sought also a freer use of melody in these operas, employing a style of writing that is akin to speech; but he had not found how to add all the other elements that make such melody significant — its accompaniment and harmonization; the latter constantly fell behind his vivid dramatic sense and his swiftness of speech. Nor, in the opinion of many, had he discovered the power of gentleness, in contrast to intensity.

In noticing such works as these of Berg's, which so far have few peers in modern music, we are again impressed with the immense difficulties confronting the modernist composer in the evolution of the new means for which he seeks. Take, for instance, the one element of speech-song which Berg carried so much further than Wagner, in this matter working clearly on the theories of his master Schönberg. We cannot even tell whether any compromise is possible between speech and song at the level for which these composers aim.

DIVERSE FOLLOWERS

The second most notable pupil of Schönberg's is Anton von Webern (*b.* 1883), whose short pieces have astonished listeners as much by their extraordinary brevity as by their bizarre quality. His five pieces for orchestra about the doings of children, timed by the stop watch, occupy respectively twenty, twenty-three, a hundred, thirty, and eighty seconds. In pursuit of what appears to be an obsession for extreme brevity, he gives out the various notes of a melody to different instruments. Ernst Křenek (*b.* 1900) has become widely known through his opera about a jazz-band leader, *Jonny spielt auf* (1927). An atonal opera, *Karl V*, is sterner stuff, less likely to appeal to those who find amusing a certain amount of satire on their gods. Kurt Weill (*b.* 1900) wrote humorous skits; also *The Rise and Fall of the City Mahagonny* and the much better known *Drei Groschen Oper*, a distant descendant of *The Beggar's Opera* of 1728, retaining some of the characters from that work (which was itself a satire).

This revival of a long-forgotten subject reminds us that the art problems of former ages are now recurring in an intensified form. Some elements of style may be workable no further; others may be. Surely, much of what is being propounded today will have to be scrapped, as composers two and a half centuries ago had to scrap some of the new ideas that had been propounded around 1600. And what of our ears — can they grow up to the new world of speech-song, of new forms in opera, of no keys, or of all keys together?

THE MUSICAL UTILITARIAN

In strong contrast to Schönberg, the theorist, stands Hindemith, the efficient pragmatic. He has based his astonishingly copious career as a composer on a solid foundation of professional experience: he has not hesitated to perform any musical task that came to his attention, under all sorts of conditions. There have been no ivory dreaming towers for him; he seems always to have been busy in the orchestral pit or on the concert platform. He has a sensible belief that music should serve its own day and generation and not bother too much about the next; so we find that his compositions are immensely busy, with few periods of rest or even repose. He has written cantatas, oratorios, chamber music, orchestral music, concertos, and vocal music, together with a quantity of "practical music" in workable combinations for a few players.[9] A great deal of his music is mechanization incarnate, immensely glib and fluent, often amusing in its salesmanlike dexterity of displaying so many lines of goods to suit all possible fancies.

[9] In 1927 Hindemith stated his creed as to *Gebrauchsmusik* ("workaday music") as follows:

"It is to be regretted that in general so little relationship exists today between the producers and the consumers of music. Today a composer should write music only when he knows the purpose for which he is writing: the days of composing for the sake of just composing are gone, perhaps forever. Nevertheless, the demand for music is great, and so composer and consumer must come to some sort of an understanding."

Included in his *Gebrauchsmusik* works are the following compositions; *Spielmusik* for strings, flutes, and oboes, Op. 43; three-part songs for singing groups; music to sing or play for amateurs and music lovers, Op. 45; a *Lesson* for two male voices, narrator, chorus, orchestra, dancer, clowns, and community singing; *Let's Build a Town,* a play with music for children; and *Plöner Musiktag,* comprising morning music for brass, table music for strings and brass, cantata for children's choir, solo, speaker, strings, wind, and percussion, and an evening concert given over to music for various instruments.

Like Schönberg, he has gone through a process of strenuous development; from writing music with a strong Wagnerian background, he passed through an atonal-cerebral period (his two operas, *Cardillac* and *Neues von Tage,* his *Concert Music* for viola and orchestra, and his oratorio, *Das Unaufhörliche,* may be said to be representative examples) to the much more human, grateful style he is using at the present time. This warmer manner of writing was first noticed in his opera *Mathis der Maler,* from which an orchestral triptych has been extracted. The *Philharmonic Dances* for orchestra and a ballet based on the life of St. Francis of Assisi, *Nobilissima visione,* are among the best things yet produced by a contemporary composer; they show an adequate mastery of the new technical resources, but do not renounce Romantic imagination. If Hindemith continues along these lines, he may prove to be the outstanding composer of his time.

THE INEVITABLE CONCLUSION

As to atonalism in general, the average listener, if not awed by names or upset by enthusiasms he cannot share, is likely to say that it may all be very well if only he could hear it as the composer (he does him the honor of believing) can. But the difficulty is, he cannot. He may be prepared to take a great deal of trouble, but he always comes out, unrefreshed, by the same door through which he entered. Sometimes he recognizes a flash of humor where it gleams amidst the great earnestness; again he may feel how apt to certain aspects of our time is this practical, no-sentimental-nonsense way of looking at things. But these are not the normal, lasting moods of the music lover; and so he goes back to his classics and his Romantics, as to his family and hobbies, after a day of grinding toil amid strangers and hard-faced men.

Toil this modern music certainly is: it would be idle to say otherwise. This is not in itself condemnation; one must toil to get the best out of the older music. But there is an immense difference in the rewards. It does not appear, by the evidence of a generation of concert programs, that modern man is at all reconciled to the so little rewarding toil of persevering with the extremer kind of modernism. It would even appear that he is learning to regard it as in no wise something sealed to this age and to be unsealed hereafter; if it is a mystery, the secret does not lie in anything that he can discover.

But we need not speculate too much on the future. We are safe in keeping to the simple test of the educated eye and ear; and when they call a halt, we can at least wave to our modernists, as they go on to fresh experiments, a cordial, if regretful, " Farewell! "

TENDENCIES IN OUR TIME

Times have changed from the times they used to be . . . old things pass away. . . . Strings would have held their ground against all the newcomers in creation. But clarinets was death. And harmonions, harmonions and barrel organs be miserable — what shall I call 'em? — miserable — miserable dumbledores!

— Thomas Hardy: *Under the Greenwood Tree*

THE BALLET

ANY attempt to describe contemporary developments in music must of necessity take into account three special forms which have arisen out of present-day interests and inventions and which therefore have proved particularly congenial to a number of contemporary composers: the ballet, film music, and a type of music written especially for radio and record reproduction.

The ballet can hardly be called a modern form; yet at no time in its long and colorful history has it shown more vitality that it possesses today. Only one phase of the long story of dancing, ballet in the modern sense may be said to have started with the founding in France, during the regime of Louis XIV, of *L'Académie Nationale de la Danse*. From that time until the present there stretches an unbroken tradition and a continuous development. Founded on ideals brought to France from Italy by Catherine de' Medici, this combination of music, spectacle, miming technique, and courtly charm was highly cultivated in France both before and after the Revolution and received the attention of a number of active performers and theorists: notably J. G. Noverre (1727–1810), who banished all the conventions which had accumulated up to his time and substituted the idea that " dancing in ballet " should be the means of expressing a dramatic idea; and Carlo Blasis, whose *Treatise on the Art of Dancing* (1803) summed up, codified, and brought to date Noverre's aesthetic and laid the foundations of what has come to be known as classic ballet technique. The academy of Blasis at Milan, with its severe course, became the model of all European dancing schools.

Afterwards there came the rise and fall of the Romantic tradition, with its attempt at escape from reality and its dramatis personae of fairies, witches, and vampires. Finally there has been the remarkable rise of the Russian school, which, starting from the reign of Catherine the Great (1762–1796), gradually absorbed all the knowledge and technique of the foreign schools until it succeeded in producing, under the great impresario Diaghilev, a type of ballet that completely revolutionized the history of the art in western Europe.

From the very inception of this art music has been its inseparable companion, sometimes as an equal partner, sometimes as a humble servant, and sometimes as a stern master. During the early days of the French ballet, composers such as Lully, Cambert, and Rameau wrote the succession of gavottes, minuets, chaconnes, bourrées, gigues, and the like, to which the court and professionals danced; in their case the music may be said to have been an equal partner. At the time of the Romantics, if we are to believe the accounts, music was the merest sort of accompaniment to an art which had become, in the words of a ballet historian, " a prelude to flirtation, the dancers nothing but grisettes and gold diggers." It was not until the advent of the first great master of modern ballet, Diaghilev, that music came into its own as a dominating factor.

At first adapting music from other sources, this discerning reformer soon saw that if he were to accomplish his ideals fully, he must have music that was created simultaneously with the choregraphic plan. So he commissioned Stravinsky to write *The Firebird,* the first work to establish the interest of serious musicians in ballet, which up to that time they had looked on as a more or less trivial art. Then came the other two great Stravinsky ballets, *Petrouchka* (1912) and *Le sacre du printemps*, the best things the composer ever wrote; later works were *The Nightingale*, *Apollo Musagetes*, and *The Wedding*, none of them outstandingly successful. Other composers to write to Diaghilev's commission were Ravel (*Daphnis et Chloé*), Strauss (*Joseph's Legend*), Falla (*The Three-cornered Hat*), and Poulenc (*Les biches*). Although Diaghilev died in 1929, his stimulating influence is still felt throughout the world — for his work became as well known in the capitals of North and South America as in those of Europe. Some other important ballet music written as the direct result of his ideals is that for *The Spider's Feast* (*Le festin de l'araignée*) by Roussel (1912), *The Wooden Prince* (*Der holzgeschnizte Prinz*) by Bartók, *The Demon* (*Der Dämon*) by Hindemith, *Job* by Vaughan Williams, *Checkmate* by Arthur Bliss, *Horoscope* by Constant Lambert, *Krazy Kat* and *Skyscrapers* by Carpenter.

The gradual development throughout the world of an enthusiastic group of balletomanes has thus had a definite effect on the history of music. These two arts — both of them expressive without the need for language — are extremely popular just now; what the ultimate results of their co-operative effect may be only time can tell. But it is bound to be important.

FILM MUSIC

No one who witnessed the first exhibitions of the little fifty-foot reels of "living pictures" shown some forty years ago at the end of vaudeville shows could have had any conception of the part which this new dramatic medium was to play in the cultural life of the future. Yet if we remind ourselves that every week some 80,000,000 persons in America and over 500,000,000 persons throughout the world see the moving pictures turned out by Hollywood alone, we cannot help realizing what a tremendous factor in contemporary life and taste the moving picture has become.

Those who saw the beginnings of this great American industry will remember that its association with music has been very close from the beginning. In the days of the silent film (prior to 1926), when often as much as a third of the total footage of the films shown consisted of subtitles explanatory of the dramatic development, the picture was always shown with some sort of musical background; this was furnished by forces ranging from a single tinny piano (in the nickelodeons) to huge orchestras equipped with machines for imitating all sorts of natural sounds — thunder, hoofbeats, birdcalls, and the like. The background music supplied for these early films was largely synchronized to the action of the film — long glissandi down to the bass, chirping birdcalls, and so on — and this kind of music, tied up with the details of the picture's action, has largely determined the general character of film music ever since. This background music was taken almost entirely from the " classics " and contemporary popular hits, the excerpts tied together with suitable cues, provided by the dozen for definite dramatic situations — hurries, adagios, sob moments, and so forth. Sometimes, when some advance-guard film was being prepared, those responsible for arranging the music would succeed in suggesting moods rather than delineating action, such as, for example, in the 1927 film, *Berlin: The Symphony of a Big City*.

When, after a great deal of experimenting, the problems of successfully reproducing and amplifying mechanically recorded sound were solved, the age of the sound pictures arrived and, beginning with 1927, a new era opened. For here, recorded on, and reproduced from, the same film as the picture itself, was an integrated musical score which made a definite contribution to the whole effect and was always the same, whether reproduced in Timbuktu or in Tokyo. Quick to sense the artistic possibilities of this new mechanical improvement, the moving-picture directors, even those in the commercialized Hollywood circles, sought the services of some well-known modern composers; and no less prominent names than those of the Europeans Kurt Weill, Eric Korngold, Ernst Toch, Shostakovich, Prokofiev, Walton, Bliss, even the great Schönberg himself, have been connected with the movie studios. Such active Americans as Virgil Thomson, George Antheil, and Marc Blitzstein have also written a number of moving-picture scores, so far with only meager artistic results, unfortunately.

There are various reasons for this. Sometimes the real heart of a composer's effort is lost through the decisions of that all-powerful court of last resort, the cutting room; the result may be that, owing to the exigencies of providing proper dramatic sequences, the composer's musical intentions are completely disregarded. Most motion-picture directors, to use one of their own phrases, are still "action crazy" and demand too literal a method of emphasizing a picture's meaning. Either that, or they go to the other extreme and react so violently against literalness that, in the case of a great many of the pictures that have been recently produced, one can but wonder why the music was ever put onto the film's sound track. Since the movies must be made for the millions, the music written for them must be simple and capable of a direct, telling effect. Such a result is not easy to achieve without being caught between the Scylla of outworn melodic clichés and the Charybdis of sterile modernism. Even the most recent of composers seem to forget the fact that they should write music capable of being well recorded by the microphone and forgo the clever tricks which they are accustomed to employ when writing for concert performance.

Slowly and painfully, as has been the case with every development in musical history, the film music of the future is being evolved. So far, the Europeans have perhaps contributed more to the solution of the problem than have the Americans, despite the fact that a great majority of the world's pictures are made in Hollywood. As this is written there are rumors of a new technique being developed, the music to be produced by "electronic" instruments in which electricity plays a primary part in tone production; this is certainly the beginning of an entirely new music, and the future possibilities are impossible to determine. But no matter what the developments of the future may bring, it is obvious enough even now that the composer interested in a wider public, the educator seeking to cultivate the general taste of the public, and the historian who would attune himself to the general cultural and emotional backgrounds of the time in which we live must study and appraise the moving picture.

MUSIC FOR RECORDS AND RADIO

In 1932 the École Supérieure de Musique in Paris appointed a Professor of the Microphone in order to " teach composers how to write for the radio as they have done for the piano, violin, and other instruments." Thus does a conservative school of music take cognizance of the rapidly growing importance of this comparatively new type of musical production, first started in 1919, when American amateurs began giving entertainments to one another over their " wireless telephones." It is only recently that those in authority in the radio world have come to realize that the microphone has opened entirely new vistas to the composer and that he should be encouraged to write special scores adapted to its possibilities and limitations.

In the United States radio commissions have been given to men like Copland, Still, Gruenberg, and Bennett, while Harris and others have written music especially designed for interpretation by phonograph records. Perhaps the most outstanding results along these lines have been the radio song plays and operas written by such composers as Blitzstein and Giannini. These, following on the experiments in vivid, self-explanatory, viewless dramas that have been successfully developed, notably by the British Broadcasting Company, seem to indicate the beginning of a new music form. We can only hope that development continues: for if any one of the older forms is completely dolorous when translated to the radio, it is opera.

These works for new mediums are far from being mere novelties; they show very clearly the trends which music is following as the twentieth century marches on and where future development is likely to come. For, no matter what the theorists and aestheticians may say to the contrary, it is as true now as it always has been that the types of art capable of reaching the greatest number of people in the end influence the history of an art most strongly. In the past these have been the opera and the symphony; in the future they may well be the music that is written for the moving picture and the radio, or for that development which lies still in the future, television.

" IN THE NATIVE GRAIN "

American Hopes

I hear America singing.

— Walt Whitman

THREE PHASES OF ACTIVITY

ACCOUNTS of American music and the place it occupies in the world of today are apt to be either fulsomely chauvinistic or contemptuously meager, according to whether the observer has leanings toward the " right " or the " left." Moreover, these accounts usually do not consider adequately the three phases which have characterized the musical activity of the United States — those of folk music, popular music, and academic or serious music. To a certain extent this is true of the majority of descriptions of nationalistic art: historians are prone to consider serious or academic art of more importance than folk or popular art. Such an account would be particularly unfortunate in the case of American music, however; for, whether we like to admit it or not, the one outstanding contribution which America has made to twentieth-century music has been in the field of popular activities — jazz, swing, or whatever name we may wish to give it. Out of the peculiar conditions of this great international melting pot, the result of a number of complex yet tremendously powerful forces, there has come the one form of American musical expression possessing real vitality, because it expresses the essential spirit of its time. The popular music of America has had a far-reaching effect on the world, for it has been as eagerly sought in Europe, in Australia, and even in the Far East as it has been in the land of its birth. In a word, it is America's most viable artistic export.

Owing to its enormous distances, the strikingly varied types of its people, the democratic character of its social organizations, and the strenuous tempo of its life, the United States seems to be producing a more widely diversified, and yet more rapidly integrating, type of art

Courtesy of The New York News

AMERICAN FUNCTIONAL ARCHITECTURE

The offices and printing plant of *The New York News* are pictured above. Architecture, more than any other art in America, has shown real results compounded of "techniques acquired from the past and a calculating eye for the practical possibilities of the present."

than any other country of the present. Nowhere else does there seem to be such a state of cultural ferment, somewhat crude as yet, but in its best estate healthy and at opposite poles from the intellectual, conscious manipulation of European art. Various elements are going into this new form of art: agelong tradition, techniques acquired from a study of the past, a calculating eye for practical possibilities, a romantic attitude toward American life compounded of a desire for expressing simple, unvarnished facts and a sort of sentimental attachment to these facts.

THE QUILTING PARTY, Anonymous, 1840–1850
The American folk spirit in art is seen in this oil painting found in Massachusetts. It is in the collection of Mrs. John D. Rockefeller, Jr., New York.

The result in some of the arts has been most salutary: in literature, men such as Lewis, Faulkner, Thomas Wolfe; in painting, Benton, Curry, Wood, Burchfield; in architecture, Sullivan and Wright — all these have produced art which may in every sense of the word be called American. In music the integration has not progressed so effectively: so far the only result that has achieved wide recognition has been American jazz and swing. These have evolved, as we shall see, out of various ingredients. There is reason to hope that this music may in turn influence the shaping of other and more important phases of American expression.

THE AMERICAN FOLK TRADITION

As its name implies, *folk music* is music that really is in the possession of the masses of the people within a country — what may be called their *musical vernacular*. It has existed among all nations, as we have observed,

Courtesy of The Metropolitan Museum of Art

THRESHING, by Joe Jones

The painting shows a characteristic American spirit and technique.

from the earliest days of music, and a great mass of it has survived in the various countries and according to the different traditions. This music belongs to a people not only because it has come into their consciousness naturally, without the process of formal instruction, but because it is so entirely within their own possibilities. A tune or a dance is a folk tune or a folk dance because it is of the sort that the average person can sing or dance easily, and moreover one which the average person enjoys singing or dancing. Obviously folk songs must be of a nature common to the great majority — they must treat of the people as they are, tell of their history, sing of their joys and sorrows, and give hopes and aspirations for their future.

It is clear enough that the traditional sources of American folk music have been drawn from the whole world: early settlers and later immigrants brought with them into the new country the songs and dances of their own lands, and many of these have survived even to this day practically

PHASES OF MUSIC

No better summary of the development of music in America could possibly be found
Lawrence Tibbett. At the extreme left is a suggestion of the music of the Negroes,
bound up with the life of the country. The left center suggests the romantic era of
the artist has painted a characteristic American farm and village church, thus inti-
center two cowboys " render " some of the music of the Western plains. The

unchanged, as is the case of the folk tunes in the isolated sections of the eastern Appalachians. Folk-song collectors have found the people there singing the old Scottish and English ballads of the time when their forebears came over from Europe and settled in these wild regions. Such music as this has, of course, been of little importance in the development of a real American folk type, since it has impinged so slightly on the general life of the country.

But a great many of these European folk ballads and dances, while preserving something of their essential nature, have taken root in the changed life of America, have been affected by its freedom, stimulated

Photograph by Juley; courtesy of Lawrence Tibbett

IN AMERICA

than this mural painted by William Yarrow for the country home of Mr. and Mrs. which, although not American in any true sense of the word, has been so closely Stephen Foster and his songs that have gone around the world; in the background mating the great role they have played in the spread of native music. In the right modern college youth and his amusement music occupies the rest of the picture.

by its struggles, and salted by its humor. The main stem of this music has been the traditional songs brought by the English-speaking peoples who settled so large a part of colonial America. But grafted on it to such an extent as to produce an entirely new fruit have been the customs and habits, the sentimentality and wit, the problems and slogans, the " lay-out and lingo " of life in a pioneer country. Adding its own flavor has been the rhythmic genius and harmonic love of color peculiar to the music of the Negroes brought into the country in the early days of its history. The result has been what Carl Sandburg, the American poet, has picturesquely called a " rag bag of strips, stripes, and streaks of color " from all parts of the earth; yet something that is as indigenous to the country as skyscrapers or Prohibition, as old as the medieval ballads brought into the Appalachians and yet as new as the latest oil-well gusher.

There are literally thousands of these ballads and ditties and dances: the best collection of them that has been made is that of Sandburg's — *The American Songbag,* a book which contains nearly three hundred of the most characteristic of these tunes and verses, gathered by the compiler and his friends from coast to coast and from the Gulf of Mexico to Canada. If one would secure the real flavor of this national folk idiom, he should go through this collection carefully, or, better still, hear Mr. Sandburg sing some of these songs. Such things as " My Name It Is Sam Hall," or " I Ride an Old Paint," or " I'm Sad and I'm Lonely," although they could have come only out of America, are as representative of the common sorrows of humanity as anything ever written or sung.

AMERICAN POPULAR MUSIC

There may be some significance to the fact that it was in the field of popular music that America made its first great success; for there can be little question that this success was achieved through the integration of certain elements from both the serious and the folk strain. The early history of popular music on the American continent shows little but a weak sort of emulation of European types. Life in America up to the time of the nineteenth century was a pretty serious, pioneering affair, with little time or opportunity for amusements, of the musical sort at least. The first popular form of amusement indigenous to the American scene was the minstrel show, a distinctly native combination of a sort of folk vaudeville with topical songs of a Negroid character.

The outstanding success of this minstrel era was the music of Stephen Foster, much of it composed for use in these shows. Foster was a talented melodist and poet of folklike lyrics which, based on Negro subjects, employed a simple sentimentality in depicting the joys and sorrows of Southern life among the blacks. Such things as " Old Folks at Home " or " Old Black Joe," with appealing texts and plaintive music, have

Courtesy of The Metropolitan Museum of Art

THE BOWERY by Marsh

Another characteristic American painting of life in a great city is reproduced here.

become popular throughout the English-speaking world and are as universal in their appeal as anything yet produced in America.

Then followed the more sophisticated variety and burlesque shows, patterned after continental models, together with the comic operas based either on the Gilbert and Sullivan types from England or on the Strauss models from Vienna. These became extremely popular during the latter part of the century, the favorite composer being Victor Herbert (1859–1924), an Irish-born musician whose style was nevertheless characteristically American. He wrote too much, and his scores are very uneven; but at its best his music possesses a melodic charm and a rhythmic verve that make it the equal of any European music written in this genre.

JAM SESSION, a lithograph by George von Physter

The lithograph is from *Down Beat*, the trade paper of the swing movement, and appears also in *Destiny*, a sketchbook of the lives of popular musicians.

Another outstanding figure in late nineteenth-century popular music was John Philip Sousa (1856–1932), whose nationalistic marches, most of them written for his own concert band, are played the world over. (It was his own opinion that a march "should make a man with a wooden leg want to step out"; his certainly do!) Nothing written in America better characterizes the "youthful spirit, optimism, and patriotic feeling" which a foreign observer felt at the time they were composed.

It was the headway gained at this time that gave impetus to the development of the peculiarly American coon song and ragtime. These rhythmic tunes and dances originated with the Negroes but soon became popular with the whites because of their happy, infectious nature. Through the infusion of other folk elements, ragtime developed into jazz, and jazz [10] into swing.

[10] Over seventy years ago W. F. Allen recorded in his *Slave Songs of the United States* a performance of Negro singing which curiously foreshadows those of jazz:

Courtesy of Hansen-Williams, Inc.

THE MOOD OF SWING

One of the most famous of swing bands, that of Duke Ellington, is shown in action.

"There is no singing in parts, as we understand it, and yet no two appear to be singing the same thing; the leading singer starts the words of each verse, often improvising, and the others, who 'base' him, as it is called, strike in with the refrain, or even join in the solo when the words are familiar. When the 'base' begins, the leader often stops, leaving the rest of the words to be guessed at, or it may be they are taken up by one of the other singers. And the 'basers' themselves seem to follow their own whims, beginning when they please and leaving off when they please, striking an octave above or below (in case they have pitched the tune too high), or hitting some other note that chords, so as to produce the effect of a marvelous complication and variety and yet with the most perfect time and rarely with any discord. And what makes it all the harder to unravel a thread of melody out of this strange network is that, like birds, they seem not infrequently to strike sounds that cannot be precisely represented by the gamut and abound in slides from one note to another and turns and cadences not in articulated notes."

Carl Sandburg in the introduction to his *American Songbag* quotes one of the earliest recorded descriptions of jazz. In a lawsuit as to the musical rights of a certain jazz composition, the plaintiff, obviously of the black persuasion, testified that one evening when his orchestra was playing in a Chicago cabaret long before the jazz vogue, "and a lady dancer started doing some fancy steps, I picks up a cornet and lets go a few pony neighs at her. The trombone come through with a few horse laughs. Then the banjos, cowbells, and sax put in a lot of 'terplitations of their own. And that was the first time the 'Livery Stable Blues' was played."

Some of the leaders in this development were accomplished musicians, thoroughly conversant with the technique of the composition and orchestration of serious music; and these carried over into their scoring for jazz and swing bands some of the principles and ideas of Rimsky-Korsakoff, Debussy, Strauss, and the rest. Thus the American popular music developed along the line of a happy combination of folk and serious influences. Among the personages in this rather astonishing development have been W. C. Handy, whose " St. Louis Blues " was one of the first of that type of Negroid songs to become popular; [11] Irving Berlin and George Gershwin, Jewish composers steeped in the New York tradition; Paul Whiteman, the orchestral leader whose pioneer work in playing " symphonic jazz " did much to bring this type of music out of the dance halls and into the theaters; Edward " Duke " Ellington, " King " Calloway, and " Prince " Armstrong, the latter three Negro royalties in the kingdom of swing.[12]

It is impossible to predict what the next innovation in jazz music will be; for one of the prices of remaining in the limelight is the necessity of popular music to find novelty at any cost. Folk and serious music, because of the breadth and variety and quality of their content, maintain their interest from generation to generation. Popular music, on the other hand, conveys a narrow and limited content: nothing is so dead as yesterday's popular song, and it is impossible to think of a people a hundred years from now exhibiting any interest, other than that of the antiquarian, in such jazz classics as happen to be popular now. Just how far this type of music can go in its development of the folk idiom it is impossible to say; but it seems doubtful that this inbred type of music of escape, erotic intoxication, and anodyne will advance much beyond its present ephemeral position.

[11] The very essence of the " blues," writes Abbe Niles, " is found in the traditional line, common property of the Negro race: ' Got de blues, but too dam' mean to cry.' "

[12] No one, even among the ardent swing enthusiasts, seems to be exactly sure of the nature of this popular American craze or its distinction from jazz. All definitions seem to agree, however, as to its having a " driving, but fluid and mechanized rhythm," over which soloists improvise as they play. Perhaps the name comes from its characteristic rhythmic abandon. This becomes " jam music " when it is simultaneously improvised by all the players.

SERIOUS MUSIC

With the exception of literature and architecture, the development of academic art in America is largely a record of serious, ambitious effort without the achievement of an art value sufficient to lift localism into world importance. Various reasons may be given in an attempt to explain this: the comparative youth of the country;[13] its necessary dependence on Europe for training and inspiration; the difficulty which all art necessarily encounters in a pioneer country where life is largely given over to earning a subsistence and developing natural resources; the impossibility of integrating so many conflicting traditions and complex idioms; etc., etc. But in spite of all this and any other American phenomena which might be submitted in explanation — the distance from Europe, the raids of the robber barons on the physical and spiritual resources of the country, and the rest — it would seem that the nervous energy and the typical assurance that are such predominant American characteristics might have produced by this time some results in serious art more commensurate with those which have been achieved in folk and popular art. There is evidence today that American workers in the visual arts are beginning to respond to their natural environment. But, so far, composers have not followed in their train.

The tale of the development of the situation of today in American music has been often and skillfully told.[14] In general it is the story of the gradual adaptation to local conditions and native soil of the ideals and principles of the body of musicians which we have described as making music for the courts, nobilities, and intelligent middle classes of Europe. It ranges from the early efforts of Francis Hopkinson (1737–1791), whom *Grove's Dictionary* calls the only native musician of distinction in early

13 When the Mayflower sailed for America, for instance, Schütz was laying the foundations of that great structure which came to be known as German music; in the early days of the colony of New York, Bach was composing his great organ and church music; and at the time of the Battle of Lexington, Mozart was 19 years old.

14 The most complete tale is Howard's *Our American Music;* the most vivacious, Kaufmann's *From Jehovah to Jazz;* the best account of modern developments, Reis's *Composers in America.*

America,[15] to that surprising social phenomenon of today, the mass distribution of good music via radio, phonograph, and sound film throughout the wide spaces of this enormous continent.

The sources of academic music in the United States may be said to be of English and German extraction. This is due to natural reasons: the fact that the English were the first settlers along the Atlantic seaboard, and their descendants long maintained whatever cultural traditions the new country possessed; and the fact that so many of the early musicians who came to this country from abroad were German, together with the natural preference shown for Germany by American students going abroad to study music. It would merely be wearisome to try to list all the influences which affected the developing taste of the young country; one of the most important was the immigration of artists which took place in the early part of the nineteenth century. After the American Revolution the musical life of the country passed, as someone has well said, from untrained native hands into the more skilled hand of the foreigner. Prominent among these early foreign musicians who affected the destinies of their adopted country were the Philadelphians Alexander Reinagle (1756–1809), an English teacher, concert manager, and composer, and Benjamin Carr (1769–1831), one of the first conductors of America to give a performance of a Beethoven symphony and who wrote, in 1796, a ballad-opera setting of Schiller's *William Tell* which antedated Rossini's famous opera by some thirty years. In New York, James Hewitt is said to have brought the music of Stamitz and Haydn to America; and in Boston, Gottlieb Graupner, a player in the orchestra which Salomon assembled for Haydn, helped found two of the country's earliest musical organizations, the Philharmonic Society (in 1810) and the Handel and Haydn Society (in 1815).

The most picturesque of these early foreigners who cast in their musical lot with America was Anthony Philip Heinrich, a rich Bohemian

[15] His contemporaries were William Billings (1746–1800), a writer of rather crude church music, and James Lyon (1735–1794), an amateur in northern Maine who made himself a church-music specialist. The early history of music in the United States was largely concerned with the music of the church, and hymn and psalm singing were by far the most vital of its musical activities clear up to the end of the nineteenth century.

merchant who lost his money and settled in Kentucky from 1818 to 1823 and who later, in New York and in Boston, wrote an almost unbelievable number of compositions, many of them demanding an orchestra of almost Berliozian dimensions.[16] As discriminating a critic as Sonneck has said that Father Heinrich, as he was called by his admirers (they also dubbed him the Beethoven of America), is easily the most commanding figure as a composer in America before 1860 and the first to display nationalistic American tendencies.

Besides the musical societies already mentioned, others were founded in American cities: the St. Cecilia Society of Charleston, founded in 1762, probably the earliest of them all; the Musical Fund Society of Philadelphia, founded in 1820; and the New York Philharmonic Orchestra, founded in 1842. In the early 1850's opera began to attract attention; there were performances of French and Italian works,[17] and after the Civil War there came an even greater variety of musical fare. That great pioneer in establishing a love of orchestral music among Americans, Theodore Thomas, made his first concert tour with his orchestra in 1869; in 1881 the Boston Symphony, the first of the American orchestras to achieve an outstanding world position, was founded; in 1884 came German opera under the aegis of Leopold Damrosch.

The entry of American music into the world arena was prepared for by John K. Paine, who studied in Germany and was the first academic professor of music in an American college, Harvard; the traditions he established were carried on by Foote, Chadwick, and Parker, the latter the most talented member of the New England group. A number of names may be included in the group of men who gradually secured a

16 Among his most characteristic works were *The Ornithological Combat of Kings, or The Condor of the Andes and The Eagle of the Cordilleras* and *The Columbial, or The Migration of American Wild Passenger Pigeons.*

17 The first opera, if it can be called such, to be produced in America was the ballad opera imported from England; Southern historians point with pride to the fact that the first work of which there is present record was *Flora, or Hob in the Well,* produced in Charleston in 1735. The first works to depart from this type were sung in French in New Orleans, where for years a most distinguished operatic tradition was cultivated. Sonneck in his *Early History of Opera in America* shows that for years adapted and arranged versions of grand opera were played on the Atlantic seaboard, together with the popular ballad works.

liberation of American music from the Germanic influences: Edgar Stillman Kelley; Edward MacDowell, the most individual of all American composers; Charles M. Loeffler, a distinguished Alsatian who made America his home during his best creative years; Frederick S. Converse, who wrote the first native opera to be produced at the Metropolitan Opera House; Henry K. Hadley, a facile writer for orchestra; Daniel Gregory Mason, grandson of Lowell Mason, one of the grand old men of American music,[18] an eminent figure in his own right; John Alden Carpenter, a vivacious composer of works with a modernistic tinge; Ernest Schelling; Arthur Shepherd; Charles Griffes, whose early death at the age of 36 robbed America of perhaps her most promising figure; and Deems Taylor, the writer of the only American operas which may in any real sense of the term be called successful.

The later generation, arising around the turn of the century, have been influenced, as were their confreres on the Continent, by general Stravinsky-Schönbergian developments and can hardly be called any more characteristically individual than their predecessors. Sowerby and Hanson are as eclectic as any others of this group, their antecedents being strongly classic; Saminsky, Ornstein, and Varèse are immigrants whose adventures in sonorities can hardly be thought of as in any sense American. Ives, Ruggles, Whithorne, Sessions, Harris, Virgil Thomson, Piston, and Antheil are well-known names among the progressives. A few years ago it seemed as if Harris showed promise of being the long-awaited great figure in American creative music; there is usually an impression of strength and suggestion of emotion in his works, but his later development has been curiously disappointing. Gruenberg and Copland have made frank use of jazz idioms in their music.

[18] The name of Mason has been closely associated with American music for three generations. Lowell Mason (1792–1872) was a banker who turned musician and composed and published a large number of well-known hymns. It has been suggested that he stands in the same relation to American sacred music that Stephen Foster does to American secular folk songs. Later he succeeded in introducing music into the public schools of Boston, thereby becoming the first of a long line of enthusiasts who have struggled to make music a part of American popular education. His grandson, Henry Lowell, helped found the firm of Mason & Hamlin, makers of fine organs and pianos. William Mason, Lowell's son, became a pupil of Liszt's and one of America's most famous pianists.

Claire Reis, in her *Composers in America*, lists nearly two hundred men as being worthy of inclusion in her book, truly an impressive number. Among these, many of the younger men show an astonishingly facile technique, without having anything particularly important to say; they may, indeed, be said to be fairly representative of all American music, in having found a voice without as yet developing anything that suggests a speech of their own. A recent criticism of an American composition in one of the metropolitan dailies might well be cited as fairly applicable to the majority of present-day native compositions:

" Mr. X's concerto, which enjoyed an admirable interpretation by the orchestra, is a work of uneven worth. It reveals certain originalities of idiom and rhythmic pattern, set down by a musician thoroughly cognizant of the orchestral means at his command. The influence of certain contemporary modes is apparent, even persistent. The first and last movements begin promisingly, but inspiration lags, and platitude and contrivance lead to a disappointing end. The slow movement has a decided harmonic strength and an almost Brahmsian weight and solidity, but little of tenderness and tranquillity. At times, it seemed as though Mr. X had tried frantically to be ' different.' "

— J. S.: *New York Herald Tribune*

One reason why up to this time America has remained so sterile in musical creation is that those who have been born or reared in one of her traditions seem to have remained so largely ignorant of the others. We have shown that whatever real vitality American music has possessed has been in the line of the folk and popular idioms; and anyone familiar with the situation will admit that there is more ability to sustain life, more characteristic personality, more distinct individuality of content in one of Stephen Foster's or Sousa's or Gershwin's works than in most of the symphonies so far composed in the country. There is no question that the works of all these men are simple and unpretentious; but they do say something that had not been said in just that way before. This is a great deal more than can be said of the works of most of their more ostentatious compatriots.

Academic, professional musicians, however — the class from which must come the effort to create serious music — too often have been disdainful of these simple idioms. They do not like either the sound or the content of traditional ballad singing or the music that the native fiddlers play for dancing; as for the banalities of jazz, most of the academics gather their skirts in contempt and pass by on the other side. The members of the other groups are almost as scornful. Thus have arisen ancient prejudices and loyalties which have negated, until very recently, the interactions and stimulations which history has shown one idiom can give to another.[19] A further disintegrating force has been the organized campaign of the professionals to " make America musical," a campaign admirable in itself but which unfortunately has tried to root out all traces of anything that seems indigenous to the American soil.

There has come a change in recent years. We find such a composer as John Powell, for instance, becoming interested in the folk music of his native state, Virginia; and a number of the younger generation, impressed by the success which has everywhere met American popular music, have not only studied it but have frankly adapted some of its technical innovations. So, paralleling the interest shown in native products by the other artists — the painters, the dramatists, the novelists — American folk and popular music has begun to permeate the national consciousness. There has been a steady increase in the use of the songs of mountain and plain, especially on the part of amateurs: the peculiar pathos and simple beauty of these " wild flowers " of music are being exploited by folk-song singers and dancers. There is likewise a revival of interest in folk dancing, a revival which has affected even the professionals of the night clubs and the cabarets. In brief, as someone has put it, urban professional music, both popular and academic, is discovering America. The result cannot help being beneficial. As Taine has said: " A new style is born when an artist's acquired technical habits are put to work in new surroundings — when interests residing in life, not in art, rouse him to personal utterance capable of imparting its flavor of direct experience."

[19] Many of the so-called international composers have, as we have seen, based their expression on the sound foundations of the traditional music of their peoples: Haydn's music certainly comes out of the simple, melodic joys of Croatian song; there is present in many of Beethoven's works an appreciation of the folk-dance idiom of the land in which he lived; Schubert may be said to have been the musical incarnation of the Viennese spirit; in almost all of Brahms there may be heard the four-square strength of the German chorale and folk song.

WHAT OF THE FUTURE?

Out of this interpenetration may result the attainment of America's coming of age, musically speaking. If all the vital forces inherent in the art of this huge, sprawling continent can be brought into some sort of interfecundation, the result is bound to be more impressive than anything it has achieved up to date. For there are certain advantages possessed by the United States which should prove of inestimable benefit, once the proper art background has been prepared. There are, for example, no problems of flaming nationalisms, no necessity to wave on high the shaky torch of patriotic propaganda. Because of its youth and enthusiasms, and the fact that it possesses a culture-eager, rather than a culture-weary, spirit, an evolution is possible in this country which, without waste of time, using atonality and all the other modern ideas, might produce a really new art. Roy Harris, who is a virile propagandist for an American style, has shown that the development of music in a new country follows a threefold cycle. The acceptance of the musical culture of an older society is followed by the dissemination of this imported music into a broad and intensive activity; this, in turn, creates a new, indigenous music that embodies the idioms and identifies and records the emotions of the people that produced it. It is apparent that America has lived through the first two periods of this cycle; it looks now as if the third might be beginning.

The tremendous activity at present to be observed in America — the stimulation of musical composition, the expansion of opera, ballet, motion pictures, and radio, the surprising changes in educational policies, and the raising of the general cultural level — indicates, according to the enthusiasts, where the future of music must lie. War has peculiarly accelerated American musical growth: it seems as if most of Europe's leading conductors, performers, composers, critics, and scholars have left their native haunts and have interjected themselves as integral factors in American musical life. What will be the result?

Whether the war has dealt European music a fatal blow, whether the black-out of opera houses and concert halls in London, Paris, Berlin,

Munich, and the rest of the great European centers means the final ending of a glorious era in music, remains to be seen. It is at least reasonable to suppose that the center of gravity in this world of artistic flux must of necessity shift across the Atlantic. The American creative artist faces a most critical period in his development: will he be able to maintain his own individuality in the face of this influx, at the same time expanding and carrying on the ideals of the great European traditions of the past? With lessons learned from history, will he be able to let his style develop easily and naturally, without forcing, find his inspiration in the life around him, and express himself simply, forcefully, and sincerely? Time alone can tell.

The music of some of the greatest composers of the past has come out of just such an interaction of forces as is now taking place in America: there is no reason why we may not hope for similar results again.

A Selective Bibliography

THE FOLLOWING BIBLIOGRAPHY is offered without apology. It makes no claim to being either complete or outstanding: it is simply a list of readable books on music in English, the perusal of which will greatly aid in acquiring a well-rounded viewpoint of the whole subject. It presupposes the availability of standard reference works — such things as *The Oxford History of Music, Grove's Dictionary of Music and Musicians,* the new *International Cyclopedia of Music and Musicians,* and *The Oxford Companion to Music;* with the exception of the last, these can hardly be called readable works, but they are necessary for reference. If French and German can be read without too much recourse to the dictionary, Combarieu's *Histoire de la musique,* Gérold's *Histoire de la musique des origines à la fin du XIV siècle,* Riemann's *Musiklexikon,* and Moser's *Musiklexikon* will be found helpful.

But the important thing is listening to, rather than reading about, music; and we rank the value of the list of recordings available for the listener's use far above that of any bibliography which might be prepared.

THE ARTS IN HISTORY

Haddon, A. C. *Evolution of Art.* New York: Charles Scribner's Sons

Sorokin, Pitirim A. "Social and Cultural Dynamics," Volume I, *Fluctuation of Forms of Art.* New York: American Book Company, 1937

THE ORIGINS OF ART

Boas, Franz. *Primitive Art.* Cambridge: Harvard University Press, 1928

O'Neill, F. R. *The Relation of Art to Life.* London: George Routledge & Sons, Ltd., 1938

Osborn, H. F. *Men of the Old Stone Age, Their Environment, Life and Art,* Third Edition. New York: Charles Scribner's Sons, 1919

Read, Herbert. *Art and Society.* New York: The Macmillan Company, 1937

MUSIC IN THE LIFE OF THE NEAR EAST

Galpin, Francis W. *Music of the Sumerians and Their Immediate Successors, the Babylonians & Assyrians.* New York: The Macmillan Company, 1937

Idelsohn, A. Z. *Jewish Music in Its Historical Development.* New York: Henry Holt and Company, Inc., 1929

Mayer, Josephine, and Prideaux, Tom. *Never to Die.* New York: The Viking Press, Inc., 1938

Ranke, Hermann (Editor). *The Art of Ancient Egypt*. New York: Oxford University Press, 1936

Saminsky, Lazare. *Music of the Ghetto and the Bible*. New York: Bloch Publishing Company, Inc., 1934

THE MUSIC OF THE HELLENIC AGE

Oates, W. J., and O'Neill, E. G. (Editors). *The Complete Greek Drama*. All the Extant Tragedies of Aeschylus, Sophocles and Euripides, and the Comedies of Aristophanes and Menander. New York: Random House, Inc., 1938

Schlesinger, Kathleen. *The Greek Aulos*. London: Methuen & Co., Ltd., 1939

Stobart, John C. *The Glory That Was Greece*, Third Revised Edition. New York: D. Appleton-Century Company, Inc., 1935

Torr, Cecil. Article on "Greek Music" in *Oxford History of Music, Introductory Volume*. New York: Oxford University Press, 1929

ROMAN AND EARLY CHRISTIAN MUSIC

Stobart, John C. *The Grandeur That Was Rome*, Third Revised Edition. New York: D. Appleton-Century Company, Inc., 1935

MONODIC MUSIC OF A THOUSAND YEARS

Chambers, E. K. *The Mediaeval Stage, Volume I*. New York: Oxford University Press, 1903

Frere, Rt. Rev. W. H. Article on "Plainsong" in *Oxford History of Music, Introductory Volume*. New York: Oxford University Press, 1929

Gray, Cecil. *The History of Music*. New York: Alfred A. Knopf, Inc., 1928

Huegle, Rev. Gregory. *A Catechism of Gregorian Chant*. New York: J. Fischer & Brother, 1928

Robertson, Alec. *The Interpretation of Plainchant*. New York: Oxford University Press, 1937

THE MUSIC OF THE MIDDLE AGES

Adams, Henry, *Mont-Saint-Michel and Chartres*. Boston: Houghton Mifflin Company, 1913

Aubry, Pierre. *Trouvères and Troubadours*. New York: G. Schirmer, 1914

Dent, E. J. "Social Aspects of Music in the Middle Ages" in *Oxford History of Music, Introductory Volume*. New York: Oxford University Press, 1929

Duncan, Edmonstoune. *The Story of Minstrelsy*. New York: Charles Scribner's Sons, 1907

Fry, Roger. *Flemish Art: A Critical Survey*. New York: Coward-McCann, Inc., 1927

Parkhurst, Helen H. *Cathedral; A Gothic Pilgrimage*. Boston: Houghton Mifflin Company, 1936

Prentice, Sartell. *The Heritage of the Cathedral; A Study of the Influence of History and Thought upon Cathedral Architecture*. New York: William Morrow & Company, Inc., 1936

Schlesinger, Kathleen. " The Significance of Musical Instruments in the Evolution of Music " in *Oxford History of Music, Introductory Volume*. New York: Oxford University Press, 1929

Sollitt, Edna R. *Dufay to Sweelinck*. New York: Ives Washburn, Inc., 1933

THE MUSIC OF THE RENAISSANCE

Burckhardt, Jakob. *The Civilization of the Renaissance in Italy*. New York: Oxford University Press, 1937

De Robeck, Nesta. *Music of the Italian Renaissance*. London: The Medici Press, 1928

Fry, Roger. *Characteristics of French Art*. New York: Coward-McCann, Inc., 1933

Gray, Cecil, and Heseltine, Philip. *Carlo Gesualdo, Prince of Venosa*. New York: Dial Press, 1926

Hargrave, Mary. *Earlier French Musicians*. London: Kegan Paul, Trench, Trubner & Co., Ltd., 1917

Lucas, Henry S. *The Renaissance and the Reformation*. New York: Harper & Brothers, 1934

Maurois, André. *The Miracle of England*. New York: Harper & Brothers, 1937

Oman, Sir Charles. *The Sixteenth Century*. New York: E. P. Dutton & Co., Inc., 1937

Trend, J. B. *The Music of Spanish History to 1600*. New York: Oxford University Press, 1926

von Rothkirch, Count Wolfgang. *Deutsche Kunst-Eine Auswahl ihrere schönsten Werke*. Berlin: Propylaen Verlag, 1934

Walker, Ernest. *History of Music in England*, Second Edition. New York: Oxford University Press, 1924

THE OVERTURE TO THE BAROQUE

Bekker, Paul. *The Changing Opera*. New York: W. W. Norton & Company, Inc., 1935

Dolmetsch, Arnold. *Interpretation of the Music of the XVIIth and XVIIIth Centuries*. New York: H. W. Gray Company, 1915

Goddard, Joseph. *The Rise and Development of Opera*. New York: Charles Scribner's Sons, 1912

Landowska, Wanda. *Music of the Past*. New York: Alfred A. Knopf, Inc., 1924

Prunières, H. *Monteverdi, His Life and Work*. New York: E. P. Dutton & Co., Inc., 1926

Rolland, Romain. *A Musical Tour through the Land of the Past*. New York: Henry Holt and Company, Inc., 1922

Rolland, Romain. *Some Musicians of Former Days*. New York: Henry Holt and Company, Inc., 1915

Sitwell, Sacheverell. *German Baroque Sculpture*. London: Gerald Duckworth & Co., Ltd., 1938

Smith, Leo. *Music of the Seventeenth and Eighteenth Centuries*. Toronto: J. M. Dent & Sons, Ltd., 1931

Streatfeild, R. A. *The Opera*, Fifth Edition. New York: E. P. Dutton & Co., Inc., 1925

THE EIGHTEENTH CENTURY

Burney, Charles. *A General History of Music from the Earliest Ages to the Present Period* (1789). New York: Harcourt, Brace and Company, Inc., 1935

Burney, Charles. *The Present State of Music in France and Italy* (1771)

Burney, Charles. *The Present State of Music in Germany, etc.* (1773)

Einstein, Alfred. *Gluck.* New York: E. P. Dutton & Co., Inc., 1936

Hayes, C. J. H. *A Political and Cultural History of Modern Europe, Volume I.* New York: The Macmillan Company, 1936

Renard, G. F., and Weulersse, Georges. *Life and Work in Modern Europe.* New York: Alfred A. Knopf, Inc., 1926

Smith, Preserved. *History of Modern Culture.* New York: Henry Holt and Company, Inc., 1930–1934

AND THERE WERE GIANTS IN THOSE DAYS

Dickinson, A. E. F. *The Art of J. S. Bach.* London: Gerald Duckworth & Co., Ltd., 1936

Flower, Newman. *George Frideric Handel.* Boston: Houghton Mifflin Company, 1923

Schweitzer, Albert. *J. S. Bach* (Translated by Ernest Newman). New York: The Macmillan Company

Terry, C. Sanford. *Bach; The Historical Approach.* New York: Oxford University Press, 1931

Williams, C. F. A. *Bach.* New York: E. P. Dutton & Co., Inc., 1934

HAYDN AND MOZART

Anderson, Emily. *The Letters of Mozart & His Family.* New York: The Macmillan Company, 1938

Bekker, Paul. *The Story of the Orchestra.* New York: W. W. Norton & Company, Inc., 1936

Carse, Adam. *History of Orchestration.* New York: E. P. Dutton & Co., Inc., 1925

Gheón, Henri. *In Search of Mozart.* London: Sheed & Ward, Inc., 1934

Hadden, James C. *Haydn.* New York: E. P. Dutton & Co., Inc., 1934

Hadow, W. H. "A Croatian Composer" in *Collected Essays.* New York: Oxford University Press, 1928

Turner, W. J. *Mozart: The Man & His Works.* New York: Alfred A. Knopf, Inc., 1938

MUSIC GROWS MORE PERSONAL

Bekker, Paul. *Beethoven.* New York: E. P. Dutton & Co., Inc.

Herriot, Edouard. *The Life and Times of Beethoven.* New York: The Macmillan Company, 1935

Locke, Arthur W. *Music and the Romantic Movement in France.* New York: E. P. Dutton & Co., Inc., 1920

Lucas, F. L. *The Decline and Fall of the Romantic Ideal.* New York: The Macmillan Company, 1936

Specht, Richard. *Beethoven as He Lived.* New York: Harrison Smith and Robert Haas, 1937
Sullivan, J. W. N. *Beethoven, His Spiritual Development.* New York: Alfred A. Knopf, Inc., 1927

THE EARLY ROMANTIC COMPOSERS AND THEIR PROBLEMS

Abraham, Gerald. *A Hundred Years of Music.* New York: Alfred A. Knopf, Inc., 1938
Berlioz, H. L. *Memoirs, from 1803 to 1865.* (Edited by Ernest Newman). New York: Tudor Publishing Company, 1935
Capell, Richard. *Schubert's Songs.* New York: E. P. Dutton & Co., Inc., 1929
Huneker, J. G. *Chopin; The Man and His Music.* New York: Charles Scribner's Sons, 1900
Kaufman, Schima. *Mendelssohn, A Second Elijah.* New York: Thomas Y. Crowell Company, 1934
Kobald, Karl. *Franz Schubert and His Times.* New York: Alfred A. Knopf, Inc., 1928
Newman, Ernest. *The Man Liszt.* New York: Charles Scribner's Sons, 1935
Niecks, F. *Robert Schumann.* New York: E. P. Dutton & Co., Inc., 1925
Sitwell, Sacheverell. *Liszt.* Boston: Houghton Mifflin Company, 1934
Wotton, T. S. *Hector Berlioz.* New York: Oxford University Press, 1935

WAGNER — HIS PREDECESSORS AND CONTEMPORARIES

Abraham, Gerald. *A Hundred Years of Music.* New York: Alfred A. Knopf, Inc., 1938
Bekker, Paul. *Richard Wagner; His Life in His Work.* New York: W. W. Norton & Company, Inc., 1931
Bekker, Paul. *The Changing Opera.* New York: W. W. Norton & Company, Inc., 1935
Gilman, Lawrence. *Wagner's Operas.* New York: Farrar & Rinehart, Inc., 1937
Hill, E. Burlingame. *Modern French Music.* Boston: Houghton Mifflin Company, 1924
Kracauer, Siegfried. *Orpheus in Paris; Offenbach and the Paris of His Time.* New York: Alfred A. Knopf, Inc., 1938
Newman, Ernest. *The Life of Richard Wagner,* Volumes I and II. New York: Alfred A. Knopf, Inc., 1933 and 1937
Newman, Ernest. *Wagner as Man and Artist.* New York: Alfred A. Knopf, Inc., 1924
Pourtalès, Guy de. *Richard Wagner; The Story of an Artist.* New York: Harper & Brothers, 1932
Seligman, V. J. *Puccini among Friends.* New York: The Macmillan Company, 1938
Sitwell, Sacheverell. *La Vie Parisienne.* Boston: Houghton Mifflin Company, 1938
Toye, Francis. *Giuseppe Verdi; His Life and Works.* New York: Alfred A. Knopf, Inc., 1931
von Weber, Max. *The Life of an Artist.* London: Chapman and Hall, 1865
Wagner, Richard. *My Life.* New York: Dodd, Mead & Company, Inc., 1931
Werfel, Franz V. *Verdi.* New York: Simon and Schuster, Inc., 1925

NATIONALISM IN ART

Abraham, Gerald. *Studies in Russian Music*. New York: Charles Scribner's Sons, 1936
Bartók, Béla. *Hungarian Folk Music*. New York: Oxford University Press, 1931
Evans, Edwin. *Tchaikovsky*. New York: E. P. Dutton & Co., Inc., 1935
Forsyth, Cecil. *Music and Nationalism*. New York: The Macmillan Company, 1911
Liszt, Franz. *The Gypsy in Music*, Volumes I and II. London: William Reeves, Bookseller, Ltd., 1926
McNaught, William. *A Short Account of Modern Music and Musicians*. New York: H. W. Gray Company, 1937
Ribera y Tarragó, Julián. *Music in Ancient Arabia and Spain*. California: Stanford University Press, 1929
Rimsky-Korsakoff, N. A. *My Musical Life*. New York: Alfred A. Knopf, Inc., 1923
Sabaneev, L. L. *Modern Russian Composers*. New York: International Publishers Co., Inc., 1927
Smyth, Ethel M. *Impressions That Remained*. New York: Longmans, Green & Co.
Trend, J. B. *Manuel de Falla and Spanish Music*. New York: Alfred A. Knopf, Inc., 1935
Trend, J. B. *The Music of Spanish History to 1600*. New York: Oxford University Press, 1926
Vaughan Williams, Ralph. *National Music*. New York: Oxford University Press, 1934

THE LATER ROMANTICS

Decsey, Ernst. *Bruckner*. Berlin: Schuster & Loeffler, 1920
Ekman, Karl. *Jean Sibelius, His Life and Personality*. New York: Alfred A. Knopf, Inc., 1938
Gray, Cecil. *Sibelius*. New York: Oxford University Press, 1931
Hill, E. Burlingame. *Modern French Music*. Boston: Houghton Mifflin Company, 1924
Hofmannsthal, H. H. *Correspondence between Richard Strauss and* [the author]. New York: Alfred A. Knopf, Inc., 1927
Indy, Vincent d'. *César Franck*. New York: Dodd, Mead & Company, Inc.
Jean-Aubry, G. *French Music of Today*. London: Kegan Paul, Trench, Trubner & Co., Ltd., 1919
Newman, Ernest. *Hugo Wolf*. London: John Lane, The Bodley Head, Ltd., 1909
Newman, Ernest, *Richard Strauss*. London: John Lane, The Bodley Head, Ltd., 1908
Reed, William H. *Elgar as I Knew Him*. London: Victor Gollancz, Ltd., 1936
Walter, Bruno. *Gustav Mahler*. London: George Routledge & Sons, Ltd., 1937
Wellesz, Egon. *Arnold Schönberg*. New York: E. P. Dutton & Co., Inc., 1925

THE MODERN REVOLT — Realism

Bell, Clive. *Landmarks in Nineteenth-century Painting*. New York: Harcourt, Brace and Company, Inc., 1927
Brandes, Georg. *Main Currents in Nineteenth Century Literature*. New York: Liveright Publishing Corporation, 1923

Mead, G. H. *Movements of Thought in the Nineteenth Century*. Chicago: University of Chicago Press, 1936

THE MUSICAL IMPRESSIONISTS

Bauer, Marion. *Twentieth Century Music*. New York: G. P. Putnam's Sons, 1934
Heseltine, Philip. *Delius*. London: John Lane, The Bodley Head, Ltd., 1923
Hill, E. Burlingame. *Modern French Music*. Boston: Houghton Mifflin Company, 1924
Mauclair, Camille. *The French Impressionists*. New York: E. P. Dutton & Co., Inc., 1903
Pannain, Guido. *Modern Composers*. New York: E. P. Dutton & Co., Inc., 1933
Thompson, Oscar. *Debussy, Man and Artist*. New York: Dodd, Mead & Company, 1937
Vallas, Léon. *Claude Debussy*. New York: Oxford University Press, 1933

THE TWENTIETH CENTURY

Cahill, H., and Barr, A. H. (Editors). *Art in America*. New York: Reynal & Hitchcock, Inc., 1935
Cheney, Sheldon, *A Primer of Modern Art*. New York: Liveright Publishing Corporation, 1935
Cowell, H. D. (Editor). *American Composers on American Music*. California: Stanford University Press, 1933
Dyson, George. *The New Music*. New York: Oxford University Press, 1926
Ewen, David. *Twentieth Century Composers*. New York: Thomas Y. Crowell Company, 1937
Howard, J. T. *Our American Music*. New York: Thomas Y. Crowell Company, 1931
Křenek, Ernst. *Music Here and Now*. New York: W. W. Norton & Company, Inc., 1939
Lambert, Constant. *Music Ho!* New York: Charles Scribner's Sons, 1934
Mumford, Lewis. *Technics and Civilization*. New York: Harcourt, Brace and Company, Inc., 1934
Reis, Claire. *Composers in America*. New York: The Macmillan Company, 1938
Scott, Cyril. *The Philosophy of Modernism*. London: Kegan Paul, Trench, Trubner & Co., Ltd., 1917
Slonimsky, Nicolas. *Music since 1900*. New York: W. W. Norton & Company, Inc., 1937
Stravinsky, Igor. *Stravinsky; An Autobiography*. New York: Simon and Schuster, Inc., 1936
Thomson, Virgil. *The State of Music*. New York: William Morrow & Co., Inc., 1939
Weissmann, Adolph. *The Problems of Modern Music*. New York: E. P. Dutton & Co., Inc., 1925
White, E. W. *Stravinsky's Sacrifice to Apollo*. London: Hogarth Press, 1930

Index

(Figures in italics refer to illustrations.)

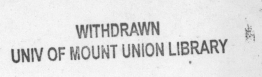